ABOUT THE AUTHOR

The author has a background in teaching, up to 'A' level and to undergraduates – in Britain and beyond. He has spent 25 years of his working life abroad, in Canada, Spain and Belgium. During this time he did considerable research into politics and society, developing conclusions on UK affairs from an external perspective. His starting point was a frustration with the narrow focus of much political and economic analysis, which led to a resolve to shed a clearer light on many common assumptions, and provide an alternative vision for the future.

Andrew Blackwood

SOCIAL CAPITALISM

*The End of Neo-Liberalism
and Where We Go Next*

AUSTIN MACAULEY PUBLISHERS™
LONDON • CAMBRIDGE • NEW YORK • SHARJAH

Copyright © Andrew Blackwood 2022

The right of Andrew Blackwood to be identified as author of this work has been asserted in accordance with section 77 and 78 of the Copyright, Designs and Patents Act 1988.

All rights reserved. No part of this publication may be reproduced, stored in a retrieval system, or transmitted in any form or by any means, electronic, mechanical, photocopying, recording, or otherwise, without the prior permission of the publishers.

Any person who commits any unauthorised act in relation to this publication may be liable to criminal prosecution and civil claims for damages.

The cover photograph, 'Cabbages and Prima Donnas – Life in Wartime Covent Garden, London, England, 1940' (IWM: D573), is in the public domain.

A CIP catalogue record for this title is available from the British Library.

ISBN 9781398453708 (Paperback)
ISBN 9781398453715 (ePub e-book)

www.austinmacauley.com

First Published 2022
Austin Macauley Publishers Ltd
1 Canada Square
Canary Wharf
London E14 5AA

*To Eleni, who was in at the beginning,
even if she didn't know it.*

And to M. for her forbearance

CONTENTS

1 Introduction – Image, Myth and Facts.. 11

2 The Individual and the Community.. 35

3 Capitalism For Ever?... 78

4 Economic Growth – the beguiling spectre?....................................... 165

5 The Market Rules – OK?... 222

6 The Great Contradiction 317

7 An Alternative Progress – for a ... *museum of anomalies* 392

8 We, the People – the Ultimate 'Resource'... 482

Index... 517

We feel that even when all possible scientific questions have been answered, the problems of life remain completely untouched.
                              LUDWIG WITTGENSTEIN

Chapter 1

INTRODUCTION – IMAGE, MYTH AND FACTS

The truth is what most people can't help thinking must be true.
                                    OLIVER WENDELL HOLMES, JR [i]

Man prefers to believe what he prefers to be true.
                                    FRANCIS BACON [ii]

There are certain doctrines which for a particular period seem not doctrines but inevitable categories of the human mind. Men do not look upon them as correct opinions, for they have become so much a part of the mind, and lie so far back, that they are never really conscious of them at all. <u>They do not see them, but other things through them.</u> It is these abstract ideas at the centre, the things which they take for granted, that characterize a period. (my emphasis)
                                    T. E. HULME [iii]

…the mind thinks with ideas, not with information. But information does not create ideas; by itself, it does not validate them or invalidate them. An idea can only be generated, revised, or unseated by another idea.
                                    THEODORE ROSZAK [iv]

The most intellectual of men are moved quite as much by the circumstances they are used to as by their own will. It is the dull traditional habit of mankind that guides most men's actions…
                                    WALTER BAGEHOT [v]

WHEN Plato's prisoners were seated in the cave, bound in such a way that they were able to see only what was shown on the wall in front of them, they believed that the images passing before their eyes were authentic reality. As Plato presented his analogy, should any of the prisoners have escaped their shackles, and been able to see the objects that threw the shadows onto the cave wall, they would have realised that what they had taken for reality were merely images of the real objects. They would have emerged into the daylight with their minds enlightened by 'truth'. However, in today's real world we have the capacity, and even the tendency to persuade ourselves that we actually prefer these reflected images; we like their shapes, their colours, their ideology, and we feel that they suit our view of the world. Even when the Plato-esque *guardians* of today's society try to show us how unreal and fanciful these distorted pictures are, we often still cling to them as *our* reality. In fact, to us they may be far more real than the objects of which they are ostensibly reflections. And there are always political leaders, journalists and image makers ready to collude in this self-deception, while at the same time being caught up themselves in the illusions of others around them. In fact, they are both victims and perpetrators of this fraudulent project, and thus, in Plato's terms, just as *destitute of philosophy* as the rest of us.

For in today's world of political and social ideas, belief is everything. True, we are told we are living in an *information society*, experiencing a revolution in which knowledge is power. In fact, an incessant barrage of information has been steadily increasing its assault on society ever since the modern media developed in the last century. But these data do not appear to make us better informed, or to help us be better equipped to come to more reasoned conclusions. We may have information overload, as many believe, leading to our being overwhelmed by conflicting detail, often contributing to apathy. We now hear that facts no longer matter, that we are now living in a world *post-truth*: the Oxford English Dictionary's word of 2016. It is certainly true that cold facts alone are not enough, even if provided in a modicum of context. But if that context is coloured by ideology, or comes with a plausible narrative, then an argument is more likely to convince. And once taken hold, popular ideas – for all their superficiality in the wider order of things – are insidious in the firm grasp they have on contemporary opinion. This explains the resistance put up when people are faced with corrective information which may in effect contradict previous suppositions. In such cases, people can cling even more strongly to their earlier beliefs, as shown by experiments conducted during the Iraq War of 2003. Despite revelations about the lack of WMDs (weapons of mass destruction), many participants of an American study remained convinced that Saddam Hussein had WMDs, which he was going to pass on to terrorists.[1] We may readily reject information which doesn't accord with our existing feelings, contradicting in our minds the arguments put before us, even while listening to them.

During the campaign leading up to Britain's EU Referendum in June 2016 it was often said that voters were starved of detailed information to help them decide on the nation's place in Europe. The two sides of the argument were accused of spreading misinformation, generating more heat than light, concentrating on fear rather than facts. But in fact the half-truths and canards put about at the time served the same purpose as more objective data. A pervasive narrative had been created over many years, promoted by wide sections of the media, which cast the European question in a very dubious light; Brussels was the nation's bogeyman. Large numbers of people had that thesis firmly in mind when hearing arguments from either the *leave* or *remain* campaigns, as if it was an accepted truth which all rhetoric had to acknowledge. It became an implicit conclusion which provided the *cognitive ease* about which Daniel Kahneman has written.[2] This is what he classifies as *System 1 Thinking*,[3] which is based primarily on intuition, where a statement, strongly linked by association to beliefs or preferences already held, appears to be true. *...when people believe a conclusion is true, they are also very likely to believe arguments that appear to support it, even when these arguments are unsound.*[4] Kahneman suggests that many people are overconfident, and tend to put too much faith in their intuitions. But when they feel comfortable and relaxed they are more likely to yield to an argument which feels familiar and true, in what is an effortless mental process. (This is in contrast to his *System 2 Thinking*, which is more likely to happen when one feels strained or less comfortable, making one more prone to be vigilant and suspicious.) At the same time, when you don't have a way to relate a statement to other things you know, you have no option but to go with the sense of *cognitive ease*.

The late US Democrat senator Daniel Moynihan once observed that everyone is entitled to their own opinion, but not to their own facts – even if Donald Trump all but demolished this notion. Of course, there are facts and there are 'facts'. While we like to think of information as factual, knowledge is more personal; it is our knowledge, our truth, no matter how distorted we may be told it is. During the 2016 US presidential election campaign cognitive scientist Steven Lewandowsky carried out some tests by giving people, Republicans and Democrats, lists of 'facts' which Donald Trump had asserted, some being true and some false.[5] It was discovered afterwards, when the participants were told which of the statements were false, that it made no difference to how they declared they would vote. In this situation Lewandowsky believed that the actual facts don't matter; they are just rhetorical tools. He saw that what was more important was how politicians speak to people, at what they feel is a deeper emotional level of truth. But the involvement of policy makers here is also to contrive to mould that truth, to synthesize perceptions with their top-down political agenda. They seek to harmonize public policy with the views of the electorate, with the propositions which people feel ought to be true, even if they are not. Thus is diffused a kind of false consciousness with which the political class falls in, to some extent duped by its own artifice, and as an accomplice readily *parroting the necessary illusions that respectability demands* – to use Noam Chomsky's phrase.[6]

But there is a sense in which facts, and therefore *truth* can be owned. Traditionally truth was authority-led, sanctioned by established elites, even if often subject to cynicism and doubt. This was the top-down pattern of data, transmitted from society's power bases; for in a more hierarchical world of *them* and *us*, knowledge and power went together, the former far more effectively controlled than in today's information society.* In this scenario, information emanates from bodies with authority, what Professor Steve Fuller has termed the *Lions*, which condition what is allowed to emerge and how it is disseminated.[7] Fuller believes that in the current internet-dominated world this model is breaking down, as information now derives from a multitude of sources. These he calls the *Foxes*, which oppose the ubiquity of a truth determined by the authority of those in power. He suggests that the *Foxes* believe the *Lions* are concealing other viable but inconvenient truths, information which hides the suspect agenda of elites, including their corrupt practices. It is the business of these elites which Donald Trump continually railed

---

* It was Nietzsche who emphasised the role of interpretation, to which most ideas and phenomena are subject. He maintained that any particular interpretation prevailing at a given time is a function of power, not of truth.

INTRODUCTION – IMAGE, MYTH AND FACTS 15

against in his campaign against so-called *fake news*, which he maintains is issued by Fuller's *Lions*. The irony is that Trump should hardly be seen as a *Fox* in this analysis; he is part of the privileged establishment whose truths he pretends to oppose, ostensibly on behalf of ordinary Americans, but principally in the cause of his own dubious populism. But in his attack on sources of established of power and influence he still, after his electoral defeat in November 2020, muddies the waters of accepted ideas, spreading doubt and dissension for his own partisan motives. Meanwhile, many other *foxes* have their own agendas.

Another very powerful influence muddying the waters and confusing belief is the post-modernist background, before which today's ideas and contentions are contested, played out, chewed over. If in the post-modern world all truths are partial, and dependent on one's subjective viewpoint, then there is scope for a multitude of opinions on any given subject – all, apparently, equally valid. And in the myriad of twenty-first century societies, with conflicting, antithetical moralities, many of them challenging conventional beliefs, relativism sits very comfortably. *Who are we to judge...* is often heard, and after all it does not do – we are told – to be too *judgemental*. *The relativist impulse* may be, as Julian Baggini maintains, *...by and large a noble one*, since it *... is opposed to the ownership of truth by one, usually privileged group; the crowding out of alternative perspectives.*[8] But this does not imply that there are no truths that we can come together on, merely that it is much harder and more complicated to do so. The profusion of views and the difficulty of testing their validity should not lead us to give up on truth. *Rather we should bring as many of these perspectives together as possible to create a fuller version of reality.*[9] No, we are not in a post-truth world; however, those who for their own purposes are resolved to create doubt and division, and undermine faith in ideas which have widespread support, have a suitably sympathetic environment, as well as any number of conducive platforms from which to fabricate their suspect schemes.

...[t]here are no conditions of life to which a man cannot get accustomed, especially if he sees them accepted by everyone around him, said Tolstoy.[10] Many would understand that this goes for ideas as well, where in fact it is evident in an even more pervasive way. For as regards

ideas, patterns of thought can easily become self-perpetuating assumptions, forming myths which take on widespread acceptance, regardless of fundamental validity. What is significant here is that *...once the myth is established it becomes a way of looking at the world. The world is seen through the myth and therefore tends to reinforce it.*[11] (My emphasis.) Alain de Botton has said that such views develop so that *...they may seem to belong to the fabric of existence as much as the trees and the sky...* even if promoted by those *...with particular practical and psychological interests to defend...* and *...may in fact be relative and open to investigation.*[12] However, once it gains credence the validity of the myth tends not to be questioned. It is, using the late Zygmunt Bauman's analysis, a *doxa: a set of assumptions ...one thinks with, but not of or about...*[13] As illustrated by T. E. Hulme's observation in the opening of this introduction, such ideas do not seem doctrines, but are accepted facets of thinking to the extent that they are almost part of the mind. As such they are taken for granted, and ideas which do not fit in with their common assumptions may be perceived but not taken in. Ideas of this kind can form themselves into an accepted ideology which, as Alain de Botton has described *...is released into society like a colourless, odourless gas. It is embedded in newspapers, advertisements, television programmes and textbooks – where it makes light of its partial, perhaps illogical or unjust take on the world; where it meekly implies that it is simply stating age-old truths with which only a fool or maniac would disagree.*[14]

Thus our contemporary world is peopled by sets of blurred assumptions, plausible half-truths, and specious illusions with which many of us are entirely comfortable. They give sufficiently convincing shape to widespread notions about social and economic development, our recent past, and expectations of the future, and it is through this veil that the modern world is viewed. Once a broad perspective of this kind is established, it forms itself into popular dogmas, gaining adherents as they develop credulity, until a whole generation is conditioned to accept them. And since they are part of a mindset, their assumptions are not easily overturned by the failure of policies and programmes launched under their auspices. For many, they will have an unshakeable veracity for some years until, with the passage of time and the transforming power of events, it becomes evident that their days are numbered. Only then will popular opinion move on to the next most plausible set of explanations through which to observe the modern age. In the meantime, the revelation that the emperor had no clothes all along is passed over; the old assumptions are forgotten, soon subsumed into new ones.

Britain's recent history is mainly seen through the lens of originally Tory perspectives about the failures of 1970s' economic policy, principally under Labour governments, and the so-called *British Disease,* which no political administration had managed to cure. The high unemployment and inflation of the '70s, the power of the trade unions, the poor economic productivity and balance of payments figures, and the humiliation visited on a Chancellor of the Exchequer by the plight of the pound sterling all contributed to an image of macro-economic failure. And economic failure became seen as social failure as well. So in 1979 the incoming Conservative government of Margaret Thatcher, giving convincing form and expression to these contemporary problems, heralded a new age. Public opinion was impressed by its particular 'New Right' interpretation of Britain's predicament, as well as by the fresh determination it showed in tackling it. The collective consciousness was already struck by the need for a fresh start, which thus prepared the ground for the acceptance of painful effects of government policies which were to follow in the 1980s. And regardless of the degree of success of those policies, the vigorous activist approach was widely approved as an attempt to answer a deep national need. Ideas about Britain's role in the world, her economic performance, and the ability of administrations to govern effectively coalesced into popular concern, which the new Tory government appeared able to interpret.

The identification of popular opinion with Conservative political remedies resulted in four election victories and eighteen years of power. This electoral success contributed directly to the rise of New Labour, the party then adjusting its programme to conform to contemporary received opinion. When in government after 1997, the Labour Party's discourse and style may have appeared fresh, but in many respects its policy solutions were disarmingly familiar, and thus helped to consolidate popular assumptions about Britain's problems and how they had come about. To borrow Judge Holmes' idea again, most people could not help thinking that, aside from the merits of particular government policies, the social and historical bases of Tory prescriptions formed in the late 1970s, and not effectively contradicted later by New Labour, must be largely true. As Voltaire once said, it requires ages to destroy a popular opinion, and now, after more than 20 years of the new century, the nation is still wrestling with the consequences of popular myths given shape by zealous New Model Tories at the start of their Thatcherite crusade. However, the failure of so many policy measures, both Conservative and Labour, have not been enough to destroy entirely the assumptions and prejudices on which they were based. The myths which have fed the rhetoric of the last generation still stubbornly persist, clouding the present and the future.

Of course, politics has long been accustomed to calculated misinterpretations of the past, perpetrated to justify partisan policy. Myths about how we got to where we are can provide convincing underpinning for political rhetoric on how to guide our future. *History – the propaganda of the victors,* wrote Ernst Toller, and there is no shortage of strategy on the part of incoming governments in co-opting their selective view of history on which to base their programmes. Political leaders, with support from sections of the media, can also rely on our common self-deception; Lebanese academic Nassim Nicholas Taleb explains how humans often fool themselves by constructing flimsy accounts of the past, believing they are true.[15] We form stories into what he terms *narrative fallacy* to explain our view of the world and our expectations of the future. The essence of the illusion here is that we believe we understand the past. A striking recent example was the common interpretation of the causes of the financial crash of 2007/08. It is still widely thought in Britain that it was due to government profligacy during the Labour years of the early 2000s. This impression was put about during the latter part of Gordon Brown's time in office, prior to the 2010 general election. And when that electoral campaign got underway Ed Miliband and the Labour hierarchy were strikingly ineffectual in combating the *narrative fallacy* it represented. The heralded light-touch financial regulation – for which all the then governments, including Labour, were responsible – was of course conveniently ignored by the Right as it tried to pin the blame on activist, *big* government.

Thus, the Conservative project in the UK, like Republican conservatism in the USA, is in fact ....*to tell a story that makes government, not lack of government, the villain.*[16] (Ronald Reagan's words in his inaugural address in 1981, that government is the problem, not the solution, still resonate.) Nobel laureate Paul Krugman, in a devastating analysis, has described how, on both sides of the Atlantic, the Right has tried to explain away the *awkward history* of how the financial crash came about.[17] Following Barry Ritholtz, he calls it the *Big Lie* of the period, the right-wing dogma which says that the growth in debt was ...*caused by liberal do-gooders and government agencies, which forced banks to lend to minority home buyers and subsidized dubious mortgages.*[18] This version of the political subterfuge, the attempt to try to make the economic facts fit our feelings and prejudices, will be very familiar in Britain. But why do conservatives so badly want to convince us that government caused the financial crisis when, as Krugman says, ...*even a cursory look at the facts*... proves otherwise ...*and the attempts to get round those facts smack of deliberate deception?*[19] To him the answer is obvious:

> ...*to believe anything else would be to admit that your political movement has been on the wrong track for decades. Modern conservatism is dedicated to the proposition that unfettered markets and the unrestricted pursuit of profit and personal gain are the keys to prosperity – and that the much-expanded role for government that emerged from the Great Depression did nothing but harm.*[20]

This perspective, the pervasive dogma of the Right which has developed since the late 1970s, is the anti-Keynesian prism through which much modern politics is viewed, and which has thwarted a realistic consensus on the origins of the crash.

No matter how bogus this narrative may be, it has gained wide credence. This is partly because it chimes with the idea that government involvement in the economy on the Keynesian model is only a stone's throw from government management of the economy in the form of socialism – itself almost a term of abuse on the political Right. Krugman puts it as: *The rhetorical amalgamation of Keynesianism with central planning and radical redistribution – although explicitly denied by Keynes himself... – is almost universal on the right, including among economists who really should know better.*[21] Corroboration for the failure of Keynesian policy even appeared to be provided by early American government response to the financial crash and credit crunch. A mild Keynesian stimulus was given to the US economy by President Obama's administration, in the *American Recovery and Reinvestment Act* of 2009. But the economic package involved did not provide the hoped-for boost in employment, and was thus taken by many voters as discrediting the whole strategy of government money to create jobs.

However, the stimulus represented less than 2% of federal government spending over a three-year period,[22] and thus its failure to deliver was more attributable to Obama's tentative approach, with a policy that fell far short of what was required to do the job. But the myth of Keynesian defectiveness was nevertheless reinforced.

When an ideology has become to appear so natural that it is, as Alain de Botton put it, almost part of *the fabric of existence,* it gathers around it a whole edifice of thought which is seen as the *status quo*. In terms of economic ideas, whole livelihoods can become bound up in the false consciousness of the age, and during the boom years of the early 2000s it seemed entirely natural for people to gravitate towards arguments which supported the accepted financial dogma. Will Hutton has highlighted the *...enormous intellectual and financial investment in the 'status quo'. Academics have built careers, reputations and tenure on a particular view of the world being right.*[23] To have challenged the dogma, to have entertained difficult questions about financial sustainability would have been tantamount to admitting that the ideological structure was built on clay. It is not just that the doctrine is propagated by vested interests, although one is reminded here of Upton Sinclair's famous quip: *It is difficult to get a man to understand something, when his salary depends on his not understanding it.* Also pervasive is the kind of inertia known as *status quo bias*; when a doctrine spreads through society like a subversive virus, it is easier to submit to it, particularly when all around you appear to be doing so. This may be seen as herd behaviour, but psychological factors undeniably influence thinking on financial matters. Referring to the period prior to the financial crash of 2008, one researcher, Robert Shiller, says, *...the most important single element... in understanding this or any other speculative boom is the 'social contagion' of boom thinking.*[24]

Numerous studies have shown much human judgement and decision-making to be biased and deeply flawed. Some of these have taken the form of conformity experiments, revealing how people's opinions can be influenced by others. The well-known studies conducted in the 1950s by Solomon Asch showed that, when asked to give answers to fairly easy tests without seeing the opinions of others, respondents almost never erred.[25] However, when everyone else in a group situation was primed to give incorrect answers, people erred more than a third of the time, thus ignoring the evidence of their own senses. These findings have been replicated in many countries and situations. Conformity effects on judgement can be quite significant. In one experiment people were asked to consider the statement: *Free speech being a privilege rather than a right, it is proper for a society to suspend free speech when it feels threatened.*[26] Asked the question individually only 19% of the group agreed, but when faced with the agreed opinions of just four other people, 58% of respondents agreed. Peer pressure as well as the need for approval may explain these apparent anomalies. But a remarkable extension of these experiments, using brain-imaging, has revealed that when people conform in these settings they actually see the situation as everyone else does.[27] As Daniel Kahneman maintains, *We know that people can maintain an unshakable faith in any proposition, however absurd, when they are sustained by a community of like-minded believers.*[28]

After all, we most of us want to fit in, in general to be in harmony with those around us, whether in terms of what we believe or how we behave. Our socialization from an early age encourages us to blend in with the community in which we find ourselves. Assimilation represents taking on the mores of our neighbours, feeling some degree of unity of outlook and congruity of purpose. Thus the social character of a society develops, and the greater the overall consensus which a society arrives at, the more harmonious is likely to be its disposition. One might say that in such circumstances Kahneman's *cognitive ease* becomes prevalent, as much in behaviour as in opinion. In modern times the equanimity of societies has been disturbed by the extreme individualism of the neo-liberal project, just as it has been by large-scale immigration where it has impacted consensus. But the tendency to be at one with those around you, to conform to majority opinion and practice is still powerful, and is to a large degree internalised. It becomes the social character of a people. The psychoanalyst and social philosopher Erich Fromm defined it many years ago:

> *It is the function of the social character to shape the energies of the members of society in such a way that their behaviour is not a matter of conscious decision as to whether or not to follow the social pattern, but one of 'wanting to act as they have to act' and at the same time finding gratification in acting according to the requirements of the culture.*[29]

Thus a kind of collective sub-consciousness becomes established – our way of seeing the world – which governs how we think and how we believe we should act.

Contemporary thinking on financial matters is part of what has been called the *ambient noise* of the free market,[30] the prevailing atmosphere governing our assumptions on the economy. A true free market doesn't exist, but this does not seem to affect the unshakable faith in its slogan. The fact that it contains the word *free* gives it a favourable gloss; in the modern world how can any of us be against freedom?! However, most would no doubt accept that some regulation of the economy is justifiable; rules to protect the environment would come under this heading. But as Cambridge economist Ha-Joon Chang says, *We accept the legitimacy of certain regulations so totally that we don't see them.*[31] (Perhaps one should more properly say that we simply see the 'free' market *through* them.) So we implicitly accept the principle of interference in the capitalist 'free' market, up to a point, but we only see it as interference when it conflicts with our cultural perspective. We *prefer* to believe that our economy is free, because it chimes with the tenor of the times. The demise of state socialism in Eastern Bloc countries after the fall of the Berlin Wall has a lot to answer for, since it has coloured our subsequent thinking on any degree of government management of the economy. The free market has thus been left apparently victorious, and all capitalist economies profess belief in it. It is now the prevailing way we look at the world; it has the complexion of an age-old truth.

As has been said, plausible ideas can maintain a powerful grip on popular opinion. Alexis De Tocqueville recognized this in the United States almost two centuries ago: commenting on American susceptibility to popular ideas he concluded that once an opinion is taken up ... *be it well or ill founded, nothing is more difficult than to eradicate it from their minds.*[32] Such opinions can stubbornly resist contradiction, which in any case can be counter-productive, especially if it emanates from official or so-called 'expert' sources. Over recent years the political establishment has been undermined to such an extent that faith in its pronouncements has been severely diluted, if not lost. Scandal, duplicity and failure have led to people putting more reliance on instinct and prejudice. One only has to recall, for example, the MPs' expenses scandal in the UK or the earlier accusations that Britain went into the Iraq war on the basis of lies. And then there was the failure to anticipate the financial debacle; in fact, in April 2007, a mere four months before the market crash, the IMF forecast that ... *world growth will continue to be strong*, and reported that economic risks had lessened since September 2006.³³ In this environment, perhaps it is not so surprising that during Britain's EU referendum campaign Michael Gove should proclaim, *I think people in this country have had enough of experts...* However, if the wisdom of experts, such as it is, is rejected and pushed aside, its place will quickly be filled by the populism of political opportunists, ready to take advantage of a disillusioned electorate. Such is the era of Donald Trump, Marine Le Pen, Nigel Farage and of course Boris Johnson himself, figures who make every effort not to sound like experts, but try to appear as authentic representatives of the people.

It could be said that there is a fine line between the otherwise reliable opinions of those expert in their fields and the views of disingenuous politicians. But this dichotomy is complicated by the fact that while the latter are elaborately tailored to fit popular taste, the authenticity of the former may not be immediately attractive. After all, expert opinion presented unadorned with any convincing ideology or compelling narrative makes it unpalatable to many in today's climate. In fact, there is now a residual suspicion of establishment opinion, especially of the political kind, for reasons cited above. A deficit of trust has been built up which feeds the populist mood, and is reminiscent of Lord Salisbury's advice to Lord Lytton at the end of the nineteenth century, that he should never trust experts: *If you believe the doctors, nothing is wholesome; if you believe the theologians, nothing is innocent; if you believe the soldier, nothing is safe. They all require to have their strong wine diluted by a very large admixture of common sense.*³⁴ For it is this apparent common sense to which populist leaders appeal, the common sense of instinct and gut feelings. Populism is proud of its lack of expertise, or at least any overt expertise which would appear to separate its leaders from those instincts and feelings. An American politician feels perfectly comfortable in declaring *...as a political candidate I'll go with how people feel, and I'll let you go with the theoreticians...*³⁵ Thus, the appeal to the mass of the population, the claim to popular authenticity, is taken to be the route to political success.

In the United States this phenomenon appears to loom larger than it does in Europe. Attempting to appear as one of the people means using a colloquial language of the most direct kind. Ronald Reagan and George W. Bush were both exponents of this practice, but Donald Trump took it much further. Sounding authoritative, though not overly so, but voicing the instincts of the people, and trying not to appear in any way remote from them – these are the objectives. One former US Congressman, Bob Inglis, puts it as, *You have to use the language of the tribe to reach the tribe.*[36] Inglis is an unusual Republican politician, one who recognizes the dangers of climate change. But he maintains that conservatives in the US have not been receptive to these concerns because they were first brought up by people *…talking liberal*. He believes that we have to show conservatives that there is a solution to global warming which is consistent with what they believe, which means, he says, *talking market forces*, not raising taxes. How you pitch the issue is crucial, and – in an extraordinary slant on expertise – he claims that he *…might sound a bit too informed*.[37] Heaven forbid that he should appear knowledgeable, and perhaps more informed than his constituents!

However, if we live in a world where expertise is not to be trusted, what can we believe? We exist at a time when a vast panoply of scientific knowledge has been developed, when cutting-edge research is daily adding to understanding of ourselves and the universe. Yet increasingly we seem inclined to rely on our untutored feelings, sensations garnered from vernacular experience and the all-too unscientific media – social and mainstream. So while we have greater knowledge of the physical and human world than ever before, there is a tendency to allow a variety of public policy to be guided by personal impressions and unsophisticated ideology, filtered through our media-dominated, digital world. In this context it is hardly surprising that facts themselves become mediated, contested, and therefore ambiguous. How can any of us be sure they are not fake? One recent study set out to examine whether or not American high school and college students could distinguish between fake and authentic online news reports. Stanford University tested the ability of 7,800 students in twelve US states to judge the credibility of online information.[38] The results showed that students were repeatedly fooled; they could not distinguish between real accounts and fake ones, or even tell serious articles from advertisements. Moreover, fewer than 20% of Middle School pupils (11 to 13 year-olds) were aware that sponsored content was not real news. It appears that in today's *information society* facts and truth are just what we make of them; belief is everything.

The question of what and how we believe is especially relevant when it comes to balance and bias. For example, judging by how the matter of climate change/global warming is often presented in the media, one might suppose that views on its existence, or on the degree of human responsibility for it, were matters of even, finely balanced judgements.

INTRODUCTION – IMAGE, MYTH AND FACTS

In discussions on radio or television a so-called *climate change denier* might be put up in opposition to a climate change scientist – yes, an *expert* – as if the encounter between the two sides were a delicate, even-handed, symmetrical argument on a highly debatable issue. The fact that the overwhelming majority of scientists in the field believe in the existence of climate change, and in human agency as a cause, often lies unobserved, dormant in the background.* Public service broadcasters usually maintain that they attempt to present debates on topical issues in a balanced way. But many current social and political problems do not lend themselves to obvious parity or equivalence, and in any case where the balance might lie on a given subject can itself often be a contested arena. During the EU referendum campaign the BBC was accused of favouring the Remain camp. Yet that pro-EU side were convinced that the corporation was guilty of false balance, most notably when a poll found that 88% of UK economists were against Brexit, while their views were frequently set against those of a tiny number of economists, often fronted by Professor Patrick Minford, who claimed Brexit would not harm the British economy.[39] In such controversies how can a balance possibly be struck; where is the mean to be found?

In international affairs there are intractable problems which present similar difficulties, exacerbated by geo-political vested interests and clouded by partisan propaganda. The Israeli/Palestinian divide, with its roots in a history formed before most people alive today were born, is now embedded in a half-submerged consciousness. Most people have grown up with the Middle East always there in the background as a perennial problem area, part of *the fabric of existence*. To the uninformed or disinterested it may well appear as a tit-for-tat conflict, a symmetrical dichotomy in which heads need to be banged together for the participants to come to their collective senses. The facts that the Israeli/Palestinian problem is above all based on invasion and occupation of Palestinian land, and that this has been condemned by United Nations resolutions for almost 50 years, are rarely dwelt upon in media

---

* Although in this case not entirely unrecognised; a report in 2011 by the BBC Trust concluded that the corporation's coverage on the subject concentrated too much on what it called ...*marginal opinio*n, reflecting the difficulty of reconciling balance and neutrality with truth. In subsequent years the BBC evidently failed to implement the findings of the 2011 review, so that the Radio 4 'Today' programme had to be censured for an interview with *denier* Lord Lawson in 2014, and in 2018 the BBC's head of news and current affairs issued a briefing note to staff on the subject admitting mistakes, and saying that it was not necessary to include a *denier* in a debate to ensure balance.

reports, this itself part of the explanation for the lack of public awareness on the subject. (In one piece of research by Glasgow University, only 9% of young people interviewed knew that the Israelis were the occupiers.[40]) Even knowledgeable observers would be unlikely to equate Israeli policy with, say, the Russian occupation of the Crimea in 2014, in spite of its obvious parallels. And yet the reasons given for protecting ethnic Russians in Ukraine are strikingly similar to Israel's defence of policies in the West Bank. It is clear that any consensus on balance or on bipartisan media coverage of political issues in far-off lands is just as problematic as it is closer to home.

These and other factors are behind the decline in trust in the media. Recent findings by the Reuters Institute put the trust index at 43% in Britain and just 38% in the USA.[41] As Reuters sees it, blame ...*deep-rooted political polarization and* perceived *mainstream media bias.* (My emphasis.) In the febrile atmosphere of recent years, heightened by the political thunderbolts of 2016, it is hardly surprising that the search for truth and probity has rarely been more hazardous. But in the era of social media, blogs and internet search engines it has now taken a turn for the worse. It appears that sections of the world wide web have been taken over by far-right groups, enabling them to disseminate their extremist ideology to many who might believe they are viewing neutral or objective platforms. Google's search engine, by far the internet's main source of information, has been accused of enabling this dissemination through its complex algorithms. For when questions on the Holocaust are entered into Google's search bar, many of the top results produced centre on Holocaust denial, and prominent among these are links to far-right, neo-Nazi websites. An 'Observer' investigation showed how these sites can engineer their hate organizations to reach the top of the search engine's list, regardless of truth and authenticity.[42] But, as the article reported, citing a leading expert on search, perhaps Google's algorithm is intended to reward popular results over authoritative ones, so that it can make more money. So do we conclude from this that the truth is for sale? If so, it is another blow against the notion of the internet as neutral and democratic. And as a phenomenon the perception is as old as it is dispiriting.

Thus many institutions and agencies in the modern world seem to have a problem with truth, and the same can be said for a wide swathe of politicians. But this has become an especially significant issue with populist leaders. Populism wants to monopolize the truth, to own the facts they share with the people. If the media report events in a manner unfavourable to such leaders, the latter may well contest or challenge the published accounts and produce their own versions. In the age of Donald Trump, who frequently denounced the news media as dishonest, this became particularly conspicuous. Soon after he took office there was disagreement between the White House and journalists over the size of the crowds at his inauguration. When a senior aide, Kellyanne Conway, was asked why the president's press secretary had lied about the crowd size, she defended him saying he was providing ...*alternative facts*. Her interviewer, Chuck Todd of NBC, replied that ....*alternative facts aren't facts; they're falsehoods*.[43] Further, a BBC journalist who reported this exchange recalled being told at a Trump event that the fact that many people believed something gave it an element of truth.[44] If truth and falsehood can be contested in this way, is authenticity not simply subjective?[45] If so, are we not truly are in a world of *post-truth*, where facts are merely *rhetorical tools*? Such is the environment of George Orwell's *1984*, or the East German Democratic Republic pre-1989.

The notion that if many people believe an idea, then that alone gives it a measure of veracity is one which became a conspicuous feature of Donald Trump's presidency, in a manner which would have seemed preposterous only a few years ago. Of course, beliefs about UFOs or views that John F. Kennedy's assassination in 1963 was the outcome of a conspiracy of the CIA, the Mafia and other agencies have been circulating for decades; to adherents, denials from official sources merely confirm their views that cover-ups are widespread and emanate from the very top of government. But now in the internet age there is an additional engine – social media – to drive dissemination of fringe opinions and proselytize those susceptible to alluring but subversive ideas. And in very recent times, condoned and even urged on by President Trump, a panoply of extreme *alternative facts* – of mainly, but not wholly right-wing, ultra-conservative conspiracy theories – have emerged. The atmosphere of fear and mistrust which developed in 2020 in the USA during the Coronavirus pandemic gave succour to a number of extravagant conceits, of which QAnon is the most powerful advocate. QAnon is the overall title of a set of internet conspiracy theories which include the belief that America is run by a cabal of Satan-worshipping paedophiles, operating a global child sex-trafficking ring, and including prominent Democrat politicians, Hollywood stars, and even Pope Francis.

Until quite recently such sensational notions, if acknowledged, would have been seen as cranky, esoteric ideas, limited to the extreme fringes of popular discourse. But when they swirl prominently around democratically elected governments in the internet age of alternative cultures, they take on a different complexion. And besides, a core QAnon conviction here is that Donald Trump was recruited by the military to break up the conspiracy and bring its members to justice, allied to which is the belief that the 'establishment' of politics and the media are controlled by this covert cabal. This was the *swamp* which Trump pledged to *drain*, once elected to the White House – even if not all those who voted for him would have been aware of the extent of the conspiracy. While many may assume this phenomenon to be a modern social aberration, in some respects it is rooted in the tradition of fabricated schemes based on false accusations and hysteria, with religious elements, going back at least to witch-hunts of the Middle Ages. Evidence and truth are irrelevant to such belief systems held by disparate groups which easily embrace apocalyptic prophecies based on the malign intent of *the other*. Recent political convulsions, a viral pandemic of almost Biblical dimensions, and fears of the effects of dynamic climate change all form a propitious backdrop for irrational, alternative movements. As the poet W. H. Auden wrote, during a previous turbulent age, *Both professor and prophet …agree in predicting a day of convulsion and vast evil…*[46]

There are parallels between today and earlier ages. The doomsday conspiracies of medieval times would have involved isolated social groups without access to the learning of the day and promoted by religious and political leaders for their own purposes. Although we now live in a hyper-scientific age, many of those subscribing to 'extreme' conspiracy theories are shielded from more rational discourse by their deriving self-reinforcing news and ideas from a few, chosen, mainly social media sources. Thus they remain in their separate information silos, wilfully secluded from pluralistic viewpoints by a uniform diet of suspect data. And in any case, contradicting or denying their strongly-held ideas would appear to confirm to them the discredited 'establishment' camp from which you come. Donald Trump himself was not prepared to disavow QAnon theories; as he said, the QAnon people like him. In fact, the publicity he fomented to the baseless suggestion a decade ago that President Obama had not been born in the USA and was not eligible to be president was typical of the undermining of credibility in public figures and institutions, all of which play into QAnon conspiracies. But QAnon has developed beyond a political movement spreading false conspiracy; it is a participatory cult, its followers congregating online to decode the latest cryptic Q posts, discuss current news, and even take part in games – all part of a kind of social bonding in a shared alternative reality. The internet allows a much greater degree of organization for trends of this kind, as well as facilitating growth in the numbers of adherents unlike anything seen previously.

The political ramifications of QAnon are a matter of deep concern to many. While some of its subject matter may be recycled from earlier conspiracy theories, its stance appears to reject reason and normal Enlightenment values, so that truth and empiricism become entirely irrelevant. Spreading suspect notions, without evidence to support them, is the chosen means to obscure right-wing ends. Thus QAnon was an influential advocate for the view that the 2020 presidential election was stolen from the Republicans by fraudulent voting in key states – by which it became mainstream thinking in the USA. It put its weight behind the scores of Republicans who – even after the shameful assault on Congress – attempted to reject the Electoral College certification of Joe Biden's election in January 2021. A constant refrain of QAnon coincided with American far right elements in their determination to *stop the steal* – the alleged theft of the election by the Democrats, in spite of the many failed attempts in the courts to overthrow results. By constantly repeating a simple lie – the long-established technique of fascist movements – the search for evidence is made to appear irrelevant by those convinced of the rightness of their cause, and to many others. In early December 2020, 41% of Republicans polled believed the presidential election result would be overturned, though this figure gradually fell over subsequent weeks.[47] Nevertheless, in late December as many as 36% of GOP voters said they believed Donald Trump should never concede victory to Joe Biden.[48]

With so much sound and fury surrounding Covid-19, climate change, and now the contested election of President Biden, the current age seems to represent the birth of a post-empiricist movement. Broad swathes of the educated populations of many nations hold 'alternative' views which defy conventional rationality. Even the arrival of vaccines to counteract Coronavirus is not wholeheartedly welcomed; many refuse to be vaccinated, and extreme views maintain that they are part of a conspiracy by the elite against the masses. There have always been minorities who have refused vaccinations when offered them, and in some respects today's resistance is no different. But widespread heretical views on a number of topical issues today are perhaps more due to online influence, which readily diffuses unconventional opinions. Yuval Noah Harari says,

> *People rarely appreciate their ignorance, because they lock themselves inside an echo chamber of like-minded friends and self-confirming newsfeeds, where their beliefs are constantly reinforced and seldom challenged. ....Bombarding people with facts and exposing their individual ignorance is likely to backfire.*[49]

Opinions formed in this way become rooted; they are very difficult to shift and presenting alternative facts, however valid, can be fruitless. Particular views, even if they defy logic, may accord with our outlook on life, conditioned by the circles in which we move. We soon become comfortable with them, and if connected with the online world we will have the solidarity of the group to support us. This is not an especially 'post-truth' age, but one perhaps more susceptible to falsehoods – or perhaps as Harari maintains, *Homo sapiens is a post-truth species, whose power depends on creating and believing fictions.*[50]

The truth we fall back on – when we search for validity, when we find the array of options too complex or incomprehensible, when we need a comfortable, plausible version to accord with our own instinctive narrative – is what we can't help thinking must be the way the world is. It also happens to be the perspective we feel we prefer. It develops into an all-pervasive false consciousness – not a Marxist false consciousness in which people come to believe in their own particular position in the social hierarchy, but a complex, symbiotic relationship between personal feelings and concepts on the one hand, and mediated ideas from the outside world on the other. The facts of a matter, however they may be determined, are less important than the impressions bearing in on us from the political, corporate and entertainment worlds filtered by mass media, social or otherwise. These, then, form part of our enduring consciousness through which we see our reality; we would not have our 'objectivity' enhanced by fresh facts. Today there is no shortage of information with which to arrive at judgements about world issues, and yet the glut of data has not apparently contributed to a better understanding of how to solve them. But pouring over data will not get us anywhere. No, it is the ...*inevitable categories of the human mind* that need to be examined. It is not what we think but how we think which has to be addressed. American author Janet Malcolm says, *We go through life mishearing and mis-seeing and misunderstanding so that the stories we tell ourselves will add up*. Attempts will be made in the following chapters to interpret these misunderstandings, in order to adjust the lens through which we see them.

END NOTES

i   Oliver Wendell Holmes Jr., *The Professor of the Breakfast-Table* (1860).
ii Francis Bacon, *Aphorisms*.
iii T. E. Hulme, *Speculations*, 1924, quoted in J. F. C. Harrison, *Late Victorian Britain, 1875-1901*, Fontana Press, London, 1990, p. 95.
iv Theodore Roszak, *The Cult of Information: A Neo-Luddite Treatise on High Tech, Artificial Intelligence, and the True Art of Thinking*, 2nd Edn., Univ. of California Press, London, 1994, p. 88.
v   Walter Bagehot, *The English Constitution*, OUP, London, 1928, pp.7-8.

1   Brendan Nyhan, in 'The New World – Nothing but the Truth', BBC Radio 4, 2/1/2017.
2   Daniel Kahneman – *Thinking, Fast and Slow*, Penguin Books, London, 2012, Chapter 5.
3   Ibid. p. 20.
4   Ibid. p. 45.
5   Steven Lewandowsky, in 'The New World – Nothing but the Truth', BBC Radio 4, 2/1/2017.
6   Noam Chomsky, *Deterring Democracy*, Vintage, London, 1991, p. 374.
7   Fuller, sociology professor at Warwick University, outlined his scenario in discussion with Laurie Taylor in "Post-Truth", on 'Thinking Allowed', BBC Radio 4, 19/9/2018.
8   Julian Baggini, *A Short History of Truth: Consolations for a Post-Truth World*, Quercus, London, 2018, p. 76.
9   Idem.
10 Quoted in Tony Judt, *Ill Fares the Land: A Treatise on Our present Discontents*, The Penguin Press, New York, 2010, p. 237.
11 Edward de Bono, *The Mechanism of Mind*, Penguin Books, 1971, p. 189.
12 Alain de Boton, *Status Anxiety*, Penguin Books, London, 2005, p. 214.
13 Zygmunt Bauman, *Does Ethics Have a Chance in a World of Consumers?* Harvard Univ. Press, London, 2008, p. 259.
14 Ibid. p. 214-5.
15 Nassim Nicholas Taleb, cited in Kahneman, op. cit. p. 199.
16 Paul Krugman, *End this Depression Now*, W. W. Norton & Co., New York, 2012, p. 66.
17 Krugman, op. cit.
18 Barry Ritholtz in Krugman, op. cit., p. 64.
19 Ibid. p. 66.
20 Idem.
21 Ibid. p. 94.
22 According to Krugman, in ibid. p. 122.

INTRODUCTION – IMAGE, MYTH AND FACTS

23 Will Hutton, *Them And Us: Changing Britain – Why We Need a Fair Society*, Little, Brown, London, 2010, p. 194.
24 Robert Shiller in Richard H. Thaler and Cass R. Sunstein, *Nudge: Improving Decisions About Health, Wealth and Happiness*, Penguin Books, London, 2009, p. 71.
25 Cited in ibid. p. 60-1.
26 Ibid. p. 64.
27 Ibid. p. 61 + end note.
28 Kahneman, op. cit. p. 217.
29 Erich Fromm, *The Sane Society*, Fawcett Publications, Greenwich, Conn., 1955, p. 77.
30 Ha-Joon Chang, *23 Things They Don't Tell You about Capitalism*, Allen Lane, London, 2010, p. 3.
31 Ibid. p. 4.
32 Alexis de Tocqueville, *Democracy in America*, (Phillips Bradley, Ed.) New York, 1945, Vol.I, p. 186.
33 Quoted in Robert Peston & Laurence Knight, *How Do We Fix This Mess? The Economic Price of Having It All and the Route to Lasting Prosperity*, Hodder & Stoughton, London, 2013, p. 123-4.
34 Lord Salisbury, quoted in Peter Vansittart, *Voices: 1870-1914*, Franklin Watts, New York, 1985, p. 71.
35 Opening of 'The New World – Nothing but the Truth', BBC Radio 4, 2/1/2017, not attributed.
36 Bob Inglis, ibid.
37 Idem.
38 Cited in John Naughton, *The internet generation can handle the truth. They just can't find it*, in 'The Observer', 11/12/2016.
39 Reported by Andrew Harrison, *Who Will Tell Us the Truth?* in 'The Observer', 6/8/2017.
40 John Pilger in the 'New Statesman', 3/6/2002.
41 Cited by Peter Preston in 'The Observer', 9/7/2017.
42 Exposé by Carole Cadwalladr in 'The Observer', 11/12/2016 & 18/12/2016.
43 Gavin Hewitt, *Trump and Truth*, from the BBC website, 24/1/2017.
44 Idem.
45 Prior to his nomination as Republican candidate for the Presidency, during a week of campaigning in the primaries Donald Trump was found to have averaged one 'misstatement' every five minutes, according to calculations by *Politico* magazine, in an analysis of his speeches and press conferences – cited in Guy Standing, *The Corruption of Capitalism*, Biteback Publishing, London, 2017, p. 266.
46 From Auden's extended poem, *The Age of Anxiety: A Baroque Eclogue*, 122, first published in 1947.
47 Data from polling on December 22nd, 2020 by 'Morning Consult', at **https://morningconsult.com/form/tracking-voter-trust-in-elections/**

48 Idem. The same survey found that, when asked to explain why the President's legal team had repeatedly failed in their challenges of the election result, 62% of all voters cited 'insufficient evidence'; 28% said the courts were biased against President Trump. It appears that many Americans, convinced by conspiracy theories, believe lack of evidence does not indicate exoneration, but is yet further 'proof' of conspiratorial manipulation by the opposition.
49 Yuval Noah Harari, *21 Lessons of the 21st Century*, Vintage, London, 2019, p. 255.
50 Ibid. pp. 271-2.

Chapter 2

THE INDIVIDUAL AND THE COMMUNITY

...the isolated asocial man is a fictitious construction.
LUDWIG VON MISES[i]

...we do not exist simply alongside and <u>with</u> others: our being, purposes and action are created socially <u>through</u> others.
GEOFF HODGSON[ii]

The social state is at once so natural, so necessary, and so habitual to man, that, except in some unusual circumstances... he never conceives himself otherwise than as a member of a body.

JOHN STUART MILL[iii]

THE *ambient noise* with which we are surrounded in the modern age contains within it an instinctive understanding that the individual is the norm, and that personal identity, autonomy, fulfilment are the precepts by which humanity should be measured. The aggregates of public policy may be looked on as serving the interests of cohorts of the population, but only insofar as it ministers to individual needs and demands. For, ultimately, people look to their own individual satisfactions – in the sense of both *id* and *ego* – as the criteria by which the success of political, economic and social programmes should be judged. Individualism is the creed, and as the atomisation of modern societies has proceeded apace, so the increasing self-regard and self-centredness of their populations has come to be thought of as the natural, *quasi* inevitable model. Particularly in the developed, *western* world we are encouraged to see our lives in the sense of personal emancipation, a process of self-realisation through which our identities are formed and re-formed, and in which personal ambition – admired and applauded – is always thought of as subjective. While there may be said to be a gradual process of global homogenisation, as nations and peoples tend to grow more similar to one another, as their expectations appear increasingly to converge, nevertheless within societies the tendency is towards distinguishing one's individual identity from that of others.

These characteristics of modern societies are relatively new historically; they certainly did not exist in the same form before the industrial revolution of the 18th century. In fact, the term *individualism* did not emerge until the 1830s, when used by the French commentator Alexis de Tocqueville, though interestingly he coined it to describe what he then saw as social isolation in the United States. But in the pre-Enlightenment era the individual was regarded quite differently. During the 16th and 17th centuries, even if the focus on the after-life was waning, religion was still very influential, and fulfilment based on personal choice was limited. Seeing life as a project to be individually designed and guided would not have been understood, while ambition was still frowned upon. Even asserting one's individuality and difference was generally disapproved of, since so-called *singularity* was not accepted.[1] However, the seeds of a different concept of the individual had already been sown. Here much academic opinion was persuaded by the ideas of Max Weber, notably his claim that the individualistic ethic arose out of Protestantism. The new Protestant ideas of 16th-century Europe certainly facilitated the rise of capitalism, and especially individual ownership which it necessitated. But the notion that, for example, land ownership rights could be possessed individually had already started to emerge before the Reformation, by the time of Henry VII's reign.² Andro Linklater points out that combining arable strips of land and taking over common grazing areas had begun by the early 15th century, and thus one might suspect that Renaissance values were more influential than religious changes in engendering this process. But the idea that private ownership of land arose out of human toil – argued by the Massachusetts Bay Colony Governor John Winthrop in 1629 – was a view which came to underpin both capitalism, and eventually a different concept of the individual.

These ideas took many decades to develop, and mainly in the Protestant world, and in the meantime the legacies of feudalism were still evident, not least in custom and tradition. The interlocking web of rights and obligations which had made up medieval society may have been eroded by the early modern age, but the residual sense of interdependence lived on. The majority of populations still remained in their allotted stations in life, even if there was increasing evidence of what we would now call social mobility, especially in England. And although nation states were emerging, and monarchs had succeeded in freeing themselves from the bonds of feudal *seigneurship*, nevertheless at a lower level personal emancipation and individual freedom did not have meaning as aspirations. A sense of interconnectedness was the norm, and life chances were circumscribed by one's social position, as well as by gender, geography and weather. Interdependence tied people to one another in terms of place, rank and occupation, and personal fulfilment was sought in only a very limited fashion. The essence of this social system was mutuality, whereby social cohesion grew out of the complex network of interrelationships. In fact, the individual would have had significance mainly through interdependence. In a more recent context the sociologist Emile Durkheim was much preoccupied with these relationships. He saw interdependence as an important element in social cohesion, and related it in a significant way to the individual: ... *social cohesion occurs because one person is always dependent upon another to achieve a feeling of completeness.*³ This perspective could suitably be applied to Medieval society and later.

During the early modern age, society in western Europe continued its trajectory towards greater emphasis on the individual, so that by the 18th century human motivation came to centre much more on personal fulfilment; Enlightenment ideas of Natural Law involved a recognition of individual rights. In a world witnessing a greater focus on the secular nature of human beings, whose enlightened self-interest concerned seeking the best for themselves, there was inevitably more scope for individual emancipation. However, this stress on the individual was in the political context of varying degrees of 18th century despotism, during Europe's *ancien regime*. Against this background, the Enlightenment taught the right of the collective of individuals to assert themselves, in societies that increasingly came to be governed by law and limited representative government, although it has to be said that the focus was on property rights, and mostly of the middle classes and the nobility. But the new liberalism which was developing was rooted in obstacles to the freedom of the individual, as David Green has contended:

All around were fetters, in economic life, in religion, in politics and in intellectual life. Liberals sought release from serfdom, government monopolies, the arbitrary power of kings, bishops and popes, and from the stultifying weight of tradition in village life and municipal guilds.[4]

From John Locke, through to the early 19th century and including Adam Smith, Reason came to confer legitimacy on the struggle of individuals against privilege and tyranny.

As is clear, context is crucial to the understanding of social developments of this kind. A new concept of the individual was taking shape in the late 18th and 19th centuries – not the thrusting, autonomous, fully emancipated version of modern ideology, but one which, on the basis of the principle of Natural Law, stood in opposition to vested interests and an overweening state. A vital element here was the liberalism of Adam Smith. His view of the individual, often held up erroneously as being on a par with neo-liberal individualism, was very much tied to his moral philosophy, as his work *The Theory of Moral Sentiments* showed. And in any case, at a time when powerful social mores framed human behaviour, Smith saw economics and morality as naturally bound together, unlike the way they are seen in today's world. His emphasis on self-interest, through which an individual, in looking after his own selfish concerns, will indirectly serve the wider interests of society, is certainly a vital principle of his economic liberalism. However, this has to be seen against the backdrop of 18th-century religious values and expectations, just as Smith's *laissez-faire* economic principles should be viewed in the light of the mercantilism and state power of his time.

Connections of a similar nature can be found in the 19th century, notably with the philosophy of John Stuart Mill. In his essay *On Liberty* he holds up individuality as needing protection from government as well as from public opinion (which he termed a *tyranny*) because, *The initiation of all wise or noble things comes and must come from individuals; generally at first from some one individual.*[5] Mill reflected the still common view of the professional classes – a legacy of Georgian England – that governments represented corruption and inefficiency. And *...whatever crushes individuality is despotism, by whatever name it may be called...*[6] At the same time he was as suspicious of democracy as he was of the power of mass opinion, both of which he thought had the tendency to invade personal life. He also feared their inclination towards mediocrity, as well as their potential to constrict individuality, from which he believed all progress stemmed. This is the wider context in which Mill's views on the individual must be seen. To this should be added the moral background, just as relevant as in Adam Smith's day. Mill emphasized the wisdom and nobility which exceptional individuals can provide, but thought it the function of government to help them to achieve their potential. And *...it is only the cultivation of individuality which produces, or can produce, well-developed human beings.*[7] Here education was vitally important to him, but he also had faith in the positive effects of voluntary co-operation, and believed in morality as a vital part of a social life where minds are receptive to improvement. His essay *Utilitarianism* is evidence of Mill's belief that morality is bound up with personal happiness; he devotes considerable space to a discussion of virtue, showing how it is inextricably linked to individual fulfilment.[8]

The first half of the 20th century saw alternating periods of austerity and laxity. World wars and depression were followed by attempts, particularly among the young, to break out, express themselves, and show rejection of the conservative traditions of their parents' generation. This was especially true of the period after 1945, when rationing and self-denial, coupled with patrician, mainly Conservative government, exerted a stifling hold on British society, in the shadow of the Cold War. But by the late 1950s, and bolstered by better economic times ushering in greater disposable income, there developed a youthful opposition to the traditions of shared purpose and consensus which their elders had thought best for Britain. Moreover, the rebellious movements of the 1960s which led the way were essentially individualistic, and mostly on the Left. They may have been mobilized in groups – of students or union members – but they asserted the needs, and especially the rights, of each individual. The 'doing your own thing' of 1960s' youth was inherently a private, personal objective, but with implications of a very politicized nature. *The politics of the '60s thus developed into an aggregation of individual claims upon society and the state,* was how Tony Judt summed it up. And *...however legitimate the claims of individuals and the importance of their rights, emphasizing these carries an unavoidable cost: the decline of a shared sense of purpose.*[9] Therefore there was a sense in which the ground was being prepared, unwittingly, for the neo-liberal project, for *...the subjectivism of private – and privately-measured – interest and desire.*[10] And ironically the then New Left was an involuntary accomplice in the subversive scheme.

In spite of the distance travelled from the concept of the individual in feudal times to the way it was viewed by Victorians, and by early 20th-century Britain, it is clear that both ends of that spectrum, as well as all stages in between, represented a distinct conceptual contrast from how we see the matter today. Since the birth of neo-liberalism in the late 1970s, a slimmed-down version of individualism has developed, with a sharp, relentless focus on personal autonomy and satisfaction. One can detect its resemblance to Victorian concepts of the individual, but is now almost entirely shorn of the moral ingredient, and has lost any element which looks to social improvement; indeed, now it is practically an idea of self without social responsibility. Thus the individual has been completely emancipated, has come of age in an era where economics holds sway, so that individualism assumes a largely economic role in a society in thrall to consumerism. Of course, there are other aspects to self, especially of a psychological kind. In a world dominated by the legacy of Sigmund Freud, for example, it is popularly thought unhealthy to inhibit the individualistic drive; repression and self-denial are no longer worthy of esteem. So free rein must be afforded to so-called *homo economicus* in order that its full potential may be realized, regardless of what *...wise or noble things...* may or may not flow from it to the benefit of wider society. Such nebulous, indirect side-effects are almost entirely incidental, in spite of what the apologists for neo-liberalism

THE INDIVIDUAL AND THE COMMUNITY

may claim. Thus present-day individualism stands alone, with limited context and few responsibilities except to self – a state perfectly corresponding to Durkheim's *anomie*.

Of course, society does not appear, from within, to be as desolate as this description would indicate. After all, in today's developed economies it is the new normal, our present-day *...way of looking at the world...* For many people in this new century, they have known no other. Our take on the individual appears to fit comfortably with our view of freedom, that panacea, goal of oppressed and marginalized peoples throughout the globe, all seemingly desperate to emulate the societies of the rich, developed, *free* world. And this whole mindset has stored within it such optimism, that any unfortunate side-effects of individualism are unlikely to be blamed on its singular culture, or attributed to systemic weaknesses in its architecture. No, they are much more likely to be put down to our own personal shortcomings; we are evidently unable to live up to its expectations, and since we are separate and alone, how can we possibly blame anyone but ourselves? We may not take any responsibility for others, but we are left with no option other than to accept full responsibility for what happens to ourselves. This is the kind of individualism towards which developed nations have been steadily moving, and which developing economies appear desperate to emulate; it is the new modernity, the new truth which *...most people can't help thinking must be true.*

Such a concept of the individual is not without antecedents, we are mistakenly assured. It is simply a revival of classical liberalism of the 18th century, made prominent by the writings of Adam Smith and other luminaries of the Scottish Enlightenment. Ever since the 1970s, when Keith Joseph found the ear of Margaret Thatcher and provided ideological justification for her untutored instincts, Smith's principles of classical economics have been used to corroborate the modern *neo-liberal* version of free market capitalism – and by extension, of today's individualism. Thus, we are given to understand that this is nothing new; approbation has been conferred on it by one of the *greats* of Britain's progressive Enlightenment. And did he not promote and justify self-interest?

> *It is not from the benevolence of the butcher, the brewer, or the baker that we expect our dinner, but from their regard to their*

own interest. We address ourselves, not to their humanity but to their self-love.[11]

Of course this – yet again – is all about appearance. Once the appropriate context (outlined above) has been provided for this expression of 18th-century values, it can be appreciated in its proper light. But this exercise would not suit the proponents of today's individualism. They are content to peddle this bogus version of historical validation to suit the materialistic objectives of their own vested interests. Thus a set of two hundred year old principles has been seized upon and given a new lease of life in an age dramatically different from the 18th century when they were first propounded.

None of this alters the fact that at the coal face of social life there is an abiding attempt to conduct personal relations in an altogether different way. There is an understanding that self-interest is far from being the only human motivation that matters; it may be important, but there are so many others. Ha-Joon Chang, in his revealing *23 Things They Don't Tell You about Capitalism*, gives us the definitive catalogue of drivers of our behaviours: ...*honesty, self-respect, altruism, love, sympathy, faith, sense of duty, solidarity, loyalty, public-spiritedness, patriotism*[12]... as if – underneath – we weren't fully aware of these. But in this post-modern age we are implicitly encouraged to believe that the majority of these are secondary values, mostly subservient to our principal *raisons d'être*. So much wool has been pulled over our eyes that we are tempted to accept the propaganda that our individual freedom need not be constrained, nor encumbered by weights of loyalty, nostalgia or tradition – sentiments of a bygone age which we should have grown out of. These subversive messages have worked their way on traditional values so that they have become almost normalized. Their insidious attraction has won the hearts of many, who in addition see them adopted by the influential opinion-formers of the day. Thus a whole layer of attitudes helps to conceal the previous normality, and any doubts harboured that the new cannot represent our true humanity are answered by vacuous slogans of choice, rights and freedom – as if these had repercussions on nothing and nobody.

Another problematic aspect of individualism is the way it relates to community. While most politicians and administrators subscribe to the warm words of community values, they mostly do not prioritise them as policy objectives; they are seen as the incidental combined results of individual aspirations, the aggregate coming together of what we want for ourselves. The understanding is that if the interests of the individual are ministered to, then those of the community will take care of themselves. There is – or at least there traditionally has been – no sense in which the well-being of community and that of the individual stand in opposition to each other. But the unscrupulous stimulation of the individualistic spirit over recent decades has left community in antagonism to it, as if it were a restraint on its freedom of action. So there can be a tendency for the two to be separated in the public mind, almost as opposites, one a hindrance to the other. This is part of the rationale for Margaret Thatcher's comment that there is no such thing as society – which she would have seen as coterminous with community. The conceptual separation of individual from community then allows them to be viewed as alternatives, as different starting points for social policy, instead of inseparable facets of human existence. Emphasising the importance of community does not deny individuality, any more than recognising distinctive individual worth is a rejection of the community from which it springs. In fact, community is more than the sum of its parts, and exclusively promoting the concerns of the individual may be to the detriment of the community as a whole. And as will be seen later, there are even situations in which serving the wider interests of community can redound to the greater benefit of the individual – a seeming paradox to our myopic age.

This placing apart of community and the individual – the interests of one in apparent opposition to those of the other – is thus a new phenomenon. No such dichotomy would have been recognized when original classical liberalism was being developed in the 18th century. Some of the explanation for this has already been outlined, but a crucial element is the new understanding of individualism. Over recent generations it has become such a powerful force that to stand in its way is to be accused of being against progress – although what one may need to stand against today is rather different from the British individualistic spirit of earlier times. The social liberalism of John Stuart Mill, for example, would certainly not have defended a liberty which exerted its autonomy at the expense of others. Neither during Mill's time nor earlier did individualism imply the untrammeled right to anything within the law, and as George Orwell once pointed out, the common acceptance of the liberty of the individual had nothing to do with the right to exploit others for profit.[13] And of course the search for personal fulfillment, such as it was, would never have been seen as principally a matter of choice. The new interpretations in this field coincide with today's mass consumer society and were promoted by the political agenda of the 1980s, now subsumed into an early 21st-century neo-liberal doctrinal amalgam to which almost all British political parties subscribe. Those who stand against it are thought political deviants, tarred with the brush of failed socialist policies – an even easier target since the collapse of European state communism.

However, the modern version of individualism represents a false ideology; it constitutes important misunderstandings as to the nature of individuality. The 20th century witnessed a progressive loosening of inhibitions on individual autonomy in social and moral areas. Meanwhile, there developed greater constraints in the form of increasing management of the economic life of industrial nations, in a complex, interdependent world; there was a burgeoning of rules and regulations. In this context it is fanciful, and largely irrelevant, to promote greater freedom of the individual as if the world still existed in some 18th-century material paradise – pre- collectivist fall. This is not to argue for state planning of economies, or indeed for wider limits on individual freedom, but simply to recognize the complex social and economic system which advanced industrial nations have developed. As Geoff Hodgson has pointed out,

> *The individualistic approach of classical liberalism is very unsatisfactory in that it has little conception of society as a system, except as a mere aggregate of individual components.*[14]

One must also stress that in the system's contemporary phase the decisions of an individual hold widening implications for society as a whole, and further choices made in the expectation of personal advantage may sometimes rebound to the distinct disadvantage of the individuals concerned, as will later be shown. However, the modern age has been persuaded to see the economic benefits to the individual of a strident free market capitalism, seemingly unaware that it is in the interests of such a system that society be fragmented into a collection of separate human entities, amenable to corporate marketising and advertising in a world of dominant consumerism. Collective or communal concerns are merely restrictive, attenuating forces in this context.

So a partial and misleading version of the individual has been promoted, encouraging one to be seen as separate from community, and all the better for it. This is part of a set of flawed premises which has formed the basis of neo-liberal, once termed New Right theory, but now integrated into the assumptions of most of the social democratic left. But in spite of the pervasiveness of this mode of thought, it represents a grossly mistaken view as to the nature of individuality. Human beings cannot be seen as autonomous creatures with entirely self-contained preferences. Our being, purposes and actions are created socially through others. And as David Marquand stresses, real people in real societies are social creatures ...*genetically programmed for sociability*.[15] Herman Daly and John Cobb, in a study of economics and community from an American perspective, also sees the individual as a social product.[16] We all come into being socially, they say, even though we have some capacity to constitute ourselves, so that we are something more than social creatures. But, ...*what more we are also depends on the character of* [our] *societies. The social character of human existence is primary.*[17] Daly sees this as representing the world of *homo sapiens* as it truly exists, in contrast to the theoretical model inhabited by what he calls *homo economicus*. *Homo economicus* behaves according to economics textbooks and differs in many vital respects from ordinary human beings, particularly in her extreme individualism. Nevertheless, the effect of political agendas over recent years – some would even say a hidden agenda – has been to weaken social and communal relations and to advance the divisive individualism to which their theories subscribe.

One aspect of this mindset – for it is a binding, implicit assumption – is the supposed sanctity of individual choice. This way of thinking does no justice to the liberal tradition, for it views individuals as entirely autonomous, self-directed beings with innate, unconnected preferences. It ignores the inescapable social nature of individuality which, as Geoff Hodgson has shown, was evident even to earlier neo-classicists such as Alfred Marshall. As individuals,

> ....*we do not exist simply alongside and <u>with</u> others; our being, purposes and action are created socially <u>through</u> others.... We perceive much of the world through language and symbols that have no meaning in an individual sense: they are purely social.*[18]

Hodgson goes on to show how this, of course, goes much deeper than the effect of advertising which, he maintains, ...*merely makes the social character of wants more obvious*.... He continues,

> ....*choice and preference do not simply become social through the existence of mass media advertising: they are social as a consequence of the social character of individuality itself.*[19]

He concludes that what was once called the New Right have basic flaws in their conception of the individual, flaws still evident, which have been accommodated by much of the political spectrum. It is vital to make clear, as Hodgson does, that none of this indicates that ultimate answers lie with governments or planners as such.

> *The fact that individuals are fundamentally social does not imply a dissolution of individuality itself, nor the absolute supremacy of a party, government or state.*[20]

However, it does mean that any discussion of markets, consumers and choice must be predicated on the understanding that individuals are not entirely atomised beings travelling light through an economic wonderland, hampered only by the extent of their means. They carry with them the full weight of their socialisation, which has already conditioned their perception of the world, their values and purposes, and even knowledge itself. Thus, freedom of choice exists only in a more limited sense, and as such is a fraudulent rallying cry for neo-liberalism or any other politics.

None of this can be fully recognized while the developed world sees society through the veil of individualism. For this is the established dogma, the frame of reference with which we think, a perspective which seems right and proper and emancipating. It is almost like a pair of black and white interlocking silhouettes; we have become so accustomed to accepting the bold outline of one of them, that the other – its mirror image, there before our eyes but unrecognized – cannot be seen. Thus collectivism does not, in any of its forms, present itself as the necessary corollary to what we see around us; quite the contrary, it is the subversive face of the enemy of the prevalent ideology. It is seen as the *other*, which would undermine our progress and devitalize individual resolve. This accords with the tenor of British life on its public, *macro* level, one which celebrates an adversarial environment in politics and business. Competition is thought to bring out the best in people in the political and economic cut and thrust, as if it were a form of organized sport, a *zero-sum* game in which winners and losers alike go home fulfilled by having taken part, with no serious impact on daily living. So the separate voter or consumer has become the standard by which – in this land of statistics and league tables – success is measured and judged. The model is one where efforts are directed towards the individual, not the community; authorities have no way of focusing on the collective, no understanding of how to deal with communal issues, except as they relate to the aggregate of isolated citizens. Their only recourse is to try to satisfy the individual, with the oblique expectation of thereby meeting the needs of society at large.

These relationships are only vaguely appreciated, dimly taken in by our peripheral vision. If at all understood by political leaders they will be studiously ignored, belief in the sanctity of the individual overriding everything; there is a pathological objection to recognizing the aggregate community which these individuals embody. Meanwhile, the *person-in-community* as a single entity, caught up in the urgent demands of small decisions, is not equipped to take responsibility for the wider association in society. In fact, there is the explicit and implicit message that this is in any case unnecessary; the community will benefit from the individual's enhanced autonomy and affluence, it is suggested by all brands of political dogma. And the criteria by which the individualistic model of economic and political theory is judged are particularly selective. Communal relationships do not figure in the indices of measurement issued by government, even though the pattern of those relationships is disrupted by the effects of government policy. If children's lives are restricted by the growth of traffic, or if a small community loses its local bus service or sees the closure of its school, these may actually feature in official statistics as increases in the standard of living or improvements in efficiency. The health of communities is beyond the intellectual reach of much political theory here. And, as Herman Daly has put it,

> *Since relationships among human beings are not part of the model with which the theory begins, the damaging of these relationships*

> is not signaled by the theory. The destruction of existing societies does not count against the success of policies designed to increase aggregate goods and services.[21]

For in a political and social climate where the philosophy of *more* is propounded more convincingly than that of *better*, any social dislocation is usually taken as an unfortunately painful but unavoidable side-effect of something called *progress*.

Of course, many proponents of unhindered individualism, unaware of the contradictions of their position, still look to have the best of both worlds, expecting their strident demands to have no adverse effect on communal life. Some, also ignorant of the incompatibility of their views, see community as subsidiary, something for others, provided that they themselves are left alone to follow their self-absorbed paths. Both courses are movements away from the real world and would ultimately benefit neither the individual nor the community. As Lester Thurow observed some years ago,

> *Societies are not merely statistical aggregations of individuals engaged in voluntary exchange, but something much more subtle and complicated. A group or community cannot be understood if the unit of analysis is the individual taken by himself.*[22]

This was recognized before the rise to prominence of neo-liberal government policies, but in the economic resurgence of the 1980s its common sense was overlooked, or denigrated as old-fashioned, un-modern. And now over thirty years later it has still not been properly reinstated. There still prevails the delusion that by serving the apparent needs of the individual, wider society will ultimately benefit. Adam Smith's so-called *invisible hand* has to accept much responsibility here: the idea that unintended social benefits will flow from self-interested actions. It has taken on a hallowed sanctity by neo-liberals and free marketeers who appear to think it applies now just as it was claimed to do in the 18th century. But as with so many aspects of the modern world, things are not what they seem.

Times have changed and economies have been transformed. In today's complex, technological and interdependent society the very opposite of the *invisible hand* thesis is frequently the case. An obvious example of where this would apply is the area of climate and the environment.

No-one seriously expects that air quality or global warming can be addressed by individual action. These are issues where co-ordination of policies is the only remedy, but a co-ordination which – in the case of climate change – must be contrived not merely at national but at international level. The world is moving closer to implicit acceptance of the idea of joint, mutual responsibility for policies which affect most nations to varying degrees, regardless of levels of wealth or extent of economic development. Thus, by the time the Paris Agreement on climate change came into force in November 2016, 169 states out of the 197 *Parties to the Convention* had ratified it, signaling common cause to limit the effects of global warming. It is patently evident to most – except perhaps to a minority of errant governments like that of Trump in the United States – that progress in this area will be achieved only through joint programmes. Individual initiative or entrepreneurship have no place here unless agreed on a global scale. In the case of the United States, policy was until recently firmly trapped within neo-liberal ideology, and the obsession with individualism and the abhorrence of regulation continue to obscure realities for millions of its population – realities accepted elsewhere.

A more parochial example of the limited application of the *invisible hand* theory would be in transport. In spite of its gradual clogging up of the British road system, the motor car is still widely accepted overall as a liberating force in modern society, as well as being for many – especially in rural areas – an absolute necessity. The majority of car users will no doubt feel that its benefits, even in diminishing returns, still outweigh the disadvantages. They well know that the problems of noise and exhaust pollution are mostly beyond their control, and will persuade themselves that in any case these will be dealt with by official policy and technological progress; they can only concern themselves with their own personal needs, fully aware of the limited effectiveness of individual decision making on the wider picture. As a Labour minister once observed, more and more people may choose to travel by car, and yet none of them chooses congested streets or polluted cities. In this example of the apparent free market in action, the sum total of individual preferences can result in an outcome that nobody chooses.[23] The supply of urban, or even rural roads cannot be indefinitely increased to meet expanding demand, while economic growth will, if anything, only exacerbate the problems. And above all, individuals with greater economic means at their disposal cannot influence matters; there is no equivalent of club class on British motorways! Only communal consensus and political action can have a positive impact in this area. The late Fred Hirsch, in a seminal study more than a generation ago, summed it up as follows: *Rather than pursuit of self-interest contributing to the social good, pursuit of the social good contributes to the satisfaction of self-interest*[24] – the very antithesis of classical economic theory.

However, these realities are not seen. The preoccupation with individualism has cast a shadow over community, so that its essence and its benefits are often not appreciated. This is a strange anomaly, since almost all of us are constituents of multiple communities. A person, after all, has many roles: member of a family or families, employee or employer, citizen of a state, resident of a local community, possibly parishioner of a church, member of a sports club or cultural group, perhaps voluntary worker – among others. The self-interested behaviour of Herman Daly's *homo economicus* does not correspond to the real-life situation of most of these roles, and in those where it has a part to play it is combined with many other feelings and motives to produce the ambiguous, conflicting stuff of ordinary existence. Economic man, as Daly points out, finds it hard even to conceive of a collective good. To provide a more realistic picture of the individual in society Daly proposes *person-in-community* as a more appropriate concept.[25] He seeks to reflect the fact that the economic system is part of the network of social, communal relations, and not vice versa, and he succeeds in presenting a picture of modern man which is far more down-to-earth than either autonomous *homo economicus* or socialist citizen in submission to state power. So much of our daily intercourse is involved with community relationships of varying kinds, and our natural affinities lead us towards mutually sustainable groupings. But all of this appears bypassed, or subordinated, by emphasis on the individual and her – limited – material objectives.

Community is in many respects family writ large. The strings which bind people in a community are the equivalent of those which link members of a family. An individual may leave either, but in doing so relinquishes something of himself or herself in the process. And the deeper the roots, the more that will be left behind when ties are broken. An individual born into a family or a community gradually forms a web of connections which are organic, not principally a matter of predilection; a child does not choose its home. Later, the choice of dwelling or workplace will influence, but not wholly determine the pattern of relationships that are formed with the local community. The village, estate, office or factory where an incomer or family settles can be evolutionary starting points for a network of communal bonds, developed not purely on the basis of self-interest, but out of an instinctive sharing of what is held in common. Whether in family or community, this is the essence of fellow-feeling. However, the communal spirit is not altruism as such, and neither can it be called selfish. David Marquand puts it as: *Communitarian loyalty is both stronger and narrower than this.*[26] Feelings of comradeship and loyalty are neither strictly self-centred nor high-minded and thus do not fit comfortably in modern economic thinking. For modern trends have assumed a *reductionist-individualist mode* of behaviour which has no way of adequately explaining community spirit. As Marquand has described, this mode ignores the three-dimensional self of the real world, a subjectivity formed by constant interaction with others, and replaces it by what he calls *the impermeable self*, which *can command, or obey, or exploit, or trade with other selves, but it cannot engage with them.*[27] The reductionist-individualist tradition which most politics today implicitly follows is both biased and incomplete, since it reflects only a narrow part of what we are.

The increasing emphasis over recent generations on purposeful individualism has thus been an important factor in the marginalizing of community in Britain. It so happens that neo-liberal economics is entirely comfortable with this development; the atomization of society is welcomed by its single-minded ideology, which sees enormous benefits accruing to social and corporate elites. In the United States, where emphasis on the individual has always been more conspicuous, matters appear to have gone a good deal further. There, under the philosophy of minimal government the public arena of infrastructure and welfare has already suffered greatly reduced funding, while the personal tax system has become more regressive, a situation which deteriorated further under the Trump administration. As the affluent have become richer, the poor – no longer concentrated mainly among the unemployed – have sunk further to form an underclass, a social feature which has since emerged in Britain. The effects of the 2007/08 financial crash in the UK and the consequent austerity were to exacerbate the marginalizing of community, heralding the abandonment of poorer individuals to their separate fates. The cuts in public spending disproportionately impacted lower socio-economic groups, which tend to rely more on the services of public provision. Whether it is the selling off of school playing fields or public parks (often of little concern to the better-off) or the closing of museums or municipal libraries, the shared, communal infrastructure is thus impoverished and the links which bind us are further weakened.

These changes were well documented a generation ago, the consequence of earlier economic developments. In one important study in the early '90s, even before the *dot-com* revolution, Professor Robert Reich, formerly President Clinton's Secretary for Labor, provided a detailed analysis of the socio-economic direction of travel.[28] He saw the higher professional and managerial groups in the USA – the decision-makers, then accounting for about 20% of jobs – going from strength to strength financially, and forming a kind of permanent elite in American society. Reich called this group *symbolic-analytic services*, their work consisting mainly of brokering and solving problems by manipulating symbols. The remainder of the workforce is made up of those involved in routine production, usually of a repetitive nature, and in person-to-person services in which pay is often a function of hours worked or amount completed.[29] These employees Reich saw as coming to form an excluded majority among which many poorer sub-classes were falling deeper into poverty, even though in work. Professor Reich's overall view was of First World societies in which symbolic analysts make up an international elite and have more in common with each other than they do with the lower forms of economic life in their respective countries. Almost 30 years on from Reich's study, this picture has become familiar, an acknowledged feature of today's world. However, these globalizing trends, encompassing the cross-border activities of transnational corporations and the free movement of executive labour, coupled with the neo-liberal policies of governments, have created a divisive social climate and a web of vested interests which have had significant effects on how we see the individual and community.

This picture of developments is very different from the future as seen from the perspective of the post-war period. In the 1950s there existed a consensus about common goals, in Britain as well as in the United States. Americans as a whole tacitly agreed on a national bargain in which government, consumers and large corporations co-operated in a joint strategy. It involved economic expansion which included reinvesting a good proportion of corporate revenues, restraint on prices and wages by the two sides of industry, and government assistance to smooth out business cycles and to provide the transport, education and housing infrastructure which the country's development required.[30] There was an unstated agreement that a measure of sacrifice of immediate gain would result in greatly enhanced benefits for all at a later date. This was similar to the *Butskellism* of 1950s Britain, where the ravages of war meant demands for even greater sacrifices. But in that environment there was a sense of working towards mutual goals in a national community which, whatever its divisions, held a common vision of the future. The neo-liberal onslaught of the 1980s, on both sides of the Atlantic, dealt severe blows to that vision, with the result that some parts of society have begun to see their future as entirely independent of others in the national community.

Robert Reich saw this phenomenon as already quite established in the USA by the early 1990s, but is even more prominent today. His *symbolic analysts* form a sub-community made up of citizens with incomes similar to their own, creating separate islands of affluence which are seen to have little to do with the rest of society. He viewed this class as accepting only a limited degree of civic responsibility, not seeing itself in the same boat as poorer people of the same country. As Reich said,

> *...symbolic analysts are quietly seceding from the large and diverse publics of America into homogeneous enclaves, within which their earnings need not be redistributed to people less fortunate than themselves.*[31]

Twenty years on from Reich's study the American sociologist Charles Murray, in his book *Coming Apart*, identified the same phenomenon, this time from the perspective of the post-crash United States.[32] He described the super-rich as a class apart, cut off from the accepted norms of American life and isolated in their gilded enclaves, which he called *super zips* – the richest post-code areas in the USA. Murray termed this class the *cognitive elite* who, through their family connections and the best education that money could buy for their children, were able to ensure continued dominance of the top professions and corporate institutions. And since the super-rich in America emerged even more wealthy after four years of recession, they have been able to maintain their hegemony and even enhance it.* As in Britain, the social mobility encompassed in the fabled American Dream is simply no more than that, a mirage holding a specious promise.

Whatever governments appeared to try to do during the financial crisis of 2008 to stave off economic Armageddon, none of it managed to share out the painful consequences of the bankers' disreputable operations. The plutocrats emerged from the wreckage largely scot-free, retaining their enormously privileged positions in their respective national economies, as separate as before from the rest of society. They are still just as likely to support the lowering of taxation, particularly income tax, which helps fund public facilities which they do not greatly use. On the other hand, they will tend to accept a level of local property taxes only to the extent that they derive a specific return in their own residential areas. One financier, said to be worth an estimated £500 million, confided to journalist Peter Oborne, *The only time I use the state is when my driver drives on public roads from the City to my country estate. I don't like it but I can't help it.*[34] This supremely affluent minority are content to fund their own services and activities – health, education, sporting – through user fees which benefit them through a direct return. Thus private clubs and associations are set up to provide exclusive facilities where this group can develop an increasingly separate identity; they can withdraw to their citadels of privilege, protected by their private guards and security systems, and fortified by their ideology of individualism and self-reliance. Meanwhile, the rest of society is encouraged to emulate their more affluent fellow-citizens but with less and less chance of being able to do so, while the communal arena of national life deteriorates as a result of a more limited tax base from which to fund its infrastructure – social and material.

Separation, moving apart, is the route to radical segregation. That is the direction of travel in which current social and economic developments are taking us – the *us* being developed economies, with developing ones not too far behind. While the power of the internet and all-pervasive social media claim to be making us more interconnected, bringing

---

* The top 1% – earning at least $394,000 a year – saw a rise in income of 31% between 2009 and 2012, while the income of the remaining 99% rose by barely 0.5%.[33]

individuals together, other more pernicious trends are splitting society along lines reminiscent of 18th-century Britain. The aristocrats of that era, secluded on their country estates or in city mansions, are today's plutocracy ensconsed in their gated communities, both with their domestic servants and hired help, and ferried around in luxurious isolation. Self-segregation of the rich – and not so rich – has been growing in both Britain and in the United States (where almost 20% of the population now live in gated communities). In the UK, numerous new gated housing complexes have sprung up, especially since 2000 and predominantly in south-east England, all with their electronic entry systems, CCTV, and often private security guards. Whether they call themselves *leisure communities*, with associated sports facilities, or *prestige developments* denoting luxury and exclusivity, they are designed to keep *the other* out. (Most residents cite greater security as the principal reason for their choice of home.) The privatisation of housing neighbourhoods may make sense to their owners, fearful of a turbulent world, but it represents the increasing fragmentation of society, principally on the basis of wealth, and will do nothing for social harmony or cohesion.

But as social friction and divisiveness have increased, attitudes to private and public space have changed, and the urge to withdraw from wider society has become commonplace. Now it is not just the well-off who aspire to exclusivity. While retirement complexes have been a feature of developed societies for many years, and *sheltered* accommodation has long been a sensible option for the elderly, the phenomenon of adults-only villages is now emerging. Developments restricted to residents over the age of 45, without children, have started to appear in Britain. Some are private ventures, while others have been built together with local authorities, and are not necessarily gated, but all are designed to exclude sections of society. Communities with limited cross-sections of the nation's population will be an attraction to some, but if pursued on a large scale will signify a break with the past, towards segregation and isolation. At least in Georgian Britain the different social classes lived side by side to a degree: ...*the lower classes still dwelled in the cottages between the vicarage and the manor house*... observed Ferdinand Mount, in spite of the ...*hauteur, resentment and condescension*...[35] which were prevalent. The increasing separation of classes in the modern age is in some respects even more pronounced; the servants of the rich certainly do not live such close, integrated lives with their employers as domestic servants would have done in former times. Today's trends denote new and significant changes, with broad implications.

The choices represented by some of these individual or family decisions might be seen as sensible personal options, appropriate to one's circumstances or to a particular stage in life. If they centre on choices about where to live, they may well not be conceptualized as issues of money or the market, but they cannot be separated from such. They happen to contribute to the further segregation of different parts of society, and by more than chance, to a demarcation largely on the basis of financial means, at the mercy of the market. This process accentuates the tendency for ...*people of affluence and people of modest means* (to) *lead increasingly separate lives*...[36] which, Michael Sandel concludes, is not a satisfying way to live. He explains his reasons:

> *Democracy does not require perfect equality, but it does require that citizens share in a common life. What matters is that people from different backgrounds and social positions encounter one another, and bump up against one another, in the course of everyday life. For this is how we learn to negotiate and abide our differences, and how we come to care for the common good.*[37]

This is the basis on which developed societies have long conducted their affairs, the default position for harmony and normal conviviality. However, this basis does not have behind it a body of ideology, one which permeates current developed societies to the point that it envelops them like a shroud. The individualistic ethic – though hardly ethical, of course – lies there in the background, implicitly inspiring our predilections and giving them an aura of modernity. So we move blindly on, choosing separateness, unconscious of our need for old-fashioned collective solutions, on the way to becoming ....*gated individuals who do not know how to share public space to common advantage.*[38]

From the perspective of the individual or family there can appear sound, *micro* arguments for the choices described above. And under neo-liberalism it is individual preference which will, it is said, see us to our destiny, as well as contributing to general well-being. But it is abundantly clear that it does not of necessity do that. If we, as separate entities, have the wherewithal to suit ourselves and do as we please, it may well have a distinctly negative effect on the community at large. Wealthy individuals putting their (apparently) hard-earned money into second homes in picturesque Cornish seaside villages, or in the leafy Cotswolds, may be seen to exercise rightful personal choices. But they cannot escape some of the unfortunate consequences their choices have on local communities: the higher house prices, restricting the ability of local people to buy in the area, or the *dark skies* effect of semi-deserted villages in winter. In examples like these, the merits of Adam Smith's *invisible hand* are hard to discern. In fact, of course, the reverse of his theory would be a more apposite interpretation; the interests of a wider cross section of individuals would be better served by communal management of the issue.* Such is the nature of today's intricate society that selfish, private preferences cannot simply be translated into public virtues. The complex interactions of daily life are not always amenable to market solutions; they must be distinguished from the economic sphere and dealt with accordingly. The ramifications of this idea will be discussed in more detail later.

The concept of communal decisions being taken in the interests of wider society, and its many individuals, does not only have to contend with ideological opposition; it is also circumscribed by money. Both these factors work against community during difficult economic times, when local and national government will often try to save money by restricting general access or by privatisation. Amenities not regarded as vital, so-called *frontline* services, previously free to the public but nevertheless incurring costs, are seen as easy targets. Thus school playing fields may be sold off, public parks privatised, libraries have their hours reduced, and previously public open spaces become restricted, private zones. Hard pressed local authorities had been selling off school playing fields for many years, in order to fund other educational improvements or plug gaps in their finances. When Labour got into government in 1997 there were hopes that the process would end, especially with Tony Blair's renowned focus on education. At the Labour Conference three years later he would announce extra funding for school sports facilities with the words, *This is not only a sports policy ...it is a health policy, an education policy, a crime policy, an anti-drugs policy.*[39] But as it turned out in subsequent years, it was not in practice a Labour policy; for the sell-off of playing fields continued, through the early 2000s and into the period of coalition government. In fact, the then Education Secretary

---

* As has been done in places such as St Ives in Cornwall and Lynton/Lynmouth in Devon, where new house purchase is now restricted to use as principal residence, and reserved exclusively for local people

Michael Gove even relaxed the regulations on this policy, thus allowing a further 118 schools to sell off their open spaces between 2010 and 2015,[40] largely against the advice of the School Playing Fields Advisory Panel.

The steady, piecemeal deterioration of school facilities which this represents will be mainly hidden from view, until a conspicuously notorious case hits the headlines. But this erosion of common patrimony not only undermines the statutory guidelines on recommended outside space for pupils; it will progressively prejudice the mass of individual children whose families do not have the resources to access private sports clubs. Furthermore, it is part of the wider trend of social infrastructure, previously held in common, being destroyed. Britain's public parks are currently facing threats not seen for generations, from spending cuts reducing expenditure on them,* to actually being sold off to developers. Green areas in towns and cities are an indispensable social amenity, the *lungs* of urban areas as they have been called. Their removal or privatisation fits an unhealthy common pattern, which now includes the selling of municipal space to private concerns; Liverpool, Bristol and Exeter have all experienced this *corporatisation*, in which development has resulted in shiny, sanitised streets and private concourses, with tight regulations and overseen by security guards. Funding cuts have also led some councils to sell off their *crown jewels:* the monuments to former civic pride in the shape of town halls and libraries, often fine, Victorian listed buildings but costly to maintain and repair.** All these features of municipal Britain, previously a visible part of the fabric of community, have been plundered in the interests of profit, while the common heritage of all citizens is steadily eroded – a trend which encapsulates the private affluence/public squalor which J. K. Galbraith wrote of in *The Affluent Society* all those years ago.

Some sections of society are attempting to counteract the trend of privatisation of public space, particularly in towns and cities, in order to make them more citizen-friendly. An attempt has been made to identify and log all privately owned public spaces (POPS), and the Ramblers Association is calling for all such spaces which come under private ownership or management to remain accessible to the public. Urban areas where people can walk and congregate enhance the common

---

* Bristol City Council has already announced that its expenditure on parks maintenance will be cut completely in 2019!
** Between 2010 and 2015 councils sold off land and property worth £10.6 billion.[41]

environment, as well as having well known health benefits. There is a recognised need for people to have more physical activity, but 'walkable' cities also create safer, more agreeable public areas which can improve social interaction. Recent developments have militated against such common sense, such as the creation in 2014 of Public Spaces Protection Orders (PSPOs), a geographically-centred version of ASBOs. These can be readily decreed by local councils in response to problems such as aggressive begging or excessive alcohol consumption in public areas. By 2016 reports indicated that 12 local authorities had prohibited loitering, or congregating in designated areas, while 11 had erected gates to close off public alleyways to pedestrians.[42] In the absence of sufficient police numbers to cope with anti-social behaviour, such measures are simply taking the cheapest, easiest way out. Apart from having an adverse impact on trading in town centres when footfall drops, they will also be to the detriment of the built environment, and to the common conviviality and sense of community which can otherwise flourish in it.

Our public inheritance is being squandered, sold off to meet the ephemeral demands of short-term exigencies, or degraded through misguided policy. We do not always realise the wealth being removed before our eyes, such is the piecemeal sleight of hand which is employed, to the plausible justification of bottom-line concerns. This gradual transfer of public wealth into private hands has been taking place progressively since the 1970s, and in many parts of the rich, developed world. In economic terms public capital has been whittled away, so that its ratio to national income has gradually reduced, the increase in the ratio of private capital to national income being its corollary. Whereas net public wealth in Britain represented around a quarter of total national wealth in the 1960s, today it stands at just a few percent; the value of private capital on the other hand has risen to levels equivalent to more than five times the national income.[43] This increase has been partly due to the wave of privatisation, initially promoted by the Conservatives in the 1980s, but later continued during New Labour's time in office. However, as Thomas Piketty has pointed out, it may be that the value of transfers of public wealth into private hands has been underestimated, particularly in view of the nature of the sell-off of large public firms in the '80s: *...privatisations that often involved notoriously low prices, which of course guaranteed that the policy would be popular with buyers.*[44] A similar strategy was adopted by the Tories with their sale of council houses, allowing them to go at prices well below market value.

Such is the profligacy of governments content to dismantle our common patrimony.

Concerns used to be expressed that private autonomy was threatened by an over-weening public sphere, that the individual was under siege from varying forms of authority. However, the opposite is the case, as the late Zygmunt Bauman emphasised some years ago: *...it is the private that colonizes the public space, squeezing out and chasing away everything which cannot be fully ...expressed in the vernacular of private concerns, worries and pursuits.*[45] He went on to say that public space is increasingly empty of public issues; for in this postmodern world there is little of value left to be mulled over, discussed and debated, since each has his/her own inviolate take on meaning, every one as valid as any other. The *agora* – which Bauman terms *...that intermediary, public/ private site where life-politics meets Politics with the capital p. ..*[46] – has given way to the marketplace. But whereas the former implies the potential for equal participation, the latter involves an entrenched demarcation of 'haves' – whether individual or corporate – and 'have-nots'. Thus the space for the concerned citizen is transformed into an arena for separate, self-absorbed consumers, all we are told masters of their fates. The myriad of phone-ins, talk shows and social internet platforms would appear to demonstrate a virtual, digital *agora*, but they mainly represent the unproductive froth of public whim, ineffectual and soon dissipated. The wider movements or campaigns which they occasionally generate may centre on popular social issues, but assuredly they will bypass the vital matters of money and power which lie out of reach of transient public opinion.

Another of the lenses through which we see – or think we see – society and the individuals of which it is composed is the area of personal responsibility, dependence and interdependence. We have grown accustomed to see the individual as the agent of accountability, the repository of ultimate liability where the buck must inevitably stop, while mutuality and dependence have assumed a distinctly negative gloss. If the life of an individual is an existential project, in which the course of her progress is almost entirely self-willed, and success or failure rests in his own hands alone, is it any wonder that interconnectedness is not celebrated? In such a world should we be surprised if dependence is denigrated, as if it were a sign that, out of inadequacy or laziness, we had not stepped up to the plate and done our bit? After all, how can responsibility reside anywhere but in us as separate individuals? But while this whole mindset may seem so right and natural in the framework of neo-liberal modernism, it of course makes no sense on a global scale. For, as Zygmunt Bauman put it, ...*contemporary drama is a humanity-wide production*.[47] Such is humankind's economic and technological hubris that our self-directed actions cannot be immune from their widespread, social, financial or environmental consequences. The fact is,

> ...*that all of us who share the planet depend on one another for our present and our future, that nothing we do or fail to do is indifferent to the fate of anybody else, and that no longer can any of us seek and find private shelter from storms that originate in any part of the globe.*[48]

Where is our autonomous individuality in this context?

Individualism is an ideological construct. As has already been shown, in its current form it is a fairly recent 'invention', and only emerged out of years of social and economic development. It is no more fixed in today's society than was the mutual interdependence of medieval feudalism, which itself lasted several centuries. In fact, for a time feudalism was a stable system of remarkable equilibrium in which – leaving aside what we would now regard as inequality – the three classes of nobility, clergy and peasantry coexisted in reciprocal interconnectedness. Each group relied on each other for their sustainability; no matter how hard the lives of the peasants, they were an indispensable element in society which neither of the others could do without. *A theory of mutual dependence held that the peasantry was no less vital and hence no less worthy of dignity than the nobility or clergy*, says Alain de Botton.[49] He justly emphasises the extent to which the poor were valued, and highlights the variety of commentators of the time who extolled their worthiness; one cleric, for example, pointed out that while society might be able to survive without nobility or clergy, it could not do so without the ploughman.[50] Pictorial representations of the three orders of society together, at the time, testify to the status which each enjoyed. The part played by the peasantry in the medieval economy was fully recognized, and accorded them a dignity which the modern working class struggles to earn, no matter how indispensable it may be to 21st-century society.* Our contemporary ideologies militate against acceptance of the interdependence of different groups in modern economies, in spite of the obvious affinities which bind them.

The rationale for the divisions in medieval society would have been plain to its members: God had sanctioned the arrangement, which suited His purpose. Of course, no such explanation serves to justify today's social disparities. No, we now have a different religious interpretation, masking itself as a modern progressive ideology, one in which interdependence is not valued. For the latter would appear to undermine personal autonomy, the theory which our political and economic system extols. There is no room left here for dependent relationships. Yet in an economy where there are a multitude of casualties, assistance is so often required to compensate for the harsh vagaries of normal existence, whether accidental or self-inflicted. The welfare system developed in the 20th century was recognition of the need for institutional support, which informal family or community resources were no longer able to provide. But as society has become more affluent, so the recipients of welfare provision have come to be seen less as deserving, and more as if they were personally responsible for their own misfortune and neediness. Thus – as Richard Sennett has pointed out in the American context – there is a new psychological relationship built into welfare systems in the western world which fails to treat welfare as a right.[51] He describes how in the United States, as time went on, an adversarial relationship developed when dealing with those in need: ...*as the country became richer, suspicion of those who remained poor increased.*[52] Thus respect diminished, regardless of the degree of indigence, as dependence became stigmatised.

It is as if the focus has now shifted from the adverse material circumstances which warrant support, onto the individual himself or herself. There is a tendency to assume that people's predicaments are a function of them as individuals, rather than being a result of inadvertently falling on hard times, perhaps through no fault of their own. Blame is attached

---

* Dignity is a quality which is insufficiently considered in modern society, and yet, significantly, Article 1 of the Universal Declaration of Human Rights, adopted by the United Nations in 1948, refers to human beings born free and equal ...*in dignity and rights.*

to them as agents of their own misfortune, instead of to their circumstances. *They are being judged as whole human beings...* says Sennett.[53] As welfare budgets have increased to meet burgeoning need, at a time of dramatically changing demographics, there has been greater urgency on the part of governments to limit expenditure. Thus the idea of dependence has become a target in itself, as if once people tackled their apparent over-reliance on state assistance all would be well. This political re-positioning is an attempt to change the debate, an oblique way – especially on the ideological right – of blaming the individual for what is always suspected as being foot-dragging recalcitrance. At the same time, attention can be conveniently deflected from the invidious circumstances of poverty, homelessness, disability, low pay, or the effects of financial cuts at a time of austerity. But even if the individual takes on full accountability, it does not mean that due respect is accorded to him or her, negotiating the bureaucratic labyrinth in an effort to access merited welfare payments. There is ample evidence of the demeaning experiences of those at the receiving end of state provision, as well as of the reluctance of many to undergo the indignities involved in applying for what they are due.

This is a far cry from an earlier era of hardship, the 1930s, when the welfare system was in its infancy, though poverty and destitution deeper and more widespread. Cynicism about the motives of welfare recipients had not yet developed, and there was an acknowledgement of the need to respect their dignity, while responding to obviously desperate need. John Maynard Keynes was one who saw that individual autonomy should not be eroded while receiving state handouts: Richard Sennett quotes Keynes' words of 1939, describing his view of a welfare system created *...to promote social and economic justice whilst respecting and protecting the individual – his freedom of choice, his faith, his mind and its expression, his enterprise and his property.*[54] Today, choice and autonomy have all but been removed from the benefits recipient, who is then asked to take responsibility for the dependence to which he/she is consigned. Furthermore, in the punitive atmosphere of the modern Anglo-Saxon welfare state, questions are frequently asked about what benefits recipients have contributed to warrant state handouts, as if not having paid to help construct the safety net made one ineligible to be saved by it. And it is significant that those posing these questions would by and large be those in society who could never imagine themselves needing this form of state assistance, which would be called on by 'the others', in this divided and unequal polity. Under neo-liberalism the individual is upheld as the ultimate agent of personal responsibility, free and emancipated, but if one lacks the vital qualifications of affluence and self-reliance then individualism is vitiated, autonomy undermined, and dignity threatened.

The perception of the kind of society we inhabit conditions the manner in which we engage with it. The myth of the coming together of the disparate elements of British society in the dark days of World War Two has had an enduring influence. The time was renowned for the social cohesion which encompassed an 'all-in-it-together' approach usually absent at less critical periods of our history. With victory the eventual outcome, this version of social solidarity has become a convincing part of national folklore, in spite of an element of self-deception in the myth. But even if the reality of that era did not entirely match the lasting perception, there was a vital unifying process in which the national cause comprehensively overshadowed the smaller concerns of the individual. The triumph of the social solidarity of the 1940s, which continued into the post-war years, was that it took in virtually the whole national community, in a manner which is usually discernible only at transcendental moments. The working classes had been a vital part of the national effort in two world wars and shared in the optimism and expectation for major social reconstruction after 1945. And there was an underlying agreement by government and the labour movement, ...*that it was unacceptable for gross material and social deprivations to exist when an unconditional commitment was being demanded to defend the nation at war.*[55] As A. J. P. Taylor observed of the post-war situation, *The governing classes were on their best behaviour, from conviction as well as calculation.*[56] The equivalent today might be the rallying round prompted by the Coronavirus pandemic, a national calamity affecting those of all social levels – though certainly not equally.

Yet periodically official attempts are made to reconstitute the social unity and togetherness of former times. The most recent serious example – part of the programme of the coalition government – was the *Big Society* idea of David Cameron. Its stated aims were to promote more community participation, return power from central to local government, and expand the scope of the voluntary sector. When launched in Liverpool in 2010, Cameron's flagship project was accompanied by the claims that ...*Only when people and communities are given more power and take more responsibility can we achieve fairness and opportunity for all...* and included the familiar mantra ...*we are all in this together.*[57] The tasks involved in this ambitious scheme were the responsibility not just of government departments, but ...*of every citizen too...* stated the launch paper. One does not have to doubt David Cameron's sincerity to imagine that, though such a policy might be offered as evidence of caring government, it would be seen as mere window dressing, especially in the context of stringent budget cuts wreaking havoc on individuals and communities whose autonomy was rapidly draining away. Then in 2017 Theresa May came out with her version of communal solidarity: *a shared society for everyone.* But few people – especially those in need of the practical assistance of real support – truly believe the rhetoric of such Conservative slogans, which are hardly likely to compensate for years of policy which has undermined cohesiveness and ingrained negative perceptions.

Woolly strategies with pretentious titles have been initiatives offered by governments of all complexions, anxious to appear modern and garner popular appeal. However, most of them accomplish little in the cause of social inclusion or communal solidarity. They are usually top-down programmes trying to give an impression of bottom-up involvement and participation. Such was the case with John Major's 'Citizen's Charter' in the '90s, promoted with the idea of empowering citizens – but, significantly, as individual consumers rather than as stakeholders in democracy. With the aim of improving the quality of public services, and providing value for money for taxpayers, the emphasis was inevitably on delivery, from above, with little focus on the public itself or with added legal entitlement for its members. Better accountability does not necessarily improve access or promote inclusion. Similar criticisms can be levelled at Tony Blair's *stakeholder capitalism*, part of the specious branding of New Labour after 1997. That particular scheme also put emphasis on the economic autonomy of consumers and shareholders, with no hint of any enhancement of social rights or extension of agency. For those on the margins of society, for the excluded, and even for many of the 'just about managing', these projects are simply theoretical niceties with little relevance. No matter how much gloss is applied to such political stratagems, most know that they do nothing for the dubious relationship between the individual and society.

Much of this was highlighted a generation ago, as was the idea that citizenship should involve a social, as well as a civil and political status. At the time of New Labour's first election victory, David Marquand cited the earlier Social Democrat position, a view which politicians still struggle to come to terms with today: *A democracy confined to the political sphere, they insisted, was no democracy. It had to embrace the social sphere as well: citizenship was indivisible.*[58] A mature democracy has to take in a form of civic inclusion that takes precedence over economic concerns, and must involve parity of dignity and status, as well as of those basic requirements of life which an affluent society has come to expect. This is the only route to greater inclusion and citizen empowerment, which politicians often speak of, but which their policies implicitly disavow. To make citizenship fully democratic, status should be reinforced independently of the constraints of the money economy. This is not to call for equality of affluence, though it must involve some financial improvement for those most prejudiced by the financial crash. But to raise the standing of the marginalized and excluded requires social emancipation in the context of discernible respect. David Marquand's comment of twenty years ago is just as relevant today: ministers *....think that citizen empowerment can go hand in hand with continued worker disempowerment.*[59] Conservative ministers also appear to believe that it can go hand in hand with cuts in welfare payments, punitive fiscal and monetary policy, and a fully flexible labour market in a global context.

The references to empowerment and inclusion lead on to discussion of the *social state*. When William Beveridge produced his report on social insurance in 1942, his vision was of a social security system for everyone, so that no-one would be allowed to fall below a minimum standard of living. While his recommendations were intended to safeguard material standards, as well as help British industry by cutting company costs, much of the inspiration for his ideas was based on social justice, of the most inclusive kind. *A state is 'social' when it promotes the principle of <u>communally endorsed</u>, collective insurance against individual misfortune and its consequences...* (author's emphasis) was Zygmunt Bauman's interpretation of Beveridge's vision.[60] Such a collective insurance can constitute a profound source of solidarity and contribute to *...a common good, shared, communally owned, and jointly cared for, thanks to the defence it provides against the twin horrors of misery and indignity...*[61] This kind of society necessarily involves commitment, mutual trust, and reciprocal dependence, from all of which derives a sense of belonging. As Bauman put it, *The social state is the ultimate modern embodiment of the idea of community...*[62] and in such circumstances the abrupt divide between the narrow interests of the individual and those of society is bridged by a recognition of an identity of purpose, in spite of material differences between citizens. In this scenario the consent of the governed becomes real and active; strength is gained by true inclusiveness.

This description will appear, to many, to be light years away from Britain as it has developed in recent times. The *social state* has been giving way to a society of 'them and us', to a punitive regime where monitoring and control have increased to meet the dangers we are led to believe are lurking everywhere, and security has taken priority over analysis or compassion. Total responsibility is thrown back onto each one of us. For as the complex infrastructure of the social state is gradually emasculated, its values undermined, so the individual becomes increasingly isolated and set adrift. Consoled by our faith in individualism, the message says, we are autonomous and invested with the freedom to choose our own paths; no excuses are accepted for our failure to take our opportunities, while complaints are seen as subversive threats. In this atomised environment policies of austerity are championed as proof of political virility, welfare cuts damaging society's most vulnerable are justified on the grounds of saving the national bacon, and tax cuts for high earners explained by recourse to the discredited *trickle-down* theory. These are the harsh realities of recent Britain: all necessitated by the effects of the financial crash, we are told, but conveniently allowing the Conservatives to follow their instincts and proceed with shrinking the state.*

As holes in the threadbare social safety net grow ever more visible, so do the dangers of a judicial system subject to financial cuts and damaging reorganisation. But even while police numbers are reduced, the probation service reconstituted, and the prison estate in crisis, the emphasis is nevertheless on a disciplinary regime, the *penal mode* as David Garland and others have termed it.[63] In this environment the spotlight is turned on security, while the earlier *welfare mode* of society becomes *...more conditional, more offence-centred, more risk conscious*[64]*...* In such circumstances both locally-generated anti-social

---

* According to Ann Pettifor, during George Osborne's time as Chancellor total managed expenditure was cut by £14 billion in real terms (2016-17 prices), exacerbated by the 3-4% rise in population, which itself was facing greater demands because of ageing.

behaviour and the threat of Islamic terrorism play into the hands of authority which, thus emboldened, feels free to extend surveillance in order to target the enemies amongst us. (These are variously said to be social security skivers, football hooligans, or disaffected youth attracted by the allure of jihadism.) Any and all of these are after all culpable, are they not, for our collective woes? The more that government can direct blame onto minorities – on *the other* around us – the greater is their freedom to call on the resources of the state to vilify and exclude, even if ostensibly to protect. Thus mental health sufferers in police cells, welfare claimants penalised for arriving late for Job Centre interviews, semi-literate petty criminals unable to access proper education or rehabilitation in prison – these are evidence of a state abdicating its responsibility to the community. The irony lost on its rulers is that supporting communities would help to bolster the rights of the individual citizen, which their ideology so reverently extols.

Another dubious myth which has increasingly clouded judgement over the last generation is the relationship between successful entrepreneurs and society at large. It is often held that these business leaders are the economy's key wealth creators, the providers of employment, whose genius drives social and material advance. We are encouraged to see them as heroes to whom we are all indebted, and without whom life for all would be so much poorer; this has become an accepted commonplace. These stars of the economic firmament must be protected, not exploited, overtaxed or frightened off, so that we can continue to benefit from their unique talents. In realty, as Cambridge economist Ha-Joon Chang says, ...*our view of entrepreneurship is too much tinged by the individualistic perspective.... In the course of capitalistic development, entrepreneurship has become an increasingly collective endeavour.*[65] But the vision of the exceptional individual, whose determination and special ability are not given to ordinary mortals, goes hand in hand, paradoxically, with the notion that we can all aspire to such heights if only we work hard enough – a vital element of the American Dream. What is excluded from the stereotype is any consideration of the whole social and scientific infrastructure which lies behind individual success. Ha-Joon Chang enumerates the collective institutions whose support entrepreneurs benefit from: the educational system, company and commercial law, a financial system enabling business people to raise capital, patent and copyright law protecting inventions, and an accessible market for their products.[66] Where would successful entrepreneurs be without these vital enabling factors of a modern economy?

The idea of the entirely autonomous entrepreneur is nevertheless ingrained in our culture, or more especially in that of the so-called *Anglo-sphere*, no matter how shaky the notion may be. A more considered approach reveals that the community around us plays a crucial part in our individual development, regardless of the life choices we make. *We are all the beneficiaries of those who went before us*, observed the late Tony Judt. But, emphasising our collective needs and responsibilities, he went on *....as well as those who will care for us in old age or ill health. We all depend upon services whose costs we share with our fellow citizens, however selfishly we conduct our economic lives.*[67] When it comes down to it, we know these to be basic truths, even if we are captivated by the romance of the idea of the untutored but charismatic individual who rises from humble beginnings to achieve great wealth and pre-eminence. And, tellingly, successful entrepreneurs themselves are conscious of the debt they owe to society around them. American business magnate Warren Buffett speaks for many when he says, *Society is responsible for a very significant percentage of what I've earned. I really wouldn't have made a difference if I were born in Bangladesh. Or if I was born here in 1700... I just got lucky as hell...*[68] Bill Gates is another hugely successful entrepreneur whose modesty recognizes the collective legacy of a mature advanced industrial society:

> *Success is a product of having been born in this country, a place where education and research are subsidised, where there is an orderly market, where the private sector reaps enormous benefits from public investment.* <u>*For someone to assert that he or she has grown wealthy in America without the benefit of substantial public investment is pure hubris.*</u>[69] *(my emphasis)*

The talents of any of us are there to be developed by our unique efforts and dedication, but we all nevertheless depend on the composition of the community around us.

The interrelationship between the individual and the community is complex and multi-faceted. It has grown yet more heterogeneous over recent generations because of the corrupted interpretation of the individual which has followed in the wake of the rise of a particular form of capitalism: market fundamentalism, or neo-liberalism. It has been difficult to counter the selfish, *harsh reality* mode of thought that has gone along with the new economic reality. For one thing, it appears to have been sanctioned by the venerable ideas of Adam Smith, giving it time-honoured authenticity, with the key principle that society as a whole will ultimately benefit from our selfishness. But also in this increasingly secular, post-modern age, it has become problematic to judge each other on moral grounds, or using practically any other criteria. For our individual preferences are somehow inviolate. That does not mean that we need to oppose the current ideology of individualism on the basis of morality; economic affairs have long been conducted on amoral terms. We would be much better off calling on age-old communal practices, which reveal the altruism and social co-operation which exist in all societies. For much of human history, and especially in prehistoric times, people existed in small, highly egalitarian communities where social cohesion and sharing were indispensable parts of economic life. Barter or exchange demonstrating overt self-interest were frowned upon as socially unacceptable, particularly before settled agriculture developed. Competition and rivalry in such societies would have been both ineffectual and anti-social.

Such examples are often taken as being irrelevant to modern industrial society, as well as said to gloss over what many see as our intrinsic selfishness and competitiveness. Popular ideas of Darwin's natural selection in which only the fittest survive, and more recently, the publicity given to our apparent innate selfishness from Richard Dawkins' immensely popular book *The Selfish Gene*, have slanted the debate. For if self-centredness is, to use contemporary terminology, hard-wired in us, then equally altruism is part of our basic nature. As individuals we only have to reflect on our own personal impulses and motivations to recognize the compatibility of this duality. We have evolved biologically to cooperate socially in our mutual interests, to show generosity by sharing with and giving succour to others, as well as to compete for our well being in a world of shortage; these instincts are rarely irreconcilable. Community life can reveal the co-existence of these different facets of our natures. The less divisive, self-centred values do not require a morality or even a communitarian ethic to flourish; they are likely to arise spontaneously out of a cohesive communal environment in which people implicitly recognize a responsibility beyond themselves. And in doing so they are fulfilling a further need which is, Susan Neiman says, *....to see our lives as stories with meaning – meanings we impose on the world, a crucial source of human dignity – without which we hold our lives to be worthless.*[70] Peoples everywhere, especially in this largely non-religious age, are anxious to attribute some significance, some dignity of status to their existence beyond – and as well as – the *getting and spending* which the poet Wordsworth believed enfeebled us.

Our regard for one another, our concern to see others around us flourish, our need to develop healthy social interaction with our neighbours are all crucial to our wellbeing. This does not easily chime with the theory, especially under neo-liberalism, that human behaviour is to be seen principally in terms of an inbuilt tendency to maximize material self-interest. But economics texts are littered with examples of studies which indicate the opposite. In Wilkinson and Pickett's important work *The Spirit Level* is a description of the 'ultimatum game', an economic experiment where volunteers are paired together while remaining anonymous to each other.[71] When given sums of money to distribute as they think fit, the exercise revealed how equally or unequally people chose to divide the cash between themselves and someone else. The results showed distinctly egalitarian preferences: as the authors point out, *...At direct cost to ourselves, we come close to sharing equally even with people we never meet and will never interact with again.*[72] Also, in their *For the Common Good* Herman Daly and John Cobb produced a detailed analysis of how the behaviour of *homo economicus* differs from that of *homo sapiens* in the real world.[73] They referred to this as *the Fallacy of Misplaced Concreteness*, after Alfred North Whitehead, where *...conclusions are drawn about the real world by deduction from abstractions with little awareness of the danger involved.*[74] When unwarranted conclusions about human behaviour are arrived at solely from examination of theoretical models it is hardly surprising that the results do not fit the contours of our familiar reality.

Nevertheless, many economists have felt the need to conduct experiments to exemplify what we have long believed, that *maximization mathematics* cannot possibly adequately explain human conduct. In their survey of such research, Daly and Cobb focus on the work of Stephen Rhoads, who has summarized some interesting studies into human behaviour and the extent to which it is guided by narrow self-interest.[75] In these studies, large groups of people are given tokens which they are told they can invest either for their own personal profit or for a return for the group as a whole. But whereas a personal investment provides a 1 cent per token return, the group exchange brings in 2.2 cents per token, although divided among everyone in the group irrespective of who invests. Thus, the group exchange provides each individual with a share of the return on his or her own investment (if any has been made) as well as the same share – related, of course, to the number in the group – of the return on what other members invested in the group exchange. In order to maximise individual benefits, which many economists suppose is the primary objective of all, participants ought not to contribute to the group exchange, since a large part of the greater total return would go to other group members. However, the results of these experiments do not bear this out: in fact, in most cases between 40% and 60% of those involved freely contributed resources to the group exchange, for the general benefit, and many participants commented that a *fair* person would give even more than they did.*

Human behaviour in such studies, as in many other respects, does not correspond with the theoretical model of maximizing personal advantage. But the tendency of economists to generalize from abstract principles is by no means new; it was variously identified in the nineteenth century for example, when even the influential commentator Walter Bagehot had a dig at the classical economist David Ricardo: *He thought he was considering actual human nature in its actual circumstances, when he was really considering a fictitious nature in fictitious circumstances.*[77] Nevertheless, in today's pragmatic, rational age it is perhaps counter-intuitive that academics and business people are still so preoccupied with theory and principle, despite the wealth of data from practical experiments displaying our more selfless, consensual instincts. It is a sign of the power of an idea, an idea based on a reductionist concept that originated over two hundred years ago, in an entirely different environment, but which has now been vigorously reaffirmed since the early 1980s. Such is the force of this overriding sense of self-interest to maximize individual gain, to the hypothetical eventual benefit

---

* Interestingly, as Daly and Cobb point out from Rhoads' findings, post-graduate students of economics taking part in the exercise contributed significantly less to the group exchange than the average person, had difficulty with the concept of fairness, and were only half as likely to indicate that fairness played a part in their decision making.[76]

of a wider public – now subsumed into market fundamentalism – that few today seem aware that it is part of an abstract ideology. In fact, to draw again on one of the themes of this book, it is an idea implicitly accepted so completely that we see life through it, without conscious thought, so that today many struggle to accept the multi-dimensional picture of *persons-in-community* that we mostly represent.

Such has been the influence of one-sided, neo-liberal thought since the 1970s that viewing economic and business life purely through the lens of self-interest is rarely questioned. This is in spite of the fact that on a daily, vernacular level, co-operation and consensus are indispensable for community and inter-community cohesion. In fact, there is little doubt that social behaviours developed in human society because they were shown to be advantageous to our evolution. There are certainly ways in which individual self-interest can lead, by the notable *invisible hand*, to favourable outcomes for wider society, but if this were to the exclusion of social co-operation or altruism – or in a modern setting, to some degree of regulation – then the successful survival of the species would have been very uncertain. And as has already been alluded to, future international problems in a globalised world are going to be much less amenable to the individualistic drive to maximize material self-interest, which is likely to be highly counter-productive. (This will be expanded on in later chapters.) No, we will have to adapt progressively to a more sharing, consensual mode if global crises are to be resolved. Of course, consensus does not necessarily have dramatic appeal, and may not be seen as attractive as a victory won from confrontation in which national character is tested. But in the ordinary, familiar context of most people's lives, consensus and compromise – coupled with the richness and variety of individual identity – are the stuff of normal existence.

Civilization would not have advanced as it has without the coming-together of individuals in community. In many respects, community could be seen as the spacial equivalent of tradition. As citizens of a country, we are indissolubly linked to its past; former custom and usage have left their imprints on modern ways and give meaning to much contemporary practice. Even recent newcomers to a society, without the same bonds of lineage, feel – perhaps unconsciously – the weight of the past, and cannot escape the encompassing reach of its influence, no matter how much they might try to preserve their own cultural identity behind their ethnic stockade. Social and cultural tradition provides a cradle in which each new generation can develop, just as community provides a nurturing environment in which families and their new members can grow and flourish. Tradition, like community, is a starting point for the socialization of each new age, carrying with it the accumulated wisdom – and prejudice – of earlier times. Generations need to come to terms with both the glory and the guilt which their history passes down, just as they need to make sense of the defects and the merits of their community, and communities. However, recent social trends are signalled by a significant break with the past in the undermining of communal values, while an individualism based on money and the market is glorified as the future – one both welcomed and said to be inevitable.

Nevertheless, surveying the panorama of modern life one might carelessly assume that the individual's relationship with the surrounding community is much as it has always been. But it does not take much delving to see the strange configuration that has developed – mainly in the last thirty to forty years. It is almost as if progress itself – *individualized ....deregulated and privatized*, as Zygmunt Bauman says[78] – were being driven only by successful individuals, whether in the economic, political or sporting arenas, so that if only we were to invest our faith in these paragons our collective future would be secured. This perspective has caught the popular imagination in this overtly media age, in spite of the fact that it is a conceit whose confused narrative, reinforced by wilful self-deception, has blurred our sight of reality. For our futures, whether on a *macro* or a local, personal level, will ultimately depend on our collective efforts. Progress will inevitably have to be made against the attitudes which have apparently beguiled so many over recent years, and especially to counter the idea that we are dominated by selfish motives, and that such motives are in the best interests of society as a whole. We will discover – in the fight against this false consciousness – that the global problems which confront us can only be tackled by enlarging the public sphere, enhancing consensus, and extending collective political power. And in that process it will become evident, to those not already aware of it, that, *the pursuit of the social good contributes to the satisfaction of self-interest,*[79] and that such communal endeavour will assuredly contribute to the greater liberation of all individuals.

END NOTES

i   Ludwig von Mises, *Human Action: A Treatise on Economics*, 1949, quoted in Geoff Hodgson, *The Democratic Economy: A new look at planning, markets and power,* Penguin, London, 1984, p. 30.
ii   Ibid. p. 30.
iii   John Stuart Mill, *Utilitarianism, Liberty and Representative Government*, J. M. Dent, London, 1910, p. 29.

1   Graham Parry, reviewing Keith Thomas, *The Ends of Life: Roads to Fulfilment in Early Modern England*, in *The Guardian*, London, 21/2/2009.
2   Andro Linklater, *Owning the Earth: The Transforming History of Land Ownership*, Bloomsbury, London, 2014, p. 18.
3   Emile Durkheim, quoted in Richard Sennett, *Respect: The Formation of Character in an Age of Inequality*, Penguin Books, London, 2004, p. 124.
4   David G. Green, *The New Right*, Harvester-Wheatsheaf, Brighton, Sussex, 1987, p. 19.
5   John Stuart Mill, *Utilitarianism, Liberty, and Representative Government*, J. M. Dent & Sons Ltd., London, 1910, p. 124.
6   Ibid. p. 121.
7   Idem.
8   Ibid., *Utilitarianism*, Chp. IV.
9   Tony Judt, *Ill Fares the Land: A Treatise On Our Present Discontents*, Penguin Books, London, 2011, p. 88.
10   Ibid. p. 89.
11   Adam Smith, *The Wealth of Nations*, Everyman Edn. Dent, London, 1977, Vol. I, p. 13.
12   Ha-Joon Chang, *23 Things They Don't Tell You about Capitalism*, Allen Lane, London, 2010, p. 46.
13   George Orwell, *The Lion and the Unicorn: Socialism and the English Genius*, Penguin Books, London, 1982, pp. 39-40.
14   Hodgson, op. cit., p. 5.
15   David Marquand, 'A Language of Community', in Ben Pimlott, Anthony Wright, Tony Flowers (Eds.), *The Alternative: Politics for a Change*, W. H. Allen, London, 1990, p. 8.
16   Herman E. Daly, John B. Cobb Jr., *For the Common Good: Redirecting the Economy towards Community, the Environment and a Sustainable Future,* Green Print, London, 1989.
17   Ibid., p. 161.
18   Hodgson, op. cit., pp.29-30.
19   Ibid. pp.30-31.
20   Idem.

21 Daly & Cobb, op. cit., p. 163.
22 Lester Thurow, 1983, quoted in ibid. p. 7.
23 Patricia Hewitt, 'Red and Green', in Ben Pimlott, Anthony Wright, Tony Flower (Eds.), *The Alternative: Politics for a Change*, W. H. Allen & Co., London, 1990.
24 Fred Hirsch, *Social Limits to Growth*, Routledge & Kegan Paul, London, 1978, p. 178.
25 Daly & Cobb, op. cit., p. 7.
26 Marquand, op. cit., p. 9.
27 Ibid., p. 8.
28 Robert Reich, *The Work of Nations*, Simon & Schuster, London, 1991.
29 Ibid., Chapter 14.
30 Ibid., Chapter 5.
31 Ibid., p. 268.
32 Charles Murray, *Coming Apart: The State of White America, 1960-2010*, Crown Forum, New York, 2012.
33 Cited in Peter Weber, 'The Week', 11/9/2013 – www.theweek.com/articles/460179/charts-how-rich-won-great-recession.
34 Peter Oborne in 'The Daily Telegraph', London, 21/1/2012.
35 Ferdinand Mount, *Mind the Gap: The New Class Divide in Britain*, Short Books, London, 2012, p. 85.
36 Michael Sandel, *What Money Can't Buy: The Moral Limits of Markets*, Allen Lane, London, 2012, p. 203.
37 Idem.
38 Judt, op. cit., p. 216.
39 Reported in *Guardian Society*, London, 3/4/2002.
40 Reported in The Observer, London, 3/7/2016.
41 Reported in 'Talk of the Town', *Walk*, Ramblers Association, London, Spring 2017 p. 25.
42 Idem.
43 Thomas Piketty, *Capital in the Twenty-first Century*, The Belknap Press of Harvard University, Cambridge, Mass., 2017, p. 229.
44 Ibid., pp. 231-2.
45 Zygmunt Bauman, *Liquid Modernity*, Polity Press, Cambridge, UK, 2000, p. 39.
46 Idem.
47 Zygmunt Bauman, *Does Ethics Have a Chance in a World of Consumers?* (Institute for Human Sciences – Vienna Lecture Series) Harvard Univ. Press, Cambridge, Mass., 2008, p. 28.
48 Ibid., p. 29.
49 Alain de Botton, *Status Anxiety*, Penguin Books, London, 2005, p. 68.
50 According to Aelfric, Abbott of Eynsham, cited in ibid., p. 69.
51 Sennett, op. cit., p. 172.
52 Ibid., p. 173,
53 Idem.
54 John Maynard Keynes, quoted in ibid. p. 174.

55 David Morgan, Mary Evans, 'The Road to Nineteen Eighty-Four: Orwell and the Post-war Reconstruction of Citizenship', in Brian Brivati, Harriet Jones (Eds.), *What Difference Did the War Make,* Leicester University Press, London, 1993, p. 50.
56 A. J. P. Taylor, quoted in ibid., p. 50.
57 David Cameron **www.gov.uk/government/publications/building-the-big-society**
58 David Marquand, *The Guardian*, London, 16/7/1997.
59 Idem.
60 Bauman, 2008, op. cit., p. 139.
61 Ibid., p. 140.
62 Ibid., p. 141.
63 David Garland, cited in Zygmunt Bauman, *Wasted Lives: Modernity and Its Outcasts*, Polity Press, Cambridge, UK, 2004, p. 68.
64 Idem.
65 Chang, op. cit., p. 165.
66 Ibid. pp. 165-6.
67 Judt, op. cit., pp. 32-3.
68 Warren Buffett, quoted in Will Hutton, *Them and Us: Changing Britain – Why We Need a Fair Society* Little, Brown, London, 2010, p. 222.
69 Bill Gates, quoted in ibid., p. 222.
70 Susan Neiman, quoted in Hutton, op. cit., p. 18.
71 Richard Wilkinson & Kate Pickett, *The Spirit Level: Why Equality is Better for Everyone*, Penguin Books, London, 2010, Chapter 14.
72 Ibid. p. 202.
73 Daly & Cobb op. cit.
74 Ibid., p. 35.
75 Stephen E. Rhoads, *The Economist's View of the World*, cited in Daly & Cobb, op.cit., p. 90.
76 Idem.
77 Walter Bagehot, quoted in Daly & Cobb, op. cit., p. 36.
78 Bauman, 2000, op. cit., p. 135.
79 Fred Hirsch, see End Note 24.

Chapter 3

CAPITALISM FOR EVER?

Has the national welfare, have the weal and happiness of the people, advanced with the increase of the circumstantial prosperity? Is the increasing number of wealthy individuals that which ought to be understood by the wealth of the nation?
SAMUEL TAYLOR COLERIDGE[i]

But the mean rapacity, the monopolizing spirit of merchants and manufacturers, who neither are, nor ought to be the rulers of mankind, though it cannot perhaps be corrected, may very easily be prevented from disturbing the tranquillity of anybody but themselves.
ADAM SMITH[ii]

....most people are not on fire with ambition; they are not wondering day and night how to get on in the world; they want if possible to enjoy a little importance in their own circle, and that is all; for the rest they like to take it easy.
J. B. PRIESTLEY[iii]

Our enormously productive economy demands that we make consumption our way of life, that we convert the buying and use of goods into rituals, that we seek our spiritual satisfactions, our ego satisfactions, in consumption. ... we need things consumed, burned up, worn out, replaced, and discarded at an ever increasing pace.
VICTOR LEBOW – 1955[iv]
(US marketing consultant)

I. When commenting on the political significance of the *Salisbury Review*, which he then edited, philosopher Roger Scruton modestly maintained, *Our influence depends entirely on the fact that people believe we have influence.*[1] But then, perhaps this had nothing to do with modesty. He may have been entirely satisfied that the illusion of importance with which his periodical surrounded itself in the 1980s was the catalyst for greater renown and influence, for which meagre quarterly sales were an irrelevance. This is rather akin to belief in the buoyancy of the stock market; for success there depends upon confidence, and confidence stems from a belief in success. As elsewhere, in the end people come to accept what is commonly believed, only tenuously connected to its validity. In fact, one might suggest that the greater degree of vested interest in a policy or idea, the less likely it is that public consciousness of its nature will conform to some approximation of reality, whatever that might be. This false consciousness, introduced in the early pages of this work, is many-faceted, but underlying it is Wendell Holmes' conviction of the power of conformity in ideas. The force of argument in the shape of facts does not often, or rapidly, undermine powerful beliefs. As Theodore Roszak says, *...it is remarkable how much in the way of dissonance and contradiction a dominant idea can absorb.*[2] It is usually the case that influential concepts with a strong hold on popular conviction are eventually overturned by new paradigms, with their own novelty and persuasive force, rather than by a fresh assemblage of facts. Accepted dogmas mostly have a certain shelf life, depending on their appeal as credible and fashionable versions of contemporary *truth,* but what is always uncertain is when their public appeal will wane.

So-called *integrating patterns*[3] of this kind have long formed shadows of misconception extending over wide areas of modern social and political life. Assumptions, for example, about the future of free market capitalism appeared bolstered by the wholesale collapse of state communism and the economic upturn of the late 1990s in North America and Europe. The world economy then suffered a major reversal during the financial crisis of 2007–08, sufficient – one would have thought – to overturn any body of economic dogma on which it rested. But the modern free market economy proved remarkably resilient: although its momentum was to a degree constrained by the banking crisis and by corporate and personal bankruptcy, ten years on saw stock markets rising and unemployment falling, despite the protectionism of Donald Trump and the commercial uncertainty caused by Brexit. So it has to be said, paraphrasing the words of Mark Twain, that stories about the imminent death of capitalism in its present form appear to have been greatly exaggerated. Economic recovery from the devastation of the Coronavirus pandemic still has a long way to go; developed economies are facing an employment revolution with the forecast increase in the use of robots; levels of public and personal debt may still be unsustainably high; and the environmental impact of climate change has the potential for widespread damage on the entire planet. Nevertheless, free market capitalism moves blithely on, apparently now the only economic game in town.

To the extent that these assumptions have taken hold of the popular imagination, there exists an implicit understanding that there are no alternatives. There has been an increasing convergence of views, to some extent aided by the perceived success of neo-liberal politics, and underpinned by the direction of world developments, towards a common ground of faith in right-of-centre market capitalism with an important, but not overriding social dimension. The modern fashion for green politics is regarded as a necessary corrective, but only in the sense of moderating the unrestricted march of capitalist progress, not altering its fundamental course or diluting its objectives. Further modernisation of national economies, higher productivity, greater enterprise at work coupled with a flexible labour market environment, as well as rigid control of inflation – these are widely accepted as prerequisites for economic development. And, of course, the crucial component of continued economic growth is still deemed vital for raising living standards. The expression *free markets* has become a short-hand description which incorporates this compendium of policies, but should also be viewed as a form of ...*Newspeak, distorting thinking and debate*.[4] In fact, Yves Smith is correct when she says that the commonly held opinion that free markets are desirable ...*creates a default position: that completely unrestricted commerce is preferable, and anyone who argues against it bears the burden of proof*.[5] But again as such, we look at life *through* this idea, not *about* it.

However, because sets of beliefs have been incorporated into the *ambient noise* of a generation, that does not imply that they are fixed in the social and economic environment, natural, like the weather. We can never take our institutions and social systems for granted, no matter how permanent they may appear; they will eventually metamorphose into something new, probably even while we cling to them. The feudal system once had an air of durability, as was shown earlier, and it was not so long ago that the Keynesian consensus appeared fixed in the economic firmament. Tony Judt pointed out that in 1940, Labour activist Evan Durbin had written that he could not conceive ...*the least alteration...* in trends towards economic planning, collective bargaining and publicly funded social services.[6] And only just over sixty years ago, Labour grandee Anthony Crosland could confidently claim in his *The Future of Socialism* that the transition *...from an uncompromising faith in individualism and self-help to a belief in group action and participation...* had been permanent.[7] Even during the long Conservative post-war government years Crosland would point to the bipartisan consensus on collective government responsibility for the direction of the national economy. The ideological tomorrow will always appear to contemporary eyes more or less like the present, and the power of societal forces is often underestimated. The tendency is to try to construct a framework for the future based on variations of the *status quo*; we are conceptually trapped by what we have become accustomed to, as well as by our lack of historical perspective, both of them hindering any wiser course of action.

For free market capitalism has become, for its adherents, a true ideology, a faith. In recent times its tenets, in the form of neo-liberal values, have taken it well beyond the practical economic system by which modern democracies have normally conducted their commercial affairs. It is no longer readily amenable to adjustments in policy, in the interests of national well-being, for its evangelists have their eyes fixed on the final prize of a world without economic regulation, a paradise from which we are all supposed to benefit. This is a recent development, which even loyal Conservative politicians once disavowed. Former Prime Minister Harold Macmillan's 1938 work *The Middle Way*, an exposition of traditional centrist Conservative values, emphasised the practical nature of capitalism, a system which had evolved over time. *Nobody ever 'invented' capitalist society*, he argued.[8] Almost all politicians then, and for many years afterwards, would have supported Macmillan's rejection of dogma:

> *If capitalism had been conducted all along as if the theory of private enterprise were a matter of principle... we should have had a civil war long ago.*[9]

The economic woes of the early 1970s contributed to the rise of conviction politics in the wake of Edward Heath's electoral defeat. One could claim that they were inaugurated by Sir Keith Joseph's speech at Preston in September 1974, in which he gave pride of place to monetarism, then the chief tenet of the new doctrine. For the next generation a fundamentalist economic creed – following the ideas of Hayek and Friedman – placed itself as an ideological polar opposite to Communism. To the many who had seen the light, they now felt they were on the true path to a promised land.

However, the rhetoric by which free market capitalism has been promoted has placed it in an intellectual position well beyond the practical views of many of its apparent adherents. But what Yves Smith calls ...*the generally approving way in which economists use "free markets"*... lends authority, she says, to the idea that completely unrestricted commerce is their preferred position.[10] Today's dominance of neo-classical economists ensures that support for free market fundamentalism is heard everywhere, in spite of the lack of substantive validation of its claims. This fits with the wider matter of the ...*limited empiricism of economics*, as Smith points out, in which theories ... *inhabit a world that isn't simply unrealistic, but wildly different from any that humans will ever occupy.*[11] In spite of this, many economists appear to believe that the rules of commerce are perfectly aligned with their doctrinal principles – wishful thinking of a perverse, self-deluding kind, but with strong religious overtones. The target is a hallowed land, where economic laws work in perfect harmony, and which we would reach if only we could attain a purity of faith and follow neo-liberal tenets unerringly. In this environment, belief in unfettered free market capitalism becomes a creed, overshadowing proper empirical science and academic rigour. Or as Ronald Wright has put it, market extremism ...*has cross-bred with evangelical messianism to fight intelligent policy on metaphysical grounds.*[12]

Nevertheless, the evangelical discourse of libertarian free markets does not have the support among economists that might be apparent. For example, when a study surveyed members of the prestigious American Economics Association in 2007, to discover their stance on the 'free market', it revealed a large proportion of participants rejecting the extreme version of the principle.[13] Only 8% of AEA members endorsed the extreme libertarian position, and barely 3% were its strong supporters.* This backs up the more commonplace view that 'free markets' do not imply an extreme stance on the matter. It also accords with the views of some of the economists most closely associated with the 'free market'. Milton Friedman himself was not at the radical end of the argument; he did not believe in a completely unregulated financial system, and even supported a negative income tax, which would involve a transfer of income to the poor. And most disciples of Adam Smith follow their mentor in accepting state intervention in economic affairs – even if, in many cases, less than he did. During the 1980s, when the role of ideology in economic affairs became more prominent, especially in Britain and the USA, it nevertheless represented more an inspiration or guiding light for Ronald Reagan and Margaret Thatcher than a strongly prescriptive creed. No, when the phrase 'free markets' is heard, it is rarely meant as a radical cry against any and all state intervention, but a much more limited statement of the need to allow free enterprise to flourish, within the scope of a practical politics incorporating a (slimmed down) welfare state.

Nevertheless, the rhetoric of neo-liberalism does imply an extreme position, regardless of the more subtle shades of interpretation which may be applied to it. Part of that extremism involves a curiously un-British submission to theory, as well as a tendency to abandon micro-managing and leave markets to regulate themselves – most notably in the period leading to the financial crash of 2007–08. With what now appears staggering complacency, faith was put in the network of complex financial instruments – some of which were not understood even by those managing them. With a religious zeal, financial markets were believed to operate in mysterious ways but, ultimately, would work to our overall benefit because – as the IMF stated in 2007 – ... *markets have shown that they can and do self-correct.*[15] It was an ideological conviction, as Robert Peston has maintained, that markets would prevent too much being lent in a reckless way – a blind faith in economic rationality which was wildly misplaced. As he concludes, *...we are the victims of the conversion of the governing and regulating class to the financial religion of market perfectability.*[16] This was

---

* A curious aspect of this survey was the way the results were written up and summarised. In a plainly biased and quite subjective manner, the authors argued that it was the responsibility of economists who supported the free market to give priority to advocating the radical version of markets. Furthermore, the article accused survey participants who do not hold extreme 'free market' views of being intellectually dishonest. As Yves Smith notes, *Bluntly, the paper measures economists' degree of adherence to a particular ideology.*[14]

very much in the Thatcher mould, where a 'hands-off' approach to the economy was supposed to foster self-reliance and provide incentives – supposedly the keys to individual and family affluence. The Thatcherites wanted to create what they saw as the appropriate conditions of economic freedom so as to liberate the latent energies of the population. Such an approach would indeed require a considerable measure of faith.

For a long period the zeal of free market fundamentalists was hidden beneath what seemed a pragmatic approach. Tory policies were presented as down-to-earth recipes for the critical economic situation which they claimed to have inherited in 1979. One of the triumphs of the Thatcherites of the 1980s and '90s was their capacity largely to conceal ideology behind a cloak of commonplace practicality, thus enabling the public to be cajoled into accepting the unpalatable medicine of Ward Sister Thatcher, and the self-denying strictures of Bank Manager Major, without being fully conscious of the delusory faiths which first inspired them. This was perhaps the only way in which the British would have stomached a theory-based politics. For the people have long been wary of philosophy, and intellectual argument remains suspect, particularly when used in public affairs. As Ralph Waldo Emerson noted after a visit to Britain in the mid-19th century, *They (the English) are impious in their scepticism of a theory, but kiss the dust before a fact.*[17] And many have pointed out the, mainly, English aversion to abstract thinking, while there has been in Britain a traditional dislike for intellectual cleverness in its leaders, just as there has been hatred of ideological fanaticism. Even in recent times the paternalistic aristocrat has often gained more respect than the conviction politician, and the only two leaders in English history who really stood for a cause, Mary Tudor and Oliver Cromwell, were both execrated.

Today, several years on from the financial crash, neo-liberal capitalism still has a powerful body of rhetoric declaiming it, even if it does not entirely inform many governments' policies.* But it is still used to rally the troops, particularly when under attack from anti-capitalist or anti-globalization forces. Thus arguments become polarised whenever

---

* The Conservative manifesto for the 2017 general election even included the words ... *we do not believe in untrammelled free markets*... and said that regulation was ...*necessary for the proper ordering of any economy.*

capitalism appears threatened, and its forces tend to group under the banner of neo-liberal fundamentalism, as if not confident they can defend a more moderate position. In the United States there was further doctrinal backtracking under the Trump administration, with the defence of capitalism conducted from a more radical, populist vantage point; the causes of low taxation, removing government regulation, and a 'small state' agenda are policies gathering popularity not just amongst the right of the Republican Party. In spite of this, since the financial crash a variety of voices have been heard forecasting the death of capitalism. In response, its proponents often withdraw behind a defence of an extreme version of its ideology, while also trying to show that free markets function in a scientific manner according to theories they claim were those of Adam Smith. David Howell argues on similar lines to Robert Peston, cited earlier, when he suggests that, in pursuit of mathematical modelling economists have ...*withdrawn into an isolated make-believe kingdom*...pretending that ...*problems which really have their roots deep in human psychology, in philosophy and in political institutions, can be isolated as semi-scientific economics and resolved by economic theory.*[18]

As arguments become more polarised, doom-laden forecasts about the future of capitalism are now frequently heard. Perhaps partly because of the lack of a systemic overhaul following the financial crash and prolonged recession, many commentators see no possibility of a change of direction to forestall future crises. ...*capitalism – unrestrained and unreformed – will die*... is a typical refrain.[19] German political economist Wolfgang Streeck is a writer who has despaired of reform; *How Will Capitalism End?* is his latest book. As a social democrat, he says he has spent many years believing that we could ...*tame the beast,* and ...*modify capitalism towards equality and social justice*...[20] but now thinks these are utopian ideals. Many see steady decline as the only possibility in the absence of comprehensive reform. Streeck himself says capitalism ...*will for the foreseeable future hang in limbo, dead or about to die from an overdose of itself*... until its ultimate demise.[21] Journalist Paul Mason, with a less overtly pessimistic view, sees capitalism as a learning organism, but is ...*a complex, adaptive system which has reached the limits of its capacity to adapt.*[22] This is a key argument in his *Post-Capitalism: A Guide to Our Future*; he believes capitalism will be abolished by creating something more dynamic. ...*capitalism's demise will be accelerated by external shocks and shaped by the emergence of a new kind of human being.*[23] He thinks this will be necessitated by a complete transformation of employment through information technology and comprehensive automation.

The apparent 'business-as-usual' environment following the latest recession has thrown up these and many other prescriptions as to how capitalism should/can be remodelled for the 21st century. Not long after the financial crash, columnist Anatole Kaletsky saw capitalism moving smoothly into an historically new, fourth phase in which pragmatism will succeed free market ideology, with the acknowledgement that both government and markets are fallible.* There appears some consensus that the economic future will involve a form of capitalism somewhere between the socialist model and neo-liberal fundamentalism; the new awareness of the extent of material inequality has placed the latter in a new light. Will Hutton, who came to prominence in the '90s with his *The State We're In*, has more recently called for a reformed capitalism, in which private enterprise accepts its obligations to the wider community of which it is an integral part.** Notwithstanding major changes to the world of work, it is highly likely that the capitalism of the near future will not differ greatly from the conformation that we presently see. Short of some unforeseen revolutionary upheaval, democratic government and capitalist free enterprise will continue to need one another; each has vested interests in the success of the other. A completely self-regulating economic system is now widely accepted as a fanciful project which would never work, and has never worked, as Polanyi asserted in his keynote work.*** At the same time, greater government control would, following the Communist experiments of the 20th century, never be accepted.

Karl Polanyi's critique of the capitalist system is important, but by no means the principal explanation for the survival of the free market in practice. His assertions that there simply is no economy without government, that society relies on a transport system, public education, judicial framework, financial environment, and other public infrastructure that only government has the ability and the legitimacy to provide, have regained wider acceptance since the economic crash over a decade ago.

---

*   Kaletsky, *Capitalism 4.0*, Bloomsbury, 2010.
** Hutton, *How Good We Can Be*, Little, Brown, 2015.
*** Karl Polanyi, *The Great Transformation: The Political and Economic Origins of Our Time*, Beacon Press, 2001 – originally published in 1944, coincidentally the same year as Hayek's *The Road to Serfdom*.

(After all, lack of regulation was an important contributory factor in the debacle.) And in any case this commonsense, un-ideological approach was precisely the view of Adam Smith:

> *The third and last duty of the sovereign or commonwealth is that of erecting and maintaining those public institutions and those public works, which, though they may be in the highest degree advantageous to a great society, are, however, of such a nature that the profit could never repay the expence to any individual or small number of individuals, and which it therefore cannot be expected that any individual or small number of individuals should erect or maintain.*[24]

Free market capitalism must never forget these truths – part of the more nuanced complexion of Smith's views that neo-liberals mostly ignore. For capitalism is not an independent machine whose complex workings should operate without supervision; it is part and parcel of society and its members, with the very contradictions and ambiguities which that implies. As Amartya Sen commented soon after the financial crash, ... *the economic crisis is partly generated by a huge overestimation of the wisdom of market processes*[25]... We should learn that lesson, so as to ensure that future market capitalism is a managed, guided system, not left to its own, far from wise devices.

One can only hope that after the last economic crisis, free marketeers will learn to temper their quasi-religious zeal, and not allow themselves to be mesmerised by theory and dogma. For such doctrinal obstinacy will only lead to future crises. Ronald Wright tells the cautionary tale of the inhabitants of Easter Island who by the time of Europe's High Middle Ages had developed an extravagant statue cult, led by a dominant warrior class.[26] The Polynesian population had by that time risen to around 10,000, supported by a rich economy: thick woodlands, rich volcanic soil and abundant seafood. The impressive stone images they began to erect to honour their ancestors developed into an obsessive cult requiring more and more wood, rope and manpower; by 1400 the woods had been completely destroyed and the people were not even able to build good, sea-worthy boats for fishing. Wright says, *The people had been seduced by a kind of progress that becomes a mania, an "ideological pathology"*, in anthropological terms.[27] When the Dutch first saw Easter Island in 1722 they were astounded at the enormous megaliths in a land without trees or major vegetation. The few remaining inhabitants lived mainly in caves. The resulting ecological and human disaster – the consequence of unrestricted population growth and profligate exploitation of natural resources – was summed up by archaeologists Paul Bahn and John Flenley as due to unlimited confidence in their religion to take care of the future.[28] Hubristic fundamentalism indeed takes many forms, all equally dangerous.

Free market capitalism is the economic arrangement by which our now globalised world has operated for several centuries, and is likely to continue for several more. It is essentially not a belief system, or a political doctrine with a body of ideology behind it as – say – communism is, and it is certainly not a religious creed to be venerated. It is a practical, quotidian pattern of affairs governing the economics of buying and selling, and of the accumulation of capital. Above all, capitalism is principally the manner by which individuals are most likely to arrange their *economic* affairs if left to their own devices, and this has been so since the late Middle Ages. It is perverse to oppose capitalism on grounds of principle, as economist Amartya Sen argues: *...to be generically against markets would be as odd as being generically against conversation. The freedom to exchange words, or goods, or gifts is part of the way human beings act with each other.*[29] But it must be reiterated that, as a mechanism for economic transactions, the free market system is an integral part of the social environment of nations; it does not have a different code of values, independent of the vernacular and communal principles which guide normal human society. (One can be sure that Adam Smith would have been amazed that this would ever need to be said.) Profit and gain may be guiding incentives, even if they do not conform to the theoretical economics of academic textbooks. However, to the extent that they are forces driving individual conduct, they nevertheless govern only limited areas of human activity, and sit alongside many other natural impulses and influences.

It has been a curious feature of recent years that political crankiness has sought to couple economic incentives with life's affective and aesthetic domains as if they represented a dominating biological instinct of *Homo sapiens*. Adam Smith may have believed that man's *...constant* concern... is *...to better his condition*, but he would not have maintained that this effort is a never-ending toil dominating all aspects of daily life. Since the rise of commercial capitalism, the norms of western culture have been influenced by a variety of principles and practices; the notion that the overriding one has been the indefatigable and unremitting pursuit of gain in the free market of life is contradicted by all practical experience. Human beings involve themselves in the business of trade and manufacture with varying degrees of energy and commitment, sometimes with zealous ambition to make money, but more often simply to earn a decent living in the context of family and communal life. Doctrinal principles have no place here – an arena of common practicality, governed by custom and precedent. Of course, regulations have been developed to provide a legal framework by which business is conducted; rules-based intercourse is a natural part of many aspects of civilization. A free-for-all in economic affairs would be just as bizarre as in other fields where competition may play a part, such as sport or intellectual property. A regulatory framework – whether brought in by government or professional bodies – is a necessary feature of human inter-involvement, ensuring legitimacy and consent.

Thus, once the principle of government intervention has been accepted, the free market as an ideological issue falls away in redundancy. The debate then centres on degree and practicality, as 19th-century Liberals acknowledged.* No, a free market in economic activity can never be a philosophical matter, and Adam Smith certainly did not view it as such. But a crucial difference between Smith's time and now is that *laissez-faire* free market economics were then – and much more than just in theory – surrounded and constrained by values of morality and community, as has already been explained. And even later, political liberals of the 19th century saw morality tied to Liberalism. In fact, as George Watson maintains, many Victorians believed a liberal form of socio-political organisation to be the only one in which moral duty could flourish.[31] This would not be a common view today, but our loss of almost any kind of general moral framework leaves economic practices adrift, with constraints on uncontrolled market activity now highly personal, random and fluctuating. From time to time there is talk of socially responsible capitalism; one even hears it said that social responsibility can save companies money; indeed, there are capitalist

---

* Hayek himself once admitted that his own values were those of Britain's 19th-century Whigs – the predecessors of the British Liberal party.[30]

organisations which accept their roles in safeguarding the environment, human rights and fair trade. But in modern economics, values are haphazard, capricious, contingent.

Apologists for a pure free market system do not appear overly concerned about this, perhaps because they have shifted the focus from personal responsibility onto the prevailing economic discipline itself. Those of the old Chicago School take moral justification from the functioning, both real and imagined, of the system's operation. The impersonal setting of price and income through the interplay of market forces is regarded in almost hallowed purity, only sullied by the intervention of the human agent. It is as if it were a natural eco-system whose delicate balance might be upset by even the merest hint of interference, such as government subsidy to an industry or its establishment of a minimum commodity price. Thus, human beings, on either the production or consumption side, are absolved of any responsibility for the functioning of free market relations, almost as if they were entirely independent of us or our social concerns. We are asked to have faith in the cause and allow the processes of ...*the most dynamic and productive economic system known to history*... to work themselves out, to our supposed ultimate benefit. However, supporters of this economic arrangement implicitly accept, and in a sense condone, the *incidental* hardships created, for long or short periods, by forces over which they would have no direct control. Problems such as unemployment or homelessness are, we are still told by the remaining hard-liners, the unfortunate side-effects of the free market and can only be exacerbated by government action. Solutions are supposed to lie in individual effort and enterprise, but the system which has necessitated remedial action is apparently sacrosanct.

It may not appear on the surface that we are vassals to an economic system, that in order to harvest the fruits of consumer capitalism we are obliged to minister to dominant, abstract free market principles. However, particularly in the so-called *Anglo-Sphere* since the 1970s, that is the abiding necessity which their practice has put upon us. But the tendency was identified well before that, in the immediate post-war period. In his 1955 work *The Sane Society*, the psychoanalyst and philosopher Erich Fromm described how we are required to behave in socially acceptable ways:

We do not choose our problems, we do not choose our products; we are pushed, we are forced – by what? By a system which has *no purpose and goal transcending it, and which makes man its appendix.*³²

The fundamentalist free market system inevitably subordinates human society, making it suitably amenable to the dictates of an economic doctrine which we have apparently sanctioned. It is part of what Fromm explained as *…the economic law which operates behind the back of man and forces him to do things without giving him the freedom to decide*³³… a disposition which he maintained had come to fruition in the twentieth century. Alongside the veneration of the market we may still imagine we have autonomy as individuals, but this is at a secondary level of commitment, and is a necessary delusion which helps underpin capitalism. *While everybody believes himself to act according to his own interest, he is actually determined by the anonymous laws of the market and of the economic machine.*³⁴ Fromm's analysis of capitalist society anticipated its early twenty-first century version of intense consumer capitalism.

In modern economics there seem to be *invisible hands* everywhere. We frequently hear from neo-liberals about the salutary indirect effects of selfish commercialism, when guided to our benefit by the *invisible hand* of the market. An even less obvious – and entirely unheralded – form of *invisible hand* is the manner by which modern free market capitalism moves inexorably forward. It certainly appears as if no human agent is capable of arresting or even slowing the march of capitalist 'progress', and of course we are led to believe that human interference would in any case not be in our best interests. Thus never-ending expansion and economic growth are allowed to continue unchecked, on the blind assumption that society will ultimately benefit – but also because no-one really knows how to stop the bandwagon. In fact, it would be dangerous to halt it because, for its protagonists, standing still would mean going backwards. As Erich Fromm pointed out many years ago,

*The individual capitalist expands his enterprise not primarily because he <u>wants</u> to, but because he <u>has</u> to, because – as (Andrew) Carnegie said in his autobiography – postponement of further expansion would mean regression. Actually as a business grows, one has to continue making it bigger, whether one wants to or not.*³⁵

Of course, proponents of the capitalist machine do not like to admit that we are all on a treadmill, with little prospect of being able to get off unscathed. Since we are not presented with any idea of a final destination to our economic progress, then we can only keep our heads down and *carry on*. Meanwhile, consumer novelties are provided to help deflect awkward questions about where we are likely to end up. Tim Jackson calls this the ...*social logic which perpetuates consumer capitalism*. As he says, *Buying more stuff keeps the economy going. The end result is a society 'locked in' to consumption growth by forces outside the control of individuals.*[36]

The lens through which we see modern capitalism also conditions how we think it should be conducted. Since the emphasis is so often placed on selfishness – often misusing the well-known words of Adam Smith – and evoking the famous *invisible hand*, the lowest common denominator interpretation of humanity has prevailed, at least in the Anglo-Sphere. For if our self-interested actions can be widely beneficial, then surely we should pursue them energetically for the greater good. Thus modern free market capitalism is given *carte blanche* to behave in as self-seeking and venal a manner as it wishes, the better to benefit society at large. Not only is *greed good*, but it has philanthropic consequences! These ideas have entered the realm of popular consciousness so that for many, and not all on the right, they have become truisms. They have been bolstered by the renown of neo-liberal policies which, it is said, rescued Britain from the disaster of the 1970s, as well as by the discrediting of socialism following the collapse of European Communism. After thirty years of the neo-liberal project, the ratification of the credentials of the Anglo-Saxon model of capitalism appeared complete. Then came the cataclysm of the financial crash, and all seemed to have changed. When American economist Nouriel Roubini's *Forbes Magazine* article appeared in February 2009, under the title 'Laissez-Faire Capitalism Has Failed', the economics terrain trembled.[37] But that was then, and now, ten years on, neo-liberalism would appear to have regained its confidence and pulled itself together.

However, no matter how successfully free market capitalism appears to have revived, the depth of the economic collapse and the length of the recession have provided the impetus for much reflection and analysis.

This has sometimes centred on the fact – already alluded to – that self-interest is by no means the dominating motive in economics, any more than it is in life in general. And looking beyond the Anglo-Saxon world, one can find plenty of evidence of how this is recognised in business, in the varying capitalist models which different cultures have developed. In the social democratic, so-called *Rhineland* version of capitalism, a much more collaborative approach is employed; stakeholders such as labour unions are more a part of the decision-making process, and social protection is thought a responsibility of business, not just of the state. In East Asia, state-sponsored capitalism is the norm, with national champions promoted, and with the awareness that business is a joint enterprise, even though the state leaves social protection to households and companies. In both cases far-sighted policies are adopted, and guaranteed long term loans are the norm. Ha-Joon Chang cites Kobe Steel (more recently involved in a data scandal), one of Japan's largest steel producers, which exemplifies businesses run on trust and loyalty rather than suspicion and individual self-seeking.[38] He quotes one of the company's top managers of the 1990s who stressed that it is nigh on impossible to run a large bureaucratic organization – in business or politics – *if you assume everyone is out for himself.*[39] He believes that one simply cannot constantly question the motives of employees if businesses are to be successful.

Many of the assumptions in the Anglo-Sphere about how business is conducted are gleaned from television – popular drama series or reality shows where dramatic effect is achieved through confrontation. And such practices can be found in companies large and small, though often not the most successful. They accord with the normalised confrontational approach in other areas of the Anglo-Saxon world, such as politics. But even in the competitive arena of American and British capitalism of popular folklore, acting in a totally selfish manner does not guarantee commercial success. Good managers understand that team work is important, connecting with employees and focusing on human motivation. This has been taken further in the so-called 'Japanese production system' which uses the latent goodwill and creativity of workers by trusting them with responsibility. Ha-Joon Chang points to the degree of control workers are given over the production line, and the encouragement they are given to come up with suggestions to increase the efficiency of work practices. As he says, *By not assuming the worst about their workers, the Japanese companies have got the best out of them.*[40] In the west over recent decades, the trend has nevertheless been contrary to this wisdom. Even so, the gradual deregulation and privatisation of the last forty years have often been counter-productive, especially in social areas like health care. Where competition has been introduced to raise efficiency, which inherent values of vocation and dedication are, apparently, inadequate to address, the effect is subversive of the more noble principles with which people enter such professions.

One might have assumed that the calamitous financial events of 2007–08 would have led to a sobering up of the business communities, to an abandonment or at least modification of some of the harsh practices of neo-liberalism. There was certainly no shortage of recipes and recommendations at the time, most of which however have disappeared without trace. But intense global rivalry, and the lack of political will on the part of politicians steeped in neo-liberal ideology, have allowed business to ride out the storm and continue much as before. Competitive pressures have seen a return to single-minded policies by CEOs in order to protect company interests, so that the phenomenon of firms maximising shareholder value but socialising losses has returned with a vengeance. Faith has been revived in deregulation and flexibility. Meanwhile, the buying up of smaller rivals and the consolidation of corporate giants has continued, helping to limit competition; the built-in natural tendency in American-style capitalism is to try to destroy competitive rivals. There are still those who approvingly echo Joseph Schumpeter's idea that economic growth and technological advance benefit from the rise of large corporations undermining competition. We may not have reached the point of commercial competition being classified as war, as Richard D'Aveni declared, but we have certainly moved even further away from any concept of a capitalism embodying a code of ethics.

This is in such stark contrast to *public interest* or *stakeholder* capitalism favoured in parts of Asia, that it is hard to believe they are both versions of free market capitalism. Charles Hampden-Turner has highlighted the contrast, focusing on the philosophy and practice of Far Eastern nations where more constructive and long-term principles tend to apply.[41] He points out that the language of *games, playing and winning* – often used in industry and commerce – is a pervasive practice in East Asian economies. Hampden-Turner draws on the ideas of James P. Carse, who distinguishes between finite and infinite games.[42]

An important difference here is between those who aim to win outright and those who want to continue playing and learning, for the long term:

> ....*the ongoing process of competing is more important than the interim results.... What is important is for an economy to keep coming up with the best ideas and for that you need multiple players, who learn from their mistakes without trauma or dislocation.... By competing you improve the ongoing process, the infinite game.*[43]

As a result most economies in South-east Asia still deplore the hostile takeover – a common feature of European and North American practice. In the Far East there is also a different concept of corporate ownership, particularly in Japan. In spite of the well-publicised economic stagnation there in the 1990s, cultural factors still influence Japanese behaviour, so that executives will still place the concerns of their employees, customers and suppliers above those of shareholders. And those shares are far more likely to be owned by collections of industrial groups, such as the famed *keiretsu*, than by pension companies, hedge funds, or other financial institutions. Anglo-Saxon business norms fly in the face of these judicious presumptions.

Another important factor is the Western custom of playing the capitalist *game* within boundaries – leaving issues like the environment, welfare and culture as *externalities*. The Anglo-Saxon model represents a business ethos in which corporate responsibility is of the most constricted kind, unlike the Far Eastern tendency towards inclusivity. In fact, policy is so single-minded that even employees, suppliers and lenders are often treated by firms as external agents to be rendered serviceable for purely selfish and short-term motives. Employees may be summarily dispensed with, contractors paid belatedly after their *credit* has been exploited, and banks sifted for as much loan funding as possible in order to leverage ambitious commercial schemes. For such policy, justification is usually claimed on the basis of shareholder interest and the success of the core company. In most Asian economies, a more all-embracing commercial approach is adopted; after all, banks and suppliers may well hold shares in the company:

> *The aim is not to make the company profitable at the supplier's expense, but to make that supply chain more profitable than other*

> *chains for all members – what is called 'shared destiny' [And regarding employees] Even where laws confine contracts to one year, custom decrees long-term relationships with employment security.*[44]

How different this evidently is from the narrow short-termism of American and British companies, where the *infinite game* would be a very eccentric concept. But, then, this is the result of the domination of market relations by neo-liberalism, as well as of the more confrontational nature of Western societies, neither of which seem to have been much alleviated by the economic problems of the last decade. There thus becomes an artificial demarcation of responsibilities, a closing off of the scope of our natural obligations – tendencies fundamentally inimical to communal, and individual, welfare.

Examining free market capitalism reveals a further odd feature of its operation. Two centuries after the western Enlightenment fostered the progress of mankind through rational action, there are still those who support an economic system whose general benefits are held to derive mainly incidentally from the selfish motivations of a minority. Not only that, but the more effective, resourceful and innovative the entrepreneurs of this minority are, the more control they gain of the levers of the economic machine. In fact, through originality, self-denial, and even luck, the efficient entrepreneur in a freely functioning capitalist system could win monopoly control of a commodity or product market. Whatever the degree of success achieved would inevitably take him/her on a path towards that point, whether or not value for money was being provided. It would be an element of the business incentive involved, and the rationale of such a market would support and encourage it. Pure ideologues of the unregulated economy would not tolerate, for example, bodies like Britain's Competition and Markets Authority, believing them to be against the public interest. But in a true *laissez-faire* economy the aims of individual entrepreneurs, legally pursued, are – if successful – ultimately against society's collective interest; the more effective the entrepreneur, the more vulnerable that interest becomes. The cut-throat competition of Anglo-Saxon capitalism can have devastating social consequences, even while it proclaims its contribution to public service.

II. In economics as in life, perception is all important. We see a world around us in which money and consumption appear the norm, but because of their dominance our world view is now refracted through a monetised prism; as a result we see a strange version of reality. It is as if all individual and social concerns relate to how they can be assessed in monetary terms. Fundamentally we know this not to be the case, but the overwhelming force of economics today, especially in rich countries, has perverted our consciousness, insisting that everything has a financial *bottom line*. Michael Sandel puts this down to the way market-oriented thinking has invaded areas of life previously conditioned by other, social norms.[45] As the role of economics has been extended to encompass the study of human behaviour, not merely issues of money, inflation, supply and demand, etc., so it has become more ambitious and far-reaching. Sandel sees it as ...*a simple but sweeping idea*:

> *In all domains of life, human behaviour can be explained by assuming that people decide what to do by weighing the costs and benefits of the options before them, and choosing the one they believe will give them the greatest welfare, or utility.*[46]

Such an idea has been an integral element of neo-liberalism, and was in at the beginning, as it were, and at the principal fountainhead: Gary Becker's *The Economic Approach to Human Behaviour* emanated from the University of Chicago in 1976 and was, according to Sandel, the most influential expression of this view.[47] Accordingly, there is no field of endeavour where monetary value does not play a part; education, personal relationships, politics, the environment, and so on – all have their price.

But a capitalist economy – if it is to be part of an egalitarian society – must rest on a framework of values which are not purely those of economics. In earlier periods, market forces operated within norms that were rooted in community, and forfeited social acceptance by going beyond these. Even in 18th-century Britain, values and economic practices had a very different interrelationship than they do today. People – mainly men – were able to pursue their own self-interest without generally damaging effects on community, aberrant practices notwithstanding,

> ...*not only because of the restrictions imposed by law, but also*

> because they were subject to built in restraint derived from morals, religion, custom and education.⁴⁸

And as many commentators have pointed out, Adam Smith's economic analysis in the *Wealth of Nations* rested largely on the social premises in his *The Theory of Moral Sentiments*. From that time on, Western European society was underpinned by Rationalism, and the belief that human nature was basically reasonable. The threads of solidarity ran imperceptibly through 19th-century Britain, bolstered by increasing government intervention and civic responsibility. But the 20th century saw a steady atomisation of society which, together with religious decline, has gradually destroyed the ethical buttressing against which commercial affairs operate. And since the 1970s especially, community has been weakened as economic transactions have taken on a purer complexion, less encumbered by values. Under the pressure of neo-liberal philosophy collective concerns have been more and more neglected; the sense of social obligation, once internalized, is steadily abandoned in the face of seductive materialistic argument.⁴⁹ After all, we are told, society is made up simply of individuals and their needs, a postulate which is both product and pre-requisite of the success of modern capitalism.

However, whatever personal, social, communal values we may think important, the strident message we hear says that they are all, fundamentally, economic values. Part of the neo-liberal project is to encourage us to see our motives as based solely on money, prices, supply and demand, since ultimately – we are told – we make choices and decisions according merely to the costs and benefits involved. This is the essence of the view summed up by Becker, because, he says *...the economic approach is a comprehensive one that is applicable to all human behaviour...*⁵⁰ (my emphasis) – even though he says we may not be aware of it. (But the extensive list he then enumerates shows that he believes this really does apply to ALL human behaviour.) And how fortuitously congruent is this bizarre notion with neo-liberal economic fundamentalism! Our whole social panorama has been transformed, for as Michael Sandel concludes, *...the last few decades have witnessed the remaking of social relations in the image of market relations.*⁵¹ So has it taken neo-liberalism to allow us to see the light, that we are conditioned by money in all of life's decisions? For, although the potency of this thesis has seemingly swept all before it, especially in rich nations, it still has to contend with centuries of complex human experience celebrating the finer feelings of family life, love and romance, philosophical and artistic endeavour, poetic sensibility, voluntary service, sporting ambition, and scientific wonder. Are we to believe that these are motivated solely by money?

It is a strange paradox that, while we are exhorted to see everything in monetary terms, our material needs have – for most people in developed economies – largely been met. We are not supposed to believe this, since we are persuaded that our needs are never likely to be fully satisfied; there will always be more 'stuff' available, more to work for, more to desire. In centuries past, it was assumed that there would eventually come a time when our basic requirements had been met, regardless of how equally they had been shared, but when we would have reached a state of wellbeing which obviated the drive for more. (Both Adam Smith and John Stuart Mill believed a *stationary state* was feasible, if not desirable.)* But with the development of heightened consumer capitalism, attitudes were transformed into a presumption that wants are unlimited, and if such wants cannot immediately be met, then a scarcity is implied. So economics becomes the study of how to manage that scarcity and how to gratify the unsatisfied desire. And keeping the engine of free market capitalism constantly running has been an indispensable part of these objectives. The Canadian economist Harry Johnson summed it up in 1960 as *...we live in a rich society, which nevertheless in many respects insists on thinking and acting as if it were a poor society.*[53] Now sixty years on, this is an appropriate description of much of the affluent world, societies with what Robert and Edward Skidelsky call *... flagrant manifestations of insatiability... in which a competitive monetized economy puts us under continual pressure to want more and more*[54]*...* a fundamentally anti-social phenomenon.

Nations and peoples have passed almost imperceptibly to this new phase of free market capitalism. Certainly, one can date from the 1970s the steady transformation to a more individualistic, merciless economic culture. But there has been not merely a change in degree, or of severity towards more ruthless competition. Any sense of arriving at individual and social improvement through collective, national resolve seems to have been lost. If selfish greed is lauded as being indirectly beneficial, then where is the link between individual motive and social utility? The

---

* It is important to note, as Robert and Edward Skidelsky remind us, that when writing of the growth of an economy Adam Smith instead used the word improvement, a term which included moral as well as material progress.[52]

abiding preoccupation with wealth and ambition has already separated off the former from the latter; they are not connected by a bond of social conscience, a sense of responsibility which was common in many societies for long before the 1970s. In Britain, the willingness of the upper classes during the Napoleonic era, already cited, to make a financial contribution to the national war effort was crucial, though not mirrored in other large states of the time. Later, the increasing responsibility of 19th-century governments for the general welfare of citizens gradually softened the raw edges of industrial capitalism. Victorian civic leadership provided municipal services which benefited not just the bourgeoisie but also large sections of the working classes. The private philanthropy of business entrepreneurs helped highlight social problems and pave the way for the beginnings of modern welfare state provision in the Edwardian period. But beyond all these, at the micro-social level of community life, lay what Priestley called that ...*reservoir of instinctive fellow-feeling,* an inheritance which he saw as a vital ingredient of the national character,[55] which to a great extent it still is.

The communal spirit and civic responsibility cited take many forms, which have always existed alongside our acquisitive and competitive tendencies. They comprise the voluntary organizations, the community self-help groups and local charities, the normal humanity of neighbour towards neighbour in the vernacular framework of common benevolence. Such motives will not be destroyed by capitalist competition, but they may have a smaller arena in which to flourish, so invasive have markets become. Meanwhile the acquisitive compulsion becomes more dominant, because, as the Skidelskys have pointed out, ...*capitalism has inflamed our innate tendency to insatiability...*[56] – always present, but formerly bound by custom and social attitudes. Running youth clubs, serving meals-on-wheels, or sitting for an afternoon with a house-bound old age pensioner do not constitute a panacea for social problems. They simply denote the customary private charitableness of those who do not seek reward for everyday humanity, around which must still exist the public provision of decent social services. It is ludicrous to assume, as the more tendentious free marketeers do, that Adam Smith's idea of the *invisible hand* indirectly advancing the interests of society means that common altruism and a developed welfare state are somehow superfluous. Nevertheless, here is the view of John Gummer, then a Conservative government minister, in a TV interview at the 1988 Tory Party conference: *It's only in a free enterprise society that one can help one's neighbour.*[57]

Such an eccentric comment appears to overlook completely any notion of civil society, which has been such an important concept since the Enlightenment. It also reinforces the perverse link between economics and human motivation which neo-liberals persist in making, and which seeks to crowd out humanitarian public spirit. There has to be scope for a vibrant civil society, a space between the individual and government authority. The Enlightenment philosophers, especially David Hume, were among the first to recognize this; Hume regarded liberty as a vital ingredient of civil society but here did not only have economic liberty in mind. And despite Adam Smith's attention to markets, he put considerable emphasis on the independent citizen, the individual who has a responsibility towards others, including the duty of safeguarding the institutions and customs which make up a free society. But whereas in Smith's time this would have been seen as a Christian duty, today it is the implicit obligation for ensuring that community can thrive in the space between market economics and government. A competitive free market in goods and services cannot provide this; in fact, if allowed to dominate, it will stifle the human instincts which help build communal solidarity. True liberalism, as opposed to neo-liberalism, makes demands on the individual; but to flourish, it requires the absence of overweening power, whether exercised by state authorities or totalitarian free markets.

However, the last generation or two have seen civic society beleaguered and maligned. Under the onslaught of market fundamentalism, perceptions have grown that selfishness itself is laudable, with a corollary creeping in that altruism is overrated. After all, is not altruism another version of self-interest?* When the beguiling metaphor of the *invisible hand* is acknowledged so widely, we are subtly induced to view our individual desires in a new light, and thus before long we become habituated to a fresh stereotype, and we look at free markets with different eyes. This perspective also happens to build on the popular impressions created by Richard Dawkins' work *The Selfish Gene*, which misleadingly conveyed a picture of humans as essentially selfish

---

* Yves Smith cites some of the contortions which neo-liberals perform in order to rationalize examples of altruism, to explain such 'anomalies' in less selfless and more individualistic terms. Even the giving of presents is stretched by interpreting it as being due to the indirect self-interest of the giver![58]

creatures. The broader reality, of a species in which both selfishness and altruism are incorporated because they both have evolutionary utility, has had far less attention paid to it. The relentless focus on the individual, to the neglect of community, also contributes to these developments. For, as consumers in a free market environment, we are encouraged to look to our own concerns, supposing that we are nobly serving the wider interests of the economy. Huge attention, and encouragement, are concentrated on our role as free-spending consumers, protected by a range of statutory consumer rights. Our responsibility as citizens of a national polity, or our roles in a political democracy, are correspondingly neglected. The unremitting focus on the free market tends to blind us to other, non-material obligations.

Another persuasive aspect of the deference accorded to economic self-interest is the notion of *trickle-down* economics. We are led to accept that by giving full rein to the so-called wealth creators in society – particularly by reducing their tax liability – their entrepreneurial acumen will not only enrich themselves, but also grow the economy so that all of us materially benefit. As the pie becomes bigger there will be increasingly larger slices even for those at the bottom of the economic pyramid. This picturesque notion – associated with Adam Smith's *invisible hand* idea – has gained considerable traction over recent decades. But it is largely myth. First of all, the clue is in the name: it signifies an actual *trickle*, a barely perceptible dribble which may or may not find its way to your bucket, if appropriately placed. The idea has been around since the late 19th century, but the term *trickle-down* itself was popularized by the American/Cherokee humourist and journalist Will Rogers in the 1930s, who joked that money also trickled up, though rather faster than in the other direction! Nevertheless, the theory of trickle-down was in effect heralded by governments of all complexions from the 1980s onwards, even the more left-leaning New Labour in Britain and the Democrats under Bill Clinton in the USA. Tax cuts for higher earners and financial deregulation have led to an upward income redistribution, proclaimed as the route to accelerating growth and greater national wealth to benefit the poor. And so the theory has passed into common folklore, an accepted principle that hardly merits scrutiny.

The misplaced belief in *trickle-down* is all the more bizarre, bearing in mind its total ineffectiveness in contributing to wealth distribution. Firstly, the policy has not led to accelerated growth over recent decades, and secondly, the impact on people on the lowest incomes in developed nations has been, if anything, negative. The evidence is so widespread it can hardly be disputed. During the so-called Golden Age of Capitalism, between 1950 and 1973 – until the crisis in higher oil prices hit western economies – growth rates were at historically high levels in the rich, developed world: around 2–3% in the USA and Britain, 4–5% in Western Europe, and even higher in Japan. From the 1970s to the financial crash of 2007–08, growth never reached such exalted levels. Yet top marginal tax rates have seen major falls, especially in the Anglo-Sphere. In the USA, for example, they came down from 70% to 28% between 1980 and 1988, and in Britain from well over 90% in the 1970s to 40% in the '90s.[59] Reductions were much smaller in countries like France and Germany. The lowering of top income tax rates and the huge rise of executive salaries, which happened simultaneously, certainly does not seem to have stimulated productivity, contrary to the predictions from the right, says Thomas Piketty.[60] In fact, Piketty maintains that no link exists between the decrease in top tax rates and the level of productivity growth since 1980. Yet the conceit of the effectiveness of *trickle-down* theory still persists.

Of course, it is often alleged that figures can be produced to prove the validity of any thesis. But when all the statistics point in the same direction there is good reason to trust their veracity. An American think-tank, the Economic Policy Institute, maintains that between 1979 and 2006 the top 1% of earners in the United States more than doubled their share of national income from 10% to almost 23%,[61] figures from a centre-left body. But the evidence comes from all quarters, especially that showing the pervasive increase in income inequality in the developed world. An ILO (International Labour Organization) report of 2008, for example, showed that income inequality rose in sixteen out of twenty advanced economies for which data had been submitted, with the USA at the head of the list.[62] And in the United States, the redistribution of wealth upwards is indicated by these startling figures: during the thirty years prior to the 2007 financial crisis, the richest 10% appropriated around three-quarters of the growth in national income.[63] In terms of GDP, income distribution is quite significant, according to researchers at the International Monetary Fund. A 2015 paper on income inequality specified that if the income share of the richest 20 percent of a country's workers increases, then GDP growth actually declines over the medium term, a clear indication that benefits do not trickle down.[64] However, tellingly, an increase in the income share of the bottom 20% is associated with higher growth.

The strong body of evidence against the effectiveness of *trickle-down* theory, and in favour of curbing the rise of top salaries, is really not in doubt. Yet popular prejudice militates against its acceptance, and reinforces the myth of the growth-enhancing effects of favouring the already well-off in society. Corporate influence – particularly its political lobbying – evidently plays its part in sustaining the illusion. And misleading dictums such as "we have to create wealth before we can share it out" appear to carry weight, implying that as things stand resources are insufficient for redistribution, and that only the rich are wealth creators. Then there is the reluctance of policy makers to challenge society's elites, and be accused of fostering the politics of envy. In Britain a predominantly right-wing press has contributed to attitudes against hand-outs to those deemed the *undeserving poor*, while the whole political campaign to reduce welfare payments has labelled many recipients as scroungers. But set against this background is the reality that, especially during an economic downturn ...*the best way to boost the economy is to redistribute wealth downward, as poorer people tend to spend a higher proportion of their incomes.*[65] Compared with this, giving more to the already well-off will always be less effective. In any case, any contributions to the rich would need to be conditional on specific measures to increase investment, and thus employment. Nevertheless, the dominant prejudice favouring the better-off appears able to *absorb* all Roszak's ...*dissonance and contradiction*... put against it,[66] leaving it relatively intact in spite of the huge body of evidence challenging it.

The maintenance of the neo-liberal *status quo* is not an option, if greater democracy and emancipation are to be achieved. And the extension of free market values into new fields will only exacerbate present problems; it will not even delegate more economic autonomy to consumers, but merely give them an illusion of greater freedom – should they have the economic wherewithal – while the market invades previously inviolate areas of their experience. Neither free market fundamentalism nor further state control over the economy will provide greater agency to individuals. It is the democratization of the entire economic system, as well as the reining in of its tendencies towards excess, which are necessary to increase personal control over those areas of everyday life where the economic motive has a legitimate part to play. However, while there is scope to extend the sovereignty of the individual over fields where the market has a need to intrude, that is not to say that the demands for market commodities can be governed entirely by the separate preferences of atomised individuals. Capitalism has moved beyond the phase where market forces generated by personal choice on a purely individual basis can be expected to provide general satisfaction. This reality has been recognized by some commentators, but almost all political leaders continue, mostly unwittingly, to expound the benefits of increased affluence and greater opportunity exercised through the market.

However, this theory is no longer fit for purpose, and has not been so for some time. For we are now at a stage where, in order to ensure that the sum outcome of private choice largely corresponds to the aggregate of individual expectations, some account has to be taken of the interaction *between* separate choices. This particularly applies in what the late Fred Hirsch first called the *positional economy* – to distinguish it from the material economy of ordinary consumer items. In an important work, Hirsch cited the example of urban workers living in the leafy suburbs, and thereby enjoying the benefits of city life in the form of access to jobs, entertainment and a variety of amenities, while escaping the more undesirable features of urban living.[67] The advantages of tranquillity, cheaper land, and easy access to rural areas can be bought with a house in the suburbs. But as general affluence increases, the attractions of this *commodity* lead to a growth in demand, a rise in property and land prices in the suburbs, and a reduction in quality of the commodity. In fact, its characteristics will be substantially changed, as Hirsch makes clear:

> *With a declining city on its inner side and another suburb rather than open country on its outer side, the essential character of a suburb will be altered and in part destroyed.*[68]

Over time, quality dilution leads to loss of satisfaction and disappointed expectations, expectations which were met at an earlier point only by the more affluent, who were able to steal a march on their fellow consumers. In these circumstances, the combined preferences of individuals produced a result that none intended, and which was worse than would have been produced by some form of interaction between individuals to co-ordinate their aims more satisfactorily.

The *invisible hand* cannot provide a solution to this predicament; neither Adam Smith's philosophy nor any bastardized neo-liberal version of it has a response to make here. Society has moved on from the day when heightened expectations could be satisfied for the few with the palliative of luxury items to answer the need for ambition or self-importance. Now it is dreams of status and lifestyle that have to be indulged, and this is mainly to be done through *positional commodities,* which by their nature can only ever be limited in supply. Before the enjoyment of these goods becomes too congested, their use can of course be restricted in the interests of the rich who acquire them first. The price mechanism of the market could be used, for example, to prevent the saturation point of suburban crowding being reached, and thus exclusively preserve the desired quality of life for the more affluent. But since this elitist approach implies that the suburban lifestyle will always remain in short supply, it permanently excludes the majority of aspirants from the prospect of being able to enjoy it. This aspect of the good life will always be out of reach, while the economic philosophy of the age encourages everyone to try to achieve it. And it emphasizes the message that under capitalism there will always be *haves* and *have-nots*, cruelly undermining upwardly-mobile ambition in the current economic system.

Thus the illusion of the promise of eventual affluence under modern free market capitalism is perpetuated, though with the myth carefully concealed behind the constant sloganeering of neo-liberal rhetoric. But these features of the system are by no means new; they were identified by Fred Hirsch and others in the 1970s. The booms and busts of fluctuating macro-economics come and go, but the promise of free market capitalism remains the same, reinforcing the message of future affluence and emancipation. And now, once the economic ravages of Covid-19 have been remedied, a revival of expansion and growth may restore belief in higher living standards, and so further enhance the demand for *positional* goods, a demand that cannot be satisfied by the majority. Meanwhile, the greater material inequalities of the present age will persist, and with individual endeavour just as separate and self-centred, so communal awareness and obligations will continue to be neglected, and much individual satisfaction will remain thwarted. The mechanism of the market, as it presently functions, cannot resolve these problems or play any part in addressing their social consequences. For some time to come, the illusion may persist that affluence and choice are the keys to personal satisfaction through the market. However, beyond the realm of most material goods it may become clearer that, as Fred Hirsch once emphasised, choice always seems more attractive before other individuals have exercised their choice.[69] It is later that disillusion may set in.

These arguments are not an apology for any economic or political ideology; they are merely an explanation of the working through of modern capitalism, unravelling the deficiencies of the market, in the post-recession world. Suggestions for a social or communal element to be incorporated into the functioning of that market are made here on the basis that some degree of co-ordination of individual choices would be able to produce a result closer to that desired by those concerned, than an atomised market process lacking any systematic arrangement. Of course, this returns the focus to the community, as the last chapter emphasised. It would involve management and regulation on the basis of consensus, whether by national or local authorities – although where feasible the principle of subsidiarity should be adopted; consensus is more easily arrived at when arrangements are made at the lowest possible administrative level. Protests against such ideas will be heard, that they are against the freedom of the individual, that greater bureaucratic regulation will restrict autonomy and stifle enterprise. Free market ideology has such a hold on the public consciousness that it forms an integral element of the prevailing *...ambient noise*, identified in the first chapter. But such myths need to be confronted if we are to achieve greater satisfaction for our own personal choices. Otherwise, returning to Fred Hirsch, *Individual choices, each made separately and thereby ... without taking account of the interaction between them,* (will) *combine to have destructive social consequences.*[70]

III. An area where the separate concerns of the self-regarding individual come up against the wider communal interests of society is tourism. In fact, the dilemmas and problems of modern world tourism perfectly exemplify Hirsch's comment, above, as well as his contention that our separate, self-directed choices, when made without co-ordination with those of others, result in outcomes that few of us would individually have chosen. Over the last fifty years, tourism has been transformed into a multi-billion pound industry, said to be the largest employer on earth; one of every eleven people now works in tourism and travel. And it is a business in which even many low earners – in developed and developing countries – can aspire to a packaged fortnight in the sun or a weekend break in a city of which they may barely have heard. The result is vast numbers of tourists beating tracks not only to Mediterranean or Caribbean beaches, but also to countless cultural, historical sites and theme-park attractions which cannot cope with either the massive influx of human beings or the intensive transport requirements to get them there. The wear and tear on cathedral steps, hillside paths, and the floors of historic houses point to the special problems faced by particular tourist sites, while the environmental stresses on coastal areas resulting from beach holidays involve wider long-term dangers.

As globalisation proceeds apace, so tourism will spread ever more widely and have yet more significant effects on communities everywhere. Recent high-profile examples of the pressures of tourism have centred on the impact of cruise liners. Southampton, Europe's busiest cruise terminal, can accommodate half a dozen gigantic vessels at the same time, all running their engines twenty four hours a day, with hugely damaging effects of pollution locally. A ship such as the gargantuan Harmony of the Seas, with almost 7000 passengers and over 2000 crew, will burn around 96,000 gallons a day of some of the most polluting diesel fuel, emitting more noxious chemicals than millions of cars. Then there is the impact of thousands of passengers disgorging themselves from these vessels onto the streets of, for example, Venice, where a fragile urban infrastructure cannot cope with such massive numbers. With locals steadily pushed out of *La Serenissima*, the population has halved to around 55,000 inhabitants, the majority of whom object to their city being swamped by tourism; in an unofficial referendum in 2017, involving 18,000 Venetians, 99% supported a ban on cruise ships. The picture is similar in many other popular Mediterranean cities, where medieval streets and ancient buildings often simply cannot cope with modern mass tourism. An $8 trillion industry will, of course, expect to provide pleasure to millions of tourists, as well as substantial employment, but is unsustainable if global expansion continues on its present trajectory.

Local opposition to growing tourist numbers has become evident over recent years. For example, in Barcelona, where 1.7 million visitors in 1990 had become 7.4 million by 2012, huge resentment has developed against the saturation of city neighbourhoods by day trippers from cruise ships, as well as against the behaviour of some younger visitors – often British. An anti-tourist group, Arran, has been blamed for vandalism targeting vehicles and luxury hotels, under the banner of 'Barcelona is not for sale'. Meanwhile, local government measures have been taken to restrict, and in Mallorca to fine, unlicensed holiday rentals. Airbnb has been a particular target; while it has had a major impact on city centre accommodation in many countries in increasing holiday letting to visitors, it has also been blamed for pushing up rents and property prices. However, the pressures of tourism are now being felt in less obvious places: residents of the Scottish island of Skye are concerned about the vast increase in tourists and their impact on the community and environment, while Cambridge – a key stop on Britain's tourist trail for foreign visitors, where a punt on the river is imperative – has made touting for punt tours a criminal offence! With tourist numbers continually rising, with the potential of millions of newly affluent visitors from the developing world, the character of tourist sites is bound to change. In fact, on a summer weekend the sight of the river Cam teeming with punts all jostling for space, might suggest that quality dilution has passed the point of no return.

The neo-liberal capitalist approach to these significant issues is to leave them to the free market to resolve. Certainly, if the costs of foreign holidays were to rise substantially, visitor numbers would likely fall, as popular locations became more exclusive. And there is no reason for tourists not to pay the full cost of the consequences of their visits. There is certainly no justification for aviation fuel continuing to escape proper taxation, or indeed for VAT not to be levied on airline tickets, while the costs of the impact that international airports have on the local environment are still largely externalized. Of course, the *polluter pays* principle should apply in these instances to its fullest extent, and charging for the effects of tourism, such as the environment tax in Mallorca, helps defray costs and does have its place. But market mechanisms can only be a short-term measure. The limited perspective of free market fundamentalists here exposes the fallacy of applying price mechanisms to every and all *goods* involving money transactions and human demand. Consumer products are made to be consumed; tourist sites are very definitely not to be treated as such, but to be passed on intact for others to enjoy. It is this qualitative difference, between mass-produced commodities with a limited lifespan and the natural, environmental and architectural attractions with unique characteristics, which exposes the absurdity of treating tourism as just another *product*.

It is the obsession with money and markets, and not just on the right, which blinds us to capitalism's limitations in resolving problems which affluence has helped create. In fact, the success of markets in raising living standards has converted itself into a myth of omnipotence, and has become one of the ....*inevitable categories of the human mind*[72]... through which we view modern issues. The problems tourism creates will require solutions of a different kind. There is no alternative to regulation, that bane of neo-liberals; in the medium to long term, sophisticated exercises in people management will have to be mounted so that mass tourism does not destroy the very attractions on which it is based, as well as despoil the human environment of residents in tourist localities. Restricting numbers through piecemeal allocation, not based on price, could be adopted in many tourist locations – even for crowded islands or beaches in summer. Local authorities will need to limit the berthing, or even size, of cruise liners at their ports, while capping numbers of beds or rental properties will be required to prevent saturation of popular destinations. Economic support should be given to poorer areas where unsustainable numbers of visitors are putting intolerable strain on water resources and sewage systems, and where sometimes even golf courses are laid out for foreign tourists in spite of the plight of the local people. Tourism must cease to be seen as simply a route to easy money or economic progress.

Rationing and control may be unpopular with people who believe their affluence gives them rights to travel without hindrance, but such policies will need to be adopted in the interests of tourist locations and especially of the residents who live there. However, measures should be carried out on an egalitarian basis, rather than privileging the more affluent travellers. For example, if overcrowding is the problem, timed tickets to popular tourist spots would be a fair method of managing excessive numbers. With boats and divers causing damage to Caribbean coral reefs, or excessive building development harming much natural habitat, limiting access by rationing will help protect vulnerable sites. Where visitor numbers are causing excessive wear and tear to areas in, say, the Lake District,* or Machu Picchu in Peru, access needs to be tightly regulated in order to conserve the attraction for future

---

* The budget for repairing paths on the fells was in 2018 put at £350,000 annually.[73]

generations. Entry may eventually have to be controlled, just as in admission arrangements to an art museum for popular exhibitions of famous paintings. The growth of so-called *eco-tourism* can have only a superficial impact on the deteriorating position. And some form of restriction may need to be applied to second home ownership, always preferably administered by the community through democratic local government. However, in the long run the management of tourism will itself have to become 'big business', and its role acknowledged by communal consensus.

In the case of public monuments of national heritage, it is especially important that democratic principles are applied. Quotas and timed entry procedures need to be adopted to regulate visitor numbers, not a demand and supply price mechanism. Entry to, for example, Windsor Castle or Canterbury Cathedral would thus be managed in the same way as buying a cinema ticket, and without a premium put on ticket prices. Using market mechanisms alone to regulate entry to cultural or historical attractions will result in unequal access to places that in many cases were handed down as legacies equal to all. And as tourist numbers rise globally, money should not be the chief criterion in regulating visits to prominent sites such as the Roman Coliseum or the Taj Mahal. As regards Mediterranean coastlines and Caribbean islands, they do not yet constitute part of the planet's natural heritage which all have a right to visit. As disposable income increases, the ensuing higher demand for world travel will eventually have to be managed, in the communal interest. No-one has the inalienable right to allow their expensive passage on a cruise liner gratuitously to despoil the resorts where it stops off, or the environment more widely. The answer of free marketeers is often to maintain that economic expansion will eventually provide opportunities for all, but this is a recipe for preserving popular tourist sites for the affluent, since in the case of *positional goods*, which are limited, no amount of economic growth will provide the less well-off with the means to emulate them.

In more economically equal societies, lack of means would not be such a key, determining factor. Social comparisons mean far less when the vast majority of one's compatriots have similar levels of wealth and income. In such environments, the stakes are not so high; the rich do not have the same incentive in paying for exclusivity when it is accessible to the majority of the population. Since status will always matter to some degree, it may continue to be looked for, but in ways which do not come at such a high monetary price. However, in a winner-take-all society with great disparities of wealth, people will concern themselves far more with expensive, exclusive *positional goods*, and be willing to pay much more for the privilege which society appears to confer on them.[74] The neo-liberal mindset, preoccupied with the notion of winners and losers, has only blunt, non-egalitarian solutions to these problems, and will find it hard to come to terms with the suggestions cited. But they are vital adjustments that economically developed nations will have to take on board. The expectations and demands of free market capitalism so often focus on numbers, ignoring the finite nature of so many aspects of the modern world. So, as the fruits of this economic system spread more widely, rationing and co-ordination will have to be enhanced in order to prevent pressure of numbers leading to damage or degradation of quality. This applies whether the attraction is free or paid for, whether it relates to the impact of tourism on dense urban living or on a pristine national park.

This brings us back to the individual and community, discussed in the last chapter. It is only management of numbers which can protect the quality of the experience which tourists or travellers have chosen. But the irony here – which should not be lost on neo-liberals – is that growing numbers can mean that the results of our choices as individuals, even for a simple visit to an urban park, are adversely affected by the similar choices of other individuals, a reality with which the hallowed sanctity of individualism cannot cope. The same is true of the transport systems required to take tourists to their chosen destinations; there has to be a presumption in favour of non-market solutions to modes of national transport, where currently the free market rules, in spite of the system of subsidies which distorts them in favour of car and lorry. The common capitalist pre-occupations with mass production for the widest possible market, and for economies of scale, are utterly inappropriate for transport systems, as well as for most tourism. Both need to involve direction and management to deal with large numbers of people, not in ideological opposition to the free market, but here recognising its practical inability to cope with excessive demand.* Above all, measures

---

* Management to co-ordinate large numbers could include an array of policies including a bias towards public transport, which might involve limiting entry to private vehicles at some tourist sites and reducing car parking – except for certain categories of the population – as well as exhorting national and local authorities to do more to co-ordinate holidays and working hours on some staggered basis so that major periods of leisure time among the population were less concentrated.

must be adopted which co-ordinate policy, rather than being left to the indiscriminate workings of an economic system based only on money; this is the way to meet the needs and interests of the largest number of individuals in an individualistic society.

IV. Of course, management, direction, rationing and quotas are terms which imply intervention in the workings of what might otherwise be a free market, (at least to the degree that modern capitalism is uncontrolled). Conceptually, this in itself is an obstacle to dealing with the problems thrown up by the workings of capitalism's current phase, as outlined above. For, even though authorities already intervene in *laissez-faire* markets in a variety of ways, objections are mounted from many quarters as soon as the term *intervention* is uttered – especially when accompanied by *state*. It is as if full-blown socialism were only a step away, and Armageddon just round the corner. The last forty years have transformed the complexion of political discourse, moving the centre of debate to the right, ensuring that government and the economy are seen through a distorted lens with a presumption that the less the former is involved in the latter, the better. How many times do we hear versions of 'government regulation – bad, *laissez-faire* – good', such as Ronald Reagan's famous declaration about government being the problem, not the solution? The previous discussion indicates that the current picture is rather more complicated. It is time to recognize that – since capitalism is not an ideological issue – problems have to be assessed on their merits and pragmatic policies adopted to deal with the complexities of global free markets which bear no comparison even with the 1950s, let alone with Adam Smith's day.

However, such a project will be by no means easy, partly because of the ingrained neo-liberal prejudices outlined above. The myth became established that *laissez-faire* capitalism was the source of Britain's successful economy and its people's affluence. The view became widespread that the untrammelled free market with little government interference was the foundation of Britain's industrial revolution, continuing through the heyday of 19th-century national economic dominance, until Labour administrations in the mid- to late 20th century enormously increased government involvement in the economy. Such is the national folklore as regards how we got to where we are. The reality is that a true free market in Britain, of full *laissez-faire* reputation, actually lasted a very brief period – *barely a generation,* according to one commentator.[75]* It had come about, says John Gray, through a combination of fortuitous circumstances and the unchecked power of Parliament. It hardly outlasted the greater democratization of the political system after the mid-nineteenth century. Indeed, government intervention had begun well before social conditions became a subject of wide public debate. Parliamentary commissions of the 1830s and '40s delved into a vast range of activities to the point that, as one historian put it, *no community in history had ever been submitted to so searching an examination.*[77] The state was evidently taking great interest in the affairs of ordinary individuals.

History shows that governments had been vigorously extending their powers *for the greatest good of the greatest number* since at least the *Hungry Forties,* so that Jeremy Bentham can lay claim to being one of the founders of the Welfare State.** Certainly, the number of Acts of Parliament regulating, among other things, factories, mines, sanitation and the environment, showed that government was pragmatically taking on responsibility for Bentham's idea of *improvement.* And the regulation of industry and commerce which these measures represented – ideological anathema to so many on the right today – was comfortably incorporated into mainstream Victorian thinking. 'The Thunderer' had already given its seal of approval to the trend: *The Times* of May 4th 1847 famously claimed that Parliament

> ....is laying aside the policeman, the gaoler, and the executioner, in exchange for the more kindly and dignified functions of the father, the schoolmaster and the friend.[78]

After the extension of the franchise in the 1860s, both major parties felt the need to bid for working-class support, and the mounting social legislation, as well as specific measures, such as the 1853 law that made it compulsory for parents to have their children vaccinated against

---

* John Gray maintains that *it was gradually legislated out of existence... ...from the 1870s onwards.*[76] To contend, as some historians have done, that Britain clung doggedly to *laissez-faire* until well into the 20th century simply does not fit the facts. The fact that Britain did not impose trade tariffs until after the First World War is a different issue, and does not undermine the present argument.

** After all, the 1848 Public Health Act was largely the work of Edwin Chadwick, a close friend and disciple of Jeremy Bentham.

smallpox within three months of birth, were steadily becoming accepted. Increasing government involvement in the social sphere, with its implications for the free market, did not face much resistance in Britain – to many eyes the citadel of *laissez-faire* in the mid-19th century.

The size, weight and expense of government in Britain had never been as great as in some Continental states, so that increasing *top-down* activity in social and economic life may, to some, be surprising. But the ease with which *laissez-faire* slackened its hold here can be partly explained by the fact that as a doctrine it did not have a firm grip on public consciousness. Classical liberalism was never an inviolate set of principles to the English mind, even to the mind of capitalism, because, as both J. S. Mill and de Tocqueville commented, that mind always had difficulty coming to terms with abstract ideas. It was an inclination for pragmatism, rather than the conscious transition from one ideology to another, which marked the gradual and cumulative increase in state involvement – the result of convenience, not principle. Any fear of overbearing power in the hands of the state was overcome by the need to answer searching social questions, as well as by a history of central government which, since the late 17th century, had been relatively benign in its effects. It should also be said that the Victorians did not closely identify individual liberty with the absence of regulation, as is often done today. Any present day invocation of Victorian *laissez-faire* by neo-liberalism of either the right or the left, should take these issues into account.

The gathering state intervention in the 19th century, then, was not alien to British ways of thinking, and its steady encroachment into the political system was not rejected, for either practical or ideological reasons. Its beginnings cannot be identified with early socialism, as some apologists of *laissez-faire* have maintained. In fact, even a venerable figure like Lord Salisbury saw central government action to remedy national problems as being firmly in keeping with British history, and had no fear of accusations of socialism: speaking in a House of Lords debate in May 1890 he said,

> *Undoubtedly we have come upon an age... ...when the action of industrial causes, the great accumulation of population and many other social and economic influences have produced great centres of misery, and have added terribly to the catalogue of the evils to which flesh is heir. It is our duty to do all we can to find*

the remedies for those evils, and <u>even if we are called socialists in attempting to do it</u>, we shall be reconciled if we can find those remedies, <u>knowing that we are undertaking no new principle, that we are striking out no new path, but are pursuing the long and healthy tradition of English legislation.</u>[79] *(My emphasis.)*

Towards the end of the 19th century, there was a growing awareness of economic problems at home, as nations like Germany and the USA caught up with British industry; talk of *national efficiency* was heard everywhere. It is perhaps surprising that government did not intervene more conspicuously to support the economy in a direct way, as other states did. But this was not down to any aversion to intervention in principle; while many emerging industrial powers were giving full support to their domestic industries, Britain was following its own separate, outward-looking path.

Britain's particular trajectory was due to pre-occupation with its vast empire, which saw capital increasingly directed away from domestic manufacture into foreign investment and loans. In 1870 overseas investment, at £1,200 million, actually overtook domestic investment;* by 1914 it had grown to £4,000 million with an annual return of £200 million, much of it from foreign railways. This financial *imperialism* – the export of capital was both a stimulus to and a result of colonial expansion – established the financial, and especially insurance, institutions of the City of London in a position of dominance which they maintained through the 20th century, and strengthened further after 1979. Manufacturing industry, on the other hand, suffering from lack of investment, was to lose its hegemony once and for all. The country never fully recovered from the depression of the 1870s and '80s, as the capital which might have been spent in helping it to meet the new conditions went abroad. And a vast amount of money flowed out at around 5% of GNP between 1870 and World War One, an astonishingly high proportion of national resources directed overseas. Britain's government had already shown its willingness to intervene in domestic social and economic affairs, but as regards looking for returns on its investments, the focus was on the empire. As W. D. Rubinstein has pointed out …

---

* That overseas investment was already greater than that in the domestic economy by 1870, before Britain had suffered the full force of international economic competition, was significant, as well as a curious phenomenon only a few years after the Great Exhibition of 1851 had shown the British the wonders of their home-grown industry.

Britain's economy was <u>always, even during the period 1815–1870</u>, primarily a commercial/ financial-oriented economy whose comparative advantage always lay in these areas...[80] (His emphasis.) For, however important a role manufacturing appeared to play in British commercial life, it was nevertheless always the poor relation.

These realities are not generally appreciated in Britain. To the extent that recent British history is understood, there is a common impression that Adam Smith's *laissez-faire, laissez-passer* held sway until well into the 20th century, when the state came to be viewed as having the best answers to national problems. The latter was a widespread assumption for a long period, according to Tony Judt, but he believes that *...we now need to liberate ourselves from the opposite notion, that the state is – by definition and always – the worst available option.*[81] He is right in the sense that we have become captive to the idea that the natural presumption should always firstly be in favour of private solutions. *This discounting of the public sector has become the default political language in much of the developed world*, Judt says.[82] This is the distorted prism through which we are encouraged to see social and economic issues, whether it be related to manufacturing, finance, or even the probation service – notwithstanding the consequences of atrocious private sector mismanagement in so many areas, of which Royal Bank of Scotland, in 2008, and the construction company Carillion more recently are only two of the most conspicuous examples. The resilience of this right-wing prejudice demonstrates again the power of a dominant idea in being able to deflect adverse publicity and counter arguments to preserve the *status quo*. In spite of the financial catastrophe of 2007–08, even the partial nationalisation of some British banks did not give government sufficient control to promote the called-for lending to business.

It is certainly time to adjust our glasses, to revise our prejudices; most of the global problems which face us today are beyond the scope of private companies to resolve. Whether it be climate change, global disparities of wealth and income, or cross-border financial transactions favouring transnational corporations, it is only the policies of nation states and co-ordination between them which can have a meaningful impact. Globalisation in the shape of a free market in goods, capital and services will not serve us, and may well exacerbate these issues, in the absence of a proper rules-based trading system which only national governments can provide. Freedom to operate globally without proper regulation lends corporate powers the capacity to distort markets, enhance their hegemony, and constrict the very free market capitalism which they profess to uphold. Of course, intervention in the dealings of private companies or individuals has to be considered and proportionate, and in most cases internationally co-ordinated. For example, not enough has yet been done to regulate the complex financial transactions which contributed to the financial crash, and Ha-Joon Chang points out that if we really are serious about strengthening financial regulations we will have to deal with tax havens. Nation states are content to act decisively when it suits them; they were more than willing to nationalise banks and to pump money into their economies when faced with global economic disaster over a decade ago. But as Chang points out, *Now that Keynes has played a useful role in saving the global economy from total collapse and …. saving the bankers and other financiers from financial ruin, he is being rapidly pushed back into the netherworld.*[83]

As regards Britain's case, the modern interventionist state was evidently developing throughout the Victorian period from a point long before the faltering national economy and newly-enfranchised working class appeared to show its exigence. On the foundations of early political reform was built the modern relationship between state and people, a bond that became increasingly intense in the 20th century. In retrospect, this should not seem surprising. There was nothing in British history which would have made it anathema to society, except occasionally practical obstacles. It became clear after both world wars that the free market could not by itself effect the national reconstruction which was required. During the twentieth century the approaches of Liberal, Conservative and Labour administrations showed varying degrees of state intervention, but the general principle did not change; activist policies were pursued to further the common good. In recent times the autonomy of central governments may have been partially constrained by EU and WTO rules. But underlying domestic policies has been a large measure of consensus that unbridled competition in society is not the best way to increase wealth or to distribute its benefits, and that government needs to play a role. Britain's history since the early days of the industrial revolution has been moving steadily towards this point. It is only since 1979 that a serious departure from consensus has been attempted. It is also a direction that goes against the grain of generations of social development.

V. One of the most powerful myths which free market capitalism incorporates is the deceptive spectacle of choice. Especially in developed economies, individuals are exhorted to choose from an increasingly dazzling array of possibilities, whether among everyday consumer items, television channels, electricity suppliers, holiday cruises, or hair colours. Choice represents freedom itself, an emancipating task – for, ironically, it is an obligation – at every step of our existence a life-affirming process that will lead to personal self-fulfilment. We have no time for doubts; choice is a prospect which we implicitly and whole-heartedly embrace, as having the capacity to provide us with the illusive autonomy we crave. The concept is not something we spend an instant thinking *about*; we simply see *through* it, to the lavish display before us, to the endless possibilities with which choice presents us in our separate, individual worlds. It is as if the host of options facing us means that we can have it all. As Big Daddy says in Tennessee Williams' play *Cat on a Hot Tin Roof*,

> *...the human animal is a beast that dies, an' if he's got money he buys and buys and buys, an' I think the reason he buys everything he can buy is that in the back of his mind he has the crazy hope that one of his purchases will be life everlastin'!*[84]

For extravagant as this thought may be, there still remains the tantalising fruition of choices well made providing us with the ultimate personal emancipation.

Nevertheless, choice remains a mirage, albeit a persuasively alluring one. It is a fancy peddled by free market evangelists, and not only those promoting neo-liberalism. As choice is increasingly to be exercised by spending money, then it is circumscribed by precisely the amount of wealth at one's disposal. With the free market constantly extended, individual autonomy becomes even more conditioned by money and earning power, so that personal control over one's *life-chances* has less and less scope outside of a purely economic framework. A narrow materialistic hierarchy of social life thus grows ever more accentuated, accompanied by a tendency to attach value principally to those items which can be assessed in monetary terms. In this process, it should be perfectly evident that wider personal control – enhanced liberation – were never to be accessible to society as a whole. The capitalist free market system has never offered sweeping material rewards, even for equal levels of effort committed to it. By its nature it is a system of winners and losers. The tangible attractions presented as prizes would not be so lavishly conspicuous if they were easily available to all. The traditional stimulus to a buoyant capitalism has been the lure of material benefit, which is implicitly equated with personal happiness. As such, the heights of pleasure – such as they are – will be accompanied by parallel degrees of distress brought on by want and privation, or so the logic of the free market dictates.

For one thing which an open capitalist economy guarantees is relative poverty, and to the extent that the attainment of life's riches is equated with economic success, so personal enjoyment outside of a purely economic domain will be restricted. Thus the more pervasive the free market, the more dependent one is on its demands, and the less control one has over personal autonomy. Contrary to the promises of the already privileged, this is the true path to serfdom, to what E. M. Forster called *the community of slaves*. In a 1946 essay he distinguished between the material world and what he termed the world of the spirit. He maintained that in the former the doctrine of *laissez-faire* would not work, whereas in the latter it was indispensable if the minds of people were not to be stunted.[85] For some time after Forster's words, progressive thought would generally have agreed with him. What has happened over recent generations is that the material world has been allowed to colonise the world of the spirit to the point where free market principles have managed to inhibit and control thought – something Forster presumed would only be brought about by censorship or a secret police. The categories Forster highlights were never mutually exclusive, but the effect of neo-liberal policies has been the impoverishment of the values and aesthetics of the world of the spirit to a critical degree. It is as if the old distinction has lost its meaning, as if the imagination is now a function of economics, as if we are now *a humanity defined by its ability to purchase.*[86]

For several decades now, terms like choice, empowerment and personal autonomy have led the rhetoric which promised greater control over one's future. In spite of the deceptive vacuousness of the concept, it nevertheless still has a strong hold on free market values, and even if there is an element here of the emperor's new clothes, few of us have the time or conviction to challenge the ideology. In fact, with noses resolutely fixed to the capitalist grindstone, time even to make considered choices, let alone reflect on the merits of the system, are luxuries few can afford. In his book *The Paradox of Choice*, Barry Schwartz highlighted the anxiety created in consumers when faced with the multiplicity of choices available[87] – even if his strategy for careful decision-making, involving a process of several considered steps, might themselves induce further anxiety. As Frances Cairncross once pointed out,

> *The result of the plethora of choice is that few people take choices in the way that economists once imagined: carefully weighing up all the costs and benefits, a cold towel wrapped around the temples, assessing all the information and reaching a rational decision.*[88]

Furthermore, it is hardly likely that our choices in the capitalist free market are going to become restricted, even if many are aware of the fraudulence involved.* One cannot imagine that the vision of self-fulfilment and autonomy held up for us is about to be diluted or modified; treadmills do not work like that. And besides, that would be the route to the undermining of the whole, neo-liberal project.

No, in fact the paraphernalia of choice is being constantly extended, as if providing even more options will compensate for the restricted potential of so many losers in the free market merry-go-round. And now new categories of choice are created, by an internet which provides us with so-called virtual worlds, most of which are ostensibly free to access, and giving the impression that one's life chances are enhanced. Over recent years social media, most notably Facebook with its 2.2 billion members as of 2018, have launched internet platforms which allow users of almost any economic means to connect with others to make 'friends' and share lives. A new range of communities has thus emerged, creating the idea that choice and empowerment have been enriched. But regardless of how idealistic Facebook's founder Mark Zuckerberg originally was, the business model which he and social media employ – sometimes called *surveillance capitalism* – is one which uses the personal data of participants to make their money. Once detailed profiles have been developed, mostly innocently, by users on internet sites, advertising can be targeted in an even more precise manner. The greater the amount of personal information which users provide, the more profit that can be

---

* Some years ago, the London Business School's Dr Patrick Barwise pointed out that when an American family are offered 55 television channels they typically watch around 13 of them a week, and that when 90 channels are available they still watch about 13.[89]

made by advertisers from their data trails. Social media involvement, mostly pleasurable but sometimes pernicious, has vastly enriched their entrepreneurs, as well as companies profiting from their members.

The targeting of internet users has now been taken yet further; commercial companies and media giants have developed complex algorithms to build more detailed profiles of us to deploy in advertising. Once we have revealed our preferences through our extensive online profiles, we are in effect advertising ourselves to the corporate entities who hope to profit from our candid innocence. Aside from the dangers of giving away personal details, making ourselves available for identity fraud, we are announcing our likes and dislikes for the profitable edification of companies, inviting them to take full advantage. The detailed patterns which these algorithms deduce will be employed to *choose* what may be offered to us in the consumer marketplace, as well as to monitor our changing tastes. For even the simplest purchase of internet shopping will confirm or add to our preferences, so that other associated items may then be offered to us. If we show that similar products appeal, we will be indicating our expanding range, advertising to companies our evolving predilections for their commercial benefit. We are frequently offered the chance to personalise what we buy, but in reality it is we who are being customized. We may believe we are special individuals with unique desires, but once advertised, our biases and tendencies can be packaged, and are invaluable to those who can exploit them. Internet users especially should be reminded of the saying *if you're not paying for it, then you're the product*, and reflect on precisely who is doing the choosing.

Indeed, the bright new future of personal self-determination offered by free market capitalism is as much of a myth as ever it was. The qualifications which circumscribe the *free* choices apparently available make a mockery of the suggestion that the market puts one's fate more firmly in one's own hands. But it is a fiction which serves the interests of the established economic system. The dedicated efforts of human beings in their roles of workers and consumers contribute to the functioning of the capitalist machine. By heeding its necessities, they are the medium through which its glory is served – a reality hidden behind the empty rhetoric which proclaims greater individual autonomy and personal freedom. As André Gorz and others have long been saying, in modern industrial capitalism the individual is a means to economic production and profitability – a role whose principal purpose is to minister to the system itself and to those who grow rich by it.⁹⁰ The human individual, whether as producer or consumer, is thereby a resource, needed on both the demand and supply sides of the economy until, because it has become too expensive (i.e. does not spend or produce enough), it is discarded.* As such, how can it be seriously accepted that neo-liberal capitalism intrinsically enhances the personal choice and autonomy of humankind? It is a sop to individualism whose participants are content to swallow it whole, blind to the lack of human nourishment it contains.

So beneath the glitter of our shiny, seductive marketplace lies much disillusion, albeit a disillusion which cannot be admitted. For if we are unable to take advantage of what is on offer, then whom are we to blame? The false hopes, the unaccountable failure representing a cruel addition to the economic disadvantage experienced by so many – these inevitably rebound on us. Where else can we look? For is not the free market system a neutral instrument, value-free and impartial? And are not our political leaders now merely disinterested managers, overseeing the capitalist operation to allow fair play, holding our coats while we get on with it? For far too many aspirants, including many of the more affluent, the outcome of this inelegant scramble for even a modest share of capitalism's goodies can be

> ...*a profound sense of paralysis, immobilism and disengagement, all of which are inadmissable in a society which aims to have enabled, motivated and involved its people as never before.*⁹²

The emptiness which is the result of so much unproductive striving stems partly from the fact that there appears to be no-one who can be held responsible – only ourselves, and the impersonal system. Thus, as Blackwell and Seabrook continue, ...*such complaints can only trail off inconclusively, as we make our peace with a system that has defeated us all.*⁹³ And so what begins as a search for greater personal autonomy according to the rules of the marketplace becomes a loss of faith in self-reliance, and a surrender of dignity.

---

* This is particularly the case with *flawed consumers*, as sociologist Zygmunt Bauman termed them, *the poor of today*, who ...*do not fulfil the most crucial of social duties*... – ... *that of being active and effective buyers of the goods and services the market offers.*⁹¹

Integral to free market fundamentalism is the concept of consumer sovereignty, whose proponents base much of their argument on the importance of individual choice. They maintain that sovereignty lies with the consumer's potential to choose between a variety of competing products, brands and companies. This line of thought easily leads to the conclusion that the more market forces are extended to new areas of social exchange, the greater becomes the degree of choice available to the individual. Madsen Pirie of the Adam Smith Institute once argued that *Those who oppose the gradual spread of market forces are forced to object to choice itself.*[94] However, society does not correspond to the theoretical and incomplete model which these notions comprise. Such theory excludes the social nature of individual choice – already examined – as well as the variety of economic factors which, as has been seen, can circumscribe personal preference to a crucial extent. On the simplest level, choice is as limited as the amount of money in one's pocket, and yet its invocation as a populist rallying cry is intended to appeal equally to all. The inexorable *tyranny of the market*, to use J. K. Galbraith's phrase, is omitted from the theorising of the right. Markets do not serve to enlighten or illuminate; they have a much narrower function. As Geoff Hodgson has said, they promote the power of money, not of ideas,[95] and as such they cannot comprehend the complexity either of individuality or of personal choice in a society which is much more than the sum of its economic parts.

The rationale for the belief in consumer sovereignty rests almost entirely on a theoretical economic model. However, capitalism today does not operate in such a neat and responsive fashion. If life were that straightforward, one can argue, government economic policy would exercise far more effective control over national affairs. In the first place, it is clear that the consumer is not the only active figure in the market, an autonomous agent to whom producers and suppliers simply react. Manufacturers themselves are continually striving to influence consumer demand through astute advertising and marketing; they would indeed be improvident to wait idly for the expression of consumer preferences to condition their corporate responses. Today, vast resources are invested by companies in attempting to influence people, not only to buy particular products, but to come to think of them as necessities. This has been especially effective in the United States: new ideas and inventions translated into established brand-name products with enormous market share. (After all, Gillette razors, Kodak cameras and Kellogg cereals could hardly be said originally to be responses to articulated public demand.) It is in the interests of manufacturing and service businesses for there to be an unwavering faith in the authenticity of consumer sovereignty, so that an ever-expanding consumer demand remains susceptible to manipulation by producers.

The more frequent and more radical the changes in hairstyle fashions, for example, the more demand there is likely to be for hairdressers' services, and hence the more successful their businesses. And it simply makes good economic sense to promote and foster rapid changes in fashion. A key to the success of consumer capitalism lies in the capacity of producers and providers to create constant novelty and change, and to encourage demand for products which were not previously thought of as necessities. Far from allowing matters to be directed by consumers, manufacturers are out to build a dependence on their products and expand market share, thus enabling them to raise levels of production and supply so that the lower unit costs achieved allow them to drop prices and consequently stimulate yet more demand. This picture of dynamic capitalism places the consumer in a relatively passive position compared with the producer, while the imperfect state of knowledge at her/his disposal further weakens the buyer's autonomy. In a technologically complex world, it is impossible to make fully enlightened decisions about the relative merits of consumer products, except in a minority of cases. And besides, the consumer is more than just a buyer in the marketplace, but will have any number of other busy roles.

There are also other factors that contradict the superficially coherent theories of many economists. Consumer sovereignty implies a considerable degree of autonomy in the hands of the buyer. However, capitalism has seen an increasing concentration of power in the successful company. There developed a system of corporate capitalism during the 20th century in which big business, the state, and in Britain – until the Thatcherite war against them – the trades unions, increasingly managed the economy. In addition, a variety of lobby organisations and interest groups forced their attentions on this *partnership* in order to benefit through pressure politics.[96] As regards the consumer, it is evident that, in spite of the rhetoric, her position has been undermined to the point where sovereignty is largely illusory. In a world with free movement of capital, giant corporations like Amazon are able to hold sway. They can arrange their affairs to minimize tax liabilities, whereas individual states may do little without international co-ordination. Indeed, many nation states have GDP levels smaller than the turnover of some transnational corporations, which thus have overweening power to strike hugely advantageous commercial bargains. The strategies of such companies, operating across frontiers, need not be greatly affected by the policies of rooted national governments, and neither are they going to be unduly influenced by consumer power, such as it is. As for investment, individual shareholders will be unable to exercise much authority over company policy in comparison with the impact of corporate investors.

Those who support the market as the overriding mechanism for the allocation of resources, goods and services like to identify the consumer's place in it as sovereign. And further, they even see individual autonomy as most effectively exercised through the economic market rather than through politics. To many, and not only those of the political right, consumer choice is the principal means by which individuals can hope to shape the world to their own designs. According to this view, everyone is enfranchised through the role of consumer in the marketplace, and all are voting repeatedly by the use they make of their spending power. Here the economic system is much more than a mere counterpart to the democratic political process; it actually supersedes it as life's main arena for the fulfilment of individual destiny. As such, the more dominant the scope of economic activity in the functioning of society, the more personal autonomy is, in theory, provided for its members. But as to the sovereignty of individual consumers, it is indeed a strange concept, for, as the late Zygmunt Bauman pointed out, it ....*has neither legislative nor executive agencies, not to mention courts of law – which are rightly viewed as the indispensable paraphernalia of the 'bona fide' sovereigns* (of) *political science textbooks.*[97] Bauman concluded that this makes the market, whose sentences are final and irrevocable, even more supreme than conventional political sovereigns, who may at least allow the right of appeal.[98]

Nevertheless, proponents of consumer sovereignty like to emphasise the democratic nature of the marketplace, in which buyers are continually able to exercise their economic *votes*. This is no more than a flimsy rationalisation, even if in an increasingly centralised state faith in conventional politics is at a low ebb. But the seductive nature of consumerism can mesmerise its adherents to see it as a panacea, compared to which democratic participation can appear an insipid, ineffectual route to self-determination. However, democracy implies equality of participation, some parity of enfranchisement. But where the power of one's vote depends on the extent of one's economic means, there cannot exist a democratic system of consumer suffrage. The effects of birth, effort, thrift and luck are all variables conditioning the authority of votes in the marketplace of capitalism. There are still tensions in society over what constitutes equality and equity, and as yet there is no consensus as to what represents fair economic gain in a system where citizens begin from a variety of starting points, except perhaps a vague understanding that some form of meritocracy is necessary. Those who want consumer capitalism to hold sway over social life in Britain have a duty to resolve these issues. For there is not much sign that human nature is transforming itself to coincide with their vision; society has not yet been successfully conditioned and systematized to the point where it sees its emancipation through consumer power as equally valid as its political representation.

Whether it be in the open marketplace of consumer goods or in social fields like health and education, in which some would like to create a free market, the individual's power is not sovereign. It is hedged in and constrained by such a variety of qualifications that little is left but the name. The hegemony of large corporations, the inequalities of purchasing power, the difficulties of applying capitalist principles to indispensable social *commodities* which do not have a price, and the random inconsistencies of market forces all conspire to make a mockery of the notion of consumer sovereignty. And the varying degrees of consumer autonomy are so disparate that it can in no way be set alongside the individual's political democratic rights as a parallel mechanism for exercising personal choice. The capitalist system would have it otherwise, and much profit is to be made if it only half succeeds in convincing us that it is right. The power of custom and routine sanctions the consumer's predicament; his/her freedom is that of an unequal partner. It bears no relation to the democratic rights connected with choosing elected representatives, for in this field the electors always have another chance to vote for something different. In democracy there is no in-built tendency towards monopoly control, in the shape of dictatorship, and the will of the electorate is sovereign in the way that the consumer's can never be. Consumer sovereignty is the slogan by which producers or their surrogates endeavour to use the open market system to become sovereign themselves.

As to the spread of market forces increasing individual choice, this is a strange, illusory perversion; in fact, overall the opposite is the case. The ever more rigid social exclusion in Britain over the last generation has come about partly due to the pervasive extension of market principles into areas previously exempt from the unbending laws of demand and supply, profit and loss.* As with so many concepts treated in this work, the appearance hides treacherous delusions. What may seem to be a cornucopia of consumer choice leads to an impoverishment of public options. The public domain, never a vibrant concept in British life, has been surreptitiously carved up over the last 40 years, first by New Right Conservatives, and later by their equally neo-liberal New Labour successors. The selling-off of school playing fields and recreation grounds – more than 5,000 during the 1990s – is the archetypal case, restricting the autonomy of individuals to spend leisure time in a healthy fashion in common public space. The whole community loses out when green areas are taken over; enhanced choice is then open only to the better-off, who can afford to use the privatised recreational facilities which may be available. In fact, the areas are more than likely to have been sold by hard-pressed local authorities for car parking space or housing – or, under New Labour, for new school classrooms (in spite of their 1997 party manifesto pledging to end the sell-offs).

The economic trends which have been allowed to develop in Britain, and which have been actively fostered by the political right, have produced a situation in which many people end up preferring the new consumer landscape. They like to use out-of-town shopping centres, easily accessible by car, and modern facilities which appear clean and safe. One study showed that urban residents with cars would choose to visit a country park or green-field garden centre on a weekend rather than walk to a local park.[99] However, these preferences represent those which have been made in the new market-focused environment of post-1970s Britain – not the natural inclinations which at another time may ideally have been preferred. They are sold as the new, progressive way of living. The old, convivial urban model has been lost; because the

---

* The spread of market forces into areas such as Britain's public utilities is often lauded as extending consumer choice. However, the myriad of, for example, available electricity companies and tariffs, or telephone suppliers, represent a bewildering array of choice among what are functional necessities – choices which often require considerable expertise and which many consumers would rather be able to do without. The time spent on selecting the most suitable options is hardly going to enhance consumer sovereignty; the whole charade denotes the victory of ideology over practicality.

original civic ideal of thriving public space has been allowed to decay, it has come to be seen as unsafe and dingy, and above all as *unmodern*. (After all, there is not much profit to be made out of city squares and urban parks!) So the effort to save money on public amenities has led to the withdrawal of their supervision, merely enhancing the vicious circle. Such a policy produces twilight environments with few people, a multitude of surveillance cameras, and little in the way of communal facilities, so driving citizens into *gated* private premises where they will spend their money.

This trend has developed further in the United States where divisions between the *haves* and *have-nots* have become more entrenched. As authors Greenhalgh and Worpole pointed out some time ago, in some American cities *...the dominant concern of the planning brief is to find ways of excluding unwanted groups.*[100] But the consequences of these attitudes were understood there over twenty years ago, lessons which Britain has still not learnt from its own misguided policies.* In New York, the Parks Commissioner summed up his thoughts after a review of policy aimed at replacing park attendants with mobile teams:

> *...the worker who appeared to be idle much of the day had in fact been lending a presence to the park that moderated disorder and gave a touch of humanity to a neighbourhood lacking in social services.*[101]

It is humanity that has been missing from much official thinking and policy. The re-colonisation of public space, areas which do not necessarily have a specific purpose and where people can just idly *be*, is a vital part of the community-based approach to public policy which the 21st century demands. But it entails a view of citizens as *partakers* and sharers in local vernacular experiences and communal space – not merely individuals with money. The consumer can only be king – or queen – with spending power, and then only within the restricted range of choices available, and with a built-in prejudice against more convivial, less market-based possibilities. Consumer sovereignty – a phrase of

---

* The attempt by railway companies to remove guards from trains, presented as superfluous, but patently a way of saving expensive 'manpower', is part and parcel of this invidious trend – doing away with the presence of personnel who might otherwise have a moderating, humanising presence on a variety of public services.

vapid, populist banality – can have only limited significance, and only as part of overall civic sovereignty in a truly inclusive society.

In a landmark work more than 45 years ago, Martin Pawley wrote of the degradation of public resources.[102] He saw consumerism as an enemy of community, and of the citizen: *The triumph of consumer society is a triumph of all private goals over all public goals.*[103] The independent, apolitical consumer – even if not sovereign – is a principal agent in a market economy, and as such is antagonistic to the individual as citizen in community. This schizophrenic relationship is lived largely unawares by individuals in free market societies; consciousness of the loss of public amenities comes to the surface on occasions, usually to be glossed over swiftly by the lure of consumer culture. Thus, education authorities will be ready with plausible economic arguments to justify the sale of school playing fields which, while perhaps helping to stretch the education budget, nevertheless represents the shrinking of the public arena in a wider sense, as does the selling of a recreation ground to make room for a new supermarket. The privatisation of public space is often viewed as *tidying up* and *sanitising* areas that were previously problematic socially. But the building of shopping malls, closed out of hours, can change the character of town centres. With their private management and security they can institute their own strict regime, aimed at maximising commercial opportunities. In the early days of one mall, in Luton, security guards tried to ensure that elderly people did not rest too long on the few available benches because, the manager was reported as saying, *Market research had shown that the general public was particularly distressed by the sight of old people sitting down.*[104] (!!) In such vivid examples, all serving the cause of extending market forces, it is difficult to discern precisely how individual choice is being promoted.

The trend – an anti-social one – towards the increasing privatisation of the public arena is driven mostly by the inexorable demand for commercial profit and individual gain. But it is part and parcel of the apparently general desire for yet greater affluence, a desire which of course can never be finally satisfied. The intense consumer culture of modern societies, predominantly in the developed world, requires an ever higher standard of – economic! – living. As Martin Pawley identified, *affluence is essential to Western societies... because ...without it, or the hope of it, they no longer possess any basis for social harmony.*[105] Pawley saw the future at a remarkably early stage in this process, before the intensity of consumerism had developed to its current pitch. But he already realised that the former communal bonds of society had been weakened in favour of a subversive monetary nexus which was allowed to be promoted on the basis of individual choice. *Affluence is vital to the social organization of the Western world because it has supplanted all the old systems of mutual obligation,* he said in 1972.[106] But the attractions of greater material affluence is not seen as a loss of anything; it is apparently a *win-win* situation, because we are led to believe that with hard work and dedication more and more of us can have it all. Here is the essence of the myth at the heart of consumer culture. We are so intent on realizing its promise that we do not see the old bonds of social accountability dissolving around us.

This takes us back to some of the discussion in Chapter 2. For consumption weakens community; it stimulates the narrow pre-occupations of the atomised individual. A unique characteristic of the role of consumer is the solitary nature of the project, for the pleasures of consumerism are *...meant ....for utterly individual, lonely enjoyment even when relished in company.*[107] There has long been a tension between the individual as citizen and the community. It is often a matter of power, such as in the cases of the privatisation of aspects of the commons, including enclosure movements, when the self-interest of landlords or entrepreneurs took precedence over subservient but wider communal concerns. In modern times government has also used its authority to enrich the national – not community – purse by selling off what had been publicly owned assets. The truly communal arena is somewhere between state and private jurisdictions, but often confused with the former. The dichotomy between them, with private interests in the blue corner and state concerns in the red, has been of such a high profile politically that the communal space in between has been pushed out of the limelight, unnoticed in the wings. Besides, in a capitalist economy, ownership is considered paramount, a requirement which cannot deal with communal assets which, as Tim Jackson points out, are *....owned by everyone and no-one at the same time.*[108] But it is here, in the non-hierarchical, market-free, apolitical mutual arena that the individual-in-community can come into its own.

The future will have to involve the revival of the communal space.

State ownership has been discredited, while further investment in the individual will not contribute to the satisfaction of our separate, personal interests – as was detailed in the previous chapter. However, investing in the community must involve a focus on organization and management, as well as on protection of communal assets. With the spread of market forces, concentration has centred on private interests, so that public amenities have too often being neglected, leading to the private wealth/public squalor syndrome, and the further denigration of the public arena. Of course, quality of resources can more easily be safeguarded when property rights are clearly delineated; thus finances have to be directed towards the jointly-owned estate in which we all have an interest, but which must be managed by communal, preferably local precept. This was the response of the late Elinor Ostrom, who in 2009 became the first female recipient of the Nobel prize for economics. She rejected the narrow options of dealing with common pool resources: either state ownership or privatisation. She recommended having faith in local communities, allowing management to be carried out by those most familiar with local conditions and requirements. In Tim Jackson's discussion of Ostrom's work he recognizes the caveats as regards common resources which are on such a scale that they clearly need management at a higher level of governance.[109]* But this does nothing to invalidate the principal argument here.

VI. To those who see no inherent weaknesses in the workings of free market capitalism, who recognize no incompatibilities between spiritual needs and the economic system *Homo sapiens* has created, the role of the autonomous consumer is significant, but so is the production of more and cheaper consumer goods. In fact, a commodity-centred society has grown up over recent years, so that as developed economies have succeeded in meeting the basic needs of their citizens (in an overall, macro-economic sense), they have produced ever more sophisticated non-essential consumer items, and managed to convince increasing

---

* Tim Jackson highlights an interesting example of public reaction to state management of a common resource: the recent British government's proposal to help reduce its financial deficit by selling off national forests, which came under the authority of the Secretary of State for the Environment. The public outcry which ensued, and which prompted the government to abandon the idea, led Jackson to comment, *The forests may have been the Minister's to own. But it turned out they were not the Minister's to sell.*[110]

numbers of us that they are necessary. At the same time, there has been a growing trend as activities, especially in the fields of sport and leisure, are commercialized and marketed as desirable commodities. There is a tendency to believe, and certainly not only by neo-liberals, that there is almost no limit to the areas of human endeavour in which demand can be catered for by packaged and marketed *products*. This has led to an implicit acceptance that individual needs can be best satisfied through the acquisition of these market commodities. Lip service is no longer paid to the idea that this is a means to an end. As Ivan Illich pointed out many years ago, politics and ethics, and even justice itself, have been reduced to a matter of the equitable distribution to the population of the goods, material and otherwise, that we produce.[111]

This is a further aspect of the willing self-delusion of modern capitalism. As societies become richer, they seize avidly on the glittering baubles of consumer culture, proud that they have the economic wherewithal to take advantage of what they see as their hard-won affluence. In the main, they do not recognize that they are serving the needs of an economic system; they do not dwell on the workings of an enterprise which is designed to increase demand to feed the capitalist demon, a being which is concerned with satisfying its own appetite, not merely the hungry desires of innocent consumers. This artifice is supported by the fact that, even now, there are still enough people in developed nations who remember times of scarcity, if not severe poverty. For those and their children it is perhaps hard to conceive of a world in which material needs are easily satisfied, and more extravagant aspirations are not entirely out of reach. It is in capitalism's interests that they do not come to realise that we exist in the midst of abundance and that, to quote the prescient words of then UN Secretary-General U Thant, even more relevant today than when he said them fifty years ago,

> *The central stupendous truth about developed economies today is that they can have – in anything but the shortest run – the kind and scale of resources they decide to have…. It is no longer resources that limit decisions.* ***It is decisions that make the resources.***[112] *(My emphasis.)*

But for those accustomed to abundance, as well as for those conditioned to scarcity, capitalist economies appear to know no future other than the ever-expanding production of non-essential commodities, in a very finite world.

In order to maintain the insatiable desire for such goods, and to keep the whole economic treadmill inexorably moving, market forces are pushed into new fields which are not inherently amenable to commercialisation. As the packaging of social life gains momentum, an intense commodity bias comes about, and an increasing proportion of daily life falls within the commercial domain. Thus the joy and freedom in taking a country walk becomes converted into a different quality of enjoyment by, for example, paying to visit a safari park, a guided nature trail, or a country estate where the *themed* amenities have been tailored to fit the supposed tastes of the modern consumer family. There is even a tendency for such *commodities* to be valued more because they have been packaged and cost money. Satisfaction gained from activities with open access, and which have not been commercialised, may be devalued, and so interest grows in leisure commodities which appear more exclusive – although of course in the process they will inevitably become less so. But in a hard-pressed world the well-off often feel a need to occupy their leisure time with *valuable*, exciting experiences. However, whereas the effects of the capitalist system may here appear benign, apparently providing greater choice and fulfilment, the reality – as Professor Hirsch has shown – is a restriction of personal freedom. By delineating property rights more strictly, open, public use becomes more controlled, and each time a common, free amenity is lost to the market, personal choice is curtailed. Liberty suffers when limited economic means restrict individual and family enjoyment.[113]

There is a further ominous significance of the effects of commodity bias and the commercialisation of social life. One sees an important disjunction between, on the one hand, those commodities or services which receive their value wholly from market forces or economic planning, and on the other, those whose value is determined by their personal or social use – that is, their vernacular value. The former help to increase the commodity intensity of society; the latter kind, defined by Ivan Illich in a striking analysis, are employed in the service of everyday, convivial, colloquial life.[114] But as this vernacular arena yields increasingly to commercialisation, such changes lead to a growing proportion of people having their needs defined more in terms of the goods or services, than through the basic human transactions of social fellowship. Technology in the shape of, for example, smart phones or computerisation can

– aside from their functional uses – serve human, colloquial purposes, but they nevertheless enhance the commodity intensity of society. And while the social media dimension of these devices may help to enlarge the vernacular domain in a virtual sense, they can also have a negative impact on personal interaction and social harmony. They in any case heighten the preoccupation with market-driven commodities and – in spite of the claims of those lauding social media – accentuate the distance between people by hindering the benevolent, humanizing effects of everyday interpersonal relations. The point has been reached where, as Illich recognised some years ago, commodity consumption is interfering with human energy and vernacular existence.[115]

Thus the notion that commodities are merely tools to personal and social enrichment has become lost, as they take on a much broader significance in the capitalist empire. The more that commodities are produced and glorified, the more fully embedded a population becomes in the consumer-producer culture. From a different perspective, political leaders are willing accomplices in this process, believing a more widespread distribution of *stuff*, helped by greater affluence, will lead to more satisfied electorates – part of the obvious modern *bread and circuses* scenario. Of course, it is in the interests of producers and sellers that personal fulfilment should be sought through purchasing goods and services. The more human wants that can be commodified, the more scope exists for profitable commercial activity. The imperial logic of modern capitalism is that it should continue to expand its domain, taking in cultural and communal elements and selling them back to its subjects – who could have obtained many of them freely before the new masters arrived. These are the more overt characteristics of consumerism, even if capitalist design would rather they were not so. But underlying the whole dynamic of free market consumerism are other, more subversive forces – ones that contradict the superficially benign veneer of commercial operations, in the ...*silent compulsion of economic relations* – to use Marx's phrase.

For buying commodities in the capitalist free market is not intended to provide deep, long-lasting fulfilment for the consumers involved. While it is designed to appear momentarily pleasurable, its purpose is also to contribute to encouraging re-purchase, and is in no way supposed to represent an end of the transactional process. An element of unsatisfied demand is a condition of a self-perpetuating consumer *culture*. Indeed, demand relies on implied dissatisfaction with what one already has, so that, as Zygmunt Bauman explained in a detailed analysis, *Consumer society thrives so long as it manages to render dissatisfaction ....permanent.*[116] And this is partly achieved, Bauman points out, by denigrating and devaluing products *....shortly after they have been hyped into the universe of consumers' desires.*[117] Consumerism requires the recurrent frustration of appetites in order to rekindle demand and restart the buying cycle; without this, faith in the market for consumer goods would not be sustainable. For this reason, Bauman was right to insist that consumerism is *...an economics of deception.*[118] We are not supposed to dwell on the underlying mechanism, or our involvement in it; we willingly comply by not wasting a moment examining the consuming process. We have allowed it to become a *category of the human mind*; we now see life *through* it and not *about* it, and its whole aura is so attractive and promising that implicitly we are more than happy to do so.

In fact, no great emotion or wide reflection is supposed to be generated by capitalist exchange; any hint of real mood or affect might destabilize the process. We need to keep our attention focused on the business of buying. In his study of the McDonald's chain and its role as a paradigm for the functioning of modern consumer capitalism, George Ritzer draws attention to the way people pass through what he calls *McDonaldized* systems*....without being touched by them; for example, customers maintain a fleeting and superficial relation with McDonald's, its employees and its products.*[119] Any sincere expression of emotion is all but eliminated, he says. *...little or no emotional bond can develop among customers, employees, managers and owners.*[120] so that the business can operate as smoothly as possible. Transactions should take place without reflection about their role in the larger scheme of things. Hence, McDonald's or similar *worlds* must be isolated and sanitised, cut off from everyday life and any harsh outside environment. Shopping malls usually lack much sense of place; they are designed as anonymous amalgams and, as Ritzer says, do not have any sense of history. He suggests how in places such as Disney World – a typical example of a 'McDonaldized' system – *People find themselves in settings that either defy attempts to be pinpointed historically or present a pastiche of many historical epochs.*[121] This management of the consumer world thus involves a relentless focus simply on the business of money changing hands. The state of mind of the buying public must be clear and unburdened; there are more commodities than ever, and capitalism demands that they be bought.

VII. The Roman writer Suetonius tells of the inventor who offered the Emperor Vespasian a large saving to take giant stone columns to the top of one of the hills of Rome where they were needed. The Emperor's reply was, *You must permit me also to let the man in the street earn his bread*.[122] Such an example of an executive policy involving the labour market might seem to many today to be either heretical, or almost quaint in its absurdity. The entrepreneurial ambition of that Roman inventor would probably have provided his Emperor a substantial financial saving, and today's neo-liberal regimes would of course have taken full advantage of such an offer, regardless of the cost of higher unemployment. Reactions to the Emperor's rejection of the inventor's enterprise might include bemusement: why on earth would a government turn down an opportunity to save on labour expenses? But this is part of a present day mindset, which accepts modern market fundamentalism as if it were part of *the fabric of existence*, as natural as the air we breathe. It finds it almost impossibly difficult to conceive of a progressive government policy which judges employment decisions on a pragmatic basis, and which does not always come down on the side of the free market and labour saving technology. The resourceful, practical, 'can-do' approach which produced Britain's industrial revolution has given way to the doctrinal fervour of ideological free market neo-liberalism.*

In our ostensibly pragmatic age theory and technology in fact rule. They both take precedence over the concerns of the wider population, condemned as it is to the invidious repercussions of government decisions taken, we are usually told, in the laudable interest of saving money. Allied to the dictates of the free market is the relentless impetus to adopt whatever technological inventions can streamline the capitalist machine – what Lewis Mumford termed *the technological imperative*.[123]** For,

---

* The inventions, such as in textiles, which led to unemployment in Britain's 18th-century cottage industry were certainly not driven by theory and ideology, but were the result of practical entrepreneurship in a period very different from our own.

** It appears that only two things have any chance of hindering the introduction of technologically viable products: money, and specific, demonstrable danger to human health – and the second not always.

advanced technology, tied inexorably to the free market, serves its dearest interests by helping cut back on expensive labour, thus reducing costs and increasing profitability – with the attendant loss felt by society as a whole. There is little opportunity to debate the merits of uncontrolled technological development, which can have far-reaching and over-rapid effects on patterns of life. The community is helpless in the face of this unrelenting advance, and the trend is set to accelerate with the further development of artificial intelligence. But these wider issues can only be decided by broad communal consensus, for which no mechanism currently exists. Unemployment is a huge expense – financial, social and personal – for the community as a whole. It cannot be shrugged off as a structural problem and is never, as a Chancellor of the Exchequer was once reported to have commented, a price worth paying. It is, in fact, closer to Leopold Kohr's description: ...*the degrading saving of manpower through the inappropriate use of advanced machinery.*[124]

In today's world of work, the interests of employees are at the mercy of external forces almost as much as they were during the nineteenth century. Only now, they toil in a working environment which – while the ideology extols the worth and emancipation of the individual – condemns them to a lottery of exigencies which may include part-time work, zero-hours contracts, bogus self-employment, increasing work intensity with high levels of pressure, and employment which does not necessarily pay a minimum living wage, based on what is required to maintain a basic decent standard of living. After the Thatcherite campaign of the '80s to shake up the labour market, to squeeze every ounce of productivity out of beleaguered employees, competitiveness and efficiency became the standard shibboleths, before which all other criteria had to give way. The severe business environment of the 1990s' recession accentuated the trend, allowing corporate management little opportunity to highlight social concerns, but in the austerity of post-crash Britain after 2007, belt-tightening took on a new, savage significance. As companies reduced staffing levels, those remaining were under greater pressure to work harder and longer. Thus a virtue was made out of a necessity, suggesting long hours were to be applauded; they even turned into a form of political correctness among the professional classes. But for thousands of others, *zero-hours* contracts and temporary or part-time work became the only option.* No longer did we hear of the proletariat; the modern version has become known as the *precariat*.

Nevertheless, the contemporary working environment is replete with conceptual confusion. We live in the world of the flexible economy, where we are free to take advantage of the *portfolio* lifestyle, break away from the dull routine of years with the same employer, 'pick and mix' our working hours in an occupational *smorgasbord*, independent of the tight control of demanding line-managers – at least, this is how the apologists of neo-liberalism would have us see it: simply a matter of choice! They want us to accept the well publicised adverse consequences of the new regime as mere incidental side-effects, few in number, the unhappy transgressions of rogue entrepreneurs who will eventually be weeded out of what is essentially a benign system; globalisation will eventually work for the benefit of all. But the phenomenon is almost all image; the reality becoming increasingly obvious includes, for example, the 7 million people – about 25% of the British labour force – who have had their work schedules regularly changed at short notice by their employer, according to a 2010 survey,** as well as the nearly one million people on zero-hours or similar contracts by 2015, reported in official figures.[127] Then there are the 13% of employees who worked more hours a week than the 48 laid down in the European Working Time Directive.[128] The evidence is ubiquitous – in the profusion of statistics as well as in the wealth of anecdotal testimony. It more than justifies the conclusion that a malign employment environment is nothing less than a systemic feature of neo-liberal capitalism.

It is not one of the tasks of the present work fully to document the iniquitous features of much contemporary employment. The drip-feed of data entering the public domain is persistent, and conveys an image that things are not right in the world of work, but this is commonly put down to competitive globalisation as well as to the demands of austerity following the financial crash. It is as if everyone – policy-makers

---

* The effect of austerity on employment is not adequately revealed by the unemployment figures, but its impact is real enough in the rigorous demands made on those still in work. As Will Hutton pointed out, British output fell by 6% during the recession (up to 2010), whereas employment fell by only 2%. The new employment picture was bleak enough to persuade many workers to accept wage freezes, new roles and even wage cuts.[125]

** Uncertainty regarding working hours and timetables is an ongoing issue, particularly among lower paid workers. One recent finding was that 29% of the lowest paid (those earning under £1,200 a month) did not know their working hours for the following month, whereas this affected only 7% of the highest income group.[126]

and citizens alike – have been struggling against these twin pressures, against circumstances over which they have little control. Despite this sophistry, a generation of deliberate political and economic choices have been directly responsible for the predicament of recent times, but glossed over by the day-to-day cut and thrust of partisan invective. Nevertheless the whole weight of policy – by Conservative and Labour governments – has been to keep taxes low (especially on companies and high earners), eschew all but essential public investment, maintain a regime of light-touch regulation, eliminate obstacles to the autonomy of transnational capital, and thus create favourable conditions for corporations to flourish, wherever they happen to reside. This approach – the very opposite of the necessary Keynesian alternative – had the attendant purposes of slimming down the state and isolating employees from sources of support, the very epitome of divide and rule. It remains to be seen how this neo-liberal regime will be impacted by the demands of economic recovery after Covid.

Thus the flexible economy – flexibility, of course, advantageous almost exclusively to employers – is a perfect instrument for the neo-liberal project. But the effect on employment is profound, transforming the traditional process of hiring labour. For example, the new so-called *digital platforms* take on staff but not in the conventional sense of employees. Rather, the companies involved work as internet market forums, matching buyers with sellers and profiting from each transaction. The workers taken on – the *taskers* – are free lance, though not strictly self-employed. They must supply their own equipment – say, vehicles in the case of the taxi platform Uber – and though they therefore may be said to own the means of production, they are dependent on the company for the number of working hours available and must follow its employment conditions, including the obligation to accept trips strictly on Uber's terms.* The so-called *gig economy* includes a variety of services – everything from food deliveries and house cleaning, to even standing in line for people queueing for theatre tickets or expensive new smart phones. They are mostly run from internet platforms,

---

* Uber's business model has been challenged in the courts in several jurisdictions. In Britain an employment court ruling went against it in 2016 by deciding that Uber's workers were employees, an appeal against which also failed. But in April 2018 a US judge in Philadelphia decided that under federal law Uber's drivers were in fact independent contractors, not employees. Eventually in February 2021, Britain's Supreme Court ruled that Uber's drivers were, while not full 'employees', at least 'workers' entitled to certain employment rights.

which maintain that their workers are not employees but independent contractors, the absurdity of which can be highlighted by cases where the *taskers* are on call. But such employment is evidently precarious where it does not qualify for normal employee rights, such as sickness benefit or holiday pay.* This represents the re-casualisation of labour – thought to have been consigned to history in developed economies.**

These trends signify a reversal of the progressive development of labour rights and conditions during the twentieth century. But it is also a continuation – of the weakening of workers' welfare which began with the attack on trades unions in the 1980s. There are now whole sections of business where workers have been uncoupled from the conventional framework of employment and set adrift in a mostly part-time environment of uncertainty and vulnerability. The increasing isolation of workers is to the benefit of large companies, whether digital platforms, brokers, or conventional firms. In his analysis of *Why Rentiers Thrive and Work Does Not Pay,* Guy Standing points out that ....*atomisation drives down wages and transfers costs, risk and uncertainty onto the precariat.*[130] Thus, as the autonomy and bargaining power of labour is further diminished, so rentier capital accrues yet greater influence – much of the funds for digital platforms deriving from venture capital from private equity firms and the like. After all, it is in the interests of capital that employment be separated and individuated so that its atomised parts can more effectively be controlled. Standing refers to ... *occupational dismantling ....the labour-related entitlements and protections built up during the twentieth century...* being steadily eroded.[131] The overwhelming flexibility which these changes represent is part of an employment model which is portrayed as modern, necessary, and above all benign – good for business and good for labour. But it is in fact just another aspect of the extravagant neo-liberal myth.

Behind such fantasy, employees are faced with the spectre of actual regression from the gains achieved by social democratic advances of

---

* In June 2018 a group of 50 Deliveroo couriers won a six-figure award from the takeaway delivery firm in an out-of-court settlement of an employment rights claim. The riders argued that they had been unlawfully denied rights, including the legal minimum wage and holiday pay, after being designated self-employed contractors. However, Deliveroo's settlement of the case did not include an admission of liability.
** A remark by Bob Bahramipour, CEO of Gigwalk, is illustrative here. (His company recruits workers for short-term tasks in retail and marketing.) He was reported to have commented, *You can hire 10,000 people for ten to fifteen minutes. When they're done, those 10,000 people just melt away.*[129]

the twentieth century. The social protections and norms which regulated employment – whether statutory or part of professional bodies or trades unions – provided a civilizing framework of ethical standards for a large part of the labour force, and prevented the emergence of what has become an insecure free-for-all. But the corporate platforms and digital start-ups of the gig economy, as well as many transnational companies, often see regulations and labour standards as impediments. They view collective agreements, and even the codes of conduct of professional bodies, as anti-business restrictive practices, and consider that ethical considerations should have no role in the marketplace. The logical extension of these attitudes would be a neo-liberal landscape of individual workers alone and detached, with only their abilities and resourcefulness to support them. We are moving in that direction, towards a scenario where stable, full-time, year-round employment would doubtless become the privilege of a minority, so that ..... *for almost half the active population, work no longer takes the form of an occupation which integrates them into a productive community and defines their place in society.*[132] (Perhaps we have already reached this point; for these words were written by André Gorz almost twenty-five years ago, as neo-liberalism gathered pace and the flexible economy started to become characteristic of many advanced economies.)

Yes, being employed is certainly a means of defining one's place in society; it has much more than a narrow, functional purpose. It helps to confer status and meaning in situations where one's role in community has become increasingly difficult to construe. For some in this new scenario this is not a matter of concern: for the single, upwardly mobile professional, a spell of *portfolio* employment may be merely a stepping stone to higher things, and may hold other attractions as representing the sleek, modern way with an Americanised gloss. But in a divided nation this is not a situation which the majority have any chance of emulating; they have more modest, fundamental expectations, one of which is to find identity in work. As Sigmund Freud said, work is the chief means of binding an individual to reality. And it encompasses

> ....*the need the individual feels to appropriate the surrounding world, to impress his or her stamp upon it and, by the objective transformations he or she effects upon it, to acquire a sense of him- or herself as an autonomous subject possessing practical freedom.*[133]

These sentiments – so obviously fundamental to identity – would have been seen as commonplace before the socio-economic changes of the last forty years. But the transformation in employment and the disintegration of community has made them appear at odds with modern capitalism. The result, André Gorz believes, is the damage to the individual's potential to form a reassuring social image, a rounded identity. Both individual and community have been sacrificed to corporate aggrandisement.

The new, flexible capitalism challenges us with questions about purpose, character and identity. But on the personal level these are rarely answered, attention invariably being focused on the macro-economic landscape. In a probing analysis some years ago, Richard Sennett examined the implications of these economic changes for personal and family existence, drawing on a variety of testimony in interviews with Americans of different social stratas.[134] He explored the disorientating effects of trying to keep up with workplace transformation and the need constantly to reinvent oneself. He asks: ...*how do we decide what is of lasting value in ourselves in a society which is impatient, which focuses on the immediate moment*? and: *How can mutual loyalties and commitments be sustained in institutions which are constantly breaking apart or continually being redesigned*?[135] Even in America, spiritual home of the flexible economy, the pain of perpetual adaptation in an ever-fluctuating labour market takes its toll of vernacular life, behind a façade of efficient modernity. Sennett conducts an in-depth examination of one family which – though previously upwardly mobile with a salary in the top 5% – then experiences the effects of downsizing, through which they adapt their way to new roles, with considerable difficulty. *Prosperous as they are, the very acme of an adaptable, mutually supportive couple, both husband and wife often fear they are on the edge of losing control over their lives.*[136] While the image of neo-liberalism offered is of a progressive, propitious force, the underlying reality in the world of work is frequently disillusion, and all too often personal tragedy.

The demands of the new labour market are more far-reaching than its proponents imagine; they go to the very heart of personal existence. For the family Sennett calls an *American Dream couple* were afraid of losing control not just in their jobs, but at a deeper level. The husband felt that... *the ways he has to live in order to survive in the modern economy have set his emotional, inner life adrift.*[137] Paid employment, running a business, or even controlling the reins of the national economy are the functional roles that fulfil our need for productive activity to sit beside the rest of life. But they are not separate from that other life, and the values inherent in work are not different from those needed at home. Change and flexibility have their places in both settings, but stability and endurance are also important. Loyalty and responsibility, long-term objectives, and working for postponed rewards – these have their roles throughout community. But as Richard Sennett asks, *How can long-term purposes be pursued in a short-term society? ... How can a human being develop a narrative of identity and life history in a society composed of episodes and fragments?*[138] One of the subjects of Sennett's book, a young executive, expresses concern that the example his own life is setting his children is entirely at odds with the values he hopes to teach them. These considerations are rarely given a high profile; the fictions endure that there is no alternative to current practices in a competitive global environment, that by working hard we can break through personal and professional restraints, and in so doing enrich both our inner and our working lives.

These experiences are replicated in other economies, particularly in the so-called Anglo-Sphere, where neo-liberalism tends to predominate. But, again, when they are highlighted, attempts are often made to explain them away as aberrations, unusual circumstances which are not the norm, or the consequence of austerity which, though painful for some, will eventually come to an end followed by a resumption of the prosperous, good life. However, the catalogue of despair and dissatisfaction cannot be dismissed so readily. British employees have some of the lowest levels of job satisfaction internationally: according to statistics reported in NatCen's latest British Social Attitudes survey, out of 20 European countries responding, only 6 were more dissatisfied than the UK.[139] Nations at the top of the rankings tended to be in northern Europe, and with high levels of taxation and social welfare infrastructure, while countries coming below the UK were principally from eastern Europe. And in another study, Britain ranked sixth out of eight major economies in a 2017 survey of 23,000 employees.[140] These findings chime with research in 2015 by the London School of Business and Finance which revealed that as many as 47% of British professionals of different age groups wanted to change their jobs, a desire for better job satisfaction cited as one of the main motives.[141] In the world of work, the glossy façade of neo-liberalism cannot easily hide the unsatisfactory experiences of so many which, far from being anomalies, are integral to a malign economic system.

In spite of the apparent dynamism and optimism of the American economy, attitudes to work there have parallels with those in Britain. The so-called *American Dream* may contain the expectation of being able to improve one's life chances through meaningful employment, but there is nevertheless much disillusion with work in the United States. An interesting survey by the research think-tank The Conference Board in 2014 showed that the majority of Americans – 52.3% – were unhappy at work. In its annual survey the Board reported that job satisfaction had fallen significantly since its first polling in 1987, when 39% expressed dissatisfaction.[142] There is ample evidence that employment status does not provide immunity from negative feelings about work, with well-remunerated professionals experiencing similar attitudes. For example, a survey of more than 17,000 US doctors carried out by Merritt Hawkins revealed that job satisfaction was declining, and around half were simply feeling burned out.[143] As a result, the on-going shortage of American physicians is likely to be worsened by around 14% of them planning to retire and a further 10% intending to switch to part-time work. Neo-liberalism has severe ramifications even for affluent, well-paid professionals in the mainly private American health care system.

In Britain, there have been repeated reports of low morale afflicting workers in the public sector, especially among the so-called *caring* professions. The well-publicised substantial salary increase awarded to NHS doctors by New Labour in 2003 has not led to sufficient numbers entering the profession, nor did it result in lasting improvement in its morale. This supports other findings which indicate that pay is by no means the decisive factor in levels of work satisfaction. Surveys have frequently shown that having interesting employment, a measure of control over work, social support in the workplace, and adequate time to do the job properly are all crucially important in determining satisfaction. Years of economic austerity significantly exacerbated neo-liberal practices, severely impacting these values. Cutbacks in the private sector have increased workloads and job intensity, while in public services reduced numbers of workers, as well as frequent, imposed system changes, have limited the capacity of employees – professional and other – to do an adequate, satisfying job. Morale is at a notoriously low ebb in many of these occupations, particularly in teaching and in the judicial system. This also is a direct result of neo-liberal policy; the deliberate reluctance to increase taxes properly to fund public services is a systemic part of the design: to promote the private sector and serve the needs of the better-off in the vain, though conspicuously half-hearted, expectation that wider society may benefit.*

VIII.   Such is the panorama of much free market capitalism during the first quarter of the twenty first century. It is based on a fundamentalist creed which demands adherence to a set of values that take precedence over their practical consequences. Faith must be placed in *invisible hands* – a theological concept indeed – in *laissez-faire*, in minimal regulation, and in what is claimed to be a system of efficient equilibrium which will lead to the optimum allocation of resources, and thus to an outcome embodying the best of all possible worlds. By increasing the commodity emphasis in society, and allowing commercial values to penetrate every nook and cranny of social existence, these neo-liberal, extremist principles will be served. The fact that economic markets do not function in this idealistically theoretical manner fails to disabuse their adherents. In this respect, also, it appears as a religion, whose followers admit their failings – weaknesses of the flesh, as it were – but remain dedicated in their resolve to reach the promised land. In other words, as fallible individuals, we fail to live up to what our faith demands. As many other religions, neo-liberal capitalism has its gurus, its time-honoured masters who were the first to reveal the truth. But in this case it is part of the fraudulent espousal of the dogma; for the ideas of Adam Smith and David Ricardo have been perverted in their modern incarnations. Enlightenment ideas have been wrenched from their historical setting, bathed in the aura of Victorian values and modern prejudices, and clumsily grafted on to contemporary political philosophy.

Because of the delusive aura of neo-liberalism over the last forty years it has been easier than might have been expected to peddle its appeal. Certainly its renown as a neutral system, without bias, fitted in well with the developing post-modern atmosphere at the close of the last century.

---

*   Appreciation of the negative effects of advanced capitalism is by no means new; they had begun to show themselves at least 25 years ago. In his book *Britain on the Couch* (1997), Oliver James pointed to the dissatisfaction and emotional malaise they induce. Although real disposable incomes rose by 80% in the quarter century after 1971, the benefits had been distributed very unevenly. The consequent relative deprivation, and the high expectations which were impossible to fulfil, led to depression, phobias and neurosis, he believed.

Meanwhile, increasing affluence following the economic open-heart surgery of the Thatcher era convinced many that neo-liberal policies had been entirely responsible – an instance of the confusion of concurrence with causation. (One must distinguish between traditional free market capitalism and the fundamentalist, neo-liberal version in a globalised setting.) And the subversive appeal of choice – discussed above – helped many believe that personal autonomy had been enhanced. However, since there is rarely any form of economic equilibrium, market information is hardly ever comprehensive, and competition is never perfect, it is entirely disingenuous to pretend that capitalism has any claim to a scientific system. Financier George Soros has criticised such attempts, saying that the *...supposedly scientific theory... turns out to be an axiomatic structure whose conclusions are contained in its assumptions.*[144] He then went on to observe, with delicious irony, *The resemblance to Marxism, which also claimed scientific status for its tenets, is too close for comfort.* Neo-liberal capitalism is merely an extreme, refined version of a free market system which has been around for several centuries, but its new conformation places profit and money above people and values.

Yet the system is content if confusion about different forms of capitalism is not removed. For when it is challenged, a defence is often mounted from a general capitalist standpoint, pretending that it is freedom of the conventional competitive market that is being attacked, by those who would advocate collectivism. A *Daily Telegraph* leader in 2012, entitled 'For Britain to flourish so must capitalism', was an apt example of this *Straw Man* defence.[145] Just a few short years after free market excesses had brought about the financial crash, it argued a case few in mainstream Britain would oppose – that there is no current viable alternative to *capitalism* as a system. But by maintaining that ... *the 20th century's failed experiments in centralised economic planning and socialist intervention...* show that ...*The alternatives don't work*, it conveyed the notion that those attacking neo-liberalism were advocating some form of socialism.[146] The polarisation of positions leaves little room for discussion of other ideas in between, and within capitalism. For example, competition being a vital ingredient of many aspects of the market does not mean that it must always dominate; there are areas of society where its presence is simply antagonistic. Margaret Heffernan exemplifies this in her work *A Bigger Prize: Why Competition Isn't Everything and How We Do Better*.[147] She shows the extent to which competition is overrated, with numerous cases of companies and organisations which have found success through collaboration, without going anywhere near collectivism.* But this is not the lens through which we generally view economics.

An essence of the challenge to modern societies is the imperial nature of such an invasive economic ideology. It purports to be a beneficent, positive kind of liberalism on which all prosperity depends, but its success relies on our feeding its voracious appetite. Its imperial ambition was summed up by the then Chairman of the American Federal Reserve in 2007: *The world is governed by market forces*, said Alan Greenspan, in a declaration which included his view that policy decisions in the US had been largely replaced by global market forces, so that it hardly mattered who became the next president.[148] The financial crash followed shortly after Greenspan's hyperbole, which certainly placed it in a special light. Nevertheless, in spite of being an illusion, this opinion is still widespread today. It encompasses an idea of society as part of global economic systems, rather than vice versa. This represents a huge gulf of understanding between neo-liberalism and its opponents: free market economics are but one component of civic society, albeit a vital one for material prosperity. There are important social, political and judicial goals which citizens demand, and they cannot all be met by competitive capitalism. George Soros, who has profited considerably from capitalist finance, is now a passionate critic of market fundamentalism. *Markets reduce everything, including human beings (labor) and nature (land), to commodities*, he says. *We can have a market economy but we cannot have a market society.*[149]

The prism through which we commonly view these ideas refracts them so that they appear binary – as if by not accepting all the fundamentalist neo-liberal baggage we are on the other side, with fully socialist credentials. This false dichotomy has become ingrained in the twenty-first-century psyche, a notion *through* which we see economics and politics, but rarely examined. And right-thinking citizens are supposed to be on the capitalist side of the divide – with little thought of the kind of capitalism desired, but ready to defend freedom against revolution. But a kind of revolution has already taken place surreptitiously over recent decades in the transition from conservatism to neo-liberalism.

---

* And in any case, the endgame of unbridled competition is to win at all costs, not necessarily to preserve the equilibrium of the rivalry in order to continue playing. The economic consequences of this ambition can often have destructive results for society as a whole.

Free markets overturn established ways of doing things, including traditional moralities, says John Gray,[150] – especially so with extremist free market systems. The future may indeed herald a major social transformation through information technology and artificial intelligence, but it is likely this will still involve a journey through versions of capitalism. And how quickly it develops will depend on its management by human beings – how much they understand the process, and how much they care. The abrupt overthrow of the capitalist system is far less likely, which in any case would likely result in the re-establishment of something like we have now – such has been the historic pattern following cataclysmic upheavals. The danger, of course, is that we will proceed imperceptibly into a more extreme, neo-liberal future, blissfully unaware of the piecemeal *primrose path* which we are following.

It is difficult to see modifications to the capitalist machine being carried out until its contradictions are more fully realised. The system's inexorable drive for economic growth and capital accumulation in a finite world, the pursuit of short-term profit over future wealth creation, and the tendency towards commodification of vernacular, social experiences, bringing them within the scope of expanding market mechanisms – all these will continue to increase instability and exacerbate social inequalities. They are also at variance with free market economics, as conventionally understood. As economist Peter Self explained, *The current market doctrine stresses the need to boost consumption by intense marketing etc., whereas the orthodox theory assumes that consumption represents the unsolicited preferences of individuals, subject only to a need for information.*[151] This dissonance is coupled with the distorted image of the private sector as being the sole repository of wealth creation. Mariana Mazzucato makes clear, in her debunking of private industry myths, that it is not the case that venture capitalists are the true entrepreneurs and risk takers: ....*to put it bluntly, this fabricated story hurts innovation and increases inequality,* she says.[152] However misleading the picture may be, it is nevertheless part of the enduring false image of modern capitalism, a commonplace notion that the public sector has had difficulty in undermining, and which – in spite of the financial crash and the economic impact of the Coronavirus pandemic – has maintained its hold on the public consciousness.

When Margaret Thatcher first came to power in 1979 she set out *....to change the approach....* as she said in an interview in 1981. She believed that *....changing the economics is the means of changing that approach.... Economics are the method; the object is to change the heart and soul.*[153] Though her approach was radical, she could not be said to have changed the heart and soul of Britain. However, by her no-nonsense, fundamentalist economics, she transformed the way capitalism was seen, and how it was conducted. The neo-liberal emphasis on the private sector and the attack on the public, communal ethos, coupled with similar changes in the USA, helped produce the divisive economic policies of the years up to the crisis of 2007–08. The task now is to counteract a whole era of economic philosophy by appealing not to dogma, but to rational common sense as well as, yes, to heart and soul. Challenging the fallacies of current free market 'philosophy', thwarting the insidious appeal of bogus consumerism, and emphasising the inherently collaborative, participatory, less Darwinian capacities of contemporary community is the only route to a better society, as well as to greater emancipation of the individual. This is the essential *change of approach* required now; far less certain are the methods to achieve it.

In view of all that has been said in this work about modern perspectives and how capitalism and individualism are commonly viewed, an indispensable starting point is to try to counteract the incessant barrage of neo-liberal rhetoric. It is easy to see why most people can't help but think that the modern free market will be our saviour,* and that its negative side-effects are incidental blips which sensible government policy and greater affluence can remedy. This has to be confronted squarely by marking out a position between neo-liberalism and socialism (no, not a Third Way!) by emphasising community involvement and decision-making at a local level, restricting the market, and tackling corporate hegemony from a national and international standpoint. A mammoth degree of rhetorical re-framing will be required to match the advocates of neo-liberalism and undermine their flawed dogma, above all among the dominant right-wing media. But we should not be cowed; what do they have to show for forty years of free market fundamentalism? Leaving aside the dubious statistical evidence, are we in Britain better off as a nation? If so, why do we – as nominally one of the world's richest – still have crises in housing, social care, prisons,

---

* Revisiting the remark of Oliver Wendell Holmes Jr. in the opening to Chapter 1.

mental health, to name but a few, as well as crumbling infrastructure affecting, for example transport, and school buildings, and of course, looming environmental disaster? These problems will not be addressed by further doses of neo-liberalism.

Thus, an alternative strategy has to be vigorously sold. A key area is the scope of the free market; it will necessarily have to be reined in, eventually to limit it to fields where demand and supply, profit (and loss) have legitimate roles to play. It cannot be allowed to rampage through society, damaging individuals and families in their efforts to negotiate their everyday concerns. There is a basic array of life's necessities which should be readily available to all – however modestly. The minimum requirements for a decent existence in a rich country have of course changed over the years, but today should include adequate housing, local transport, sports facilities and internet access, all at affordable prices, as well as greater emphasis on stable employment at a proper living wage. These elements are vital to ensure not necessarily equality of affluence, but parity of dignity and status in a society where all need to believe they have a fair share. They are indispensable priorities which cannot be put on hold while the delusional promises of *trickle-down* theory are indulged, so that – like a mirage in the desert – they remain indefinitely a nebulous phantom on the horizon. Such basic needs take precedence over the freedom of individuals to exploit others for profit, or the right to massive remuneration for running essential public utilities. The primary objective would be – while acknowledging its autonomy with non-essential items – to put a limit to the scope of the free market, restricting its capacity to do harm in a rich economy where there is plenty to go around.*

---

*   In 1944, in the final months of Franklin D. Roosevelt's presidency, he was too ill to deliver his state of the union address to Congress, and so broadcast it by radio. It was not thought to have been filmed, until activist Michael Moore discovered a filmed recording – not shown at the time – in a lost university archive in 2009. It contained Roosevelt's proposal for a second bill of rights – a new vision of a better American future – including a guarantee of employment at a living wage, a decent home, medical provision, protection against destitution in sickness and old age, and even freedom from unfair monopolies. None of these remarkable elements of his speech was broadcast at the time, and today would all be widely condemned in the US as an overtly socialist manifesto. But most of them are simply the vital requisites of any society with an advanced economy.[154]

It is not the business of this work to provide a detailed programme of reforms, economic or otherwise. Nevertheless, there are broad outlines – to be elaborated in Chapter 7. For example, an acceptance of higher levels of taxation will inevitably be required. A progressive wealth tax would be a priority, accompanied by increases in inheritance and corporation tax, as well as higher income tax rates on top salaries. Britain has become accustomed to levels of tax well below what were common in the 1970s, as well as less than those of many other successful, advanced economies today. But in order to have the decent society citizens have a right to expect, more of the national wealth has of course to be redistributed, along Keynesian lines. And while the disposable incomes of, at least, the top 5% will be reduced, the revenues thus generated would be invested in public infrastructure of all kinds – material and social – increasing employment and therefore tax receipts in the process. Much of this investment, such as in renewable energy or in public amenities, can be revenue-generating; such schemes must take precedence over expensive, ill-advised projects like HS2, which will produce little return on vast investment, other than a marginal saving of travelling time between north and south. Social investment by local and central government has to pay due regard to overall quality of life, in what must essentially be a low-carbon future, and not only to narrow, short-term profit.

As regards the basic essentials of life's material infrastructure, such as utilities and local transport, there should not be the potential for profit by private companies – or in the case of some current train franchises, by foreign states! It is ludicrous to maintain that indispensable services such as water or electricity cannot be provided efficiently by communally-owned enterprises, without the need for vast executive salaries being paid at public expense. Over time, some privatised services will have to be brought back under government control, while a much more rigorous approach will need to be applied by the regulatory authorities of those concerns remaining in private hands, as well as a greater role for employee participation in the running of companies of all kinds. This does not mean wholesale nationalisation of the means of production, for the focus is not on means, but on outcomes. But helping to keep the expenses of the vital necessities of individual and family life to a minimum, and preventing advantage being accrued by allowing these to be exploited, would inevitably require the reversal of some earlier privatisation. To take one example, how can a society condone a situation where an unemployed citizen wishing to travel to a job interview, but without car access, cannot afford the exorbitant cost of 'public' transport or does not have a regular local service?* Such inequities do not impinge on the national consciousness as major disasters, but nevertheless represent significant personal and communal dislocation: the result of inappropriate dogma.

Rich countries have the wherewithal to remedy such failings, but in Britain this is prevented by a view that sees principle as more important than outcome, often coupled with a prejudice against those seen as the undeserving poor. It is such judgements which must be contested, with – in the case just cited – the provision of an affordable, regular, subsidised bus or train service. For the absence of this, especially in rural areas, is a form of exclusion from what can be considered civic claims on the national patrimony – necessities which would not be pondered even for a moment by the more affluent in the population. It is here that there must be parity of status, a form of equal rights.** After all, we do not require citizens to be means-tested to judge their fitness for equal treatment by the police or fire services, or for protection in wartime or a national emergency. In these situations we can call on the resources of the nation to come to our assistance, and such principle should also be applied to the provision of basic living standards, without which there is no civic equality, by which we are all demeaned. It is only our cramped perspective which prevents this approach being readily accepted, the result of years of free market evangelizing. And what is the current homelessness crisis but a national emergency, exacerbated by economic austerity, as well as by forty years of misguided housing policy? Today's society demands inclusiveness to minimize the effects of amoral, indifferent economic theory.

Restricting the unbridled autonomy of the capitalist free market could make a contribution to these objectives. By limiting its range, particularly with regard to life's essential commodities, citizens would be less at the mercy of indiscriminate capitalist ambition, which would help to reduce vulnerability. Recent decades in Britain have seen moves in the opposite direction, for the abiding logic of capitalism is to expand the scope of the free market, commodifying more and more of society.

---

* In January 2019, around 25% of people in Britain were without access to a private car for their own use.

** Peter Self, following William Galston, argues that a liberal society is ...*a joint cooperative project*, and as such should contribute to the satisfaction of the basic needs of its citizens, who should have a reasonable claim on the allocation of society's resources. Without this, liberty would remain merely a theoretical concept, he believed.[155]

This must be reversed; it is socially divisive and increases inequality. Market forces are not sacrosanct, and so must be kept in their place, their freedom of movement restrained. One effect of the trend to put a monetary value on more and more goods and services is, as the Skidelskys warned, that .... *capitalism constantly enlarges the sphere of monetary measurement and thus the ease of direct comparison.*[156] By limiting the scope of such measurement, and reducing the range of goods by which comparison can be made, the hazards of material life are more likely to be contained. There will still be plenty of opportunity for families to compare themselves with their neighbours, and try to emulate the 'Joneses', but there is no reason for such comparison to reach down to life's necessities, with the consequent exclusion and humiliation.* Recognition of a family's failure to be able to afford to go on holiday, or buy a new second-hand car, is far more bearable than the stigma of having to go to food banks or needing to apply for free school meals.

Thus, by reining in the market, the liability of ordinary people to the vagaries of advanced capitalism would be reduced. The economic stakes in life would be lowered for those less well off, and the competitive money economy would therefore have less chance of impacting their quality of life on a daily basis. Of course, this would have to be accompanied by wage levels which would guarantee a decent, minimum standard of living, without the need for welfare top-ups. At the same time, if more of life's ordinary vernacular intercourse were to be available either free or at minimal cost, then modest incomes would not mean exclusion from the accepted norms of the national experience. An aspect of what some view as 'progress' has been the steady development of *commodities* such as good health, the use of open country spaces, and a safe, secure childhood environment becoming dependent on economic means. These trends limit choice for the many, while the affluent move blithely on, their freedoms untouched, their quality of life unaffected. As such, society becomes stratified into different economic levels, each with different experiences of life. Times have moved on considerably from, say, the 1930s when some of the effects of poverty and inequality might be mitigated by the consolations of family or community. Today,

---

* Just as some items in a free market system have come to be sidelined from normal demand and supply, even though they carry costs to produce – such as ballpoint pens or many local newspapers – so must more significant commodities, such as local public transport, be taken beyond the worst consequences of the market. The poorest members of a rich nation should not have to worry themselves because they cannot afford the price of a local bus journey for their families.

the philosophy of consumerism preaches inclusion and access, while the lived reality is division and exclusion. If life chances are to be almost wholly dependent on purchasing power, then social mobility is frustrated, leaving a nation permanently divided.

Neo-liberal capitalism has had the effect of intensifying economic competition. By increasing the commodity emphasis in society and by enlarging its commercial sector, values have become dominated by economic standards. And since living with the free market has come to be seen as an exciting project in which there is much to gain, even if also much to lose, time has borne out the two potentialities in success and failure, invigoration and enervation, but inevitably with a more divided society. An ideology of affluence and acquisition, supposed to empower all individuals, has weakened and impoverished many, while undue preoccupation with commodities has constricted human potential even if, ironically, the rhetoric proclaims their power to liberate. As greater affluence raises the material condition of society – though grossly unequally – so more and more people seek to buy advantage, status or exclusivity, particularly in the field of leisure activity. But whereas manufactured commodities can easily be increased in supply, this cannot be achieved likewise with positional goods such as exclusive ski resorts, road space, or top executive positions in public life. Neither separate individual decisions nor endless economic growth can deal with these issues, which have an important social element. In many respects distributional issues need to be organised on a communal basis in order to satisfy individual demand more efficiently; only concerted actions among individuals in community can produce effective solutions to meet individual needs.

The impact of capitalist economics should, in fact, be lowered for all in society, including those better off. Individual satisfaction will not be enhanced by further competition; for as prosperity enables the affluent to accumulate more of the market's luxuries, so rivalry for positional goods becomes more intense. But the striving of rugged individualism will not prove effective here. Heightening the struggle between individuals for the positional prizes of capitalism is the sure path to frustration and disillusion. To return to Fred Hirsch's argument, touched on in the last chapter, rivalry among competing individuals for the fruits of an economic system will, at the present stage of capitalism, only worsen the position for all. *The disease, in brief, is the blight on individual action as an effective means to individually desired results*, says Hirsch.[157] Part of the answer must be to reduce the competition for status and exclusivity by taking positional goods, as far as is possible, out of the commercial field, ...*making them more available through public access or public allocation on a non-market basis.*[158] In order to dilute the connection between education and wealth, as Fred Hirsch recommended, remuneration for executive roles should be lowered, and the monetary allure of high positional jobs should be separated from the attractions of status and job satisfaction. The focus on money has perverted society and undermined values about the worth and purpose of work – problems which might be mitigated in a world where all had a decent basic standard of living.*

None of this suggests that modern capitalism should be overthrown; it will continue, though cannot do so in its current form. However, its next stage must include a re-evaluation of the relationship of the individual to her communal and environmental surroundings. The early days of industrialism were times of scarcity, while the individualistic drive – such as it then was – was embedded in an elaborate ethical framework. Today, in the absence of the latter, and with the increasing ineffectiveness of strident individualism in achieving expected outcomes, communal mechanisms will have to be developed to allow individuals more control over their own lives. For the sense of impotence of many in society, and not just those at the bottom of the socio-economic scale, can lead to bitterness and resentment which are themselves socially divisive. Such feelings no doubt contributed to the result of the 2016 EU referendum, fuelled by vivid awareness of the casualties of the financial crash. Meanwhile, in a world of abundance the dominating ideology should not be a materialistic one; economics is but one element in communal and family affairs, and quality of life does not arise automatically out of material quantity. Fulfilling human potential and pursuing individual ambition can take many forms, but it is by no means limited to material value, as we all know. But under current arrangements money and profit are given vastly undue prominence, while indispensable values like dignity, respect and equality of opportunity are dangerously neglected.

There is no point in calling for the end of capitalism without a viable system to replace it, and when so many obvious reforms to its workings could be undertaken. There are plenty of examples of responsible

---

* After all, there have been times in Britain – the 1920s and '30s, for example – when socially valued occupations, such as teaching, attracted social status while by no means being well remunerated.

free market practices by which to modify our current corrupted model, whether they be features of Asian paradigms or the essentials of Adam Smith's recommendations tailored to a twenty-first-century environment. As Nobel Prize recipient and Harvard Professor Amartya Sen suggested in the aftermath of the crash,

> *If we were to look for a new approach to the organization of economic activity that included a pragmatic choice of a variety of public services and well-considered regulations, we would be following rather than departing from the agenda of reform that Smith outlined as he both defended and criticized capitalism.*[159]

(After all, Smith's published works taken together show that he stood for much more than merely free enterprise and minimal state activity.) No, capitalism is not about to come to an end; it will still be the accepted, familiar way of doing business. And if neither financial crash nor global pandemic can bring it to its knees, then future crises are unlikely to overthrow it entirely. What is now indispensable is, of course, reform of the system, in order for it to concentrate on serving the interests of humanity as a whole. The idle speculation about the imminent demise of free market capitalism never appears to recognize its embedded nature in modern society, and above all fails to recognize its indispensable connection with liberal democracy and social freedom which the descendants of Adam Smith and John Stuart Mill have always accepted.

However, time is short. Still today the rapid pace of neo-liberal 'progress' and the further consolidation of consumer capitalism is generally considered inevitable, and not entirely unwelcome. But without doubt modern economic and social trends are carrying forward the developed world – and soon the rest – into a savage new era. The inexorable spread of market forces, the blind adherence to growth philosophy, the subversive propaganda of consumer sovereignty and the commodity saturation of modern societies are all portents of a future dominated even more by money and institutionalised economic power. And with technology rampant and efficiency the guiding light of development, basic human needs will be pushed even further down the list of life priorities. For, however rapidly we approach that spectre, such trends constitute a deep-seated incompatibility with underlying values, social needs and what it means to be human. It is evident that a profound inconsonance exists between the direction of contemporary societies and the individual and communal requirements of modern *Homo sapiens*. Greek economist and former Finance Minister Yanis Varoufakis described the emergence of market societies as *exchange* values were triumphing over *experiential* values, a triumph that has produced unimaginable wealth and untold misery. But, he says ...*it accomplished something else too: it put us, as a species, on a collision course with Earth's capacity to maintain life.*[160]

END NOTES

i   Samuel Taylor Coleridge, *On the Constitution of Church and State*, 1837.
ii   Adam Smith, *The Wealth of Nations*, Book IV, Chp. III, Pt. 2.
iii J. B. Priestley, *The English*, Heinemann, London, 1973, p. 21.
iv Victor Lebow, 'Price competition in 1955', quoted in Tim Jackson, *Prosperity Without Growth: Foundations for the Economy of Tomorrow*, 2nd Edition, Routledge, Abingdon, Oxon., 2017, p. 120.

1. Roger Scruton, in *The Observer*, London, 29/12/1985
2. Theodore Roszak, *The Cult of Information*, University of California Press, London, 1994, p. 90.
3. Ibid. p. 93.
4. Yves Smith, *ECONNED: How 'Unenlightened' Self Interest Undermined Democracy and Corrupted Capitalism*, Palgrave Macmillan, New York, 2011, p. 106.
5. Idem.
6. Quoted in Tony Judt, *Ill Fares the Land: A Treatise on Our Present Discontents*, Penguin Books, London, 2011, p. 48.
7. Quoted in Ibid. pp. 48-9.
8. Quoted in Richard Sennett, *Respect: The Formation of Character in a World of Inequality*, Penguin Books, London, 2004, p. 161.
9. Harold Macmillan, in *The Sunday Times*, London, 10/2/1980.
10. Yves Smith, op. cit., p. 106.
11. Yves Smith, op. cit., pp. 106-7.
12. Ronald Wright, *A Short History of Progress*, Canongate Books, Edinburgh, 2006, p. 129.
13. Cited in Yves Smith, op. cit., p. 107.
14. Yves Smith goes further than these brief conclusions in her damning analysis of the AEA's 2007 study entitled "Is There a Free-Market Economist in the House? The Policy Views of American Economics Association Members." op. cit. pp. 107–9.
15. Quoted in Robert Peston & Laurence Knight, *How Do We Fix This Mess? The Economic Price of Having It All and the Route to Lasting Prosperity*, Hodder & Stoughton, London, 2013, p. 19.
16. Ibid. p. 227.
17. Ralph Waldo Emerson, *English Traits*, Unit Library Ltd., London, 1902, p. 47.
18. David Howell quoted in John Gray, "The Gale of Destruction", in *New Statesman*, London, 18/9/2000.
19. Aditya Chakrabortty in *Guardian Review*, London, 10/12/2016.

20 Wolfgang Streeck, quoted in ibid.
21 Idem.
22 Paul Mason, *PostCapitalism: A Guide to Our Future*, Allen Lane, London, 2015, p. xiii.
23 Ibid. p. xiv.
24 Adam Smith, op. cit., Book IV, Chp. III, v. 1.
25 Amartya Sen, "Capitalism Beyond the Crisis", *New York Review of Books*, 14/3/2009.
26 Ronald Wright, op. cit., Chp. III.
27 Ibid. p. 61.
28 Cited in ibid. p. 63.
29 Amartya Sen, from his *Development as Freedom*, quoted in "Soros: May Day Protestors do Have a Point", in *The Observer*, London, 6/5/2001.
30 Cited by Andro Linklater, *Owning the Earth: The Transforming History of Land Ownership*, Bloomsbury, London, 2014, p. 357.
31 George Watson, *Politics and Literature in Modern Britain*, Macmillan, London, 1977, Chp.10.
32 Erich Fromm, *The Sane Society*, Fawcett Publications, Greenwich, Conn., 1955, p. 83.
33 Idem.
34 Ibid. p. 82.
35 Ibid. pp. 82-3.
36 Tim Jackson, op. cit., p. 195.
37 https://www.forbes.com/2009/02/18/depression-financial-crisis-capitalism-opinions-columnists_recession_stimulus.html#1c64154222ef
38 Ha-Joon Chang, 'Thing 5' in *23 Things They Don't Tell You about Capitalism*, Allen Lane, London, 2010.
39 Ibid. p. 43.
40 Ibid. p. 47.
41 Charles Hampden-Turner, 'Masters of the Infinite Game', in Geoff Mulgan (Ed.), *Life After Politics : New Thinking for the Twenty-First Century*, Fontana Press, London, 1997.
42 Ibid. p. 363.
43 Ibid. p. 365.
44 Ibid. p. 366.
45 Michael Sandel, *What Money Can't Buy: The Moral Limits of Markets*, Allen Lane, London, 2012, p. 48.
46 Idem.
47 Gary Becker's *The Economic Approach to Human Behavior*, Univ. of Chicago Press, Chicago, 1976, which Sandel highlights as a forceful, materialist, unsentimental analysis of human beings in relation to the market, in ibid., pp. 49–51.
48 Fred Hirsch, *Social Limits to Growth*, Routledge & Kegan Paul, London, 1978, p. 137. In my analysis of modern capitalism I am indebted to the ideas of the late Professor Fred Hirsch, in particular as set out in this indispensable text. It has been unduly neglected, even though its arguments are increasingly relevant to today's situation.

49 Idem.
50 Sandel, op. cit., p. 49.
51 Ibid. p. 51.
52 Cited in Robert Skidelsky & Edward Skidelsky, *How Much Is Enough? The Love of Money and the Case for the Good Life*, Penguin Books, London, 2013, p. 53.
53 Quoted in ibid. p. 12.
54 Ibid. p. 13.
55 J. B. Priestley, op. cit., p. 240.
56 R. & E. Skidelsky, op. cit., p. 40.
57 John Gummer interviewed by Vivian White, BBC TV, Brighton, 18/10/1988.
58 Yves Smith, op. cit., p. 98.
59 Thomas Piketty, *Capital in the Twenty-first Century*, The Belknap Press of Harvard University, Cambridge, Mass., 2017, p. 639.
60 Ibid. p. 656.
61 Ha-Joon Chang, op. cit., p. 144.
62 Ibid. pp. 143-4.
63 Thomas Piketty, op. cit., p. 373.
64 Era Dabla-Norris; Kalpana Kochhar; Nujin Suphaphiphat; Frantisek Ricka; Evridiki Tsounta, *Causes and Consequences of Income Inequality: A Global Perspective*. (SDN/15/13) International Monetary Fund, Washington D.C., June 2015.
65 According to Ha-Joon Chang in op. cit., p. 146.
66 Theodore Roszak, quoted earlier in more detail, op. cit., endnote 2.
67 Fred Hirsch, op. cit.
68 Ibid. p. 37.
69 Ibid. p. 52.
70 Ibid. p. 37.
71 www.ethicalconsumer.org/commentanalysis/ethicaleconomics/taxhavensinthesky
72 T. E. Hulme, quoted in Chp. I, note iii.
73 www.fixthefells.co.uk/what-we-do/funding/
74 Robert H. Frank & Philip J. Cook, *The Winner-Take-All Society: Why the Few at the Top Get So Much More Than the Rest of Us*, Virgin Books, London, 2010, pp. 57-8.
75 John Gray, *False Dawn: The Delusions of Global Capitalism*, Granta Books, London, 1999, p. 212.
76 Idem.
77 G. M. Young, quoted in John Bowle, *England: A Portrait*, Readers Union/Ernest Benn, London, 1968, p. 165.
78 *The Times*, London, 4 May 1847, quoted in William C. Lubenow, *The Politics of Government Growth*, Newton Abbot, 1971, p. 15.
79 Third Marquess of Salisbury, quoted in B. W. Clapp, H. E. S. Fisher, A. R. J. Jurica (Eds.), *Documents in English Economic History*, G. Bell & Sons, London, 1976, p. 435.
80 W. D. Rubinstein, *Capitalism, Culture, and Decline in Britain, 1750-1990*, Routledge, London, 1994, p. 25.
81 Tony Judt, op. cit., p. 202.

82. Ibid. p. 198.
83. Ha-Joon Chang, 'The revival – and the retreat – of the state?' in *Red Pepper*, London, April/May 2011.
84. Tennessee Williams, *Cat on a Hot Tin Roof*, Act II.
85. E. M. Forster, *Two Cheers for Democracy*, Harcourt, Brace & Co., New York, 1951, p. 57.
86. Trevor Blackwell, Jeremy Seabrook, *The Revolt Against Change: Towards a Conserving Radicalism*, Vintage, London, 1993, p. 58.
87. Barry Schwartz, *The Paradox of Choice*, Harper Perennial, New York, 2004.
88. Frances Cairncross, 'The Curse of the Chinese Menu', *New Statesman*, London, 24 July 2000.
89. Cited in ibid.
90. See André Gorz, *Strategy for Labour*, Beacon Press, London, 1967.
91. Zygmunt Bauman, *Consuming Life*, Polity Press, Cambridge, 2007, p. 126.
92. Blackwell, Seabrook, op. cit., p. 62.
93. Idem.
94. Madsen Pirie, quoted in *The Sunday Times*, London, 8/1/1989.
95. Geoff Hodgson, *The Democratic Economy: A new look at planning, markets and power*, Penguin, London, 1984, p. 31.
96. Ibid. pp. 124–5.
97. Zygmunt Bauman, 2007, op. cit., p. 65.
98. Idem.
99. Liz Greenhalgh & Ken Worpole, 'The Convivial City', in Geoff Mulgan (Ed.), op. cit., p. 168.
100. Ibid., p. 170.
101. Ibid., p. 171.
102. Martin Pawley, *The Private Future: Causes and Consequences of Community Collapse in the West*, Thames and Hudson, London, 1973.
103. Ibid. p. 61.
104. BBC Radio 4, 'File on Four', 1/3/1994, quoted in Will Hutton, *The State We're In*, Vintage, London, 1996, p. 219.
105. Martin Pawley, op. cit., p. 13.
106. Ibid. p. 179.
107. Zygmunt Bauman, *Does Ethics Have a Chance in a World of Consumers?* (Institute for Human Sciences – Vienna Lecture Series) Harvard Univ. Press, Cambridge, Mass., 2008, p. 28.
108. Tim Jackson, op. cit., p. 190.
109. Ibid., p. 192.
110. Idem.
111. Ivan Illich, in *The Schumacher Lectures*, Vol.I, Satish Kumar (Ed.), Blond & Briggs, London, 1980, Chp. III.
112. United Nations Secretary-General U Thant, quoted in Alvin Toffler, *Future Shock*, Bantam Books, New York 1971, p. 96.
113. Fred Hirsch, op. cit., p. 92.
114. Ivan Illich, op. cit., Chp. III.
115. Idem.
116. Bauman, 2008, op. cit., p. 170.

117 Idem.
118 Ibid. p. 171.
119 George Ritzer, *The McDonaldization of Society*, Pine Forge Press, Thousand Oaks, California, 1996, p. 156.
120 Ibid. 157.
121 Ibid. 158.
122 Quoted by Leopold Kohr, in his 'Tribute to Ernst Schumacher' in *The Schumacher Lectures*, Blond & Briggs, London, 1980, p. xiv.
123 Lewis Mumford, in *The Listener*, London, 16/10/1971.
124 Leopold Kohr, op. cit., p. xii.
125 Will Hutton, *Them and Us: Changing Britain – Why We Need a Fairer Society*, Little, Brown, London, 2010, p. 365.
126 Revealed in the 2018 British Social Attitudes report, at – http://www.bsa.natcen.ac.uk/media/39254/bsa35_work.pdf.
127 Both data cited in Guy Standing, *The Corruption of Capitalism: Why Rentiers Thrive and Work Does Not Pay*, Biteback Publishing, London, 2017, p. 228.
128 According to analysis by the TUC – https://www.tuc.org.uk/news/workers-uk-put-%C2%A3336-billion-worth-unpaid-overtime-year
129 Quoted in Guy Standing, op. cit., p. 214.
130 Ibid. p. 239.
131 Ibid. pp. 228–9.
132 André Gorz, *Capitalism, Socialism, Ecology*, Verso, London, 1994, p. 46.
133 Ibid. p. 55.
134 Richard Sennett, *The Corrosion of Character: The Personal Consequences of Work in the New Capitalism*, W. W. Norton & Co., New York, 1998. I have drawn on this revealing and insightful work for some of my comments on the effects of flexible capitalism.
135 Ibid. p. 10.
136 Ibid. p. 19.
137 Ibid. p. 20.
138 Ibid. p. 26.
139 http://www.bsa.natcen.ac.uk/media/39254/bsa35_work.pdf
140 Reported in the *Daily Express*, https://www.express.co.uk/life-style/life/821892/UK-workers-job-satisfaction-rank-low-employee
141 https://lsbf.org.uk/infographics/career-change
142 https://www.conference-board.org/publications/publicationdetail.cfm?publicationid=2785
143 A wide-ranging survey carried out in the USA on behalf of The Physicians Foundation, found at https://www.staffcare.com/physician-job-satisfaction-declining-new-survey-reveals/
144 George Soros, 'The Capitalist Threat', at https://www.theatlantic.com/magazine/archive/1997/02/the-capitalist-threat/376773/
145 The *Daily Telegraph*, London, 21/1/2012.
146 Ibid.
147 Margaret Heffernan, *A Bigger Prize: Why Competition Isn't Everything and How We Do Better*, Simon & Schuster, London, 2014.

148 Alan Greenspan, quoted in 'Beyond the Crash' by Adam Tooze in the *Observer*, London, 29/7/2018.
149 George Soros, 'Toward a Global Open Society' at **https://www.theatlantic.com/magazine/archive/1998/01/toward-a-global-open-society/307878/**. This article was partly in response to the reaction to his previous contribution (in *The Atlantic* magazine in February 1997) to the debate in the late 1990s, though still hugely relevant today.
150 John Gray, *Gray's Anatomy: Selected Writings*, Penguin Books, London, 2010, p. 6.
151 Peter Self, *Rolling Back the Market: Economic Dogma and Political Choice*, Macmillan Press, London, 2000, p. 164.
152 Mariana Mazzucato, *The Entrepreneurial State: Debunking Public vs Private Sector Myths*, Anthem Press, London, 2013, p. 4.
153 Margaret Thatcher, interview in the *Sunday Times*, London, 3/5/1981.
154 From a filmed recording by FDR in 1944, unearthed by Michael Moore and shown in his film *Capitalism: A Love Story*, Overture Films/Paramount Vantage, 2009.
155 Peter Self, op. cit., p. 61.
156 R. & E. Skidelsky, op. cit., p. 41.
157 Fred Hirsch, op. cit., p. 181.
158 Ibid., p. 185.
159 Amartya Sen, 2009, op. cit.
160 Yanis Varoufakis, *Talking to My Daughter: A Brief History of Capitalism*, Vintage, London, 2019, p. 167.

Chapter 4

ECONOMIC GROWTH – THE BEGUILING SPECTRE?

As long as you don't stop climbing, the stairs won't end; under your climbing feet they will go on growing upwards.
FRANZ KAFKA[i]

Growth for the sake of growth is the ideology of the cancer cell.
EDWARD ABBEY[ii]

It must always have been seen.... by political economists, that the increase of wealth is not boundless: that at the end of what they term the progressive state lies the stationary state, that all progress in wealth is but a postponement of this, and that each step in advance is an approach to it.
JOHN STUART MILL[iii]

To assess a nation through its economic data is a little like re-envisaging oneself via the results of a blood test, whereby the traditional markers of personality and character are set aside and it is made clear that one is at base, where it really counts, a creatinine level of 3.2, a lactate dehydrogenase of 927, a leukocyte (per field) of 2 and a C-reactive protein of 2.42.
ALAIN DE BOTTON[iv]

I absolutely think we've got to stop iconizing the maximization of our GDP per capita growth. It's not the case that we can rely on growth alone to deliver relentless improvements in human welfare.
ADAIR TURNER[v]

TREADMILLS are currently extremely popular. Carry out an internet search and you will be presented with a multitude of ergonomic fitness machines for the home or office, most measuring heart rate, calories burned, distance covered, and some with MP3 and USB outlets and even a WiFi connection. (Why not check your emails or watch a movie while exercising?!) Do these devices represent progress being made? For individuals trying to keep fit, they will serve a useful purpose since, however expensive they may be and regardless of what others in the population may be doing, they enable users to keep fit. Thus, personal well-being is enhanced in an absolute sense: the greater the use of such machines by the wider population, and not just fitness fanatics, the healthier are likely to be the majority of people – or at least those who can afford the price of the treadmill, if not working out in some other, possibly 'lower-tech' manner. But the expense and effort may be regarded by many as well worthwhile even if, for those without machines carrying all the advanced bells and whistles, the treadmill process seems... *monotonous, wearisome routine*, as dictionaries define it. Whilst remaining in the same position, its users will have advanced in terms of their own fitness, and possibly even stolen a march on many of their fellow citizens.

The metaphorical treadmills on which most world economies are firmly entrenched are similarly continuous, moving beltways, which demand resolute dedication to the cause of national fitness. Each country's population is exhorted to expand their efforts to increase economic productivity and raise the growth rate of the economy. Gross Domestic Product (GDP) has become the standard by which economies are measured (having taken over from GNP – Gross National Product – by the early 1990s), and an ever-rising index has become the principal indication of a successful economy. Standing still, without the numbers constantly moving upwards, represents stagnation, which signifies failure, and so focusing the nation's attentions on the targets ahead keeps it tied to the perpetual motion of the treadmill. There is apparently no possibility of getting off the machine, for to do so would imply abject surrender to the economic challenge, appeasement in the face of international rivalry. By such striving, nations may – or may not – improve the welfare of their peoples in an absolute sense, albeit rarely raising standards equally. However, sitting back and enjoying progress already achieved is seen as unacceptable national conduct, for there is no end to the exertions required to increase economic growth; as a nation we can never be fully fit. And, as Martin Pawley observed almost fifty years ago, ...*'perpetual motion' proves a better tranquillizer than any attempt to arrest the whole process.*[1] He believed that any impediment to growth might impact social stability: ...*like trying to stand still on a bicycle, the trick is harder than continuing to ride.*[2]

The benign view of the matter – unpleasant as this unending toil on the treadmill of economic life may be – is that it is a means to a worthwhile end. For, the pay-off will be a better life for all in higher living standards, though this *better* is a vague promise, its precise nature constantly shrouded in mystery as to what it will look like and when it will come into view. The accepted certainty is that higher economic growth is the route to an improved future, and this assumption has long taken on the characteristics of an unshakeable dogma which only the deranged or heretical would question. The faith in economic growth as a macro-policy target has become one of those *categories of the human mind* examined in Chapter 1, part of a subliminal pervasive narrative which is taken for granted, its status as a national objective almost never considered. When referenced by politicians or commentators of practically any complexion its value is rarely questioned, the focus always being on how to increase it. Attempts to raise GDP are a constant of economic life; apparently we can never have enough. This brings to mind Michael Young's dystopian society in *The Rise of the Meritocracy*, in which the effort to raise national production was an ever-present preoccupation, which subversives would undermine:

> *The agitators speak as if ... the Age of Plenty had arrived at last. Nothing could be further from the truth. The country needs every scrap of human and material capital it can save if it is to contend with other great nations in the battle for survival. We are all poor, and shall always remain so...*[3]

That Young's depiction was set in only 2033 should help concentrate minds today.

However, faith in the cause of economic growth is unlikely to be easily shaken. It withstood the vicissitudes of the 2007/08 financial crash, and in the bleak aftermath even consolidated its position as the principal target of national economies in an increasingly globalised world. And in spite of evidence to the contrary, there appears no sign of its dominance waning. As a significant national index, economic growth has only a tenuous relationship with social well-being – a fact long pointed out but not given widespread prominence. Policy-makers, and even professional economists, appear transfixed by the target of higher growth, although many are fully aware of the problems with its criteria and the way it bypasses standards of individual welfare. Scouring the pages of conventional economic textbooks would not reveal any established correlation between well-being and growth. In fact, numerous studies have identified the loose, and in some cases negative, relationship between economic growth and factors such as life expectancy, material equality, or social welfare (some of which will be looked at later). It is almost as if economists and politicians cannot think of any other worthwhile objective for macro-economic policy, or perhaps no other which provides such a suitable, readily comprehensible criterion. So we are left with an index which most people *can't help thinking* must be the right and sensible way of measuring our national performance – in all its variable conformations.

However, doubts about its validity are by no means new. One of the first economists to lay out conclusions about GDP and GNP was Simon Kuznets – later a Nobel laureate – in the report he prepared for the US Senate in 1934. His analysis of the early years of the American Depression was remarkably detailed, although the report is notable for the numerous caveats added to Kuznets' remarks. He suggested that statements about national income, particularly international comparisons, *...can be true only when qualified by a host of "ifs"...* and *...The welfare of a nation can, therefore, scarcely be inferred from a measurement of national income...*[4] Nevertheless, after the Second World War values of economic growth became the principal measure of a country's economy, part of the post-war financial settlement following the Bretton Woods conference in 1944. And during the years of economic reconstruction in the 1950s and '60s, with GNP and GDP figures rising by, in many cases, 4 or 5% annually, fewer doubts were raised about the validity of the statistics.* Steady economic expansion appeared to be translated into higher living standards, and thus a better quality of life. A direct causal relationship between the two was widely accepted in most countries; in Britain it was confidently assumed that if growth

---

* The financial markets were also booming: Wall Street returned an annual growth rate of almost 10% between 1950 and 1973, while Britain's financial sector saw steady rises of about 8% a year during the 1950s and '60s, in spite of a closely regulated economy and high tax regime.[5]

were maintained, then Harold Macmillan's *never had it so good* years of the 1950s would continue.

The global problems of the 1970s, following the oil crisis early in the decade, threw up doubts about the direction of economic progress. Uncertainty and self-reflection replaced the buoyancy of the 1960s, but these concerns were expressed more by commentators at the time than by policy makers. Engineer and physicist Dennis Gabor pointed out in 1972 that *Growth addiction has become the universal creed of our world.*[6]* He maintained that dynamic growth could not continue indefinitely, and forecast that as its end approached, the transition to a new economic order would be neither stable nor happy. Two years later Ralf Dahrendorf, in his BBC Reith Lectures, called for the drive for continued expansion to be channelled into efforts at improvement: quality not quantity should be the objective. He was not against economic growth as such, but thought it should be subject to much greater direction and political influence in order to serve wider interests of life.[7] But the governments which came to power in London and Washington in 1979/81 had no such misgivings about economic growth, and resolved to deal with the problems plaguing Western economies with hard-edged, so-called New Right policies, which took no prisoners. Quality of life assumed second place to driving economies forward in an uncompromising, lean and mean numbers game which inevitably involved casualties. The evangelists of the Thatcher and Reagan administrations were on a crusade to reinvigorate their economies, and higher growth was one of their main objectives.

Thus the right-wing policies of the 1980s were in some respects a reaffirmation of the economic direction which had produced the successful record of the post-war period (almost a version of making Britain and America great again!). The neo-liberals now in power concentrated on re-energising free market capitalism, promoting entrepreneurship (in true Schumpeterian fashion) and limiting the involvement of trades unions and the state in the economy – in other words, returning to the situation which policy-makers 'perceived' had been responsible for the post-war boom. But conditions were now very different from the period after 1945, when dedication to the cause of national revival from

---

*   Gabor, a Nobel laureate for his invention of holography, had published *Inventing the Future* (1963) in which he outlined his concerns about the future of mankind. He later became a member of the Club of Rome, set up to promote understanding of the perils facing the planet. Its first report, *The Limits to Growth*, became a landmark.

war-time devastation and a willingness to forgo immediate reward and invest for the future provided a unique economic environment. And while neo-liberals dutifully followed the ideas of one of their mentors, Friedrich Hayek, they neglected those of Hayek's fellow Austrian Joseph Schumpeter, who forecast the demise of capitalism. Any notions that capitalism might overreach itself and decline, perhaps as a result of its own success, were not contemplated. Confidence in free market capitalism was further reinforced at the end of the 1980s by the collapse of state communism in the USSR and Eastern Europe, which appeared to vindicate not only the resolute foreign policy of NATO and the West, but also the strident, uncompromising neo-liberalism of Margaret Thatcher and Ronald Reagan.

Thus the millennium approached with capitalism apparently triumphant and with no apparent rivals. In spite of the fact that the free market's largesse was by no means benefiting its constituents in any fair or equal manner, with the result that serious social problems were mounting, nevertheless viable alternatives to the dominant economic system were not on the horizon. Neo-liberal capitalism was here to stay, it seemed, and – as its adherents expected – would continue to spread its reach throughout the globe. The triumphalism of the period was reflected in the hubris of new Chancellor of the Exchequer Gordon Brown, who ended the '90s with claims that the British economy had broken through the barrier to lasting low inflation and sustained economic growth. Such assertions were gaining adherents, in spite of the growing social and economic problems which, many were suggesting, were caused by contemporary capitalist practice. In 1999 a book by Edward Luttwak came out which highlighted these problems and the losers of the compelling momentum he termed *turbo-capitalism*: .... *almost all Western governments have had no better plan than to allow turbo-capitalism to advance without limit, while hoping that faster growth will remedy all its shortcomings.*[8] But New Labour – taking advantage of a combination of fortuitous circumstances – now claimed to have solved the riddle of economic success and ended cycles of boom and bust. The sunny uplands of prosperity had it seemed been reached, and Britain at least was on the plateau of permanent progress.

Again, it is doubtful if any politicians were bothering themselves with the ideas of Joseph Schumpeter. He had maintained that capitalism was constantly evolving, and did not believe there was anything permanent about free market arrangements, forecasting the eventual collapse of the system. However, while he agreed with Marx that capitalism would eventually be replaced by some form of socialism, he thought this would come about through capitalism's decay from within, as resentment against the foundation of its success grew stronger, rather than by overthrow in violent revolution. Schumpeter was famous for his emphasis on the importance of inventive entrepreneurship to keep capitalism vibrant and progressive. But though he believed this was vital for its future, he nevertheless also saw it as the essence of the *creative destruction* which would eventually undermine the whole capitalist edifice. The restless enterprise of the digital age, which has led to the emergence of today's giant technology and social media companies, conforms to Schumpeter's picture of constant innovation driving capitalism forward and sustaining economic growth. However, the excesses which produced the financial crash of 2007/08, which might have led to the final undermining of capitalism itself according to Schumpeterian logic, have had no such effect. He might have been surprised at the capacity of the system to recover from the cataclysm, rediscover its faith in material progress, and refocus attention on economic growth as the key measure of success.

The second decade of the twenty-first century ended with maintenance of the *status quo*, higher economic growth remaining the principal hope for future prosperity, and especially for emancipation from the mountain of debt which has been the consequence of the Coronavirus pandemic. Not that much attention is focused on economic targets: the need to protect employment and livelihoods has required vast government borrowing, which has overshadowed conventional Treasury planning – in effect 'kicking the can' of harsh decisions on tax way down the road. Besides, constant preoccupation with Covid-19 and the urgent need to be vaccinated have narrowed the public's focus of attention. Meanwhile, the complex fallout from Brexit, ongoing fears over the planet's environment, the still critical condition of Britain's social care sector, and the remaining scourge of right-wing populism even after Donald Trump's defeat – these take up the majority of available mental bandwidth. Behind this façade, the well-off get on with the business of making money, and the remainder struggle to make sense of a sea of inequality in a bleak economic landscape. There will remain concerns about unemployment, about the long working hours culture or job insecurity, about the ever-disappearing mirage of civic equality, about the widening fractures in social harmony, and the co-existence of private enrichment with public squalor – all to be washed over by a bath of facile political rhetoric and enfeebling consumerism. But apparently, everything will be alright if only economic growth can be maintained.

As usual, so much of the national panorama is about perception. Since life is taken up with day-to-day preoccupations, the constant reiteration of economic values and targets lies in the background, out of focus. Thus the evidence against economic growth as a worthwhile value is unlikely to be examined. Over recent years a variety of arguments – among them moral, practical, environmental – have been raised against targeting continued growth, but governments have been in the hands of leaders with vision restricted by past experience, and increasingly circumscribed by populism. They speak as if unaware of either the practical or mathematical difficulties with growth statistics. For example, the exploitation of finite natural resources can serve to raise GDP, and so can the increased sale of drugs needed to cope with diseases contracted by affluent societies. Growth figures do not distinguish between the destructive and the creative; all add incremental points to the index. Environmental scientist Ernst von Weizsäcker cites the example of two cars passing on a country road, not generating much economic activity. But if one of the drivers inadvertently crosses into the path of the other, causing a serious accident, national GDP is affected:

> ... air ambulances, doctors, nurses, breakdown services, car repairs or a new car, legal battles, visits from relatives to the injured, compensation for loss of earnings, insurance agents, newspaper reports, tidying up the roadside trees – all these are regarded as formal, professional activities which have to be paid for. Even if no party involved gains an improvement in his or her standard of living, and some actually suffer considerable loss, our 'wealth', namely our GDP, still increases.[9]

Such anomalies should raise doubts about the usefulness of growth as a valuation.

After all, economic growth as a measure of the market value of all goods and services during a given time period will exclude some activities, as well as including others which do not signify progress in any sense. GDP ignores functions which are not provided through the market, such as housework, volunteering, or other unpaid services such as caring. As Chilean economist Manfred Max-Neef explains:

> ...consider the situation of two neighbours, who each have five children and work hard all day at home. They have no economic value whatever, but suppose one day Mary says to Jane, "Look, why don't we do this: from tomorrow I will do all the things in your house, and you will do all the things in my house, and at the end of the month I'll pay you $500 and you'll pay me $500." If they do that the GNP grows. Furthermore, if a man marries his housekeeper the GNP goes down because she becomes a wife who has no value, whereas as a housekeeper she does.[10]*

Attempts have been made to estimate the value of the range of unpaid work, in some cases putting it as high as 50% of GDP. Figures vary enormously depending on the methodology used, so that they do not greatly inform the debate. Nevertheless, calls have been made for household labour to be included in GDP calculations since, some maintain, it is a substitute for services that have monetary value, and might otherwise be purchased. Examples such as these are obviously not merely minor anomalies in an otherwise sensible system; they throw doubt on the value of growth statistics and thus undermine the basis of modern economic computing.

There are many features of national income and patrimony which simply do not lend themselves to being assessed in any economically meaningful way. Some of these, if amenable to computation, might add value to national statistics; some others may need to be subtracted from the figures. For example, while the increase in industrial production can grow GDP, any resulting negative externalities, such as pollution, will not be counted. However, while the economic activity involved in cleaning up the pollution, as well as the potential health costs for people affected all have to be paid for, they may well be reflected in higher GDP figures. And after all, a more dangerous, less secure society will no

---

* In the 1980s some economists, such as Max-Neef, were still highlighting Gross National, rather than Domestic Product. However, the point he makes has significance regardless of the criterion used.

doubt enhance GDP statistics as a result of the growth in sales of security devices, and the proliferation of locksmith's businesses. An interesting development in Britain was the setting up in 2013 of a 'Natural Capital Committee', charged with safeguarding and promoting nature with a 25-year environmental plan. Its remit included *transforming the natural environment*, and passing on to our children a *more resilient natural inheritance*, but it also showed support for higher GDP, saying ...*a healthy environment is the basis of sustainable economic growth*.[11] There will even be an attempt to measure progress on natural capital improvement, with a set of national accounts for the purpose.* Whether such ambitious objectives can ever bear fruit is highly problematic. Making investment decisions for the future based on the market is normal in the private sector, but with natural capital, values are not easily assessed relying on market prices.

Such noises emanating from government may sound encouraging. But from a global, environmental point of view they represent a tiny pinprick, hardly likely to hinder the march of economic growth which continues as strongly as ever. For some years, most political parties in Britain made lukewarm efforts to establish their *green* credentials, without producing significant policies to match the rhetoric, and in any case policy measures here have usually been thought of only as minor correctives to sustained economic expansion. Few political leaders have accepted the radical changes necessary, or the importance of investing in green technologies – which may have a growth momentum of their own. Some believe growth itself is the answer; as journalist Walter Schwarz once observed, ironically, ...*we shall need yet more growth to provide money to clean up the effects of growth.*[12] As regards pollution, the *polluter pays* principle was once popular, predicated on the assumption that everything can continue as before, except for some incidental expenses borne by the miscreants who dirty the environment. As with global warming, there is always a tendency to assume it is someone else's responsibility, rather than examining the lifestyles that developed societies have come to demand – or at least that their leaders say they demand. The problem, as Walter Schwarz said thirty years ago, ... *lies in the extravagant way we live and the still more extravagant way we hope to live next year.*[13]

---

* The Office for National Statistics (ONS) was committed to producing a comprehensive set of national accounts by 2020. How these will be used, combined with or alongside GDP figures (?) has yet to be revealed.

In spite of many dissenting voices over recent years warning of environmental dangers, economic growth is still regarded as a fundamental objective of modern societies, and economic productivity as an important criterion of national well-being. Whether the discussion centres on imposing limits to the use of scarce natural resources, on reducing amounts of waste which societies produce, on protection of the rain forests, or now, especially, on the dangers of climate change – the arguments all skirt around the subject of economic growth, leaving it as an unquestioned target for today's world, which all other matters must accommodate. It is assumed that when GDP rises, then benefits will accrue to some or other economic and social measures, while the incidental and unwanted side-effects of growth are a separate issue which will be dealt with when the time is right. But when GDP doesn't rise, or does so only modestly, politicians and many economists take fright and see it as a sign of approaching disaster. Forecasts of impending doom may lead to companies cutting back on investment, issuing profit warnings, and even laying off staff, such is the prophetic significance of the hallowed index. It apparently contains within it all we need to know about how we are all doing in this life, and how we will do in the future. Meanwhile, urgent environmental concerns patiently await our distracted attention.

The principal environmental issue which we struggle to focus on is, of course, global warming and the climate change which – most scientists accept – it is inducing. Concerns about the heating up of the planet have been growing since the 1980s. The Intergovernmental Panel on Climate Change (IPCC) had lobbied for some years before the significant report Nicholas Stern produced for the British government in 2006. It made headlines, particularly due to its warnings that without urgent action the costs of climate change could amount to losing at least 5% of global GDP each year, *now and forever*.[14] This worrying evidence received far more attention than what the report suggested were the costs of acting: in order to reduce greenhouse gas emissions to avoid the worst effects of climate change the price was likely to be limited to around 1% of global GDP annually. But what might have appeared to be a 'good deal' then did not galvanise nations into action. Stern had warned of the risk of major social and economic disruption – on a par with that affecting the planet during world wars, and that climate change might be difficult or impossible to reverse. Nevertheless, years passed and meetings came and went, before a conference in 2016 produced the Paris Agreement on climate action, which set a target of keeping a global temperature rise this century well below 2 degrees Celsius above pre-industrial levels.* But how would this objective be accommodated within economic growth strategies?

For, the enduring problem is that whereas attempts to raise GDP should be downgraded, subsumed within overall aims of reducing global warming (apart from other important social purposes), it is these other objectives which are made to give way to the overriding aim of higher GDP. Such is the fixation with economic growth that there is a comprehensive confusion of ends with means. It has become such an abiding *category of the human mind* that GDP statistics have become an obsessive end in themselves. If this is maintained, the world may well see continued growth for a period, until the cumulative effects of climate change, as well as of critical inequality and social dislocation, demand attention requiring such vast resources as to make a mockery of previous economic growth. And all this is despite the burgeoning evidence of the benefits of investing in measures to combat global warming. A United Nations report in 2018 found significant under-estimation of the advantages of *climate-smart* growth. It declared, *Bold climate action could deliver at least US $26 trillion in economic benefits through to 2030, compared with business-as-usual.*[15] UN Secretary-General António Guterres, commenting at the launch of the report in New York said,

> *Climate action and socio-economic progress are mutually supportive. Yet, despite some encouraging momentum, we are not making progress fast enough. Climate change is running faster than we are. ... Runaway climate change is a real possibility, with severe implications for communities, economies, peace and the security of nations. Climate change has been proven to amplify and exacerbate other risks.*[16] *(My emphasis.)*

But even potential financial benefits of this magnitude may do little to undermine the obsessive conviction that the overwhelming prerequisite is higher economic growth.

The precise nature and extent of the dangers of climate change are not the principal concern for us here, worrying as they certainly are.

---

* and to pursue efforts to limit the temperature increase even further, to 1.5 degrees Celsius. By early 2020 189 nations out of the 197 signatories to the agreement had ratified it.

The bizarre conviction that continued economic growth will answer the significant global problems which confront us is the underlying conundrum – one of the psychological muddles which comments in Chapter 1 of this work attempt to explain. Because we see the question of economic growth *through* the veil of our pressing needs and threats to existing lifestyles, we pin our hopes on its capacity to deliver us from them, and carry us into a fuller, safer future. A further aspect of the conundrum is why government leaders and policy makers connive at our delusions, giving tacit approval of our aspirations. Perhaps they have simply acquiesced in a form of populism in which satisfying our needs as consumers has taken precedence over responsible leadership, so that their collusion has led to their own self-deception. How else can we interpret the constant publicity given to GDP figures which, if converted into aspirations on a global level, would lead to exponential economic expansion with apocalyptic consequences? Since the world economy has grown by an average of over 3.5% annually since the middle of the twentieth century, continued expansion at this rate would produce a global economy more than 200 times larger than that of 1950 by the year 2100.[17] And this does not even take into account the effects of a possibly more economically equal world.

The failure on the part of many major governments to come to terms with such possibilities is due, of course, to a variety of factors. A preoccupation with what appear to be more pressing issues has certainly constricted the attention of political leaders, while they realise that the policy implications of serious action would be unpopular with electorates. Many hope that paying lip service to potential reforms will suffice in the short-term, knowing that their constituents also hope the problem will either go away or be remedied by new emerging technologies. It does not help that the USA, one of the largest emitters of greenhouse gases,* was led until early 2021 by a populist president determined even to turn the clock back, attempting to revive the coal industry. Yet China, the economy with the largest carbon footprint, has been accelerating attempts at carbon reduction, in spite of its resolve to catch up with 'Western' industrial leadership. It announced in 2018 that it had already achieved its emissions reduction targets for 2020. Then President Xi Jinping, in an announcement at the United Nations in September

---

* The US was responsible for a rise in carbon pollution in 2018, for the first time in five years.

2020, came out with an ambitious pledge to reach 'peak carbon' before 2030, and drive down emissions to virtually zero by 2060.[18] Of course, the Chinese government does not have to contend with the kind of pressures exerted by Western electorates, and to that extent escapes the same tendencies towards populism. But its policies may increasingly highlight the failure of its rivals to adopt the radical measures needed to combat global warming.*

The longer that major economies postpone adopting policies adequate to the scale of the problem, the harder it is for developing countries to follow suit. And all the while, poorer nations will hope to emulate the rich with their apparently glamorous, highly mobile, energy-intensive lifestyles. They will be persuaded that limitless economic ambition – the example set by advanced nations – is the route to higher living standards, and have reason to resent entreaties to cut carbon emissions without major economies doing much more themselves.** The fact that a potential future world in which all have the level of affluence of the West would be entirely unsustainable should energise rich nations to do far more to rein in their own ambitions; so far progress has been painfully slow. A key element is obviously to abandon growth targets. But as Tim Jackson says, while ... *the idea of a continually growing economy is anathema to an ecologist, ... the idea of a non-growing economy... can be a problem for economists.*[19] But these attitudes are likely to endure as long as the fixation with growth remains part of the narrow focus on material prosperity. Industrial and technological progress has given us so much materially over the last two hundred-odd years that a fuller perspective on life, including ecology and overall well-being, is easily neglected and overlooked. Dennis Gabor, writing as long ago as the early '70s, put it less charitably: *The conquest of Nature by rational man... has brought us face to face with the basic irrationality of man.*[20]

Indeed, much of the discussion of economic growth is based on the premise that it will lead to greater prosperity in the form of higher material living standards. This is always the promise, the incentive to encourage us to buckle down and keep going, towards that bright future which

---

* It is now accepted that global carbon dioxide levels in the atmosphere are higher than they have been for millions of years.

** That poorer nations are pro-active to any extent, contributing to reducing global warming with their own UN Nationally Determined Contributions (NDCs), is no doubt largely due, in many cases, to their greater susceptibility to dangers such as rising sea levels.

awaits – the perennial *jam tomorrow*. In the sense that economic growth will result in a larger economy, and therefore a greater overall national income, this has an element of veracity.* We are repeatedly told that growth is indispensable to provide the extra money needed to fund the NHS, education, etc. Thus, a vibrant, expanding economy, to which all must dedicate themselves, is seen as the panacea, the answer to remaining social ills and a remedy for the enduring poverty still evident in Britain today. The metaphor of *raising all boats* is often used to suggest that becoming a wealthier country will benefit everyone. But this begs the significant question as to why years of past economic growth have not had that precise effect. From the inauguration of neo-liberalism in the early 1980s to the beginnings of the financial crash in 2007, the average annual rate of GDP growth in the UK was 2.53%.** Surely such cumulative expansion of the economy should have been sufficient to solve the range of social and economic problems which faced the incoming Thatcher government in 1979? And surely degrading poverty would have been eliminated from the national landscape well before 2007, enabling the country better to cope with financial crash and economic recession?!

The fact that we remain in a critical state as a nation, with widespread poverty, homelessness and social dislocation (all exacerbated by leaving the EU), should be answered by thoroughgoing national introspection. Where has all the increased wealth gone, what went so wrong with the promises of neo-liberalism, and where will the money come from to remedy the parlous state of so many citizens? For, according to the OECD, the average per capita annual income in Britain in 2016 was US$42,943 – twelve times greater than in 1970[22] – roughly on a par with comparable developed nations which mostly do not see the levels of poverty present in the UK. Distributed more fairly and taxed more appropriately, such current income levels would be sufficient to render an adequate standard of living for all. But of course a key aspect here is that while all *boats* may have been *raised*, to varying degrees, the difference between the heights raised by the affluent boats and those of the poorer ones is immense. It is the distribution of national income

---

* always assuming that population growth does not negate the increase in GDP; for although economic growth will make the numbers appear larger, national productivity will be no greater if the population is rising to a commensurate degree.

** certainly creditable, even if not as high as the 2.96% average between 1961 and 1979 – which of course encompasses the 1970s, the decade which the Right in general continues to malign.[21]

which is more significant than average figures as such, as the words of R. H. Tawney indicate at the opening of this chapter. But countries following neo-liberal practices have seen a disproportionate amount of their increased income going to the better-off. Thomas Piketty has shown that in the USA, the foremost example, the share of national income going to the wealthiest Americans rose dramatically between 1976 and 2007, so that 58% of US growth during that period was appropriated by 1% of the population.[23.] And this escalated to 65% between 2002 and 2007!

In the light of this shabby picture – none of it particularly hidden or enigmatic – it is truly remarkable that the promise of economic growth retains its firm hold on economists and policy makers. Is it a sordid confidence trick to allow further material advantage to accrue to the already well-off? Have we been entirely hoodwinked to accept the propaganda that the high-flyers who run major corporations and financial institutions are special people whom we cannot do without, and who must be pampered and cosseted, else they desert our shores? Or have we been ensnared by the quaint metaphor of *trickle-down* or other picturesque but equally vacuous notions which theorists and commentators use to get *hoi polloi* on side? GDP figures are not magic numbers with special powers – though the devotion to them would almost make us believe they are. They have been used in their current form for barely a century, and their significance will wane. But in the meantime we must not repeat past errors by staking everything on economic growth. Its gains have vastly enriched the few, raised the mean level of material standards, and trained our sights on a hollow phantom of a number, but it has not made us better off. If regular economic growth over the last half century has still left us with poverty, with health, education, social services and a judicial system all crying out for investment, and a police service unable to ensure our safety, then how can it make any sense to call for further growth? It is time we faced up to this bizarre delusion.

This is not to suggest that we should try to prevent the growth of the economy, or call for de-growth.* The issue is not one of economic contraction, aspiring to reduce GDP. If the British economy is larger this

---

* A de-growth movement with a range of ideas has developed in recent years. It encompasses views on how to devise sustainable alternatives to growth-based development, as well as aims to undermine the whole edifice of modern economics with a very different post-growth scenario. The **6th International Conference: Degrowth for Ecological Sustainability and Social Equity,** took place in Malmö, Sweden, in August 2018.

year than last, then the questions centre on why that is so, where does the added productivity come from, how is it shared out amongst the citizenry, and above all how does it enhance the well-being of the nation. If these questions can be answered satisfactorily, and if the growth is based on a stable trajectory and is environmentally sustainable, then well and good. And this scenario is certainly feasible. But when the focus is entirely on enlarging the economy, which is thought necessarily and inevitably to be the route to higher economic standards and therefore *a good thing* for the country, then we are on a dangerous path. For that way lies environmental disaster, an increasingly unequal society with a wealthy super-elite, an inappropriately flexible labour market with a continuing long hours employment scene, and insufficient investment in health, education and social services with ongoing repercussions on society's most vulnerable – all of which would most definitely not be *a good thing*. This is the unfortunate avenue which countries – notably those of the so-called *Anglo-Sphere* – have been following by adopting neo-liberal policies in an effort to increase wealth. The panorama of personal, social and environmental ills evident in these nations is what this strategy has produced.

We have to learn above all that economic growth based on such policies over the last two generations, especially in America and Britain, has not worked – and will not do so in the future. This is where psychology again comes in – a matter of expectations and comparisons. For the main issue in Britain today is relative material differences between people of contrasting economic fortunes, but differences which nevertheless loom large in the goldfish bowl world of contemporary times. So imagine a typical mid-nineteenth-century skilled worker in Britain, possibly in the textile industry, earning about 20 shillings for a 72-hour working week. This would have barely covered life's simple necessities for his family – i.e. a diet with meat only on Sundays, no fruit, potatoes the only vegetable, perhaps 5% of income going on soap and candles, and for any children, possibly being able to afford the cost of reading at school, but not writing. If told of the material possessions, opportunities, and leisure of a modern, so-called working-class British family in 2021, with income derived from unskilled labour, this nineteenth-century worker could only marvel at such undreamt-of luxury. But the wide social and economic gulf between rich and poor existing in today's Britain would hardly impress the worker from earlier times, when such differences were the norm. To poor nineteenth-century families, whose health and nutrition was always prejudiced, scarcity meant absolute deprivation.

Therefore, from the perspective of that nineteenth-century family, the particular level of affluence of its modern successor would evidently mean far more than the social and economic gap between rich and poor which they would discover exists in Britain today. Now, even though deprivation and real poverty exist, the main problem is relative differences and increasing inequality. Most families have the basic economic means to ensure a reasonable level of health, comfort and security, but many do not *feel* well off. With publicity given to stratospheric levels of executive remuneration, while basic pay levels stagnate, material differences become ever more glaring and pronounced. The undreamt-of luxury for families of modest means today is here with us, in the material possessions and lifestyles of the very affluent. Though well out of reach for most ordinary people, nevertheless it often exists close by, cheek by jowl with poverty, in many modern cities. However, looking ahead in vain to the anticipated improvements provided by economic growth, there would be little point most modern families settling for the standard of living, and lifestyle, of their counterparts one hundred years from now, if in some Faustian fantasy they were offered it. If they did, they would still be in the same position of relative poverty as they are today (with, heaven forbid, twenty-second-century quasi-neo-liberals telling them of the boundless opportunities which existed, if only they would work for them!)

We return to the question of perception. What would be the point of all of us shifting up the economic ladder? Some of us would still remain at the bottom end, as conscious as ever of the wealth of those at the top. If this is what more economic growth leads to – addressing the *amounts* not the *proportions* – then progress will not have been made. The economic psychology will have to change; it is absurd to persist with a course of action which has failed us for forty years. But the psychological mindset is a major stumbling block. If the economic progress, such as it is, of the last generation is doubted or challenged, then the riposte is to point to current standards of living, or to the technological advances which have been made: in other words, highlighting absolute amounts. This is often followed by exhortations to redouble efforts to raise material standards further, so to eliminate poverty – this the enduring fallacy, exposed above. There comes a point when a developed nation has reached a level of general affluence which allows its members to be comfortably off, provided that overall wealth is fairly distributed and society's most vulnerable are catered for. This still leaves room, as it must, for entrepreneurial ambition, to devise new social programmes, create new technologies, and – yes – sell new products, but not at the expense of the general welfare.* One is reminded of Irish writer John McGahern, speaking of his upbringing in 1930s rural Ireland. Poverty, he said, was the lot of 90% of the people, … *but it did not feel poor.* Today as a nation we are no longer poor, even if we act as if we are, and we should start organising our economy accordingly.

Another factor militating against this advice is the insatiability that develops in affluent societies. The psychology of economic life is indelibly connected with forward movement, with looking ahead to higher figures, better standards, and more *stuff*. The fact that the aim of sustained economic growth, as well as the socio-economic system surrounding it, was developed in an age of scarcity is lost on modern generations. But scarcity and how to deal with it is the business of economics, so that our perception is of the constant need to overcome it. It is time that perception caught up with reality here; even before the birth of neo-liberalism UN Secretary-General U Thant saw the future, when he declared, *It is no longer resources that limit decisions. It is decisions that make the resources.*[25] The constant desire for more money appears to be the mark of an affluent society, with its insatiable drive for novelty and heightened experience. Some of this contains an element of envy, or a need to emulate others, while there is also the common idea that we should try to give our children a better standard of living than we experienced. The result is the tendency for each generation to want greater purchasing power than the previous one, regardless – it seems – of the quality of life (to be discussed further later) which results. Britain, as a rich country, is not alone in being able easily to satisfy the needs of its population, but the insatiability of wants puts a large psychological spanner in the works and helps maintain the wholly inappropriate emphasis on the desire for more economic growth.

However, the concentration on economic growth and the resolve to see the figures constantly rising preceded the phenomenon of insatiability of contemporary consumer capitalism. There has long been a desire to acquire more *things* – partly a confirmation of status, a symbol of

---

* As Robert and Edward Skidelsky so rightly observe, *It is only our culture's poverty of imagination which leads it to believe that all creativity and innovation….needs to be stimulated by money.*[24]

one's achieving a measure of success in life. But the acquisitive drive for *more* has been greatly intensified, not so much by capitalism – as Robert and Edward Skidelsky maintain[26] – but by its modern neo-liberal version.* There is undeniably a human tendency to compare our situation with that of our neighbours, but this is not the dominant, overriding urge in societies where socio-economic differences are not so wide and so glaring (of which more will be said later). There are many more factors influencing individual and family ambition than mere acquisition, some of which were explored in Chapter 2. It is too attenuated to say that it is in the nature of human beings never to be satisfied with what they have. Recall the words of J. B. Priestley in the opening of Chapter 3: writing in the early 1970s, he believed that people were not generally consumed with ambition. ... *they want if possible to enjoy a little importance in their own circle... for the rest they like to take it easy.*[28] These sentiments, apparently now out of fashion, are much more in tune with traditional attitudes than the driven instincts of many today. In any case, the restlessness which can be part of insatiability is often sublimated into a search for stimulation and adventure, for which a richer nation is not necessarily a requirement.

The fixation with economic growth in the neo-liberal era has spawned a variety of prejudices about developed economies and how they should be organised in order to facilitate higher GDP. A conspicuous one is that higher government expenditure, particularly in the form of so-called 'unproductive' welfare payments, represents a drain on economic productivity, thus limiting the capacity for GDP growth.** It is often believed that by reducing the size of the state and its considerable expenses, greater economic dynamism will result. But as in so

---

* The Skidelskys later refine their analysis, correctly saying ... *In retrospect, it was the shift to a market-based philosophy of growth rather than to a growth-based philosophy as such which inflamed the insatiability of wants we identified in Chapter 1.*[27]

** The considerable drain on national resources – in the form of social, psychological and physical health services, and even potentially for the judicial system – which can result from meagre handouts to the poor or vulnerable almost never figure in discussions of this kind. Adequate welfare payments where needed allow the better functioning of rich, developed societies, whereas much expensive remedial assistance will be required to compensate for the lack of a proper safety net. In this sense, severely limiting welfare payments is itself a significantly unproductive, even 'counter-productive' policy. The consequences of the casualties of a miserly welfare system are always underestimated.

many respects, these common perceptions do not conform to reality in a simple causal relationship. Several commentators have observed that over recent generations the United States has grown more slowly than most European countries, despite having a much smaller welfare state. Ha-Joon Chang points out that in 1980 13.3% of American GDP went on public social expenditure, compared to an average of 19.9% for the then fifteen EU nations, with ratios as high as 28.6% in Sweden and 24.1% in the Netherlands.[28] Nevertheless, the USA grew more slowly than Europe between 1950 and 1987, income per head rising by only 1.9% – while in (West) Germany during this period it rose by 3.8% and in Sweden by 2.7%.[29] Expenditure on social welfare is, of course, one element among many affecting GDP growth, but the contention that a large welfare state is a significant drag on productivity is undermined by these and many other statistics.

The way in which common political and economic assumptions differ from sober reality is an enduring and fascinating phenomenon – part of the thesis laid out in Chapter 1. Habitual prejudices easily become lasting myths, which ... *most people can't help thinking must be true.* There is little doubt of the veracity of the facts cited above. Yet under neo-liberalism a consistent theme – especially in the *Anglo-Sphere* but predominantly in the United States – has been the corrosive effect on the nation of 'big' government. Most American presidents since Ronald Reagan have railed against it, and eulogized the idea of setting the people free from the shackles of Washington's political administration: *laissez-faire* meant what it said. But the rhetoric of the 1980s was in contrast to the practice of the 1950s and '60s. First, Eisenhower's government launched a huge public works programme, continuing the theme of Roosevelt's New Deal, followed by the enormously expensive NASA moon landing project under John F. Kennedy. Later in the decade Lyndon Johnson's 'Great Society' put considerable resources into medical care for the elderly and poorer families. Inevitably, taxes had to rise to pay for such ambitious schemes. However, the irony, no doubt later lost on neo-liberals, is that during this earlier period the American economy grew at 3.7% annually until the oil crisis of 1973, and meanwhile Wall Street boomed, in what was in effect a golden age. Such was the success of the highly regulated and heavily taxed post-war American economy.[30]*

---

*   Another interesting observation, pointed out by Andro Linklater, concerns a nation's

The less than impressive record of the United States on economic productivity in relation to welfare spending during the later 1970s and '80s continued during the 1990s and after. In spite of an improving economic performance during the Clinton boom years, at a time when European economies were doing less well, the start of the new millennium saw high-spending European governments growing at a similar pace to the US, at around 1.8%. In fact, evidence shows that in the period 2000–2008, prior to the financial crash, Scandinavian countries with some of the highest welfare spending, such as Sweden (at over 30% of GDP) and Finland (at 22.5%) were growing considerably faster than the USA.* *Were the free market economists right about the detrimental effects of the welfare state on work ethic and incentives for wealth creation, this kind of thing should not happen*, says Ha-Joon Chang.[33] Similar right-wing prejudice has influenced opinion in Britain, with Tory views of the sclerotic effects on productivity of high welfare spending, and the dangers of so-called *welfare dependency*. These largely baseless assumptions go back to the 1970s, when poor economic performance in Britain was attributed to the lack of dynamism which a large welfare state was said to induce – another *big lie* which became an enduring legacy of the Thatcher years. After the Conservative electoral triumphs of the '80s such attitudes became ingrained in popular thinking, part of the myth of neo-liberal policy curing the nation of the *British Disease*.

With the weight of these right-wing arguments, and the economic success they profess to have produced, it is hardly surprising that the obverse of such thinking – in the shape of the reduced enterprise and dynamism which hardship and insecurity are themselves likely to engender – has never gained credibility. But by promoting greater financial security, a more comprehensive welfare state can help foster openness, ambition, and a more vigorous, forward-looking workforce, as Scandinavian examples testify.** Nevertheless, the uncomplicated myth of the dangers of *big* government and high state spending has endured

---

capacity for wealth creation: during that same era of high taxation and government regulation (in fact from 1951 to 1976) 23 of the largest global corporations were born in America, three more than in the longer time period of low taxation and light regulation between 1976 and 2007.[31]

* Average annual growth rates during that period were Sweden, 2.4%, Finland 2.8%, but the USA only 1.8%.[32]

** It is also worth pointing out that, for most benefit recipients, a larger proportion of income is spent than is the case with the better off, thus injecting taxpayer-funded money back into the economy.

well into the twenty-first century; it seems to have become an accepted commonplace which cannot be readily overturned, in spite of the successful European economies which have exposed its duplicity. In America, Donald Trump reinforced its potency with continual attacks before and during his presidency on an overweening state – represented by what he called the *swamp* of the Washington establishment which he pledged to *drain*. However in the USA, being against high government spending does not necessarily mean being opposed to government deficits. In fact, Republican attitudes had often viewed federal surpluses as dangerous, since they were likely to motivate further government expenditure. Deficits would help to curtail these tendencies; *starving the beast* had been the phrase used during Ronald Reagan's presidency.*

Donald Trump finally managed to get his huge federal tax-cutting bill through Congress at the end of 2017. It increased the size of the government deficit, raising it from 3.2% of GDP in 2016 to 3.9% in 2018. But the large reductions in income tax, and especially corporation tax, were heralded as being self-funding, as a result of the boost which it was said would increase economic activity and raise growth. Adam Tooze has pointed out the telling fact that in 2009, when economic expansion was badly needed to deal with the worst effects of the financial crash, Republicans in Congress all lined up against Barak Obama's stimulus package. Yet eight years later, at a time of lower unemployment, they were supporting President Trump in trying to get a ten-year $1.4 trillion economic boost enacted.[34] With the passing of this measure the Republicans had fresh motivation to back huge spending reductions which were part of the 2018 budget: cuts of more than $50 billion affected many social programmes, and were accompanied by increases in funding for defence to the tune of $66 billion. The result of these budgetary and fiscal changes would leave the federal government's proportion of GDP at only 17% – ... *a figure befitting an emerging market state rather than the government of an advanced economy...* comments Adam Tooze.[35] However, despite Trump's forecast of a more dynamic US economy, the reductions in tax and federal expenditure did not boost

---

*   The budget surpluses built up during Bill Clinton's presidency in the late 1990s were soon demolished during George W. Bush's first administration, initially by his substantial June 2001 tax-cutting measure, and then by huge increases in defence and security spending in the wake of the 9/11 terrorist attacks.

GDP significantly, with annual growth under his presidency unable to match the 3.1% increase achieved in 2015, under his predecessor Barak Obama.*

During all the long years when economic growth has been held up as the target to aim at, the focus has always been on material standards of living. Lip service is occasionally paid to the aim of improving conditions and raising levels of well-being, but the core of the argument is perpetually about macro-economic numbers, a narrow concentration on money, output, productivity, and value added (or subtracted). This is of course inevitable: Gross Domestic Product signifies the value of what the country has produced in economic terms, and measured in pounds or dollars. It does not, and is not supposed to, assess happiness, psychological well-being, or environmental equilibrium. The problem is that these criteria are often conflated with economic standards, and discussed as if they were part and parcel of the same overall assessment of how satisfied and successful we are as a nation. In 2014 the *Daily Telegraph* reported an initiative by the Office for National Statistics to supplement GDP figures with a set of well-being measures, to give broader indications of our economic welfare.[37] It was a good example of the blending of values which perpetuates this muddying of waters. Under the headline *What does GDP really tell us about economic growth?* was the question as to whether GDP is a good measure of the economic recovery. But this was immediately followed by another question: ... *is GDP a false measure of our well-being?* In other words, economic well-being and overall human welfare are used interchangeably as if they amounted to the same evaluation.

So even attempting to broaden the methods used to assess well-being will run into difficulties as to precisely what kind of thing is being judged. *Per capita* GDP does indeed tell us about the expansion or otherwise of the whole country's economy, although of course bearing

---

* – and with annual average growth of around 2.5% (barely above Obama's) before Covid-19 struck. Nobel laureate Paul Krugman points to the wealth of research into the effects of fiscal policy on productivity, principally demonstrating the strong connection between increased government spending and higher GDP growth. He says, *The evidence is stronger than it has ever been that fiscal policy matters – that fiscal stimulus helps the economy add jobs, and that reducing the budget deficit lowers growth at least in the near term.*[36]

in mind – as described above – that growth in some economic categories may not be good for us. However as an example, while a person newly finding employment in a precarious, possibly part-time post with irregular hours of work will help enhance GDP statistics, nevertheless the nature of that job for the employee concerned may well involve uncertainty, stress and a constant struggle to make ends meet. These malign circumstances would likely more than offset the personal well-being gained from feelings of self-worth and dignity derived from working for one's living and contributing to society. Thus, this small instance might be said to result in a loss of overall, national well-being, although hardly susceptible to being measured. There has long been a tendency to believe that non-economic problems can be solved by economic remedies – this, the *econo-think* which Alvin Toffler saw America suffering from forty years ago. And, perversely, there is still an understanding that quality of life, in all its varied richness, will flow from higher levels (quantity) of material affluence. It is time to separate entirely economic statistics from measures of national well-being and accept that, however difficult the latter are to assess, they are the true criteria of how we are doing as a people.

The project to de-couple economic measures from underlying quality of life will come up against ingrained assumptions about how we evaluate success; our sense of *cognitive ease* (described in Chapter 1) ensures that we rely on comfortable conventions and prevent our tackling difficult or unsettling tasks of definition. But what are growth statistics for? If they cannot furnish us with meaningful indications of our social, human progress, then we must find others that will. And of course we need to have a clear notion of what we should be progressing towards, in order to know what to measure. Ideas about the good life have been around for centuries, from at least the time of the ancient Greeks, up to the twentieth century when Keynes looked ahead to a future of greatly increased leisure, due to higher capitalist productivity. But most views of that ideal life involved time, away from daily toil, to devote to personal and family interests, unconnected with the material means to arrive at them. In today's world – at least in economically developed societies – there is no conceptual separation between productive leisure and the economic means to come by it. It is as if we need to spend money to validate our time off and give it meaning – even to prove to others that we have a significant share in the good life, because whatever glimpses we have of it we are certainly paying a lot for. And because so many leisure pursuits have been commodified, their attractions become heightened as they form integral elements in consumer capitalism, for which long hours appear willing to pay.

It is not that we *need* to work long hours to enjoy leisure time; it is extreme consumer capitalism which leads us to want expensive free-time activities to endorse the dedication and hours spent in being required to earn them. Thus ends and means become confused. The sense of work being a means to enjoying indispensable time off has been replaced by an insatiable drive to earn as much as possible in order to be able to fill the limited free time available with intense, market-orientated, probably expensive distractions. The requirements of neo-liberal capitalism direct us to demand what is on offer, even though it may not be what our natural tendencies lead us towards. So, as Robert and Edward Skidelsky aptly put it, ... *we adapt our preferences, ending up wanting what we get, not getting what we want*.[38] As regards economic growth, filling our spare time with market-based pursuits may enhance GDP figures, but is unlikely to improve overall well-being or increase levels of happiness. There is considerable evidence from several 'Western' countries that many people would prefer to work fewer hours, even if it meant less pay. But in most cases this option is not available, while many lower-paid workers could not in any case afford to work less, in what may be their two or three different menial jobs. There is also the kudos which comes from having a busy, professional life, with no time to spare, the epitome of employment modernity. A half-empty diary and a surfeit of leisure time are not likely to attract admiration from fellow workers and gain social status.

Further growth in the economy through increased productivity will not modify this process; it will merely intensify competition and extend the imperial expansion of market forces. Leisure time will continue to be of marginal wider significance, unless it is amenable to commodification; as such, it will be a means to a marketable end, not a worthwhile objective in its own right to be relished in its human, vernacular essence. Most basic leisure pursuits, even organised sport, have been intrinsic to most societies for millennia and centre on shared cultural and folk experiences. They can be undermined by being packaged and marketed. But above all, these activities are largely independent of economic fortunes, so that higher GDP or greater purchasing power per head will not usually result in their being enjoyed the more. And these observations are linked with doubts sometimes expressed about the whole concept of *developed* or *advanced* countries which, as Chilean economist Manfred Max-Neef points out, may be lagging behind so-called *underdeveloped* societies in the satisfaction of fundamental human needs.³⁹ In many of these, he says, *the needs of 'being' are probably more important and better satisfied than in the rich countries, which concentrate mainly on satisfying the needs of 'having'*. He goes on,

> *... in poverty-stricken areas you often find forms of solidarity and mutual aid that satisfy at a very high level the needs for protection, affection and participation. In a highly competitive system it is precisely those needs that are undersatisfied...*⁴⁰

Such basic human satisfactions form part of the needs of all societies, and should be the focus of any assessment of quality of life, but are left ignored or neglected.

Because aspects of the good life are so often conflated with economic criteria, it is worth considering whether judgements about well-being, personal satisfaction or happiness have any close relationship with economic growth or GDP per head. For, in view of the common prejudices about the effects of affluence, the rises in GDP in most wealthy nations over the last fifty years might lead one to expect significantly increased subjective feelings of well-being.* There has been considerable research here – to add to the wealth of anecdotal evidence – particularly since Richard Easterlin's famous 1974 paper, 'Does Economic Growth Improve the Human Lot?' His conclusion, based on surveys in a number of countries, that it probably does not, was regarded as puzzling, leading it to be called the *Easterlin paradox*. But to see it as such is a reflection of the assumption, still influential today, which presupposes a causal relationship between affluence and happiness or contentment. Within countries there does appear to be a link here, in the sense that higher

---

* Many doubts have been expressed about happiness surveys and the ways happiness is measured, particularly as *happiness economics* has grown as a specialism. There are different methods of assessing subjective well-being as well as different components to the concept itself; affective and cognitive appraisals of life are seen to figure within the evaluation of overall happiness. Then there are cultural differences which determine how we define happiness, and even the extent to which we are willing to admit to it. However, defined as the degree to which an individual judges the overall quality of his/her life-as-a-whole favourably, happiness evaluations can have valid significance (always assuming people know how happy they are!) to set beside more objective material criteria, such as income or GDP. Fortunately, there is enough appreciation of the meaning of happiness to regard surveys as sufficiently meaningful.

income groups in society do generally report greater levels of happiness than those on low incomes. This seems to be a consistent pattern internationally, and accords with conceptions of the various advantages that a higher income could provide, in terms of status, opportunities and a less constricting financial situation. Such phenomena relate to relative differences in income, which might be said to be a constant in the relationship between happier, better-off citizens at one end of society and less happy, poorer ones at the other.

However, looking at developments over time, there appears little correlation between happiness and levels of national income. In Britain's case, the Skidelskys have noted that a near doubling of *per capita* GDP between 1973 and the financial crash was accompanied by very little change in what is termed *life satisfaction*.[41] (In other words, when averaged out, the varying degrees of satisfaction at different income levels remain fairly stable over the period.) This finding has been replicated elsewhere. In the United States, for example, where data on life-satisfaction have been recorded since the 1940s, Easterlin noted very little change in attitudes between that period and the 1970s, when he was doing his research, although real US *per capita* income had grown substantially in the first two post-war decades.[42] Also, Tim Jackson has pointed to figures showing a decline in the UK of people reporting themselves very happy – down from 52% in 1957 to 36% in 2005, during a period when real incomes had more than doubled.[43] All these findings can appear enigmatic, even contradictory, to those – economists and others – expecting a clear correlation between money and happiness. This is an indication of the conditioned assumptions of advanced industrial societies, caught up as they are in a consumer culture embodying the invidious tendency to confer a price on almost everything of value. The money nexus has become such an integral part of modern life that we cannot but see all else *through* it.

So modern economies appear unable to avoid the expectation that a higher income will inevitably lead to greater personal well-being; otherwise, one might think, why would so much attention be devoted to money, statistics, GDP? Of course, as has already been noted, the latter is a convenient, broad measure, as well as an index with international acceptance. But though its supporters cling doggedly to its significance, it is nevertheless too narrow and unsophisticated to stand as an all-purpose guide to personal well-being. Steven Pinker's recent, celebrated book *Enlightenment Now* included the exhortation, *Let's* *agree that the citizens of developed countries are not as happy as they ought to be, given the fantastic progress in their fortunes and freedom.*[44] This *ought* might be said to indicate a simplistic view of the life satisfactions of our species, implicitly ignoring a host of factors which make up the composite picture of what makes us happy. There is a curious presumptuousness about declarations which set so much store by affluence – an understandable but essentially narrow perspective, originating in rich societies.* Naturally, the effect of substantial rises in GDP in poorer countries – if spread sufficiently widely – can lead to rapid improvements in material well-being, and therefore to a rise in subjective satisfactions. The same increases in rich nations, where affluence is the norm, will have only a marginal impact, and may even disappoint because greater improvements were expected.

In fact, expectations are a crucial part of what makes people happy. If one lives in a society where social mobility is lauded and promoted, then there may be a general optimism that things will improve materially, and a feeling of well-being derived from this. There again, in a society where little social change is possible, there may be a sense of resignation, which may not necessarily produce overt dissatisfaction with one's lot – provided one's lot is not that of unremitting, grinding poverty. Another factor has been observed: a form of *regression to the mean*; in situations where GDP grows and national and/or personal income rises, there may be an initial improvement in subjective happiness which, over time, may settle back to one's accustomed level of personal well-being. Reflecting on this, one knows that there is commonly an habitual, day-to-day level of subjective happiness, part of one's prevailing psychological make-up, which can vary to some extent depending on outside circumstances. This is especially the case in reasonably well-off societies where a desperate struggle for life's basic necessities is not the norm. (In most situations, people form judgements based on their national surroundings, not globally compared with other countries.) All these characteristics are rather uncertain and nebulous, which helps explain the difficulties in arriving at agreed criteria for evaluating social progress. So economists cling to a concrete, measurable economic value – GDP.

---

* Curiously, Robert and Edward Skidelsky in their excellent *How Much Is Enough?* also at times appear wedded to the need for GDP growth to have greater significance. They say, *Happiness economists .... are rightly alarmed by the divorce of economic growth from any humanly intelligible end...*[45] While this comment is mostly pertinent to affluent nations, the *divorce* should make economists look for more meaningful ways to measure human purpose, rather than seek to mend the relationship.

Thus one has to say that the relationship between economic growth and overall personal well-being or happiness is indeterminate. The considerable economic progress in Europe and North America in the 1950s and '60s, with rising growth figures and improving material conditions of life, were accompanied by negligible changes in subjective life satisfaction. However, equivalent economic progress in poorer societies has often led initially to considerable improvements in such expressed satisfaction. The so-called *happiness curve* shows a levelling off in degrees of happiness – just as it does, incidentally, in figures for life expectancy after earlier rises – as countries get progressively richer. In their work *The Spirit Level* Wilkinson and Pickett show this to be a consistent pattern involving numerous nations, with the curve flattening out at around $25,000 *per capita* in the early years of this century.* As the authors point out, ... *the richer a country gets, the less getting still richer adds to the population's happiness.*[46] Most people might be inclined to say that the same phenomenon would apply to them individually. But that isn't to say that progress in other areas – more in social than in economic fields – may not maintain the increase in a population's happiness; there is certainly much room for improvement, even in the richest nations. The focus now should be on using the economic wealth of a country to invest in aspects of society which collectively would improve the quality of life for all.

Therefore, accepting the fact that beyond a certain point increases in economic growth are somewhat meaningless in relation to happiness, might it not be wiser to focus directly on improvements in well-being? For it appears pointless to address issues of human welfare obliquely by a concentration on economics. For example, in some rich nations increases in GDP over recent decades have been accompanied by an intensification of work practices so that employees are often working longer hours (even, because of so-called *presenteeism*, longer than they have to). At the same time, in many families two incomes are indispensable to pay the mortgage and make ends meet, with the associated demands on time, parenting and family life from long working hours – exacerbated yet further in one-parent families. These pressures may even themselves be part of the explanation in Britain for disaffected

---

* although they do suggest that the income level at which this occurs is likely to rise over time. The authors also show that similar degrees of happiness are experienced in countries with vastly contrasting levels of national *per capita* income – Tanzania and Indonesia, for example, being on a par with nations like Norway and Switzerland.

youth, school exclusions, and adolescent delinquency – including the current wave of knife crime – with which reduced social services are presently inadequate to cope. In a society concentrating on growth, economic efficiency and competitiveness in order to increase resources – with the *indirect* purpose of being able to afford to address such social issues – these pressures are unlikely to be reduced in anything but the long term. Leisure time, an increasingly expensive commodity in such societies but surely one of civilization's basic objectives, can only be made more available by ... *the structuring of our collective existence so as to facilitate the good life.*[47]

But of course, our perception – our prejudice, in fact – is that money is the answer to most problems. The pressures described above will inevitably have multiple origins, some with culturally specific roots. However, evidence suggests that numerous key social problems in modern societies are independent of a country's wealth, once it has reached a certain level of affluence, and that trying to increase national income further will not necessarily raise indices of well-being. In general, health improves and life expectancy rises with increases in national wealth, the statistical correlation being closer at earlier stages of development. But to take specific examples, two stable, democratic countries, Chile and Costa Rica, have managed to raise their life expectancy figures at birth to around 80 years, but on the basis of *per capita* incomes barely more than a fifth of that of the USA – where people on average do not even live as long as in these poorer nations.* A similar apparent discrepancy appears as regards years of schooling in countries with different levels of national income. In his analysis Tim Jackson points to the high rates of educational participation in Eastern Europe; as an example, Estonia achieves more mean years of schooling than the more developed Japan, Norway or Ireland, countries with income levels four or five times higher.[49] It is evident that cultural and social factors have a considerable bearing on these matters, and concentrating on economic growth will not necessarily lead to the desired outcomes in terms of social progress or well-being.

---

* This leads to the conclusion that if the much richer USA wished to enhance its figures for life expectancy, it might well concern itself with addressing wider social, medical and cultural issues, instead of trying to increase GDP further. (It is also worth noting that countries with fairly similar levels of GDP *per capita*, such as, say, Swaziland and China, have markedly different figures for life expectancy.)[48]

With the aim of achieving improvements in overall human well-being, particularly in societies which have already reached a modicum of material affluence, efforts aimed specifically at raising GDP should be abandoned. If such an index is to be maintained (and it could still serve a limited economic purpose), its statistics should be given much less prominence, since they are not good guides to general progress. It is high time other assessments were drawn on to provide a clearer indication of human welfare, and it is not as if many of these have not already been suggested. Some of them originated over thirty years ago, long before neo-liberalism became so firmly embedded in government policies. The idea of sustainable development with controlled growth became popular in the 1980s; it was the Brundtland Commission, chaired by a former Norwegian Prime Minister, which in 1987 recommended that the world economic system transform priorities so that the global environment bequeathed to future generations be in a similar state to that inherited from previous ones. Doubts about the significance of GDP (or at the time GNP) had already surfaced; the discrepancies between it and human welfare had prompted economists William Nordhaus and the late James Tobin, as early as 1972, to devise the 'Measure of Economic Welfare', incorporating certain quality of life measurements to give a wider picture of human progress.[50]* Nordhaus, at least, must no doubt be astonished to see the hold that GDP still has over modern government policy nearly fifty years on.

The intervening years until now have seen a variety of proposals put forward as alternative evaluations to judge these matters. For example, in the late 1980s after much detailed research, Herman Daly and John Cobb came out with a measure they called the 'Index of Sustainable Economic Welfare' (ISEW).[51] It included an assessment of economic progress but only within the context of overall human well-being, which had to take into account aspects of social or environmental concern which may or may not have any impact on GDP. The ISEW incorporated data on the distributional inequality of incomes,** as

---

* For example, the authors believed – in keeping with modern reservations about the usefulness of GDP – that there were negative externalities connected with economic growth which should be factored into evaluations of social welfare. One instance, higher salaries paid to urban workers, could be considered – they thought – as compensation for what they saw as the *disamenities* of urban life and work.

** which in the USA, incidentally, had been falling from 1950 to the end of the 1960s, when it began a steady rise. By 1980 the figure for income inequality was almost back up to the level of thirty years earlier.[52]

well as figures for commuting costs, the loss of wetlands, the net stock of roadways, and many other elements affecting human welfare. It is significant that in the post-war United States measures of ISEW *per capita* showed a parallel rise to those of GNP until about 1970, after which the ISEW index fluctuated but in a generally downward direction, while conventional figures for national wealth continued to rise.[53] (There is everything to suggest that these data would be replicated in Britain.) Similar trends are evident when figures for GDP *per capita* are put alongside measurements of the Genuine Progress Indicator (GPI)* – the result of studies carried out in 18 countries with a combined total of around 50% of global GDP: that after two decades of growth the GPI began a slow decline in the late 1970s, whereas GDP continued rising until the financial crash of 2007/08.[54]

This kind of evidence confirms the contention, made in several chapters of this work, that modern capitalism is now in a different phase from the immediate post-war period, and that macro-economic growth ceased to have close correlation with general social progress from at least the late 1970s. While economic growth provided broad benefits to developed nations for a generation after World War II, all indications show its divergence from measurements of human welfare thereafter, in spite of the persuasive rhetoric from self-interested parties proclaiming the comprehensive bounty provided by ever rising GDP. This illustrates again the major departure taken by governments from the late '70s onwards in their adopting of neo-liberal policies – privatisation, deregulation, tax reductions (mainly for corporations and the already affluent), and an emphasis on heightened competition in a winner-take-all marketplace of intense consumerism. Yet while the governments of Margaret Thatcher and Ronald Reagan were heralding economic emancipation on the march into the *bright, sunlit uplands*, behind the gloss lay the reality of many deprived and less well-off constituents who were not benefiting from a resurgent economy. For some while they remained hidden behind headline macro-statistics which appeared to tell a quite different story – of economic renaissance promoted by neo-liberalism, the deceptive aura of which had yet to be fully exposed. The lack of

---

* In its calculations the GPI includes unpaid elements and non-market services not computed in conventional GDP – such as housework – as well as accounting for financial depreciation, while taking out many external factors such as the costs of crime and resource depletion.

wider measurements of social progress allowed stock market, inflation and GDP headlines to command the heights.

Popular ideas are always hard to undermine, especially if they appear plausible and predictive, and are accepted by the experts. And growth figures have the added advantage of being standardized and understood internationally. Wider measures of life satisfaction or happiness do not yet have common, accepted standards, in spite of many versions being put forward both before and after the financial crash. Even the UN's 'Human Development Index' (HDI), inspired in the early 1990s by the work of Nobel laureate Amartya Sen, is not seen as a real rival to GDP. While not covering all aspects of human welfare, the HDI focused on the key areas of longevity, education and knowledge, and standard of living, striving to uphold people and their capabilities as more important criteria than simply economic growth, albeit GDP was one of HDI's components. Together with Joseph Stiglitz and Jean-Paul Fitoussi, Sen was also part of the Commission on the Measurement of Economic Performance and Social Progress set up in 2008 at the instigation of French President Sarkozy. The Commission's three-hundred-page report identified the limits of GDP and suggested criteria of social progress more relevant to the modern age. Similarly, the OECD's *Guidelines on Measuring Subjective Well-being*, produced in 2013, were intended as a more appropriate framework for non-economic aspects of well-being.[55] It is time for economists and policy-makers to stop using GDP as a summary of a nation's overall well-being and examine these other criteria more closely.

Deciding what features of personal and communal life are important to us would, of course, determine which ones are measured, the prominence they received, and thereafter the policy decisions to which they led. But the concentration on economic statistics relegates social factors to optional extras, interest in which provides a sideline curiosity but never regarded with the seriousness afforded economic growth. When New Labour came into government in 1997, they suggested that quality of life be included in assessments of national progress. John Prescott famously (famous for its novelty value) proposed a list of factors of collective well-being, including a survey of numbers of songbirds in the countryside. Such a suggestion might provide extra pleasing detail on the state of the nation but would neither replace economic criteria as the key measure nor act as a meaningful corrective to them. Even the incoming government under David Cameron in 2010 wanted to bring in a 'well-being index'; where does that now figure in national statistics a decade on, one might ask? Economic giant Japan publishes Net National Welfare statistics, which include the effects of environmental damage, but no-one suggests they could possibly 'compete' with narrow economic figures. However, the tentative nature of these steps towards new criteria are still no reason for persisting with a substantially flawed, even if widely accepted measure: GDP.

The 'hard-nosed' economics of developed nations, especially of the *Anglo-Sphere*, seem unlikely to embrace any of the suggestions for measuring quality of life, fanciful or otherwise. Their pride and self-importance, based largely on generations of economic pre-eminence, would appear to make them especially resistant to contemplating progressive measures – even if they might enhance the welfare of their peoples. And in spite of much innovative thought from writers and academics, it will be difficult to reach a consensus on agreed criteria for overall human well-being, and even harder to imagine governments accepting them. Fresh ideas are more likely to come from smaller, less hide-bound countries, especially from those with more to lose from the current economic fixation. For example, the tiny Himalayan kingdom of Bhutan has adopted a measure of what they call Gross National Happiness (GNH). Facing existential threats to its culture from 'westernization', and following the global financial crash, it developed a complex model of well-being involving the four *pillars* of economy, culture, the environment and good governance. These are divided into nine domains as part of the GNH index, even extending to how much time a person spends with family, at work, etc. And every two years the indicators are reassessed through a nationwide survey. One minister warned of insatiable human greed and the dangers of over-concentration on economics, illustrated by the global economic crisis: *You see what a complete dedication to economic development ends up in.*[56]

As is evident, ideas of this kind have been around a long time, yet they have not made significant inroads into conventional economic thinking in developed nations. Doubts are often cast on the practicalities of measuring quality of life, compared with the (apparent) ease and intelligibility of GDP, and objections are put forward as to methodology. For example, should the 'Cantril Ladder' be employed, whereby respondents are asked to say on which of ten steps of a ladder they personally feel they currently stand (the top representing the very best, and the bottom the worst possible life)?* Many social scientists researching subjective well-being adopt the familiar four category framework common to many questionnaires: the options being 'very ', 'fairly', 'not very', or 'not at all' in response to, for example, the question of how satisfied people are with the life they lead. But practical issues of methodology, as well as what features of quality of life should be assessed, all lie on the periphery, at some remove from the central question of Gross Domestic Product – the overwhelming economic judgement. The problem is a conceptual one – of the dominant fixation with an outmoded value which, while not fit for purpose, appears immune to modification. Faith in it is sustained through the ubiquitous incantation of its mantra, so that people only see *through* it, to what they expect to derive from it. Its resilience is due to the psychological hold it has over politics and economics, tied to an excessive reverence for individual affluence and corporate profitability – NOT to its validity.

Another area where myth and confusion abounds is the relationship between economic growth and social and economic inequality. It is often said that further or faster growth is necessary if inequalities are to be reduced, that enlarging the national cake will lead to greater affluence lower down the economic scale and contribute to more equality. Well, the cake has certainly grown over the last forty years, albeit at a slower rate than previously, but this has been accompanied by yet greater inequality, as the largest gains have been made by the already well-off (the myth of the benefits of *trickle-down* having been exposed in the last chapter). It was when growth in developed 'Western' economies stalled in the 1970s that the fiction was promulgated that a cause was high taxation (together with over-regulation), thus insufficient incentive being accorded to society's 'wealth-makers'. The neo-liberal policies which were concocted certainly increased the share of income going to the investing class, but with the consequence of worsening social inequalities.** Attributing the 1970s' economic slowdown to inci-

---

* This method is used for the annual World Happiness Report, launched by professors John Helliwell, Richard Layard and Jeffrey Sachs, and conducted by Gallup since 2012 for the United Nations Sustainable Development Solutions Network. Surveys are carried out in 156 countries and in over 100 languages.

** The significance of the high economic growth of the years 1950 to 1973 in most

dental factors and devising right-wing, monetarist policies to address matters was wilfully to ignore this relationship as well as a generation's economic experience. Joseph Stiglitz states unequivocally what we now know: *It is no accident that the periods ... when inequality* (in America) *has been reduced, partly as a result of progressive taxation – have been the periods in which the US economy has grown the fastest.*[58] This equally applies to Britain, particularly post-World War II.

Certainly, if the appropriate policies are adopted to reduce inequalities in society, economic growth may well accompany them. However, the last forty years in most developed nations have seen stratospheric rises in incomes for the top earners, stagnating average wages, and mounting inequality coexisting with only modest GDP growth. But, ignoring the message this picture gives us, the neo-liberals insist all the while that we stick to their rigid prescriptions – irrespective of their efficacy or the fact that many of them fly in the face of standard economic thought. Some of their advocates even suggest that issues of productivity and growth should be separated from the distribution of wealth, implying that the latter should be left to ethics and politics – which would coincide precisely with the impression that the economic Right does not accept the merest responsibility for society's poorer members. But the incomes, and therefore the fates, of rich and poor are inextricably tied together, and linked to growth in the economy. Distributing money from the poor to the rich, as has happened over recent generations, in fact lowers consumption and therefore growth, because high-income earners spend less as a proportion of their incomes than do lower-income earners. As Joseph Stiglitz makes clear, *The relationship is straightforward and ironclad: as more money becomes concentrated at the top, aggregate demand goes into decline.* Only extra government involvement can help redress the situation – *which is exactly what those at the top are hoping to curb.*[59]

This brings us back to Keynes and Keynesianism, the recently much maligned theories which did so much for global economies in the earlier twentieth century. They require the very opposite of the upward redistribution of income which has been the practice under neo-liberalism. Income inequality has risen substantially in most advanced economies, especially up to the financial crash. Ha-Joon Chang cites an ILO

---

wealthy capitalist economies, being accompanied by high tax regimes, extensive government regulation and increasing economic equality, has already been well highlighted.

(International Labour Organization) report of 2008 which showed that of the twenty of these countries for which data was available, between 1990 and 2000 income inequality rose in sixteen of them[60] – and this during a period when economic growth had slowed following the market liberalisation of the 1980s. When economic inequality leaves less in the pockets of poorer citizens, then less gets spent, demand is reduced, and the economy suffers. So income redistribution downwards will not only give the less well-off a better life, but will increase consumption and help stimulate economic activity. Higher GDP as a consequence would be welcomed, provided the whole of society shared the benefit, in an environment of sustained growth without negative externalities – but economic growth is not the principal target. In fact, as Richard Wilkinson and Kate Pickett show ... *greater equality makes growth much less necessary*, and can be ... *a precondition for a steady-state economy.*[61] The whole relationship between inequality and GDP has to be re-examined in order to extricate ourselves from the misleading dogma – the 'fake news', even – of recent decades.*

The years since the financial crash have, of course, seen the dissemination of the idea that government spending has to be reined in to cope with the consequences of the disaster. But this was a political decision, by politicians of the Right who were still resolved to protect the upper echelons of society more than those below them. Exhorting people to tighten their belts may *sound* sensible at times of financial stringency, but it is clear who will suffer more if this is achieved and who will find the process relatively painless. Reducing expenditure is counter-productive for the economy as a whole, and especially damaging to its poorer citizens. And ironically for the adherents of this policy, it is also particularly harmful to economic growth. However, it is presented as an appeal to the common sense of 'ordinary' household economics – even though these have little to do with the national arena. The views of pro-austerity economists and politicians – at once muddled and partisan – can only exacerbate a dire situation. For, as Paul Krugman maintains, they do not grasp the fact that ... *your spending is my income, and my spending is your income.*[62] Austerity leads to demand in the economy being held back, restricting what is produced, preventing growth, but

---

* This is part of the whole confusion which mixes up ends and means: the widely-held assumption that higher economic growth will benefit poorer sections of society and reduce inequalities should be turned on its head. The focus has to be on reducing those inequalities, which may incidentally lead to higher growth.

above all harming the interests of the majority of the population. This is a political choice, presented as the moral option, which represents the semi-literate economic argument behind which the wealth of the better-off remains protected.*

To reiterate, this is not an argument for promoting economic growth: the objective is to improve the national economy as a whole by helping low-income families and reducing inequality, irrespective of the effect on macro-economic numbers. An end must be put to oblique, indirect policies whose benefits for society's under-privileged or even 'just-about-managing' are so incidental or long-term as to be almost fruitless. It is no use waiting for future GDP growth to remedy material inequalities, while the beneficiaries of inequality move blithely on, even if bolstered by the vacuous rationale of *trickle-down*. After all, GDP is an indiscriminate, aggregate measure, which – like an innocent bystander – knows nothing of income distribution. Direct, targeted policies, such as a more progressive tax system, are likely to prove far more productive in reducing inequalities and, contrary to the rhetoric of the Right, do not necessarily impact negatively macro-economic efficiency. Robert Frank and Philip Cook make much of this argument in their analysis of hyper-competitive economies: *The time-honored trade-off between equity and efficiency is far less agonizing than it appears*, they say, because ... *the very same policies that promote both fiscal integrity and equality are also likely to spur economic growth*.[63] But overtly pushing for more growth itself will be far less effective, since it may not promote equality, and continues to overlook the non-marketable goods which form an indispensable part of life satisfaction – outlined above – and which may even be damaged by it.

There is another principal flaw in modern capitalism's continuing obsession with economic growth: that, at least in developed economies, it cannot go on extending its provision of the 'good life' to increasing numbers of aspiring consumers. Even in the most benign circumstances there are obstacles to the market's bounty being distributed as widely as capitalism's ideology suggests, regardless of the efforts of its suitors.

---

* It is interesting to note that inequality increases the pressure to consume which, with personal financial means severely restricted, can lead only to rising levels of debt and to unsustainable consumption, the concrete evidence of which is all around us.

Our economic system has gone beyond the stage where it can hope to provide for all its adherents the lifestyle of the present wealthy few, although this is its implicit promise. In the formative period of industrial capitalism, expansion and growth were able to raise living standards of whole swathes of society; through its productiveness material privation was gradually overcome, even if very unequally. But, as Professor Fred Hirsch has shown in a crucially important study,

> *As demands for purely private goods are increasingly satisfied, demands for goods and facilities with a public (social) character become increasingly active.*[64]

Once material needs have been largely met there is a tendency for individuals and families to direct themselves outwards towards the consumption of services and facilities with an important, or even dominant social element – the enjoyment of which will be affected by their *consumption* by others. The satisfaction of these individual preferences will alter the situation for those following afterwards, who wish to satisfy similar wants.

At earlier stages of market capitalism, when scarcity was more prominent, output of goods and services could be increased to meet rising demand without diluting quality for individual consumers. But the production of goods with a predominantly social character cannot usually be raised in this way. The increasing demand for cinema seats, for example, can largely be satisfied without restricting access or unduly harming the enjoyment of films for others. However, to take fairly basic aspirations, the capacity to enjoy walking in the National Parks or even basking on Britain's beaches would be seriously prejudiced if many thousands more people were to spend their leisure time in such a way. And significantly, the same would be true of more exclusive aspirations: activities like sailing, grouse-shooting on Scottish moors, the purchase of second homes in the country, membership of exclusive clubs and private airport lounges. Further economic growth leading to greater affluence and opportunity can only increase demand for consumption of a more social nature – what Fred Hirsch termed *positional* commodities. The gradual commodity saturation of modern societies will further heighten this process; in fact, the satisfaction of individual preferences directed towards positional goods will seriously impact the enjoyment of others with similar aspirations. *What each of us can achieve, all cannot*, Hirsch says.⁶⁵ Economic growth has no answer to these perplexing perversities.

Education is another *commodity* with an important social quality, though in a slightly different sense. The utilitarian value of education to a person does not depend solely on the absolute level reached, but also on how well others are educated and the qualifications they achieve, particularly in competition for specific jobs. And so, since scarcity will inevitably continue in many areas of employment, what is possible for a single individual will not be possible for all, and, as Fred Hirsch points out, would not be possible even if all possessed equal talent.⁶⁶ As with poverty, it is the relative quantity which is the crucial element in education, and no matter to what extent educational opportunities are developed, or economic growth and affluence increased, this will remain the situation. The prospect is that while growth raises expectations widely, it fails to satisfy them as a whole. It can only do so for those who raise their position relatively in the economic and social hierarchy; for the majority, there is likely to be disappointment and frustration as they see their positions raised – at most – equally. In this sense, Hirsch says, the distributional struggle returns, merely heightened by the process of dynamic growth – an exact opposite of what politicians promise that growth will produce. Hence the paradox of affluence.⁶⁷

In a society dominated by money there is likely to be even fiercer competition for top jobs in the future. Qualifications inflation has been a consequence of the expansion of university places over recent decades, with more and more students obtaining undergraduate degrees, albeit of varying standards. This will inevitably lead to heightened demand for professional and advanced employment, though with a higher qualification, such as a university degree, required where once British 'A' Levels would have been sufficient. And for posts where numerous applicants have similar qualifications, intensified competition will mean greater screening used to select the best candidates. If further economic growth increases affluence, even if shared more equitably, then this competition for top jobs will be further invigorated. Desperate scrambling to gain even the slightest advantage, such as via expensive private schools and sought-after unpaid internships, will be the route the better-off will endeavour to follow. The best way to begin countering these tendencies is to enhance the intrinsic attraction of posts and the status they carry, while scaling back their remuneration. This would contribute to education courses being chosen more for their inherent worth and less for the high salaries to which they may lead, one of the more invidious aspects of *positional* competition. Limiting the high-profile salaries of top jobs would lower the stakes in education, and could even reduce the costs of investment in qualifications. But all of this is to follow an entirely separate, more enlightened path, far from the blind alley of fruitless economic growth.

Thus, the developed economies of the 'Western' world which industrialized in the nineteenth century have reached the point where the system of economic liberalism which served them in their formative years has outlived its usefulness. Individual drive and endeavour were once able to translate self-interest into wider social and individual benefit. This is no longer necessarily the case and will, if pursued in the future, only exacerbate the dissatisfaction arising out of high expectations which will often be unmet. But this failure to deliver is not the result of excessive demand. As Professor Hirsch makes clear, it is not a matter of exhorting individual consumers to increase their efforts in terms of output and to exercise restraint in their claims for reward.[68] The benefits to be derived from the economic system will not continue to accrue in this way, though this is what the public is usually told by governments while waiting for their policies to bear fruit. Patience in the face of the vagaries of macro-economic cycles will not even bring delayed reward. The truth is that economic growth cannot deliver what its apologists promise. The growing conflict between individualistic actions and the satisfaction of individual preferences is not understood, though its relevance is ever more significant. However, the heart of the problem is the ambiguity of economic growth, at once a panacea for free marketeers and a dangerous mirage, ultimately, for us all.

Our inability even to be aware that we are on a treadmill, and certainly to be conscious of convincing scenarios to replace it, continues to puzzle those who consider the matter. But it is part of the strange, rigid mindset already examined earlier in this work. Analyses come and go, books full of exhaustive research and arresting prognoses occasionally hit the headlines, and are even highlighted in the media by politicians and commentators, until they slip quietly from our flickering gaze – their novelty soon replaced by new, provocative ideas with dubious relevance to anything significant. But all the while economic growth is constantly held before us as the answer to any high-profile issue, demanding our acquiescence. And so we do not think to question it; it is part of the accepted dogma through which national problems are interpreted. After all, practically all authorities on the subject tell us that raising GDP will expand our economic possibilities, and give us more of what we want and need. It is a bit like the fraudulent promise in Britain on the side of the 'Vote Leave' bus in 2016, though without the precise figure to tell us exactly how much better off we shall be with higher GDP. But the promise of economic growth is even more persuasive, since we think we have evidence of what it has previously given us – don't we? We want more of the same, and so what is there to be questioned?

A strange aspect of this is that prior to the current phase of economic development, the endless forward movement of industrialism and economic growth had periodically been subject to doubt. Almost a century and a half ago, well before mass consumerism and a population in thrall to economic statistics, John Stuart Mill had reflected upon the development of human society and where it was being led. He asked, *Towards what ultimate point is society tending by its industrial progress?* (We may add here ... *and economic growth.*) *When the progress ceases, in what condition are we to expect that it will leave mankind?*[69] What indeed?! But then who today is contemplating the cessation of economic growth? This is a concept which may not be expressed, at least not, perhaps, until we are all as wealthy as the richest today or until developing nations are on a par with the developed. This brings to mind the thought that the term *progress* itself is meaningless unless the endpoint, towards which progress is working, is identified. Today, of course, no-one can say where it is leading or what the destination will look like. After all, treadmills do not take you anywhere; you merely work very hard to remain on the same spot. Certainly, individuals or families will have their own targets and many of them will be reached, but this is the common lot of human kind, to be renewed with the next generation. However, the endless forward movement of our economic striving is not part of any cycle of life and, taken as a whole, is leading us nowhere.

The neo-classical economists of the eighteenth century believed growth was a process of improvement which would make everyone better off, and not just in material terms. They envisaged a plateau upon which humankind would alight, almost a kind of promised land, to which the industrial advances of the time would carry us – and yes, it did convey a religious sense, almost as a kind of vindication of our prowess as a God-given species. But they did not see the advance as never ending. John Stuart Mill later commented at length on this; he regarded nineteenth-century industrialism as a necessary stage in the progress of civilization, but he did not believe that what he termed *... the mere increase of production and accumulation... was ... its ultimate type.*[70] He saw industrial progress leading on to *a stationary state*, what he called *... an irresistible necessity...* which ultimately it would be impossible to avoid, in spite of the fact that, as he saw it, the political economists of his time identified *... all that is economically desirable with the progressive state, and with that alone.*[71] (Just as most contemporary politicians and economists would now maintain.) And in another uncanny parallel with today, Mill thought Victorians had *... been led to recognize that this ultimate goal was ... near enough to be fully in view; that we are always on the verge of it, and that if we have not reached it long ago, it is because the goal itself flies before us.*[72] The goal of growth-driven national prosperity, moving ever in front of us, plays this role faultlessly in the twenty-first century.

In the later nineteenth century, through the Edwardian period, the aftermath of World War I, and until the Great Depression, industrial progress and technological advance appeared to be spreading capitalist prosperity more widely than ever. Notions of a stationary state had been put into cold storage, as it were, only later to be revived by John Maynard Keynes. In an essay of 1930, before the worst consequences of the Depression had been felt, Keynes had looked ahead to the benefits which an intensely productive capitalist system might bring, if technological progress continued.[73] He saw huge savings for labour, so that almost all workers would enjoy greatly increased leisure time. In fact, he thought that – in the absence of wars and major increases in population – what he termed *the economic problem* would be solved within a hundred years. While he acknowledged that human needs may be insatiable, he suggested that once capitalism had succeeded in providing our basic needs, we would then turn our energies to non-economic purposes. Although capitalist productivity has been more prodigious than even Keynes imagined, in spite of major wars and a significant increase in population, we are still far from working an average of a 15-hour week, let alone solving *the economic problem*. Thus, against all logic, we feel compelled to push for higher growth and further productivity to bring us to that perfect hypothetical state that we blindly seek. If Keynes were to return today he would no doubt be bewildered to see what we have made of capitalism – and what it has done to us.

Of course, the devastation wrought by the Second World War necessitated an economic revival of huge proportions. The growth of economic activity in the nations affected relied on dedicated efforts to rebuild infrastructure, regenerate markets, and create employment: economic expansion was both a prerequisite and a consequence of a process which sustained much of the world until the early 1970s. Confidence in free market capitalism had been re-found, and few paid attention to ideas of limits, or to the potential dangers of rapid economic growth, while the notion that capitalism was engaged in energetically stimulating demand for consumer products, and not just responding to existing preferences, had not gained wide currency. Nevertheless, when economic progress stuttered in the '70s it was the signal for doubts to be raised in many quarters. At that time Herman Daly, one-time senior economist at the World Bank, was one of the first to promote the idea of a *steady-state economy*. Concerns in the 1980s then centred mainly on sustainability and the finite nature of resources, as misgivings about economic growth spread. As Daly said in *For the Common Good*, *Continuous growth in the scale of the aggregate economy could only make sense in the context of an unlimited environment.*[74] His ideas were further set out in an updated edition of his *Steady-State Economics* in 1991,[75] and have since come to be part of the mission of the Center for the Advancement of the Steady State Economy (CASSE), where Daly is a board member.[76]

However, more recently the focus of proponents of a steady-state economy has been on the dangers of climate instability as economic growth continues apace. The exigence for action here is made all the more pressing by the geopolitical effects of global warming. The disruption caused by climate change may in the future impact stability by increasing international resentment and rivalry, while developing nations seeking to grow their economies in order to raise living standards as well as to increase their military power will often see calls to abandon growth as unreasonable demands from an already rich and powerful 'first world'. But as CASSE maintains ... *in an overgrown global economy, economic sustainability is more conducive to diplomacy and stability among nations.*[77] Unfortunately, climate change will not await a more equitable world; a global steady-state economy is in the interests of all nations now, in order to begin safeguarding the planet's environment as well as for reasons outlined at length earlier in this chapter. When John Stuart Mill deplored the relentless struggle of *getting on* by fighting for one's own advancement by damaging that of others, he saw it as part of only one, somewhat primitive phase of industrial development, out of which British society would, in time, pass. But Mill was not contemplating the global aspects of this process, or the length of time required for poorer nations to work their way through development, the implications of which we have yet to grapple with.

But grapple with them we must; on the whole the dangers of inaction are likely to impact poorer countries more severely than richer ones. An holistic approach is indispensable in facing the consequences of climate change. While remedial measures should be adopted to mitigate poverty in the Third World, abandoning economic growth targets has to become global policy. Believing that 'efficiencies' can bring about sustainable growth, or even so-called *decoupling*, will not do. Efficiencies in one area may merely allow extra expenditure elsewhere. And if industry uses resources more efficiently, it may claim that smarter growth is being achieved, while more input may still be allocated to production, and the emphasis on growth will remain. Resource use must be limited in an absolute sense, regardless of what happens to output and incomes, above all bearing in mind, to reiterate, that more does not mean better, as this chapter has tried to illustrate.* Besides, there is simply no sustainable, just way that, with a growing global population, world incomes can continue to rise over coming decades; the result would be environmental catastrophe later this century. To forestall such disaster, there are no alternatives to reducing fossil fuel use and carbon intensity, curtailing primary resource extraction, and concentrating on meeting climate change commitments, while ignoring the effects these policies may have on economic growth.** The latter is no valid measure of economic or human progress and is almost entirely incidental to the vast challenges facing the planet.

---

*   This is one of the main theses of Bill McKibben in his book *Deep Economy*. He calls for a reorientation of the market economy, abandoning economic growth and nurturing community and our essential humanity.[78]

**   The result should at least usher in *absolute decoupling*, where resource use and emissions decline in absolute terms, even if economic output continues rising – an advance on *relative decoupling*, where material or emission intensity falls, though without necessarily using fewer materials. Under the title 'The Myth of Decoupling' Tim Jackson analyses the two scenarios, concluding that neither is sufficient to deal fully with our problems.[79]

Of course, reverting to a steady-state economy – in which the objective of economic growth is rescinded, though may occur – will require a transformed economy and a different kind of society, one which is presently hard to envisage. For, as was laid out at the beginning of this work, so much of what will be demanded of us is to do with perception; the current political landscape has conditioned us to accept implicitly the requirements of the market as overriding, so that its assumptions lie out of sight, almost out of mind. They only surface to be defended unthinkingly when challenged, by what is then seen as tendentious dogma which would vainly defy our prevailing certainties. For example, our perspective which sees capitalist production as a positive benefit, the more of which the better, must be transformed into an emphasis on production as a cost to us all. When resources are devoted to producing consumer items, or even some basic necessities, there are wider prices to be paid, so that judgements have to be made as to whether these costs can be borne without eroding the capacity for similar economic activity in the future. Dynamic equilibrium must be maintained; overuse of scarce resources, production which results in externalized costs – such as environmental degradation, the relentless increase in consumption, and the erosion of vital material capital which cannot be renewed – all these will harm economic and ecological balance and must be abandoned, so that the regenerative capacities of societies and the ecosystem may be restored.

The conceptual adjustments required to transform society will test some of our basic secular faiths and customs – ones which many believe to be their natural birthrights. But this is the result of a kind of macro-economic self-delusion, leading to the *cognitive ease* described in Chapter 1. However, before industrialisation a steady-state economy had existed for thousands of years, even if the concept was not then appreciated, during which much innovation and change was brought about. For, none of the requirements outlined above means that society would stagnate or decline; it is only the poverty of our imagination and our ingrained conviction which restricts our vision. In fact, moving to a steady-state economy could, and must, release a wave of creative innovation, just as the coming end of fossil fuel use has produced a range of inventive, carbon-free, green technologies. Perhaps reassurance could even be derived from the words of John Stuart Mill, more than a century and a half ago:

> *It is scarcely necessary to remark that a stationary condition of capital and population implies no stationary state of human improvement. There would be as much scope as ever for all kinds of mental culture, and moral and social progress; as much room for improving the Art of Living, and much more likelihood of its being improved, when minds ceased to be engrossed by the art of getting on.*[80]

– not that the aim of *getting on* would cease in the new environment, but ambition would necessarily be hedged about with the variety of social and ecological concerns which a changed awareness would require. Above all, it is our perception, our mindset which will need to change, out of which can come a wealth of creative progress.

At present, however, changing the outlook, removing economic growth figures and targets from their centre-stage prominence appears a daunting prospect. And while the majority of the bandwidth of policy-makers and commentators is absorbed by the repercussions of Covid-19, Brexit, climate change, global terrorism, and right-wing populism, dabbling in the murky terrain of economic concepts and measurement might appear absurdly perverse. But how we view our economic and social futures is absolutely central to dealing with these over-arching global issues. Economic growth and its misrepresentation is bound up with how we see one another and treat one another – with social harmony. The whole capitalist enterprise is currently run as a kind of zero-sum project – all movement and individualist effort – the casualties of which hope to pick up incidental crumbs from the self-interested striving of others. Little of this provides lasting satisfaction to those at either end of the economic spectrum – in spite of the promises of what growth can deliver at some indeterminate point in the future. But it is often maintained that dissatisfaction is built into the system, an integral aspect of its functioning, helping to drive us forward. Economist E. J. Mishan believed restlessness and discontent to be product and pre-condition of sustained economic growth.[81] After all, if contentment and equanimity were to have at least equal status with ambition and energetic endeavour, the promise of economic growth might lose its power to energise. And then where would we be?!

In a healthier place is of course the answer, but one which would place the obligation on policy-makers to devote themselves to rectifying problems of poverty, inequality and homelessness now, without waiting

ECONOMIC GROWTH – THE BEGUILING SPECTRE?

forlornly for growth to bear fruit – the economic version of Godot. As the situation currently exists, dealing with national problems can always be postponed, ostensibly leaving them to the future when growth is expected to deliver its bounty. In this respect, economic growth is a proxy to which we can transfer responsibility in order to exonerate us of our failings. In the early stages of late capitalism, Henry Wallich, a former governor of the American Federal Reserve, expressed this quite boldly: *Growth is a substitute for equality of income. So long as there is growth there is hope, and that makes large income differentials tolerable.*[82] But researchers Wilkinson and Pickett, who quote Wallich's words in their important analysis of equality in *The Spirit Level*, turn this around decisively: *It is not just that growth is a substitute for equality, it is that greater equality makes growth much less necessary.*[83] In fact, greater equality would be a preliminary step to a host of social and economic improvements, as their work amply illustrates – and which will be examined in a later chapter. But in the current climate the prevailing sentiment is with Wallich's words, which represent a total inversion – and subversion – of the misunderstood reality.

Thus the case against concentrating on economic growth is overwhelming. However, the extent to which it is ingrained in the global psyche indicates that the concept will not be easily overwhelmed. A small exchange in a BBC Radio discussion in 2016 gives a sense of what we are up against.[84] Juliet Michaelson, of the 'New Economics Foundation', gave an eminently sensible, progressive view on growth:

> *Growth is the wrong thing to focus on. We tend to treat it as a proxy for what people want. But people want jobs, a decent standard of living, health and happiness. But we haven't approached the thing from the other angle: what level and what type of growth is compatible with achieving those outcomes. How can we have an economy that delivers what people want – not just how can we grow.*

One of the panellists, entrepreneur Luke Johnson, came in straightaway with the comment ... *That sounds like a centrally planned economy to me. Capitalism works with millions of entrepreneurs to raise money and make businesses work, and when state starts to intervene then it goes wrong.* This kind of knee-jerk reaction is common, as if the implications of doubts about GDP lead on a short, straight path to authoritarian socialism. But it has long been in the interests of neo-liberals to eschew the nuances of economic theory and paint opponents of growth as anti-business, conveniently ignoring the adverse consequences of the lack of state involvement – most notably leading to the financial crash over a decade ago. Much more publicity needs to be given to these failings, and their sombre implications.

Mr Johnson's view is by no means unusual, but it is part of a dangerous and outdated creed, one that eulogizes the limitless forward movement of free market capitalism. As a free-enterprise system, capitalism is likely to be with us for some time, but the intense, neo-liberal *hyper* version, whose inexorable drive comes at the expense of humanity, will be overtaken by a more humane variety – one which recognises limits. Almost all early traditional societies saw the need to live within boundaries – physical and social – and those which succumbed to hubris and went beyond them courted disaster, as did classic Mayan civilization in early-tenth-century Central America. Ronald Wright explained how Mayan society degenerated as militarism took hold, while the leaders indulged themselves building ever more extravagant stone monoliths.[85] Evidence has shown that overpopulation, agrarian failure, a growing gulf between rich and poor and falling life expectancy resulted in the demise of Mayan civilization. As Wright put it, *In modern terms, the Maya elite became extremists, or ultra-conservatives, squeezing the last drops of profit from nature and humanity.*[86] Modern industrial society has come so far from its rural past and is in danger of being threatened by an equivalent catalogue of ills, headed conspicuously by climate change. But whereas the hubris of ancient civilizations affected merely their own limited societies, the risks inherent in surpassing our own well-recognised boundaries today may come at the expense of the whole planet – currently our only home.

It is not as if today's world is intellectually unaware of the finite nature of our planet, of our lives themselves. But at the level of subliminal consciousness, in both developed and developing societies, there lies a focus on striving, on expansion, on looking ahead to more and bigger- not just on better. The last two hundred years or so of industrial development have instilled a sense that there need be no frontiers, that human possibilities are almost endless, and that dominion of the planet and eventually of areas beyond will fulfil this potential. It is as if the busy exploitation of nature itself sanctifies the species' course of domination, one which has been fed by the modern creed of individualism and the loosening of religious and psychological restraints. *Besides, development is part of our paradigm of unspoken assumptions*, says Walter Schwarz. *We need to feel we have progressed from our pre-industrial days and that the non-industrialized world 'needs' to go the same way.*[87] We tell our children they can be anyone, do anything, travel anywhere – as if we can have total agency. We act as if the unimpeded exercise of will is to be the source of human salvation; yet it is this misplaced trust which has led to the predicament in which we find ourselves. This abiding faith in economic growth having the capacity to solve our problems means that our attention is invariably turned away from the present, overriding the pressing need to deal with current problems in the here and now. Like the novelist Flaubert, we constantly feel that we are about to live.

Homo sapiens may be *infinite in faculty*, but yet is as limited in its ultimate possibilities as in its individual lives. Here again, societies have lost a sense of proportion: death is no longer implicitly accepted as part of nature, but rather as an enemy, an aberration almost. Because of this, it is becoming ever harder to submit to it with dignity. Serge Latouche goes as far as to refer to the *cult of life*, from which death must be entirely shut out.[88] This is in marked contrast to traditional societies which accept our mortality, without attempting to transcend it. The irony is that in their endeavours to emulate the rich world, many developing countries are turning their backs on ways of living which previously sustained them, and which today could offer examples from which the first world could learn. But the latter has come so far from its own indigenous, rural past that it has lost that recognition of limits on which traditional societies were almost always based.* As a result, essential harmony has been lost. The trouble is that recognising limits imposes restrictions on our freedoms, and here we are back in the conceptual world of ideas, rights and destinies, in which we invest so much rhetoric. One might say that it is easier to rally the crowd behind the ideology of rights and freedoms than against the practical, disabling scourges of poverty or inequality – perhaps because the former do

---

* This accords perfectly with the philosophy of the market. As Karl Marx pointed out, capitalism is a machine for demolishing limits. It is not comfortable working within finite boundaries.

not appear to threaten anyone's economic interests, whereas the latter appear an indelible fact of existence.

Economic growth represents our comfortable illusions: aspiring to raise GDP seems always to have been with us, so that we are satisfied with its promise. How could its potential be destructive? It is hard to imagine NOT moving forward with our attention concentrated on high profile statistics, which, surely, must indicate progress and enhanced well-being? But we have to abandon the *cognitive ease* of recent times and recognise that devoting macro-economic policy to raising the growth index does not guarantee higher standards of human welfare, and nowadays does not even necessarily carry the consolation of raising employment levels with it. After all, in the British case income *per capita* has more than doubled since the mid-1970s, and yet our well-being could hardly be said to be at twice the level of forty-odd years ago. Economic growth is largely an incidental factor in our aim for a better quality of life, a distraction which measures the wrong components. A future world needs to be one in which mention of GDP figures would be an incidental occurrence, little publicised and certainly not made the basis for policy decisions.* And it would be surrounded by caveats and qualifications, justified by its limited, partial relevance. The focus would be on indices which matter, in terms of prosperity, employment, economic stability, environmental sustainability, and psychological well-being. These measures of human success cannot be assessed by economic growth statistics.

If we put our efforts into raising economic growth, then we may well grow the size of the economy – for all the good it may do us. But size hardly matters here; we do not need a bigger economy to be better-off. Indeed, it is plainly possible to achieve admirable levels of health, life expectancy, and education on much lower incomes than those of the wealthiest 'Western' nations, as will become evident in a later chapter. It is time we devoted our ambition to improving the **quality** of lives – something at least which need not be restrained by limits – rather than waiting for the uncertain, indirect contingencies of economic growth, with all its unfortunate side-effects. Over fifty years ago, in the year he

---

* Lord Adair Turner, former Director-General of the Confederation of British Industry, put it like this in his 2010 Robbins Lectures: growth ... *should not be considered the 'objective' of economic policy, but rather the highly likely outcome ... of two things desirable in themselves – economic freedom to make choices, and a spirit of continual enquiry and desire for change.*[89]

was assassinated when campaigning for the United States presidency, Robert Kennedy made a speech at the University of Kansas which included these words, which I believe are worth quoting at length:

> ... *for too long, we seemed to have surrendered personal excellence and community values in the mere accumulation of material things.*
>
> *Our Gross National Product, now, is over $800 billion dollars a year, but that Gross National Product – if we judge the United States of America by that – that Gross National Product counts air pollution and cigarette advertising, and ambulances to clear our highways of carnage. It counts special locks for our doors and the jails for the people who break them. It counts the destruction of the redwood and the loss of our natural wonder in chaotic sprawl. It counts napalm and counts nuclear warheads and armoured cars for the police to fight the riots in our cities. It counts Whitman's rifle and Speck's knife,* and the television programs which glorify violence in order to sell toys to our children.*
>
> *Yet the gross national product does not allow for the health of our children, the quality of their education or the joy of their play. It does not include the beauty of our poetry or the strength of our marriages, the intelligence of our public debate or the integrity of our public officials. It measures neither our wit nor our courage, neither our wisdom nor our learning, neither our compassion nor our devotion to our country, it measures everything in short, except that which makes life worthwhile.*
>
> *And it can tell us everything about America except why we are proud that we are Americans. If this is true here at home, so it is true elsewhere in the world.*
>
> *And:* **Even if we act to erase material poverty, there is another greater task, it is to confront the poverty of satisfaction – purpose and dignity – that afflicts us all.**[90] *(My emphasis.)*

---

*   Kennedy was referring to two horrifying acts of mass-murder from two years earlier: Charles Whitman's indiscriminate shooting from a tower of the University of Texas building on 1 August 1966, which killed 13 and wounded many others; and Richard Speck's murder of eight student nurses in their dormitory three weeks earlier.

END NOTES

i Franz Kafka, from "Advocates", quoted in Zygmunt Bauman, *Does Ethics Have a Chance in a World of Consumers*, Harvard Univ. Press, Cambridge, Mass., 2008, p. 257.
ii Edward Abbey,'The Second Rape of the West' in *The Journey Home: Some Words in Defense of the American West*, Dutton, New York, 1977, p. 183.
iii John Stuart Mill, *Principles of Political Economy with some of their Applications to Social Philosophy*, Longmans, London, 1909, Seventh Edition, Book IV, Chp. VI, Pt. 2.
iv Alain de Botton, *The News: A User's Manual*, Penguin Books, London, 2015, p. 127-8.
v Lord Adair Turner, on BBC Radio 4, May 9th, 2016.

1 Martin Pawley, *The Private Future: Causes and consequences of community collapse in the West*, Thames and Hudson, London, 1973, p. 32.
2 Idem.
3 Michael Young, *The Rise of the Meritocracy, 1870-2033*, Thames & Hudson, London, 1958, pp. 128-9.
4 Simon Kuznets, 'National Income: 1929-1932.' Division of Economic Research, Bureau of Foreign and Domestic Commerce, Washington D.C., 1934, p. 7, at **https://fraser.stlouisfed.org/title/971/toc/227058**. (FRASER is a digital library of US economic, financial, and banking history—particularly the history of the Federal Reserve System.)
5 Cited in Andro Linklater, *Owning the Earth: The Transforming History of Land Ownership*, Bloomsbury, London, 2014, p. 359.
6 Dennis Gabor, *The Mature Society*, Secker & Warburg, London, 1972, p. 2.
7 Ralf Dahrendorf, *The New Liberty*, Routledge & Kegan Paul, London, 1975, Chp. V.
8 Edward Luttwak, *Turbo-Capitalism: Winners and Losers in the Global Economy*, Harper Collins, New York, 1999, quoted in *The Ecologist*, London, Vol.29, No.5, Aug./Sept. 1999.
9 Ernst von Weizsäcker, Amory B. Lovins, L. Hunter Lovins, *Factor Four: Doubling Wealth – Halving Resource Use*, Earthscan Publications, London, 1997, p. 271. (A further report to the Club of Rome.)
10 Manfred Max-Neef, 'Reflections on a Paradigm Shift in Economics', in Mary Inglis & Sandra Kramer (Eds.), *The New Economic Agenda*, The Findhorn Press, Forres, Scotland, 1985, pp. 151-152.
11 'Natural Capital Committee – Advice to Government on the 25 year Environmental Plan' – London, Sept. 2017, p. 2, at: **https://assets.publishing. service.gov.uk/government/uploads/system/uploads/attachment_data/ file/677872/ncc-advice-on-25-year-environment-plan-180131.pdf**
12 Walter Schwarz in *The Guardian Weekly*, London, 3/9/1989.

13 Idem.
14 The Stern Review, 'The Economics of Climate Change', 2006, p. vi, at http://mudancasclimaticas.cptec.inpe.br/~rmclima/pdfs/destaques/sternreview_report_complete.pdf
15 Report by the Global Commission on the Economy and Climate, Sept. 2018, at https://unfccc.int/news/climate-smart-growth-could-deliver-26-trillion-usd-to-2030-finds-global-commission
16 Idem.
17 Tim Jackson, *Prosperity Without Growth: Foundations For The Economy of Tomorrow*, 2nd Edn., Routledge, Abingdon, Oxon., 2017, p. 20.
18 See also UN Climate Change News, Dec. 2018, in a series of country updates on national performance and actions to reduce carbon emissions, at https://unfccc.int/news/countries-present-updates-on-their-pre-2020-climate-actions-at-cop24
19 Tim Jackson, op. cit., p. 21.
20 Dennis Gabor, op. cit., p. 4.
21 See https://data.worldbank.org/indicator/NY.GDP.MKTP.CD?locations=GB
22 Measured in 2016 prices and PPPs. See https://data.oecd.org/gdp/gross-domestic-product-gdp.htm
23 Thomas Piketty, 'Enough of GDP, Let's Go Back to National Income', in *Chronicles On Our Troubled Times*, Penguin Books, London, 2017, p. 44.
24 Robert & Edward Skidelsky, *How Much Is Enough? The Love of Money, and the Case for the Good Life*, Penguin Books, London, 2013, p. 9.
25 U Thant, quoted more fully in Chapter 3, p. 74, End Note 112.
26 Robert & Edward Skidelsky op. cit., p. 3.
27 Ibid. p. 183.
28 J. B. Priestley, quoted in the opening to Chapter 3, End Note iii.
28 Cited by Ha-Joon Chang, *23 Things They Don't Tell You about Capitalism*, Allen Lane, London, 2010, p. 228.
29 Ibid. pp. 228-9.
30 Andro Linklater, op. cit., gives an illuminating account of the US and British situations during the post-war years, in the context of changing economic and political ideology, 358ff.
31 Ibid. p. 381.
32 According to figures cited by Ha-Joon Chang, op. cit., p. 229.
33 Idem.
34 Adam Tooze, *Crashed: How a Decade of Financial Crises Changed the World*, Allen Lane, London, 2018, p. 584.
35 Idem.
36 Paul Krugman, *End This Depression Now*, W. W. Norton & Co., New York, 2012, p. 238.
37 "What does GDP really tell us about economic growth?", *The Daily Telegraph*, London, 15/10/2014.
38 Robert & Edward Skidelsky, op. cit., p. 33.
39 Manfred Max-Neef, op. cit.

40 Ibid. pp. 150-1.
41 Robert & Edward Skidelsky, op. cit., p. 103. The Skidelskys draw on the vast 'World Database of Happiness' at Erasmus University in the Netherlands: **https://worlddatabaseofhappiness.eur.nl/** It has a wealth of research findings on ... *subjective enjoyment of life*.
42 Cited in Tim Jackson, op. cit., p. 56.
43 Idem.
44 Steven Pinker, *Englightenment NOW: The Case for Reason, Science, Humanism and Progress*, Allen Lane, London, 2018, p. 268
45 Robert & Edward Skidelsky, op. cit., p. 97.
46 Richard Wilkinson and Kate Pickett, *The Spirit Level: Why Equality is Better for Everyone*, Penguin Books, London, 2010, pp. 8-9.
47 As Robert & Edward Skidelsky have put it, in op. cit., p. 179.
48 For the statistical evidence shown here I have drawn on Tim Jackson's analysis of life expectancy in relation to GDP, and the data from the Human Development Index which he cites, in Tim Jackson, op. cit., p. 74.
49 Ibid. p. 76.
50 William Nordhaus and James Tobin, "Is Growth Obsolete?" in *Economic Growth*, National Bureau of Economic Research General Series, no. 96E, Columbia Univ. Press, New York, 1972.
51 Herman E. Daly and John B. Cobb Jr., *For the Common Good: Redirecting the Economy towards Community, the Environment, and a Sustainable Future*, Green Print, London, 1990, pp.418-9. A detailed explanation of the index is set out in the Appendix, pp. 401ff.
52 Ibid. p. 418.
53 Ernst von Weizsäcker, Amory B. Lovins, L. Hunter Lovins, op. cit., p. 273.
54 Tim Jackson, op. cit., pp.54-5.
55 At **http://www.oecd.org/statistics/oecd-guidelines-on-measuring-subjective-well-being-9789264191655-en.htm**
56 Kinley Dorji, Bhutan Secretary of Information and Communications, quoted in *The Observer*, New York Times section, London, 17/5/2009.
57 This is the common practice of questionnaires carried out for the World Values Survey **www.worldvaluessurvey.org** The WVS is the most extensive non-commercial, cross-national, time series body of research into human beliefs and values ever conducted.
58 Joseph E Stiglitz, *The Great Divide*, Penguin Books, London, 2016, pp. 96-7.
59 Ibid. p. 97.
60 Ha-Joon Chang, op. cit., p. 143.
61 Richard Wilkinson and Kate Pickett, op. cit., p. 226.
62 Paul Krugman, op. cit., p. 28.
63 Robert H. Frank & Philip J. Cook, *The Winner-Take-All Society: Why the Few at the Top Get So Much More Than the Rest of Us*, Virgin Books, London, 2010, p. 22.
64 Fred Hirsch, *Social Limits to Growth*, Routledge & Kegan Paul, London, 1978, p. 4.
65 Ibid. p. 5.
66 Ibid. p. 6.
67 Ibid. p. 7.

68 Ibid. pp. 8-9.
69 John Stuart Mill op. cit., Book IV, Chp. VI, Pt. 1.
70 Ibid. Book IV, Chp. VI, Pt. 6.
71 Ibid. Book IV, Chp. VI, Pt. 3.
72 Ibid. Book IV, Chp. VI, Pt. 2.
73 John Maynard Keynes, 'Economic Possibilities for Our Grandchildren', in *Essays in Persuasion*, W. W. Norton & Co., New York, 1963, p. 358.
74 Herman E. Daly and John B. Cobb Jr., op. cit., p. 145.
75 Herman E. Daly, *Steady-State Economics*, Island Press, Washington DC, 1991.
76 Center for the Advancement of the Steady State Economy (CASSE) at **https://steadystate.org**
77 In 'Downsides of Growth', at ibid.
78 Bill McKibben, *Deep Economy: The Wealth of Communities and the Durable Future*, Henry Holt & Co., New York, 2007.
79 Tim Jackson, op. cit., Chapter 5.
80 John Stuart Mill, op. cit., Book IV, Chp. VI, Pt. 8.
81 E. J. Mishan, *Economic Efficiency and Social Welfare*, Allen & Unwin, London, 1981, pp. 275-6.
82 H. C. Wallich, 'Zero Growth', Newsweek, 24/1/1972, quoted in Richard Wilkinson and Kate Pickett, op. cit., p. 226.
83 Richard Wilkinson and Kate Pickett, idem.
84 From a panel discussion in 'Free Thinking' on BBC Radio 3, 7th April 2016, with panellists Matt Wolf, MPs Liam Byrne & John Redwood, Juliet Michaelson and Luke Johnson.
85 Ronald Wright, *A Short History of Progress*, Canongate Books, Edinburgh, 2006.
86 Ibid. p. 102.
87 Walter Schwarz in *The Guardian Weekly*, London, 26/7/1992.
88 In Serge Latouche, *Farewell to Growth*, Polity Press, London, 2009.
89 Lord Turner, 'Economic Growth, Human Welfare and Inequality', Lecture 1, Lionel Robbins Memorial Lectures, London School of Economics, October 2010, quoted in Robert & Edward Skidelsky, op. cit., p. 170.
90 At **https://www.jfklibrary.org/learn/about-jfk/the-kennedy-family/robert-f-kennedy/robert-f-kennedy-speeches/remarks-at-the-university-of-kansas-march-18-1968** in which Kennedy used the then common value of GNP, rather than the now usual GDP.

Chapter 5

THE MARKET RULES – OK?

People of the same trade seldom meet together, even for merriment and diversion, but the conversation ends in a conspiracy against the publick, or in some contrivance to raise prices...
                                        ADAM SMITH[i]

... the idea, which is popular with rich men, that industrial disputes would disappear if only the output of wealth were doubled, and everyone were twice as well off, not only is refuted by all practical experience, but is in its very nature founded upon an illusion. <u>For the question is not one of amounts but of proportions</u>. (My emphasis.)
                                        R. H. TAWNEY[ii]

It was ... an established fact that Mr. Melmotte had made his wealth in France. He no doubt had had enormous dealings in other countries, as to which stories were told which must surely have been exaggerated. It was said that he had made a railway across Russia, that he provisioned the Southern army in the American civil war, that he had supplied Austria with arms, and had at one time bought up all the iron in England. He could make or mar any company by buying or selling stock, and could make money cheap or dear as he pleased. All this was said of him in his praise – but it was also said that he was regarded in Paris as the most gigantic swindler that ever lived; that he had made that city too hot to hold him; that he had endeavoured to establish himself in Vienna, but had been warned away by the police; and that he had at length found that British freedom would alone allow him to enjoy, without persecution, the fruits of his industry.
                                        ANTHONY TROLLOPE[iii]

We must make our choice. We can have democracy in this country or we can have great wealth concentrated in the hands of a few, but we can't have both.
                                        JUSTICE LOUIS D. BRANDEIS[iv]

I. The maelstrom which is the North African *souk* (more exactly *souq*) is the epitome of the bustling centre of Arabic commerce, the hub of constant movement of barter and exchange whose history goes back at least 2,500 years. Stepping into the famed Marrakech *souk* via Djemaa el Fna, for example, is to enter a world of hectic vibrancy where the senses are assaulted by the vast array of exotic sights, smells*, and a cacophony of noise, as well as by a feeling of invigorating, infectious energy. The merchants' specialties – leather, scarves, jewellery, aromatic spices, oils (above all the argan oil), dried fruits, ceramics, rugs etc. – cover every available metre of the tightly packed stalls. *Souks* have always been part and parcel not just of commercial affairs, but of the vernacular culture of everyday life, where families, friends and vendors interact, eager to present their wares and exchange the latest news – the gregarious, beating heart of Middle Eastern human reciprocity. Originally thought to have been established at locations where incoming caravans stopped for refreshments, *souks* then became regular features of local festivals, eventually forming networks linking major settlements, and even leading to breaks in tribal conflicts being declared to allow for periods of unhampered commercial operations.

Markets in this respect – physical commercial centres where what goes on extends well beyond buying and selling – are like the Greek *agora*, the Persian *bazaar*, or the Roman *forum*, originally versions of open-air markets in which judicial and political business was conducted as well as family interaction being carried on. Everyday commercial activity is transacted around and within a market setting, in an open communal arena which becomes a multi-purpose venue. But basic commerce – no matter how vital to family livelihoods – is only one feature of the social interaction which forms the underpinning of communal relations. And, crucially, the motivations and procedures which govern trading practices in the *souk* – if managed correctly – do not pervade quotidian social interchange, or the affective domain of which it is a part. Commercial motives are but one aspect of the means to making a living and to personal and family fulfilment; buying and selling, demand and supply constitute only a limited part of those ambitions. When, nearly fifty years ago, Alvin Toffler declared ... *the*

---

* The distinctive smell of a *souk* tannery will be detected well before one is spotted; the stink emanating from vats of diluted bird excrement, in which animal hides are dipped for a month to soften them, is not easily forgotten. Merchants hand visitors sprigs of mint in case the stench becomes too strong to tolerate.

aims of progress reach beyond economics, his comments came at the time economic forces were beginning their phase of ideological expansion, when market relations were moving into personal, non-commercial areas with the devastating consequences which we have since witnessed.[1]. That we need to be reminded of Toffler's words today is an indication of how far we have travelled.

It was established in Chapter 3 that capitalism is the natural result of free economic exchange in an open society, and does not require a body of ideology to justify its existence. However, it is crucial to accept that it is nevertheless only one element of that society, albeit at times with voracious tendencies to extend its reach. But it is principally a means to the gratification of basic human need, as well as to the satisfaction of our more ambitious, acquisitive propensities. When it surpasses these limited, natural inclinations of humankind, when it assumes such a dominant character that it unreasonably exacerbates existing economic inequalities in society as well as fomenting new ones, then it becomes a dangerous, predaceous organ oblivious to the deeper interests of civilization. In more balanced, rooted, self-conscious societies than are found in most of today's developed world, these dangers would be more readily apparent and would be more rigorously questioned. But contemporary free market capitalism has such a firm grip on modern thinking that challenges are easily deflected, principally on the grounds that – while it may have weaknesses – it is the best system available and we should try and shape up to it. Its protagonists do not allow distinction to be drawn between capitalism as conducted during the 1950s and '60s, and its modern neo-liberal conformation in which market forces and unbridled competition are given almost free rein over economic affairs, as well as undue influence in areas of social and vernacular relations.

The success which proponents of neo-liberalism have had in painting free market capitalism as one homogeneous system has assisted the propagation of their extreme policies. Together with the traditional lack of historical perspective, it has encouraged the mistaken view that capitalist values have remained largely unchanged, and that the growing demands of globalization – and more recently of austerity – have simply required a more vigorous application of those principles to continue to make our way in the world. Thus we are expected to view capitalist economics through one unclouded lens, when in fact the perspective has radically changed since the 1970s. George Orwell observed that an illusion can easily become a half-truth; a mask can change the expression of a face.[2.] And no great conspiracy needs to be perpetrated to bring this about – merely sufficient self-delusion, plausible rhetoric, and willing acquiescence. The mask of the modern capitalist system indeed has a benign aura: it shows itself as an agent to enhance personal freedom, liberate the consumer, and increase human choice, and if these ambitions face obstacles we should look elsewhere for solutions, not blame the impersonal system which, we are assured, is the best one around. From here it is but a small step to widespread acceptance, that the monolithic free market is true capitalism and we must make the best of it, for the only alternative is the discredited command economy, and we know where that leads!

Thus, unfettered free market principles, beset on all sides – we are told – by those who would subvert them and take us down collectivist paths, are painted as the *sine qua non* of our species' future. They are presented as all or nothing; since neither government action nor our inherent, benevolent disposition is sufficiently competent to arrange the fair distribution of material goods and services in society, we should leave the job to the 'impartial' conduct of market forces. And we are advised that the market has superior credentials for the task: it is supposedly governed by the price mechanism in a self-regulating, self-correcting manner which will thereby allocate resources more efficiently* – whether in times of scarcity or abundance – than any other system. It has the added merit, we understand, of being a neutral player in the economic arena, uncontaminated by our grubby, partisan, venal impulses which can only interfere with the freedom of market forces and hamper their tendencies towards equilibrium.** One academic writer expresses such theory as ... *By equilibrium market economists mean the state of perfect co-ordination of economic action in which the price structure reveals no further possibility of improvement*, albeit accepting this as an ideal *rarely* seen in the real world.[3] Indeed! Terms such as *impartiality, neutrality* and *equilibrium* are best confined to textbooks of economic theory, but then so much of this discussion covers scenarios not found in the real world: systems and theories have a far too prominent place in any consideration of economic free markets.

In fact, from the era of the gradual revival of free market ideas after

---

* In the light of the consequences of the 2008 financial crash, and government responses to it, it is hardly surprising if these claims are currently met only with howls of laughter and derision.
** Ditto!

World War II, following the ascendancy of Keynesianism, until the full flowering of neo-liberalism more recently, theory and ideology have had strange and undue influence. Proponents such as Friedrich Hayek and Milton Friedman played key roles, although both departing significantly from the neo-classical economics of Adam Smith. Yet both carried weight with the nascent New Right thinking in the 1970s. In the case of Hayek, initially with his landmark *The Road to Serfdom,* his theorizing was an attempt to warn against the socialist trends which were sweeping intellectual circles during the Second World War. But his arguments in this, and later in *The Constitution of Liberty* (1960), one of Margaret Thatcher's 'bibles', contained ideas which – through the author's attempts at political persuasion – deviated some way from everyday macro-economics. Meanwhile, his preoccupation with individualism led to a conflating of its wider theory with economic freedom, and thus to confusion between the whole and the parts (such as was taken to task in Chapter 2). Open, free -market operations being essential to a liberal democracy do not merit the construction of theoretical models to justify their ideal functioning, as if they were part of a delicate system of perpetual motion which human interference might easily destabilize. They are simply part of the everyday interchange of goods and services, with all the inherent frailties of the human beings who operate them.

Markets are dynamic, ever-changing meeting-points where human agents, their products and ideas come together. They can never be perfect, and are rarely in any form of equilibrium – which, in any case, is itself a subjective matter when it comes to economics and human relations. It is all very well speaking of factors of production being paid just enough to keep them operating efficiently, with no-one able to influence price, so that everything is in balance and market failure minimized; this is not practical, applied market economics. And as for neutrality, that is another fiction. As Robert and Edward Skidelsky sum up: *... A 'neutral' state simply hands power to the guardians of capital to manipulate public taste in their own interests.*[5] While free markets can confer undoubted benefits on their participants and the wider public, their perverse consequences must always be open to examination. The tendency to retreat into ideology in the face of valid criticism must be resisted; resorting to a *straw man* argument, claiming an attack on any aspect of market forces is a left-wing plot, part of a proxy advocacy for some form of socialist planning, will just not do. Many human agents and authorities intervene in market relations, for better and/or worse as well as to varying degrees. If in doing so they 'distort' this rough-hewn series of relationships in malign fashion, or manage to shape their workings to their own designs, then further intervention is legitimate, and probably required.

Although Adam Smith wrote of a *system of natural liberty*, markets are not systems. Certainly they are an explanation of how people tend to conduct their economic affairs when unhindered by authority, just as other forms of human behaviour are a result of our natural propensities. For example, we do not need to systematize our affective interpersonal relationships or attribute to them any kind of self-correction or equilibrium – until, perhaps, the law is required to intervene as a result of abuse or ill-treatment. We do not justify allowing people to conduct their own interpersonal affairs in a decentralized, unregulated manner – beyond the influence of political authority – on the grounds that it is more efficient than a system guided by the state; there is no *invisible hand* governing our love lives. It is simply a matter of what has been called *negative* liberalism being allowed free rein in the conduct of our natural preferences and partialities, whether it is as to whom we might choose as a partner or mate, with whom we decide to do business, or how we might make our living.* All these matters are ultimately subject to the law of the land, but that law should only intervene when damage is inflicted as a consequence of the unrestrained action of a person or group. Both monopoly corporate power and the modern state have the capacity to coerce, control, or even tyrannize, which is why arenas of freedom, economic or otherwise, need boundaries as well as regulation – none of which need hamper the legitimate operation of the free market.

However, as certain as one might be of the validity of this characterisation, it is one far removed from the perspective and ideology of neo-liberals. The right-wing dogma of the last forty years has taken its toll

---

*   Peter Self follows Isaiah Berlin's separation of *positive* and *negative* liberty, the latter ... *meaning the absence of external restraints upon an individual's freedom to act as she chooses*... whereas the former involves ... *improvements in the opportunities available for using her freedom more effectively*... and is thus more sympathetic to calling on government action for this purpose.[4] *Negative* liberty has been in the ascendancy for the past two generations, now reinforced by populist leaders in several countries who, like President Trump in the USA, have begun to dismantle some of the legislation favouring *positive* liberal action.

of the more open-hearted sensibilities of populations in many western democracies. The destructive effects of the strident, modern version of free market capitalism have subverted solidarities and ways of living and undermined relationships – at work, at home, and in community. *... intermediary social institutions and the informal social controls of community life are weakened by market-driven economic change*, concludes John Gray.[6] And, perhaps even more significantly, they have changed the way we see free market economics. There appears no room in our short memories for a wider appreciation of how market capitalism was once conducted, when greater social responsibility was assumed and individualism did not mean self-absorbed egotism. Seduced by neo-liberalism, we now find it difficult to see economics through any other veil, so that we are trapped by popular, stereotyped assumptions formed forty years ago. As was laid out in Chapter 1, the insidiousness of popular ideas can become all pervasive, so that they develop into unconsidered, self-generating commonplaces. In fact, a plausible idea becomes ... *so much a part of the cultural consensus, that it sinks out of awareness, becoming an invisible thread in the fabric of thought*.[7] As such, an idea will then subtly expand by assembling its body of corroborating facts; for, as Theodore Roszak maintains, ideas create information, not vice versa.[8]

But what we perceive today as the norm, as the way we think economic business should be done – because that is the way it **is** now done – emerged almost imperceptibly following the oil crises of the 1970s. Certainly it was given impetus by the popular capitalism crusade of Margaret Thatcher and Ronald Reagan, who had circumstances in their favour. The appeal of apparently fresh ideas depends very much on timing, and upon the extent to which their form and expression – but to a lesser degree their content – fashionably explain contemporary developments. The economic woes of the period – high unemployment, inflation, powerful trades unions and sluggish national performance – played into the hands of the New Right zealots, who responded with monetarism, privatisation, deregulation and the emasculation of the unions. One might see it as an example of Marx's contention that the broad transformations of society over time arise from changes in economic conditions. But the ideological metamorphosis was reinforced by the deceptive populism of Margaret Thatcher; as she put it at a Tory party conference, *Popular capitalism is nothing less than a crusade to enfranchise the many in the economic life of the nation. We Conservatives are* *returning power to the people.*⁹ Thus neo-liberalism became established, and a hard-edged, Janus-faced dogma, aided and abetted by the harsher climate of the 1980s and '90s, gradually ingratiated itself into contemporary thinking.

The modern domination of the idea of the market can be seen in other ways. While most economists and politicians accept some degree of intervention in free markets, the tendency to promote the *freedom* of economic exchange, as if it were sacrosanct, appears to support a much more radical position. And references in the media indicate changing emphasis and attitudes. Writer Yves Smith points out that in the 1960s it would not have been common to view markets as virtuous; *even the stock exchange*, she says, *had a whiff of disrepute*.[10] She proceeds with an interesting analysis of how this was reflected in the press, pointing out that in 1965 *The New York Times* had sixty-six articles including the phrase *free market*, and almost twice as many with the expression *free enterprise*. Meanwhile, 1,131 stories in that year mentioned *citizen*, and 1,342, *consumer*. By contrast, in 2008 the use of *free market* had risen almost 500% to three hundred stories, and *free enterprise* had dropped by more than half to forty-three. But the mention of *citizen* in 2008 – an election year she points out – had fallen from 1965 levels to 964, while those including *consumer* had more than doubled to 3,203.[11] Another small, but significant symbol was a 1961 article in *Time* magazine in which two prominently conservative economists, Milton Friedman and Arthur Burns, showed support for federal aid to education.[12] Recently, right-wing free marketeers in the USA have more often been opposed to tax funds going to public education. We are now in an era substantially different from the 1950s and '60s.

After the initial shock tactics of conservative administrations on both sides of the Atlantic, the imaginative assimilation of this extended concept of free markets developed steadily over the following decades. There was no one specific moment when ideology and policy changed, as a result of a new government with a new manifesto for a dramatically revised agenda. Yet, gradually, attitudes to many social and political questions were transformed into a new norm, and younger generations easily adjusted to a different environment in which the moral and social sympathies of earlier periods, and of earlier liberal thinkers, have been jettisoned. In their place has grown what Peter Self calls ... *a politically influential but intellectually thin set of ideas ... a bare individualism.*[13] Where Adam Smith was acutely conscious of the mutual responsibilities of a society in which religious faith was a binding element, modern proponents of economic liberalism – Friedrich Hayek, Robert Nozick, Milton Friedman – rationalized on a much narrower, purely material basis. This effectively eliminates concern for social justice which, they maintain, has no place within modern concepts of economic self-interest. And the emergence of the new dogma has been welcomed by business, which has much to gain from – and has helped to promote – a slimmed-down liberalism. This may seem to some a logical, an organic ideology, but a contributory factor was, as the Skidelskys have argued, that *In effect, the governments of Reagan and Thatcher handed economies back to the businessmen.*[14]

II. Much has been said in this work about the myths with which we surround ourselves, the misguided notions which dominate our presumptions about social and economic issues. But, as was laid out in Chapter 1, these are not conscious beliefs which carry reasoned, if mistaken arguments about values or social policy; if they were, perhaps they could be challenged more easily, and a brighter light shone on the fallacies of much contemporary thinking. No, they lie at a more hidden, deeper level; the subliminal nature of assumptions which drift unnoticed in the murky waters of public discourse means that they are never taken to task for their deception and sophistry, of which indeed even many of their advocates are unaware. They are threads of credence which run imperceptibly through our tendentious rhetoric, so that we think *through* them and not *about* them, forever leaving them lying in the unspoken premises of our discussions. Another example of these perceptions which has consolidated its place in the public consciousness, especially since the financial crash, is the connection between national finance and household economics. The idea that a government's accounts are much like that of a family, that building up high amounts of personal or household debt – living beyond one's means – is just as problematic for a government as for an ordinary family, has become firmly embedded in popular thinking. It is supposedly nothing other than a sensible, valid interpretation of modern economics – a perversion which requires determined unravelling.

There is a connection between personal and government finance, but it resides in the origin of the term *economics*. The prefix *eco,* deriving from the Greek *oikos*, stood for connected but moveable concepts of household, family and the family's property – even extending to its slaves. The Hispanic world has a related notion represented by the term *hacienda*, meaning a large landed estate, as well as a business enterprise, or even property or possessions (linguistically, 'what has been *made*'). Interestingly, in Spain and some of its former colonies it is also the government department for tax collection. But here the connections between family and government cease. Family households are encompassed WITHIN overall national financial arrangements, not in any way parallel or analogous to them. Taking on debt by borrowing is the normal practice for government, as well as for businesses investing for future production and profit. National economies can withstand being constantly in debt and financing interest payments on a regular, sustainable basis, something which individual households cannot manage for very long. As Nobel laureate Paul Krugman points out ... *debt does not make society as a whole poorer: one person's debt is another person's asset*.[15] As such, total wealth is not affected by the amount of overall debt, certainly at the global level, although the size of some nations' liabilities may make them vulnerable in a crisis situation. However, none of this relates to cases of household finance, where constant debt is likely to have crippling effects.

Of course, when families get into debt the sensible advice is for them to cut back, so that expenditure comes into balance with income – otherwise, as in Mr Micawber's day, the result will be *misery*. But if consumers drastically rein in spending in order to pay off credit card debt, the result could be a shrinking economy with job losses, and eventually even greater consumer debt and possibly general deflation. Krugman quotes the then Vice Chair of the US Federal Reserve, Janet Yellen, on ... *the paradox of deleveraging, in which precautions which may be smart for individuals and firms – and indeed essential to return the economy to a normal state – nevertheless magnify the distress of the economy as a whole*.[16] Krugman accepts that people ... *are trying to buy less stuff than they are capable of producing, to spend less than they earn*. However, *That's possible for an individual, but not for the world as a whole*.[17] For what is often misunderstood among politicians and policy makers, he says, is the fact that ... *your spending is my income, and my spending is your income*.[18] But in spite of these realities we are encouraged to believe in an apparently down-to-earth common sense which maintains that the same ordinary logic of household finances should be applied to national economics. And there is even a hint here that this homespun wisdom, which no-one could fail to understand, is superior to the advice of *so-called* financial experts and civil servants' departments.

Analogies of this nature became a noticeable part of discussions after the financial crash, especially on how to devise measures to rescue national economies. They served the interests of those proposing policies of severe financial austerity (of which more will be said later) in order to balance government books and recoup the vast amounts spent on bailing out the banks. Thus, erroneous interpretations of a nation's finances become established, their simplistic assumptions not to be questioned or analysed. It is firmly in the interests of those driving forward such policies that they consist of easy stereotypes with popular appeal, so that they come to form what the linguist and philosopher George Lakoff calls *cognitive frames*.[19] These are the perspectives through which we come to view common issues – as was laid out in Chapter 1 of this work. Once commonplace assumptions – which suit the atmosphere and prejudice of the moment – settle in the public domain and pervade media and social circles, they soon sink beyond the horizon into a comfortable complacency, forming part of what Alain de Botton calls the *fabric of existence*.[20] In the case of the fallacy of linking household finances to government balance-sheets, the frame through which the matter was viewed during the period 2010 to 2015 became a serious obstacle to those arguing against austerity measures, and especially to politicians opposing Conservative Party rhetoric for electoral purposes. This unconscious *cognitive frame* became a new norm and, as is its nature, was not to be shifted by reason or argument.

The myths which form themselves into *cognitive frames*, through which we view contemporary society, sometimes clarify themselves to us. We may even assume they are the perspectives of others all around us. But then there are other areas where our underlying assumptions are more clouded and indistinct, where we have a much more hazy impression of where we stand. And as regards the economic arena it may well be that those in power or authority are eminently happy with this uncertainty. The question of the extent to which market forces should be permitted to permeate modern societies is undoubtedly one of these. It suits the interests of the drivers of neo-liberalism if there is some ambivalence over how far the market should spread into social and personal life: confusion as to appropriateness, limits, and morality serves the purposes of money. In Chapter 3, the principle of free economic exchange under capitalism was accepted, but whether any boundaries should restrict the reach of market forces – howsoever free they may be – and where such boundaries should be placed, are far more nebulous issues. This is largely a matter of the thin, and growing, end of a seemingly benign wedge, since markets are seen to have a range of positive effects on societies. But as such, they cannot be readily assessed on principle. In order to decide on the acceptable extent of their operations, value judgements constantly have to be made on ethical and social grounds.

However, society has a conspicuous reluctance to pronounce on the degree to which human activities should be subject to market forces. In the current social environment there may be topics at the margins where there would be a fair amount of consensus. For example, most people in Britain would not condone direct product advertising or sponsorship in schools or prisons. But in difficult financial times corporate advertising in, say, the classrooms of teenagers – already savvy consumers in their own right – could bring in much-needed funds for education. And why not accept sponsorship from, perhaps, Sports Direct for the Science Department and its teachers in a secondary school, with the accompanying logos, posters, and science projects linked with the company?* With the growing purchasing power of children, firms involved would certainly find the captive nature of this particular audience especially attractive. However, this example of the potential scope for market activity highlights our dilemmas as regards where limits on it should be placed. For even now, most societies would recoil from accepting as normal commercial advertising in the classroom – *a pernicious presence*, Michael Sandel calls it. Why? – because, he says ... *it is at odds with the purpose of schools*, which is ... *to cultivate citizens*, whereas ... *the purpose of advertising is to recruit consumers*.[22] So, according to this analysis, although advertising is an accepted part of modern society,

---

* Examples of this kind are not at all far-fetched: Michael Sandel has cited the American example of an entrepreneur who in 1989 offered schools free TVs, video equipment and a satellite link in exchange for an agreement to show a twelve-minute, commercial-sponsored news programme (including two minutes of adverts) everyday, and require students to watch it. By the year 2000 it reached over 40% of US teenagers.[21]

market forces are far from neutral, since they have their own particular agendas and may in some spheres be injurious.

There are evidently fields where the public in general would be opposed to giving market forces free scope, such as the NHS, but there are also grey areas where consensus is harder to reach.* However, there is little opportunity to debate such matters and come to principled public decisions as to the permissible extent of market forces. There is certainly a sense that commercial activity can be corrupting in some circumstances, so that it would be helpful for some form of communal consensus on the market. But the hegemony of free market capitalism appears to leave no room for discussion, let alone agreement. Its advocates maintain that it is neutral in terms of social or moral values, which itself makes it attractive to adherents wishing to avoid being encumbered by difficult ethical questions. Its more malign tendencies in terms of, for example, exploited workers or poor labour conditions are often well publicised, but in a world of *out-sourcing* where should the blame be laid? Producers and consumers alike, though for different reasons, may well disclaim responsibility, while the free market system itself is too nebulous and disparate to assume culpability. Besides, in today's subliminally post-modern atmosphere, where freedom reigns, there is a tendency to avoid value judgements on economic questions; to be 'judgemental' now has distinctly prejudicial connotations. Market forces are a slippery target – at once the esteemed source of our prosperity and an invasive, predatory power.

III. Perhaps there is something latent in particularly the British psyche which allows for an acceptance of extremes once a principle has been admitted. In the case of the free market, since its bounty is so often extolled, why not extend its scope to more, or even all areas of human activity? *Surely it can only be beneficial*, is the train of thought. Competition, for example, an essential element of market forces, is thought to bring about the best of economic results and therefore should be widened – goes the unthinking thinking – to take in areas beyond conventional private enterprise. Adam Smith believed in competitive markets as a

---

* It was significant that one of former President Trump's impromptu remarks during his state visit to Britain in 2019 contained the hint that the even the NHS would be up for debate during eventual trade talks with the UK.

bulwark against government as well as corporate monopoly power – the latter often in league with the former – but he accepted the need for a regulatory framework. He was fully aware of the tendency for rapacious entrepreneurs to try to corner the market, undermining competition and harming society's interests. And in a free environment, self-interested individuals, competing with one another in the marketplace, led to socially beneficial outcomes, provided that competition – in effect a neutral regulator – was conducted on a level playing field. Extreme greed and selfishness would thus be held in check, a restraint on the capacity of the unscrupulous to take advantage of others. But Smith was not naïve enough to assume free competition could be *perfect*, except in rare cases and then not for very long. Yet this idea gained adherents as time went on.

The default view in neo-liberal economies, particularly in the *Anglo-Sphere*, is that competition is the best mechanism for producing desired outcomes. Of course, we are told, there may be those who do less well from a competitive free market, but that is down to individual differences and personal responsibility. After all, goes the argument, is not competition part of our instinctive nature, evident in all aspects of human society and centred on our *selfish gene*?* But this is not a true picture of our species, only partisan rhetoric to serve the cause of the further marketisation of everyday life. For there is an important distinction to be drawn between a society with markets – the common situation stretching back into the mists of time – and our present 'market society' ... *where exchange value rules supreme*.[23] Economist Yanis Varoufakis has explained how the latter developed out of the former over recent centuries, during which most productive activities were gradually routed through markets and became commodities with *exchange value* – the *Great Transformation*, he calls it.[24] In this process fewer and fewer of life's bounties would be judged by what he terms their *experiential* value, activities or items not normally measured in terms of the market. The increasing tendency to judge goods with exchange value more highly than experiences with no market price has accompanied this development. But the reciprocal, vernacular relationships, untouched

---

*   This fallacious stereotype, examined in connection with individualism in Chapter 2, is the reductive position which neo-liberals take up. Part of the sloganeering of the dogma, it is not always borne out in practice when applied to 'hard cases'. In the USA, that bastion of the free market, many neo-liberals support the minimum wage and would be against a race to the bottom in terms of the labour market.

by exchange value, which carry on alongside a steadily commodified society, still represent the vital bonds of families, friends and communities; price and profit do not normally figure in these.

However, as more and more goods and activities become commodified, it becomes harder to separate life's essence in terms of enjoyable, quotidian experiences from marketable products. The division between the two becomes increasingly blurred on the public level, while the question as to whether this commodification should be allowed to proceed is overshadowed by the dominance of the all-hallowed free market. What criteria should be used to determine how far market forces should be permitted to spread? And where should markers be laid down, restricting further potential for employment, productivity and profit? In an environment where the competitive market is seen as such an important route to prosperity, and where money has become more than a means to an end, these questions have no obvious answers. In addition, they are not part of any public debate, though one is sorely needed. So much of life is now seen *through* market relations that this perspective has become the norm, but this was not always so. It was the Thatcherite crusade of the late 1970s and '80s, deliberately trying to engineer a *popular capitalism*, which gave implicit approval to the extension of market forces. Behind the apparently benign slogan of a *property-owning democracy* were the Thatcher government's attempts to re-design the electorate and direct it towards strict neo-liberal values, all of which has left us abandoned on a continuum which has no obvious end point.

It was not always like this. Today's emphasis in the competitive free market is resolutely on the individual and what she can obtain in the hyper-consumerist world of contemporary capitalism. And since authorities have little capacity to enhance goods with *experiential* value, the focus is ever on enlarging the scope for satisfaction of commodities with *exchange* value. The isolated individual, set adrift with nothing but her economic means, has recourse to herself alone for all other attributes of a meaningful life. As laid out in Chapter 2, this is a false interpretation of individuality, but is nevertheless how a modern economy is viewed in these neo-liberal times. Producers are seen to have a very narrow range of responsibilities, social obligations rarely among them. So with competition paramount, co-operation and solidarity are not highly regarded, their roles seemingly out of place in today's harsh economic environment. In this respect, companies which attempt a more collaborative approach are not common. The success of the John Lewis Partnership, the UK's largest employee-owned business, thus appears an anomaly. But being able to feel part of the company you work for and benefiting from a share of profits are attractions to employees and do not appear to detract from profitability. (*When you're part of it you put your heart into it...* is the slogan conveying their philosophy.) It is surprising, perhaps, that more companies have not followed this model, but most eschew what can appear woolly benevolence which is not the path to maximizing profits and shareholder value.*

Of course, co-operation or collaboration within the free market are by no means new or recent developments. When Welsh textile manufacturer Robert Owen took over the cotton mills at New Lanark on the Clyde in 1799, he began putting into practice theories of human resources management which were well ahead of his time. There, the largest cotton-spinning complex in Britain was the centre of a community of over 2000 people, where Owen's ambitious business plans were allied to efforts to improve the health, education, and rights of his workers, and thus create a better society for all. Although criticised at the time, he influenced reformers after him with his progressive policies, which he later took to the USA, with the less successful model community at New Harmony, Indiana. Through improvements to conditions for his workers, Owen became a beacon in early Utopian Socialism, as well as being a co-founder of the Co-operative movement. His idealism was based on his belief in the vital formative powers of early education and humane working practices. Now, over two centuries on, there still seems a reluctance fully to embrace these ideas which are widely recognised as beneficial to economic development. In fact, due to austerity-led public spending cuts there has been a kind of neo-liberal retrenchment: the now much-reduced but supremely valuable Sure Start programme for early childhood, and the outdated long-hours working culture, both

---

*   Blackwell bookshops and jam maker Wilkin & Sons are two of the better known companies with considerable employee ownership, of which more than 100 exist. However, studies show that such companies typically outperform those organisations where employees do not have an ownership stake or any right to participate in decision-making. And during the recession following the crash of 2007/08, employee-owned businesses had a higher rate of sales growth and job creation than firms under more conventional ownership.

stand in stark contrast to Owen's ambitious ideals over two hundred years ago.

However, there is a tension between the individualistic, competitive thrust of neo-liberal economics – the American business model, as it is often called – and the collaborative approach of a system in which the role of the state is more than merely the protection of property rights and the enforcement of contracts. This dichotomy is in evidence in many economies, and in spite of the hubris which led to the financial crash is unlikely to be resolved easily or soon. Co-operation and collaboration in business are seen everywhere, even though – as John Kay points out – economists find it hard to fathom ... *why there is so much more co-operative behaviour in the world than the pursuit of self-interest would imply.*[25] A wider appreciation of our species and its economics, which this work has tried to provide, would indicate that this is not at all surprising; it is the domination by neo-liberal values and their apologists over recent years which have clouded the issues and allowed a warped, one-sided vision of society to prevail. In fact, it is more surprising that many economic entities have managed to remain successfully profitable with this narrow interpretation of their employees and consumers. Kay highlights redistributive market liberalism, a less fundamentalist market capitalism, in which individuals seek their own self-interest – within the constraints of tax and regulation – while nevertheless accepting the need for publicly funded redistribution,[26] a system which has already gained wide social consensus.

However, this does not go far enough. To reflect the true nature of society and its individuals – as outlined in Chapter 2 – market forces need to take on a fuller responsibility towards society as a whole. For as Kay says, ... *market economies function only by virtue of being embedded in a social context.*[27] One cannot support a model in which a cut-throat, winner-take-all mentality is sanctioned in market economics but is shunned in social contexts.* Solidarity (though not of the us-against-them variety) as well as loyalty are to be valued wherever they are found, and are necessary for organisations to become effective. We are nevertheless going through a phase where, for many employees as well as most consumers, loyalty is regarded as entirely dispensable,

---

* In any case, extreme competition leading to zero-sum situations is destructive of the competitive environment itself, in economics as in life generally. As Richard Sennett says, the winner needs to leave something for the loser, so that they can engage again. *Such strict markets resemble sports; you don't want the losers to disband as a result of defeat.*[28]

and even as a handicap to productive competition; such trends can truly be socially destructive. As has already been emphasised, capitalism is part of society, not *vice versa*, and if their symbiosis is to work they must share the same values. For example, the short-termism and fragmentation of much modern capitalism is at odds with the needs of building families, communities, careers. And both the prevailing economic system and its parent society need rituals ... *to relieve and resolve anxiety*, as Sennett maintains, by directing people away from a detached solitariness towards *shared, symbolic acts*.[29] These ritual ties must be strengthened, in order to provide deeper co-operative meaning than the narrow, self-absorbed individualism which fundamentalist free market values demand of us.

IV. An area where waters have been deliberately muddied over recent decades is the question of the extent to which the free market should be regulated. Where once norms and guidelines had a recognised, and in many cases statutory, role in guiding the operation of market forces, today they are frequently criticised – and not just by neo-liberals – as hampering the workings of the economy. This has contributed to their being weakened and diluted, to the benefit mainly of private companies. Although those proclaiming the need for unfettered free markets often do so as a kind of rallying cry, behind which a more nuanced approach to corporate policy is normally conducted, nevertheless the slogan carries weight: it is part of the neo-liberal message that regulation is an unnecessary bureaucratic impediment, hindering competitiveness and, it is thus implied, our increased prosperity. And since the financial crash over a decade ago – to which a lack of appropriate regulation itself had contributed – government austerity has led to the further weakening of monitoring and policing of private firms. One might have thought that after the cataclysm of 2007/08, and the major remedial policies which it entailed, the vital need for such regulation would have been recognized – by private enterprise as well as government. But it has come to be seen as an optional extra, not vital, something which cannot always be afforded and which in any case will hamper full economic recovery.

But of course memories are short, and financial concerns often prefer them to be so. Business leaders as well as the general public soon become accustomed to the prevailing environment, so that the deregulation of the 1980s and '90s is a long-forgotten phase of economic history – certainly not part of today's truth. Whereas it might be supposed that this area of practical economics should be based on just that – practicality – in actual fact it is an arena dominated by ideology. When in the 1980s the privatisation of public monopolies got underway it was largely motivated by the neo-liberal dogma of the time, which also inspired the deregulation of the finance industry. The 'Big Bang' sparked off by the 1986 Financial Services Act ushered in a system of self-regulation allowing finance firms greater autonomy, such as freedom to set their own liquidity ratios and widening the range of products they could offer. Thus the traditional hegemony of Britain's financial sector was enhanced by the further financialisation of its economy. Not that concerns were not voiced at the time, even by those within the Conservative Party: in the mid-'80s, MP David Willets expressed reservations about the measures allowing the City of London to become more competitive. And doubts were also raised within Mrs Thatcher's own circle: Cabinet Secretary Sir Robert Armstrong wrote to Nigel Wicks – then the Prime Minister's PPS – with concerns about ... *the way in which corners are being cut and money is being made in ways that are at the least bordering on the unscrupulous.*[30]

However, in the heady days of 1980s Britain, an optimistic wave, falsely justified by neo-liberal wishful thinking, was carrying the country into a self-deluding euphoria not witnessed since the 1920s. The same trend was evident in the USA under Ronald Reagan, and maintained with Bill Clinton's (albeit Democratic) administration a few years later. The important Glass-Steagall Act of 1933, which had kept retail banking and mortgages separate from investment banking, was eventually repealed in 1997, and the deregulation of the finance industry was continued by the Financial Services Modernization Act (the Gramm-Leach-Billey Act) two years later. What had been fairly secure financial sectors soon became rife with speculation and risky procedures, and, as Andro Linklater has put it, ... *the industrial home, driver of the consumer economy, became once more what it had been in the Roaring Twenties, a functional adjunct to Wall Street.*[31] Measures which had protected the public from the worst predations of irresponsible finance were swept away on a tide of ideological fervour and positive thinking. In Britain, where the finance industry is an even larger proportion of the national economy, the boom years up to the financial crash saw lending to property companies soaring, while the amount of credit banks provided to businesses fell as a percentage of GDP, inhibiting investment in manufacturing. Such were the repercussions of liberating British finance.*

It is almost as if we are compelled to go through the full spectrum of a cultural or financial trend before we can extricate ourselves from it and come out on the other side. Ideas have to be worked through before they can be discarded, as we settle on the next set of prejudices which absorb us – and which before long we believe to be indispensable to our economic survival. We are currently in the phase which says untrammelled free markets good, stifling government-imposed regulation bad, while its cheer-leaders chant this one-sided refrain as if life were a question of extremes – and all this a decade or so after the financial meltdown which should have brought the gatekeepers to their senses for a generation. But no, we are in the hands of leaders who respond to years of boom with an almost total lack of caution or scepticism, caught up as all are in the feverish excitement of the age. Thus when disaster strikes they are as spellbound as the rest of us, ... *in a state of shocked disbelief...* as former US Chairman of the Federal Reserve, Alan Greenspan, professed to be following the 2007/08 crash.[33] The conviction that government should keep out of private enterprise and allow companies to conduct their affairs unmolested, for the wider benefit of society as a whole, still pervades the *Anglo-sphere*; political involvement in business has yet to regain trust. And with no plausible, fresh ideas appearing on the horizon, there appears nowhere else for our faith to be placed.

Yet, while the notion of the untrustworthiness of government interference is constantly put about, and with a dearth of new ways to counteract it, the evidence for corporate culpability accumulates. Even reputable companies like Volkswagen have shown their disparagement for necessary regulation with the vehicle emissions scandal which surfaced in 2015. The American Environmental Protection Agency had discovered that many VW diesel cars sold in the United States and elsewhere were fitted with a software *defeat device*, which subverted results of laboratory emissions tests; these caused the engines to emit 40 times less NO_x during testing than in normal driving conditions. The German automobile giant later admitted cheating, by devising techniques which meant their engines could in effect tell when they were being tested. Such

---

* Robert Peston and Laurence Knight give an insightful, comprehensive account of these trends and how they led us into the *mess* of the financial crash and its aftermath (and make us wonder why so few saw it coming).[32]

corporate irresponsibility on a vital matter of public health makes the ongoing demands in the private sector for no more than self-regulation even more implausible. But whether it is devising ways of undermining existing regulations or trying to forestall new ones, many firms will put efficiency and profitability before regulation, especially that imposed by government. And in the current climate companies have the support of business-friendly political authorities. The Conservatives often speak of regulation as if it were part of a socialist conspiracy. As Prime Minister David Cameron had pledged to abolish the *albatross of over-regulation*, and after the Tory victory in 2015 the new Business Secretary Sajid Javid launched the Cutting Red Tape initiative.

Once the Conservatives were again the sole party of government in 2015, they pressed resolutely on with their cost-cutting and anti-red-tape agenda. An aspect of this was reducing regulations on new-build properties, one feature of which was to limit the time taken carrying out fire safety inspections. It was reported then, in 2017, that for some companies the time had been reduced from six hours to forty-five minutes, for which government ministers congratulated themselves, on the basis that managers could more quickly get back to their 'real' jobs.[34] However, its timing could not have been more significant, for in June that year a devastating fire in the Grenfell Tower apartment block in west London killed 72 people, raising questions once again about regulation – unnecessary bureaucracy or vital health & safety legislation? Yet strident calls have been heard, especially from right-wing media outlets, for a *bonfire of regulations* – not the most appropriate of metaphors – following Britain's exit from the EU. This again feeds the false impression – on both sides of the Atlantic – that we are over-regulated and much of it is anti-business. Just one example puts a strong counterweight on the other side: in late 2018 unidentified drone activity near Gatwick Airport caused a thousand flights to be affected by the shutdown of the airport, and even the army to be deployed to tackle the problem. The lack of adequate protective measures and a proper regulatory framework led to Gatwick spending £5 million on preventive action before normal flights were eventually resumed after two weeks.

Nevertheless, the bandwagon carrying the right-wing ideologues and their fellow travellers still has momentum. Even after high-profile cases in which a lack of regulation has been implicated, there is still a prejudice against rules and measures, usually supported by the right-wing media, and frequently linked to Britain's exit from the EU. The attitude is ingrained in popular thinking, consistently developed over time, corresponding to George Lakoff's *framing* analysis, cited earlier.[35] If the debate centres on *regulation*, an abstract term conveying restriction, bureaucracy, anti-freedom, then the key element of *protection* – the *raison d'être* for much guidance and legislation – is ignored or bypassed. And most analysis to determine the impact of such regulation is focused on business, not on the agents whom the regulations are designed to *protect*. So that when David Cameron said in 2012 that his government would … *kill off the health and safety culture for good*, it was more likely to bring to mind examples like children being stopped from playing conkers, or Morris dancing being banned on safety grounds, than the risks of important legislation protecting employees being overturned. But the danger of the indispensable being lumped together with the frivolous or the unnecessary, in the interests of business efficiency, is all too real. In this light, the 'one in one out' rule to control the amount of new regulation and abolish some existing measures, which the government introduced in 2010, can be seen as arbitrary policy to promote business interests.

Thus the clamour to cut back on regulation has not abated. One Conservative MP, Stephen Hammond, mused in 2011 about *wholesale regulatory deletion*, possibly with … *a Minister of State for Deregulation, specifically tasked to remove regulations, redefine regulatory impact assessments, and demolish the health and safety culture.*[36]* After the EU referendum of 2016 the focus was on how leaving the EU would liberate government and allow – as Andrea Leadsom, then Environment Secretary, said in 2017 – for the slashing of rules which hold back farmers. However, a report in 2018 by the CBI employers' group, examining 23 sectors of industry, indicated that diverging from EU rules after Brexit would mean more costs than benefits.[38] Any advantages to areas such as agriculture, shipping and tourism, it said, would be vastly outweighed by the impact on other sectors of the economy. CBI Director-General Carolyn Fairburn said business was not interested in a bonfire of regulations, emphasising that … *diverging from EU rules and regulations will make* (businesses) *less globally competitive, and so should only be done where the evidence is clear that the benefits outweigh the costs.*[39]** Calls for evidence-based policy one does not

---

\:u2003As regards the 'one in one out' rule, Hammond's flippant (?) remark was that … *for the more radically inclined… this could be boosted – for example, 'one in three out'.*[37]

**\:u2003The CBI's view was supported by The Financial Conduct Authority. The FCA's

often hear from the Right, more often unsubstantiated claims that the bonfire of red tape will stimulate economic growth, accompanied by the deluge of repetitive, sweeping assertions that Britain's economy is tied up with the stuff and simply cannot function.

There would not appear to be clearer evidence for the need for strict regulation than the fire which ravaged Grenfell Tower. Initial findings in the independent report of the inquiry into the fire declared the whole system and practice of building regulation in the UK *unfit for purpose. The mindset of doing things as cheaply as possible must stop* was the damning comment of Dame Judith Hackett, chair of the committee of inquiry. No doubt she had in mind the failure of the mandatory fitting of sprinklers, to make homes and schools safer, after the measure had been recommended. And as regards the combustible cladding on Grenfell Tower and numerous other blocks, the government eventually introduced – long after the event – a ban on its use in new high-rise buildings in late 2018. However, after the report on Phase 1 of the public inquiry was published in October 2019, and with Phase 2 hearings still ongoing, a full improved regulatory system is still awaited. In opening a debate in the House of Lords in July 2017, soon after the fire, Baroness Andrews cited the ... *fatal obsession with deregulation... across Whitehall... which ... has been pursued with no regard for consequences, other than the benefits to business.*[41] In a fulsome indictment of the campaign to reduce government regulation, the Baroness blamed governments since 2010, which had come to a position ... *where deregulation is an ideological and political choice – where, indeed, it has turned into a battle cry.*[42]

Austerity has, of course, played a key part in this sorry picture. During a decade of budget cuts, which according to various estimates reduced local authority budgets by an average of 40%, staff involved in checks regarding food protection and pollution control were severely reduced, while there has been a substantial fall in the number of enforcement notices issued by local authorities as well as the Health and Safety Executive. In the House of Lords debate cited above, Baroness Andrews commented on Sajid Javed's claim, during the 2015 election campaign,

---

Christopher Woolard warned that a bonfire of regulations would not be in the interests of financial services. In evidence to a House of Lords committee in October 2017 he emphasised that many standards were now set globally, and that the majority of business is done ... *in pretty rough enforcement jurisdictions. ... This is a system of international standards where money tends to have a flight to quality.*[40]

that due to cuts in red tape thousands of businesses no longer faced health and safety inspections, by declaring ... *how right he was...* then proceeding to cite a TUC survey of April 2016 which found that half of all workplaces had never been visited by a safety inspector(!).[43] There has been much discussion about the budgetary cuts and how necessary they were for Britain's economic revival after 2008, but there is little doubt about where they fell and their consequences – although the latter is often disputed by government. However, the bias towards private enterprise has been significant, in accordance with neo-liberal prejudice. In spite of high-profile cases of the failure of private companies, as a result of fraud, mismanagement or sheer incompetence, the benefit of the doubt is frequently accorded to the private sector, in spite of its record: Enron, WorldCom, Lehman Brothers, Northern Rock, RBS, Carillion, as well as all the many, many scandals which did not lead to corporate collapse.

Nevertheless, conservative governments – including those of New Labour – show their true colours by their undue bias towards the private sector. Perhaps they are seduced by their own dogma that state-run services are invariably inefficient and expensive and private industry can always do a better job. So when it came to welfare reform, a major part of the coalition government's programme after 2010, the inevitable plan was to award contracts to private companies, which would receive large amounts of public money to administer the changes. For key elements of the programme, such as the welfare-to-work scheme involving 3.2 million people being assessed as to whether they could rejoin the workforce, lucrative five-year contracts were being awarded to successful companies. But a report at the time revealed that allegations of fraud against these private firms were growing; MPs on the Public Accounts Committee had received numerous complaints from whistle-blowers.[44] Yet in March 2012, the Department for Work and Pensions had only 49 investigators to examine such potential fraud – a reduction of 20 on two years previously. In the same period the number of investigators looking into fraud allegations against benefit claimants rose from 2,760 to 2,876[45] – the notoriety of such cases attracting more colourful publicity from their exposure in the right-wing tabloids, to which government gleefully responded.* Regulations, and the staff to

---

* Efforts to get welfare claimants registered as disabled back into work were part of the reforms. However, in 2018 as many as 70% of the 'disabled' judged fit for work succeeded in overturning the decision on appeal.

police them, do appear to find favour with populist authorities when it suits their interests.

Neo-liberal governments and their fundamentalist free market allies remain resolute in observing a conceptual separation between the idea of an open market system and its proclaimed benefits on the one hand, and its many weaknesses and harmful repercussions on the other. They attempt to explain away the latter, variously, as incidental side-effects, or due to bureaucratic restraints or government interference, and even down to personal failings by rogue elements not characteristic of corporate practice. But they refuse to acknowledge that private enterprise has inherent failings, due to the nature of the human beings who run it, for this would imply that it naturally requires regulation, just like any other branch of human endeavour. But of course the regulation in place has to be effective. The hodge-podge of private train companies which run Britain's railways have inflicted a variety of indignities on the travelling public, with cancellations, delays, and huge disruption. Yet neither the rail regulator nor ideologically-driven transport ministers have managed to come to grips with the situation. The original, flawed model of privatisation over twenty years ago, inspired by neo-liberal conviction rather than practicality, has not been managed in the public interest, but failure does not necessarily mean a company will have its franchise withdrawn.* In 2018, increased problems with trains and/or crews, plus a timetable fiasco, led to soaring cancellations, but the resistance to re-nationalising the railways remains a red line for Conservative governments.**

Nothing must be allowed to disparage the ideals of free market economics or the often unearned profitability which results from it. In the case of Britain's railways, both are allowed to take precedence over efficient management of a *public service*, given large handouts of *public* money, and which most authorities agree badly needs a central organising authority. Regulation in the airline industry is an even more critical issue. Within five months in 2018–19 two disastrous plane crashes of

---

*   Unless the company runs out of money, as Virgin Trains East Coast did in June 2018, putting London North Eastern Railway back in the hands of the state.

**   Among a host of franchise failings, FirstGroup's running of GWR since 2006 stands out: in spite of exiting its contract in 2013, owing £800 million to the government, it was allowed to continue running the service, since when it has received a number of short-term contract extensions. The latest, in November 2018, meant the Department for Transport has allowed it to continue operations until at least 2022, which will mean that FirstGroup has been awarded a rail franchise for almost 10 years without a competitive tendering process.

Boeing 737 Max 8 aircraft led to the grounding of all such airliners worldwide.* Pilots were reported to have struggled when the plane's computer system automatically pushed the plane's nose down when it was at risk of stalling, a fault which was implicated in both crashes. It had been suggested that when Boeing decided to adapt its 737 airliners with heavier, more fuel-efficient engines, instead of wholly redesigning the plane, the fresh re-certification procedure which should have taken place did not happen. Had Boeing opted for a complete overhaul of the Max 8's design, it would have taken several years before certification and verification by a third party had been completed. Whether or not budget cuts to the US Federal Aviation Authority played any part in Boeing's decisions is unclear, but the FAA's standing, with its exemplary technical reputation, is not helped by the libertarian onslaught in the United States against regulation, which in this field is so crucial to passenger safety.

One of the contentions of parties in favour of Britain's exit from the European Union was that freedom from EU regulation would provide a boost to the British economy. It was often alleged that stifling European bureaucracy hampered Britain's performance, especially as regards freeing up the labour market. However, on closer examination it appears the potential for change is to be more limited. For example, labour market protection and the freedom to dismiss workers vary considerably across the EU; being a member did not prevent Britain from having one of the most flexible labour markets in the world. OECD data show that UK workers have less protection than most EU states, particularly with regard to individual and collective dismissal, more on a par with other countries in the *Anglo-sphere*.[46] Thus British employers have had the kind of flexibility many say was lacking, and the restrictive burden on them was far less than claimed. It was a similar picture for numbers of working hours, in view of the UK's right to opt out of the EU's Working Time Directive limiting the working week to 48 hours. John Springford of the Centre for European Reform maintained that as for product and services markets EU rules do not generally impose strict harmonisation on the union. In fact here, he showed that the level of regulation moved towards Britain's liberal model, rather than *vice*

---

* Although the United States was the very last jurisdiction to ground its planes.

versa, so that *A post-Brexit bonfire of EU rules would hardly be enough to warm a pot of tea.*⁴⁷*

However, these realities come up against the mindset which sees regulation as an ideological issue. The fundamentalist Right has succeeded in having it framed as a struggle between those who uphold the freedom of wealth-creating private companies on the one hand, and those promoting regulation and restriction on behalf of anti-capitalist forces on the other. Neo-liberals eschew an empirical, reality-based approach and they certainly don't do *grey*. As economist and law professor Neil Buchanan says, commenting on the American context,

> *The radicalized version of the Republican Party ... has long since decided that reality is for chumps. ... Just as they do with taxes, Republicans like to pretend that the opposite of their absolutist opposition to all regulations can only be for Democrats to be in favor of all regulations.*⁴⁸

Once this form of *truth* is established it is hard to contest, and it becomes a widely accepted interpretation. As Buchanan says, in the United States the Democrats are not anti-business; they are just *not quite as pro-business* as the Republicans. Like the more left-leaning political parties in Britain, they are more aware of the impact of narrow cost-benefit corporate decisions on the rest of us, and ... *are keenly aware of the dangers of allowing the pursuit of short-term profits to cause long-term problems.*⁴⁹ Most political parties in a capitalist free market system want companies to succeed and grow, but that has to be within a rules-based environment where the costs of success are not borne by society at large; externalities have to be taken into account.

The many failures of business practice, scandals involving firms circumventing regulatory regimes, the lack of a framework of

---

*   Many supporters of Britain's leaving the EU, especially those who viewed with alacrity the prospect of exiting without an agreed deal, appeared to think forging trade agreements with all and sundry would be simple matters. But they underestimated the advantages of belonging to the EU's Single Market, which itself deals with the variety of trade barriers arising from different national regulations. Thus, Britain's future negotiations are likely to be long and tortuous, having to come to terms with the myriad of national rules and requirements to arrive at satisfactory trading arrangements. A single market differs from a free trade agreement because it seeks to tackle barriers to trade that arise from diverse national regulations. Even countries outside the EU, but with different degrees of single market access – such as Turkey or Norway – are obliged to sign up to certain parts of the *acquis communitaire* in order to benefit from relatively regulation-free trade with the EU.

requirements guiding vulnerable free market operations, or the absence of inspection regimes to monitor them and control risk – all are familiar features of today's capitalism. Yet none seems to undermine the pervasive neo-liberal conviction that markets work best when unfettered by regulators or politicians, principally because we see these as aberrations *through* the indelible assumption of our world-view. They are unfortunate, incidental side-effects which must not be allowed to subvert our faith. Alongside this belief in the sanctity of market forces, and underpinning it, is the idea that in business people act rationally in their own respectable interests, through which – *à la* Adam Smith – others will indirectly benefit. Such is the influence of economic theory that it is accepted that unregulated, competitive market forces are, in the jargon, *optimal* for us all and will result in the best outcomes. However, this is far from an analysis of the world as it is. This was demonstrated in an entertaining and trenchant work by two Nobel laureates in economics, George Akerlof and Robert Shiller, who maintain that an unregulated economy produces much manipulation and deception.* They believe insufficient attention is paid to these, which are usually thought of as anomalies rather than systemic aspects of the market, and as a result regulation is unjustly denigrated.

In practice, says Robert Shiller, *The success of the United States economy – and of those similar to it – can be attributed both to the relative freedom of its markets and to the fact that common-sense regulation has been imposed on them.*[50] And because recent innovation has led to products and systems that make deceiving the public easier, regulation has become even more crucial. But the textbook theory still insists that each individual is able to safeguard his/her own welfare through maximising their *utility* to produce an optimal economic outcome. Nevertheless, no matter how much elegant mathematical shaping is used to explain such a rationale, this is just not how human society behaves. We all know how much emotion is involved when we engage in the market, as well as how little we really know about the options on offer and their relative merits. And as far as always looking after our own best interests, well…! In fact, just a century ago the American economist Irving Fisher argued that, because of the errors and uncertainties people are subject to when making purchases, the term *wantability* would be

---

* George A. Akerlof & Robert J. Shiller, *Phishing for Phools: The Economics of Manipulation and Deception*, Princeton Univ. Press, Princeton, New Jersey, 2015.

preferable to *utility* in describing their motivations.⁵¹ He believed that consumers were in a relatively passive position and could easily be taken advantage of by producers and sellers. As participants in markets we are ... *often emotional, excitable and ignorant,* says Robert Peston, *never all-seeing, all-knowing.*⁵²

V. Just as neo-liberals and market fundamentalists demand minimal government regulation in the workings of capitalist free enterprise, they claim a general *hands-off* approach by the state to be beneficial to private business and – it is implied – to consumers. And in most free market economies today this is the common view, which has in fact become a widespread prejudice. But government intervention in such economies has a long, if not entirely familiar history. As outlined in Chapter 3, there was a steady increase in state involvement during the nineteenth century, as the worst effects of early industrialism were mitigated, and in spite of the reputation Britain had for *laissez-faire* capitalism. During the twentieth century any socialist-style planning and centralised direction of capitalist economies has long since lost any credibility, its cause finally ended by the collapse of state communism. And since the 1970s the neo-liberal view has gained ground that state-run enterprises are inefficient and that the market knows best. However, this has not prevented even right-wing governments in many countries from intervening in their economies to regulate firms, subsidise chosen sectors, and pick 'national champions'. Even in the citadel of free enterprise, the USA, says Tony Judt, where state involvement is most maligned,

> *Whatever Americans fondly believe, their government has always had its fingers in the economic pie.* What distinguishes the USA from every other developed country has been the widespread belief to the contrary.*⁵⁴

Both rhetoric and appearances can be wholly deceptive.

The prejudice against government interference in the economy is part of the ideological justification private enterprise employs to rationalize

---

* Judt cites railway barons, wheat farmers, car manufacturers, the aircraft industry, steel works as having been supported or even subsidized by the US Federal government.⁵³

its demand for freedom of action. But that does not mean that private business cannot flourish in regimes with considerable government involvement of different kinds. In fact, imposing requirements on individual companies may promote the collective interests of business, or even of the economy as a whole. Ha-Joon Chang points to the success of Asian economies in producing rapid growth in spite of being heavily regulated. He cites the example of South Korea, which by the 1990s had experienced over 6% *per capita* growth for more than thirty years, in spite of the enormous burden of hundreds of permits needed just to open a factory there.[55] Other free market regimes like Japan and Taiwan had, at an earlier stage, similarly developed successful, fast-growing economies in spite of heavy regulation, which did not prevent some home-grown companies becoming major global corporations. Chang contrasts this situation with Latin America and Sub-Saharan Africa where many countries, in spite of having deregulated their economies, grew more slowly in the 1980s and '90s than they had in the more heavily regulated 1960s and '70s.[56] There is more to the economic success of a nation than its level of government involvement, the ideology of which is irrelevant.

What is beneficial for one private company may not necessarily be good for the entire economy, and vice versa. Standards which national regulatory regimes establish can enhance the economy as a whole, including the quality of its products and the welfare of its consumers. Yet some individual firms may take objection to such regulation, believing lower standards would give them a competitive advantage in terms of productivity, and thence for their bottom line. But of course they are more likely to justify their stance on the basis of free market ideology – so familiar to neo-liberal audiences – rather than admitting to the practical matter of narrow, short-term self-interest. This is all about pulling wool over our eyes, so that in developed Western countries we continue to put our unwavering support behind free enterprise. This is another enduring myth – that our prosperity depends on the risky innovation of brave entrepreneurs who are responsible for the wealth creation from which the rest of us benefit. To show our gratitude we are expected to help these *masters of the universe* by keeping their taxes low and minimizing restraints on them, so that capitalism's bounty can continue to flow from their 'superhuman' efforts. Undoubtedly figures such as these do exist, but overall this is a false picture, an exaggerated ideological construct that serves the interests of private capital and its protagonists.

The notion that CEOs, entrepreneurs, and bankers have to be protected – because our prosperity depends on them – is allied to the idea that their companies need support, and THAT they certainly do receive. Behind the flimsy pretence that the state is no more than a mere facilitator, setting out the ground rules and safeguarding commercial fair play, is a whole panoply of intervention, subsidies, corporate promotion, fiscal breaks and basic research from which companies later benefit. The constant rhetoric emanating from boardrooms and right-wing politicians nevertheless conveys a message that governments should keep out – except perhaps when its help is desperately needed!* When Royal Bank of Scotland and Northern Rock got into difficulties during the financial crash of 2007/08, where would these *too-big-to-fail* corporations turn for help, but to the state? And after the initial gigantic bailout, who would be behind government to pick up the unprecedented bill during long years of austerity, but the ordinary citizen? In their blind hubris and misplaced confidence the bankers did not have the imagination to see where their reckless financial speculation might lead, but no doubt firmly in the back of their minds was the assurance that they would not be allowed to go to the wall. And so it proved: colossal amounts of taxpayers' money provided in rescues – such as the £45.5 billion to RBS and £20.5 billion to Lloyds, the largest bailout in British history to ensure these banks survived.[57]

Taxpayers' funds to support large corporations can take many forms, but the money provided to banks as loans might be better employed going straight to businesses and households rather than via intermediaries. For example the £80 billion of subsidised loans to British banks in 2013 was put into the Funding for Lending scheme, instead of being made directly available as credit to borrowers. The banks are still indispensable institutions which have to be sustained. But in view of their vital role in society they should be seen as public bodies, particularly the largest ones, since there is an implicit commitment that *in extremis* they will be supported. As such, more control should be exercised over them. Otherwise we have what has been termed *ersatz capitalism*, where autonomous private companies gain full benefit from their profitable activity when times are propitious, but know they can depend on outside authorities when in difficulties – i.e. a form of capitalism ...

---

* As the American humorist Will Rogers put it: *The business of government is to keep the government out of business – that is unless business needs government aid.* – Not so funny after the experiences of recent times.

in which losses are socialised and profits privatised.[58] But public money may be needed whether a company is bailed out or even files for bankruptcy. In the case of the giant contractor and services firm Carillion, which collapsed in early 2018, taxpayers face a bill which may eventually amount to £150 million. The government has been accused of insufficient oversight of a corporation working on many Whitehall-commissioned contracts to build roads, hospitals and schools with, it was said, new ones being offered even when the company was in financial difficulties.

Private-sector firms do often seek to have the best of both worlds: unrestrained freedom to profit from their activities and the assurance that their ultimate liabilities will be limited if their businesses fail. And since many large concerns are embedded in the social fabric of the nation, or involved in contracts of national significance, they know they can rely on government in worst-case scenarios. Companies like Serco, Atos and Capita have flourished with millions in public money from government contracts. But the many cases of corporate failure often demonstrate a lack of supervision and accountability by government and statutory bodies, resulting in public services being let down at further public cost. Thus when G4S, contracted to supply security personnel for the London 2012 Olympics, failed to provide them, the situation was redressed by the mobilising of 3,500 soldiers, government again riding to the rescue.* However, even with G4S shares dropping 15% in just over a week, examples like these do not put a significant dent in the reputation of private enterprise, bolstered as it is by incessant right-wing propaganda. The shortcomings of the private sector are those of the human beings who work in it; there is no systemic virtue which places it above publicly-run provision of vital services. And while ideologues of the Right like to castigate government for bureaucracy, even where such criticism is valid, it is more than matched by the potential for abuse in companies desperate for short-term profit.

The selling-off of Royal Mail – a state-run operation for almost 500 years – was completed in 2015 and presented as another triumph of clever government business by the Tory/Lib Dem administration. Yet

---

*   In vital areas like health, supervision is even more important, which makes the failure of Serco in its long-term contract (worth an estimated £32 million) to supply out-of-hours GP services in Cornwall even more critical. It took whistle-blowers in 2012 to reveal concerns about the running of the service. Serco had been unable to fill all necessary clinical shifts, and it was discovered that their staff had altered data reported to the primary care trust, thereby overstating their performance.[59]

closer examination puts it squarely in Joseph Stiglitz's category of *ersatz capitalism* cited above. Specious arguments were used to justify a sell-off which the coalition government had set its heart on; no, it did not need to become privatised in order to access private capital, as public-run Network Rail had already shown. So the new company took on a thriving business with rising profits, and gained for a price – eventually totalling £3.3 billion – considered by experts to be a severe under-valuation. In fact, the National Audit Office's view was that the government had been far too cautious ... *the price of which was borne by the taxpayer*... to the tune of £750 million.[60] It was generally agreed that this privatisation had only been made possible by the British government accepting responsibility for Royal Mail's pension fund, estimated at £37.5 billion – a burden whose liability would have to be met by future taxpayers, but certainly not by George Osborne or Vince Cable, architects of the deal. Thus, we have a perfect example of a company primed to benefit from the perfect start as a privatised entity, having been divested of troublesome debts which might circumscribe its profit-making potential. It remains to be seen how it will fare in the free market and whether comprehensive postal deliveries will be fully protected, particularly once the commitment to a six-day service ends in 2022.

Privatised Royal Mail, with currently all the advantages of an indispensable service, and with the burgeoning postal/courier business needed by online shopping, may in time become a highly profitable company. But in that case little notice is likely to be taken of the wholly benign circumstances of its birth. Such is the pattern with much private enterprise: advantageous platforms being provided by the state so that free market players are given the perfect launch pad to thrive. Regardless of the motives behind this kind of state support, it represents an unheralded role of government – a form of sponsoring of private firms, while retaining the reputation as mere facilitator or regulator, beyond which neo-liberals profess they do not wish the state to go. However, in practice they do in fact go well beyond this position. The decisive revelations in Mariana Mazzucato's *The Entrepreneurial State* show the extent to which government policy, particularly in the United States, has aided private business, enabling it to profit from state investment and research in a wide spectrum of sectors.[61] Despite perceptions to the contrary, the US has been proactive in funding development and commercialisation of new technology in areas like aeronautics, space and aircraft industries in the twentieth century, as well as nanotechnology, computers, and pharmaceuticals then and later. Nevertheless, the picture of the true wealth creators being risk-taking entrepreneurs in the private sector has endured.

Perhaps government sponsored technological development by state agencies with dull acronyms does not have the inspirational appeal of famous individual entrepreneurs. Nevertheless, huge amounts of research and development, especially in the United States, by government-funded and directed projects has allowed many start-up companies to become viable, as well as enabling established firms to profit from research funding and promotion initiated by the state. DARPA (the Defense Advanced Research Project Agency), set up in the 1950s, contributed to many fields of research, going well beyond military requirements, such as semiconductors, computer networking and graphical user interfaces in information technology, and more recently mass cargo transport and neuroscience. Mazzucato says that this involves the state in an entrepreneurial role in fields in which the private sector would not invest, even if it had the resources – ... *the courageous risk-taking visionary role of the state has been ignored*, she says.[62] She also points to the role played by President Reagan who, contrary to his free market credentials, built on DARPA's policy by setting up the SBIR (Small Business Innovation Research) in 1982, composed of different agencies promoting research. By rewarding innovative policies in chosen companies, says Mazzucato ... *the US has spent the last few decades using active interventionist policies to drive private sector innovation in pursuit of broad public policy goals.*[63]

So the American government has gone well beyond merely facilitating and regulating private enterprise, contrary to the claims of neo-liberals, and despite the disparagement of government as inefficient and sclerotic. Mazzucato highlights the pharmaceutical industry where, despite popular impressions, government research has made a huge contribution to the development of vital new drugs. She notes that 75% of NMEs (new molecular entities) can be traced back to research by publicly funded NIH labs – the National Institutes of Health – rather than private companies.[64]* Instead of acknowledging this, the private sector often prefers to eulogize its own contribution, claiming it would be even greater if only it could be left to its own devices. Mazzucato

---

* It was pointed out that the budget for research at the National Institutes of Health had been rising annually – to almost $30.9 billion in 2012 – at a time when some big pharmaceutical firms were shutting their R&D units.[65]

quotes Andrew Witty, CEO of GlaxoSmithKline until 2017: *The pharmaceutical industry is hugely innovative ... If governments work to support, not stifle innovation, the industry will deliver the next era of revolutionary medicine.* This is the typical rhetoric of *Big Pharma* executives, to which Mazzucato retorts,

> It is the revolutionary spirit of the State labs, producing 75% of the radical new drugs, that is allowing Witty and his fellow CEOs to spend most of their time focusing on how to boost their stock prices (e.g. through stock repurchase programmes).[66]

She adds that the US government undertakes the riskiest research but *Big Pharma*, preferring to invest in less risky variations of existing drugs, has through favourable federal policy reaped the major rewards.[67]

Therefore it is not just that private enterprise benefits from the whole panoply of state infrastructure – in education, transportation, the legal system and the rule of law, including the enforcement of intellectual property rights. It has been assisted in a variety of ways, from the early nineteenth century on, even in the United States, that bastion of the free market. Government-sponsored research at American universities laid the foundations for the agricultural revolution there, small business loans have long helped firms start up and flourish,[68] while more recently it was the foundations laid by government funding which enabled the development of the internet, wireless networks, GPS, and micro-electronics.[69] Yet all this is carried on behind a deceptive façade, on both sides of the Atlantic, that commercial creativity and innovation are the result of individual brilliance and dedication, independent of government. Who is aware, asks Mariana Mazzucato, that work which set up the initial algorithm that led to Google's success was aided by a public National Science Foundation grant?[70]* Of course, modern nations are mostly mixed economies, and could not flourish without interaction between public and private, but the idea that government is a hindrance to economic success, or that we need to allow the private sector more autonomy and less oversight, are ludicrous suggestions in view of how today's free market operates.

---

    *   Joseph Stiglitz points out that Newton had the modesty to acknowledge that he stood on the shoulders of giants, whereas today's ... *titans of industry have no compunction about being free riders...*[71]

VI. Another reflection of the discrepancy between the image of free enterprise conveyed by the market fundamentalists and the reality of free market operations is the existence of subsidies to private companies – both direct and indirect. There is a huge range of financial assistance provided by central and regional government – staggering in both its proportions and its complexity. Yet entrepreneurs and executives never cease parroting the mantra of free, unfettered competition and the autonomy of thrusting, innovative corporations in furnishing our prosperity. The vast funds provided to the banks following the financial crash have already been cited, but – whether justified or not – those were a response to a crisis situation which had the potential to develop into a catastrophe. However, the far more routine and regular *hand-outs* to business have a much lower profile, their extent and variety remaining largely under the radar; it would not do to undermine the accepted fiction of a self-reliant, independent private sector!* According to one assessment, the total of all subsidies amounts to over 6% of GDP in most rich countries, and probably more in developing states.[72] This is 'corporate welfarism', generally unearned, and in the case of the biggest financial institutions it is a true safety net. In fact, that description is more appropriate for the *too-big-to-fail* corporations than for the poorer recipients of welfare for whom it is normally used; for in countries where neo-liberalism is dominant, their proclaimed safety net is too threadbare to justify the term.

It is remarkable, when company executives stress the need for government to maintain a *hands-off* approach to business, how little is said about the financial aid they receive from that very source. In the United States, where political involvement in the economy has been much maligned ever since Ronald Reagan's oft-quoted words about government being the problem, not a solution, private enterprise has benefited to the tune of billions of dollars. Boeing, for example, over the last twenty-five years has received around $14.5 billion from federal, state and local sources, just in grants and tax credits, while this figure can be multiplied fivefold if the full range of loans, guarantees, and bond financing measures is included.[73] During roughly the same period the company has been recorded as having donated around $17 million

---

* This is not to impugn the millions of small, independent companies, struggling to survive and maintain market share, mostly without outside assistance, while – as so often happens – the giant corporations benefit from hand-outs, tax breaks, preferential loans and other incentives.

to the two main political parties in America.⁷⁴ And despite the fact that small businesses account for over half of all sales in the United States, the vast majority of subsidies go to the biggest corporations. For example, two thirds of the $68 billion in US grants and tax credits between 2000 and 2015 were awarded to around 600 large companies.⁷⁵* Rich tech giants like Intel and Google have no qualms about applying for public money, the latter having received over $600 million from two US states – Oregon and North Carolina – during 2006–07 alone.⁷⁷ Even wealthy finance companies – not quite on the breadline – manage to secure huge state grants, such as the $600 million or so Goldman Sachs has received over the last twenty years, mainly from New York State.⁷⁸

The first reliable, comprehensive assessment of what is handed out in the UK to companies in terms of grants and tax breaks came in 2015. Businesses were estimated to be receiving as much as £93 billion annually from the taxpayer – more than £3,500 from each household.⁷⁹ This amount of corporate welfare was certainly reinforcing David Cameron's pledge to make Britain the most open, welcoming, business-friendly country in the world. But while no general public approval of such a policy has ever been given, and no informed debate ever held, the amounts of public money involved are never likely to be widely publicised. And although corporate subsidies may bring certain benefits in terms of domestic investment and extra employment – and thus higher amounts of employers' national insurance – the deals are invariably to the overwhelming advantage of the companies involved. In fact, tax receipts are in any case suffering, due to the rates of corporation tax which recent governments – both Tory and Coalition – have progressively lowered.** While politicians often proclaim the benefits of incentives offered to overseas corporations to do business in the UK, the financial advantages are more dubious. For example, in the year 2012–13 government subsidies, grants and corporate tax benefits amounted to £58.2 billion, in comparison with collecting just £41.3 billion in corporation taxes.⁸¹ The other financial benefits from granting

---

* It is also instructive to observe corporate policy of certain firms receiving taxpayer hand-outs. For example, soon after benefiting from $32 million in government subsidies in 2012, the huge Eaton Corporation moved its registered head office to Ireland.⁷⁶

** Now at 19%, UK corporation tax is one of the lowest in Europe, and the Conservatives have plans to reduce it further, though not as low as the 12.5% which Ireland currently levies. Nevertheless, some companies manage to avoid such rates altogether; a *Sunday Times* report maintained that in 2014, six of the ten biggest British companies paid nothing in corporation tax in spite of the £30 billion combined profits they made.⁸⁰

such largesse, mainly to large corporations, would indeed need to be substantial to allow this to be seen as an attractive bargain.

Many of the figures for government subsidies are hard to calculate because there is no official source in the UK for support to business. The amounts quoted here are the results of considerable research, but if anything are likely to be conservative assessments. However, the £14.5 billion in subsidies and grants cited in Kevin Farnsworth's data is a figure used by the Treasury itself; it covers a variety of support including money for defence firms as well as cash for the train operating companies.[82] In fact, transport gains considerably from government policy, as Farnsworth shows, including the benefit to airlines for not having to pay tax on fuel. This may amount to as much as £8.5 billion a year, according to the Commons select committee on transport.[83] Traditionally, energy companies have also done well out of subsidies from government. Yet with the acute considerations of climate change in mind one might have expected greater support for renewable energy. Paradoxically, this area of subsidy appears to be in decline: government grants for solar panels in the UK ended in 2015, and those who have already installed them have, since April 2019, no longer received payments for generating electricity and supplying it to the grid – the so-called Feed-in Tariff. Meanwhile, vast sums of public money are being used to try to ensure future energy supplies, from nuclear power, with the building of Britain's first nuclear plant for twenty-five years – but not due to be ready before 2025.

The paradoxes of energy supply in Britain defy reasoned analysis, not helped by the somewhat opaque nature of government support for the sector. In fact, according to a parliamentary committee, not all handouts to energy firms are fully disclosed: *The variation in definitions of subsidy allows the government to resist acknowledging subsidy in many areas.*[84] However, we know that renewable energy now receives miserly government support, much less than elsewhere in Europe, in spite of it being largely a success story for the private sector, with falling costs and great potential. Nuclear is an entirely different matter. Hinkley Point C, the UK's latest nuclear plant, currently under construction, could eventually cost as much as £37 billion, and may only be viable if the wholesale price of electricity in the later 2020s is considerably more than it is now – otherwise electricity consumers (i.e. all taxpayers) will have to make up the difference.* Then there are the vast costs of decommissioning old plants coming to the end of their productive lives over the next decade. When the Nuclear Decommissioning Authority came into being in 2004 it was awarded an initial £19 billion.[85] It puts its planned expenditure for the year 2018–19 at £3.1 billion, of which over £2.2 billion is taxpayers' money; the Authority claims that cleaning up Britain's earliest nuclear sites is being carried out *cost-effectively*.[86] How much more cost-effective would decent subsidies for renewable energy appear by comparison?!

As regards the potential for nuclear mishaps – accidents or more sinister events – the cost implications are staggering. Disaster insurance is obligatory for nuclear operators, but in no cases are premiums set at a sufficiently realistic level to cover the expected costs of major incidents. If they were, it would simply make nuclear energy uncompetitive. The reform of Europe's nuclear insurance regime in 2016 led to raising the cap on liability for operators to 1.2 billion Euro, in the case of an accident. But in view of the vast ongoing costs of the Japanese nuclear disaster at Fukushima in 2011, possibly rising to $US ½ trillion over thirty to forty years, that figure would appear remarkably modest. And the estimated costs of dealing with the Chernobyl accident in 1986 have also been around 450 billion Euro. Because it is unrealistic for operators to be insured for the full potential damage from a disaster, maximum liability tends to be capped, so that any serious incident is likely to lead to a substantial proportion of costs being socialized, and thus paid for by the taxpayer. The costs and benefits of nuclear energy cannot ignore the potential costs from disasters which, however, rare, are an ongoing danger.** No matter how clean this energy may appear on a routine basis, the possibility of a terrorist incident or a geologically-induced disaster puts it in a different perspective, as well as making renewable energy sources far more viable and attractive – in fact, in the long run almost always cheaper.

The range and complexity of subsidies to the private sector is far wider than is commonly believed. The incessant message put about from neo-liberals is that the free market is hampered and restrained,

---

* The wholesale price dropped considerably after George Osborne signed the deal with EDF, but has soared recently.

** There are also the complications of the cross-border consequences of nuclear accidents. For example, while still exporting nuclear energy to some neighbouring countries from its domestic plants, Germany has decided to phase out nuclear as a source of energy at home. Meanwhile, it has increased its demand for electricity from foreign plants, mainly in France.[87]

and needs to be set free of government shackles, whereas in fact it has a symbiotic relationship with political authorities which – particularly in the *Anglo-Sphere* – overwhelmingly benefits the corporate sector. Certain advantages it gains from government may be transparent, such as some direct subsidies, while the value or even the existence of others – perhaps inducements to invest, preferential loans, grants for research, or credit guarantees – may remain concealed from public attention or even from commercial rivals, possibly through accounting subterfuge. However, tax breaks awarded to private enterprise can be even more opaque, since they represent government income forfeited, and thus do not appear as expenditure. Corporation tax has already been mentioned, but a more general benefit is the tax credit system which is a valuable indirect subsidy to capital. The costs of working and child tax credits in Britain had risen to around £30 billion a year by 2015, by which time there were over 3.3 million working people dependent on tax credits to make up their meagre incomes.[88] Such government *hand-outs* have the effect of suppressing wages, which of course affects competitiveness. For all its talk of the importance of the market, it seems that the private sector is somewhat relaxed about a distorted labour market which is anything but free.

VII. When state-run firms are privatised, it normally involves a subsidy – not the conventional form of help for the private sector, but an unearned grant nonetheless. Initially, privatisation in Britain was part of the Thatcherite campaign of the 1980s to cut public expenditure by off-loading inefficient nationalised businesses, while trying to build what was called a *share-owning democracy*. So the sale of major British *flag-ships* such as British Aerospace, Rolls-Royce and British Airways, as well as public utilities – gas, electricity, telecoms and water – was a vital element in attempting to raise the country's economic performance, as well as chiming with the emerging neo-liberal ideology. The latter provided the driving force for privatisation – the conviction that companies always thrive better as private entities, a view hardened by the experience of the '70s: ineffectual state-run industries dominated by union power. Privatisation would also contribute to reducing the power of public sector workers, mitigating wage pressures, and thus in theory making investment more attractive. But to ensure that the sale of these state-owned assets was a success, Tory governments of the time offered them at a considerable discount, just as with the sale of Royal Mail more recently, often writing off a company's debts before flotation.* But while the take-up of the new shares was thought a success, the government was not able to hide the dubious process it had conducted. In fact, a poll of 1989 revealed that 18% of those surveyed considered privatisation the worst policy of the Thatcher years.[90]

The conviction about the virtues of private enterprise has outlasted the zeal of Thatcherism, and has been corroborated by governments of different complexions – including New Labour – since that era. And while there are cases where privatisation of state-run enterprises may make sense, such as where there are potential gains from true economic competition, the drive to privatise has been motivated by ideology and has been pursued in areas where competition is virtually non-existent, but where this or other countervailing arguments are ignored. The Conservative governments of the 1990s were determined to privatise British Rail, in spite of its utter unsuitability by almost any measure. The division of train operating companies from track and infrastructure never made sense, merely adding cost and complexity. The myriad of train companies using the network – cited earlier in the chapter – struggle to provide a decent public service, not helped by the ease with which firms can walk away if they find insufficient profitability from their franchises. Re-nationalisation has much public support as a result of widespread, and often personal, awareness of the railways' systemic issues.** And in this case it is not a matter of public perceptions clouded by misinterpretation and long-held assumptions. Inertia, vested interests, continuing neo-liberal ideology, a prejudice against state-run business, and above all a refusal to admit privatisation has failed, all result in a system impervious to change.

The influence of neo-liberal values has much to answer for here. Forty years of propaganda has taught that all businesses must make a profit, so that we often view society purely on the bases of efficiency, demand and supply, monetary gain and profit margins. In a

---

* As happened with the privatisation of the water companies in 1989, when the government assumed responsibility for their debts of £5 billion. These companies were also put up for sale very cheaply, at a price estimated as equal to 22% of their true market value – measured as the difference between the initial price of the privatised shares and the share price after the first week of trading.[89]

** As well as cynicism at the approximately £2 billion in dividends paid out annually on the privatised companies, even that not ensuring public accountability.[91]

hyper-consumerist world it has become the common way of looking at life, our default perspective. But there are aspects of society which do not conform to this description, and public transport is one of them, since it has vital non-monetary requirements of a social nature. Getting about, particularly at a local level, has to stand as a public service, in which factors such as efficiency and competition take on an entirely different meaning. Here, normal free market principles have to be modified, and any attempt to make them a conventional feature of a public transport system will be problematic – certainly as far as railways and local buses are concerned.* For example, as Tony Judt points out, ... *the better* (public transport) *does its job the less 'efficient' it may be.*[92] For, if buses only served the most direct routes they could no doubt make a good profit, while leaving more remote areas without a 'service' altogether. By excluding less populated regions, a company will likely be commercially viable, but as a social amenity it will be highly inefficient. And this is the crux of the issue: society has to come to a judgement as to the limits of the free market, and where social, community concerns should take precedence over it.

Of course, the implication of the above is that some form of subsidy has to be involved. Whether local bus services should be fully nationalised or run as not-for-profit companies with injections of public money, they cannot be left to the vagaries of the free market, which are oblivious to community concerns. But whereas transport has a somewhat ambiguous position as regards community, there is a much wider consensus in relation to the health – with an overwhelming majority of the British in favour of a state-run service free at the point of need. Yet private companies are always looking for opportunities to create a market in health care. They have won numerous contracts for services outsourced by the NHS, mainly those not seen as core functions, but Hinchingbrooke Hospital in Cambridgeshire became the first hospital to be run by a private company when Circle Health took it over in 2012, signing a ten-year contract. They evidently saw considerable financial potential, in spite of taking on the existing debts of the struggling hospital. With the prospect of a sizeable profit, in effect a state subsidy, the company bargained robustly – and probably too ambitiously in terms of its

---

* Long-distance travel, especially by air, is excluded here, although even in this area the workings of the free market can have unfortunate repercussions. The social and climatic externalities are simply not being taken sufficiently into account, so that market functions are heavily weighted in favour of the commercial airlines.

pricing – to reach a deal. Nevertheless, after some early success Circle decided that its franchise was no longer viable; it withdrew from its contract in early 2015, just as the Care Quality Commission had rated the hospital *inadequate*.* Evidently, the over-optimism which Circle Health had displayed was a result of their assessment of the potential windfall to be made from the National Health Service.[93]

The private sector is always ready to take advantage of opportunities in areas of buoyant consumer demand. And in an era of an ageing population, and increasingly technologically intensive treatments, health is undoubtedly one of these. It requires ever more money to meet these demands, and governments are reluctant to increase taxation to raise the necessary funds. This is why PFI (Private Finance Initiative) schemes suited their purposes, as well as being enthusiastically seized on by private companies. If the government commissions a contractor to deliver an infrastructure project, with the firm borrowing to finance the job, government doesn't have to raise money from taxes or borrow funds itself – which may all sound appealing. However, since the state then has to pay the contractor over what may be many years, in effect the government is leasing the project – hospital or prison, for example – instead of owning it as an asset outright. In theory, the private company involved takes on the risks associated with costs and deadlines, as well as later being liable for maintaining the asset, all of which would otherwise be borne by government. Such schemes were based on the enduring prejudice of the greater efficiency of the private sector over government departments in delivering major building projects. The idea of PFI, imported from Australia, was initially employed by the Major government after 1992, but it was under New Labour that such schemes were fully exploited; by the early 2000s more than fifty PFI contracts were being signed each year.

Up until the financial crisis PFIs were supremely popular vehicles for private enterprise. The alacrity with which it signed up for them was due to considerable benefits, including the prospect of raking in substantial repayments over 25 to 30 years. But the schemes were attractive to central government as well, particularly in the short term, since private

---

* As early as September 2012 a National Audit Office report noted that Circle was already missing its own financial targets for the contract, and also warned that the company's projected savings of £311 million over 10 years were unprecedented as a proportion of annual turnover in the NHS. The over-ambition of Circle Health evidently contributed to its failure; subsequently, the hospital, now run by Hinchingbrooke Health Care NHS Trust, recovered enough to be awarded a rating of good overall by the CQC.

finance debt does not figure on the balance sheets of national accounts.*
As the National Audit Office wrote in its 2018 report, PFIs lead to:

> ... *lower recorded levels of government debt and public spending in the short term. Unlike conventional procurement, debt raised to construct assets does not feature in government debt figures, and the capital investment is not recorded as public spending...*[94]

which could be an attractive scenario for any government, particularly during post-crash austerity, allowing public authorities to initiate capital projects when they do not have the available funds. But whereas the Treasury's budgetary regulations are not infringed by most PFI deals, because the costs are spread out over time, it is the long pay-back period which imposes such a heavy financial burden on the commissioning body. Such was the reason behind Northumberland Healthcare NHS Foundation Trust's decision in 2014 to buy out the PFI contract that had funded a local hospital in 2003. By paying off the private contractors early, it was reported that the trust would save about £3.5 million each year for the remaining 19 years of the contract.[95]

There were still more than 700 PFI contracts in operation in early 2018, with a capital value of around £60 billion. But whereas they had been seen as the answer to the prayers of cash-strapped local authorities surveying their decaying infrastructure, it became increasingly clear that they could be very expensive. After all, loans setting up PFIs cost more than more conventional public investment because the private sector has to pay more than government to borrow from the markets. With this in mind, it has been very difficult to assess whether or not PFI schemes have been value for money for the taxpayer; as the National Audit Office points out, governments have not conducted any systematic evaluation of them. Of course, these contracts can only benefit the public financially if the profits made by private firms are no greater than the amount saved by not keeping the projects 'in house', and having the work carried out by public bodies. But they undoubtedly appear attractive to the private sector; with changes in the global economy, investment in infrastructure has become more appealing to international capital. Then there is another lucrative wheeze: the chance for PFI companies

---

* Although PFIs began under the Conservatives, they later used this aspect of the schemes to attack New Labour for their expansion of the use of the device, saying they were concealing the true extent of public borrowing.

to increase their investment by *flipping* – selling on contracts to other investors in the early years of a lengthy term. However it is achieved, sizeable profits can be derived from public projects. The annual repayment bill for PFI deals amounted to £10.3 billion in 2016–17, and with no new contracts entered into, charges which continue until the 2040s will still amount to £199 billion.[96]

Since the financial crisis PFIs have become less popular, while the collapse of Carillion – the UK's second largest construction business, with a broad portfolio of these contracts – brought them under greater scrutiny. Thus, in October 2018 Chancellor Philip Hammond announced that no new PFI deals would be entered into. They were principally a legacy of the New Labour years, and represented the way the authorities can draw on the free market, and large amounts of unused private capital, to fund public projects, while at the same time keeping the full implications of the contracts from public gaze. They can play into the hands of government by creating the impression that, for example, health and education budgets are being generously funded, whereas much of the money is going to pay off debt created through often invidious corporate deals. And the acclaim accorded the private sector is part of neo-liberalism's disparagement of the public domain and undermining of confidence in the effectiveness of public administration. Allowing private companies a major role in public schemes feeds the voracious appetite of international capital, while serving to corroborate the view that the public sector is less effective than private enterprise in mounting large infrastructure projects. There is little basis for this, even if it is one of those *truths* that has gained popular credence, adding to evidence for the contention that PFIs have an ideological dimension in eroding the public ethos and hollowing out public services in the interests of transnational corporations.*

VIII. One of the principal cultural and ideological divisions between neo-liberals and the rest of us is over the question of ownership, not only of individual consumer items, but also of our common heritage.

---

* The case against the public sector, that private companies are more efficient, quicker, and cheaper in completing large infrastructure projects, is largely demolished by Dexter Whitfield in his wide-ranging analysis of public-private partnerships and what he concludes is a very unequal relationship between the two.[97]

The trends of the last two generations have seen a clearer delineation of goods – material and other – into privatised commodities on the one hand, and those without such obvious exchange value on the other, but with the former always trying to make inroads into the latter. This has been part of the imperialistic drive of market forces, to make more and more *goods* into saleable *commodities,* thus adding to potential profit. And this is integral to society's increasing individualisation; it is the individual, above all, who profits by more commodification. Once the focus is on the satisfaction of separate, individual preferences in a consumer society, the inevitable logic drives the tendency to make more and more goods marketable. And this trend does not stop at the frontier of conventional consumer items; its momentum carries it into territory where *goods* had not hitherto been available for sale or privatisation – such as public municipal space – which had previously been seen as part of our mutual *commons*. Nineteenth-century legislation in Britain had ensured that streets and other public areas should come under the control of local authorities, not be part of the private fiefdoms of aristocratic landlords, as had often happened in Georgian times. This movement has now seen an ominous reversal.[98]

Are market fundamentalists seeking to do away with any sense of communal, collective assets? For this is their route to greater material gain. The idea of *the commons* goes back into the mists of time, even to the birth of agriculture, formalised by the Romans as *res communis*. It represented the common heritage of a society or of mankind as a whole, as distinct from *res nullius* which stood for goods not belonging to anyone, but available to be owned. *Res communis* is a concept still used in international law, and stands for the capital of our common inheritance over which no-one individually has rights, and in which everyone in theory has a stake.* Many societies once had domestic customs which laid out the communal terrain covered by this notion, but in modern times the concept has been undermined, as the philosophy of the market has gained ground. The partisan simplification which seeks privatisation of the somewhat vague, problematic area of our shared patrimony accords with the simple-minded endeavours of neo-liberals. But such limitations restrict options and are inadequate for modern developed society, as is the too easy solution of state ownership. A

---

*   The idea has been employed in Antarctica as well as for outer space. The 1967 Outer Space Treaty classified space as a *res communis omnium*, and designated its use and exploration as the ..*province of all mankind*.

form of communal management and regulation is required, as outlined by the work of Elinor Ostrom, cited in Chapter 3. The degradation of *common-pool* resources – famously highlighted by Garrett Hardin – can be avoided with responsible, delegated management, out of reach of both the state and the market.*

In today's world, in which many global issues can be tackled only by joint international action, there is even more need for communal solutions. The massive problem of climate change is only the most obvious and most significant. But others, such as harmonizing fiscal regimes to prevent individuals or corporations from taking financial advantage of disparate national regulations, will have their day. In terms of the domestic arena, communal arrangements of ownership and management need to be established, probably set up through statutory instrument, and overseen by the lowest level of administration feasible in each particular case, the principle of subsidiarity being essential. The privatisation of municipal space, such as in cities like Liverpool where whole swathes of its urban centre have been sold off to private companies for regeneration, uses the free market model to profit from local communal resources which were always thought of as our common heritage.** While public rights of way there may currently be guaranteed, they may not be so secure in perpetuity; who is to say that cash-strapped local authorities will not again be forced to submit to corporate power at some point in the future? More vibrant and well funded local politics would help withstand such pressures, while a statutory framework for our *commons* – whether urban or rural, natural or man-made – would protect their rights from the predations of market forces.

The changed environment over the last thirty years has brought us to a point where regimes of communal management are even more appropriate and necessary. The looming requirements of global crises have started to concentrate minds and emphasise our interconnectedness as never before. But at home, also, regulatory systems of management of our collective inheritance, in between the state and the market, have to be the answer to the twin problems of a voracious free market and a remote, bureaucratic and top-heavy central government. In Elinor

---

* American ecologist Hardin revived a 19th-century idea in his 1968 article 'The Tragedy of the Commons', in the magazine *Science*, in which he warned of the dangers of shared but unregulated common resources deteriorating for lack of proper management when no individual or communal body was responsible for them.

** The entire site of Liverpool One is leased to the Duke of Westminster's Grosvenor Estate for 250 years.

Ostrom's *Governing the Commons*, which came out in 1990, she mainly used developing economies' examples of common-pool resources, over which no-one has private property rights – such as fisheries, grazing lands and groundwater, all vulnerable to exploitation and degradation if not managed responsibly.[99] But the same principles can be applied in developed societies, where property rights are even more fiercely demarcated. Urban public space, for example, if not adequately protected by municipal authorities, should come under some other form of communal management, and the same could apply to Britain's elaborate network of public footpaths. As regards the environment, air quality, cleanliness of water, and the availability of green areas, these must all be safeguarded. As Aristotle is said to have remarked, *What is common to the greatest number has the least care bestowed upon it.*[100]

The main principle for *the commons* is that where rights are common to all, independently of market forces, and where all have right of access, protection must be guaranteed by some form of communal regulation, and inclusiveness assured. The pressure of central government-imposed austerity has led to local authorities having to sell off school playing fields to make ends meet – Westminster party-political decisions thus having a detrimental impact on access to sport and exercise, affecting above all the poorest in society. A body set up to protect parks, playing fields and other green urban spaces would require official, probably statutory status, with wide participation from central and local government and community groups, and with broad social remit – above all to defend the green spaces of a crowded island and help promote the health, in the widest sense, of the national community. Such an authority would act as a kind of independent regulator answerable principally to its local constituency, but where funds were required it would need to draw on the national treasury. And as regards funding, a similar practice should be adopted with, for example, flood management. With the increasing incidence of freak weather events due to global warming, communities – often in coastal areas – will suffer the damaging consequences of behaviour for which we must all accept responsibility; the expense of remedial action should not have to be borne by a local community alone.*

---

* In time to come, when there is perhaps greater global agreement and cohesion, this principle will need to be applied internationally. In terms of climate change in particular, the policies and practices of far-off nations often make major negative contributions to events on our own doorsteps – and *vice versa*.

Official communal authorities of this kind would contribute to the drawing of red lines in society, over which neither the market nor partisan, short-term politics would be able to cross. They would constitute a new species of not-for-profit organism, a form of trust, with responsibility to the public good of the relevant community involved. There may well be scepticism for what appears to be another branch of bureaucracy, particularly when notions of *the commons* and sharing are put about. But what some may see as idealism not suited to today's harsh realities can be a rigorous model to safeguard the public interest of individuals in that communal space between market fundamentalism and discredited national politics. And as yet, no other viable mechanism has been put forward to accomplish this; certainly, the limited horizons of transitory political administrations, swayed by populism and influenced by corporate greed, are not fit for this purpose. So a fresh concept of this nature will have the effect of re-focusing on the community – the route to which the individual can be better served. As earlier sections in this work have outlined (particularly Chapter 3), the complexities of today's world mean that, ironically, the welfare of individuals can in many respects be better promoted by considering the interests of the wider community – the antithesis of Adam Smith's *invisible hand* as identified by Fred Hirsch over forty years ago.

It would be constructive if elements antagonistic to such suggestions were to produce ideas of their own. But no, neo-liberalism's concerns are money and profit; it is not in the business of coming up with new ideas. Its tired dogma of market fundamentalism is incapable of providing answers to the pressing social problems generated by modern capitalism. Its only recourse is to redouble its efforts to colonise more and more of our vernacular terrain. Like a cancer, it eats away at the *body communal*, progressively taking over national society, which capitulates piecemeal to its venal impulses. This trend can especially be seen in the erosion of the public realm by much modern urban development in Britain, already cited above. Even the phrase *private-public spaces* is implicit acknowledgement of the convenient blurring of lines, where social amenity crosses with commercial opportunity. Yet this is openly admitted: *The trading environment is the public realm and the public realm is the trading environment*, says Jacquie Reilly, Project Director of National BIDs (Business Improvement Districts).[101]* There we have it:

---

* BIDs are an ingenious corporate contrivance of which many local councils are keen

the personal and social nature of our common, vernacular environment synonymous with the marketplace. And developers do not feel they need to hide their agreement. One – the property firm Argent, responsible for the huge King's Cross development project – candidly declared,

> *As the role of public authorities in the public realm has declined, the role of development companies has grown stronger, and the public realm, in many instances, has become more of a commodity.*[102]

Since 2010, when the Conservative-dominated Coalition government came in, the public realm has been under further threat from private sector development. For the previous sixty years, since the Town and Country Planning Act of 1947, markers had been laid down to control development, especially urban sprawl, and ensure that local authorities could examine projects before permission for them was granted. The principle that ownership of land was not in itself enough to allow its development became the accepted norm. But this was far too restrictive for David Cameron and his corporate allies. The innocent-sounding National Planning Policy Framework (NPPF), introduced in the spring of 2012, significantly changed the planning landscape. In particular, the framework brought in a new, rather ill-defined measure recommending *the presumption in favour of sustainable development.* This signified at least an amber light to increase development in the countryside, confirmed in media reports at the time: according to the *Daily Telegraph,* in a secret meeting before the plans were published an aide to David Cameron privately told builders that the new NPPF would *trigger more development.*[103] According to the paper, the government's controversial plans would replace 1,300 pages of planning regulations with just 52 pages of the new NPPF. It also appeared that the wording had undergone changes before publication, to the extent that not all of the team who had devised the original regulations were ultimately willing to stand by the final document.[104]

It became clear that the emphasis was now going to be on promoting and facilitating more building development, to the principal advantage

---

to take advantage. Money from a development company and local business funds a particular urban district in order to build a profitable, exclusionary consumer environment, similar to an indoor shopping mall but covering a broad urban location. These centres can then be regulated, policed and sanitised for the benefit of, mainly, large retail companies.

of private industry. The public interest – often interpreted by neo-liberals as an economic benefit – was thus to be threatened by corporate power allied to government policy.* Following the introduction of the NPPF, its principles were tested in a number of court cases in which local opposition to development was contested by property firms. These culminated in an Appeal Court decision in 2017 which confirmed the scope of the presumption in favour of sustainable development.[105] The verdict did specify that where a local authority had an up-to-date local plan which included the identification of sites sufficient to meet five years' worth of housing need, then the presumption in favour of development would not necessarily apply. However, local councils will need to be scrupulous in ensuring they have watertight cases in order to withstand the power of corporate legal teams. As one planning law expert warned, *Other material considerations ... may be powerful enough to justify a decision otherwise than in accordance with the* (local) *development plan.*[106] It is clear enough where the balance of power lies. Of course, a responsible house building programme is badly needed, but the principles of sustainability – social, economic and environmental – have to be rigorously assessed, without bias towards any particular commercial interest.

All of this points to a conceptual problem: what does *land* represent? Our famed *green and pleasant* environment becomes, especially under neo-liberalism, a commodity to be bought up and exploited for short-term profit, rather than protected as a finite resource, a precious amenity, an element in our psychological well-being, and a finely-balanced ecology which is our common inheritance. Its benefits have to be ring-fenced – literally and ideologically – to preserve them for us and for future generations. How we see our land and our landscape is a significant indication of who we are as a people; if we pursue the logic of neo-liberal values, we show our basic requirements as a species to be up for sale, for short-sighted, superficial greed. As such, voracious folly prevents us from recognizing that the market has limits. But as regards land ownership, Britain's predominantly urban populace is not generally aware of recent changes. The nation's distinctly odd lack of mandatory registration of property title – common almost everywhere else – prevents transparency, while the widespread sale of land by the

---

* After all, senior members of the property and construction industry as well as the head of policy at 10 Downing Street were conspicuous by their presence at the original meeting in June 2011 to discuss the new planning framework.

state over the last forty years is not fully appreciated. Brett Christophers' book *The New Enclosure* in 2018 gave an estimate of a staggering 10% of the land area of Britain as having been sold off during that period – Forestry Commission land, Ministry of Defence residential property, school playing fields, and even land owned by the NHS, to cite a few examples.[107]

These developments are representative of the increasing commodification of assets, which has been synonymous with neo-liberalism. But beyond that there are not many parallels; for land is in a different category of *goods*. Regardless of the fact that it has commercial, exchange value, it is still in a class of its own, for reasons cited above. In his history of land ownership, Andro Linklater quotes a 1906 campaign speech of Winston Churchill in which the latter declares that the fundamental conditions of land mean that it ... *differs from all other forms of property*.[108] A century later, this is still the case. Of course, circumstances have moved on from those which prevailed in medieval times, when land was not seen as having exchange value. But even after the decline of feudalism led to land becoming capital by the seventeenth century, its full, unscrupulous exploitation had to wait until the late twentieth century. However, increases in population, a scarcity of land, and the new environmental awareness all favour the reversal of this trend. As regards the housing shortage, policy must focus initially on brown-field sites, empty properties and local authority policies. The lazy recourse to market solutions – the default neo-liberal mindset which crowds out proper analysis – must come to an end. In fact, the presumption in favour of the cautionary principle must become established procedure, so that the onus is on commercial concerns to prove that their short-term demands do nothing to prejudice our wider collective interests.

So it is imperative that our view of the market and its relationship with society changes to embrace the *commons*, the community, the communal. Not only is our joint common inheritance threatened by the extension of market forces, but so is our capacity to tackle common global issues which are no longer confined within national borders. The latter is easily understood, only limited in its implications by myopic greed. But remedying the former comes up against the barrier of capitalist ideology, centred on the individual, which continually thwarts progressive policy. To return to ideas set out in the early pages of this work, we see society *through* the veil of cost-effectiveness, demand and supply, profit and loss. This is the *frame* which conditions our perspective, regardless of facts or evidence. And as George Lakoff maintains, once a frame is set, ... *if the facts do not fit a frame, the frame stays and the facts bounce off.*[109] Thus the force of market philosophy appears to make it immune to modification. As regards the *commons*, ... *the idea of a common inheritance and of using it for the public good is not yet part of the frame structure that most people use every day.*[110] But one way or another it will eventually have to be so, and this is not a matter of ideology. For the demand of commonality will increase; in an interdependent world of instantaneous news, and in which our lives carry such immediate transparency, individualistic solutions will become increasingly obsolete.

Part of the major conceptual and ideological adjustment required will involve expanding the notion of *res communis*. A category of commonality will have to be laid out – a terrain which takes in not only our common patrimony, material and other, but also our joint, communal requirements, those which are not satisfied by narrow individualistic solutions. Health services, basic housing, local buses, urban as well as national parks, a universal postal service, a full network of libraries,* and access to the internet are just some of the categories of need which occupy this common ground, over which no-one individually should have rights, especially the right to profit. Everyone has a stake in the proper functioning of these areas, all of which – as well as others – should be sacrosanct, beyond market forces. James Meek has called these *universal networks*; in *Private Island* he identified a range of them – health, energy, education, transport, etc. – which form the basis of the modern state, and all of which originated with a security network: the defence of the nation against a hostile world, transcending separate, individual concerns.[112] Lakoff has a similar take on *the commons*, which he says covers the electromagnetic spectrum (bandwidths) as much as it does the earth's atmosphere.[113] In a rich modern polity like the United Kingdom, expectation demands equal qualification for everyday

---

* The author Philip Pullman was defending far more than a comprehensive public library service, and ... *that great democratic space that opens up between you and the book... when he said ... there are things above profit, things that profit knows nothing about, things that have the power to baffle the greedy ghost of market fundamentalism, things that stand for civic decency and public respect for imagination and knowledge and the value of simple delight.*[111]

services, which as such takes precedence over the right to make profit or enrich oneself.

It is only with parity of access to the accepted necessities of contemporary living in developed societies that national commonality can be maintained. It is here that an equality of dignity and inclusivity must be assured, so that feelings of discrimination can be mitigated and a sense of belonging can be extended to all socio-economic groups. Society has to come together to agree on how far universal networks should reach, but as James Meek has put it, ... *once a private, optional network makes the jump to being a universal network, it ceases to be possible for it to belong exclusively to that free market world.*[114]* And apart from elements on the periphery, it should not be difficult to arrive at a common acknowledgement of what constitutes goods and services which modern society – whether rich or poor – can reasonably expect the nation as a whole to provide. For example, no-one without their own transport should be prevented from getting to a job interview because of the cost of bus fares, any more than one should be excluded from internet access by exorbitant monthly charges. And no family should be consigned to semi-permanent bed and breakfast accommodation, or to insecure, extortionate private renting, because of an inability of local and central government to facilitate adequate housing. These are basic necessities of modern living which society has to find ways to remedy. The free market cannot be permitted alone to condition such fundamental requirements of life.

None of this will undermine the principles of contemporary capitalism; it will merely serve to contain it within decent bounds, and allow citizens the scope for basic, human living, without the winner-take-all logic of neo-liberalism to divide and rule. After all, there is plenty of scope for individual enrichment and exclusivity in the wide world of the free market, beyond what everyone requires for a normal, decent existence under modern conditions. How far and how quickly this can be accepted is principally a matter of judgement and perception, as so many of the arguments in this work have shown. Danish society, for example, approves a high level of personal taxation to pay for a comprehensive range of services, many of which elsewhere in neo-liberal conditions have to be paid for – or not – through the free market. A consensus does

---

* Or perhaps one should demand that it loses any right to belong to that free market world at all.

not yet exist in Britain, and even less so in the USA, which would countenance free comprehensive child care costs being borne by the state through taxation. But this is a matter of how we see life's necessities and the obligations of the community to each one of us, and of course this is partly dependent – as George Lakoff has shown us – on the way the matter is *framed*. The strength of free market dogma currently mitigates against a more generous, inclusive view of vernacular living, framing such issues in terms of *free-riding, personal responsibility, taxation and big government*. This perspective requires wholesale realignment.

A notable example of where the line is drawn between the free market and *the commons* concerns sport. The glue which holds together a society on the broadest, unspoken levels binds wide areas of popular culture, shared traditions and national customs, and nowadays includes professional sport. In fact, the major sports have become very much a part of the common currency of national culture, attracting a following across social classes and genders more than ever before. And as they have gained popularity, they have increasingly become targets for marketing opportunities for commercial sponsorship and the mass media. Capitalising on neo-liberal trends, business has exploited the mass appeal of sport, both at live events and on television, by repackaging its image and profiting out of new forms of exclusivity. Satellite TV, pay-to-view events, the merchandising of sportswear and corporate hospitality at sporting venues are modern devices to maximise revenues from activities which, nevertheless, have always had community at their heart. They are not ordinary commercial products from which consumers may choose, like brands of breakfast cereal, even if one TV executive once justified their marketing as such.* Under the dubious slogan of choice, sports fans are invited to spend more on televised events, and associated products, or perhaps risk losing the chance to watch them at all. Thus, sports occasions become more and more removed from the vernacular arena and reserved for an exclusive audience, leaving others only to listen or read about them.

Free market principles like supply and demand do not easily apply to the world of professional sport. There is only one Grand National horse race; few football fans of Manchester United would conceivably abandon their team for another which had cheaper entrance charges;

---

* David Elstein, when Director of Programming for BSkyB, rationalised Sky's monopoly of the broadcasting of the 1995 Ryder Cup golf tournament on the basis of the viewing public having a choice – like buying Marks and Spencer's food products.[115]

an England cricket supporter during an Ashes Test series does not have the option of switching her allegiance to another country if unable to watch the matches on television. Custom, sentiment and romance, undying *brand loyalty*, and a sense of belonging have been key ingredients in sporting allegiance since long before sport became big business, but these are patently open to manipulation by those, including sports organisers and promoters, whose principal loyalty is to profit. Professional sports clubs, such as in national games like soccer, are acting from monopoly positions in what is anything but a free market – selling a *product* which is like few other commodities; their followers are simply not ordinary consumers. But as publicly quoted companies, many clubs are changing their ethos, transforming themselves into money-making concerns with an entertainment dimension. In this manner, values of community and allegiance may well decline in significance, altering the role of sport in Britain. The less affluent will find it harder to afford gate prices at successful clubs, and an economic hierarchy will gradually establish itself. Meanwhile, the interests of corporate customers will put status above community. Organised sport will eventually cease to belong to a broad national culture – a socializing, constructive force – and ally itself purely to highly paid entertainment and big business.

These realities are important enough, but when they impinge on patriotism and national identity they become even more significant. Some sporting events, such as supremely traditional occasions like the Grand National or the Wimbledon tennis tournament attract an extra dimension of support by appealing to a broader cross-section of the nation, often including some people not usually interested in sport. Even more significant are competitions involving representative national teams. The football or rugby world cups and cricket test matches – when involving the home countries – as well as the Ryder Cup golf tournament, are examples of events which have meaning beyond competitive sport, and as such should not be able to be exploited by a minority for advantage or profit. A citizen is perfectly entitled, for international matches, to claim that since the national team is ostensibly representing **her**, then she has a right to watch the games on free-to-air television. Guaranteeing certain events for a broad television audience has been officially recognised in the compiling of a range of *Listed and Designated events*, first devised by the government in 1991, which must be available on terrestrial television for at least 95% of the country. However, these so-called *crown jewels* of sport are not chosen on the basis of the key principle, namely that national teams representing **us** must be available to be watched by **us**. The latest review of the list in 2019 still failed to recognise the transcendental significance of representative sport and its link to national identity.

The point here is that the principle of ensuring viewing access to one's national teams, representing the collective body of the people, entirely trumps the requirement of raising funds to distribute to grassroots sporting organisations – the argument often used to justify pay-to-view sports on television.* National events of a sporting, heritage or even political nature, which have meaning to the British tribe, should not be able to be monopolised for commercial gain, to the restriction of general access. (After all, would the buying up by satellite television of a crucially important spectacle such as the coronation of the British monarch – even with the proceeds going to charitable causes perhaps – be acceptable commercial practice?!) Television has long been, for all intents and purposes, outside of the normal demands of the market economy in terms of viewing access, a medium which crosses all socio-economic boundaries equally. The welfare of the community as a collective body must take precedence over financial profit or media monopoly dressed up as the sanctity of market forces. A nation, like a family, is more than the sum of its parts, and gains cohesion by an all-embracing inclusiveness, which gives it stature regardless of economic means. If celebrations of national integrality are to be further undermined by money and material gain, then our collective cohesion will be further eroded and as individuals we will become even more culturally devitalized.

It is a reflection of the hold which neo-liberalism has over common values that important sporting occasions can be put up for sale to the highest bidder, to general public acquiescence. Organisers of national events have a responsibility to the whole nation – all of us – just as a small, local football club must answer to the surrounding community, its extended family members. But market fundamentalism has come to override community values – partly because we have allowed the distinction between consumerism and our collective vernacular sentiments to

---

* Besides, this argument does not withstand scrutiny; the claim that such funds would expand participation is distinctly short on evidence. One important example indicates trends in the opposite direction: Sport England was reported to have shown that those aged over 16 playing cricket at least fortnightly had fallen by 20% between 2016 and 2019, and those who play it just once a year had fallen by 8%.[116]

become lost. Michael Sandel is writing of the American context when he says, ... *money in sports has been crowding out the community*.[117] He discusses the proliferation of corporate sponsorship in the USA, in particular the naming of sports stadiums – civic landmarks whose meaning he believes is altered by a change of name. Sandel highlights the broader significance of sports venues, which give a sense of being all in it together, where civic pride can be shared. But ... *as stadiums become less like landmarks and more like billboards, their public character fades. So, perhaps, do the social bonds and civic sentiments they inspire.*[118] In Britain, money in the form of higher gate prices, especially at top soccer matches, has also had the effect of marginalizing community, and leading to crowds of a more exclusive, middle-class character. All these examples reflect the way market impulses smother the collective values which are at the heart of most organised sport.

There is one final feature of *the commons* which requires attention here: Britain's National Health Service. This is an institution which is certainly recognised as part of the nation's common heritage, our *res communis* in which we all have a stake, an even more crucial one since the onset of Covid-19.* Political parties of different persuasions often disagree over the extent to which the NHS should allow entry to market forces, but all know that a health service free at the point of use has the overwhelming support of the mass of the population. It is widely acknowledged as part of our common inheritance, over which no-one individually has rights beyond their claims for health care when needed. However, this should be taken further and enhanced. As an example of a vital *universal network* it should be accorded special status, in order to protect it from the predations of political interests unwilling – for ideological or financial reasons – to devote sufficient public money to its cause. It should not be permitted to become simply one more element in the everyday cut and thrust of political horse trading. The increasing costs of a rapidly ageing population with ever more complex health needs and expensive treatments have been recognized by government lip service, but not in terms of the financial commitment they have been willing to devote to the national health budget.

So the NHS should be disengaged from direct political influence and

---

* Even those who in normal circumstances pay privately for health care, to avoid waiting times or to ensure they have a private room in hospital, know that the NHS is there to fall back on in case of emergency need. Not all private hospitals have the range of 24-hour nursing and technological support available to the NHS.

given separate status, rather as does the BBC, with possibly a board of trustees answerable to the Health Secretary, who would have ultimate oversight. And to avoid wrangling over finance a budget should be agreed upon in bi-partisan fashion, a specified proportion of GDP which governments would be obliged to invest for a particular period.* Sufficient funds for an ongoing health budget should thus be made available, and long term planning devised, to avoid the perennial predicament of staff shortages – of, for example, around 40,000 nurses at the end of 2019. Of course, recent governments have been dominated by Brexit, and now consumed by the consequences of Covid-19, and have taken their eyes off many balls, but there is no justification for what has been in effect an incompetent central administration responsible for the unchecked, random repercussions of austerity following the financial crash, both negatively impacting the health budget. The results are evident in Britain's poor position, relatively, when it comes to investment in health.** Health spending needs to be apportioned according to need, with consistent, guaranteed provision, protected from party political and ideological infighting, so often accompanied by statistical manipulation giving a false impression of the exact size of the health budget. And this would also help to protect it from the further incursion of market forces.

IX. Much has been said in this work about the relationship between ideas and facts – a problematic relationship, to say the least. In a *macro* sense the facts are usually in a subservient role to the ideas which hold sway, and which influence the public's assumptions; that is, the over-arching ideologies of the time will take precedence over, and guide the policy detail, as well as the 'facts' garnered to support it. This is

---

*   A figure could be arrived at by looking at comparable wealthy countries, so that a percentage which was, say, at least an average of European or OECD nations' budgets became the established norm for health investment.
**   The UK was ranked last of twelve comparable developed nations for per capita health expenditure in 2017.[119] Also, it was the second lowest per capita spender amongst the G7 group of large, developed economies in that year, national expenditure having slipped from 9.8% as a proportion of GDP in 2013 to 9.6% in 2017, while four of the remaining six G7 countries saw their spending rise during that period.[120] Furthermore, the UK has fewer doctors per head of population than most OECD nations. Their data rank the UK 22nd out of 33 countries, and the only European states with fewer doctors per head are Poland and Slovenia.[121]

nowhere more relevant than in economic fields of finance, taxation, remuneration, and the policies of so-called austerity. Whatever the facts of these matters, certain ideas have driven public policy for many years, ideas which fall into line with neo-liberalism. For example, government direction on inflation and taxation has favoured the better-off in society – those with high salaries and substantial savings – behind which is the notion that high earners, especially entrepreneurs, are the principal wealth creators in the economy whose autonomy must be protected. Segments of society well beyond hard-core neo-liberals are persuaded of the force of this conviction which, while times are hard, they are told, must take priority over more expansionist policies. But it is the force of the prevailing ideas, the ideology, which convinces adherents, not the facts which are used to underpin it. As Theodore Roszak pointed out (quoted on the opening page of Chapter 1), the mind does not think with information, but with ideas. *Ideas come first,* he said, *because ideas define, contain, and eventually produce information.*[122]

However, this is not how policy or politics are presented; the barrage of facts which are used to influence the public in democratic societies are presented as if they justify and authenticate some set of ideas for which they stand. But in fact the detail, and – crucially – the way in which it is *framed*, is merely to make the ideology more concrete, more easily comprehensible. The facts are props and costumes used to give convincing shape to the overriding ideological message – which is not reliant on information at all. *Master ideas are based on no information whatever.*[123] Once the strength of a prevailing idea has been established it tends, for a period, to carry all before it, and contesting it with evidence can be a fruitless task. As George Lakoff pointed out (see p. 274), *the facts bounce off* what becomes an impregnable set of convictions. Such is the case with economic austerity: in the wake of the financial crash, many were persuaded of the need for desperate measures. A severe and resolute response was seen as vital to forestall yet further damage to the global economy, as well as to prevent further bankruptcies of major financial institutions. So the mantra of the vital necessity of austerity – regardless of its damaging side-effects – became fixed in the public mind. Its potency began to weaken at the end of Theresa May's administration, though the ideology behind it – temporarily shelved – has yet to be entirely overturned by a new way of thinking.

The austerity syndrome and its associated prejudices which have dominated policy over the last decade still remain, albeit sidelined for the moment by the Covid emergency. This recent period has been part of a neo-liberal continuum, going back to the late 1970s and the aftermath of unproductive industry and overweening union power – of renown. The loosening of restraint ushered in by Thatcherite commercial deregulation and the financial Big Bang was part of a moralistic crusade which sought to free up the drivers of the economy, particularly financial institutions, but fostering a winner-take-all, sink or swim attitude – the essence of neo-liberalism. It may have been couched in terms of *personal responsibility* and *sound household economics*, seemingly designed to benefit everyone, but in fact winners were the sleek suits of the City of London and the sharp elbows of ambitious service industries' entrepreneurs. This was the general thrust of the 1980s' policy in the USA as well as Britain; it involved a conservative message, but behind this the less conservatively inclined, aided by the removal of financial restraints, could press on with the business of making money. The framing of the issues was crucial in packaging the neo-liberal doctrine and making it palatable to the ordinary constituent, and it characterised the period up to 2007/08, including the decade of neo-liberal New Labour. Meanwhile, behind a veneer of responsibility and efficiency, reckless risk-taking was widespread.*

Thus, hidden by the seeming rectitude of Thatcherite economics, was a financial 'wild west', more recently termed *casino capitalism*. And while its excited participants remained glued to their computer screens, absorbed with their credit default swaps and their spot trading, looking for short-term gains from trillions of impatient capital sloshing around the world, the myth circulated that Britain's economy was booming. So by the turn of the millennium the false consciousness of the age centred on finance: not only had ordinary citizens been hoodwinked by plausible financial gurus and a booming stock market, but these same experts had succeeded in deluding themselves. Everyone appeared convinced that an increasingly financialised economy, with the famed *light-touch* regulation, had put an end to *boom and bust* cycles. But the new financial

---

* The pre-eminence of the finance sector is in the British tradition; the relationship between a subservient manufacturing industry and the City of London had endured from the end of the nineteenth century, when the former had already lost its hegemony. The result was an economy dominated by finance in which – in contrast to other major economies – the focus of capital was external. And apart from brief periods, such as in the special conditions of wartime, this pattern has continued for over a century. The only difference in the last thirty-odd years has been the financial deregulation which has led to rampant risk-taking – hubris on a grand scale.

instruments which deregulation had spawned were not fully understood even by some of those using them, and the misguided belief in their perfectability was a recipe for disaster. A new reflection on expertise would be suggested by the then Chairman of the US Federal Reserve, just two years before the financial crash:

> *These increasingly complex financial instruments have contributed to the development of a far more flexible, efficient, and hence resilient financial system than the one that existed just a quarter-century ago.*[124]

Alan Greenspan was regarded as the expert of experts, but what he thought of as strengths, Paul Krugman says, were just what led to the collapse of the system.

People very often see what they want to see: when authorities give approval for open, deregulated markets, and that old *invisible hand* argument seems to corroborate the prevailing thesis, few are disposed to question it. And when economic indices are mostly moving upwards, amongst extravagant, frothy talk of a new world for a new millennium, national self-delusion is understandable. The *Cool Britannia* of New Labour appeared to provide validation – of course entirely spurious – that we were in a new era, with even the economic problems of the early '90s (exchange rate issues forcing Britain out of the ERM, etc.) a distant memory. The booming financial sector, exemplified by the colourful, even romantic images of City traders, helped consolidate impressions. The fact that the profitability of financial companies, which had risen markedly since deregulation, was not matched by that of non-financial firms on either side of the Atlantic did not gain wide attention.* In fact, as industrial activity declined, in many developed countries, so manufacturing firms often *financialised* operations by expanding their financial arms. While such policies may have had some commercial basis, the belief in the benefits of finance and its profitability has more to do with image and faith – a degree of self-delusion coupled with the residual belief in light-touch government and the *invisible hand*. Add to this the

---

* The disparity in Britain between the finance industry and the rest of the economy is exemplified by data such as (i) between 1990 and 2006 the pay of top bankers in the UK went up between ten and twenty-fold, whereas average annual gross pay rose from £13,760 to £24,134 – not even double, (ii) in the 2007/08 tax year, financial services reaped 45% of all bonuses paid out in Britain, around £19 billion, even though the sector comprised only 3.7% of the national workforce.[125]

years of benign economic conditions and we become accustomed to a new norm, so that any sense of the old risks recedes further and further from our consciousness.[126]

The fact that all this has much more to do with ideology and image than with economic reality was also supported by a document which emerged from a meeting of more than thirty top economists from finance, government and academia convened by the British Academy in 2009. Their remit was to try to explain why a financial debâcle on the scale of the 2007/08 crash had not been anticipated, and was prompted by a visit to the Academy by the Queen the previous year, when she had asked that very question. The conclusions of the Forum were sent to the Queen in a letter in July 2009 and contained some intriguing, if not surprising conclusions.[127] The top brains assembled at the meeting believed the root of the problem was mainly ... *a failure of the collective imagination of many bright people*... to understand the risks to the system – and that in spite of the banks being awash with risk managers, reputedly as many as 4000 at one major British bank. Economist Ha-Joon Chang picked up on this curious analysis: he could not recall much discussion about *imagination* in economics, he wrote, since markets are supposed to function through our individualistic and rational motives.[128] Yet the economists appeared to be admitting that considerable creative cogitation by non-economic expertise might have helped avoid the financial catastrophe which inflicted so much damage on so many national economies.

It does not take much innovative thinking to realise that responsible economic management requires more than (mere) economic expertise. Economics is far from being an exact science and – as has already been shown – apparent rational motivation is not enough to explain its direction of travel. Besides, behind the markets of the financial front line were economists and politicians responsible for creating the conditions for the events of 2007/08 in the first place – all with their own ideological agendas. And the signatories to the British Academy letter noted that the booming conditions of expanding businesses, bumper bonuses, and high tax revenues going into health and education, were all ... *bound to create a psychology of denial. It was a cycle fuelled... not by virtue but by delusion.* They went on to say that the financial industry had ... *some of the best mathematical minds in our country and abroad. But they frequently lost sight of the bigger picture.* And ... *It is difficult to recall a greater example of wishful thinking combined with hubris.*

Then, referring to those who should have been overseeing our welfare, protecting the national economy from policy hubris, they concluded, *Politicians of all types were charmed by the market.*[129] Charmed they may have been, but when they were progressively dismantling the regulations which had earlier protected the finance industry, on both sides of the Atlantic, from reckless over-indulgence, they were motivated by the myopic ideology of neo-liberalism.*

The period of economic austerity in Britain, following the financial crash of 2007/08, is still a period marred by misunderstanding and blighted perceptions. Firstly, there is the misplaced culpability for the debâcle: attributed particularly in Britain and America to the irresponsibility of governments. Paul Krugman, following fund manager and blogger Barry Ritholtz, refers to this as the *Big Lie* of the financial crisis: ... *the right-wing dogma which says ... debt growth was caused by liberal do-gooders and government agencies, which forced banks to lend to minority home buyers and subsidized dubious mortgages.*[130] This version – completely ignoring the fact that the crash originated in a banking failure on Wall Street – is mere deceit, as Krugman's demolition of it clearly shows, but that has not prevented it from gaining credibility. Those on the Right have invested much in it; they cannot afford to let go of the message that markets flourish best with light-touch regulation and governments which shun intervention, and thus need to paint politicians, particularly those on the Left, as the villains. In Britain, the fact that Labour were in power at the time of the crash helped sustain the fraud, while the failure of the Labour leadership during the 2010 election campaign effectively to challenge it contributed to their failure to retain power. This false consciousness has been exploited in the UK not only to justify austerity, but also to blame it on the party on the other side of the political divide.

---

* The politicians started changing the ground rules from as early as 1980, when in the USA the Monetary Control Act was passed under President Carter. But bankers took full advantage of the new political environment. The various iterations of the complicated Basel Rules on banking were fully exploited by the banks over the following twenty-five years, all in the cause of short-term profit. They progressively increased their leverage by lending vastly more money relative to their capital reserves, and were therefore – largely unseen by regulators – taking on much greater financial risk. At the extreme end was Northern Rock in Britain, which in 2007 had a capital-to-assets ratio of just 1.7%!

The reasons for the policy of austerity being accepted in Britain, and by sections of society well beyond just neo-liberals, centre largely on the way it was framed. For it did gain approval as a necessary evil, a set of measures seen as indispensable to rescue a grossly indebted nation. But that was because the Right of the political debate managed to frame it as the responsible, mature response to the crisis. George Lakoff explains this as the *strict father morality* model, appealing to the public on the basis of independence, self-reliance and discipline as the route to individual prosperity and well-being.[131] Standing on one's own two feet to pursue one's self-interest is the way to become a 'good' person, proclaims the message, and this easily translates to the national stage. The converse of this is the irresponsibility of not developing self-discipline, and therefore becoming dependent and living off others' resources. In the context of a country in serious debt, this kind of moral message easily rings true. It also chimes with the idea of budget cuts, even those affecting welfare payments, which after all only help people to become more dependent – so the argument continues – and less worthy as a result. And if promoting social programmes is wrong, because they foster an immoral reliance on others and undermine personal autonomy, then rewarding the independent, self-reliant with, perhaps, tax cuts will be a constructive, positive, and entirely moral policy – or so the theory goes.[132]

Lakoff sees this conservative world view as applying equally in business and politics as in individual and family life. So: spending beyond one's income, welfare dependence, national indebtedness – BAD; cutting one's coat according to one's cloth, self-reliance, and national belt-tightening to pay off debt – GOOD. There is certainly a moral element in these messages, and it ends with the implication that individual poverty is one's own responsibility, not that of the state. On the national scale, soaring indebtedness cannot be tolerated, and if dealing with it involves personal sacrifice, then so be it. The polarisation of positions was reinforced by the increasing stigmatization of benefits recipients, compounded by George Osborne's comment about those on their way to work looking up at the closed curtains of those he implied were the idle unemployed. It was sustained also by the continual reference to *welfare dependency*, as if being on benefits was simply a wilful endeavour to avoid work. To many on the Left, austerity policy was nothing more than an excuse to cut back state expenditure – while charging New Labour with profligacy – and limit the size of government, part of neo-liberalism's agenda. But that agenda happened to synchronize with the ethos of meritocracy: if one prospered by one's own effort and ability, then failure to succeed, to the point of needing to rely on benefits, implied personal inadequacy – which, neo-liberals believed, should never be indulged.

As a result of these attitudes, financial stringency represented to many not only the necessary policy to reduce indebtedness but also the correct moral path to regain national respectability. The consequence of not following austerity – it was repeatedly implied – would be to condone extravagance and perpetuate living beyond one's means, both personally and nationally. And colourful examples, such as the note left at the Treasury by the outgoing Labour government in 2010, saying that the money had run out, all contributed to the Conservative message and the implication of New Labour's irresponsibility.* Thus George Osborne's time as Chancellor was marked by much moralising in order to hammer home the partisan message by which austerity was justified. During this period it was not difficult to keep the Labour opposition on the back foot, since they found it problematic to secure ideological purchase to counteract the government's message; they failed to frame it in their interests. And the scale of the financial crash had been such that it was not hard to push what were seen as emergency measures onto a shell-shocked public; a national crisis was presented as requiring nothing less. To a people raised with the folk memory of wartime self-denial, the response to economic calamity could almost be presented as the equivalent of the spirit of the Blitz. As a result, it was hard to challenge the demands made on the populace, fallacious and misjudged as they happened to be.

However, no amount of rationalizing or sophistry can alter the fact that austerity as applied in Britain was more a political programme than an economic policy. Despite the fraudulence of the analogy, austerity was interpreted in homely terms, as the equivalent of what a family should do when in debt – anything to conceal the fact that in economic respects austerity can be self-defeating, as the IMF has suggested. John Maynard Keynes himself argued in the 1930s that cutting state

---

* Liam Byrne, the outgoing Chief Secretary to the Treasury in 2010 had – in line with the convention for departing ministers to leave a perhaps cryptic or amusing message for their successors – left a note saying, *I'm sorry to tell you there's no money left,* which Byrne forever regretted. The government under Gordon Brown, having helped save the country from the financial abyss following the crash, which had reduced national tax revenues by more than £40 billion, inevitably had to resort to large-scale borrowing.

spending in a downturn can produce a depression out of what could be a short-lived recession. After all, it makes perfect sense to borrow when interest rates are low – and they have been at historically low levels since the crash. But the new dogma maintains that austerity will itself contribute to a return to growth; such airy optimism can only be for public consumption, for after a decade there was still little sign of the promised turnaround. Meanwhile, a policy endures which hurts the poor much more than the better off. Austerity has exacerbated the debt burden on ordinary households while the private wealth of the affluent has continued to grow.* Keynes believed inflation was the fairest way to reduce public debt, a course which assisted many national economies in the mid-twentieth century, but of course such a policy is anathema to the Right. As an alternative Piketty favours taxes on capital – by far the best answer, he says: *The worst solution in terms of both justice and efficiency is a prolonged dose of austerity...* and yet that is the cause to which Europe is dedicated.[134]

Any analysis of modern economies, especially since the financial crash, has been bedevilled by the same false consciousness described earlier. The official response to austerity has been presented as the reasonable, commonsense approach which any of us in a crisis would apply to our own financial shortcomings – except that the two situations are just not comparable. Nevertheless, this same explanation has been peddled since the start of the austerity programme. Yet, as Guy Standing says, *The austerity rhetoric is a confidence trick, aimed at convincing people that they must accept lower incomes in the interest of national recovery...*[135] So the specious message is couched in terms of morality as well as economics. But the warnings of those on the Right that austerity is necessary, that further government borrowing will just put up interest rates, are not based on sound economics; they may be a convincing argument in times of near full employment, but certainly not during a severe recession with interest rates at an all time low, as Keynes knew. Paul Krugman points out that extra government borrowing gives somewhere for all the excess savings to go, which helps increase demand and thus raise GDP. *The bottom line... is that the plausible-sounding*

---

* Thomas Piketty points out that the increase in private wealth in rich countries has seen it rise from a level of between two and three and a half years' worth of national income in the early 1970s to a 2010 ratio of between four and seven times income, in spite of economic bubbles, stock market falls, and the financial crash – *the emergence of a new patrimonial capitalism*, he calls it.[133]

argument that debt can't cure debt is just wrong. On the contrary, it can.[136] The prime example of this is the period of World War II and its aftermath. Krugman concludes...

> *Finally, there's the continuing urge to make the economic crisis a morality play, a tale in which a depression is the necessary consequence of prior sins and must not be alleviated. Deficit spending and low interest rates just seem 'wrong' to many people, perhaps especially to central bankers and other financial officials, whose sense of self-worth is bound up with the idea of being the grown-ups who say no.*[137]

X. Hovering in the background of any discussion of national economics is the question of taxation. But a crucial aspect of this subject – like many others – is how it is perceived. The political Right in the *Anglo-Sphere* has no doubt as to how it should be viewed: *Frankly, I don't really like any taxes*, David Cameron blithely told the Federation of Small Businesses in 2014, in true populist fashion.[138] This is how they would have us see modern society: an arena in which tax is an evil and government revenue derived from it should be whittled down to a minimum, so that we focus on individual endeavour, which has all the answers. The fact that it doesn't have answers to financing, say, the health service or the armed forces is conveniently glossed over. Would neo-liberals perhaps prefer we have a national whip-round when funds are needed for a new aircraft carrier, a new hospital, or locally for a new fire engine? To view taxes as a *burden*, from which we need *relief*, can be understood in vernacular terms by a hard-pressed populace, especially in times of recession, but in defence of decent public services and vital national infrastructure progressive taxation must be supported by political leaders. It has to be *framed*, as George Lakoff has stressed, as a necessary requirement – even sacrifice – for the greater good of a modern civilization. But the difficulty here is one which Lakoff terms *hypocognition*: that there is no succinct phrase or idea which encapsulates the sense of taxation as a benefit, in the same way as *tax relief* works for conservatives.[139]

Of course, the public's view of taxation depends partly on where one is in the salary scale and how much of it one pays to the exchequer.

There is a natural tendency to see the matter in quite parochial terms, as well as to seize on prejudicial stories in the tabloid press. It is quite common to hear that as a nation we are overtaxed, when in fact tax revenue as a share of UK national income – somewhat under 34% – is lower than that of the average of G7 or OECD nations, as well as lower than in almost all European countries.[140] As a subject, taxation is surrounded by misconceptions, many highlighted by colourful media stories, apocryphal and other. To glean some insight into what high earners thought about remuneration, journalists Polly Toynbee and David Walker, in conjunction with Ipsos Mori, carried out interviews with senior staff at a world-famous law firm and well known merchant banks in London in 2007. The respondents were major high-fliers in the top 0.1% of earners in the UK, accustomed to dealing in large amounts of money. But their knowledge of salaries in Britain (to be highlighted later) was remarkably limited. And as regards taxes, their attitudes were pejorative and dismissive, rationalizing their high salaries by criticising the system, belittling the idea of tax redistribution and condemning the *politics of envy* – views not a considerable distance from the more high-profile examples in the popular press.[141]

For example, when confronted with the fact, at that time, that the top tenth of income earners in the UK were paying a lower proportion of their total income in tax than the bottom 10%, the interviewees simply pointed out how much more they paid in cash, implicitly denying the purpose of a progressive tax system. They also resorted to criticisms of the levels of welfare benefits, the costs of the tax credit system, and the whole idea of providing extra money directly to poorer people. Their knowledge of costs involved was decidedly shaky, and they had exaggerated ideas of the levels of welfare benefits paid out. *But*, the authors point out, *their ignorance was delivered with all the aplomb of power.*[142] The bankers and lawyers questioned appeared to have little contact with officials, which might have made them better informed; their views seemed mainly based on hearsay or on limited dealings with people outside their own circles. Another common theme deriving from these interviewees was the view that their tax pounds would only be wasted; they thought public money would always be misspent, thus seemingly justifying their reluctance to pay more tax. They also had scathing opinions of the abilities of the public officials dealing with public money, as well as of the efficiency and accountability of the systems they employed.

As a result, they did not believe that government should be trusted with more of their money.

Some developed nations – especially those in the so-called *Anglo-Sphere* – are in a very curious position with regard to taxation. Popular acceptance of the range and level of taxes, as well as public understanding of the fairness of current tax regimes, are skewed by the populist policies of governments, especially the neo-liberal bias of tax distribution. In general the trend has been towards a less progressive tax system, which has benefited mainly the well-off, but it has not contributed to more vibrant economies. As has already been cited, GDP figures have certainly not grown any faster during the neo-liberal era, since the 1980s, while the creation of large, successful corporations was a more prominent feature of the post-war period up to the 1970s, than more recently. But this is not the image portrayed by the apologists of the Right, who have persistently advocated a low-tax regime in the interests, they say, of a growing economy and general prosperity. Thus, a version of *trickle-down* economics is supposed to derive from lowering corporation tax, whereas the main consequence is the race-to-the-bottom syndrome of *inversions*, whereby companies gravitate towards low tax regimes to minimize their tax liabilities, thereby reducing legitimate tax revenues elsewhere. The same argument is used to defend low taxes on rich business people: by supporting creative, innovative entrepreneurs and protecting their autonomy we help our economies to flourish, we are told.

Once citizens get accustomed to the particular fiscal environment of their nation, they tend to think of it as the norm, perhaps entirely unaware of significant national variations elsewhere. Every country has its own preferences, influenced by its history and mores, so that attitudes to tax are largely culturally determined. Danish society is, according to surveys conducted there, comfortable with tax contributions amounting to around 46% of national income, while the average for all Scandinavian nations is over 40%. Such figures have gained approval, in part no doubt due to the high level of social services they buy. And in the late twentieth century the top rate of tax in Sweden was over 90%, without apparent adverse effects on national economic performance. The Institute for Fiscal Studies has stated what has become patently clear as regards economic performance: *Other countries show that it is possible to operate successfully with much higher levels of tax.* But this is ignored – for both ideological as well as practical reasons – by regimes which nevertheless badly need more tax revenue.[143] But the political persuasion of decision-makers has often placed ideology above financial practicality. The personal tax rates for top earners in many countries were substantially lowered from the 1980s onwards – roughly halved in the case of the USA, down to 35%. The resulting shortfall in revenue there, needed particularly for wars in the Middle East after 2001, led to an increase in American national debt during George W. Bush's presidency of $5 trillion.[144]

However, while perceptions regarding taxation are often quite subjective and frequently based on misconceptions or ideological preferences, not all high-earners are happy with the *status quo*. In the USA in 2011, the hugely wealthy Warren Buffett called for an increase in taxes on millionaires, to cease protecting them as if they were an endangered species. *Americans are rapidly losing faith in the ability of Congress to deal with our country's fiscal problems*, he said.[145] In Britain in 2008, headmaster Nigel Richardson – then Chair of the Headmasters Conference and about to retire as head of a top private school – deplored the growing gap between rich and poor:

> *I don't think it can go on like this. I think we heads should get together and say enough is enough, it's time to intervene. We need higher taxation and we need to use the money to make society more equitable. How do you stop politicians promising more tax cuts, when we need more spent?*[146]

The better-off in society will sometimes acknowledge their good fortune while accepting their social responsibilities. But in Britain it has to be recognized that many middle-income earners too have prospered under the current tax regime, even though the common perception is that it is mainly the rich who need to be taxed more. As the IFS points out, *In most cases, average tax rates would be higher for both median and high-income earners if the UK implemented the income tax and SSC (Social Security) system from one of the EU15 countries that raise more tax than the UK.*[147]

But Britain is unlikely to follow the example of EU countries, particularly now outside the European Union. Neo-liberal instincts will see no need to draw back from a fiscal regime which is notably more regressive than that in continental nations. A lower than typical level of tax on median incomes in the UK is partly compensated for by higher indirect taxes, such as VAT, which have a disproportionate impact on the less well-off. And as for income tax revenue in Britain, at just over 9% of national income it is one of the lowest in the developed world, but politically it will be difficult to increase this significantly. As for increasing National Insurance Contributions (NICs) which as regards the employers' element are also lower than in many tax regimes, British politicians have generally been opposed to it. In fact, in their rivalry for leadership of the Conservative Party in 2019, both Jeremy Hunt and Boris Johnson pledged to raise the income level at which NICs would start, which would make the UK even more of a fiscal outlier. Recent trends have been to increase personal allowances to take even more people out of income tax altogether: laudable enough for those on the lowest incomes, but coupled with increasing the starting point of NICs this can get very expensive very quickly, the IFS says. All these plans are in the context of an ageing society with increasing pressures on health, social care and pensions, and now the vastly larger national debt incurred by the unprecedented spending to protect the economy from yet greater devastation caused by Coronavirus.

Nevertheless, public perceptions of the fairness or otherwise of Britain's tax system will not be conditioned by these factors alone. They may well continue to be framed by the pejorative yet plausible-sounding utterances of right-wing politicians, who meanwhile will profess dedication to investing in health and social programmes which all know are desperately required. Yet while there are those on the Right who want to have it both ways – low taxes and a comprehensive social infrastructure – there is also the subversive strategy of those who would undermine public services by demolishing the tax base which funds them. The more persuasive the conservatives are in steering the debate on taxation, the less likely it is that public services will receive the financial support they need.[148] But it is not as if – beyond these confines – there is not an abundance of proposals about how to address the fiscal shortfall. Most notably, Thomas Piketty recommends a progressive tax on capital, an annual levy on the net value of individual assets, similar to taxes on wealth current in places like Switzerland and Spain. The scale of the tax he advocates would bring in revenues at about 2% of Europe's GDP, which would cut the level of European debt significantly.* This is the

---

* Before the situation was exacerbated by increasing debt to combat the Covid-19 pandemic, Piketty pointed out that rich nations in Europe had debt levels averaging about a year of national income (or 90% of GDP) – more indebted than at any time since 1945. His

only way, Piketty says, of controlling rising levels of wealth and inequality (which he calls a ... *potentially explosive process*) ... *while preserving entrepreneurial dynamism and international economic openness.*[150]

There is also the matter of ensuring that the full extent of legitimate taxes is collected. Even those supporting tax cuts would not on the whole take exception to such efforts, which could raise hundreds of billions in extra revenue. Joseph Stiglitz has pointed out (in 2015) that US companies paid tax at just 13% of reported worldwide income, much lower than the official rate of corporate taxes which would be due.[151] Steps could be taken by eliminating loopholes and minimizing evasion,* but the key solution Stiglitz and others call for would have corporations pay taxes in the countries where their production and sales are located, i.e. where they do business. This would help reduce tax avoidance through outsourcing production and locating company headquarters abroad. If all nations took this approach in a co-ordinated manner corporate tax takes everywhere would rise. Any such measures would have to face the equivocal rhetoric arguing that tax cuts, even if they increase budget deficits, will stimulate growth and thus eventually lead to higher government revenue. It was on this basis that in 2017 President Trump raised the estate tax threshold in the USA to $11 million, and made swingeing cuts to business taxes – even though the top quintile of US income distribution already owned 90% of corporate equity.[152]** Populism can be disarmingly deceptive, even if it does not serve *the people*, but it will have to be confronted ... *if democracy is to regain control over the globalized financial capitalism of this century...* and ... *to avoid an endless inegalitarian spiral.*[153]

XI. One of the reasons that taxation has had a high profile in Britain in recent times is the publicity of pay levels and their glaring disparities. Popular feelings about remuneration are somewhat mixed and ambivalent. On the one hand, there is a fascination with astronomical salaries, the people who earn them, and their lifestyles, linked to the

---

recommendations then were calculated to bring these down to around 70% of GDP, closer, he says, to the 60% which was the designated maximum set by the Europe Union![149]

* Through avoidance and evasion HMRC has said that the shortfall of tax owed could be as high as 15% of liabilities, while the USA has admitted to a figure almost as high.

** Trump's 2017 tax-cutting bill was, incidentally, rammed through Congress without a single hearing.

preoccupation with celebrity and wealth. On the other hand, there is widespread concern about the growing social and financial divisions in the country and their impact on national well-being. And as the traditional British reticence about ostentation has become diluted, displays of wealth and the luxurious lifestyles which accompany them have become more conspicuous. So our way of looking at the world, what we assume is the norm and normal, has been coloured by money and our dreams of acquiring more of it – for our dream home, our holiday of a lifetime, a no-expense-spared wedding with all the trappings of luxury, to be remembered forever. Living standards have risen and many have much more disposable income than a generation ago. Thus the extravagant flashiness of the 1980s has been transformed into an expectation that affluence is within reach of all, while the belief in meritocracy has convinced us that we deserve it. Nevertheless, that considerable poverty endures and the austerity programme has blighted ambitions for a decade are factors imposing often insurmountable restraints on the realisation of what is left of an abiding vision.

However, all of this exists beside some rather anomalous and paradoxical assumptions about levels of income, their acceptability and consequences. When the renowned, old-established travel firm Thomas Cook collapsed in the autumn of 2019, it threw up some of the typical issues of executive pay. The departing CEO Peter Fankhauser and his predecessors had been remunerated extremely well: paid around £35 million over the previous twelve years, while Fankhauser had received £1.7 million in 'bonuses' over five years. When questioned by a crossparty House of Commons committee in October 2019, he was asked – in the light of the difficulties which the firm had already been known to be experiencing – if he intended to return any of his recent £500,000 bonus, to help mitigate the costs to taxpayers of the vast repatriation programme of Thomas Cook holidaymakers stranded abroad; he declared he hadn't yet decided.* As for responsibility for the demise of the company, Fankhauser would not accept that it was down to him, telling the committee *multiple parties* were involved (although believing his pay was appropriate for a FTSE 250 company). Many are the examples of major companies – from banks to BHS, Carrillion, etc. – which

---

* Following (Sir) Fred Goodwin's disastrous stewardship as CEO of Royal Bank of Scotland, and its near collapse in 2008, his reluctance to return any of his huge pension eventually changed after intense negative publicity, and he agreed to give up more than £200,000 a year in pension rights.

have often gone into administration leaving gaping holes in pension funds, with departing executives who invariably retain their massive salaries and bonuses. Such is the way of the invidious neo-liberal business world and its hallowed free market.

It has not always been thus, certainly in its degree of inequity, and the data indicating this have been well documented. The increase in the remuneration of company bosses – including bonuses and long-term incentives – since the late 1980s has been remarkable, so that by 2011 they were taking home 184 times the average full-time pay of a British worker, whereas in 1989 the ratio had been 19.1 times. Thus, the average paid to CEOs of companies listed in the FTSE 100 in 2011 was £4.8 million, compared with the £26,000 which the average worker earned at that time.[154] And a large proportion of this increase had been achieved in the few years after the financial crash. Ha-Joon Chang cites similar evidence in the USA, where the ratio of CEO remuneration to that of the average worker was around 30 or 40 to 1 in the 1960s and '70s. This had risen to a staggering 300–400 to 1 by the 2000s.[155] Thomas Piketty says that the rise of what he calls the *supermanager* is mainly a feature of the *Anglo-Sphere*, including Canada and Australia. The top centile's share of national income in these four nations was broadly similar at 6-8% of national income in the 1970s, and yet thirty years later had risen to nearly 20% in the USA, and to 14–15% in Canada and the UK. He contrasts this with the situation in other wealthy countries, where increases have been much more modest since 1980: from about 7 to 9% in Japan, France and Italy, and from 9 to 11% in Germany.[156] Such data highlight the divergence of these English-speaking nations from the rest of the affluent *West*.

This is an area of the free market apparently immune to normal reason and rationality, so that we see the subject of pay through a veil of prejudice and polemics even more than usual. What many like to believe is reasonable is often muddled and contentious, and appears to reinforce social divisions, certainly in Britain. Yet it is a bizarre curiosity that soaring salaries and benefits can be paid to top business leaders, when earnings of the average worker barely keep pace with inflation.* Why would Jeff Fairburn of housebuilder Persimmon, for example, accept/need/want a salary of £47 million, 22 times his pay in 2016, or Simon Peckham of Melrose Industries take home £42.8 million, 43

---

* They rose by just 1.7% in 2017 according to the High Pay Centre's annual review.

times that of the previous year? And should Emma Walmsley, CEO of GlaxoSmithKline CEO and the highest paid woman at a FTSE 100 company, not feel seriously aggrieved at receiving *only* £4.9 million?[157] These executives may indeed believe they provide unique expertise, but it is more likely, as Peter Fankhauser admitted, that *multiple parties* determine the success, or otherwise, of their companies? And as regards the figures involved, what does an extra few million pounds provide for an executive, of which doing without would deprive him or her? The ramifications of excessively high salaries evidently do not occur to most who receive them; so the impact on the dignity and self-worth, let alone on the standard of living of ordinary working people, is unlikely to ruffle their equanimity.

Defence of excessively high pay invariably comes down to the market, whose workings are said to be neutral and impartial, with no *skin in the game*,* and therefore not to be interfered with by mortals. Thus apparently, the inviolate rules of economics take precedence over their impact on the human condition. Of course this is a dubious basis on which to organize a society. But the hands-off approach to executive pay is accompanied by a number of other arguments, mostly fallacious. It is often said that top executives will add huge value to their companies, and that they are therefore more than worth their high salaries. Evidence does not support this, as a couple of examples readily indicate. A study by the British section of the CFA Institute of investment professionals found that the link between executive pay and company performance was *negligible*. Their research showed that CEOs of the leading 350 companies in Britain received a median pay package of £1.9 million in 2014, up 82% from 2001. However, the performance of their firms, in terms of the return on invested capital (the CFA's preferred measure), had risen by barely 1%.[158] *Our findings suggest a material disconnect between pay and fundamental value generation*, the report said – the same disconnect, one might say, as that between the rhetoric of corporate bosses and the more down-to-earth perceptions of the majority of employees.

The evidence above is corroborated by numerous other pieces of research, with negligible testimony to contradict it. When the consultancy firm Obermatt was commissioned by the BBC to carry out

---

* As expounded by Nassim Nicholas Taleb in his celebrated *Skin in the Game: Hidden Asymmetries in Daily Life*.

research over the period 2008 to 2010, they found precisely zero correlation between company bosses' remuneration and the performance of their businesses, in terms of shareholder return and growth in profits.[159] According to Obermatt, a similar lack of correlation had been shown in their studies in the USA, Germany and Switzerland.* With such weak, documented evidence of value to their companies, it might seem surprising that so much is invested in these executives, to keep them at their firms. But another argument is just that: since they are highly mobile, if they are not paid well enough they may easily migrate elsewhere, perhaps to a rival. Warnings are often heard – usually from the rich or their apologists – that if we tax highly paid executives too much they will leave. The evidence is to the contrary. Cristobal Young, the author of *The Myth of Millionaire Tax Flight*, has proved that for highly paid bosses place still very much matters.** He compiled research based on 13 years of tax data for every American millionaire. Only about 2.4% of them moved, even to new states, each year and not all went to lower-tax states. *Here's the bottom line,* he says. *Overall, millionaires are deeply embedded in place.*[161]

Young also analysed the list of global billionaires from Forbes magazine to judge movement of the wealthiest executives. He discovered that about 84% of them still live in the countries of their birth, and that of those who live abroad, the majority moved there well before they became rich. He says, *Higher income earners show low migration levels because they are not searching for economic success – they've already found it.*[162] Only about 5% of the world's billionaires moved after they had become successful, because – Young points out – *places are sticky*: it is not so easy to move once you have built a career somewhere, particularly if you have a family[163] – ordinary life impacting rich and not-so-rich alike. This may not fit with the common picture of rich, jet-setting executives, or the occasional notorious examples of their lifestyles which hit the headlines and appear to confirm the stereotype. But the majority of company bosses have a more mundane existence, most having worked their way up through their firms rather than having created cutting-edge, multi-billion pound organizations from scratch,

---

* And other similar data are frequently published. For example, the High Pay Centre showed that between 2000 and 2013 remuneration for directors of FTSE 350 companies increased more than twice as fast as profits and four times as fast as corporate market value.[160]

** *The Myth of Millionaire Tax Flight: How Place Still Matters for the Rich*, Stanford Univ. Press, Stanford, CA, USA, 2017.

through risk-taking ambition. It is also the case that top executives are often headhunted, their posts and salaries rarely advertised, not being open to all and sundry. Another factor often noted is that most executives see pay as a competitive issue in relation to their peers, but are not as focused on the actual amounts they are paid *per se*.

During the 1970s, after the Golden Age of successful capitalism following World War II, many economies began slowing down. Part of early neo-liberalism's response to this was to attribute it to a lack of dynamism in the economy and to high taxation inhibiting entrepreneurial ambition. If only our corporate leaders among the investing class could be adequately rewarded, freeing them from fiscal repression, then our economies would thrive and all would benefit – was the mantra. Higher top salaries, lower taxes, financial deregulation and a smaller state were to be the panaceas for national revival. But the result, instead, was a new class of super-rich, much greater economic and social inequality, and a fall in global economic growth between 1980 and the financial crash, to around half what it had been in the previous era. *The rich got a bigger slice of the pie all right, but they have actually 'reduced' the pace at which the pie is growing*, was how economist Ha-Joon Chang put it.[164] From all that has been said, it seems difficult to find any worthwhile justification for high pay and bonuses for top executives. Yet not even the sobering realities of the financial crash appeared to moderate their demands; for the years after 2008 saw continuing high remuneration – at least among the companies that survived! Tim Jackson highlights the $2.6 billion in end-of-year bonuses Goldman Sachs paid their staff in 2008, even though they had been bailed out with $6 billion from the US government.[165]*

One might conclude that these top earners have considerable power and influence in commercial and political circles – or is it that none of the economic woes of the early twenty-first century can be pinned on their narrow shoulders, that they have to be cosseted and protected at all costs? Could it also be that we have become so inured to exorbitant executive salaries that they are now the norm, a permanent mask which conceals the true face of corporate affairs, including their negative effects on the rest of society? For although there was considerable animosity towards business and its bosses in the wake of the crash, they have

---

* The bonus culture was still going strong some years later. Jackson cites the statistics for 2013, when some 2,600 banking employees in Britain received a total of £3.4 billion – £1.3 million each on average, and about 50 times the average yearly British salary.[166]

largely ridden out the storm to the extent that they have returned to their old ways. Pressure has grown on shareholders to challenge excessive pay, but not enough to vote down the report or remuneration policy of any FTSE 100 company. In fact, most pay packages in 2018 were voted through with levels of support of 90% or more.* The negative impact of excessive pay for executives is increasingly recognised, but not as yet sufficient to overcome the presumption in favour of *laissez-faire*. After a survey of employee attitudes in 2015 the Chartered Institute of Personnel and Development, the HR professionals body, demanded a *fundamental rethink* on the pay of CEOs, since the growing pay gap between boardroom and workforce was actually found to demotivate staff. Almost 60% of employees in the study believed this was the effect of excessive pay at the top, and over half thought it was bad for the reputations of their firms.[168]**

Certainly anyone struggling to make ends meet in the UK is not going to be heartened by publicity surrounding *Fat Cat Day*, which in 2019 fell on Friday January 4th. A few years ago the date was calculated by which the chief executive of a FTSE 100 company would have earned the equivalent of the gross annual average pay of a full-time British worker. Thus, at 1pm on Fat Cat Friday, after three working days of 2019, the CEO on an average (median) salary of £3.9 million will surpass the £29,574 which the average worker earns for the entire year. Caught up in the daily routine of work and family, the ordinary worker will hardly have time to dwell on such detail, but the headline figures glaring out from the media will be hard to miss. However, the high earners at the top looking down appear less well informed. In 2007, the lawyers and bankers surveyed by Polly Toynbee and David Walker in the study cited above (p. 290) did not have a good grasp of relative salaries. When asked about the poverty threshold in Britain, they assumed it was around £22,000, a figure which was in fact close to the median pay of full-time earners, £23,764 at that time; the poverty line for a childless couple was less than half that. They also found it hard to

---

* And this at a time when opinion was flowing the other way. One survey, the Edelman Trust Barometer 2019 for the independent non-party High Pay Centre, found that 62% of respondents believed addressing high pay and bonuses for senior management and business leaders to be either important or very important.[167]

** This mirrored an earlier study, in 2007, when nearly all of a group of human resources professionals said they thought that over-paying executives led to poor employee relations, eventually harming an organization's effectiveness. Interestingly, they believed an acceptable salary ratio should not be more than 14:1.[169]

believe that only about £40,000 would put someone in the top tax band – among the top 10% of UK taxpayers. They thought the figure needed would be four times that, at around £162,000.[170]* And while admitting to enjoying their high salaries, the majority of those questioned nevertheless refused to admit that they were rich.[172]

Earnings are not just a matter of economics. Salaries are determined by a variety of factors – politics, custom, prejudice, and diverse national perceptions. (The latter helps to explain the discrepancies between executive pay in Britain and the USA, and that in continental Europe and Japan.) But fairness, or what workers deserve to be paid, does not seem to figure in this discussion. In fact, the feeling of making a valuable contribution to family or society would appear unrelated to pay received, almost as if it is reward in itself. Certainly, vocation is still a vital motivating factor today, especially in the professions, in spite of the steady battering of morale and status by market ideology. And the millions of hours of overtime worked, paid or unpaid though largely unrecognized, are of immense social benefit to the national community. They derive from the resolve to complete the task, do a job well, and to fulfil obligations – above all in people-orientated occupations. But if neo-liberals had their way, the cash nexus would entirely replace the ethic of service, that vital element of social adhesion which proponents of market dominion implicitly devalue. Here is the late Milton Friedman, an early guru of Thatcherism, pandering to basic instincts: *If your income will be the same whether you work hard or not, why should you work hard?*[173] Many neo-liberals would like to purify work in that way and limit everything to effort, money and profit, to the detriment of social need or human welfare.

Reflecting on Friedman's simplistic notion, one might wonder what would have happened to British society during the last decade or so of austerity – when earnings stagnated for the majority of ordinary workers – if they had ceased to work hard. There is more pride in doing a worthwhile job of work than is dreamt of in the stunted philosophy of neo-liberalism. Employment is more than a matter of livelihood; it also helps define one's role in society, one's self-worth, and, yes, one's dignity. And these sentiments have to contend with the high-pay culture

---

* Similar misapprehensions are to be found in the United States. Paul Krugman cites the results of a survey which found that Americans, on average, believe the salaries of business CEOs to be about thirty times that of ordinary workers, which hasn't been the case for over forty years. In fact the ratio is about ten times that.[171]

which, by implication, maligns the significance of the working roles of millions. In fact, job satisfaction is one element of work which most aspire to regardless of level of salary – albeit threatened by pressures exerted by fewer employees often resulting in the same amount of work being done by a reduced workforce. American journalist Bernard Nossiter identified a feature of the British working environment of the 1970s which he termed *satisficing* – attempting to do a satisfactory job of work within the confines of limited income – rather than aiming at *optimizing*.[174] (If this is at all prevalent today it could be said to be a result of *force majeure*.) But the money element and demands for higher wages have assumed such a bold profile over the generations partly because, as Gordon Rattray Taylor noted many years ago, motives tend to become *monetized*. He says, *People have been taught that money is the key to satisfaction, so that when they feel that something is wrong with their lives they naturally ask for more money*.[175]

F. Scott Fitzgerald's short story 'The Rich Boy' opens with the words *They are different from you and me*. While once upon a time the rich, especially those with 'old money', could be classed as a race apart, it cannot be said today, in more egalitarian societies, that the rich are different from us; on the whole they just have more money. And their wealth may often derive from no greater ability, effort or productivity. Should we care if large corporations wish to pay their leaders vast salaries and perks? Such decisions are the result of market forces, they say, and the money would not be otherwise employed to benefit the general welfare; so does it matter? But here is another error: market forces – such as have any role here at all – are not separate from humanity. They are not natural phenomena, and are open to change. Since we are also told that we are all in this national community together, and must all contribute when disasters such as the financial crash strike, then yes, these inflated pay packets concern us all. In fact, in view of the evidence of the equivocal contribution to the economy of highly paid executives, cited above, there would be justification for reducing their remuneration substantially – as well as taxing them much more appropriately. This subject has significance well beyond economics; the current situation is an affront to the lower paid, but often far more valuable roles in society of those who believe in the ethic of service and contribute massively to national well-being.*

---

*   As regards productivity in employment, it is precisely those caring professions, the

THE MARKET RULES – OK? 303

XII. The gap between the kind of free market recommended in this chapter and the way market forces currently operate under neo-liberalism may not appear such a huge gulf. However, conceptually it is a chasm, and its consequences for society and community are immense, and all the more dangerous for the imperceptible nature of their progress. Behind what may appear an innocent, neutral set of economic practices by which buying and selling, production and consumption are carried on, the detrimental impact on all of us is growing insidiously so that our common culture and sensibilities are being corroded. Many people growing up today may assume that how we now do things is the way it has always been, and should they study the matter, looking back they will find it hard to identify a moment or event when things changed. But change they did, and have continued to do so since the 1970s, as market principles have colonised more and more of our experience.* Today almost everything is for sale; we have gradually come to look at life *through* a transactional prism, which we are encouraged to accept is the norm, so that exchange value gets applied to all relationships, whether commercially based or not. Without being rationalised or justified this has become the default perspective, one that we are not to dwell on, since it is seen as a natural, benign social development which is supposed to represent modern progress and, above all, will undoubtedly enrich us.

Philosopher Michael Sandel has pointed to some of the more unusual items which are for sale today, somewhere, such as prison cell upgrades, or obtaining your GP's mobile phone number. Apparently some American prisons, such as in Santa Ana, California, offer non-violent inmates a clean, quiet jail cell away from the rougher parts of the prison, for perhaps $82 a night. Also in the USA, being able to phone your doctor for special *concierge* service, such as same-day appointments, might be available for annual fees ranging from $1,500 to $25,000.[178] And what about plastering the walls of your entire house with the advertising material of a major company, to enhance your family income, or

---

labour intensive work in the NHS and social care (as well as in the creative 'industries') where productivity is somewhat irrelevant. Time spent with clients and patients is the essence of the work, which in many cases cannot be hurried to meet the arbitrary demands of efficiency and accountability. *Time is quality*, says Tim Jackson.[176]

* Thomas Piketty reminds us of the watershed which the mid-1970s represented. People felt that capitalism had been overcome and that inequality and class society had been relegated to the past... which, he says, explains the dismay in Europe later at the ending of social progress after 1980.[177]

allowing hard-pressed local authorities to charge user fees for library books or public footpaths? No, these last two examples have not been tried – as far as is known – but could they not contribute to alleviating debt, improving local services, helping to reduce levels of council tax? Would promoting commercial sponsorship in education, with widespread advertising by pupils and staff alike, including naming rights for schools and departments, be steps too far? Should we not be somewhat more imaginative, and flexible about methods of fund raising during austere times? Or should we – in this era of creeping commodification and monetisation of almost anything which moves – retain some red lines, which should never be crossed by market forces? Such questions are not being addressed.

There is both a reluctance to face up to these issues, as well as a feeling in some quarters that they do not merit discussion. This is partly due to the tendency to think that market forces are not a matter of values, where difficult dilemmas have to be faced, but to see them as a-moral, a-social, and separate from questions of ethics or taste. To some extent this explains the absence of discussion as to how far market forces should be allowed to colonise everyday life. Since their seemingly neutral position chimes perfectly well with post-modern attitudes, there appears nothing to seize on, nothing to condemn. As Michael Sandel says, *Markets don't wag fingers. ... This nonjudgmental stance toward values lies at the heart of market reasoning and explains much of its appeal.*[179] This aspect certainly appeals to right-wing politicians since they can – at least ostensibly – wash their hands of any involvement in the free market, as well as absolve themselves of any blame for its consequences. So the public realm is free of debate on the subject – except perhaps when the NHS appears under threat from market forces; at such moments the political Right tends to steer clear of controversy over this 'national treasure'. Thus acquisition and profit, the driving impulses of market forces, are left to their own devices, with a momentum which leaves them immune from censure, a kind of non-stick economic mechanism to which no blame attaches itself so that it gets away scot-free.

None of this alters the fact that unregulated market forces – regardless of the extent to which they may enhance affluence – can have a merciless impact on citizens and their settled ways of life. But these negative effects are mostly attributed to human error or weakness, rather than to the supposedly impartial and impersonal system. This can be true in the manner in which markets can influence morality,

THE MARKET RULES – OK?

in their corrosive tendencies on the human agents who manage them. During the financial crash, the philanthropic Templeton Foundation in the USA held a symposium on that subject, with a variety of contributors, including Professor Michael Walzer:

> *Competition in the market puts people under great pressure to break the ordinary rules of decent conduct and then to produce good reasons for doing so. It is these rationalizations – the endless self-deception necessary to meet the bottom line and still feel O.K. about it – that corrode moral character.*[180]

This encapsulates the influence on executives to bend the rules and lower their moral threshold to keep pace with successful rivals, or be at a commercial disadvantage. And since distortion and manipulation of markets will inevitably be employed to some degree – something which with technological sophistication can only increase – the expected optimal outcomes in terms of economic theory cannot be ensured. So we should stop glorifying the market and apply proper, measured and effective regulation.

As well as morality there are also other factors which should govern our decisions as to the valid boundaries of market forces, such as aesthetics, community values and citizenship. The example of covering one's house in advertising, cited above, would if widely adopted change the appearance of communities in a way of which few would approve. And as regards the community sustenance derived from sport, substantially raising ticket prices for Premiership football teams in Britain would likely still fill stadiums, but would narrow the social base of spectators by excluding many of the less well-off.* The principal objective of professional clubs is surely sporting success, no matter how wealthy they are, but there are avenues they could follow to bring in more money, such as moving home matches to grounds in richer areas. Raising revenue sometimes seems more important to the biggest, quoted clubs, but the more they pursue this objective, the further they take the game away from the core community values where they began. Furthermore if, as the neo-liberals tell us, private enterprise is always more efficient than state run activities, could not the Foreign Office hire firms of mercenaries to

---

* This has already begun to happen, consigning many to watching their teams only on TV, provided they can afford the prices of subscription television.

replace units of the armed forces for military operations, thus saving money, and perhaps British lives? Civic respectability or honour renders the impropriety of this idea immediately obvious (even if some nations have employed the policy). But no, by no means is everything for sale.

In spite of the invasive nature of market forces, we know deep down that there are parts of our lives which we would not part with for any price. We have a range of sentiments and motivations which do not come within the scope of financial consideration, even if outside attempts are sometimes made to cost them, for others' gain. In fact commercialising a *good* – perhaps a social *good* – and putting a price on it may influence buyers or sellers: the commercialization effect. Michael Sandel gives the example of The American Association of Retired Persons which asked a group of lawyers if they would provide a particular legal service to needy retirees at a discount. The lawyers refused, but when asked if they would provide the advice for free, they then agreed.[181] They evidently saw that carrying out the work as a charitable service put it in a different, non-transactional category. This exemplifies the converse of normal market mechanisms in that monetary reward can, in some cases, be counter-productive. Its potential can demotivate us, so that we reject the benefits of the transaction on offer – indicating yet again that we are stimulated by so much more than material gain. This was illustrated famously by sociologist Richard Titmuss in the 1960s when he examined the systems of giving blood in Britain and the USA. In his book *The Gift Relationship* he argued that the British system of voluntary blood donation was superior to that in the US, where blood was bought and sold.*

The principal objections Titmuss held against the sale of blood centred on ethical and social questions, though he also maintained that donation was safer, avoided shortages, and did not exploit the poorest in society. It limited the danger of blood being contaminated, and avoided the tendency for most blood to be supplied by the poor and desperate. However, he was most concerned about the effect of a market in blood on people's natural altruism to donate freely. He believed it would weaken their sense of social obligation and impair the gift relationship, an element in the civic glue which held decent societies together. Titmuss perfectly exemplified the variety of impulses which govern our

---

* Richard M. Titmuss, *The Gift Relationship: From Human Blood to Social Policy*, Allen & Unwin, London, 1970.

behaviour; we do not respond only to monetary incentives. In fact, in the blood donation example we reject them in favour of what can be seen as motives of a higher order. There is much discussion of incentives in economic theory, but not enough appreciation of the non-material factors which drive human instincts and behaviour. Just because the free market has been the principal vehicle for raising material living standards since the industrial revolution does not mean it should be given untrammelled authority over all aspects of our lives. Human society is much more subtle and complex than economic theory assumes.* Recognition of this will allow us to challenge the reductive absurdity of neo-liberalism and make space for communal, social and moral values in economic decision-making.

It is sometimes pointed out that no new framework of economic thought has been devised since the rise of neo-liberalism and the demise of state communism, no new *'ism'* for political theorists and activists of the Left to rally around. Thus it appears that market fundamentalism is unopposed and triumphant. But this is analogous to the triumph of political and social freedom in democracies since the Enlightenment; we accept its prevalence and ubiquity but do not give individuals free rein to exploit others. For example, *à la J. S. Mill*, we do not generally allow the exercise of one person's autonomy to impair the freedom of others, a principle our legal system upholds. And neither should we allow unrestrained market forces to inflict serious material disadvantage on others. Democracies profess civic equality, whereas under market forces there is no equality, either in theory or in practice. (In fact there is what Piketty calls *meritocratic extremism*, the need of modern societies to designate some individuals as winners, and reward them excessively for their apparent qualities.[182]) We do not need a new political or economic philosophy to underpin modern capitalism, but merely a managed system of fairness and decency to ensure that it serves all in society. Both liberal democracy and capitalist free markets have their weaknesses, and from time to time require new regulatory mechanisms to improve and modernise them. But they do not need fresh theoretical

---

* Theorists sometimes discuss the matter of present giving, and whether or not giving cash is acceptable, rather than gifts in-kind. To maximize utility, giving cash could be seen as the best kind of present, as some economists have argued. However, the stigma attached to cash presents, especially between friends, spouses, etc., tells us that there is a higher reasoning than mere efficiency. On reflection we all recognise this.

frameworks to vindicate their existence – simply humane and equitable operations in the context of Enlightenment values.

The difficulty is that there is a vacuum at the heart of Western societies created by the dissipation of ideology to support social and economic progress. The working-through of the Western Enlightenment has, after two and half centuries, left material advancement and individualism high and dry, their only justification being the efficacy of their own existence. In the march towards economic plenty and personal emancipation, much traditional ethical and social baggage has been shed. The emphasis on mankind, his potentiality and perfectibility outside of a purely religious context, and the reform of human society, have become drained of their essence. What has been left is a mechanistic drive towards greater productivity, for quantity without purpose in a world where a human being's function is being reduced to an economic one. And all that remains of the noble pursuits of happiness and personal fulfilment is the attempt to acquire as many as possible of the material fruits of an economic system. The fact that the system has even now failed to produce an equitable distribution of these goods, and want has not been overcome, results only in a vigorous struggle to squeeze every last ounce from an economic machine whose design dare not be examined. In the absence of a common ethical culture, we must return to holistic values – ecological, humanitarian and equitable, not merely market-driven. Then, in the vacuum created by the emptiness of modern progress, the tide may turn, and human society in its unsatisfying state of *middle happiness*, to borrow George Steiner's term, may begin to search for something better.

END NOTES

i   Adam Smith, *The Wealth Of Nations*, Book I, Chp. Xc, para. 27, p. 145.
ii   R. H. Tawney, quoted in Dr. Laurence J. Peter (Ed.), *Ideas for Our Time*, Bantam Books, New York, 1979.
iii Anthony Trollope, *The Way We Live Now*, Volume 1, Chapter 4.
iv Justice Louis D. Brandeis, US Supreme Court Justice, quoted by Raymond Lonergan (otherwise Edward Keating) in *Mr. Justice Brandeis, Great American*, 1941, p. 42

1. Alvin Toffler, *Future Shock*, Bantam Books, New York 1971, p. 458.
2. George Orwell, *The Lion and the Unicorn: Socialism and the English Genius*, Penguin, London, 1982, p. 45.
3. Norman Barry, 'Understanding the Market', in *The State or the Market: Politics and Welfare in Contemporary Britain*, 2nd Edn., Sage Publications/The Open University, London, 1991, p. 233.
4. Peter Self, *Rolling Back the Market: Economic Dogma and Political Choice*, Macmillan, London, 2000, Chapter 2.
5. Robert & Edward Skidelsky, *How Much Is Enough? The Love of Money, and the Case for the Good Life*, Penguin Books, London, 2013, p. 12.
6. John Gray, *False Dawn: The Delusions of Global Capitalism*, Granta Books, London, 1998, p. 32.
7. Theodore Roszak, *The Cult of Information: A Neo-Luddite Treatise on High Tech, Artificial Intelligence, and the True Art of Thinking*, Univ. of California Press, London, 1994, p. 105.
8. Idem.
9. Margaret Thatcher, at the Conservative Party Conference, Bournemouth, October 1986.
10. Yves Smith, *Econned: How Unenlightened Self Interest Undermined Democracy And Corrupted Capitalism*, Palgrave Macmillan, New York, 2010, p. 112.
11. Idem.
12. Idem.
13. Peter Self, op. cit., p. 58.
14. Robert & Edward Skidelsky, op. cit., p. 184.
15. Paul Krugman, *End This Depression Now*, W. W. Norton & Co., New York, 2012, p. 43.
16. Janet Yellen from "A Minsky Meltdown: Lessons for Central Bankers", 16/4/2009, quoted in Ibid. p. 41.
17. Paul Krugman, op. cit., p. 30.
18. Ibid. p. 28.

19 George Lakoff has been working on linguistics and human cognition for several decades, looking at metaphors, our conceptual system, and how we build our understanding of reality. Works such as *Metaphors We Live By* (with Mark Johnson), *Moral Politics: What Conservatives Know that Liberals Don't*, and more recently his best seller, *Don't Think of an Elephant! Know your Values and Frame the Debate* constitute important analysis in this field. He maintains that our use of frames is always unconscious and automatic. This followed on from the influential sociologist Erving Goffman's *Frame Analysis*, published in 1974.
20 See Chapter 1, p. 7.
21 Michael Sandel, *What Money Can't Buy: The Moral Limits of Markets*, Allen Lane, London, 2012, pp. 196-7.
22 Ibid. p. 200.
23 Yanis Varoufakis, *Talking to My Daughter: A Brief History of Capitalism*, Vintage, London, 2019, p. 38.
24 Ibid. Chapter 2.
25 John Kay, *The Truth About Markets: Why Some nations are Rich but Most Remain Poor*, Penguin Books, London, 2004, p. 245.
26 Ibid. pp. 234–5.
27 Ibid. p. 336.
28 Richard Sennett, *Together: The Rituals, Pleasures and Politics of Cooperation*, Allen Lane, London, 2012, p. 84. Sennett's brilliant analysis of the evolution, rituals and varied character of co-operation comes to the conclusion that, in spite of today's need to engage with people unlike ourselves, such co-operative bonding is slowly waning.
29 Ibid. p. 280.
30 Cited by the Political Economy Research Centre at Goldsmiths, Univ. of London – at http://www.perc.org.uk/project_posts/remembering-big-bang-financial-deregulation-30-years/
31 Andro Linklater, *Owning the Earth: The Transforming History of Land Ownership*, Bloomsbury, London, 2014, p. 362.
32 Robert Peston and Laurence Knight, *How Do We Fix This Mess: The Economic Price of Having It All and the Route to Lasting Prosperity*, Hodder & Stoughton, London, 2013.
33 Alan Greenspan, in testimony to the Congressional Committee on Oversight and Government Reform in October 2008, quoted in ibid. p. 221. The authors say that Greenspan all but accepted that financial leaders at the time were mesmerised by the ideology of unfettered markets.
34 At **https://metro.co.uk/2017/06/16/government-ministers-congratulated-themselves-for-cutting-fire-regulations-6713967/?ito=cbshare**
35 See *cognitive frames*, p. 14.
36 From Conservative Home, at: **https://www.conservativehome.com/platform/2011/11/stephen-hammond-mp-a-bonfire-of-the-regulations.html**
37 Ibid.
38 Reported by the BBC, at **https://www.bbc.co.uk/news/business-43719924**
39 Ibid.

40	Woolard, the FCA's Director of Strategy and Competition said, *What looks like a good plan to deregulate in certain circumstances comes back to bite people years later when the compensation scheme kicks in.* At https://www.ftadviser.com/regulation/2017/10/10/fca-rules-out-brexit-bonfire-of-regulation/
41	'Deregulation: Public Services and Health and Safety' in House of Lords, 13th July 2017, at https://hansard.parliament.uk/Lords/2017-07-13/debates/C9D8A1B9-A494-4E16-A147-D501D3AD3B48/DeregulationPublicServicesAndHealthAndSafety
42	Ibid.
43	Ibid.
44	Reported under 'Coalition cuts fraud investigators as private welfare contracts grow', in the *Guardian*, London, 31/3/2012.
45	Ibid.
46	OECD data, Chart 2 at https://www.cer.eu/publications/archive/policy-brief/2016/brexit-and-eu-regulation-bonfire-vanities
47	John Springford, Senior Research Fellow at the Centre for European Reform, at ibid.
48	Neil H. Buchanan, 'Why the Bonfire of Business Regulations is a Big Business Scam', in *Newsweek*, 16/1/2018, at https://www.newsweek.com/why-bonfire-business-regulations-big-business-scam-781938
49	Ibid.
50	Professor Robert Shiller, 'Faith in an Unregulated Free Market? Don't Fall for It', in the *New York Times*, 9/10/2015, at https://www.nytimes.com/2015/10/11/upshot/faith-in-an-unregulated-free market-dont-fall-for-it.html?searchResultPosition=1
51	According to Robert Shiller, at ibid.
52	Robert Peston and Laurence Knight, op. cit., p. 220.
53	Tony Judt, *Ill Fares the Land: A Treatise On Our Present Discontents*, Penguin Books, London, 2011, pp. 199-200.
54	Ibid. p. 200.
55	Ha-Joon Chang, *23 Things They Don't Tell You about Capitalism*, Allen Lane, London, 2010, p. 196.
56	Ibid. pp. 196–7.
57	Robert Peston gives an account of some of the subsidies provided to British banks, while nevertheless showing that after the crash government was minded to keep them as private bodies and at arms length, in Robert Peston and Laurence Knight, op. cit., pp. 370–4.
58	Joseph Stiglitz, *The Great Divide*, Penguin Books, London, 2016, p. 194.
59	Serco's contract was transferred from the primary care trust to the local Clinical Commissioning Group in April 2013, just after the National Audit Office had reported on the concerns raised about the company, available at https://www.nao.org.uk/wp-content/uploads/2013/03/Out-of-hours-GP-services-Cornwall-Full-Report.pdf
60	According to Amyas Morse, head of the National Audit Office, at https://www.nao.org.uk/report/privatisation-of-royal-mail-plc/
61	Mariana Mazzucato, *The Entrepreneurial State: Debunking Public vs. Private Sector Myths*, Penguin Books, London, 2018.
62	Ibid. p. 30.

63 Ibid. p. 89.
64 Ibid. p. 72.
65 Ibid. p. 194.
66 Ibid. pp. 72–3.
67 Ibid. p. 196.
68 Joseph Stiglitz op. cit. pp. 203–4, 408–9.
69 Mariana Mazzucato op. cit. p. 202.
70 Ibid. p. 27.
71 Joseph Stiglitz op. cit., p. 204.
72 Guy Standing, *The Corruption of Capitalism: Why Rentiers Thrive and Work Does Not Pay,* Biteback Publishing, London, 2017, p. 85.
73 According to one source, a non-profit research centre on economic development subsidies – https://subsidytracker.goodjobsfirst.org/parent/boeing
74 Recorded by the nonpartisan, not-for-profit National Institute on Money in Politics, at https://www.followthemoney.org/entity-details?eid=385
75 Out of a total of about $18 trillion awarded during that period, from figures published in August 2017, at https://www.equities.com/news/corporate-welfare-how-big-business-lives-off-government-subsidies
76 Ibid.
77 From https://www.mic.com/articles/85101/10-corporations-receiving-massive-public-subsidies-from-taxpayers using data from Subsidy Tracker at https://www.goodjobsfirst.org/corporate-subsidy-watch
78 Ibid.
79 In research carried out by Kevin Farnsworth, Senior Lecturer at York University, published in the *Guardian,* London, 7/7/2015, as 'The £93bn Handshake: businesses pocket huge subsidies and tax breaks'. Farnsworth stresses that this £93 billion is a conservative estimate.
80 The *Sunday Times,* 31/1/2016, cited in Guy Standing op. cit., p. 90.
81 The *Guardian,* 7/7/2015 op. cit.
82 Ibid.
83 Ibid.
84 The House of Commons Environmental Audit Select Committee, quoted in Ibid.
85 According to Corporate Welfare Watch, at http://www.corporate-welfare-watch.org.uk/wp/database_awards_table-2/database-or/
86 At https://www.gov.uk/government/organisations/nuclear-decommissioning-authority/about#budget
87 There is more on this at https://theecologist.org/2014/feb/06/true-cost-disaster-insurance-makes-nuclear-power-uncompetitive
88 Cited in Guy Standing, op. cit., p. 110.
89 According to The Centre for Public Impact, at https://www.centreforpublicimpact.org/case-study/privatisation-uk-companies-1970s/
90 An Ipsos MORI poll, cited at ibid.
91 According to Karel Williams, Professor of Accounting and Political Economy at Manchester Business School, writing in the *Observer,* London, 7/1/2018.
92 Tony Judt, op. cit., p. 209.
93 For more on this see https://www.nhsforsale.info/private-providers/circle-new/
94 See https://www.nao.org.uk/wp-content/uploads/2018/01/PFI-and-PF2.pdf

95 The *Independent*, London, 9/6/2014.
96 According to figures provided by the National Audit Office. See https://www.nao.org.uk/report/pfi-and-pf2/
97 Dexter Whitfield, *Global Auction of Public Assets: Public sector alternatives to the infrastructure market & Public Private Partnerships*, Spokesman Books, Nottingham, 2010.
98 Journalist Anna Minton has researched and written on the subject of the privatisation of public space with illuminating effect, notably in her book *Ground Control* (Penguin, London, 2012). In this instance I have drawn on her paper 'Common Good(s) – Redefining the public interest and the common good', 2013.
99 Elinor Ostrom, *Governing the Commons: The evolution of institutions for collective action*, CUP, Cambridge UK, 1990.
100 Quoted in Ibid. p. 2.
101 Quoted in Anna Minton, 'What kind of world are we building? The privatisation of public space', report for the Royal Institution of Chartered Surveyors, London, May 2006, p. 26.
102 In Argent's public realm strategy for King's Cross, quoted in idem.
103 The *Daily Telegraph*, London, 23/9/2011.
104 Reported in ibid.
105 See https://www.pinsentmasons.com/out-law/news/appeal-court-confirms-scope-of-presumption-in-favour-of-sustainable-development
106 According to Clare Mirfin at law firm Pinsent Masons, at ibid.
107 Brett Christophers, *The New Enclosure: the Appropriation of Public Land in Neo-liberal Britain*, Verso, London, 2018.
108 Andro Linklater, op. cit., p. 12.
109 George Lakoff, *Don't Think of an Elephant: Know Your Values and Frame the Debate*, Chelsea Green Publishing, White River Junction, Vt., USA, 2014, p. 15.
110 Ibid. p. 151.
111 Philip Pullman, 'Market fanatics will kill what makes our libraries precious', in the *Guardian*, London, 29/1/2011.
112 James Meek, *Private Island: Why Britain Now Belongs to Someone Else*, Verso, London, 2014.
113 George Lakoff, 2014, op. cit., p. 151.
114 James Meek, on access, privatisation and vital services, in the *Guardian*, London, 28/4/2015.
115 David Elstein on the 'Today' programme, BBC Radio 4, 25/9/1995.
116 Reported by Andy Bull in the *Guardian*, London, 13/7/2019.
117 Michael Sandel, op. cit., p. 172.
118 Ibid. P. 173.
119 Cited at https://www.healthsystemtracker.org/cha83rt-collection/health-spending-u-s-compare-countries/ (Figures PPP adjusted).
120 According to Britain's Office for National Statistics, at https://www.ons.gov.uk/peoplepopulationandcommunity/healthandsocialcare/healthcaresystem/articles/howdoesukhealthcarespendingcomparewithothercountries/2019-08-29
121 Data cited by the *BMJ* at https://www.bmj.com/content/357/bmj.j2940
122 Theodore Roszak, op. cit., p. 88.

123 Ibid. p. 91.
124 Alan Greenspan in October 2005, quoted in Paul Krugman, op. cit., p. 54.
125 Cited in Robert Peston and Laurence Knight op. cit., p. 46.
126 Suggested in ibid. p. 225.
127 Letter on behalf of The British Academy, written by Professors Tim Besley and Peter Hennessey at https://www.thebritishacademy.ac.uk/publications/british-academy-review/global-financial-crisis-why-didnt-anybody-notice
128 Ha-Joon Chang op. cit., p. 247.
129 All by Professors Tim Besley and Peter Hennessey, The British Academy, op. cit.
130 Paul Krugman, op. cit., p. 64.
131 George Lakoff, 2014, op. cit., Chapter 1.
132 Ibid. p. 6. Lakoff believes that the success of conservative political parties recently has been largely based on the conclusion that people vote less for their economic self-interest than for their values and self-identity.
133 Thomas Piketty, *Capital in the Twenty-first Century*, The Belknap Press of Harvard University, Cambridge, Mass., 2017, p. 215.
134 Ibid. p. 701.
135 Guy Standing, op. cit., p. 35.
136 Paul Krugman, op. cit., p. 148.
137 Ibid. p. 207.
138 David Cameron at https://www.gov.uk/government/speeches/supporting-small-businesses-david-camerons-qa-at-the-federation-of-small-businesses
139 George Lakoff, 2014, op. cit., p. 21. Lakoff discusses hypocognition and its origins on pp. 21–2. He highlights the fact that progressives have suffered from serious hypocognition for many years, while conservatives – who once experienced it – have learnt framing, and thus avoid it. But *What is taxation?* he asks. *Taxation is what you pay to live in a civilized country.*
140 Shown by data of the Institute of Fiscal Studies, at www.ifs.org.uk/publications/14256 The share of UK national income raised in tax has fluctuated between 30 and 35% since 1945. It has been on the rise since the early 1990s, perhaps not surprising in view of the growing impact of an ageing society on the costs of health, social care and pensions.
141 Described in Polly Toynbee & David Walker, *Unjust Rewards: Exposing Greed and Inequality in Britain Today*, Granta Books, London, 2008, pp. 32–5. (Research sponsored by the Joseph Rowntree Foundation.)
142 Ibid. p. 35.
143 'Observation', for the Institute for Fiscal Studies, 'Cutting taxes on income would make UK more unusual relative to other countries', 19/7/2019 at www.ifs.org.uk/publications/14258
144 According to Andro Linklater, op. cit., p. 378.
145 Quoted in ibid. pp. 381–2.
146 Quoted in Polly Toynbee & David Walker, op. cit., p. 67.
147 Report by the Institute for Fiscal Studies, 'How do other countries raise more in tax than the UK', July 2019 at www.ifs.org.uk/publications/14256
148 For this argument, see Lakoff's analysis in George Lakoff, 2014, op. cit., pp. 54-5.
149 See Thomas Piketty, op. cit., p. 705.

150 Ibid. p. 562.
151 Cited in Joseph Stiglitz, op. cit., p. 111.
152 Cited in Adam Tooze, *Crashed: How a Decade of Financial Crisis Changed the World*, Allen Lane, London, 2018, p. 583.
153 According to Thomas Piketty, op. cit., p. 663.
154 According to a survey by Manifest/MM&K all of which cited in Robert Peston and Laurence Knight, op. cit., p. 410.
155 Cited in Ha-Joon Chang, op. cit., p. 150. The author adds to what he calls a *bleak picture* with further data on pp. 150-1.
156 Cited in Thomas Piketty, op. cit., pp. 398-401.
157 http://highpaycentre.org/pubs/high-pay-centre-cipd-executive-pay-survey-2018
158 A survey by the CFA UK, reported as 'Negligible link between executive pay and firm's performance, says study', – in the *Guardian*, London, 27/12/2016.
159 Cited in Robert Peston and Laurence Knight, op. cit., p. 410.
160 See http://highpaycentre.org/blog/new-high-pay-centre-report-performance-related-pay-is-nothing-of-the-sort
161 See 'Taxes Don't Make Millionaires Move', in *CommonWealth* magazine, June 2017, at www.commonwealthmagazine.org/economy/taxes-dont-make-millionaires-move/
162 Cristobal Young, 'If you tax the rich they won't leave: US data contradicts millionaires' threats', in the *Guardian*, London, 20/11/2017.
163 Ibid.
164 Ha-Joon Chang, op. cit., p. 145.
165 Tim Jackson, *Prosperity Without Growth: Foundations For The Economy of Tomorrow*, 2nd Edn., Routledge, Abingdon, Oxon., 2017, p. 37.
166 Ibid. pp. 234-5.
167 'Executive Pay in the FTSE 100 – September 2019' at http://highpaycentre.org/blog/what-next-on-top-pay-reflections-on-recent-trends-in-executive-pay
168 'The view from below: What employees really think about their CEO's pay packet', at https://www.cipd.co.uk/about/media/press/181215-exec-pay
169 Cited in Polly Toynbee & David Walker, op. cit., p. 45.
170 Ibid. pp. 24–5. And see endnote here 140.
171 Cited by Paul Krugman, in 'Bernie Sanders and the Myth of the 1%', in the *New York Times*, New York, 18/4/2019, from data at https://journals.sagepub.com/doi/abs/10.1177/1745691614549773
172 In Polly Toynbee & David Walker, op. cit., p. 30.
173 Milton and Rose Friedman, *Free to Choose: A Personal Statement*, Harcourt Brace Jovanovich, New York, 1980, p. 23.
174 In Bernard D. Nossiter, *Britain: A Future That Works*, André Deutsch, London, 1978, p. 88.
175 Gordon Rattray Taylor, quoted in J. A. C. Brown's classic study, *The Social Psychology of Industry*, Penguin, London, 1954, pp. 201-2.
176 See his discussion of the subject in Tim Jackson, op. cit., pp. 147-8.
177 Thomas Piketty, op. cit., p. 441.
178 Michael Sandel, op. cit., p. 3-4.
179 Ibid. p. 14.

180 Michael Walzer, Professor Emeritus at The Institute for Advanced Study, Princeton, NJ, quoted in Catherine Rampell, 'Free Markets and Morality', the *New York Times*, New York, 6th October 2008.
181 In Michael Sandel, op. cit., p. 121.
182 Thomas Piketty, op. cit., p. 421.

Chapter 6

THE GREAT CONTRADICTION[*]

Among democratic nations, men easily attain a certain equality of condition, but they can never attain as much as they desire. It perpetually retires from before them, yet without hiding itself from their sight, and in retiring draws them on. At every moment they think they are about to grasp it; it escapes at every moment from their hold.
ALEXIS DE TOCQUEVILLE[ii]

Equality is in general and in every sphere foreign and antagonistic to the Englishman. Equality is a demand of rationalism and logical thought, to which the Englishman, with his individualistic perception of differences and readiness to emphasize and accentuate them, is a stranger.
PAUL COHEN-PORTHEIM, 1930[iii]

One of the regrettable... effects of extreme inequality... is its tendency to weaken the capacity for impartial judgment. It pads the lives of its beneficiaries with a soft down of consideration, while relieving them of the vulgar necessity of justifying their pretensions, and secures that, if they fall, they fall on cushions.
R. H. TAWNEY[iv]

We've always had rich and poor. But money is increasingly something that enables the rich... to live a life apart from the poor. And the rich and semi-rich increasingly seem to want to live a life apart, in part because they are increasingly terrified of the poor, because they increasingly seem to feel that they deserve such a life, that they are in some sense superior to those with less. An especially precious type of equality – equality not of money but in the way we treat each other and live our lives – seems to be disappearing.
MICKEY KAUS, journalist[v]

---

[*] What economist Yanis Varoufakis terms *...the coexistence of unimaginable new wealth and unspeakable suffering.*[i]

THE Englishman, Tolstoy wrote, ... *is self-assured as being a citizen of the best organized state in the world.*[1] Informed public opinion in the Britain of the second half of the nineteenth century certainly believed that the nation had the finest government and administration anywhere in the world; they saw it as the best regulated and the most modern of any country. British civilization with its huge empire, its industrial and technological prowess, its rising national prosperity, and its developing representative democracy, saw itself as tolerant, progressive, magnanimous – an example for all others to emulate. This edifice of Victorian stability radiated a confidence in which the majority of the population shared, and which instilled an overriding sense of optimism throughout the nation – a belief in human progress with Britain in its vanguard. These sentiments survived the relative economic and industrial decline towards the end of the century, and were implicitly reaffirmed by victory in the Great War. Thus, prior to the 1929 crash latent British feelings of self-satisfaction and superiority were still part of the national psyche, epitomized in politics by the words of former prime minister Arthur Balfour:

> ... *it is evident that our whole political machinery pre-supposes a people so fundamentally at one that they can safely afford to bicker; and so sure of their own moderation that they are not dangerously disturbed by the never-ending din of political conflict. May it always be so.*[2]

Almost one hundred years on, Britain finds itself in a very different place. Nevertheless, overcoming the might of the Axis powers in World War II and the economic revival of the post-war years reasserted national confidence in a transformed world – loss of empire notwithstanding. And the country rallied economically as a result of – and in spite of – the shock tactics of the 1980s' government policies. So by the turn of the century the United Kingdom still sat, somewhat surprisingly, among the group of richest nations – according to headline figures.*
However, beneath the surface was a society far from at ease with itself. Political and social scandals, as well as the financial crash of 2007/08, helped to reveal a country of desperate need coupled with conspicuous

---

* With less than 1% of the world's population, and in spite of the emergence of huge economies like those of China and India, the UK is still the 5th or 6th largest global economy, depending on which indices are used.

wealth, to lay bare the dire consequences of under-investment in social services and the NHS, and to highlight the effects of over-reliance on a free market with inadequate regulation. A nation now in the process of turning its back on the EU is as divided as it has been for two hundred years, and scarred with social problems which unparalleled affluence and the welfare state were supposed to have consigned to history. On the one hand are heard the voices harking back to the past, emphasising the deep capacity of the British to survive and prosper, alone if necessary. On the other, are those calling urgently for full social and political regeneration to bring the nation up to the level of modern 21st-century societies.

So for any of the variety of peoples in these British islands who believe its venerable civilization has reason to rest on its laurels, to sit back and reflect on past achievements and the distance travelled – let us see: if we compare society in the United Kingdom today with the situation in a number of other countries, such as those in Scandinavia or Japan, we come across some very unflattering differences. People in the UK are less likely to be helpful to others; people there trust each other less; in Britain violence is more common than in these other nations; also UK social mobility is less, while people are less likely to marry across social classes; signs of status and class have become increasingly important in the UK by comparison, and status anxiety is higher at all levels of British society, so that people spend more on status goods; citizens work longer hours than do people in these other nations, but get into debt more easily, as they try to appear successful; the UK sends more people to prison *per capita*, and for less serious offences, than do the other nations cited; a more punitive climate of opinion prevails in Britain, and longer prison sentences are handed down. The United Kingdom compares distinctly unfavourably with the Scandinavian nations and Japan on all these, and numerous other measures, so that the clear evidence is of a more troubled society, with all the associated costs – personal and financial – that these problems would imply.[3]

This list of shortcomings conveys a picture of British society as in many respects somewhat backward compared to Japanese and Scandinavian societies. These nations have been highlighted because they mostly fall at one end of a spectrum of the incidence of conspicuous social issues. Some other European countries, like Germany and the Netherlands, are not far behind on many of the comparisons cited above. (The UK, incidentally, is on these terms usually a mid-point between on the one hand, most of Europe, and on the other the USA, which by all these criteria is worse off.) While the differences are painted here in broad-brush terms, they form part of extensive and statistically documented accounts comparing Britain with other advanced industrial societies. By almost every measure, these other societies could be said to be more socially developed than that of the UK, though mostly not any richer. To pick out one prominent example, as regards child well-being Britain does decidedly worse than Japan, the Scandinavian nations, Germany and the Netherlands, as well as ranking below several other European states.[4] For the nation which pioneered better working conditions and reduced hours for children, with the Factory and Mines Acts of the 1840s, but which now lags behind many other modern states in child welfare, what has happened? And why does the United Kingdom now compare unfavourably with these – otherwise apparently similar – nations on so many different criteria?

The British state has so often stood alone from the rest of the world, once linked closely with its worldwide empire, but invariably apart from the European continent. As long ago as the Middle Ages the English (then) had stood out as being differentiated from continental peoples, noted frequently by European ambassadors to the Court of St James. As George Orwell pointed out, *When you come back to England from any foreign country, you have immediately the sensation of breathing a different air.*[5]* More recently, the British have often prided themselves on going it alone, ideas bolstered by sentiments arising from the Battle of Britain and the Blitz. When to this separateness is added the legacy of early twentieth-century feelings of superiority, it results in a latent prejudice that ... *we know best*, and ... *other countries cannot show us how to do things* – when the evidence is that very often they can. *Splendid isolation* still trumps 'best practice' when it comes to how to organise a society; it has never been the British 'way' to pick from good working examples abroad. It is usually thought preferable to muddle through, with trial and error, to our own home-grown arrangement which will attract domestic loyalty. As we can see from the examples above, this is no longer good enough.

It is remarkable that there exists in Britain an abiding refusal to accept that many comparable nations can, and have, ordered their affairs

---

* Or as John Maynard Keynes declared in 1919, *Europe is apart and England is not of her flesh and body.*

more progressively and humanely than has happened in the UK. The British-centric focus appears to eschew admiration for foreign practices, even where they appear evidently superior to those at home. And there appears little interest in analysing the reasons for the consistent pattern of success that some European nations achieve in dealing with modern social problems. For example, at a time when many British prisons are at crisis point, and recidivism is all too common, there is a reluctance to examine other models of penal policy or incarceration. Progressive foreign measures in this area, such as those of Norway or Portugal, may occasionally feature in BBC documentaries, but are rarely taken seriously enough to inform public policy. It is as if we were still living in the days of empire, when Britain appeared to have all the answers and foreign visitors arrived to witness social and economic practices they thought represented the future. And perhaps there are still those who would privately echo the quizzical words of Dickens' Mr Podsnap in *Our Mutual Friend*: when asked by *the foreign gentleman* how other countries fare, 'They do, Sir', returned Mr Podsnap, gravely shaking his head, 'they do – I am sorry to be obliged to say it – as they do.'

The plain fact is that on a whole range of social measures Britain compares distinctly unfavourably today with many developed nations around the world, most of which do not benefit from more advantageous economic conditions than the UK. It is hard to discern why and how has this come about. There is no lack of British expertise to create the policy and social infrastructure to remedy national problems, but the gulf between principles, concern for others, and progressive policy, on the one hand, and political will on the other is glaring, with the result that practical solutions do not emerge. The ... *we're all in it together* sentiment is simply no more than that. The British profess to believe in evidence-based policy for tackling political and social issues, priding themselves on a supposedly rational and scientific modernism; this appears a fiction when faced with dire national need. There is undoubtedly an element of leaving outcomes to the market, putting ideology before welfare, indulging economic theory regardless of how long its workings take to bear fruit. And how many times in Britain does one hear the mantra that only by growing the economy will there be the extra resources to improve health and social services, as if the nation were not already one of the world's richest? Yet the failings in so many aspects of social well-being in Britain resolutely endure, in one of the most advanced of nations.

The discrepancies in performance can certainly not be down to overall national income; the UK is economically on a par with most of the nations which come out better in the social comparisons cited on pages 319-20, above. It currently has a *per capita* GDP figure at a similar level to Finland, and higher than that of France or Japan.[6] And near the top of the tables for national income is the United States, far wealthier than most European states, but which nevertheless fares worse on almost all the categories of social comparisons cited. It is also evident in the richest countries that the expected results of higher expenditure – public or private – on a range of social issues often fail to materialize. For example, the striking contrasts in health outcomes between the USA and Cuba have long been noted. While US *per capita* spending on health care is more than ten times that of Cuba,[7] it still lags behind that nation in figures for infant mortality, and is only marginally ahead in terms of life expectancy.* The amounts which nations devote to different elements of social expenditure, either total or per head of population, are – perhaps paradoxically – not a good indication of likely outcomes for the overall health or success of their societies.

Moreover, as indicated above, national income statistics give little indication of how well a society manages to order its affairs; affluence itself is not a reliable guide to social cohesion, community health, psychological well-being, or whether a society is at ease with itself. This is perfectly exemplified by one of the world's richest nations, the United States, which has a questionable record in many social areas. Choosing three particular matters – child well-being, problem gambling, and adult literacy – a clear picture emerges. In these three respects, important measures of progress in modern, developed societies, the USA performs worse than many developed economies, as well as many less advanced ones. On the 2016 UNICEF Child Well-being Index the US is ranked 18th overall, out of 41 rich nations, on four indications of child welfare.[10]** As regards problem gambling, research shows the USA with a noticeably higher incidence than thirteen other rich nations, with only Australia and Singapore ahead of it.[12] The results are similar for literacy proficiency among adults, where the US ranks 18th, about

---

* 2013 figures indicate that in spite of the enormous gulf in expenditure on health, Cuba recorded 5.8 deaths per 1000 live births, in comparison with 6.2 in the USA.[8] Cuba's life expectancy in that year was 78.4, slightly below that of the US at 79.7.[9]

** It is also noteworthy that the United States is the only OECD country without nationwide, statutory, paid maternity leave, paternity leave or parental leave.[11]

the mid-point in a table of well-off countries, below the OECD average as well as lower than poorer nations like Russia and Slovakia.[13] So as regards educational attainment in adults, as well as the other two issues cited, the vast riches of the United States have not resulted in commensurate social outcomes. On the contrary, they appear to show a less fully developed, less harmonious, less modern society than might be expected.

Such is the environment of the 21st century world that money is often thought the solution to all social and economic problems – as well as to personal happiness. And as this work has tried to show, the atmosphere engendered by neo-liberal policies has exacerbated this tendency, so that materialism has become the universal creed. Nations, as well as individuals, are held in high esteem according to their level of affluence. High-income countries – even if some of this income is generated by debt – are assumed to be able to look after their peoples; where the proceeds of the empty theory of *trickle-down* are awaited, government programmes are still thought capable of safeguarding basic welfare standards. Countries like the United States, and to a lesser extent the United Kingdom, both with severe social problems and flimsy safety nets, could be classed as anomalies, outliers, which seem to defy the norms of modern market economies in that their riches bear little relation to the priority they appear to attach to social well-being. For neither their substantial gross national incomes, nor the amounts they devote to social programmes (most conspicuously in the case of USA health spending, outlined above) succeed in raising their peoples to the level of many other more harmonious, more contented, more socially equal societies.

In order to appreciate the seeming discrepancies of wealthy countries which nevertheless have severe, even intractable social problems, one has to look at those apparently more cohesive, happier societies which were highlighted earlier in this chapter. There are some significant contrasts between these nations – Japan and the northern European states – and countries of the so-called *Anglo-Sphere*, like Britain and the United States. The most crucial difference is equality – specifically income equality. It is here where we must look to understand what has gone wrong in the last forty years of burgeoning neo-liberalism.

Nations – predominantly advanced, developed economies – which have a greater degree of equality of incomes tend to have a lower incidence of a wide range of social problems, from mental illness, status anxiety and adult literacy, to social mobility, child bullying and life expectancy. These and a variety of other social, educational and health matters all represent more prominent, worrying issues where inequality of income is more extreme. The evidence for these contentions has been set out by Richard Wilkinson and Kate Pickett in a huge body of exhaustive research, published in numerous articles and reports as well as in two comprehensive works, *The Spirit Level* (2010) and *The Inner Level* (2018), already cited. The results and implications of their conclusive, compelling evidence will be examined during this chapter.

Wilkinson and Pickett have convincingly established that the degree of income inequality is the key unifying element in the majority of societal failings. From their work, and that of other researchers, it is clear that this variable is more important than factors such as how rich a nation is in macro-economic terms, or than the average level of income per head of population. Even expenditure on social programmes – though relevant in many areas – seems less important than this decisive factor: how a nation's total income is shared amongst its population. How citizens are remunerated, in terms of incomes from private or public sources, their rewards from productive employment or rental gains from the return on capital, as well as the results of fiscal and welfare policies – these amount to crucial measures which condition the degree of equality or inequality of income. And the overall pattern of that inequality has an extensive impact on the whole of society; … *living in a more unequal society changes how we think and feel and how we relate to each other.*[14] Apologists for neo-liberalism will always maintain that growing the economy as a whole will help improve standards generally, reduce poverty and mitigate its consequences – the *raise all boats* scenario. However, the significance of equality of incomes, and the improved social conditions which accompany it in so many countries, entirely undermine that argument.

In countries of the *Anglo-Sphere* the whole broad subject of equality is a very troubled one – at the same time lauded and misinterpreted. In the United States, in spite of the fine words of the American Declaration of Independence there is no national aspiration towards material or economic equality, merely a sense of civic equality before the law.* In fact, one might argue that equality is more a part of the social and political atmosphere than a value or principle. And as regards individual emancipation there is an implicit faith in equality of opportunity in spite of the lack of substance to the ideal, with the narrowing scope of social mobility in recent decades. But to many Americans equality has socialist connotations, the idea of an enforced levelling which would be contrary to freedom. In the UK in these still neo-liberal times, a vague sense of equality of opportunity as a laudable objective pervades society, but without the energy to create a level playing field as an equal point of departure for society's young. In the nineteenth century Disraeli distinguished two kinds of equality: ... *the equality that levels and destroys and the equality that elevates and creates.*[15] He believed the latter sort compatible with British values, and such is the thinking today, so that in theory there is no obstacle to individual drive and ambition beyond inherent, personal limitations. Thus, an equal starting point is implied, from which there is the freedom to aspire to one's own particular, unique heights.

Such is the theory, from where reality marks a major departure. For the situation on the ground, in the known world of everyday living in the economies pursuing neo-liberalism, is one of severe and growing inequalities, as well as the ever-vanishing mirage of social mobility – a theory still held before us, but now almost a relic from a more optimistic age. Publicity given to nations which have refused to follow this divisive economic path, thus avoiding these extremes, is resolutely ignored – unless 'exceptionalism' is claimed, suggesting that their examples would anyway not apply at home. The egocentric national media generally approve this myopic approach, proclaiming the virtues of what we know, blind to the notion that citizens of, say, Denmark or Sweden or Japan, etc., might have found a better, more fulfilling path. In both Britain and the United States it is implied that we are in the vanguard of history, following the right and only path to greater national emancipation, and that current social problems are merely blips on the road to this goal. This is a programme in self-deception, but the ideological stance of the *Anglo-Sphere* endorses it, so that many of its constituents subscribe to the national direction taken. This returns us to the opening

---

* There is, incidentally, no mention of *equality* in the original American constitution, signed just before the emergence of the French Revolution's motto of *Liberté, égalité, fraternité*.

chapter of this work, to the implicit acceptance of ideas which become part of the fabric of national existence – assumed but not dwelt upon – and against which a body of dissenting voices struggles to make an impression.

Examples from the past are sometimes used to endorse the direction of right-wing ideology and the narrow conception of *economic man* which it represents, as if history is on its side. This is part of the notion of historical evolution as progress – an inevitable, steady advance towards human emancipation on Enlightenment lines, with greater prosperity and equality in prospect. It has taken cultural research to show how false this picture has become. In pre-historic times hunter-gatherer societies had a certain degree of leisure, since their search for food took only a few hours a day. In a famous extended essay 'The Original Affluent Society', cultural anthropologist Marshall Sahlins highlights how these primitive peoples followed what he considered a Zen strategy to affluence, achieving material plenty even with a low standard of living.[16] Through having few and finite wants coupled with the adequate, albeit unchanging technical means to provide for themselves, they remained free of the obsession of scarcity. They had few possessions but were not poor. And crucially, these pre-historic communities were for the most part egalitarian in organisation. In fact, for the vast majority of human history – that is, up to about 10,000 years ago – equality was the norm, since ... *only egalitarian societies existed on our planet*.[17]

This reality contradicts the Hobbesian notion of conflict, which necessitates hierarchical arrangements and strong leaders, and the view that competition and tendencies towards dominance are inherent elements of our species. It suits the purposes of neo-liberalism to promote an image of *homo sapiens* as naturally competitive, and even that it was this characteristic which gave rise to social and economic progress, and to the eventual affluence of industrial society. But the research evidence shows early 'man' as egalitarian, collaborative, resisting any inclination towards hierarchy or subjugation by dominant figures. Anthropologist Christopher Boehm has compiled a huge collection of accounts of hunter-gatherer societies on different continents; he analysed 48 of these in order to judge whether humans are predisposed to co-exist as equals. He concludes that egalitarianism may not be part of our genetic code, but that our *behavioural propensities* predisposed the earliest groups and tribes towards maintaining parity among adults. In fact, *This belief was so strong that males who turned into selfish bullies, or even tried* to boss others around for reasons useful to the group, were treated brutally, as moral deviants.[18] These factors, Boehm believed, militated against these societies becoming hierarchical. As other researchers have maintained, ... *there is no dominance hierarchy among hunter-gatherers... and ... rank is simply not discernible among hunter-gatherers.*[19]*

Thus, hierarchy is not an inherent characteristic of human communities; it is now thought to have emerged with the development of agriculture. But it has certainly become a feature of almost all the post-prehistoric world up to the present. Stratified societies, with wealth and power concentrated at the top, usually rationalized by religion or ideology, became the norm for civilizations, so that any kind of real social equality would have been a bizarre anomaly. Later, egalitarian values were part of the 18th-century western Enlightenment, the ultimate of which was represented by Jean-Jacques Rousseau's declaration that ... *the fruits of the earth belong to us all, and the earth itself to nobody.* His 'Discourse on the Origin of Inequality' (1754), like other Enlightenment texts, went back to first principles and so-called Natural Law to castigate the iniquities of social arrangements at that time. But writers then had not only Enlightenment philosophy and the revolutions of the late 18th century to inspire them, but also the examples of native populations of North America. From the sixteenth century on, reports of these indigenous self-governing communities of Indians showed remarkably harmonious, stable, egalitarian groups run on the basis of consensus. English trader James Adair, writing of the Cherokees in 1775, declared, *Their whole constitution breathes nothing but liberty.*[21]

The egalitarian customs of native Americans did not escape the notice of the Founding Fathers of the United States. Benjamin Franklin was impressed by the mode of government of the Iroquois Confederacy, of upper New York and southern Canada. Their system of participatory democracy invested considerable authority in clan and village chiefs, and arrived at decisions on the basis of consensus. Franklin's admiration prompted him to recommend that the Thirteen Colonies take on some of their practices.[22] Property and power also concerned the political leaders of the nascent United States, particularly Thomas Jefferson. While US

---

* Canadian anthropologist Richard B. Lee, famous for his studies of Bushmen of the Kalahari over several decades, gives a picturesque example of the egalitarian approach of the Ju/'hoansi people: *When a young man kills much meat he comes to think of himself as a chief or a big man and he thinks of the rest of us as his servants or inferiors. We can't accept this... So we always speak of his meat as worthless. This way we cool his heart and make him gentle.*[20] (To be contrasted with our treatment of productive CEOs of market capitalism?)

Minister to France in the 1780s, Jefferson was struck by the poverty and inequality he saw there, and this subject continued to preoccupy him for the rest of his life. He believed it was a responsibility of government to prevent too great a concentration of power and wealth in large, often inherited landed estates. In a famous letter to James Madison, Jefferson wrote,

> *I am conscious that an equal division of property is impracticable. But the consequences of this enormous inequality producing so much misery to the bulk of mankind, legislators cannot invent too many devices for subdividing property...*

He called for higher taxation on large estates, since ... *Whenever there is in any country uncultivated lands and unemployed poor it is clear that the laws of property have been so far extended as to violate natural right.*[23]

Jefferson came, of course, from a wealthy Virginia family and benefited all his life from a privileged position, owning large estates as well as around 200 slaves. But he had nevertheless imbibed Enlightenment values; he believed in government intervention, including taxation, to ensure that property – the main source of wealth at the time – was distributed as widely as possible. No-one, he thought, had a natural right to own unlimited tracts of land, and democratic government had a responsibility to protect its citizens' interests. *The small landowners are the most precious part of a state...* Jefferson said, believing that an unfettered licence to ownership could not be compatible with individual rights. However, in spite of a degree of levelling in society since his time, and frequent expressions of the injustice of social disparities, the last forty years have seen a return to the perversion of widening inequalities. This does not now amount to a *religion*, as Matthew Arnold maintained, since the social ethos is against it, but its adherents are nevertheless resolute in their opposition to its demolition. When R. H. Tawney revived Arnold's phrase in his 1931 lectures 'Equality', he said that Arnold would have been amazed to see the persistence of inequality fifty years on – to which we can add our faith that Tawney's astonishment would be even more profound were he to return from the grave to witness today's social divisions.*

---

*   Matthew Arnold used the phrase *the religion of inequality* in a speech at the Royal

Many citizens of the United Kingdom and the United States, more especially those old enough to have witnessed the advances of the 1960s and '70s, are equally amazed at the economic and social inequalities of today. The figures are staggering: in Europe 35% of total income, and in the USA 50%, going to the top 10% of earners in 2010[25] – proportions which have been maintained in the aftermath of the financial crash when those on low incomes have been suffering particularly. Thomas Picketty identifies the core of the problem: the rate of return on capital exceeding the rate of growth of output and incomes. But can this disparity be sustained indefinitely? Not according to Picketty, who believes it will have a destabilizing effect on society: ... *capitalism generates arbitrary and unsustainable inequalities that radically undermine the meritocratic values on which democratic societies are based*.[26] President Obama also warned of a worsening social crisis. After his first administration, the worst years following the crash, he said ... *the basic bargain at the heart of our economy has frayed. ... The combined trends of increased inequality and decreasing mobility pose a fundamental threat to the American Dream, our way of life and what we stand for around the globe.* He defined inequality as ... *the defining challenge of our time.*[27] Could this assessment similarly be applied to the United Kingdom?

In February 1988 the then British Home Secretary Douglas Hurd, speaking at Tamworth on the bicentenary of the birth of Sir Robert Peel, gave an address in which he highlighted ... *the amazing social cohesion of England formed under Peel and the Victorians.* This cohesion was certainly remarkable, all the more so because of the strains in British society caused by the industrial revolution, but it is a characteristic present long after the epoch Mr Hurd was describing. Social stability and cohesion have been traditional features of English, and to some extent British identity. They are part of an inner equilibrium of the people which commentators have described,* involving a collective harmony linked to satisfaction with life's outcomes. Individuals

---

Institution in 1878. R. H. Tawney used it as the title of one of the chapters in *Equality*, the publication of his 1929 Halley Stewart Lectures.[24]

* Such as the Spanish-American philosopher George Santayana who wrote expressively about this on a visit to England during the First World War: *The Englishman establishes a sort of satisfaction and equilibrium in his inner man, and from that citadel of rightness he easily measures the value of everything that comes within his moral horizon.*[28]

are bound together by their interdependence and complementarity, although perhaps integration is now supported more by strength of tradition than by consciousness of *kind and kin*.[29] Cohesion includes a respect for legality and constitutionalism, a belief in the law as above state and above the individual. As George Orwell pointed out, this *law* may be something cruel and stupid, may even involve one law for the rich and another for the poor, but it has traditionally been seen as incorruptible[30] – a view which itself has had to withstand severe body blows in recent times. But even now, the idea that power is more important than law has not taken root. Although it has long been thought acceptable to flout laws perceived as unfair, it is still nevertheless taken for granted that the law will be respected.

Social cohesion is to some extent founded on settled ways of living, on the longevity and seeming permanence of English civilization. It is also the converse face of a well known feature of the English – that they have never troubled to define their national identity. Englishness, now uneasily promoted into a loose Britishness, has been a matter of subliminal understanding, which stood for itself – all the more reason why its future may be at risk under its metamorphosis by the dominance of neo-liberal economics and the fracturing of the body politic. The consequences of the 2016 EU referendum have left a seriously divided nation, such as elections, war, and depression have never done. Communities and families have been split along lines which are not easily defined, but the undermining of cohesion and equanimity has been the result. And since poverty and privilege are elements in the social rupture, their ramifications will have to be dealt with if some form of cohesion is to be restored. The earlier brand which developed during the nineteenth and twentieth centuries had a somewhat uncharted, implicit evolution, but was forged by wartime experience and thus an undeniable 'all-in-it-together' ethos, as well as assisted, as Anthony Burgess said, by a patience and philosophical resignation.[31] Whether this can be recreated in the face of glaring social and economic inequalities remains in serious doubt.

In the past, at times of similarly serious inequalities, other factors contributed to social stability, one of which – perhaps ironically – was a culture of patrician liberalism. It became established in the 18th century and later enabled aristocracy and gentry to maintain a dominance over society and state.[32] In spite of economic fluctuations and social divisions, paternalism allowed the elite to remain in control by, as Lawrence and

Jeanne Stone have said ... *co-opting psychologically those below.*[33] But as these authors have shown, the social integration of *those below* was maintained by a self-conscious policy arising from a sense of duty as well as from a desire to augment local prestige. Although the poor had to bear the greatest burden of taxation through the excise, the landed elite were willing to impose a land tax on themselves, and in the war years 1793–1815 accepted large increases in taxes on luxury goods. At the same time, welfare for the poor provided a wider and more humane service than elsewhere in Europe before 1834, and the elite were generous in their support of local charities: schools, hospitals and almshouses.[34] In rapidly changing times, a controlling paternalism was sustained through the nineteenth century by a promise of democratic emancipation and a share of the new affluence. Thus cohesion was preserved into the 20th century, as all classes adjusted to new economic and political realities. Recovery from the Depression, victory in war, expanding social mobility, and the *never-had-it-so-good* years of the post-war period all abetted a form of social consensus.

So, until well into the twentieth century the upper classes accepted what the Stones refer to as ... *a culture of legalistic obligation,*[35] while the middle and lower ranks of society were either accomplices or acquiescent partners in the unequal relationship. In any event, a web of relationships had been created which helped bind the disparate and potentially conflicting elements of the community into a stable social network, of which equality was not a part. Indeed, equality was not then vital for cohesion. As Douglas Hurd declared in his Tamworth speech, social cohesion is quite different from social equality; the concept of the latter is too problematic for the British, whose pragmatism has traditionally made more sense of ideas of fairness. In the Edwardian era Britain was a cohesive, strongly-knit nation, but with considerable inequality. The bonds of unity were largely concealed beneath marked social divisions, but yet were nevertheless strong, as the previous outline would imply. Although few like to accept that Britain is a deeply stratified society today, vestiges of hierarchy and deference still remain, and may be explained in terms of traces of deep-rooted paternalism and legalism. But these are constantly being overtaken by the modern ethos of rights and entitlements which has become so pervasive. And in a culture of consumerism and strident individualism the social emblems of the past are being demolished.

However, while prodigious social change may be undermining old certainties, it does not lead on naturally to greater equality in society. Governments come and go, sombre pronouncements are repeated, national expenditure continues to rise, and much wringing of hands takes place, but gross social disparities endure and their sad consequences escalate. It is not that serious inequalities in economic conditions are in principle accepted, but their continued existence means they are condoned – which amounts to the same thing. Beyond equality of opportunity there is no meaningful concept for the public in the *Anglo-Sphere* to get hold of, but there is a notion of what constitutes justice, which to the British amounts to fairness. Old Labour stalwart Roy Hattersley suggested *fair* as what he called a *gentle pseudonym for 'equal'*, which chimes with much ordinary opinion. Perceived injustice or unfairness – vague and subjective as these values may seem – mean more in Britain than estimations of theoretical equality. When, two hundred years ago, Tom Paine railed against ... *the contrast of affluence and wretchedness continually meeting and offending the eye,* he called not for equality or charity, but for justice.[36] Today, calls for justice, for those at both ends of the iniquitous economic divide, will have greater appeal than demanding charity or equality. In the collective of the nation all are demeaned by gross injustice.

The social responsibility of the upper classes, *the culture of legalistic obligation* cited above, has now in the twenty-first century worn very thin. It appears that any remaining paternalism is steadily disappearing. In fact, according to recent studies there appears to be a tendency for better-off citizens to act in anti-social ways but, strikingly, this phenomenon was not found in more equal nations. In places with more income equality like Japan, Germany and Holland, richer people are no less likely than the poor to be trusting and generous.* By drawing on different bodies of research Wilkinson and Pickett demonstrate the contrast between countries with greater and those with less income inequality in the way they treat others. ... *inequality renders whole societies less empathetic,* they declare, as that environment contributes to a loss of the feeling of all being in it together.[38] And an extensive study of 26

---

* This from a 2015 American study entitled 'High income inequality leads higher-income individuals to be less generous'.[37] The study even discovered a tendency for citizens in the US with high incomes to be less generous, but only in more unequal American states.

European nations found a significant tendency for people in the more equal ones to be more willing to help others.[39] Moreover, it appears that people in more unequal countries, irrespective of their own incomes, were less disposed to helping their fellow citizens. Evidence is gradually building to indicate the importance of the relationship between the degree of income equality in a society and its cohesion, demonstrated by its level of neighbourliness and mutual solidarity.

Fairness, solidarity, cohesion, neighbourliness – these are all desirable qualities, but which seem hard to grasp. We know when they are not there, but how to create them in their absence would be an obscure, nebulous objective. They may appear abstract characteristics unrelated to money, but it nevertheless seems that the level of income equality in a society does have a significant bearing on their prevalence. How we behave as nations and peoples, and how we relate to one another are evidently impacted by society around us and especially by how we see others – their status, income, wealth, and behaviour. And how we relate to each other is also conditioned by our view of society, our concept of what it is to live together in the same polity – our mutual coexistence. So it comes down to a question of relationships; these have a vital bearing on our attitudes and principles, and are just as important as material elements in our lives. In this materialist age, when economics is elevated almost to a religion, it is easy to underestimate the interpersonal relations which govern so much of what we do and who we are. Being rich or poor, or living in a society of severe or modest income equality, these matters are about the inter-play between different sets of people. As Marshall Sahlins said, *Poverty is not a certain small amount of goods, nor is it just a relation between means and ends; above all it is a relation between people. Poverty is a social status.*[40] – Just as equality is a matter of status.

Another difficulty here is one of perception. Though paternalism has all but dwindled in this more classless age, a degree of cohesion and solidarity among and between the different levels of society has hung on, a legacy of bygone ages. But it continually has to struggle against the neo-liberal spirit that is weakening the social glue which hitherto bound people. In 1940 George Orwell referred to the *emotional unity* which he thought held the nation together by *an invisible chain,* in spite of the class-bound nature of the country.[41] This has not entirely disappeared, even if there is now little unity of outlook and purpose, and the new elite have little interest in reassuring the 'lower orders'. The changed environment brought on by Brexit and the revived socio-economic inequalities are aspects that many citizens have yet to get to grips with conceptually. They do not know how to address the altered national landscape; there is no theoretical reasoning which would justify opposition.* And all this has crept up on the populace over the last forty years, while families have raised their children, the ambitious have got on with earning money and feathering their nests, and inequality has widened. It was not supposed to be like this, but in Britain in particular many have not yet adjusted to the new reality that, contrary to Tolstoy's assertion over a century ago, the nation is far from well run. There remains the illusion that it is progressively modern, but beneath the waterline much has changed.

Some years ago essayist and commentator Tom Nairn declared that the triumph of the modern industrial state ... *lay in evolving a system which both Dukes and dustmen could like, or at least find tolerable.*[44] This had to do with a degree of common identity which contributed to national cohesion. For the last forty years the dukes, duchesses, dustmen and women have moved progressively apart. But in any society there is a need for some form of common purpose – some kind of *fraternity*, the late Tony Judt said.[45] However pluralistic a community becomes there has to be a binding force in the sense of some mutual identity and interdependence. Otherwise it can hardly be termed a community. The increasing dominance of market forces in vernacular life threatens this very fraternity. Above all, after the divisive process of Brexit major cleavages have appeared in British society, within and between families and communities, particularly over concepts of national destiny. The widening socio-economic inequalities merely exacerbate these divisions. Transcendental occasions such as the 2012 London Olympics and important international cricket and football rivalries do create social bridges, and may help rally the nation in opposition to *the other*, but common purpose and solidarity require more than chauvinistic sport and abiding materialism to unite national sentiments.

Today's neo-liberal regimes are retreating from social cohesion. By

---

* In any case, as has already been mentioned, the British are not good at theory or ideology. Orwell expressed it as ... *the lack of philosophical faculty, the absence in nearly all Englishmen of any need for an ordered system of thought or even for the use of logic.*[42] Another interesting slant on this was provided in the 1930s by a German commentator: *A great many things are thinkable in England that would be impossible elsewhere, and the logically inconceivable is none the less perfectly possible if only it stands the test of practice.*[43]

the very nature of their fundamentalist market policies they implicitly deny the importance of the collective, in stark contradiction to their occasional warm words on community. They foster division and segregation, the sense of living in separate communities, so that we ... *confine our advantages to ourselves and our families: the pathology of the age*, as Tony Judt termed it.[46] If society were not so socially and economically unequal such trends would not develop; there would not be the need or the desire for them. For inequality of income is the demon, around which there is so much prejudice, and so much in the way of rhetoric and polemics. As outlined above, the inequalities found in some rich nations are associated with considerable social dysfunction of different kinds; the greater the inequality the deeper and more prevalent are a wide range of social problems. This is not to call for complete equality – as neo-liberals often dishonestly attribute to opponents. But a community needs an *equality of being* to maintain a common culture (which does not mean an equal culture), as Raymond Williams said sixty years ago.[47] He believed a genuinely common national experience was essential for a society to survive, and an equality of being was vital for this.

> *The inequality that is evil is inequality which denies the essential quality of being. Such inequality, in any of its forms, ... rejects, depersonalizes, degrades in grading, other human beings. On such practice a structure of cruelty, exploitation, and the crippling of human energy is easily raised.*[48]

Williams believed that there are many inequalities – such as those of skills or abilities – which do not harm this vital equality. Discrimination as regards distinctions of merit or value does not point to inequality of being. However, the inequalities which are not acceptable are those which lead to segregation and domination. It is these which have mushroomed over recent years, with the result that social and economic divisions – notably in the *Anglo-Sphere* – have implicitly denied essential parities, and thus vitiated a true common culture. The destructive effects of extreme market pressures have riven community and undermined equality of being, because the market has taken precedence over that latter. A hundred years ago, a grudging acceptance of the *status quo* was accompanied by a multitude of solidarities; now the strident message is that all rewards and consolations are embodied in affluence, the new social ethic. Now, inequality, as well as – indirectly – poverty and unemployment, must be tackled in its proper central role, not half-ignored as a bi-product of modern economics affecting society peripherally. Only by correcting income inequalities and social status will a sense of shared identity be re-established. This is not the same as the shared goal of individual affluence within the framework of a materialistic way of life – the rainbow's end of today's damaged, atomised societies.

There has traditionally been much discussion in philosophy and in politics of the relationship between equality and liberty. Right-wing tracts have tended to warn of the dangers to liberty of trying to engineer greater social and economic equality in society. Even some centre-left voices have concurred: writing in the '90s, Will Hutton said, in a section entitled 'Inequality hurts us all',

> *However effectively equality can be created it is always at the expense of individual liberty. The wealth and freedom of action of the better-off are qualified by state intervention, constraining their liberty in a vain attempt to promote equality.*[49]

This is akin to Walter Bagehot's fear in the 1860s that Britain might catch the *French disease*, whereby liberty would be sacrificed to equality. However, much recent research has confounded this fear. There is now considerable evidence, particularly in works like *The Spirit Level* and *The Inner Level*,* that quality of life as well as liberty are enhanced by greater overall economic equality. In the latter work, in what they call one of their more surprising findings, Wilkinson and Pickett give examples of how inequality impacts the population as a whole. They say that the well-educated in society, with good jobs and incomes, would be better off in a number of ways if they lived, with those same jobs and incomes, in a more equal society.[50] For example, they would be likely to live longer, would less likely become victims of violence, and their children would do better at school and be less likely to develop serious drug problems.

These findings are crucially important, as well as possibly surprising to many. They are beginning to be replicated widely and have serious

---

* Both by Richard Wilkinson and Kate Pickett, cited above.

implications for public policy and for all of us. The evidence is gathering that even the materially well-off would benefit from a more equal society, and as such would not see their liberty curtailed, which opponents of levelling usually claim would be the result. The latter betrays the common, limited understanding of the relationship between the individual and the wider society – as was outlined in Chapter 2. The issue is ... *not so much whether more unequal countries do or do not have more poor people, but the way larger income differences across a society immerse everyone more deeply in issues of status competition and insecurity.*[51] It turns out that the greater interdependence of the modern world reaches deep into societies, so that their overall configuration has implications for both rich and poor – in some cases positively for both at the same time. Thus, in more equal societies the data shows that community life is stronger, trust in others is greater, while status anxiety and violence both decrease.[52] So by limiting material differences, well-being could be improved throughout society, and agency enhanced for all. However, if liberty is extended only for the better-off – by tax cuts, status enhancement, and increased rights – the greater inequality which ensues will be at the expense of the less well-off, and may well rebound against the rich later on. A more divided society has repercussions on us all.

This thesis is diametrically opposed by many – and not just neo-liberals – in a free market economy. They resolutely cling to the empty notion of *trickle-down*, lauding the supposedly positive contribution of the well-off, the so-called wealth creators, to society as a whole. However, we now know that this is not what is meant by the interconnectedness of modern developed nations; there are deeper and, to some, paradoxical affiliations between the different segments of society. If the quality of life of the most affluent can be enhanced by reducing income disparities as a whole, then where does that leave the renowned *invisible hand*? But these connections, already emerging some years ago,* are now becoming more widely accepted as a result of recent analysis, though still resisted by much of the political Right, which will eventually have to yield to the new reality. For, to reiterate, it is not just that gross material inequalities have a negative impact on communal relations and social harmony; it is now clear that they result in a host of

---

* A whole generation ago some of these relationships were becoming known. In 1994 the British Medical Journal reported that ... *there is evidence to suggest that national infant mortality rises if the rich get richer while the real incomes of the poor remain constant.*[53]

economic, social and medical problems for ALL strata of society. Deliberations on the interaction between liberty and equality are becoming redundant; extending the latter does not have predictable consequences for the former. But in current market economies, enriching the better-off on the misguided assumption that it will assist the poor means that the welfare, and indeed liberty, of all classes are being sacrificed to a mythical ideology.

Thus the theoretical relationship between equality and liberty can be left to philosophers. The great Isaiah Berlin spent time pondering the question before accepting that perfect equality is not compatible with perfect liberty.[54] This was one facet of his view that the ideal of true perfection was not merely unattainable but inconceivable, and this is how we should approach the relationship in the complex, practical, everyday world. Of course perfect liberty would be deeply anti-social, and is for that reason alone inconceivable. Extending liberty for the better-off will adversely impact the poor, whereas curtailing it can have beneficial social effects on both rich and poor – though much work will need to be done to convince the well-off that their interests lie in that direction. And this involves pragmatic politics, not theorizing. Will Hutton's assertions that *The distribution of income and living standards in society should be left to the market: here as elsewhere there is only trouble in store for those that meddle with market processes...*[55] was the accepted view a generation ago. But important advocate as he is for a fairer society, Hutton will be aware that it was the lack of *meddling* during the 1980s and '90s which led on to today's gross inequalities. The hands-off approach to markets vastly enriched the better-off, but did not make them happier, more secure or more socially responsible. In the landscape of today government interposition is required to deal with the resulting inequalities, so that quality of life can be improved for both rich and poor.

The idea of equality has excited advocates of many ideologies, not just socialism; there is no reason to undermine its inspiration as an ideal to energize peoples towards a more humane social environment. This is nothing to do with a faith that human beings are equal in character and attributes – what R. H. Tawney called a *romantic illusion* – and people have a right to their own personal disparities. And there is no point in searching for unrealistic, arbitrary extremes. After all, as Herman Daly and John Cobb declared,

> *Complete equality is the collectivist's denial of true differences in community. Unlimited inequality is the individualist's denial of interdependence and true solidarity in community.*[56]

But accepting existing inequalities, which help generate so many social pathologies as evidenced above, will only result in further internal division and in the development of even greater security resources devoted to protecting what the 'haves' have acquired. Reducing inequalities is not only socially just as well as economically functional, but can raise many of the indices which define the so-called good society (more of which will be outlined later). And thus R. H. Tawney's words almost a century ago are particularly appropriate:

> *... while their natural endowments differ profoundly, it is the mark of a civilized society to aim at eliminating such inequalities as have their source, not in individual differences, but in its own organization, and that individual differences, which are a source of social energy, are more likely to ripen and find expression if social inequalities are ... diminished.*[57]

The iniquities of severe social and economic divisions in developed societies are deplored by many sections of the populace. Beyond that, attitudes vary according to political views, how poverty and disadvantage are seen, and to opinions on welfare and dependence. But there is a general understanding that opportunities exist to rise from humble beginnings, and with determination and hard work to build a successful life. Famous examples of so-called *self-made* women, but mostly men, help sustain the idea that with single-minded dedication the upwardly-mobile path is there for us all, and our failure to take it is down to our own inadequacies or simply complacency. The focus on individualism puts the onus on us to make the best of our lot, and not blame society or its economic system for our lack of progress – this being entirely congruent with neo-liberalism's acceptance of the inevitability of the gulf between rich and poor. So although social inequalities are there for all to see, some belief in equality of opportunity has survived in most modern economies, despite the reality of severely restricted social mobility in many of them. The actual extent of opportunity in the real world certainly does not match its popular image; the subject is still seen through the lens of the optimistic 1950s and '60s, while the rhetoric of free market capitalism is there to sustain the perception – now more of a myth than ever.

In some respects societies in the *Anglo-Sphere* now have a situation which can be summed up as the worst of both worlds. For while social mobility is limited, and equality of opportunity largely a mirage, nevertheless their theories continue to be advanced for all to exploit. And in this theoretical scenario those who do not take advantage of the opportunities available are seen as complicit in their own failure. This was not the social picture in earlier times, when class privilege and old money meant that ability and intelligence were not synonymous with position in society. Then, it was not claimed that status was deservedly earned through talent or virtue. But where there is a belief that career opportunities are indeed open to those with education and ability, then responsibility appears to rest with the individual, however unjust this may be. Britain has long been a place where reality and illusion have sat side by side. For, what Will Hutton calls the *people's touching faith in social mobility* is almost entirely unjustified. He cites one intergenerational mobility study comparing boys from different social backgrounds born in 1958 and 1970, indicating how privilege and disadvantage had become even more entrenched by the latter date.[58] This regression flies in the face of the myth of mobility, even while many still cling to the fallacies it represents.* In fact, research has shown that social mobility is related to income inequality, in that it is reduced in places where such inequality is greatest.[60]

While the post-World War II period was noted for movement towards a more open, egalitarian society with greater social mobility, progress here gradually petered out over two or three decades, and steady retrenchment took place. Privilege reasserted itself, so that while it may not have been based mainly on class, it depended just as much as previously on money, connections and – increasingly – education at the right schools. When in the early 2000s former Labour minister Alan Milburn produced his report on social mobility, it provided a striking indictment of how little had been achieved in creating an open-access society.[61] The twenty-first century dawned with top positions in the law, civil service and finance still mainly in the hands of the privately educated scions of wealthy families; the upwardly mobile, grammar-schooled children of

---

*   Nobel laureate Joseph Stiglitz cites evidence from the Brookings Institution in the USA which shows that only 6% of Americans born into the bottom fifth of income earners manage to move into the top fifth.[59]

the middle classes made only limited inroads into this exclusive world. This will not see great change until opportunities are more equitable, but since most personal wealth is still obtained through inheritance, the autonomy of families and individuals is circumscribed in that, as Geoff Hodgson pointed out, *The unequal distribution of inherited wealth imposes a pattern of choice upon succeeding generations that is largely beyond their control.*[62] Thus, while all are forced to breathe the bogus atmosphere of inclusivity and opportunity, the Two (at least) Nation society of Victorian repute is recreated in defiance of basic national aspirations.

Perhaps even more important than privilege or inherited wealth in mature, developed economies is now education, which can also be said to circumscribe the opportunities of families and individuals. Far from being a route out of poverty, deprivation or low status, it has become a limitation on the potential of many. The well-off professional classes can ensure that their children receive the best education at private or top state schools – working the system as regards family connections and residence location. They can also afford the extra tutoring which may be necessary for their offspring to gain entry to prestigious universities, as well as placement at the valuable internships ideal for raising employment prospects. In the information age, good university degrees and the shrewd awareness of how to exploit them are serious advantages for professional advancement. Increasingly wealth and education go together, as white-collar families get richer as well as ever more astute at navigating the educational system; a new form of privilege is passed down from parents to children, consolidating status in a new educated class – an invaluable inheritance not liable to taxation. Meanwhile, those excluded from the knowledge economy will more and more be consigned to menial employment, often in service industries, without much prospect of high earnings (as might have been the case in the previous industrial age) or the chance of advancing their own children.

The result of these trends is that in the current employment market education has the effect of accentuating, and even widening the class divide. Higher education in particular helps to solidify status and rank, provided that the degree qualification is used to further one's career path.* In this way there is an increasing concentration at the top of

---

* In Britain at least, where close on half the school population goes on to university, the qualifications obtained there are by no means equal. Inferior class degrees do not always enhance employment prospects, while many degree subjects are less marketable in the jobs arena.

society of an elite, almost an aristocracy of the rich and educated, a self-reinforcing class with little likelihood of any downward social mobility. Meanwhile, a large proportion of the rest of society is left behind, without the wherewithal to raise themselves in an education system, unless they have particularly dedicated, ambitious parents and considerable luck.* Many of this *left-behind*, excluded majority formed part of the swelling numbers of Brexiteers and Trump supporters in 2016. But apart from the fact that there is no equal starting point for the different classes, this system may appear to some to be meritocratic, conferring advancement on the bright and educated. However, it has been called a *Meritocracy Trap*. In a book describing the American situation Daniel Markovits portrays merit as a false rationalization constructed to justify unfair exploitation of their class position.[64] Whereas once, one's position in the social hierarchy was accepted as unchanging, almost God-given, today's privileged class status – and the chasm separating it from those below – is increasingly being justified on the basis of due reward for perceived merit.

Meritocracy may represent a trap, but if so it is one in which its beneficiaries are supremely content to be caught. Their status within it has apparently been won through talent and hard work, and any claim that a privileged background played a part in their success would need to be quickly repudiated, lest it undermine their proud achievements. *Education*, says Kenan Malik, *has come to be a marker of the values one holds and the place one possesses in society.*[65] It is almost as if we are acting out a version of Michael Young's dystopian satire *The Rise of the Meritocracy*, in which

> Now that people are classified by ability, the gap between the classes has inevitably become wider. Gone are the days when ... clever members of the upper classes had as much in common with clever members of the lower classes as they did with stupid members of their own.[66]

As for the lower classes, Young writes, they know they have had every

---

* In fact the role of parents can be crucial in access to higher education, particularly as regards family income. In the United States research has shown that the chances of young people going on to higher education are largely determined by parental income. There, children of the poorest parents in the 2010s had only a 20 to 30% chance of getting to university. This increased in a steady, linear fashion to the point where the probability of children of the richest parents attending university was 90%.[63]

chance, because they are tested again and again (a familiar scenario?), to the point where they are obliged to recognize their inferior status – *not as in the past because they were denied opportunity, but because they are inferior. For the first time in human history the inferior man has no ready buttress for his self-regard.*[67] This was Young's fictitious end point which he contrasted with an imaginary situation in the early twenty-first century when ... *Educational injustice enabled people to preserve their illusions; inequality of opportunity fostered the myth of human equality.*[68] Are we now engaged in a similar historical process to the one Young depicts: *The Rise of the Elite?**

Today there is ambivalence as to whether or not the status and high earnings of those at the top of society are deserved. A common awareness has emerged that their levels of remuneration are very often excessive, especially with regard to executives in the finance sector who appeared to survive the financial crisis unscathed. And when the salaries of rank and file workers have seen only stagnation, it is easy to understand the resentment of those with high, and rising earnings. This was certainly not the case in Young's fictional Britain of 2034, where if someone ... *fought his way up the educational ladder and received a high salary for doing it, why then he probably deserved it.*[69] Such faith in meritocracy endorsed the social gulf between classes, and the salary differentials involved, in a way which doesn't (yet?) exist today. What is clear now is that high earners have substantial incomes and corresponding status as a fulsome *buttress for their self-regard*, whether deserved or not, and in a great many cases it appears they do believe they deserve it. People at the top often think they are there by right, because of their value to their organisation. It is easy for them to fall in with the idea that they are successful products of equality of opportunity in a dynamic free market capitalism which distributes its largesse to those *beneath* them through its *invisible hand*; people at the bottom are almost as easily persuaded that their low status is rightly due to their own inadequacy – neither of which is empirically sound.

But meritocratic values do play a role in appearing to vindicate

---

*   It is worth remembering that one of the key indications of attitudes to both Donald Trump and Brexit is education.

inequalities in today's societies, in the top echelons of which are those who have every reason to subscribe to them. French economist Thomas Piketty cites a study of the late 1980s based on hundreds of in-depth interviews with upper middle class high earners in various cities of France and the USA.[70] They were asked about their careers, how they saw they place in society and what differentiated them from other social groups. A key finding of the study was the way this elite class chose mainly to emphasise their abilities and moral qualities, using terms like *rigour, patience*, and *effort*, as well as *tolerance* and *kindness*. Piketty also points to the many American TV series with *super-qualified characters*, and based on values endorsing meritocratic hierarchies. Our own common sense as well as research evidence can tell us that where people end up in life is far more unpredictable than Michael Young's famous formula, IQ + Effort = Merit, would suggest; chance plays a much more important role in our outcomes than the well-off are usually prepared to admit. In fact, Wilkinson and Pickett maintain that:

> *Rather than different endowments of talents determining position in the hierarchy, it is much nearer the truth to say that <u>position in the hierarchy determines abilities, interests and talents</u>.*[71] *(My emphasis.)*

Any cursory analysis of our own situations reveals the random twists and turns of life's fortunes, and the key role played by the starting point of our home background.

Nevertheless, many at the top of society persist in wrapping themselves in the elitist garb of superiority to rationalize their status, claiming it is merited through their having taken up available opportunities. Those who have risen from modest beginnings often laud a system of equality of opportunity which their rise appears to exemplify. At the same time, many will suggest that the fact that more do not similarly climb up through society's ranks is evidence of the sheer difficulty of achieving greater equality. Prime Minister Boris Johnson is evidently one of these; in a speech in 2013 he stressed that economic equality would never be possible, citing the low IQ of a major segment of the population as a contributory factor.[72] He acknowledged the intense competition which he believed accentuated inequality, bearing in mind, he said, that human beings are ... *very far from equal in raw ability, if not spiritual worth*.[73] Johnson displayed the ignorance typical of many, apparently oblivious of the far greater equality which some societies – notably in Scandinavia and Japan – have achieved. He then added the tendentious conceit that ... *some measure of inequality is essential for the spirit of envy and keeping up with the Joneses that is, like greed, a valuable spur to economic activity.*[74] An informed appreciation of how society functions has moved on from this simplistic prejudice and, one might say, Johnson should know better.*

But of course many of the Prime Minister's ideological persuasion wish to have it both ways: they like to tell themselves, and us, that equality of opportunity exists, while implying that our inherent diverse attributes will ensure that an equal society remains an impossible dream. So they may continue blithely to pay lip service to the notion, feeling secure in the faith that equality will not be brought about. Some neo-liberals, though, like their late arch-guru Milton Friedman, have taken a bolder approach by declaring that in any case equality of opportunity, like personal equality before God, should not be interpreted literally.[76] Friedman saw it as an ideal which by its very nature cannot be fully realised – which of course effectively undermines claims free market fundamentalism may profess to promote social justice. But whenever prominent figures emerge who have risen in the social hierarchy from humble origins, they are taken by the Right as exemplars of equality of opportunity – proof that opportunity exists, perhaps, but not of course that it is in any way equal. Similarly, Friedman, at an early stage of the neo-liberal project, accepted social mobility as alive and well, taking the rise in social position of *various less privileged groups* as indicating that obstacles to progress *were by no means insurmountable,* since they were availing themselves of opportunities.[77] One might say that Friedman was easily satisfied, but this illustrates the difficulty of measuring the degree of equality of opportunity which actually prevails in society.

Degrees of social mobility, as well as the extent of take-up of socio-economic opportunities, are quite variable across different societies. One reason for this is the contrasting starting points for individuals, which denote playing fields that are far from level at the formative stage of their development. Whatever plausible rhetoric is used to uphold equality of opportunity, it cannot be said to exist if young people set

---

* Numerous economists have pointed out the negative effect inequality can have on economic growth and its role in promoting instability. Nobel laureate Joseph Stiglitz, for example, says, *Even the International Monetary Fund, not known for its radical economic stances, has come to recognize the adverse effects of inequality on economic performance.*[75]

out on life's journey from such vastly different family origins and early experiences. Of course, character and personal responsibility play a part, but those whose starting point is poverty and severe disadvantage are ill-equipped to compete with their more fortunate peers; they will be unable to seize opportunities even if they recognize their existence. So they will rarely manage to achieve parity at a later stage, particularly in a neo-liberal, winner-take-all culture. But there are dangers in policy makers extolling the tangible rewards of equality of opportunity, since it implies an obligation on their part to try to remove obstacles to opportunity, such as large disparities of inherited wealth, unequal educational provision, poor housing conditions and even – one might say – nutritional disadvantages. As Ha-Joon Chang has pointed out, without some equality of outcome, at least in terms of parental income, the poor are simply unable to take advantage of opportunities which do exist.[78]

Thus we arrive at the anomalous situation where it is highly unlikely that opportunity will be evened up until there is greater economic equality in the first place. But where will the affirmative action to further such an objective come from? There is certainly no appetite for this on the part of most political parties, while neo-liberals would be ideologically against it – since, like Boris Johnson, they see inequality (erroneously) as a *valuable spur to economic activity*. So, in this situation, how can we assess equality of opportunity, particularly as many individuals are unable to take advantage of its promise? How can opportunity be extended, and how will we know when this has been achieved? Do we need to evaluate whether people have reached their true potential, and how could this be done? To take the case of gender parity, what proportion of key positions in political life, in business, the law, etc., do women need to occupy before they are seen to have achieved an acceptable degree of equality with men? For, evidence of equal opportunity is far too nebulous and variable to be a satisfactory indication of progress. Indeed, the only real sign that true opportunity exists is, in fact, if it is exploited, thus allowing human potential to be realised and achieving greater social equality in the process. Under current conditions this is simply not going to happen. No, the only way for equality of opportunity to be judged effectively, and to be promoted, is by extending equality of outcome.

The accepted view in modern, developed nations is that education is the key to bringing out the best in the young and raising them to be productive citizens able to make a constructive contribution to their families and to society. And part of this notion is the belief that if we provide people with equal opportunities, and encourage them to realise their potential, we will in the process contribute to a more egalitarian society. It is usually thought that beyond eliminating poverty and ensuring certain basic standards of living it is not the role of the state to engineer greater equality, but that an equality of opportunity – as well as serving those who take advantage of it – will be conducive to this end. It now turns out that we have been getting these ideas entirely the wrong way round. For, paradoxical as this may sound, the only route to improving social justice, to affording the young some parity of opportunity in life to make the best of their talents and potential, is for society to be much more equal in the first place, above all in terms of income, living standards and status. We should forget about affirmative action: trying to correct disadvantage by increasing numbers of poorer students at top universities, for example, or mandating quotas for racial or gender disparities in boardrooms. No, it is not opportunity which needs to be equalised in order to produce a fairer, more just, more egalitarian society; it is a more equal society which will help bring about greater equality of opportunity for all.

When 13-year-old Andrew Carnegie left Scotland with his family to emigrate to America, following the failure of Chartism in 1848, he was a poor, barely-educated teenager but with immense determination and ambition. His rise from cotton mill worker earning $1.20 a week to huge wealth as owner of the world's largest steel manufacturing company was due to intelligence and drive. However, his renown today stems not only from his prodigious philanthropy, but from a less salubrious reputation as a ruthless steel magnate responsible for cut-throat business practices and violent strike-breaking. And while his widespread 'good works' can be applauded, one would prefer that the socio-economic circumstances surrounding Carnegie's rise had not existed, so that his struggle from poverty had not been required. If Carnegie had been born more recently into a relatively egalitarian society, without the need for his family to emigrate in order to better their circumstances, he could still have found an opening for his energy and ambition – but from a much happier starting point.* And a future social environment of greater equality will still afford ample opportunity for those with unusual energy, inventiveness and ambition to make something more of themselves, to raise their sights above the conventional and the mundane. We should remember that for the few exceptional figures who, like Carnegie, have risen from poverty to wealth and prominence, there will be many thousands more who find it impossible to escape the handicap of their blighted origins.

Were this not the case, and societies were generally more equal, there might well be a much narrower focus on social mobility. The need to rise in the social scale would be far less relevant where disparities of status, wealth and income were more limited. In fact, the whole question of moving up or down socially would assume a different significance if the gap in income and status between those at the top and bottom of society were much reduced. The potential distance of social travel would be far smaller, and consequently attention would cease to centre on *mobility*; movement as such just wouldn't be an important preoccupation. Emphasis could then rest with questions of personal fulfilment, making the most of one's abilities, education and potential, and mapping out individual and career paths to maximize life's satisfactions – enterprises so often ill-fated where the departure point is poverty and disadvantage. After all, the concept of social mobility has meaning mainly in unequal, stratified societies where, because of the sad contrasts in standards of living, people need its promise as a vital aspiration. We are accustomed – even encouraged – to compare ourselves with others on different rungs of the social ladder. A point of bitter irony here is that more unequal countries tend to have lower social mobility, Britain and the USA being notable examples.** In both cases social mobility has fallen over the last forty years, precisely the period when they have become more unequal.

As in so many respects in this work, perception here is crucial, and just as relevant as the facts of the matter. Today, how we see our standard of living depends on that of others around us, as well as on those further up and down the social scale, and our opinions are conditioned by these relationships. In earlier times the tendency of the poor would have been to discount the huge differences between themselves and the better-off in society – and not just because the latter's lifestyles would

---

* In his The Gospel of Wealth Carnegie wrote, ...*the emigrant is the capable, energetic, ambitious, <u>discontented</u> man.* (My emphasis.)

** This relates to intergenerational income mobility – the income of parents when a child is born compared to the child's income at the age of 30.[79]

not have been readily visible to them. It would have been unusual to condemn the social disparities between the aristocracy and the peasantry when the class system appeared to be fixed and immutable, almost ordained by God.* But one outcome of the Enlightenment was a change in our view of the human condition. From this has developed a focus on the individual and his/her inexhaustible potential, so that today our whole social ethos – enhanced by education, media and government – encourages us to make comparisons with those beyond ourselves. Meanwhile, an unending stream of comparative statistics from official and non-governmental sources feeds our propensity to differentiate ourselves, raising expectations as to what kind of life might be possible – expectations which in the *Anglo-Sphere* will so often be betrayed by the inflexibility of its extreme free market system. And so major social inequalities become ever more firmly embedded, even while they become harder to justify or explain away.

It is characteristic of more unequal countries that people spend even more time looking around and comparing themselves with others. Judging by the research evidence, status and the income differences which highlight it have a major effect on people's lives, influencing how they value themselves. More glaring income disparities make differences in status more significant, and impact a person's self-worth. As Marshall Sahlins pointed out (see p. 333 above), inequality as well as poverty are matters of status. Concerns regarding how we are seen by others – the so-called *social-evaluative threat* – is, according to Wilkinson and Pickett, now one of the main burdens on people in rich countries, more especially so where inequality is greater. The threat is measured in terms of stress, anxiety and depression, as well as in worse physical health.[81] Symptoms of stress and social anxiety have become much more prevalent in places like Britain and the US than in the 1950s and '60s.** But it must be emphasised here that in spite of the degree of hardship which is still present in the more unequal societies, the impact of inequalities on citizens as regards their place in community is just as important as poverty and material deprivation as such. In this respect the degrading, corrosive effects of inequality are having serious consequences on

---

* *Princes or kings are simply a different category of human to which you cannot aspire by the definition of your society,* Oliver James points out.[80]

** Wilkinson and Pickett cite significant research highlighting these issues: 1) a study at Kings College, London, found teenagers in 2006 had much higher levels of serious emotional problems than 20 years earlier, and 2) American research indicated that the average child there in the 1980s reported more anxiety than child psychiatric patients in the 1950s.[82]

quality of life in countries which overall have never been so materially well-off.

So nations with great disparities of income experience a wide, complex range of effects, many of which do not immediately appear related to material circumstances. More unequal societies, regardless of their level of macro-economic wealth, become more fragmented as social distances widen. As Wilkinson and Pickett indicate ... *participation in community life declines with increased inequality... due to ... the increased social evaluative threat: people withdraw from social life as they find it more stressful.*[83] The same authors point out that there is also a close correlation in Europe between income inequality and the degree of participation in civic affairs; on a steady gradient, belonging to groups and clubs of many different kinds is noticeably lower in more unequal societies.[84] People thus have a tendency to withdraw into themselves, worried about appearances, and therefore become less neighbourly. But feeling unable to take part in normal activities consigns one to a humiliating social exclusion, in that it marks one as inferior in the eyes of others – and often in one's own. A report of such experience has shown that in Britain the most socially excluded groups are ten times more likely to die early than people in the general population.[85] The lead author of the study commented that the disparities exposed *something toxic in our society*. Excluded people were more likely to be murdered or commit suicide, as well as to die from accidents, cancers, and infectious diseases.*

Drawing parallels with others is a natural tendency of human beings. However, in the present social environment in countries with more extreme free market systems much greater personal investment is being concentrated in one's status and level of income. As a result, social anxiety at all levels of society – including the wealthiest – will be higher where income inequalities are greater.[86] And in a rich, developed economy – supposedly one homogeneous polity and increasingly a common culture – we are unlikely, as was once common, to discount glaring disparities. They prevent us from coming together and signify that we are far from being *in this* as a collective. It has been said that

---

* This certainly bodes ill for the victims of the current Coronavirus pandemic, in terms of the numbers of various excluded groups in Britain who succumb to the disease. At the same time, as the proportion of the British population living alone continues to increase (presently at over 10%) there will be implications for those whose vulnerability will be accentuated by social exclusion.

resentment and envy are more likely to be provoked by those of our own small circle who manage to rise beyond us in status and income. But these are largely harmless sentiments, which perhaps say more about us as individuals than the socio-economic system by which we live. In a fairly egalitarian society, one at ease with itself, they certainly need not cause the heightened anxieties found in today's rich but grossly unequal economies, where status and income have become so intrinsic to self-worth; the smaller, less meaningful differences of status will not result in social exclusion and degradation for those at the bottom of society.

For this has to be the direction of travel: to make our lives less in thrall to a primitive fight for economic survival and getting on – the lot of so many in today's more unequal nations. After all, while this struggle is iniquitous for those at the bottom of the economic heap, it does not have salutary effects on the better off either. In what are seen as meritocracies, the incapacity of some to free themselves from poverty and deprivation appears to confirm to the rich that they are responsible for their own predicament. Because of the social and economic divisions in neo-liberal regimes, prejudicial attitudes are engendered towards the less well-off which would not exist were egalitarianism the norm; there is less and less appreciation of what it means to be at the foot of society. Eldar Shafir and colleagues have written about the psychology of scarcity, the way it...

> *... captures the mind. ... (it) is more than just the displeasure of having very little. It changes how we think. It imposes itself on our minds... making us ... less insightful, less controlled.*[87]

The better-off will rarely have experienced true poverty, but one of its less discussed consequences is a legacy of cognitive impoverishment, in that being poor has a major impact on the psychology of coping. It alters the capacity to deal with one's predicament. Shafir stresses that *... people who don't do things well when they are poor do things much better when they are less poor.*[88]

Social studies often point to the desire for more control over one's life, one's time, one's workplace practices and conditions. However, one of the effects of extreme free market capitalism on the poor is a degree of induced helplessness, a feeling that no matter what action is taken it will make no difference to the outcome – a total contrast with the sense of enhanced agency derived from wealth and power. But the well-off will mostly have little conception of the mindset which comes with not having enough. George Orwell understood it well since, although from the upper classes himself, he saw the reality of poverty with his own eyes in 1930s Lancashire. One of its *peculiar evils*, he wrote, is that ... *the less money you have, the less inclined you feel to spend it on wholesome food*[89] – an attitude for which poorer people have been blamed more recently. And his following comment would also be familiar to many today:

> *When you are unemployed, which is to say when you are underfed, harassed, bored, and miserable, you don't <u>want</u> to eat dull, wholesome food. You want something a little bit 'tasty'. ... <u>That</u> is how your mind works when you are at the P.A.C. level.*[90] *(P.A.C. – The Public Assistance Committees responsible for poor relief in the 1930s.)*

But judging by the resourcefulness of the working classes in the 1930s, such as the *scrambling for coal* from moving trains which Orwell witnessed, feelings of impotence or learned helplessness, so common today, were not always induced by poverty. No doubt some comparative *discounting* was still in evidence in poor communities then.

However in the modern era, when the gulf in living standards between rich and poor is so conspicuous, deprivation can be truly debilitating, effectively narrowing the mental 'bandwidth' of those concerned. The greater the degree of inequality in society, the more important money becomes as a signifier for status and value, while shame and opprobrium become attached to those who demonstrate their lack of it. Thus a vicious circle ensues whereby, as deprivation becomes entrenched, the victims become less and less capable of coping with it. And this is exacerbated by exclusion from access and participation in the public sphere which accompanies it. Zygmunt Bauman summed up the meaning of poverty as *a social and psychological condition*, which can be judged *... by the standards of decent life practised by any given society. ... Poverty means being excluded from whatever passes for a 'normal' life.*[91] Pronouncements by the authorities, especially on the Right, or by the better-off, rarely take account of these realities, and especially of the psychology of poverty and exclusion. Their claims that meritocracy can be an answer to this situation display their lack of understanding and outdated faith in a discredited idea. A humane society cannot make progress on the basis of perpetual social divisiveness, leaving the welfare of its citizens to the random workings of vacuous free market theories of meritocracy, *trickle-down*, or even to the wishful fruits of future economic growth.

However, the psychology of those at the bottom of society has not been a focus of government. It was certainly not a priority of Labour ministers in the early years of the new century. In fact, the emphasis then seemed to be mostly on the rich – various cabinet ministers talking up the virtues of the new money makers. Peter Mandelson famously admitted being *intensely relaxed* about people getting *filthy rich* which, even though followed by the proviso ... *as long as they pay their taxes*, did not go down well with those struggling to feed their families. Then there was John Hutton's comment in 2008 when Business Secretary: ... *rather than questioning whether huge salaries are morally justified, we should celebrate the fact that people can be enormously successful in this country.*[92] The irresponsibility of the *enormously successful* bankers, then in the process of precipitating the financial crash, highlighted such crass, specious, irrelevant remarks. But then eulogizing the wealthy fits alongside the misleading faith in the theory of meritocracy. Whether the riches are gained through productive activities leading to an over-remunerated, *hypermeritocratic* elite, or by *rentier* capitalism in what Thomas Piketty calls a *hyperpatrimonial* society, they both lead to a supremely unequal distribution of income.[93] Economies with neo-liberal policies tend to have the worst-case scenario – a combination of the two.

So, contrary to all that has been said and published about the malign effects of severe social and income inequalities, there appears little appetite on the part of policy makers actively to reduce them. Whether they are modified somewhat, or remain much the same, and regardless of their extreme consequences which come to light, in both the UK and the USA the national moods are not sufficiently strong to call for government action to eradicate them. And besides, active, interventionist policies are often thought inappropriate *meddling*, counterproductive and contrary to neo-liberal, *laissez-faire* norms. It is not that attitudes are dismissive of inequality; the British, at least, appear suspicious of it. The results of a 2018 study showed that more than half (55%) of respondents thought that to be a fair society disparities in living standards should be *small*, though 53% believed large differences of income were acceptable *to reward talent and effort*.⁹⁴ (This was down from 64% just prior to the financial crash.) Almost two-thirds of interviewees acknowledged that there was *quite a lot* of poverty in the UK, a rise of over 10% from when the question was posed in 2006. Further, 62% believed that poverty had increased over the previous decade, about the same number anticipating a further increase over the next decade. Extreme free market ideology has infiltrated national sensibilities so that perceptions of fairness are combined with a lingering faith in *laissez-faire* economics, and still a misguided conviction that a true meritocracy would serve us all.

But of course, even if a restricted form of meritocracy may be part of a neo-liberal culture, we know that a more meritocratic society is not the prerequisite for less inequality. In fact there are those who see it as promoting a new kind of elite. Hannah Arendt believed that meritocracy ran counter to principles of equality, and if pursued – as she perceived was happening in 1950s Britain – was just as likely to result in another form of aristocracy or oligarchy.* As Ross Douthat has pointed out in the American context, ... *the meritocratic ideal ends up being just as undemocratic as the old emphasis on inheritance and tradition...* He goes on to say that meritocracy:

> ... *forges an elite that has an aristocracy's vices (privilege, insularity, arrogance) without the sense of duty, self-restraint and noblesse oblige. ... and ... the meritocratic elite inevitably tends back toward aristocracy, because any definition of "merit" you choose will be easier for the children of these self-segregated meritocrats to achieve.*⁹⁵

This could be an apt description of the super-rich in their gilded enclaves, as well as of many others who strive to emulate them. It also brings to mind the 'Gilded Age' of the late nineteenth century, when extreme free market capitalism resulted in excessive wealth, wild consumerism with its *conspicuous consumption*, and of course severe poverty. Then, just as now, the few who managed to escape poverty were the exceptions in an otherwise firmly stratified society. Today the aristocracy of wealth in neo-liberal democracies is constituted differently from its make-up

---

* See endnote 69.

in the 19th century, but the same hierarchical arrangement is becoming embedded in society in Britain and, above all, in the United States, as intergenerational mobility declines.

History can repeat itself, even though the second iteration may appear very different from the original. But when – at the end of the previous 'Gilded Age' referred to above – Irving Fisher gave his presidential address to the American Economics Association in 1919 he was highlighting an issue with which we are all too familiar. He spoke of the inequality in American society, saying that the increasing concentration of wealth was the nation's most important economic problem.[96] Today a century on, in the midst of the Coronavirus pandemic which provides huge economic challenges of its own, we are surrounded by inequalities of a similar magnitude. And since their 'modesty' can be partly hidden behind the fig-leaf of meritocracy,[97] and with the plausible reassurance of a welfare state, perhaps they seem less unacceptable than in earlier times. But, again, so much of this is bound up with perception: it appears easy and comfortable to rationalize the social gulfs around us on the basis of our faith in free market capitalism, and the conviction of our economic and technological superiority over previous eras. Thus are poverty and inequality legitimized, whilst any suggestions to mitigate them face a barrier of neo-liberal ideology and restrictive macro-economics constructed to rationalize it. This edifice represents a huge obstacle to progressive measures which could reduce inequality even while enhancing macro-economic performance.

The 'Gilded Age' of the late nineteenth century, and arguably of today, is very different from the so-called Golden Age of Capitalism between about 1950 and the 1973 oil crisis. During that quarter century, what glittered was the expanding capitalist economies of the 'western' world, growing at 2-3% in the USA and Britain, and 4-5% in Western Europe.[98] But what also flourished was the living standards of people of modest means in these countries, by means of progressive taxes and spending on social programmes which gained widespread public approval. Perceptions then were that this was the route to enhancing the welfare of whole societies. But the landscape began to look different when economic growth in major capitalist countries slackened during the 1970s. Then, as Ha-Joon Chang put it, *... the free marketeers dusted off their nineteenth century rhetoric and managed to convince others that the reduction in the share of income going to the investing class was the reason for the slowdown.*[99] Thus was inaugurated the neo-liberal age, soon to have a whole body of theoretical justification behind it, to provide the gloss on a deteriorating economic performance. For, the consequences of the new regime saw slower economic growth, larger shares of national income leeching upwards to the already rich, and a reduction going to those at the bottom.* And even after the cataclysm of the financial crash, that is more or less where we are today – and in the midst of a viral pandemic.

As for inequality in the British context, nothing much has changed. Perhaps senses have been numbed by the attention absorbed by Brexit, by attempts to recover from the years of financial austerity, and now by the all-consuming consequences of Covid-19. So as we enter the third decade of the new century there is scarcely enough mental bandwidth in the country to cope with these unprecedented events, let alone consider divisions of income and status. Should we worry about how much people earn and whether it is more or less than us; should we not put off such concerns until we have reached the other side of these crises? We know deep down that we are not *all in this together*, even if we are heartened by the apparent national unity on behalf of the National Health Service in the face of a killer disease. And the resentment we may harbour over our unequal society may be softened by the news of the high-profile wealthy forgoing some of their colossal earnings in support of the national cause. So we burrow down, care for our own, and try to get to grips with a new kind of austerity. In the meantime we might reflect on whether the consequences of the war against Coronavirus might help put an end to this *gilded age* of neo-liberalism, just as the First World War finally saw off the excesses of the Edwardian era.

During the current crisis talk is heard of a new era – societies transformed by the sobering effects of 'lockdown' so that peoples re-evaluate their priorities and rediscover their true human, interpersonal concerns. But many 'spots' will have to be changed for this to be transformational. We are still the same individuals who allowed a fractured, divided

---

* This pattern was common in many countries, especially those adopting neo-liberal policies, but the evidence was particularly stark in the United States. According to Thomas Piketty, the share of primary income going to the bottom 50% of the American population nearly halved in the 40 years after 1970, while the share going to the top 1% doubled during this time. Meanwhile, the federal minimum wage in the USA lost 30% of its purchasing power in the 50 years following its peak of 1968-70.[100]

society to develop, and stood aside while high earners piled massive bonus upon exorbitant salary and fed us specious rationalization. Part of that rationalization has always been that inequality is the price we pay for a dynamic, capitalist economy to function well – except, of course, that it does not function well and had not done so for a generation before the financial crash of 2007/08. In fact, defences of inequalities have been systematically demolished in endless publications over many years, so that the system that produces them has barely a leg to stand on. Yet, propped up by governments of all persuasions, they obstinately endure. So when we learn of the latest CEO to be awarded astronomical remuneration we blink, pause, and then see that it is business as usual. Late in 2019 Denise Coates, multibillionaire founder of the gambling company Bet365, was reported as receiving £323 million the previous year – the highest salary paid to the boss of a British company and equivalent to 9,500 times the average British salary.[101] Meanwhile, there are currently at least six food banks in the Stoke-on-Trent area where Bet365 is based.

Leaving aside the source of Bet365's revenue – and the propriety of its business in an environment in which problem gambling is a major social concern – one might ask why Denise Coates would want to pay herself an income of that size. What could she do with £323 million which at, say, £50 million she would be obliged to forgo? The neo-liberal response may be that if her company can afford it, then why should one object? Others may say that if she built up the business from scratch then she must have earned whatever recompense the firm can bear. These arguments all bypass the more complex concerns regarding the wider culture which such excess unwittingly promotes. One effect of inequality and excessive pay has been called an *expenditure cascade*, as the rich raise their expenditure simply because they have more money. In their analysis of the 'winner-take-all' society, Robert Frank and Philip Cook show how more spent on housing by the wealthy raises the bar for the next echelon of wealth and income, and so on all the way down the ladder.[102] For the average earner the stakes are raised as prices for median properties go up. Such *expenditure cascades* occur in numerous markets, such as fashion, with the same impact on buyers below the top rank of income, as the frame of reference shifts in inflationary manner. Frank and Cook maintain that much of the extra spending which results is simply wasteful, since beyond a certain point *only relative consumption matters*.[103]*

Excessively high pay is often spoken of as if it is merely the concern of the business which pays it, and is somehow unrelated to the wider economy or the public in general. But the example above is part of an inflationary culture which impacts many ordinary people, as executives and others vie for the prestige which goes with higher and higher salary packages – the precise figures being an irrelevance since it is the relative level which matters. Prior to the financial crash this became particularly conspicuous in the finance industry, and its vestiges still remain. The financial bonanza years of the early 2000s were a time of speculation in complex, innovative products, some of which were not understood even by those dealing in them. The bravado with which investors, obscure hedge funds, and commodity traders wheeled and dealt – vastly enriching their protagonists in the process – was often presented as if it operated in a rarefied world unconnected to the concerns of ordinary mortals. But in fact, it can have a significant impact on the cost of basic household goods and services. Robert Peston has stressed, for example, the way that betting on commodity and energy prices can affect the costs of bread and petrol; these can be determined not only by real demand and supply, but also by speculation on the part of a range of commodity traders and financial institutions.[105]

Judging by the way the remuneration of top executives has been negotiated, both before and after the financial crash, it certainly appears they see themselves as separate from the rest of society. In their book *Unjust Rewards*, which came out in 2008 at the onset of that crisis, Polly Toynbee and David Walker examined the huge pay differentials of the time and interviewed people across the earnings spectrum, among them Sir Philip Hampton, then chairman of J. Sainsbury plc. Hampton, who the authors call a *liberal-minded tycoon*, called for pay transparency, maintaining that salary inflation was due to the remuneration consultants who help set the standards: ... *Pay is remorselessly benchmarked with big fat books about what everyone else has got and what's the median, the average, the top decile and the bottom quartile. It's almost implicit that it leads to a natural trading up.*[106] It is evident that

---

* There is also the effect of the behaviour, and especially consumption of the rich on the rest of the population, in particular the way in which it can reduce the satisfaction of others in their purchases, devaluing them by implication. Robert Frank has written of this in his book *Falling Behind*.[104]

this practice has not disappeared; it is a symbol of an endemic culture of bosses who, once they reach a certain position in the hierarchy, lose the sense of a connection between themselves and the corporate rank and file. Their high pay may be financially sustainable within the organization, but they do not appreciate that vast pay differentials and the inequality they embody have detrimental consequences on the majority in a society which aspires to be 'one nation'.

However, there appears little to prevent the current situation from continuing largely unchanged. One can detect an appetite in society – particularly noticeable during the Coronavirus lockdown – for the *all in it together* mantra to have some real substance. But those able to influence public policy have no idea how to achieve it. In fact many of them expect matters to sort themselves out independently – because that is the way neo-liberalism is supposed to work, with disinterested 'managers' paving the way, setting the ground-rules, and leaving the dynamic forces of the economy to work themselves out to mutual benefit. It is being explained to them repeatedly that for the last generation or so this has not happened, and that the increasing inequality is in part due to money being channelled upwards. Apparently this has been a surprise to some. One right-winger was given to declare frankly, *We did not expect this and most of us are at a loss to understand what has happened.*[107] These were the remarks of Ferdinand Mount, aristocratic stalwart of conservative think-tanks and former adviser to Margaret Thatcher, who came to the realisation that *trickle-down* theory doesn't work and that not all boats are raised by the rising tide. In his 2012 book he admitted that the super-rich *oligarchs ... hardly belong to the society they flit through* – precisely the elitist phenomenon we have seen develop steadily over the last forty years.[108]

Mount is an unusual phenomenon of his own – a humane, one-nation, thinking conservative on the *wetter* side of the Tory Party from a very privileged background (a baronet, no less) who deplores the more extreme consequences of the governments for which he worked in the 1980s. As regards post-crash inequality, he considers a pay ratio between CEOs and their staff of 20:1 to be sufficient. Like many on the soft Right he is far from supportive of the huge social divisions in modern Britain, but does not have detailed answers to remedy them. It is as if the events of the last forty years have just crept up on us all, conservatives included, with social inequality an unfortunate, unexpected side-effect of clever, well-intended, thought-through policy – a kind of hapless Laurel and Hardy moment. Now and again figures from the Right pop up and look bewildered, questioning a state of affairs which has become familiar to almost all, the result of a combination of conspiracy and cock-up, as well as negligence. But the perpetrators of our current predicament can hardly say that they weren't in the room – over the last few decades – when the fateful decisions were being taken. For, yes, they were deliberate policies that got us into this mess. From the 1980s onwards, calculated measures were devised, initially by the Thatcher and Reagan governments, which would result in unemployment, slower growth, *casino capitalism*, and – in the deluded expectation that it would benefit the economy – in a more divided society.

So inequality has been no accident. As Joseph Stiglitz says of the US situation, which has so many direct parallels with the United Kingdom,

> *We make 'political' choices about how we spend our money – whether on tax breaks for the rich or on education for ordinary Americans; whether on weapons that don't work against enemies that don't exist or on health care for the poor; whether on subsidies for rich cotton farmers or on food stamps to reduce hunger among the poor. We could even raise tax revenues by simply making (major companies) pay the taxes they already should be paying.* [109]

It seems counter-intuitive that neo-liberals will not accept that a fairer society would also be a more economically productive one, with higher consumption and growth. As Stiglitz points out, when too much money is concentrated at the top of society, spending of the average citizen is reduced; moreover, higher-income earners spend a smaller proportion of their income than do lower-income individuals.[110] A more equal society would be optimal economically, enabling human resources to be employed for the fullest benefit of the nation, as well as for the personal fulfilment of citizens. The current situation amounts to a dysfunctional economy, with a wastage of talent and humanity – those at the bottom of society so often feeling useless and superfluous, and those at the top striving to profit from a level of productivity which could potentially be so much greater.

Seriously unequal economies like those of Britain and the United States, inefficient and feckless in so many respects, have a range of other features which co-exist with severe social divisions, and help to perpetuate them. These are factors which – though they occasionally hit the headlines as worrying social problems – mostly do not earn publicity as regards their connection with income inequality. For example, the well-being of children, a matter of great concern to all one would assume, varies considerably across developed nations.* But its variations do not, it seems, depend principally on wealth and income, as one might expect. Richard Sennett cites a UNICEF report when he says, *...there is no obvious relationship between levels of child well-being and GDP per capita.*[111] As an example Sennett points to the Czech Republic which is placed higher in the table of well-being than wealthier Austria next door. However, there is a significantly close correlation between child well-being and the level of income equality in their home countries, as shown by Richard Wilkinson and Kate Pickett. Putting the UNICEF index of child well-being alongside data on income reveals that, on a steady gradient, the USA with its severe income disparities but low well-being ranking, is at the opposite extreme from Japan, Scandinavia and the Netherlands, which are all much more equal but perform best on child well-being.[112]

This connection indicates once again that it is not a nation's wealth or its level of consumption which is significant, but the relationship between the incomes of different individuals and sections of society. Again as regards the young, there is a strong link between income inequality and the degree of conflict between children. Data show that the more unequal a society in terms of income, the more fighting and bullying children will report they have experienced; the UK performs very poorly in this regard.[113] Yet this is the pattern with so many social issues which trouble the rich, developed countries – that they are distinctly more problematic where there are higher levels of income inequality. Wilkinson and Pickett's compelling research points to wide areas of society where this relationship is prominent: rates of mental illness are five times higher in the most unequal societies, compared with the least equal; people are likewise five times more likely to be imprisoned, and six times more likely to suffer from clinical obesity in more unequal environments; and murder rates will be significantly higher there too.[114] In unequal societies it is a broad cross-section of

---

* This subject was touched on earlier in this chapter. See page 322, and Endnote 10.

their populations which are impacted by these problems, which partly explains why the disparities are so great. The notorious 1% may feel they are immune, but they too will pay a price, both in terms of social issues as well as in a poorer functioning economy.

This is a crux of the matter: nations which tolerate high levels of income inequality suffer their effects throughout their populations. To many of the highest earners in a society this may seem counter-intuitive. They would no doubt think of poverty and disadvantage when the subject of inequality is raised, and would find it hard to accept that they are implicated in the repercussions of income disparities. But judging by the list of social problems which accompany inequalities of income, they should perhaps pay more attention. In his *Inequality and the 1%*, academic Danny Dorling includes a detailed chart showing the incidence of various social and political issues in four countries – the UK and the USA with severe income inequalities, and Japan and Sweden, two of the least unequal developed nations.[115] Whether it is teenage pregnancy, infant mortality, social mobility, life expectancy, or the degree of trust citizens show in one another,* the unequal nations – especially the United States – perform much worse than the more equal ones. As Wilkinson and Pickett remark, *Inequality seems to make countries socially dysfunctional across a wide range of outcomes* – and incomes.[116] As for the young, Richard Sennett says that in wealthy but unequal Britain and the USA ... *childhood appears to be socially impoverished*.[117] It is almost as if inequality was devised as a predictive factor for some of the worst social features of modern life, many of which have no respect for wealth or status.

Another curious phenomenon linked here, which can affect people of all economic levels, is the tendency to *big* themselves up, exaggerate what they see as their good aspects in order to promote themselves. This has become more noticeable over recent decades, but more especially in certain environments: viz., those countries which happen to have greater inequality of income. Where status anxiety is more significant, stemming from a greater social-evaluative threat, there is evidence that the inclination towards *self-enhancement* is stronger, in order to maintain and project the required self-image. Wilkinson and Pickett

---

* This factor, an important indication of social cohesion, has significant implications for the rich where trust is low, in the expensive arrangements they may feel compelled to make for their security, while potentially costing us all more in terms of policing and the security apparatus of the state.

cite a wealth of data, including one comprehensive study of fifteen nations, which show close correlation between *self-enhancement bias* and income inequality.[118] In their earlier work, the same authors highlight the contrast between a very equal society, Japan, and the United States, one of the most unequal, pointing out that Americans are far more likely to put their successes down to their own abilities, but their failures to external forces.[119] The Japanese on the other hand, according to evidence from numerous studies, tend to do precisely the opposite. Of course there may be other cultural factors at play here, but it appears that across more equal societies people feel less need to project themselves as superior or above average; in fact, they even identify luck as playing an important part in their achievements.

So it appears that people in societies which do not harbour major economic disparities are generally more at ease with their self-image and how they believe they are seen by others. There will be a degree of status anxiety, especially at lower socio-economic levels, in all societies, but in the more equal ones there will be less concern about status and income differences, and thus a reduced sense of a social-evaluative threat. Where there are vast differentials in incomes there is inevitably going to be an impact on how people feel they are valued, and these subjective impressions are felt, to a greater or lesser degree, to almost the very top of the social hierarchy. People in these environments appear to need to convey a positive image of themselves, and this even extends to physical health. It emerged that when people were asked to assess their own levels of health, those in more unequal countries – where physical health is actually worse, and life expectancy lower – rated themselves more highly than did respondents in more equal nations.[120] For example, 80% of Americans in the study believed their health was *good*, whereas in Japan, a nation with one of the highest figures for life expectancy, only 54% gave themselves this rating. It seems that unequal societies induce citizens to display confidence in themselves and assert their self-perceived strengths, a need which is far less noticeable where there is more equality.

It is hard to know to what extent these attitudes are genuine and honest or to some extent for public, or at least outward consumption. After all, appearing confident and optimistic is a common feature especially in dynamic free market economies. In the United States, for example, displaying positive thinking and overt optimism is almost a requirement of *getting on*; pessimism is not seen as politically correct, one might say, and modesty not highly valued. In the competitive arenas of business, politics and sport it is believed vital to exude resilient, self-confident enthusiasm, without which you are thought far less likely to succeed. This self-confidence tends to be reinforced, Daniel Kahneman says, by the admiration of others – leading on to his hypothesis that it is optimistic, overconfident people who have the greatest influence on the lives of others, but in doing so are likely to take more risks than they realize.[121] These kinds of people have got where they are, he says, by seeking challenges and taking risks, but are often luckier than they believe. People usually find confidence in others persuasive, whereas uncertainty or diffidence will not be trusted.* But excess confidence can be dangerous, especially in business and finance – where we have ample evidence of its destructive effects. Nevertheless, projecting a forceful, capable image may inspire a following, regardless of how illusory the substance.

Judging by the public pronouncements of leaders of seriously unequal nations like Britain or the United States, one would not believe that inequality of income was a particularly conspicuous problem which required priority action. The subject is often reported in the media, but news of homelessness, childhood poverty, and food banks make for more dramatic headlines, and seem more prominent in stirring empathy in the wider public. It is partly a matter of perception, but perhaps these issues appear readily *fixable* – not that social policy appears ready to jump into action on them with big budget measures, particularly at a time when a global pandemic has devastated economies. And income inequality certainly seems far less amenable to government action and will – it is thought – resolve itself if these other issues are tackled properly first. The public is more likely to feel the *cognitive ease*** of agreeing that something must be done about child poverty, whereas the challenge of severe income inequalities is a far more nebulous, perplexing issue which throws up moral questions and value judgements. While it might be accepted that the welfare of children cannot afford to await a slow improvement in macro-economic fortunes, social disparities stemming from income differences are seen as issues which can be addressed *all in good time* when the economy comes right.

---

* Uncertainty or doubt on the part of apparent experts, particularly medical ones, will not inspire confidence. But as Kahneman says, *An unbiased appreciation of uncertainty is a cornerstone of rationality – but it is not what people and organizations want.*[122]

** Daniel Kahenman's explanation of *System 1 thinking*, outlined in Chapter 1.

However, this is not how it must be allowed to happen; all these considerations amount to putting the cart well and truly before the horse. It has all been heard before, many, many times, and still the erroneous canards are put before us – the neo-liberal fallacies which get wheeled out to postpone any day of reckoning. The mounting data from a range of disciplines make little impression on policy makers, especially in the *Anglo-Sphere*. They are so steeped in ideas born in the 1970s, and so convinced of their rectitude, that the ideology forms an invisible defensive shield around them. And they can rely on the complicity of the wider public; the prejudices of two generations have seeped into national consciousness so that they lie there, accepted albeit discredited. Meanwhile, practical answers and policies from which all could benefit remain ready and available, endorsed in many a more enlightened jurisdiction, but up against a mental obstacle of resolute false consciousness in the neo-liberal world. A fixed idea – as Theodore Roszak maintained – can only be unseated or replaced by another idea.* Yet the serviceable alternative does not constitute an ideology, merely a powerful body of evidence-based data and empirical examples which could well bring about a social revolution by shaking up the damaging inequalities of hide-bound regimes.

It is here where change must begin. The only practical, worthwhile way forward is for countries like Britain and the United States to aim as their single most important social and economic priority to reduce income inequality in their societies. So to start with, an advantage which would appeal to most free marketers: greater equality could help economic growth. As Chapter 4 laboured to show, growth as a target makes little sense and as a measure of economic or social progress is not credible. However, if conservative politicians and economists want a reason to reduce inequality, one they could live with, they could focus on this. An IMF paper of 2015 posed the question, *Why would widening income disparities matter for growth?* Its own response was,

> *Higher inequality lowers growth by depriving the ability of lower-income households to stay healthy and accumulate physical and human capital. For instance, it can lead to underinvestment in education as poor children end up in lower-quality schools and are*

---

* See Roszak's words at the opening to Chapter 1.

*less able to go on to college. As a result, labor productivity could be lower than it would have been in a more equitable world.*¹²³

For too long, governments – and not just those of the neo-liberal variety – have focused on economic growth as the solution to most social and economic problems. The conventional wisdom has been that enlarging the economic pie will provide more for all to share. But advanced free market capitalism has now gone beyond this; increasing economic equality should now be the top priority to improve overall welfare, and if healthy economic growth happens to accompany this, then so be it.*

If countries with extreme income inequalities can be induced to bring in a policy to lower them substantially, then a host of benign consequences may flow from this – benefits which would accrue to the whole of society. It is here where the data are often met with scepticism. When Richard Wilkinson and Kate Pickett came out with their work *The Spirit Level* in 2009, its huge body of conclusive research did not receive the attention it deserved. Yes, it was acknowledged that reducing social inequality might help to tackle some persistent social problems of rich, capitalist economies. But in spite of the book's sub-title, *Why Equality is Better for Everyone,* the idea that the benefits of reducing inequality would accrue to all, even to the better-off, was skirted around almost as if it was a subversive dogma. It certainly did not make a significant impression on the rich and powerful – testimony, again, to the power of collective ideology which forms a buttress against reasoned argument. It was not that the evidence of Wilkinson and Pickett's conclusions was not convincing, but that it could not penetrate the solid mindset of extreme free market thinking which had become ... *an inevitable category of the human mind.*** As the authors so aptly declared, what they believed were the necessary political changes would only gain wide support once the perspectives in their work had ... *permeated the public mind.*¹²⁴

So this is what we are up against – populations unsuspectingly rooted in their comfortable, time-worn prejudices which implicitly favour

---

* As laid out in Chapter 4 above, economic growth is not *per se* injurious to social welfare, although some of the factors which go into its measurement may well be so. It is important to devise constructive public policy which enhances the welfare of all; if some increase in GDP accompanies such measures in an ecologically sustainable and globally just manner, then this incidental growth should not be rejected.

** See T. E. Hulme's remarks in the opening of Chapter 1. As explained further in that chapter, these *categories of the human mind* are not seen or properly appreciated; other things are seen *through them.*

a mainly neo-liberal stance which they assume will eventually bring about a better society. One of the positive characteristics which such people would no doubt like to see more of is trust. A society of greater cohesion and communal harmony is something most people say they value. During the Coronavirus lock-down of 2020, comment was often heard about an increase in camaraderie and solidarity, a harking back to wartime conditions when people felt united in a common purpose. It remains to be seen whether the severe demands of the pandemic will result in a higher incidence of trust in others. When respondents have been asked if they think most people can be trusted, as opposed to whether ... *you can't be too careful dealing with people* (the standard wording for this type of question), the percentage figures in Britain have fluctuated between the high 30s and the mid-40s over the last generation – with a slight rise in the last five years.[125] In the USA, in response to the same question, less than a third of Americans said that most people can be trusted, down from around 50% in the early 1970s.[126] (It is interesting that in the United States in particular, crime rates fell in the 1990s and 2000s but nevertheless Americans grew less trusting.) Significantly, many societies today record higher levels of trust than does the Anglo-Saxon world.

American academic Eric Uslaner has written and researched extensively on the subject of trust in society. He has found that places with more trusting populations have better functioning governments and more open markets, as well as more redistributive policies. He also indicates a clear link between trust and inequality: *what distinguishes countries that are trusting from those that are not is the level of economic equality ... which he maintains is ... the strongest determinant of trust.*[127] Social solidarity appears a casualty of increasing inequality, and of course it is in the interests of neo-liberal economics that people separate out into atomised units for the benefit of individualized consumer targeting (as was outlined in earlier chapters). So greater social and economic inequality leads to a more segregated society as people become more wary of others and trust each other less; thus inclusiveness and empathy suffer. Of course, the poorer members of the population will be affected more deeply, but the phenomenon will nevertheless have repercussions on the better-off, in more divisive social attitudes and a less secure environment. But falling levels of trust can also impact government in that they undermine legitimacy, a legitimacy hitherto earned by the promises of the *social state* to defend its citizens against ... *exclusion and rejection ... and the ... random blows of fate*, as Zygmunt Bauman put it.[128]

The unquestionably strong links between social and economic inequalities and a variety of prominent issues in society should have a far greater impact on national consciousness than has been the case. In an increasingly globalised world people still focus almost exclusively on their own insular concerns, reluctant to pay attention to alien examples or embrace foreign practices. Nevertheless, better models of society abound, and could find favour in less divisive, partisan times. All in society would surely welcome a reduction in the incidence of mental illness, which has been shown to be three times more prevalent in severely unequal nations such as the USA and UK than in much more equal ones like Japan.[129] The countries affected most by the wave of mental health problems feel the effects across the whole of their populations. For although there is more mental illness the further you go down the social gradient, nevertheless a survey of men in England, for example, showed the extent of the impact of depression on the second richest 20% income group.[130] And the scepticism as to whether less mental illness in more equal nations could be due to the resources spent in tackling it was answered by a comprehensive European study which found no evidence for this.[131] But the same research did point to the link in these countries between better mental health and a lower incidence of status anxiety, as well as more participation in social networks that involve reciprocity, trust and co-operation.[132]

Ever since the 18th century, Enlightenment values have stood behind a range of social and medical improvements, among them raising life expectancy and lowering infant mortality. Today these are significant indications of the social progress made by developing countries, as they endeavour to raise welfare standards. It might be expected that statistics for these factors would be fairly uniform among rich nations, which have experienced decades of economic and social evolution; yet this is not the case. The latest figures show a sizeable gap between, for example, Japan with an expected life span at birth of 84.6 years, and the USA with 78.8 years, more on a par with some eastern European countries. The United States is considerably richer than Japan, as well as much better off than countries like Sweden, France or Spain, whose citizens all have a life expectancy averaging over 80 years.* But what these

---

*   OECD figures for *per capita* national income in 2018: USA – $63.600, Sweden

other nations have in common is societies which are far more equal in terms of wealth and income than in the USA (which actually recorded a slight decrease in life expectancy between 2016 and 2017). In fact, there is a distinct correlation between lower life expectancy and high income inequality in many countries, and this same relationship exists among states within the United States, people in the more equal ones living longer on average.[134] One 2016 research study noted that income inequality within the USA had led to a discrepancy of ten to fifteen years of life expectancy.[135]

In order to make a direct comparison between countries, a study of mortality was carried out some years ago in Sweden and Britain using the same (British) class classification system by occupation.[136] It emerged that death rates among working-age men in more egalitarian Sweden were lower at all occupational levels than in England and Wales. Furthermore, Sweden's highest mortality, that of the lowest social class (V), was lower than that in the highest class level (I) in England and Wales – evidence once again that more equal societies are better for people of all occupational and income levels. A similar pattern emerges with infant mortality: nations with greater income equality tend to have lower figures for infant deaths. For example, a striking contrast between the wealthier, but much more unequal United States, and less unequal Japan is shown by 2018 figures: 5.8 deaths per 1000 live births in the former, compared with only 1.9 deaths in the latter.[137] The figure for the USA, on a par with that of Russia, is considerably higher than those of many developed and less developed countries – including most of Europe – all of which are far more equal than American society. Contrary to what many of the rich assume, believing that their individualistic striving is above all the way to benefit themselves, it is evident that the poorer performance of the most unequal countries on a whole series of social issues has an impact across the full range of their societies, to the very top of the social scale.

Many governments are finding it very difficult to adjust to the new realities. Brought up in times of economic uncertainty, when the national focus had to be on efficiency and expanding the economy, leaders cannot see that relationships within societies now are just as important as GDP or national income. Once a certain level of overall affluence has been

---

– $54.800, France – $47.300, Spain – $40.600, Japan – $43.000[133] It is also noteworthy that life expectancy is not related to the amount spent on health care in rich nations.

reached, the success or otherwise of a nation appears to rest on these inter-communal relationships, in particular those between people at different income levels. Wealthy countries with greater income inequality simply do not function as well as more equal ones; they generally have a greater incidence of a range of poor health and social outcomes. Opponents may question the lack of specific causal connections, but the data are so consistent across a broad spectrum of issues to the point that there can be no doubt that the degree of income equality in a society is the key to its social success; it is the only credible unifying factor. And since the initial connections were made between equality and various aspects of health, a large number of international studies in different environments have since supported the contention that more equal societies are in the widest sense healthier. And Wilkinson and Pickett confirm the augural nature of these relationships:

If – for instance – a country does badly on health, you can predict with some confidence that it will also imprison a larger proportion of its population, have more teenage pregnancies, lower literacy scores, more obesity, worse mental health, and so on.[138]

As human creatures we are most of us gullible and susceptible, prisoners of our biased assumptions and our backgrounds. And our recent collective background since the Industrial Revolution has been an evolution from scarcity to abundance, from pre-development to affluence. But now we find it difficult to accept the notion that 'more' does not necessarily mean 'better', even if the perspective of the *middling sort* and the poor looking up seems to indicate that it does. We cannot get to grips with the new prospect that increasing our income – family or national – may well not make us materially any better off. We have got used to the assumption that only by growing the economy will more resources become available for valuable social services – this now a supposed fact of life which we rarely dwell on, but simply think *through*. But these are all facets of the old way, before the decisions were capable of engineering the resources. The new reality, that it is the relationships between people and between different sectors of the population, and the decisions we take to harmonize them, which will determine our prosperity – financial and social – is still not appreciated. Some may think that they can go it alone and enrich themselves without affecting others, but in the new world of interdependence it turns out that how we relate to one another is more important than outdated individualism.

Over recent years questions of capitalism, growth, inequality and poverty have been the focus of many research papers as well as media debates. An example of the latter was an edition of BBC World Service's 'Inquiry' Programme in 2016, in which a panel of four experts in the field gave their views on the question *How Much Inequality Is Too Much?*[139] One of the contributions, from Professor Deirdre McCloskey of the University of Illinois, was of a kind that has been heard on a number of occasions – exonerating inequality by defending capitalism. By praising economic progress since 1800, individual striving, and capitalism in general she justified inequality, implying that it is simply part of normal economic development, and something she admitted to being relaxed about. Thus the debate becomes polarised, as if opposing inequality puts one firmly in the anti-capitalist camp.* Then there is the question of degree; it is the extremes of inequality which have become so damaging in certain jurisdictions over recent decades, not the existence of moderate disparities based on difference. So when Professor McCloskey writes, with rhetorical flourish ... *if a brain surgeon and a taxi driver earn the same amount, we won't have enough brain surgeons. Why bother?* it does not advance the debate.[141] The blessings of the free market must be distinguished from the retrogression in certain economies over the last forty years: lower growth and productivity, greater income disparities and reduced social mobility.

The increasingly interdependent world has implications for all within societies, where attitudes and ambitions are closely connected and reinforcing. The middle classes and the poor are part of a national culture today to a greater degree than when nations were growing their economies in the 19th century, at an earlier stage of capitalist development. And though reformers at that time were trying to humanise

---

* This is a rhetorical device common to economists and politicians on the Right; Boris Johnson has employed the same refrain. In a speech in 2013 he followed remarks on inequality by saying, ... *what has been really striking about the last five or six years is that no one on the left – no one from Paul Krugman to Joe Stiglitz to Will Hutton, let alone Ed Miliband – has come up with any other way for an economy to operate except by capitalism. ...the free market is the only show in town.*[140] Such spurious rhetoric is, of course, part of a different argument. Capitalism is likely to be around for a long time to come (as was justified in earlier chapters) but inequality on the current level in the UK and USA is certainly not the only show in town.

industrialism, societies were still firmly demarcated, and the modern mass media had not yet emerged. But by the post-World War II period capitalism had reached a level of maturity within the context of a welfare state and much greater social inclusiveness. Most developed economies had come to a point where citizens had broadly similar material aspirations, and in this sense a *one nation* ethos could be said to characterize their societies. At the same time wider education and a more extensive mass media now helped foster a consciousness of how others lived. This had not generally been the case even in the pre-war period; while many – notably domestic servants – would then have been aware of vast differences of wealth and status, the ruling classes often had little conception of the ordinary lives of the majority. In Britain, Prime Minister Neville Chamberlain's comment in 1939, on learning of the malnutrition of evacuated children, was emblematic: *I never knew such conditions existed, and I feel ashamed of having been so ignorant of my neighbour.*[142] (Chamberlain had been Minister of Health in several earlier governments!)*

By the late twentieth century, individuals and families of all social levels were encouraged to expect more from government, whose remit was so much broader than a century before. Of course, material standards were, and are important, but what those in authority usually fail to appreciate is that dignity is as important as the living standards which a certain level of income or wealth can provide. This stems from self-respect which parity of recognition helps create – another way of defining equality of being. But dignity is easily vitiated by material poverty, and as such, shame is then not far away. More widely, deprivation exists in an inability to take part in everyday community life. In Adam Smith's famous example of what constitutes normal life, he notes that a linen shirt is not an absolute necessity, but that a labourer who appeared in public without one would be attracting opprobrium to himself and his family. Thus would he be labelled and would be unable to escape social shame. In the open, goldfish bowl of twenty-first-century society, involvement in normal life – thus avoiding shame – consists in having a diverse range of familiar goods. As Tim Jackson says, *The baseline for proper social functioning is always the current level of commodities.*[144]

---

*   Later, Winston Churchill was fond of identifying with the British people, though was not necessarily well placed to understand their requirements. As his wife was once said to have remarked, *He knows nothing of the life of ordinary people. He's never been on a bus and only once on the Underground.*[143]

However, it is crucial to appreciate that participation also exists in having the wherewithal to communicate, travel, and to join the networks of social intercourse which are part of everyday vernacular existence.*

So the need is not for complete material equality but for an equality of treatment and respect, which cannot be assured when poverty of existence ranges from insufficient goods and amenities, to a lack of agency and autonomy to be part of everyday communal life. Only by rectifying these forms of deprivation can shame be avoided. After all, we know from psychology that seeking respect from others, and from it dignity in existence, are fundamental drivers of human behaviour. The shame of poverty comes from not being able to enjoy what most people regard as everyday necessities – and these are by no means only physical commodities. Respect cannot be earned by remaining excluded from common activities. However, the increasing commodification of modern life erects barriers to entry; the more activities which are subject to market forces the more will those at the bottom of society be excluded from normal social interaction. If this process could be progressively reined in, and access therefore made less dependent on financial means, then poorer citizens would have the potential to be more involved in society's participatory norms. Even without extending purchasing power this could lead to more respect from others and for oneself – in fact, to more equality of being. This would contribute to eradicating the grossly invidious phenomenon, *the profound 'indecency'*, as Tony Judt put it ... *of defining civic status as a function of economic good fortune.*[145]

While calling for absolute equality would be absurd, and unjust, reducing the current extremes of inequality in the *Anglo-sphere* is a prerequisite to creating an equivalence of status. This would go towards helping restore self-respect to a deprived underclass, many of whom have lost dignity. One should not be held responsible for being poorly educated or unemployed, and need should be seen for what it is. But the suspicion and distrust which permeate the welfare system in both Britain and the US have grown with the harsher demands of extreme market capitalism. Enhancing the self-respect of those at the bottom

---

* To take one example, countries which prioritise the private car – with the associated expensive infrastructure paid for out of general taxation – neglect vital investment in public transport, especially buses. This bias in transport policy implicitly favours the better-off, and is also environmentally damaging. The deregulation of bus services in Britain in the 1980s represented clear discrimination against sections of the population – the worse off, students, the elderly, and the disabled – which helped embed inequality of access to basic needs which has lasted to this day.

of society was a corollary of the building of welfare states in the 20th century, but under neo-liberalism the stigma of *undeserving*, as opposed to *deserving*, poor has returned; thus dignity and inclusiveness can be the casualties. Dependence is vilified, even if there is no other recourse for those involved, and as Richard Sennett points out in the USA, the relationships which develop in such welfare systems do not treat welfare as a right.[146]* In these circumstances a general level of civic equality is very hard to achieve, for it relies on a mutuality of respect. During the lockdown required by the Covid-19 pandemic, there emerged in Britain a different outlook, almost a sense of Orwell's underlying *emotional unity*, manifested in huge affection for the NHS and respect for workers in poorly paid, caring services; but how long this outlasts the crisis is far from certain.

According respect to the disadvantaged, to those who for whatever reason are unable to contribute much to society, and even to those who kick out against its norms, is the route to inclusiveness and civic equality. This does not imply admiration or even approval, but conceding parity of being is a way of ensuring dignity on the part of the other – which helps foster responsibility, and is an essential condition of mature developed society. Withholding respect for others and denying them dignity will diminish and ultimately destroy their self-respect, as the Nazis calculated all too effectively during the Holocaust. But in societies which allow extremes of social inequality, severe deprivation as well as forced dependence on others removes agency and undermines self-respect, particularly since it is implicit in neo-liberalism that one's predicament should not be blamed on anyone or anything else. Increasing materialism, the commodification of amenities not previously subject to market forces, and an ever-widening income gap all contribute to defining and restricting someone's worth to money and status. And the intensity of this process will have familiar consequences for mental health, such as depression, status anxiety and the social-evaluative threat, outlined earlier in this chapter.** It will also, under chronic individualism, lead to more isolation as society becomes more fragmented.

Late free market capitalism will not easily be shifted from its

---

* Sennett notes that suspicion of the poor in the United States increased as the country became more prosperous.

** It is significant that it appears that one's income rank is more important than level of income *per se* in relation to predicting mental distress. Wilkinson and Pickett cite studies in Britain and the United States which show that someone's income within a social comparison group, not income itself, is the key determinant, even allowing for differences of age, gender,

ill-judged confrontational path. Since competition is such an integral driving force of its operations, particularly in Anglo-Saxon capitalism, it seems difficult to exclude it from everyday social and interpersonal affairs. But consensus and collaboration will be able to be harmonized with the new capitalism, once neo-liberalism has been confronted. In fact, the more inclusive social environment of the future could well enhance free market productivity. Entrepreneurs today are mostly wedded to the idea of the thrusting, striving enterprise of the so-called 'wealth creators' and the rewards they are said to deserve; how much more energy, innovation and creativity might follow from those now at the foot of society, should they be emancipated from penury and the constant effort to make ends meet. Their potential for productive enterprise lies dormant, currently masked by the poor self-esteem, under-education and lack of opportunity which a severely unequal society guarantees.* But these prospects are ignored while all the focus is on the monied executives at the top, and the simplistic notion that they alone can drive the economy forward. It is time to bring the whole of society into the national effort and learn – what pupils are always told in school – that all have something to offer the collective. If we did not understand this before, then the response to the Coronavirus pandemic has shown us all its importance.

Finally, equality of being will more easily be established and appreciated in a fully integrated society. Countries with extremes of inequality tend to develop rich, self-selected, segregated communities, as their occupants try to shield themselves from perceived threats to their affluence and security. Meanwhile, poorer citizens gravitate by default to their own separate neighbourhoods, where they may live only a stone's throw from their wealthy compatriots. But in such circumstances their contribution to the wider community is consistently undervalued; their seclusion from mainstream affluent society ensures that it will remain invisible. A wholesome community needs a mutuality of respect, some bonds of citizenship, however unequal the contributions of its different elements. The further down the road of inequality and segregation society travels, the less sustainable it is as a community. The poor must

---

education and other factors.[147] Again, even with a question of finance like this, it is relationships which are the meaningful element in the impact on personal well-being.

* As the OECD so aptly put it, in its 2015 paper *In it together: Why Less Inequality Benefits All*: ... *lower-income people cannot realise their human capital potential, which is bad for the economy as a whole.*[148]

not be excluded, and the rich must not be allowed to exclude themselves, as if they were not part of normal society – unless, that is, they agree to avoid using public transport and public roads, state education, locally provided emergency services, refuse collection, and all the other services paid for by the community as a whole. Of course, the end point of that would be the denial that all citizens are part of the web of communities to which we all belong, and thus to national disintegration.

We are nowhere near this point in Europe, but the trends in the United States are showing us the way there. It comes down to our concept of what society is, not what a national economy represents, and how we see our fellow citizens is a key to conceptualizing the whole. In feudal times the contribution to society of the peasants was overtly recognized, as outlined earlier in this chapter. We need to discover some equivalent – and not just at times of national crisis. As for the rich, they are not a separate, self-created species. Tony Judt points out that the notion anyone could be entirely 'self-made' disappeared with 19th-century individualism. He reiterates a common theme: *We are all the beneficiaries of those who went before us, as well as those who will care for us in old age or ill health.*[149] We must accept, yes, dependence, especially upon services which we all jointly provide and fund. George Lakoff emphasises the relationship between public – government – resources and private benefit: *Every great corporate innovation story simply burnishes the truth that the private depends on the public*, he says.[150] The efforts of the whole of society striving together can promote innovation, sustainable expansion, and affluence, such that a privileged, rich elite and a demoralized underclass can never achieve. But to this end the relationship of the individual to society needs to be reassessed, to correct the neo-liberal bias and reassert the social nature of individuality, as suggested in Chapter 2.

When Bernie Sanders was campaigning for the Democratic Party's nomination in the USA in 2016 he highlighted inequality by citing a report which pointed out that the twenty richest people in America owned more wealth than the bottom 50% of the population – 57 million households. This fact was so staggering that many doubted its veracity, but it was confirmed by, among others, 'Patriotic Millionaire' Chuck Collins who co-authored the report.[151] When figures of such astounding magnitude are cited they almost cease to have significance to ordinary citizens, to whom they represent a distant world beyond their experience. In fact, statistics from many sources can be churned out to demonstrate the degree of severe inequality in societies like Britain or the USA; these may or may not make an impression, depending on the lived existence of those examining them. But numbers are important, principally because – as this chapter has highlighted – it is the *degree* of inequality which distinguishes the period since the 1970s from the immediate postwar era. The social market capitalism of that earlier period, with high taxation, rapid economic growth and near-full employment, gained popular legitimacy and considerable cross-party political consensus in most of Western Europe and the United States. It was also marked by historically low social and economic inequalities within nations.

The economic difficulties of the '70s then led to a gradual transformation of the political landscape over the following years. With right-wing governments in power in many countries, opportunities emerged for the so-called New Right and neo-liberal principles to transform priorities and oversee widening social and economic divisions. In Britain these divisions continued to expand under governments of different complexions up to the financial crash, so that the figure for inequality on the Gini index reached 0.386 (i.e. 38.6%) in 2008. In spite of a correction during the economic downturn and the period of austerity, income inequality has since started to rise again. The latest government figures show a slight increase to 0.347 in the two years ending in 2019 – on a par with the level of 2011.[152]* According to OECD data, the United Kingdom was placed 26th for inequality in a list of developed nations, with a Gini coefficient of almost 0.35 in 2017, whereas Nordic and some central European states were at the head of the rankings with barely 0.25.[153] These seeming innocuous numbers hide major differences between advanced, developed nations which otherwise show many social and economic similarities. However, their trajectories in terms of how their national incomes have been distributed among individuals and sectors, over many years, indicate significant contrasts in political and economic priorities, and, ultimately, in ideology and national consciousness.

---

*   These figures represent considerable social divisions. On the Gini scale, where '0' would signify complete income equality throughout the population, and '1' (100%) would indicate a person earning the whole nation's income alone, the USA's figure of nearly 0.4 stands out as a prodigious level of inequality, surpassed by very few developed states. The UK's inequality is at a mid-point between that and the more progressive nations.

It is perhaps surprising in this increasingly homogenised world that national awareness in comparable countries could vary so much. But not all 'western' nations, for example, see society in the same way; more progressive ones appear much more accepting of high taxation to fund comprehensive social services and do not generally baulk at paying for ones they do not use. In such cases a binding social solidarity takes precedence over narrow individualism, and such ideological forces that exist do not promote the latter at the expense of the former. However, the nations of the *Anglo-Sphere*, once with societies closer to that model, have since diverged and followed a separate ideological path, many of their constituents unaware of how different and radical their direction of travel. But the consequences of that political course begun in the 1970s are now unmistakeable, littering the national landscape like so much social detritus, severe inequalities one of its most egregious features. Nevertheless, because the inequalities have developed piecemeal over several decades, with no obvious, sudden break with the past, successive generations have progressively accustomed themselves to new *status quos* – every fresh set of figures representing a new normal, to be defended by the usual ideological 'culprits'. During this process, voters as a whole have not been sufficiently conscious of the developing scenario to halt it by rejecting policies which allow it, any more than the frog in the fable will be sufficiently aware of the slowly boiling water to take evasive action and try to jump out.

This has been the pattern in the United States and Britain, as well as to a lesser extent Australia, New Zealand and others. In these jurisdictions the casualties of neo-liberal policy, however strictly applied, have often come to be seen as incidental side-effects of otherwise necessary and salutary measures, rather than defects inherent in the premises on which it is based. And thus its adherents have relaxed in the implicit understanding that its policies are right and just – a self-righteous mindset not to be upset by adverse publicity or reverses of fortune. So *cognitive ease* sets in, a form of relaxed, casual thinking which does not want to be challenged by disturbing, rational argument.* In this way, trust is placed in existing prejudices, fortified by political rhetoric but not examined or analysed. In fact, challenges to firmly-held beliefs are not felt or even taken in. Perhaps only direct, personal impacts to our livelihoods or our families would make an impression on our deep

---

* See again Daniel Kahneman's 'System 1' thinking, examined in Chapter 1.

inner suppositions. So in spite of the cataclysm of the financial crash of 2007/08, years of economic austerity, a macro-economic performance which for a generation has been unable to match that of the 1950s and '60s, and numerous examples around us of more successful societies – nevertheless, the pernicious bias towards neo-liberalism is maintained.

All modern, capitalist societies are to a degree dysfunctional, but those with extremes of social and income inequality are conspicuously more dysfunctional than the others; however successful their macro-economies may be, they are social failures. Yet apologists for neo-liberalism would have us believe that inequality is indispensable for economic dynamism, while maintaining that the incidental casualties of capitalist efficiency are a small price to pay for affluence.* But the casualties are emblematic of extreme free market capitalism, a permanent disfigurement on the face of modern society. Economic cycles may come and go but inequalities remain – only to grow wider and more intransigent. The late Zygmunt Bauman pointed out that ... *no one plans collateral casualties of economic progress, let alone draws in advance the line separating the damned from the saved.*[154] That is why poverty, like inequality, is said to be incidental to capitalism, but nevertheless allowed and condoned. No-one will take responsibility for it because no person can be found to blame – only the system itself. Bauman illustrates this with the bewildered hero of Steinbeck's novel *The Grapes of Wrath*, who tries to defend his farm which is no longer viable:

> ... *he could not find a single malevolent perpetrator of his torment and distress to shoot. Being but a sideline of economic progress, the production of human waste has all the markings of an impersonal, purely technical issue.*[155]

In spite of this the *all-in-it-together* mantra has become an oft-repeated refrain over recent times. During the national 'lockdowns' prompted by the Coronavirus pandemic, it has been both a call for unity, as well as a felt sentiment reflecting the collective desire to combine in a joint effort to combat a crisis affecting rich and poor indiscriminately.** In order for

---

* Yes, the reader may indeed wonder what on earth justifies descriptions of *efficiency* or *dynamism*, especially in recent times, but this indicates the conceptual gulf between reality and the extravagant imaginings of neo-liberals, who have no alternative but to continue to peddle their bogus message.

** While wealth provides no immunity against a new virus, the worse, more crowded conditions in which many poorer people – as well as some ethnic minority communities – live

lockdown to succeed, it requires solidarity, even if partly prompted by fear of catching the disease. Adherence to government norms becomes a demonstration of support for national efforts, as well as for the dedicated health professionals in the front line. In Britain there has been almost a sense of relief at the spirit generated by the publicity of how the public is responding to the crisis – reflecting the long-held yearning amongst broad swathes of the population for more communal unity. In spite of some breaches of government regulations, and protests against the severity of the restrictions, there has been widespread observance of an imposed regime unlike anything seen outside of wartime. The feeling of inclusivity may not extend to the whole population – including the more affluent attempting to escape to their second homes – and in any case may well not last much beyond the health emergency. But in Britain, at least, it has revived a national consciousness which allows citizens to see themselves, in a social sense, on the same level.

There is in fact a direct parallel between the endemic income inequality in countries with neo-liberal policies and the Covid-19 pandemic. In both cases a return to greater national health could be facilitated if all in society were to restrain their uninhibited impulses in support of the general good – which would also redound to serve individual interests. As regards Coronavirus, resenting and failing to observe government restrictions may not benefit those determined to assert their freedoms, since it can put them at greater risk of contracting the disease. As for nations with gross income inequalities, it has already been shown that reducing them will improve many social and economic conditions and enhance quality of life at all levels of the population – including the rich. However, while there is a demonstrable benefit in following official guidelines in a pandemic, it appears that much more is needed to convince the affluent classes that greater income equality can benefit even them, in a better quality of life.* But when the evidence of this is shown to high-income earners, or to policy-makers in government, it still usually fails to convince; they remain tightly wedded to the dogma of materialism and still cannot see that social life is more complicated

---

will inevitably facilitate the spread of the contagion and thus lead to a higher level of mortality amongst them.

 * The negative effects of gross income inequalities have now become mainstream, many official sources and research bodies testifying to the dangers they pose to the planet, and especially to the bottom 40% of the population who are increasingly getting left behind. Less inequality would benefit all, reiterates the OECD, but in neo-liberal circles one wonders if anyone is listening. (See Endnote 123.)

than that. As we have seen, the authority of ideology can appear more powerful than reasoned argument; it will need a significant conjunction of forces, as well as some vigorous advocates, to overcome it.

However, it is at times of crisis that the tectonic plates of ideological rigidity and blind adherence to unfounded dogma may start to shift. The financial crash and the years of austerity which followed were evidently not sufficient to provide a truly seismic shock and to change underlying assumptions. Nevertheless, things may be different when the world eventually recovers from the impact of the Covid-19 pandemic which is ravaging societies and economies. It appears likely to have global consequences equivalent to those of a major war – if not in the numbers of victims, then in the devastation wrought on economic fortunes. In the changes to everyday social life which it has already precipitated, it has started to alter perspectives. While its effects on the poor, particularly in the Third World, are especially severe, it is forcing even people of the rich world to reassess priorities – as regards employment, time, and perhaps values. The work done by low-paid employees – emptying refuse bins, caring for the elderly, delivering door-to-door – is being reconsidered. Affluent societies cannot do without the basic, mundane services which keep the wheels of modern civilization turning.* The current crisis may help persuade the affluent that those responsible for these tasks should be better remunerated, even if the wider benefits of greater equality are not yet conceded. But this could be an important step to a wider understanding – which will eventually come.

Over twenty years ago, newspapers highlighted the inequalities in society which had spiralled during the long years of Conservative government. *Britain stuck with a two-tier society...* was a typical headline in 1997.[157] That one appeared above an article citing a new book, *Inequality*, which had just come out. But the article noted the new Labour government's intention to remedy the matter by concentrating on education, training and welfare-to-work schemes – NOT, by more immediate, direct policies. Then, New Labour's nervous determination to stick to tight spending plans, with insufficient investment in the public

---

* In his interesting *Utopia for Realists*, Rutger Bregman contrasts the strike of New York's 'sanitation workers' in 1968 with that of Irish bankers in 1970. When the American garbage crews walked out, New York's mayor, with the support of the local press, tried to hold out, but the mountains of rubbish and stench in the streets forced him into declaring a state of emergency, before giving way to the strikers' demands after only nine days. However, Ireland survived for a full six months when their bankers went on strike two years later, apparently without it having a major effect on the Irish economy.[156]

sphere, had little impact on underlying income disparities. And under Labour, Tory/Lib Dem, or Tory administrations, that was the pattern for 23 years, until Coronavirus prompted a cascade of government cash to forestall economic ruin. The evidence of the growing inequalities over that period, and their resistance to half-hearted, peripheral measures, have never once prompted governments to tackle them head on. They have always been left to resolve themselves indirectly through promises of a growing economy, higher employment, *trickle-down* mechanisms, and so on. None of these has succeeded because neither overall national wealth nor higher GDP, neither greater numbers of people in work nor a higher *per capita* average income, neither macro-economic improvement nor piecemeal social tinkering can in themselves provide solutions to the problem of inequality – which was, and remains, an issue not of *amounts*, but of *proportions*.

This chapter has been an attempt to expose some of the misunderstandings surrounding inequality, and to explain its impact on modern societies. It is not a static feature of modern life, but can vary greatly over time and in different places; it is not the result of unvarying, timeless natural laws, but a phenomenon created by human beings. Its position today has evolved since the mid-20th century, when in most countries of the developed world much greater equality was the norm. But from the 1970s onwards a divergence took place. In jurisdictions under the sway of extreme free market forces, inequalities were allowed to become more exaggerated; in others, where social market policies were adopted, and where public services were more developed, inequalities usually remained fairly constant or grew only slightly. The result is a world of contrasting fortunes, but one in which very unequal societies have been censured. Their deep inequalities – not their poverty – have been criticised by international bodies, think-tanks and NGOs, humanitarian charities, and numerous political figures of the Centre and the Left – to almost no avail. For progress will be achieved only by engineering greater income – and as a consequence social – equality. Voices are heard calling for poverty to be tackled first, as a more important target which in any case will reduce inequality.* But no – addressing

---

* These voices emanate not just from the fields of politics or economics. For example, celebrated Harvard cognitive psychologist Steven Pinker maintained that combating poverty of those at the bottom of the social ladder in developed nations was far more important than reducing inequality.[158] Pinker's popular works such as *The Better Angels of Our Nature* (2011) and *Enlightenment Now* (2018) have been very influential in propagating a positive, optimistic view of human civilization today.

inequality has to be the first, urgent, overriding priority, from which other benefits will follow, the means to greater human fulfilment.

END NOTES

i   This chapter's title is taken from Yanis Varoufakis, in *Talking to My Daughter: A Brief History of Capitalism,* Vintage, London, 2017, p. 48. He defines it as ... *the coexistence of unimaginable new wealth and unspeakable suffering* – the spectacular increase in inequality.

ii.   Alexis de Tocqueville, from *On Democracy in America*, 1835.

iii.   Paul Cohen-Portheim, *England, The Unknown Isle*, translated from the German by Alan Harris, Duckworth, London, 1930, pp. 143-4.

iv.   R. H. Tawney, *Equality*, George Allen & Unwin, London, 1931, p. 31.

v.   Mickey Kaus, *The End of Equality*, Basic Books, New York, 1992, pp. 5-6.

1. Quoted in George Watson, *The English Ideology*, Allen Lane, London, 1973, p. 29.
2. Conservative peer Arthur Balfour, then Lord President of the Council, in his Introduction to Walter Bagehot, *The English Constitution*, Oxford University Press, Oxford, 1928 edn., pp. xxiii-xxiv.
3. I have taken some of my analysis from two key texts by researchers Richard Wilkinson and Kate Pickett: *The Spirit Level: Why Equality is Better for Everyone*, Penguin Books, London, 2010, and *The Inner Level: How More Equal Societies Reduce Stress, Restore Sanity and Improve Everyone's Well-being*, Allen Lane, London, 2018. The amount of documented evidence in these works is remarkable – almost as remarkable is the lack of attention paid to it by media and policy makers. The data I have drawn on for this paragraph come largely from *The Inner Level*, Chapter 7.
4. According to the UNICEF index of child well-being, 2013, cited in Richard Wilkinson & Kate Pickett, 2018, op. cit., p. 107. Of 21 developed nations figuring in the data, only Greece is ranked below the USA for standards of child well-being.
5. George Orwell, 'England your England', in *The Lion and the Unicorn: Socialism and the English Genius*, Penguin Books, London, 1982, p. 36.
6. According to the latest OECD country statistics (January 2020) at **https://data.oecd.org/**
7. WHO figures for 2016 put total annual US spending at $9,870, and Cuba at $970. See **https://data.worldbank.org/indicator/SH.XPD.CHEX.PC.CD?name_desc=false**
8. At **https://www.infoplease.com/world/health-and-social-statistics/infant-mortality-rates-countries**
9. At **https://www.infoplease.com/world/health-and-social-statistics/life-expectancy-countries-0**

10 See *Innocenti Report Card 13, Fairness for Children: A league table of inequality in child well-being in rich countries*, at https://www.unicef-irc.org/publications/pdf/RC13_eng.pdf. Dr. Sarah Cook, Director of the UNICEF Office of Research – Innocenti, commented, "The Report Card provides a clear reminder that the well-being of children in any country is not an inevitable outcome of individual circumstances or of the level of economic development but is **shaped by policy choices.**" (My emphasis.)

11 See https://www.unicef-irc.org/publications/pdf/Family-Friendly-Policies-Research_UNICEF_%202019.pdf

12 As shown by Richard Wilkinson & Kate Pickett, 2018, op. cit., p. 97, based on their article 'The enemy between us: the psychological and social costs of inequality', in *European Journal of Social Psychology* 2017; 47: 11-24.

13 From OECD (2016), 'Skills Matter: Further Results from the Survey of Adult Skills', OECD Skills Studies, OECD Publishing, Paris, at https://www.oecd.org/skills/piaac/Skills_Matter_Further_Results_from_the_Survey_of_Adult_Skills.pdf Official site of full report – http://dx.doi.org/10.1787/9789264258051-en

14 Wilkinson & Pickett, 2018, op. cit., p. xvii.

15 From Benjamin Disraeli's *Vindication of the English Constitution*, quoted in Ferdinand Mount, *Mind The Gap: The New Class Divide in Britain*, Short Books, London, 2012, p. 46.

16 'The Original Affluent Society', in Marshall Sahlins, *Stone Age Economics*, Aldine-Atherton, Chicago, 1972.

17 Says cultural anthropologist Christopher Boehm is his 2007 article 'Political Primates', at https://greatergood.berkeley.edu/article/item/political_primates/

18 Ibid. See also Christopher Boehm, *Moral Origins: The Evolution of Virtue, Altruism, and Shame*, Basic Books, New York, 2012.

19 D. Erdal and A. Whiten, 'Egalitarianism and Machiavellian intelligence in human evolution', quoted in Wilkinson and Pickett, 2018, op. cit., p. 122.

20 Quoted by James Suzman in 'Why the Kalahari Bushmen are Earth's most successful civilization', in *The Observer*, London, 29/10/2017. In his article he draws on Richard B. Lee's groundbreaking *The Dobe Ju/'hoansi*, now in its 4th edition (Wadsworth/Cenage, Boston, 2013). Suzman's own recent work is *Affluence without Abundance: The Disappearing World of the Bushmen*, Bloomsbury, London, 2017 – based on over twenty years of work in the field.

21 Quoted in Ronald Wright, *A Short History of Progress*, Canongate, Edinburgh, 2006, p. 116.

22 Suggests Ronald Wright in idem.

23 Letter from Thomas Jefferson to James Madison, 28th October 1785, in George L. Abernethy, *The Idea of Equality: An Anthology*, John Knox Press, Richmond, VA, USA, 1959, pp. 151-2. See also Andro Linklater's discussion of private property in *Owning the Earth: The Transforming History of Land Ownership*, Bloomsbury, London, 2014, pp. 208-11.

24 R. H. Tawney, op. cit., Chp. II.

25 According to figures in Thomas Piketty, *Capital in the Twenty-First Century*, The Belknap Press of Harvard University Press, Cambridge, Mass., 2017, p. 311.

26 Ibid. p. 1.

27 President Obama in a speech at a Washington D.C. community centre in Dec. 2013, quoted in Adam Tooze, *Crashed: How a Decade of Financial Crisis Changed the World*, Allen Lane, London, 2018, p. 456.

28   George Santayana, *Soliloquies in England*, quoted in J. B. Priestley, *The English*, Heinemann, London, 1973, p. 32.
29   A. H. Halsey's analysis in *Change in British Society*, 3rd. Edition, OUP, Oxford, 1986, p. 148.
30   George Orwell, 'The Lion and the Unicorn: Socialism and the English Genius', in *The Collected Essays, Journalism, & Letters of George Orwell*, Vol. II, Secker & Warburg, London, 1968, pp. 61-2.
31   Anthony Burgess, *El País*, Madrid, 26/4/1987.
32   A. H. Halsey, op. cit., p. 150.
33   Lawrence Stone, Jeanne C. Fawtier Stone, *An Open Elite? England 1540-1880*, Oxford University Press, New York, 1986, Abridged Edn., p. 293.
34   Ibid. p. 296.
35   Ibid. p. 297.
36   Tom Paine, 'Agrarian Justice', Part 3, 1795.
37   Research by S. Côté, J. House and R. Willer cited in Richard Wilkinson & Kate Pickett, 2018, op. cit., p. 82.
38   In ibid., p. 84.
39   Research conducted by M. Paskov and C. Dewilde into people's willingness to contribute to the welfare of others, cited in ibid., p. 86.
40   Marshall Sahlins, op. cit., p. 37.
41   George Orwell, 1968, op. cit., p. 68.
42   George Orwell, 1982, op. cit. p. 50.
43   Paul Cohen-Portheim, op. cit., p. 123.
44   Tom Nairn, *The Break-up of Britain*, Verso, London, 1981, p. 51.
45   Tony Judt, *Ill Fares the Land: A Treatise On Our Present Discontents*, Penguin Books, London, 2011, p. 185.
46   Idem.
47   Raymond Williams, *Culture and Society, 1780-1950*, Penguin Books, London, 1961, p. 304.
48   Idem. This is a crucially important discussion of cultural issues, especially on pp. 304-6.
49   Will Hutton, *The State We're In*, Vintage, London, 1996, p. 173.
50   Richard Wilkinson & Kate Pickett, 2018, op. cit., p. xxi.
51   Idem.
52   Ibid., p. 150.
53   Editorial in issue of *The British Medical Journal*, 1994, quoted in Oliver James, *Britain on the Couch: Treating a Low Serotonin Society*, Arrow Books, London, 1998, p. 93.
54   See Isaiah Berlin, an interesting discussion of the subject in 'The First and the Last', Granta Magazine, extracted in *The Daily Telegraph*, London, 9/10/99.
55   Will Hutton, op. cit., p. 173.
56   Herman E. Daly, John B. Cobb Jr., *For the Common Good: Redirecting the Economy towards Community, the Environment and a Sustainable Future*, Green Print, London, 1989, p. 331.
57   R. H. Tawney, op. cit., p. 63.

58   Research by Jo Blanden and Stephen Machin, cited in Will Hutton, *Them and Us: Changing Britain – Why We Need a Fair Society*, Little, Brown, London, 2010, pp. 283-4.
59   Joseph E. Stiglitz, *The Great Divide*, Penguin Books, London, 2016, p. 160
60   See Richard Wilkinson & Kate Pickett, 2018, op. cit., p. 151.
61   The Cabinet Office, *Unleashing Aspiration: The Final Report of the Panel on Fair Access to the Professions*, HMSO, 2009.
62   Geoff Hodgson, *The Democratic Economy*, Penguin, London, 1984, p. 25.
63   Cited in Thomas Piketty, *Capital and Ideology*, The Belknap Press of Harvard University Press, Cambridge, Mass., 2020, p. 535, + graphic p. 35.
64   Daniel Markovits, *The Meritocracy Trap: How America's Foundational Myth Feeds Inequality, Dismantles the Middle Class, and Devours the Elite*, Penguin Books, London, 2019.
65   Kenan Malik, 'Posh is so passé – today's elite prefers the myth of the meritocracy', in *The Observer*, London, 30/12/2018.
66   Michael Young, *The Rise of the Meritocracy 1870-2033: An Essay on Education and Equality*, Thames & Hudson, London, 1958, p. 85.
67   Ibid. pp. 86-7.
68   Ibid. p. 85.
69   Ibid. p. 123. It is also interesting that the philosopher Hannah Arendt criticised the concept of meritocracy in her 1958 extended essay 'The Crisis in Education'. Although referring mainly to American education, she pointed to the selective 11+ exam in Britain through which, she believed ...*What is aimed at in England is meritocracy*. Nevertheless, she maintained, *Meritocracy contradicts the principle of equality*.
70   Michele Lamont, *Money, Morals and Manners: The Culture of the French and the American Upper-Middle Class*, Univ. of Chicago Press, Chicago, Ill., 1992, cited in Thomas Piketty, 2017, op. cit., p. 529.
71   Richard Wilkinson & Kate Pickett, 2018, op. cit., p. 153.
72   See The Third Margaret Thatcher Lecture, for the Centre for Policy Studies, at https://www.cps.org.uk/files/factsheets/original/131128144200-Thatcherlecturev2.pdf
73   Idem.
74   Idem.
75   Joseph Stiglitz, op. cit., p. 420.
76   Milton Friedman, *Free to Choose: A Personal Statement*, Harcourt Brace Jovanovich, New York, 1980, p.132.
77   Ibid. p. 134.
78   Ha-Joon Chang, *23 Things They Don't Tell you About Capitalism*, Allen Lane, London, 2010, p. 219.
79   Evidence cited by Richard Wilkinson & Kate Pickett, 2018, op. cit., p. 177. Their graph of major nations shows the UK & the USA as having greater income inequality than many of the usual European *suspects* already cited (Scandinavia etc.), but with much less social mobility.
80   Oliver James, op. cit., p. 88.
81   See Richard Wilkinson & Kate Pickett, 2018, op. cit., p. 4.
82   Cited in ibid. p. 8.
83   Ibid. p. 58.

84 Research published in *Social Science Research*, 2012, cited in ibid. p. 57.
85 Research by University College, London, the charity Pathway, and an international team of experts, published in *The Lancet*, 12/11/2017, reported in *The Observer*, London, 12/11/2017.
86 Shown graphically in Richard Wilkinson & Kate Pickett, 2018, op. cit., p. 34.
87 Sendhil Mullainathan and Eldar Shafir, *Scarcity: The True Cost of Not Having Enough*, Penguin Books, London, 2014, p. 7.
88 Eldar Shafir, in discussion in front of an audience at the Blavatnik School of Government at Oxford University, broadcast in 'Analysis', BBC Radio 4, 23/3/2014.
89 George Orwell, *The Road to Wigan Pier*, Penguin Books, Harmondsworth, 1962, p. 86.
90 Idem.
91 Zygmunt Bauman, *Work, Consumerism and the New Poor*, Open University Press, Buckingham, 1998, p. 37.
92 Quoted in Polly Toynbee & David Walker, *Unjust Rewards: Exposing Greed and Inequality in Britain Today*, Granta Books, London, 2008, p. 15.
93 See Piketty's categories of cases for unequal income distribution in Thomas Piketty, 2017, op. cit., p. 331.
94 The figures in this paragraph are taken from the reliable, annual British Social Attitudes Survey, cited at https://www.bsa.natcen.ac.uk/media/39288/6_bsa36_poverty-and-inequality.pdf
95 Columnist Ross Douthat, 'The Case Against Meritocracy: An aristocracy that can't admit it', in *The New York Times*, New York, 8/12/2018.
96 Described in Thomas Piketty, 2017, op. cit., p. 649 – Fisher's comment not too dissimilar to President Obama's claim in 2013 that inequality is ...*the defining challenge of our time*. See p. 329 of this chapter.
97 This is part of Jo Littler's thesis in her *Against Meritocracy: Culture, Power and Myths of Mobility*, Routledge, London, 2017.
98 Figures cited in Ha-Joon Chang, op. cit., p. 142.
99 Ibid. pp. 142-3.
100 Cited in Thomas Piketty, 2020, op. cit., pp. 528, 531.
101 Reported in *The Guardian*, London, 19/12/2019, which also noted that the Denise Coates Foundation makes major donations to medical and education charities, though not apparently to gambling or addiction charities.
102 Robert H. Frank & Philip J. Cook, *The Winner-Take-All Society: Why the Few at the Top Get So Much More Than the Rest of Us*, Virgin Books, London, 2010, p. xvi.
103 Ibid. pp. xvi-xvii.
104 Robert H. Frank, *Falling Behind: How rising inequality harms the middle class*, University of California Press, Berkeley, CA, 2007.
105 Robert Peston and Laurence Knight, *How Do We Fix This Mess? The Economic Price of Having It All and the Route to Lasting Prosperity*, Hodder & Stoughton, London, 2013, p. 92.
106 Quoted in Polly Toynbee and David Walker, op. cit., p. 55.
107 Ferdinand Mount, from his *The New Few, Or a Very British Oligarchy*, Simon & Schuster, London, 2012, quoted in Polly Toynbee, 'They're all in it together', *The Spectator*, London, 5/5/2012.

108 Idem. But it took the political and economic earthquakes of 2020/21 for President Biden to utter these words – in effect an ideological bombshell – in his address to Congress at the end of his first 100 days in April 2021: *My fellow Americans, trickle-down economics has never worked.* (!)
109 Joseph E. Stiglitz, op. cit., pp. 75-6.
110 Ibid. p. 97.
111 Richard Sennett, *Together: The Rituals, Pleasures and Politics of Cooperation*, Allen Lane, London, 2012, p. 138, and see https://www.unicef-irc.org/publications/pdf/RC13_eng.pdf
112 Richard Wilkinson & Kate Pickett, 2018, op. cit., p. 104, and graph, p. 107.
113 Richard Wilkinson & Kate Pickett, 2010, op. cit., p. 139.
114 Ibid. p. 176.
115 From 'The Equality Trust', 2012, cited in Danny Dorling, *Inequality and the 1%*, Verso, London, 2014, p. 181.
116 Richard Wilkinson & Kate Pickett, 2010, op. cit., p. 174.
117 Richard Sennett, op. cit., p. 141.
118 Richard Wilkinson & Kate Pickett, 2018, op. cit., pp. 63-4.
119 Richard Wilkinson & Kate Pickett, 2010, op. cit., p. 44.
120 Richard Wilkinson & Kate Pickett, 2018, op. cit., pp. 61-2.
121 Daniel Kahneman, *Thinking Fast And Slow*, Penguin Books, London, 2012, p. 256.
122 Ibid. p. 263.
123 'Causes and Consequences of Income Inequality: A Global perspective', (SDN/15/13) by Era Dabla-Norris, Kalpana Kochhar, Nujin Suphaphiphat, Frantisek Ricka, Evridiki Tsounta, at https://www.imf.org/en/Publications/Staff-Discussion-Notes/Issues/2016/12/31/Causes-and-Consequences-of-Income-Inequality-A-Global-Perspective-42986. IMF Staff Discussion Notes showcase the latest policy-related analysis and research. The OECD also emphasises the negative effect of inequality on economic growth. In their 2015 report, *In it together: Why Less Inequality Benefits All*, they say, … *the rise of income inequality between 1985 and 2005, for example, is estimated to have knocked 4.7% points off cumulative growth between 1990 and 2010, on average across OECD countries…* See: OECD (2015), *In it together: Why Less Inequality Benefits All*, OECD Publishing, Paris. At http://dx.doi.org/10.1787/9789264235120-en.
124 Richard Wilkinson & Kate Pickett, 2010, op. cit., p. xii.
125 According to the results of the annual British Social Attitudes survey, available at https://www.bsa.natcen.ac.uk/media/39278/bsa35_social_trust.pdf
126 The USA's General Social Survey (NORC at the University of Chicago) has been carried out since 1972. See https://gssdataexplorer.norc.org/variables/441/vshow
127 Eric M. Uslaner, from his article 'The Moral Foundations of Trust' (September 2002), available at SSRN: https://ssrn.com/abstract=824504 or http://dx.doi.org/10.2139/ssrn.824504 This is also the title of Uslaner's book, *The Moral Foundations of Trust*, CUP, Cambridge UK, 2002.
128 Zygmunt Bauman, *Wasted Lives: Modernity and its Outcasts*, Polity Press, Cambridge, UK, 2004, p. 89.
129 Richard Wilkinson & Kate Pickett, 2018, op. cit., p. 36.
130 Research for the NHS Information Centre, 2009, cited in ibid. p. 40.

131 Article in *European Sociological Review*, 2012, cited in ibid. p. 44.
132 Idem.
133 https://data.oecd.org/natincome/gross-national-income.htm
134 As shown in Wilkinson & Pickett, 2010, op. cit., p. 83.
135 Research at Massachusetts Institute of Technology's Economics Department. Michael Stepner there said, "When we think about income inequality in the United States, we think that low-income Americans can't afford to purchase the same homes, live in the same neighborhoods, and buy the same goods and services as higher-income Americans. But the fact that they can on average expect to have 10 or 15 fewer years of life really demonstrates the level of inequality we've had in the United States." https://news.mit.edu/2016/study-rich-poor-huge-mortality-gap-us-0411
136. Research by D. Vagero and O. Lundberg cited in Richard Wilkinson & Kate Pickett, 2010, op. cit., p. 178.
137 See https://data.oecd.org/healthstat/infant-mortality-rates.htm
138 Richard Wilkinson & Kate Pickett, 2010, op. cit., pp. 173-4.
139 'How Much Inequality is Too Much?', subject of BBC World Service 'Inquiry' programme, broadcast 8/1/2016. Professor Deirdre McCloskey's contribution: 'Capitalism is not the enemy'.
140 https://www.cps.org.uk/events/q/date/2013/11/27/the-2013-margaret-thatcher-lecture-boris-johnson/
141 Professor Deirdre N. McCloskey, 'Growth, Not Forced Equality, Saves the Poor', in the *New York Times*, New York, 23/12/2016.
142 A. Sinfield, *Literature, Politics and Culture in Post-War Britain*, (1989) quoted in David Morgan and Mary Evans, 'The Road to *Nineteen Eighty-Four*: Orwell and the post-war reconstruction of citizenship', in Brian Brivati and Harriet Jones (Eds.), *What Difference Did the War Make?* Leicester University Press, London, 1993, p.51.
143 M. Soames, *Clementine Churchill*, (1981) quoted in ibid.
144 Tim Jackson, *Prosperity Without Growth: Foundations For The Economy of Tomorrow*, 2nd Edn., Routledge, Abingdon, Oxon., 2017, p. 124. Jackson references the marvellous work of Indian economist Amartya Sen in this field. See notes p. 249.
145 Tony Judt, op. cit., p. 25.
146 Richard Sennett, *Respect: The Formation of Character in an Age of Inequality*, Penguin Books, London, 2004, p. 172.
147 Richard Wilkinson & Kate Pickett, 2018, op. cit., pp. 50-1.
148 OECD (2015), op. cit., at http://dx.doi.org/10.1787/9789264235120-en
149 Tony Judt, op. cit., p. 31.
150 George Lakoff, *Don't Think of an Elephant: Know Your Values and Frame the Debate*, Chelsea Green Publishing, White River Junction, Vt., USA, 2014, p. 91.
151 'Billionaire Bonanza: The Forbes 400 and the Rest of Us', The Institute for Policy Studies, at https://ips-dc.org/billionaire-bonanza/ and 'Patriotic Millionaires', at https://patrioticmillionaires.org/2016/02/02/global-inequality-american-inequality/ The (mainly) American 'Patriotic Millionaires' also drew on Oxfam's

paper 'An Economy for the 1%', at https://www.oxfamamerica.org/explore/research-publications/an-economy-for-the-1/. Data on inequality emerging from these two sources prompted 'Patriotic Millionaires' to conclude that the problem was ... *disgusting, alarming, immoral and un-American.*

152 https://www.ons.gov.uk/peoplepopulationandcommunity/personalandhouseholdfinances/incomeandwealth/bulletins/householdincomeinequalityfinancial/financialyearending2019. There are other measures of income inequality, such as the S80/S20 ratio, comparing the total income of the richest 20% of the populations with the bottom 20% of earners, and also the Palma ratio, comparing the income share of the richest 10% of people with that of the poorest 40%. Both of these ratios have seen a rise in inequality in Britain in recent years. Furthermore, the richest 1% of the population accounted for an average of 7.6% of total income between 2011 and 2019, though still not back to the high of 8.8% between the years 2007 and 2009.

153 The OECD national rankings are based on Gini coefficients for 2017, (or latest available) accessed at https://www.equalitytrust.org.uk/scale-economic-inequality-uk

154 Zygmunt Bauman, 2004, op. cit., p. 40.

155 Idem.

156 Rutger Bregman, *Utopia for Realists – and How We Can Get There*, Bloomsbury, London, 2018, Chapter 7.

157 'Britain stuck with a two-tier society', by Paul Johnson, *The Guardian Weekly*, 3/8/1997. The book cited: Alissa Goodman, Paul Johnson, Steven Webb, *Inequality*, OUP, Oxford, 1997.

158 Steven Pinker, interview in *The Observer*, London, 11/2/2018.

Chapter 7

AN ALTERNATIVE PROGRESS – FOR A ... *MUSEUM OF ANOMALIES**

The certainties of one age are the problems of the next.
R. H. TAWNEY

There is no building for the future any more in the traditional sense, no putting away for later rainy days like those of the past – the only certainty is now. ... Use what you've got today – tomorrow you might find it obsolete, irrelevant, or worse, a strangling noose around your neck. The most precious thing in the world is now, because it's the only thing in your grasp. Your existential posturing will constantly shift – reality is only temporary. ... Never has the future been more NOW.
LONDON ARCHITECTURAL STUDENT, 1970[ii]

Belief in progress is the Prozac of the thinking classes. ... The core of the idea of progress is the belief that human life becomes better with the growth of knowledge. The error is not in thinking that human life can improve. Rather, it is imagining that improvement can ever be cumulative.
JOHN GRAY[iii]

"*If machines produce everything we need, the outcome will depend on how things are distributed. Everyone can enjoy a life of luxurious leisure if the machine-produced wealth is shared, or most people can end up miserably poor if the machine-owners successfully lobby against wealth redistribution. So far, the trend seems to be toward the second option, with technology driving ever-increasing inequality.*"
STEPHEN HAWKING[iv]

Does inventing an online bookstore really render your human worth greater than that of 42 million Ukrainians combined?
LUKE HILDYARD.[v]

---

*   Ralph Waldo Emerson's summing up of the nation in his *English Traits*, first published in 1856.[i]

AN ALTERNATIVE PROGRESS

IT was the year 2016 when significant parts of the world disappeared down a metaphorical rabbit-hole, following the United Kingdom's EU referendum and the presidential election in the United States. These nations, as well as others which came within the political orbit of the bizarre consequences of these events, found themselves in a preposterous, almost unrecognisable environment, one which the most imaginative novelist would have been hard pressed to invent. For it was a strange, eccentric world peopled not with white rabbits, March Hares or even Mad Hatters (of the conventional kind), but with Donald Trumps, Boris Johnsons, Jair Bolsonaros,* George Floyds, inflammatory rhetoric and provocative conduct. Anti-racial movements were sweeping the globe, demonstrations cropping up in all continents, and in 2020 a dangerous virus emerged to produce a worldwide pandemic, destroying lives and livelihoods. With large parts of the planet under lockdown in an attempt to contain the disease, with vulnerable people confined to their homes for weeks on end, and many more with their jobs or businesses extinguished, there were many waking each morning amazed at the dystopian spectacle confronting them. And now, with a vaccination programme well underway, do we think there will ever be a return to familiar normality, or has the old world gone for ever?

However, while we may ponder almost wistfully the memories of solid (albeit flawed) political leaders, reliable and mutually beneficial international alliances, worthwhile employment – even if insecure or poorly paid – and everyday, companionable social intercourse, before we were obliged to keep our distance, there are nevertheless features around us which do not change. The consequences of decades of neo-liberal government policy have not left us: endemic material deprivation alongside excessive riches, severe social inequalities, homelessness, promotion of private concerns and neglect of the public realm, and delusional economic programmes built on false promises. These and numerous other iniquities have made steady inroads into British national equanimity for more than forty years, undermining social bonds and encouraging us to be a harder, less generous society. And while the virus allowed the politics of austerity to be suddenly cast off as if it were eminently superfluous, all know that this is the result of irresistible *force majeure*. The financial cascade from the Treasury has

---

* For each has his acolytes who strive to match their mentors for divisive language and extravagant behaviour.

been turned on through dire national exigence, to forestall yet greater economic disaster; it will just as readily be turned off when circumstances appear to warrant it – such as when debt becomes frighteningly large and/or the adverse effects of Brexit, hidden behind the fig leaf of the ravages of Covid-19, demand action. It is not as if the punitive rationale behind austerity has been renounced, or that the malign motivation of its protagonists has been diluted.

Indeed, the realm of political and economic ideas is little changed by the cataclysmic events of the last four years; it now has a different backdrop before which they can be played out. Extraordinary measures are put forward to deal with unprecedented circumstances, and the Coronavirus emergency gives considerable latitude to official policy. But the instincts and prejudices of right-wing governments of recent years resolutely endure, and will become more prominent in informing conventional policy when occasion allows. For the time being, the global pandemic has relegated populations to a kind of nether-world, where behaviours and expectations have been transformed and normal service has been suspended. And all the while, as we struggle to do what is asked of us, we are thinking, as Alice did, ... *couriouser and couriouser*! It has been suggested that the demands placed on health and emergency services, the caring sector, and communal, voluntary initiatives will have a lasting legacy – in a kinder, more altruistic society. And the outpouring of open-hearted humanitarianism in Britain and many societies, prompted by the crisis, has shown the potential for such a transformation. But the vernacular, coal-face arena of ordinary lives is unlikely, on its own, to be able to drive future developments. Once material instincts re-assert themselves, it will be hard to resist the slide towards business as usual, as neo-liberal governments return to a world they understand.

In a sense, the repercussions of Covid-19 provide a window of opportunity. The politics of the last few decades have contributed to the establishment of a hard-edged *status quo*, which has gained the glinting hallmarks of permanence – neo-liberalism, the currency of the age. It is a struggle to see the nation trading in any other medium. Because an implicit acceptance has developed that there is no alternative, belief has spread in many quarters that faith in market fundamentalism will endure – to the material benefit of all – so that we must adapt or suffer. But in economics, as in life, confidence in the medium of exchange is vital for it to be sustained. No amount of hardship or inequality, or even a financial crisis, has been able decisively to undermine trust in the currency of neo-liberalism, but the consequences of the global pandemic may yet lead to a questioning of its rectitude. The display of goodwill and voluntary humanitarianism, as well as unmistakeable professional dedication, have illustrated another side to our species, an alternative to *homo economicus* – always present, but lately obscured behind the noise and swagger of individualistic materialism. It is just that the acceptance of neo-liberalism – such as it has been – developed into one of Hulme's *categories of the human mind*, described in Chapter 1, a powerful notion underlying much government policy, which many could not help but think must be the true way of progress: attractive, modern, smart.

For, as outlined at the start of this work, our implicit perception of the world around us is crucial in conditioning our responses to society and its norms. The dominant economic values of the 1980s became the prevailing perspective, notably in Britain and the United States – the *ambient noise* of several generations through which we tuned in to policy and practice. Emerging out of neo-liberalism was a whole panoply of assumptions which developed into the extravagant myths of the age, and were absorbed subliminally. We allowed ourselves to be convinced by the tales we were told, and reinforced them with our own rationalizing – of the need for stern, uncompromising policies in a hostile world of fierce competition. And any contrary suggestions were rejected as being soft, unrealistic, or worse: socialistic statism. In fact, there has been a refusal to engage with alternative ideas – something which has been termed *knowledge resistance*. In a recent book, Mikael Klintman laid out the terrain in which people in like-minded groups instinctively form *knowledge tribes* with their own sets of rigid beliefs, and become resistant to opposing opinions.[1] And the greater the deviation of the group's views from those of others, the stronger their collective cohesion becomes, thus establishing an impermeable defence against doctrinal infiltration. Thus many of us remain shielded from contrasting perspectives and stay rooted in our narrow, self-reinforcing silos.

For some time now there has been a desperate need for change, something to shake the mindset of complacent, largely unspoken assumptions, and let in the fresh air of new thinking. For neo-liberalism has not been working – and neither will the 'one-last-push' line of reasoning produce the intended outcome of lasting prosperity and national renewal. In fact, the economic cataclysm of Coronavirus has pushed the promised land even further over the horizon. Change is required – not to overthrow an economic system, but to mould it to suit the needs of the twenty-first century, as well as the latent characteristics of British society. To this end, a concentration on dogma and principles is a worthless exercise: the modern era has had enough of ideology. In any case, the British inclination towards pragmatism has rarely required practical politics to have a strong underpinning of values; policy does not have to be dressed up in fancy theoretical garb.* But such may be the transforming power of dramatic events like a viral pandemic that new avenues may be able to be laid out. The shake-up to established patterns of living, which it has precipitated, may allow eyes to be opened and new possibilities entertained. The starting point must not be ideology or even morality, but practical prescriptions which connect with established ways of living, with community, and – rejecting the bogus representation of *homo economicus* – with a realistic conception of modern humanity.

So the task in the following pages is to outline future directions for Britain – suggestions some of which might apply to other neo-liberal regimes, with obvious modifications required for different national contexts. These recommendations, compatible with free market capitalism, amount to an alternative to the divisive, anti-social, free market fundamentalism on neo-liberal lines which has plagued Britain and similar societies over recent decades. That is not to suggest a radical shake-up of political structure or a new form of government. But because no dramatic break with the past is advocated, or prescriptive doctrine proposed, it may well not be easy to conceptualize the avenues outlined. This is not a revolutionary manifesto and does not amount to a new *-ism* – beyond what is in the title of the work. There is enough evidence around the globe of the effects of political upheavals – usually leading to a return to a version of the *status quo*, but only after considerable suffering. No, the subtle requirements needed to change the bases of extreme market capitalism cannot be easily summarised, except perhaps as a kind of pragmatic, humanitarian, communal strategy with an emphasis on what can work. Enough has been set out in the preceding chapters to indicate the widespread malfunctioning of British society

---

* One might say that the lack of interest in Britain in abstract ideas has helped preserve freedom and privacy. As Professor John Carey once said, *If the English had valued ideas, they would have started locking one another up for having the wrong ones...*[2] (Although lately, some anti-terrorist measures have come close to this.)

and its casualties. The following prescriptions – albeit hampered for some time to come by the effects of Covid-19 – are designed to remedy this dire situation.

Project One: Towards Social Capitalism: Reining in the free market.

Much has been said over many years about the end of capitalism and its replacement with a new economic system – most of it irrelevant and unrealistic. Talk is heard of its substitution with some non-market-based arrangement, following its demise through hubris and hyper-consumerism. And the shadow of Marx still hovers over ideas of a transformation through a form of Hegelian evolution, by which the existing system is faced with an antithetical convulsion, leading to an entirely new kind of economy. However, the contention here is that the free market is so enmeshed in global economic arrangements, and is so much a part of democratic politics, that such expectations are unrealistic. That is not to say that capitalism will not evolve, or that it could not decay from within, as economists like Joseph Schumpeter believed. There are plenty of current signs of its protagonists over-reaching themselves in their efforts to exploit it for all its worth; after all, Golden Geese have been killed before. This is all the more reason why markets have to be guided and managed to maintain their proper functioning for the benefit of all. Wheels do not need to be re-invented; there was a time not long ago when the free market shared its bounty more fairly with all socio-economic levels. In a competitive environment there will always be some economic entities that do not survive, but human needs require that capitalism must not be solely a Darwinian struggle for existence.

So, again, how we conceptualise capitalism will condition its future direction. Its function within wider society has to be properly appreciated. In the years after the Second World War, western free market systems, alongside sensible worker representation and comprehensive welfare states, functioned for the benefit of most in society, and social inequalities were reduced. But since the 1980s the market has increasingly favoured the already affluent, and has allowed vast socio-economic gulfs to emerge. In other words, capitalism has come to dominate society, and severely prejudice its poorer members, to the extent that neo-liberals see social existence as a component of capitalist economics.

This is not only false, but dangerous, since it encourages the view of human beings as economic entities, rather than an holistic concept of humanity in which materialism is but one element. As George Soros pointed out, quoted in Chapter 3, *We can have a market economy but we cannot have a market society*. The free market needs to be kept in its place, both strategically and conceptually. Otherwise we belittle our humanity and over-rate the acquisitive part of our nature. By endeavouring to keep free market instincts subordinate, and their roles limited within prescribed boundaries, we will enhance our perspectives on life and contribute to a return to a pre-existing form of capitalism.

The task of reining in the free market will be made easier if its proper role is appreciated. Human existence cannot be defined purely in economic terms, any more than social life can be explained by reference only to the individual. The fact that these realities are often ignored has been responsible for much social dislocation of recent years. As John Kay pointed out, quoted in Chapter 5, ... *market economies function only by virtue of being embedded in a social context*. The complex social paraphernalia of democratic states which underpin the free market are essential for its optimal operation; without the legal, commercial, and educational framework of capitalist economies – within existing communal norms – markets would be even more anti-social and dysfunctional.* However, in spite of this important context, neo-liberal regimes like the UK and USA still need to build consensus toward the further containment of free market autonomy in the interests of social harmony and equality. For, neither community nor custom, neither morality nor sentiment have been able to exercise sufficient restraint on efficiency and the drive for profit – as might have been the case when the idea of the *invisible hand* was first propounded. We cannot allow further evolution of rule by the market – *economic totalitarianism*, as it was once called.[3] The sweeping certainties of material self-interest must ultimately have to give way to social and cultural considerations, and above all to dignity.

Market forces will need to be contained within social boundaries, for the benefit of the population as a whole. As the prevailing economic system of advanced democracies it has to be nurtured and guided. Its role in the production, distribution and sale of commodities is essential,

---

* One only has to compare the functioning of the free market in modern Russia with its situation in western democracies to realise the importance of the social and political context as well as a regulatory framework.

but that does not mean it can be allowed full authority over all goods and services in a society in terms of demand and supply, pricing and availability, regardless of the economic and social outcomes which may ensue. The existence of comprehensive welfare states and various fiscal measures to protect poorer citizens in advanced societies shows that this is already recognized in principle. But the so-called 'safety net' is seen as security for those who fail to take advantage of the largesse of market economics, rather than as compensation for the limitations of the system – its inability to function for the benefit of all. Of course, the market does not exist to serve individual or social needs; it is amoral and disinterested in the consequences of its operations (which is one of its advantages, many of its proponents will argue). We hear it said that *... the markets will decide*, or that *... we should not interfere but leave it to the market*. And of course this policy conveniently absolves participants from responsibility for unfortunate outcomes. But neo-liberalism has no interest in modifying free market economics because it does not accept obligations to wider society.*

This is where society must step in. Time is past when populations must be obliged to endure the random consequences of a man-made (yes, by 'men') economic system which serves the interests of humans only incidentally. And of course the resolve of neo-liberals is to keep hands off (they mean the hands of others!) the levers of capitalism, and certainly not guide market forces towards desirable social outcomes. Even the classical liberal John Stuart Mill accepted that interference in the economy was necessary to remedy the inhumane features of capitalism, although prior to the development of sociology as a discipline he did not have the lexicon to express in modern terms the relationship between freedom and the individual as a member of society. Nevertheless, he supported legislation in order to ensure personal liberty, which is what is required today in neo-liberal environments where market dominance severely hampers the living standards of many individuals, curtailing their liberty in the process. The role of the free market has to be re-fashioned in order to restrict its destructive power by limiting the domains in which it freely operates. While free market operations are not crucial to individuals of modest means in fields like luxury

---

* – because its master is money, not people; the greater the freedom of expression of free market capitalism and the more limited the social restrictions placed on its autonomy, the more it embodies true neo-liberalism and the greater its dominance in the interests of capital, especially institutional capital and its rich capitalists.

cars, jewellery, or long-haul holiday destinations, they certainly are as regards food, medicines and winter fuel. It is here that the community has to be involved.

Thus the project to rein in the market must involve a process of containment. Goods essential to everyday, vernacular life must be protected from the indiscriminate forces of market economics. In a rich, developed society commodities which most citizens really need, or reasonably require, should not be subject to the full force of free market economics. Essential foodstuffs, health care, local public transport, nursery education and child care, basic sports facilities, access to decent broadband as well as to museums and other sites of national heritage, and the availability of legal redress – these are the principal items which ought not to be denied to individuals because, under the demands of modern capitalist practice, they cannot afford them. Level of income should not be a crucial, determining factor in, for example, whether one is able to leave a child well cared for while a parent goes to work, afford a nutritious diet for oneself as well as one's children, or take part in everyday sports. In twenty-first-century Britain or America, these are often out of reach. Yet all these goods and facilities are integral to national life; as such, they should form a prerogative, contributing to the socialization of the young in society and helping provide a sense of commonality among its members. National art treasures should be as accessible as free education, and a cheap, frequent, local public transport service should be guaranteed as are democratic rights and free speech.

In fact, the private exploitation of, and personal profit from services and facilities such as these are deeply anti-social; they should not be part of the normal market economy. The wider principle encompassing this has by implication already been approved: subsidised school meals or an NHS free at the point of use are obvious examples. And householders in remote country areas do not – yet! – have to pay the full cost of having their mail delivered. Of course, opposing the autonomy of market operations in some fields will attract charges of being anti-capitalist. But limiting the power of money and the market in what – in this day and age – are the essential requirements of respectable modern life is merely what all in a decent society have a right to expect. It represents the primacy of humanity, and the subordination of raw economic forces to individual and communal needs. Acceptance of the market mechanism does not mean it should be allowed unrestricted licence to expand its reach in imperialistic fashion, at the cost of standards and livelihoods. Otherwise, what has been the purpose of the years of growth and productivity which have enriched us as nations? And beyond the realm of essential material needs, there is ample scope for capitalism and its individualistic drive to operate through ambition, innovation, entrepreneurial spirit, and simple money-making.

Containment and limitations of this kind could contribute to placing the so-called 'good life' within reach of more of the population. By raising the material standards of the poor and the 'barely getting by' in society – abolishing the penury and desperation of so many – there would be a wider commonality of experience amongst the population. All would have more time and opportunity to assess the true value of what are currently held up as commodities to covet and goals to emulate. The problem here is that we have lost the sense of aspiring towards the 'good life' – part of our abandonment of the notion of limits. As Robert and Edward Skidelsky point out, ... *having discarded the concept of the good life, modern economics can make no sense of the distinction between needs and wants.*[4] We find it hard to differentiate between necessities and luxuries. Hyper-consumerism and increasing commodification have blurred our appreciation of value and priorities. The late Zygmunt Bauman wrote perceptively of the invidious trends this represents:

> *The market penetrates areas of life which had stayed outside the realm of monetary exchange until recently. It relentlessly hammers home the message that everything is or could be a commodity, or if it is still short of becoming a commodity, that it should be handled like a commodity.*[5]

Thus the current direction of travel is the wrong way: creeping colonisation of communal, vernacular territory extends market reach, and often creates commercial areas where competition is artificial, mainly serving large corporate interests.

However, if the scope of market forces were reined in, it would not prevent those wishing to enrich themselves from trying to do so – EXCEPT, not at the expense of the living standards and self-respect of swathes of the population. These concerns have to take precedence over corporate interests; it is intolerable to hear that profit and shareholder value should be protected in sectors involving essential commodities, when raising prices will have a dire impact on poorer citizens. Of course, employment is bound up with company performance, but concern for living standards must take priority, and in any case a decent level of welfare provision will help mitigate the effects of unemployment. Rich, advanced economies have gone beyond the stage where growth and productivity can come at the expense of human welfare. Even – and especially – during crises such as that caused by Covid-19, the money economy must not be permitted to prejudice further the lives of ordinary people; it needs to have a much lower profile in the social scheme of things. There are still those who maintain that any negative consequences of market forces are mere anomalies – incidental side-effects of our vital engine of affluence. This form of denial has become part of the assumptions of capitalism's benefits, whereas – as Martin Pawley said fifty years ago – its afflictions are in fact ... *the predictable result of things being arranged as they are.*[6]

There will always be discussion as to what items should be regarded as essential elements of modern life in a rich society. Those mentioned above in this chapter go beyond the vital requisites of existence in terms of sustenance, shelter, warmth, etc., for reasons already cited. Adam Smith understood this over two hundred years ago, when he gave the example of a labourer's linen shirt – not an absolute necessity of life, but the obvious lack of which would be a mark of dishonour in his community (outlined in Chapter 5). For some form of parity of existence, one needs the wherewithal to lead a normal life, earn the self-respect of one's peers and neighbours, and possess sufficient mental *bandwidth* to be able to cope with the demands of employment, health, education, child care, and so on. It becomes a question of whether one can take part in everyday life on the same terms as one's neighbours, and of course this is a matter of psychology, morale and dignity. One can exist without an occasional visit to the cinema, or even a television – neither of which is crucial to keep body and soul together. But not being able to afford such basic non-necessities places one at the very margins of society, with all the implications for self-respect and mental health. When the free market impinges on such aspects of personal well-being among segments of a rich nation, then it is a sign of a dysfunctional economic system.

None of this is very new, but the means to achieve it – in an age of market fundamentalism – will need to be novel and imaginative. Before the birth of neo-liberalism in the late 1970s, and even during the Great Depression of forty years before, attention had been focused on guaranteeing minimum living standards within a free market system. In 1950s' Britain there was a form of Keynesian consensus in the *Butskellism* of Labour and Conservative governments, both accepting the principles of a welfare state and high tax regime.* Earlier, in 1944, President Franklin Roosevelt's ideas for a second bill of rights – only recently unearthed by activist Michael Moore (outlined in Chapter 3) – contained proposals which would have granted health provision, employment at a living wage, and a welfare system with protection in sickness and old age, as rights. It is instructive to note that even now not all such guarantees are accepted throughout Europe, almost eighty years on, and would mostly be rejected by a majority of voters in the United States. Such is the tenor of modern times in an era of market fundamentalism. But what is recommended here is not more *statism* – greater control of the levers of the economy on socialist lines. It is to limit the effects of excessive market dominance, which so often gives undue advantage to those already wealthy. Reining in the scope of market forces would emancipate those who have little from the constraints of poverty – widening their elbow-room and their horizons.

There is no reason why the economy could not be arranged so that vital services and commodities were not entirely subject to normal market operations – often at prohibitive cost, in order that they be more fairly available. Nobel prize-winning economist James Tobin had a similar idea before neo-liberalism became established. As he put it, *The social conscience is more offended by severe inequality in nutrition, basic shelter, or access to medical care or to legal assistance, than by inequality in automobiles, books, clothes, furniture, boats.*[7] The specific items to be included will vary over time according to economic circumstances, but Tobin's definition in 1970 was the ... *non-market egalitarian distributions of commodities essential to life and citizenship.*[8] In today's more inclusive world that *life* must take in items which fifty years ago would not have been thought essential, but *citizenship* conveys the sense of participation in society in the fullest sense – from which many of the marginalised poor are today excluded. Tobin acknowledged the role for incentives in market forces, but believed that the necessities of life

---

* *Butskellism* signified the remarkable convergence of the centrist economic policies of R. A. Butler and Hugh Gaitskell, respectively Tory and Labour Chancellors of the Exchequer during the decade.

should remain outside the scope of the common striving for personal enrichment. The free market would continue to operate as usual, but its more thrusting, divisive tendencies would no longer be able to prejudice significantly the welfare of ordinary people.

A way of limiting the areas of life where cost and income have a decisive bearing would be to divide market domains into spheres. Philosopher Michael Walzer suggested this in the 1980s as part of his notion of *complex equality*. In some spheres of life one's level of income would be severely prejudicial, but in others one would be on a more equal footing with fellow citizens, and status would not depend on purchasing power alone.[9] Once agreement is arrived at, as regards what items must be accessible on an equal basis regardless of income, there would be a clear and lasting demarcation which would not allow poverty to restrict access. Some of the lines separating out these spheres of life have already been suggested, and they are by no means limited to consumer goods. It is clear that the domains where access should be equal must include those where significant stigma is attached to exclusion, as well as those which involve civic or social rights. So, affordable housing rents and winter fuel will come under the same banner as access to legal aid ensuring equality before the law. However, expensive SUVs or long-haul overseas holidays, for example, would not be subject to market constraints or government intervention; their lack of affordability for those on low incomes is a more tolerable feature of market economics. But in this context, with *multiple inequalities* in different spheres of life, no-one would be entirely at the mercy of the market 'game' and its grievously high stakes, as previously.

How such proposals could be achieved will be outlined in the coming pages. Of course, this amounts to interference in the so-called 'free' market. However, various kinds of intervention in capitalist operations have taken place through the years, some of it manipulation by parties bent on their own enrichment, and often by governments attempting to protect individuals from the worst effects of indiscriminate market forces. For example, the introduction of Working Tax Credits in Britain by New Labour (now superseded by Universal Credit) was one policy designed to compensate for the low pay individuals earned in what is in effect a dysfunctional labour market, which in many cases fails to pay a living wage. As already mentioned, markets work in random fashion, with no built-in security for those without sufficient capital – human or financial – from which to prosper. And for the many who are unable to earn an adequate income, even from full-time employment, then the community as a whole – in the form of central and/or local government – has to become involved to provide the necessary compensation. And while acknowledging that this represents a call on the collective resources of the nation, one must emphasise the overall benefit which it would provide to the community. In lowering the stakes of daily existence and lightening the pressures on individuals and families, it would be economically and socially highly functional, improving morale as well as productivity.

The contribution of the community as a whole to ensure certain commodities and services are more accessible to poorer members of society would also be mutually beneficial. Raising living standards for the lowest echelons in the population in this way would have the effect of enhancing their coping strategies and addressing the psychology of scarcity (explained in Chapter 6) which is all too common, especially in more unequal societies. This would make the least well-off more capable of dealing with other challenges: reinforcing status, and bolstering self-esteem by reducing the *social-evaluative threat* – all more significant for severely stratified communities than even poverty itself. The incidence of mental health issues – particularly status anxiety, also impacting physical health – is considerably higher in nations where income inequality is greater. However, enhancing living standards, as well as status, of the poorest will reduce inequality as well as improving the mental welfare of the majority of the population. These outcomes would eventually ensure a citizen's undiluted claim on a range of provision, highlighted above, which would be largely unaffected by personal means. Such a development could have a liberating effect on the community, countering the inequality of status and constant demands of just endeavouring to make ends meet, which can crowd out participation in civic life.

These measures would not be an attempt to engineer overall economic equality in society, although reducing the level of income inequality is an important target which would be both socially and economically beneficial for all – as outlined in Chapter 6. But their primary objective would be to mitigate the evils of neo-liberalism in its impact on those unable to cope with unrestrained market competition. *Specific egalitarianism*, James Tobin called this. Raising standards for the poorest in society would not help those alone; due to the inter-relationship of different socio-economic levels – outlined in the last chapter – such a policy would enhance well-being throughout society. This phenomenon is still not appreciated, and amongst those on the Right of politics mostly not accepted. Furthermore, this is the only route to increasing equality of opportunity; by creating a less unequal society in the first place, a more level playing field will embody the starting point, from which will follow more equal life chances across the community. By reducing the economic stakes of life in order to make sheer survival, or even 'getting on', less of a constant preoccupation, the space can be generated for horizons to be broadened for those at all socio-economic levels. But – as the last chapter emphasised – for this to be achieved, the free market has to take up less room in our daily endeavours, in our lives as well as in our minds.

Project Two: Damage Reduction: limiting the malign effects of the free market.

In societies like those of the United Kingdom or the United States over recent decades, there have settled certain myths about how economies should be run. A broad and implicit consensus that a neo-liberal stance is appropriate has become established – whether or not its implications are fully understood. Since the early 1980s the approaches of right-wing parties like the Conservatives in Britain or the Republicans in the US were joined almost seamlessly by New Labour and the Democrats under Bill Clinton. While some social measures have been brought in, to provide a more human gloss to a hard-edged capitalism, the system nevertheless stands rigidly by a regime of extreme free market forces, privatisation of state enterprises, low taxation and inflation, restricted welfare provision, a long-hours culture, and a flexible labour market with limited worker protection – all favouring corporate capital and the already well-off. Of course, these features are not generally viewed as deliberately malign policies, a not-so-hidden agenda with a distinct political bias. None the less, the instinctive reflex of many in the population is to support this overall approach which, whenever challenged, is answered with reminders of the need for austerity to cope with financial crisis, terrorist threats, indispensable foreign wars or national economic emergency. And it may not be long before the relinquishing of austerity due to the Covid-19 emergency is reversed, with a return to business as usual.

However, the capitalism of the future will have to be different: a system which distinguishes commodities one from another, whether goods or services, in that some may continue to be subject to normal market forces and others must certainly be not. There are a number of ways in which this could be done, but they rely on acceptance that there are different spheres of life – some of which are essential elements which almost everybody may need to access at some point. These would be protected domains, what James Meek calls *universal networks* (as outlined in Chapter 5), available to all, and would require mechanisms to ring-fence them from the open free market. They would be areas where the right to profit, if permitted, would be contained within strict limits. To the extent that these would be 'markets', they would be obliged to function for the benefit of society, and as such would be part of the jointly-owned *res communis*.* There would need to be consensus as to the items included, but the precise list is less significant at this point than acknowledgement of the principle that there should exist protected domains in which all have a right to share, regardless of means. This would ensure equivalence of status, and eventually the elimination of stigma. Of course addressing these issues will be expensive, but not a serious obstacle for a rich nation with, at present, one of the lowest tax regimes in Europe.

With the current social climate in Britain, and even more so in the United States, arriving at a form of communal agreement as to what should constitute these different spheres will not be easy. It will certainly require far-sighted political leadership, nowadays in short supply. But in order for a nation to see itself as a community it has to possess a number of things in common, and these must include access to essential commodities as well as a capacity to share in common endeavours and in those with *experiential* value, particularly in relation to national patrimony (as defined in Chapter 5). There is a tendency in neo-liberal circles to want to restrict benefit claimants to a bare minimum in the belief that they will then make more effort to, for example, find work, learn now to economize, but above all pull themselves together so that they are less of a drain on the state. This approach is a denial of the need for, or even the existence of a national commonality, let alone a common culture. More than two centuries ago, Adam Smith recognized that basic living requirements were not merely ... *those commodities*

---

*   As set out in Chapter 5.

which are indispensably necessary for the support of life, but whatever the custom of the country renders it indecent for creditable people, even of the lowest order, to be without. And as Will Hutton suggests, this indicated that Smith acknowledged that poverty was *socially determined*, and was aware that luxuries would, in time, become necessities.[10]

The *custom of the country* will vary over time, according to the propensities of the people and their perspectives on life. When in 1936 Seebohm Rowntree, son of philanthropist Joseph, updated his 1899 survey of poverty in York, he reconsidered what should be regarded as essential commodities people needed. In his new list he included items not vital for survival, explaining that ... *newspapers, books, radios, beer, tobacco, holidays and presents were fundamental to a meaningful life.*[11] But thoughts as to fundamentals have included some less accommodating views about what people should be entitled to: Stephen Armstrong cites the case in the United States in 2011 when it was suggested that for those classed as living in relative poverty, owning a refrigerator should carry a substantial tax increase.[12] Unlike in earlier times, today the common way of life and conventional standards in advanced capitalist economies are well known, even if there is not agreement that all are entitled to these norms. However, in spite of prejudices, and protestations about the resources available, it is vital to reach some general acceptance as to what our *customs* indicate should be the vital 'commodities' which *creditable people* – of whatever social order – must not have to go without. There will inevitably be argument at the margins, but that does not invalidate the principle, on which the health of the national community depends.

Differentiating pure market domains from protected social spheres

Thus the following ideas are put forward – proposals to modify the current free market system in the interests of equity and humanity, and to put a brake on the further 'marketization' of society. Some of them have been suggested before, often to be dismissed as impracticable or idealistic, but mostly to be rejected because they do not conform to the neo-liberal framework – and even less to its ethos. And this is the problem underlying fresh notions of how an economy might be organized and society better served: the prevailing mindset of existing free market practice is one which rejects outside involvement. This is so deeply ingrained that most observers can't help thinking of it as an inviolable principle, one continually reinforced by neo-liberals. And as outlined in Chapter 1, once these assumptions become the prevailing myths of the age they are seriously difficult to counteract, until transformed by the force of dramatic events or shifts of power. So even though the following may, in isolation, appear sensible, plausible recommendations, once seen in the context of current economic prejudice and forty years of rhetoric they can take on the spectre of dangerous heresy. Thus an important issue is not the question of their validity, but of their credibility.

There are already, of course, areas staked out which point to acknowledgement of the rights of the population to certain services – in Britain most notably in health care. After the response of the National Health Service to the Covid-19 crisis, and the enormous esteem in which the NHS is held, this is a domain where free use of the service has broad approval. Here discussion remains only at the periphery, such as to whether there should be charges – and if so how much – for medical prescriptions or dental treatment. Then there is the matter of the extent to which ancillary services, such as hospital cleaning, should be privatised, which of course should come down to cost and effectiveness and not ideology. Mental health services must also come within this same domain, as must the social care sector. The former has been grossly underfunded, with the result that mental health victims have often had to be dealt with by the police, whereas the latter has become a high-profile issue after the number of Covid-19 deaths in residential care homes. With an increasingly elderly population, the status of social care needs to be enhanced with proper funding as well as made fully professional, as many now accept. In Britain, at least on the question of principle, so far so easy; it is hard to see capitalism in the United States pulling back from health care provision to allow what many there call *socialised medicine* to become the norm.

Another key area of 'commodities' would be utilities and services which are part of everyday life at the current stage of the twenty-first century. The supply of water and energy utilities, as well as telecommunications and digital services, must all be supplied at economic cost. It is not crucial whether the suppliers are state providers or private companies, but if the latter they must be strictly regulated. The privatisation of companies like British Gas or BT in the 1980s was carried out mainly for ideological reasons, imposing competition in markets where there was little opportunity for product differentiation, and tempting the public with cut-price shares in the newly privatised concerns. Since most citizens simply require their gas, electricity, landline telephone and broadband to be supplied uninterrupted and at reasonable cost, how this is arrived at is more of a technical issue than a matter of principle. But in order to ensure that the consumer is protected, comprehensive regulation is required in what is ultimately an artificial market created by Conservative dogma. So the regulators – Ofgem in the case of energy supply – may need to impose price caps to protect buyers, as well as to simplify a 'market' which presently involves much unnecessary switching between suppliers. The companies involved have a responsibility to the public which is far less relevant in the case of less *universal* consumer goods.

One would not wish to start from here, but clocks cannot be turned back. Going to the expense of nationalizing private utilities – particularly on grounds of principle – would not be justified, unless poor management and ineffective regulation demanded it in the interests of the consumer. But at the very least a check will need to be kept on unnecessary profits from what are indispensable goods.* This example denotes where the boundary lies – between the open free market and the protected domains of essential commodities. In the modern, digital world the latter extends to another vital service: a consistent, fast broadband connection to all properties. With increasing numbers of people working from home, and with more and more activities carried out online, this becomes a necessity. It is the responsibility of government to ensure this service, which falls within the same category as energy supply. The powers of the regulator Ofcom should be reinforced, and emphasis placed on access at modest cost; even if competition between companies, carefully monitored, is maintained, it should not continue to be part of Ofcom's remit to promote. Proper regulation is indispensable to influence the free market wherever it allows gains to be made from products which are essential commodities; the capitalist presumption of

---

* If these companies remain in private hands they should be far more tightly regulated. For example, it should be mandated that a majority of profits be ploughed back into the business, leaving only a minimal amount for shareholder dividends. For example, British Gas profits rose by almost a third during 2015, to more than £500 million. But the fluctuating fortunes of its parent company, Centrica, which suffered a loss of more than £1 billion in 2019, even before the impact of Coronavirus, and which had earlier led it to make thousands of staff redundant in early 2018, are a consequence of an entirely unnecessary and artificial 'market' in a product sector which people can hardly avoid.

competition and profit has to be replaced here with a social ethos of decent public provision.

Regulation of these services will have to encompass careful oversight of costs and prices. However, other mechanisms may be employed, especially fiscal ones; for example, the reduced VAT rate of 5% which the UK applies to domestic energy bills should be abolished, as well as that on energy-saving materials. VAT is one of the most regressive taxes, needlessly adding to costs for poorer people. And why should VAT be charged on the installation of items such as solar panels, heat pumps and buildings insulation, at this critical time of rapid climate change? Taxation, which will be examined further later, is one of the important expedients which will have to be employed in distinguishing between protected domains and normal free market operations. It is required both to cushion those on the lowest incomes from rising costs in essential product areas, as well as to raise the necessary funds to provide a respectable range of services such as in transport or cultural areas. This latter is also one of the spheres which must be protected for all citizens, so that access to a comprehensive library service, public museums and art galleries, as well as sites of national historical significance are available regardless of means. Such a prerogative is integral to one's civic entitlement in the communal realm, and can contribute to the education and socialization of the young; it should not be denied on the basis of cost.

As regards transport, this has long been a contentious issue. Ever since the early 1960s, when the 'modern' way forward was seen to be car travel and expanding the road network – especially with the start of motorway building – the emphasis has been on private transport, to the neglect of public provision. The Beeching cuts to the expensive, creaking British rail network – an apparently rational response at the time to increasing car ownership – had the effect of actually promoting greater car use. But the privatisation and deregulation of bus services by the Conservative government in 1986 had an even more serious impact on local travel, especially in rural areas and on poorer residents. Semi-monopoly positions by a small number of subsidised bus companies had contributed to a broad network of provincial public transport until the fierce winds of Thatcherite competition shook up the system.

Deregulation, one of the totems of neo-liberal policies, was to produce a bracing atmosphere of enterprise. But the consequences included higher fares, new bus operators fighting over old routes, increased traffic congestion, especially in towns, and reduced provision, leaving some communities with barely minimal services. Such were the prices paid for allowing ideology to override common sense. For the new bus companies bent on efficiency and profit, some remote routes were evidently uneconomic; for many poorer residents, their isolated, rural existence was itself, in effect, uneconomic!

In many respects public transport is a paradigm for the ineffectiveness, even irrelevance, of market forces in serving communal needs under modern capitalism. While one may understand the role of competition between airlines for passengers making for holiday destinations, public, particularly local, transport is of an entirely different order. In fact, it comes under the heading of a common public domain, a universal *network* as outlined above, which is part of a broad communal entitlement funded by local authorities or their agencies.* While remote country living inevitably comes with increased transport costs, subsidised public transport is crucial for rural areas – even if lacking the comprehensive service towns and cities enjoy. Without public transport links rural life becomes increasingly problematic; the vicious spiral of recent generations has seen higher property prices, greater distances being travelled to work, and a greater reliance on motor cars – for those with access to one.** The main victims of this situation are, as usual, older and less affluent people, as well as the disabled – adding to isolation and social exclusion. And inevitably the trend towards greater car ownership will increase, whenever it is affordable, at a time when climate change demands less private vehicle use for the benefit of the wider community – both nationally and globally. So here again, the well being of the wider population is being sacrificed to the interests of more affluent individuals and empty right-wing dogma.

I'll get you on the bus, says Prescott... was the waggish newspaper headline just two months after Labour's 1997 election victory.[15] In the

---

* This form of public provision would be available at modest cost, or even in some environments free at the point of use, as happens in many other countries.[13] Limited town centre areas, or even small off-shore islands, would benefit from rapid, mass-transit systems operating frequent shuttle services without immediate charge.

** According to official figures, 6-7% of residents in rural/village areas had no access to a car or van in 2017; the figure for 'vehicle-less' people living in rural towns, or on the fringe of them, rose to around 13% – overall, a sizeable proportion of the population.[14]

aftermath of the electoral success of an apparently progressive, centre-left party, it seemed as if official policy might now be to provide proper support for public transport. But the transformation did not materialise. Although the time of New Labour's first triumph coincided with the 1997 Kyoto Climate Change Conference, minds were evidently not concentrated enough to produce a transport policy which could contribute to the mitigation of global warming and cater to British transport needs at all income levels. The Labour Party of that era was so concerned to burnish its free market credentials and break with its collectivist past that it abandoned a holistic approach and made its peace with neo-liberal requirements. Thus the following years were ones of continued neglect of public transport at a time when, for a host of social, environmental and health reasons, it should have been a priority for government policy. So, bus passenger numbers continued falling, while the last twenty years have seen fares rise inexorably, faster even than the increase in railway or motoring costs, as well as inflation. And even though buses still account for more than half of all public transport journeys in Britain, and lower income groups rely on bus use much more than the more affluent, nevertheless local authority funding for buses has fallen substantially since 2010.

It is hardly surprising that during the years of central government-imposed austerity local authorities should have found it so difficult to fund local bus transport adequately. But neglect of important community services fits with the ideological stance of government since 2010 – the moderating influence of the Liberal Democrats to 2015 notwithstanding. Creating an artificial market in local transport and lauding competition was exactly what deregulation brought in. Even the most recent legislation, the Bus Services Act of 2017, follows the same policy. For, although it gives local councils the powers to promote franchise networks, it still, perversely, prohibits them from forming companies for the purpose of providing local bus services – i.e. reversing deregulation – when the evidence shows that this could substantially improve public provision. So we now have the anomalous situation whereby anyone has the right to start up a private bus company with limited notice, while elected councils – with the on-going interests of their constituents at heart – are forbidden from doing so.* After all, it is local government

---

*   Well-run municipal bus companies, such as those of Nottingham and Reading which pre-dated deregulation, could help save local authorities money at a time of severe budgetary

that will be there for the long term, endeavouring to manage travel requirements for local people, as well as having responsibility for the environment and other transport modes, matters with which private operators are not obliged to concern themselves.

Local bus services will rarely be able to pay for themselves, and ever more expensive fares cannot be the answer when, outside the metropolitan regions, the passengers are very often less well-off travellers and those with concessionary tickets. With climate change, traffic congestion, and co-ordination of different transport modes all pressing issues, public management and public money are necessary to deal with the travel demands of the twenty-first century. The £2.2 billion subsidy buses received in England (of which London alone gets £801 million) in 2018–19 may appear substantial,[16] but should be seen in the light of the large sums bus companies are able to pay their shareholders – £2.8 billion in dividends between 2003 and 2013.[17] This seems an extraordinary way of operating what is essentially a public service: sizeable profits made by private concerns which have no responsibility to consult passengers or funding sources about the nature of the bus network – i.e. little accountability as to how public money is spent. In contrast, the twelve local authorities in England with municipally-owned bus providers are able to plough back profits into services. Of course, some bus operators do reap rewards for the state: viz, where companies are partly or wholly owned by foreign governments. It was pointed out in 2018 that in Epsom and Ewell, the then Transport Secretary Chris Grayling's constituency, *Most of the profits from bus fares… are reinvested in French and German public services.*[18] One wonders what these other governments make of this curious phenomenon.

Local public transport should be designated one of these separate, protected domains, beyond the reach of private firms to exploit. After all, it encompasses wider communal concerns than money and profit. Properly regulated bus services, with connections and timetables fully co-ordinated with other forms of transport would help address poverty, inequality and social exclusion. Families on low incomes, where perhaps one member of the household needs the only vehicle to get to work, can easily be isolated, above all in rural areas, lacking the means to access education, healthcare, job interviews and civic involvement. It

---

cuts by central government, as well as co-ordinate all the different modes of local public transport in an area to help compete with car travel.

is invidious to allow private profit to ignore such deprivation. And at a critical time in the development of global warming, only comprehensive public management and investment will succeed in getting people out of their cars (if indeed they have one) and using public transport more.* But what we often hear from the wings is that this approach is *uneconomic*. This is the neo-liberal fallacy which can only operate in narrow financial terms, and which eschews the joined-up thinking desperately needed to tackle the huge social and environmental challenges facing us. In place of current policy, which benefits only the few, the new *invisible hand* of the future will operate in reverse, by collective, communal measures serving individuals – of all social classes as well as the planet (which will never be able to make sense of 'our' economics).

Thus in the future there will need to exist systems of public transport managed in the communal interest, beyond market forces, because we all have a stake in their proper functioning. There used to be a saying in the United States, in simpler times, that what was good for General Motors was good for America. That was in the days before globalization on the current scale, when the interconnectedness between us all and the global environment was not appreciated. But now we know that what might be considered 'uneconomic' for a local private bus company, trying to operate between far-flung villages, can be beneficial and just for society as a whole and its environment, provided their disparate needs are integrated and there is sufficient collective investment.** Extreme entrepreneurial capitalism cannot cope with these issues; it can only harm more people than it serves, while creating division and exclusion. Communal management in these cases will effectively assist more people to achieve their individual goals than would be possible if matters were left to the market and individuated choice. Capitalism may be able to bear an almost infinite variety of brands of potato crisps or tablet computers, but it cannot work with rival bus companies ignoring social values in attempting to maximize their returns, and with the further growth of private cars, without severe damage to society and the planet.

---

*   All this was known more than a generation ago. It is over 25 years now since John Whitelegg's important *Transport for a Sustainable Future: The Case for Europe*, John Wiley & Sons, Chichester, 1994.
**   For example, separate shuttle bus services could be arranged to link outlying areas with health centres, local shops, and child care facilities to supplement the voluntary schemes which often already exist.

In considering the social spheres which must be kept sacrosanct, free as far as possible from the complicating motives of money and profit, it is clear that caring for people should be a crucial one. But as far as adult social care in the UK is concerned, for almost forty years the trend has been for authorities to outsource provision to private companies – usually for financial reasons. In 1979, almost two-thirds of beds in residential and nursing homes were provided by local authorities or the NHS; this had fallen to just 6% by 2012.* Without any real debate, and largely unchecked, this process of privatisation gathered pace over the years, allowing profit to be made from the institutionalised care of our dearest, often most vulnerable, mainly elderly relatives. And while this model of privatised care has become embedded in Britain, local authorities still retain responsibility for subsidising adult social care in their areas – while not being obliged to subsidise local buses! In an increasingly ageing society, and with many disabled younger adults living longer, the care home sector now caters to over 400,000 residents, but greater demand did not prevent spending on social care from falling by almost 10% in the seven years of austerity after 2010. With dozens of competing care providers in an ever tighter financial environment, it is hard to see this model of care flourishing in the post-Covid-19 future – and why should it?

However, over the years a variety of financial concerns – hedge funds, venture capital companies, equity investors, etc. – have entered what they evidently believed was a lucrative 'market'. And with rising numbers of elderly people, it may have appeared that there was ample scope for profit, so that investors were eager – often at the cost of considerable debt – to get involved in the sector. As it turned out, many companies discovered social care to be an expensive business, and it became evident that it was a fragile market without easy pickings. Of course, the costs of failure of private companies in such a sensitive social sphere go far beyond finance. The repercussions of providers going bust include the political implications in what is a controversial market area, as well as the obvious uncertainty for thousands of mostly elderly care home residents. The fragility in the sector was shown by the collapse of Southern Cross in 2011, the first major casualty, a social care provider with almost 10% of the 'market' nationally. Many of that company's

---

* In the case of domiciliary care the reduction was even greater: from well over 90% to about 11%.

homes were taken on by one of the largest private providers in the UK, Four Seasons Health Care, which itself went into administration in 2019. The comment at that time by the Care Quality Commission, the sector's regulator, that it did not expect any disruption to the lives of the provider's 17,000 residents in over 300 homes, was hardly likely to provide much reassurance for them or their families.

One might have expected residential care – of which a proportion of the national population will eventually have to avail themselves – to be part of a tightly regulated sector, with stable social providers acting in the broad communal interest. While, like most others, it cannot be an area entirely free from financial restraints, nevertheless a responsible society should surely be able to provide a service without money being leeched to private companies – often abroad – profiting from vital care for human beings. A funding model, often based on frequently restructured debt, held by financial institutions with little relevance to the care 'business', hardly seems appropriate to social care services of which the state is a major commissioner. For example, private equity firm Terra Firma Capital Partners took over Four Seasons for £825 million in 2012 through huge borrowing, so that when their finances later deteriorated the basis of their investment became unsustainable. Most of the debt was taken on by one of their lenders, H/2 Capital Partners, a US-based hedge fund, which has been in control of the company since late 2017, whilst Four Seasons have been handing over some care homes to rivals, intending to sell others as going concerns. By late 2019 the broader situation was summed up by the *Financial Times* as follows:

> *Britain's four largest privately owned care home operators — HC-One, Four Seasons Health Care, Barchester Healthcare, and Care UK — have racked up debts of £40,000 a bed, meaning their annual interest charges alone absorb eight weeks of average fees paid by local authorities on behalf of residents....*[19]

British governments have for many years struggled with the issue of how to fund and organise residential social care – while the numbers of elderly in the population have continued to rise. While lack of funding from central and local government authorities has been a perennial problem, private providers have come to dominate the field during this period. And though some of them may originally have started up care homes as small businesses for the purest of motives, once ownership becomes consolidated, and the interests of capital exert their authority, the impulses of finance firms can only be seen as being entirely at odds with those of the residents – their customers. Government has been fully aware of the urgency of finding over-arching solutions, which a decade ago prompted the launching of a major study of the social care sector, by the Dilnot Commission. Although its remit did not include examining private companies' management of care homes, the recommendations in their report, published in 2011, would at least have put funding on a sounder basis and produced a more robust business, capping contributions from residents to no more than 30% of assets, and at a cost to the state of no more than 0.25% of GDP. But though widely welcomed, and with government legislation promised, the report languished, its measures not enacted. Such is the timidity and lack of resolve of successive governments, reluctant to take the tough decisions society deserves.

But necessary though the measures in the Dilnot report were, matters have to be taken further. Funding on the lines of its recommendations would be a positive step, but since residential care should have some protection from exploitation by private firms, there should be a gradual attempt to limit their involvement. If this sector were acknowledged for what it is, an essential social network, then more responsibility would perhaps be accepted by the community, and thus by government. Then, commissioning of providers could be carried out more carefully so that residential homes did not change hands so frequently, ensuring greater stability in the business. Further, though privatisation of social care is unlikely to be rapidly reversed, at least private ownership can be enhanced by greater transparency of contracts; there needs to be much greater openness with the origin of funds as well as assurances as to the extent private companies are discharging their tax duties, especially if they are foreign entities. While many private providers will carry out their social care responsibilities faithfully, the tests for compliance and ownership must be based on ethics – and this applies to domiciliary care as much as residential institutions. It is dogma, the ideological muddle that authorities have got into over recent generations, which is mainly responsible for the lack of rigour in policy, and the failure to recognize where public provision should take precedence over private enterprise.

However, the proper funding and regulation of social care which are needed for citizens towards the end of their lives should be matched by similar attention to care for the very young. And if there is a social domain in which all have an acute interest, it is young children, especially in their first five or six years. How they fare at that age, the socio-economic conditions which govern their early family life, and relationships with their peers will have an intimate bearing not only on their futures, but also on those of others they come into contact with. Their health, well-being and behaviour will depend on conditions established at that time, after which they will be set on a steady trajectory. Therefore, early-years child care should be accessible to all parents regardless of economic circumstances, and not conditioned by market forces. This is a basic universal network which would help create a measure of equality at the start of life. Some nations, such as in Scandinavia, have taken this approach by subsidising child care so that it is widely accessible. In Sweden, where it is the norm for parents to return to work after childbirth, children will usually attend nursery full-time until they start school at age seven, which costs parents a maximum of 3% of salary, currently capped at the equivalent of about £115 a month. But in spite of Sweden's high tax regime, it is significant that very few Swedish taxpayers appear to resent subsidising child care costs for working parents.

In Denmark the situation is similar, with a variety of options – day nurseries from ages one to three, and kindergartens from three until school starts at age six. All families are offered childcare, mostly guaranteed from age one, with a maximum parental contribution of around 30% of the actual cost, although low-income families and single parents pay less. British parents do not have the benefit of such generous arrangements, nor of course the greater tax burden to pay for them. The Childcare Act in the UK is a latecomer in European terms (September 2017), introducing limited free child care of only 30 hours per week over 38 weeks of the year (or 22 hours a week over the whole school year) to three- and four-year-olds of working parents.* So in Britain, social inequality is incorporated from an early age, with many parents without sufficient earning power unable to afford child care, thus not able to return to work unless they can find informal arrangements for

---

* What appeared at least to be a good start with subsidised child care soon turned out to be a less encouraging reality: after just a year there were many complaints that the scheme was severely underfunded. One typical study found that nearly half of parents taking up the 30 hours a week offer had been asked to pay additional fees; that just over a third of child care providers planned further increases in parent fees for non-funded hours over the next year; and that 40% of nurseries and child minders feared that they may have to close over the following year because of the scheme – consequences of poorly planned and underfunded government policy.[20]

their children. There is as yet no clear consensus in the UK which would approve more general support for working parents and their young children, no acknowledgement that this should be a common right, which would help create a more equal starting point for the life chances of the young. Britain's individualistic culture still mostly expects families to be entirely independent, oblivious of the fact that common conditions for children at the beginning would contribute to social harmony and a mitigation of many expensive health, employment, and law and order issues which currently plague society. (Outlined in Chapter 6.)

It is curious that public attitudes should vary so much between neighbouring societies. But in Britain there appears to be a general resistance to the equalising of life chances – particularly if public money is committed to it – as well as disregard for the huge inequalities which young children experience in their early lives. In many parts of Europe there is a more inclusive public attitude which sees child rearing and child care as generally beneficial to the future of society as a whole. The United Kingdom did take a major step forward with the introduction by New Labour of the Sure Start programme in 1999. This was an ambitious 'flagship' policy launched to give support and advice to families of young children regarding health, parenting, money, and even employment – a broad national scheme but based on local centres at 'pram-pushing' distance, initially targeted at the 20% of poorest wards in the country. This is exactly the kind of overall programme which, if well funded, can help further the life chances of the very young. The focus on parenting, so crucial in today's disconnected world, can provide the mainspring of so much positive social development. There was some early evidence for the positive impact of Sure Start centres in terms of behaviour and well-being, but more recently research by the Institute for Fiscal Studies demonstrated clear health benefits, especially in a drop in the numbers of children's hospital visits, delivering significant savings to the NHS.*

So aside from the wealth of anecdotal evidence from families, especially in deprived areas, and the positive feedback from local authorities about the benefits which schemes like Sure Start can provide, there is likely to be worthwhile savings to the NHS budget in the UK. Nevertheless, the programme has been run down since Labour left office a

---

* The report suggested that providing a centre per thousand children under five would mean around 5,500 fewer eleven-year-olds being hospitalised each year.[21]

decade ago, with at least a thousand centres closing and a spending cut of about two-thirds. Now that the Sure Start budget is no longer ring-fenced, but merged with other schemes, it can easily be whittled away surreptitiously by governments obstinately opposed to broad social schemes. And under the specious approach of localism, responsibility is hived off to local councils which central government starves of funds. Sure Start had the merits of being a national scheme for all parents, not means-tested so that no stigma was attached to participation, and local enough to be easily accessible.* As such, it fits perfectly into the category of a universal service which not only helps to equalize the life chances of the very young, but also to alleviate some of the dire social problems which can stem from inadequate parenting and dysfunctional families struggling to cope with deprivation. Supporting young families, especially in very unequal societies, with communal policies unrelated to income or status, means that problems which otherwise end up in police cells, youth courts, poor child health, and severe educational inequalities can be addressed and mitigated.

Finally, the over-arching subject of housing should be mentioned, as one of the crucial social pillars which a decent society should ensure for all. This cannot be classed as one of the essential domains as such, beyond the reach of market forces, but has to be regarded as a vital requirement to which legislation and strict regulation must be applied. While many would consider it a 'right' in a rich society like Britain, there is little point in according it such status when no government or institution is in a position to act on such a demand, even if disposed to do so. Housing policy in Britain has long been a disaster area; for the last fifty years, while the country has got richer, the availability of housing has fluctuated, as have the numbers on housing waiting lists and those sleeping rough. So, one of the world's wealthiest nations is incapable of ensuring that all its people have roofs over their heads – not because of lack of economic means, but through inappropriate policy and market failure. Right wing political parties eulogize competition and the market, but

---

* As writer Frank Cottrell Boyce put it, on noting the decline in Sure Start centres, *Children's centres are a place to turn for help without having to submit to the idea that you are a basket case or that your community is a war zone. A place where people could share vulnerabilities, pool resources and thus create durable bonds.*[22]

for many decades the only periods when available properties have approached demand have been when governments have intervened. So a hundred years after Lloyd George made housing a national responsibility, with his promise of *homes fit for heroes* and the first housing act in 1919, the UK cannot house its citizens.

This is, of course, one of the vital arenas in which all have a stake, and has to form a priority matter which government must address. The concept of *res communis*, cited earlier, should be widened here to encompass the sense that the common heritage of a developed nation should include an expectation of a permanent home of one's own. In material terms, the wealth of the national community – built up over the centuries, even if not always salubriously – constitutes the accumulated stock of the collective and is available to be called on by its citizens, not necessarily in monetary form, but certainly as a civic responsibility which commits governing authorities to ensure a range of basic, agreed standards of life. Of these, housing is one of the most crucial, and where normal market mechanisms cannot facilitate this, there public institutions must step in. Many bodies are at last coming to see housing as a vital 'service', part of a common prerogative. The Social Prosperity Network at University College London has done considerable research on universal basic services and believes they would help combat rising inequality and strengthen social cohesion. Furthermore, it maintains that, contrary to popular assumptions, basic services as a whole are well within the scope of reasonable expenditures.* The analysis concludes that decent housing – as one key element of these services – is essential for full participation in a modern developed economy.

This has been, over the years, part of the rationale behind social housing, a requirement for those unable to buy their own homes or afford high private rents. Council house building was the mechanism – especially after the sacrifices of world wars and depression, and the demolition of slums – for widening the property base. This lasted until the final quarter of the twentieth century, when manipulation by over-reaching central government effectively halted progress. Ever since the Thatcher administration extended the sale of council houses with

---

* Jonathan Portes and his co-authors at the Global Prosperity Institute admit their analysis is based on broad-brush assumptions, with much work still to be done, but nevertheless calculated (prior to Covid-19) that a range of basic services would cost in aggregate around 2.3% of GDP, but that by reducing the personal tax allowance to £4,300 a year, and leaving the benefit system untouched, the scheme could be revenue neutral.[23]

their Right to Buy scheme in 1980 – bogus egalitarianism popular with many council tenants – there has been an increasing shortage of social housing. Partly due to the restrictions on what local councils could do with the proceeds of house sales, there has been a lasting failure to build sufficient homes. This reached a point in 2014 where 11,000 council houses were sold in Britain, but only 1,180 built, and according to the same source the number of households waiting for social housing at that time was 1.8 million.[24] Since market forces have done nothing to remedy this national scandal, legislation has to mandate government to intervene – with substantial house building, stricter management of the private rented sector, policies to regulate second homes and empty properties, and proper exploitation of brown-field sites. Much can be done to circumscribe damaging market forces in the interests of providing homes for the whole population.*

All of this is eminently feasible for a rich country like the United Kingdom, and would already have been accomplished were it not for the obsession with market ideology and the prejudice against government intervention. Other, less prosperous nations have achieved much more with much less. So, for authorities to commit to providing homes for all they will need to acknowledge the responsibility which Lloyd George implicitly assumed a century ago. The conceptual adjustment needed will mean accepting housing as a basic universal requirement; there is no point in speaking of rights, but of collective responsibilities, yes, there has to be recognition. Once this point has been reached, political will has to follow. It seemed remarkable how quickly rough sleeping – an apparently intractable social problem – was largely cleared from British streets during the early months of the Coronavirus pandemic in 2020. Resolve of a similar kind is needed for the far bigger project of providing homes, a duty which must not be evaded. In different times it might have been expected that the vast sums paid out in housing benefit in Britain, and publicity about the huge numbers for people unable to find a decent place to live,** or perhaps the scandal of rich oligarchs

---

* Research for the Social Prosperity Network, cited earlier, suggests a feasible doubling of the current social housing stock by funding 1.5 million new housing units using 30-year Treasury Bonds at the then (2017) market rates (little changed since). Much of this kind of modelling is clearly practicable, although in the light of the economic impact of Covid-19 will need considerable re-working.[25]

** According to research in 2019 for the National Housing Federation, in the first ever 'state of the nation' report on the housing crisis, an estimated 8.4 million people in England – about one in seven – live in insecure, unaffordable, or unsuitable homes.[26]

buying up London property, promoting house price inflation, would have spurred action by government, but no. This indicates the magnitude of the problem, which only a major mental readjustment will begin to address.

Thus, a major project of the years ahead is to enhance social provision for the whole population by limiting market influence. This will involve two broad categories: firstly, market intrusion must be entirely excluded from the supply of goods and services in certain essential spheres, such as health care or local public transport, where extracting profit from the general public would be inappropriate and anti-social. Secondly, the free market must be contained and tightly regulated in areas like housing, energy, and digital communication utilities, etc. It is the responsibility of government to intervene in order to ensure, for example, sufficient social housing as well as a properly regulated rental market, especially to protect the rights of those needing long-term tenancies. And while there will still be plenty of scope for house builders to run profitable businesses, and for landlords to secure adequate rental income, they must not be at the expense of the poorest in society. Furthermore, in an open, free society it is not suggested that private health care or independent education should be prohibited, but they should not be able to benefit from any form of state aid. There will always be potential for private firms to offer alternatives for those with the resources to pay for them – provided this would not dilute or degrade the provision of free universal services to those who require them. It is a question of priorities; market forces must never be allowed to prejudice vital social need.*

So, where essential commodities and services are concerned there will be a range of the degree of involvement to which the free market will be permitted. As outlined above, certain goods will be entirely free for the user, and in other cases a regulated market will allow access to vital everyday items at minimal cost. Such changes would contribute to reducing social inequalities, in that they would be a force for redistribution. Anna Coote at the New Economics Foundation makes a strong case for such policies, quoting Oxfam data which suggest that public

---

* And neither must the free market be allowed to come before the demands of combating climate change, nor – in a crowded island like Great Britain – ahead of the need to protect the countryside.

services provide the poorest in society with the equivalent of 76% of their post-tax income.²⁷ As users and consumers, those on the lowest incomes would be relieved of the greatest economic burden by having, at the very least, an affordable home, low cost energy, digital/information services, child care at nominal cost, and free local transport, as well as the public services of health and education already available in the UK. This would represent in effect a 'social wage', which the Social Prosperity Network at UCL has calculated – according to the elements they include – as worth £126 a week to all who use the services.²⁸ And apart from reducing the often crippling stake such citizens are otherwise obliged to have in the free market, the availability of free or cheap transport and information services would enhance their potential to access employment – as well as improve morale and psychological well-being.

The categories above do not constitute an exhaustive list of essential goods and services. For example, access to legal aid is a vital 'commodity' which has been severely curtailed over recent years, thus limiting the civic rights of many citizens, not just the poorest. The financing of such legal rights is a collective duty to which government must respond. Like child care services in a properly resourced society, it cannot be allowed to be degraded as a result of a policy of austerity which expects those on low incomes to bear an inequitable burden for national economic problems. Similarly, access to sporting facilities must not be restricted by allowing playing fields and green spaces to be sold off by local councils, when the main impact will be on those unable to afford private clubs and gym membership. In all these respects the interests of the less well-off must be protected; ongoing universal provision of essentials is the way to achieve this. As for food, the other major area not covered above, the purchasing power of those on low incomes will benefit if the other goods and services mentioned can be provided at little or no cost – i.e. if the so-called 'social wage' is guaranteed. Also, raising the national minimum wage, as well as fiscal measures, can help protect living standards of the poorest, and allow them to circumvent the worst consequences of market forces in that most basic need of all – to be able to feed one's family.*

It has been argued that improving access to goods and services in

---

* It is still the case in Britain, one of the world's richest nations, that there are thousands who go hungry. Over recent times, huge numbers have been forced to use food banks to feed themselves, while in 2015 it was reported that more than 2,000 cases of malnutrition were recorded by 43 hospital trusts in a 12-month period.²⁹

the manner outlined above is more effective in economic redistribution than direct transfers of cash or targeted benefits. Because it involves open entry, without the need for any form of means testing, it serves to protect dignity by avoiding labelling. It can also help foster social solidarity by bringing people together through making a broad range of basic requirements available to all, regardless of means. This is certainly needed, since British culture is a long way from that prevailing in Scandinavian nations, where high taxation to pay for comprehensive social services is generally accepted. The schemes proposed here would contribute to a more participatory common culture in which citizens of varying levels of affluence would be likely to bump up against each other – sharing and enhancing community – in an environment where relationships matter more than buying and selling. This was precisely what had begun to happen in the early years of the Sure Start programme until, later, resources began to be more directly focused on deprived families, and the original open, all-inclusive environment was compromised. There will be those who criticize all of this for being idealistic, but the initial success of Sure Start demonstrated idealism in practice. And besides, idealism is exactly what is required in these bleak times.

Just precisely which spheres of life – particularly those at the margins – should be shielded from the full rigour of market forces is a matter for debate and ultimately consensus. But once agreement has been reached they can be recognized as a kind of protected species. In British sport there are certain prescribed events which must be available on free-to-air television – a list of the so-called 'crown jewels' of games and competitions which must not be shown exclusively on pay-only TV channels. An equivalent concept should apply in wider society to a range of essential goods and services which must be protected for general availability, and not be subject to market forces alone. It is not important that they be state-run, by central or regional authorities – although administration at a local level, influenced by local knowledge, is always preferred. Nationalisation of private entities, such as energy companies, is not vital, provided they are regulated adequately and profits reinvested into the business. As regards the provision of essential services it is not who runs them but how they are run which is key.* There will still be

---

*   The dogged ideology of neo-liberals in always favouring private enterprise has resulted in strange anomalies, such as in rail and bus transport, where profits are made from what are essential services, but where competition is artificial and not even punctuality can be guaranteed. The much criticised franchise system on the railways, for example, unable to

those who decry the suggestions above, insisting that the productivity and dynamism of free market capitalism can benefit the least well-off in society. But earlier sections of this work have already made the case against this; in any case, if the substantial increase in national wealth of the last 30 years has still left us with a huge residue of deprivation, what chance is there that a yet richer economy can overcome it, without a major social or macro-economic corrective of the kind most of us once believed in?

Project Three: Regulating the economy in the public interest

When Benjamin Disraeli was returned to office at the head of a Conservative government in 1874, the third plank of his election platform had been ... *improvement of the conditions of the people*. The practical policies which flowed from that manifesto ranged from municipal authority over housing to consumer protection, and this followed important reforms in education and health which had marked Gladstone's ministry which Disraeli's replaced. Increasing government involvement in social and economic affairs had developed through the 19th century and was to be a feature of the next hundred years. It was only with neo-liberalism that state intervention was given a bad name and 'big government' became a term of abuse – in spite of much enduring economic involvement which continued behind this façade. But this deceit is part of the myth of unrestrained *laissez-faire* policies, outlined in Chapter 3, which were reputed to have underpinned government's approach in Britain throughout the 19th century and beyond. A more activist state was accepted as necessary by a wide body of political opinion in Disraeli's era, and even more so at the end of the century after Charles Booth had published his *Life and Labour of the People of London*, highlighting a degree of poverty which no amount of private philanthropy was going to solve.

Over a century on from Booth's inquiry a different kind of government action is required to remedy the accumulated deprivation and inequality – which no amount of capitalist neo-liberal policy is going to solve. This would not amount to major national appropriation of

---

withstand the stress test of Covid-19, was finally consigned to history in September 2020, while emergency measures were put in place and new models of financing considered.

private firms, but it does involve circumscribing the free market – as described above – and directing it in ways which benefit society to a much broader extent then hitherto. As part of this project, there will need to be greater, and more refined regulation of the national economy in order to ensure that businesses function better, that more progressive taxation serves society, leading to a fuller range of public provision, that more attention is paid to employment in an age of increasing automation, and that remuneration is kept within bounds of decency and dignity. Of course, none of this will be easy; because we have had the neo-liberal view thrust at us for two generations, the veil of misleading prejudice and assumption has long clouded understanding. So whenever regulation has been mentioned it has been cast as the enemy of incentives, opportunity, freedom, instead of in its role as enhancing these aspects of the economy and society. This false dichotomy is responsible for much simplistic thinking; however, if regulation is mentioned in connection with, say, the Grenfell Tower fire in London in 2017, or the shortage of meat inspectors potentially affecting food security in the UK, then, *Ah*, they say, *that's different*.

But if it is not the alleged restraint on economic activity which is claimed to be the main consequence of increased regulation, then it is the difficulty the authorities profess they face in intervening in the affairs of private, and even public companies. (*Impossibilism is the enemy of social change*, says Tim Jackson.[30]) These and other kinds of justification will be wheeled out to impede the proper management of the economy in terms of good corporate governance, responsible taxation, and socially accountable levels of remuneration. The inventiveness of neo-liberals knows no limits here, and when challenged they invariably fall back on the charge of 'big government', believing this to be the clinching argument, regardless what the greater government activity is for – as usual, ideology before practicality. To treat rules and regulations emanating from government as an encumbrance inhibiting individual and corporate autonomy is part of the mindset which sees society as merely a collection of atomised beings, and businesses as separate entities with few responsibilities.* However, both individuals and companies need a framework of mutually reinforcing relationships,

---

* The longevity of the myths blaming government for economic problems is truly remarkable: viz. the wilful persistence of neo-liberals in erroneously attributing the 2007/08 financial crisis to government 'meddling', exemplified by renowned economist Arthur Laffer in his recent comment, quoted in Chapter 1.

including duties as well as rights, and democratic government is the body to provide this. Leopold Kohr's metaphor is a way of summing this up: ... *as the snail must carry the burden of the shell, so must the citizen carry on his shoulders the burden of the state if he wants to derive any benefit from it.*[31]

In order to argue convincingly for suitable government regulation – national and local – to build a better functioning system, it must be framed in the right terms. How it is explained and justified is almost as important as the obvious, sensible appropriateness of the measures. George Lakoff explains how, when US President in the 1990s, Bill Clinton framed his rhetoric to use conservative language, giving the impression of eschewing a larger role for government, and talking about *welfare reform.*[32] How policy is presented is crucial to its acceptance. Employing reams of facts and statistics will often be counter-productive, the data just gliding off already-held basic assumptions and, as Daniel Kahneman pointed out, simply not absorbed.[33] This is why rhetoric of a progressive kind, while necessary, is not sufficient on its own, particularly when it comes up against a conservative mindset which, for example, represents tax as an imposition curtailing ability to dispose of one's earnings as one sees fit – the old 'freedom' argument. This is one of many underlying conceits which reach beyond right-wing circles, so that they become part of the everyday furniture of familiar discourse, left lying there while we talk around them, almost invisible to the naked mind. In order to contest them, a deft presentation of the advantages of tax revenues to the whole population is needed here, chiefly avoiding statistics and framing the discussion in terms of benefits not burdens.

One approach to these issues is to use the analogy of professional domains like education or health provision, which have specific, recognised purposes in serving their clients. In most cases here there is less division of loyalties as pertains in business where there is a three-fold responsibility – to shareholders, as well as employees and customers. But the roles of doctor or teacher are fully comprehensible, and legitimate in the sense that they are socially useful; they are public services, whereas private companies, leaving aside the matter of the profit motive, play a much more equivocal role in society. The element of 'service' should be recognised more prominently, but under neo-liberalism this is hampered by the notion of capitalist enterprises as entirely separate, independent entities which owe nothing to the wider community – even if this is by no means the view of all their executives and directors. But a more holistic concept of society needs to become much more mainstream in the public mind, which will be made easier by thinking of capitalism more as a contributor to general well-being – and not just as a purveyor of consumer goods to those with means. Entrepreneurs may seek to enrich themselves, but they must not lose sight of the broader role their enterprises play for and amongst all of us.* This is the frame in which productive capitalism must be viewed – in its full social, public dimension.

Thus the following suggestions – general outlines, many of which have been aired before – would form part of a more inclusive concept of national community, with the necessary coordination of its different elements. For example, hindsight shows us that greater regulation of the banking sector is now overdue. The hubris of the early years of the century led to financial disaster, partly due to the famed 'light-touch' regulation helped by the 2004 Basel banking rules (Basel 2), which allowed greater self-regulation of financial institutions. The clever management of diversified risk, which it was then claimed would safeguard the huge expansion of credit, patently failed, but this has not been sufficiently remedied in the intervening years. So there is a clear need for greater regulation in this sector, with more rules on the amount of credit banks hold in relation to their assets, a reinforcement of regulations governing the separation of conventional retail banking from investment finance (which came in in 2019), and stipulation regarding the amount banks lend to productive businesses.** The incentives for *casino capitalism*, which benefits only a financial plutocracy, have to be curtailed, and greater stimulus provided to socially useful enterprises which assume wider obligations.

In fact, it is clear that greater regulation is precisely what financial institutions should be subjected to when their only purpose is to enrich themselves. The freedom to build wealth by slick mechanisms which manipulate the money of others for one's own benefit – a form of 'rent-seeking' – cannot be classed in the same category as risk-taking entrepreneurship which provides employment and results in products

---

* Earlier chapters have already emphasised the debt, notably in developed countries, which companies owe to their host societies with regard to infrastructure, education, patent and intellectual property rights, and the general rule of law, openly acknowledged by some – though insufficient – prominent, successful entrepreneurs.

** Government provided huge financial sums to major banks, on both sides of the Atlantic, following the financial crash of 2008, but notoriously little found its way to businesses – a source of complaint ever since.

people want. (Many are the stories of businesses with innovative schemes struggling to access finance to get their ideas off the ground.) While free market capitalism has a wholly valid place in a democratic society, it is not the job of government to facilitate inordinate profit-seeking, especially in grossly unequal societies. In fact, its task should be to prevent it, and to endeavour to direct finance and entrepreneurship into more productive fields.* For, where the private sector can create wealth and employment for the wider community, government should provide full support. This will be helped if the notion that value to the economy is added only by entrepreneurs and private companies is challenged, and the huge wealth generated by ordinary workers in numerous occupations duly acknowledged. The New Economics Foundation has calculated the value to society generated by, for example, hospital cleaners and child care workers as being between £7 and £10 for every £1 they are paid, showing how we underpay work that has a high social value, and considerable personal value to us all.[34]

On the other hand, many workers in the finance industry are vastly overpaid, in spite of the meagre social benefit they provide to the community. Many cannot even be said to be involved in constructive financial work. In foreign exchange markets, for example, a large volume of the trading has been pure speculation, serving no wider economic purpose. Robert Peston pointed out that while foreign exchange trading has increased by a factor of 234 since 1977, world economic output has risen only 7 times in that period.[35] Difficult as it may be to achieve, it is in areas like this that supervision should be increased in the form of, perhaps, an extra transaction tax to attempt to limit socially useless financial activity and promote that which benefits the broader economy. At the same time, more inclusive oversight of the sector would improve financial practice as well as enhance transparency. Will Hutton has written of the narrow range of expertise involved in supervising financial services.[36] He cites the Bischoff Inquiry into the City's international competitiveness after the financial crash: of the total 662 years of work experience of its membership, 75% had been spent in City occupations or enterprises servicing them. Hutton contrasts this with earlier inquiries

---

* Further regulation of financial institutions is yet needed, in both Britain and the USA, to prevent another calamity of the kind they produced in 2007/08. And however beneficial the financial sector is to the British economy, if it had a lower profile in society, then more ambitious, clever young people might find their way into socially useful economic businesses, instead of being dazzled by the glamour of the City of London.

into the City, like the 1931 Macmillan Committee or the 1980s Wilson Committee which contained members from the wider business community and even from trade unions.

Of course, these issues are hard to legislate for, especially those involving attitudes and motivation, but in most cases it is government which must take the lead; they have many tools at their disposal. During the heady years leading up to the 2007/08 financial crash, it appears as if many authorities had lost their way – or at least lost any sense of rigour or caution, believing that the financial good times could not be jeopardized. It has been pointed out that during the eighteen months to July 2007, during a period of major profligate lending, the 61 major topics discussed by the board of the Financial Services Authority included only one connected to prudential risks taken by banks.[37] The view that market conditions were so propitious that nothing could go wrong had evidently led experts and non-experts alike into a fools' paradise. But although the FSA was dissolved in 2013 and two new bodies created in its place, there are still accusations that regulation of the financial sector has still not gone far enough to forestall another major crisis in future.* Further reform of capital markets is still needed to ensure macro-economic stability; financial practices which destabilise the wider economy must be banished, and their operations penalised. Sensible taxation of speculative, short-term financial operations should be introduced – possibly a version of the well-known Tobin Tax – as well as measures to combat predatory lending. (More will be said about tax later.)

One of the issues which lurks in the background of any discussion of finance is the question of limited liability, one of the pillars of the free market. However, while it became a vital feature of industrialism in the nineteenth century, which made modern capitalism possible, its exploitation under neo-liberalism, pushing *casino capitalism* to its extremes, has led to its being put under the microscope in many quarters. The productive power of industrialism was facilitated by limited liability, which in its early days was indispensable to reducing the dangers of entrepreneurship, allowing capital accumulation and large

---

* It remains to be seen whether the new Financial Conduct Authority (responsible for the functioning of the financial markets in Britain) and the Prudential Regulation Authority (regulating banks, insurance and investment firms) are able better to manage the UK's financial operations than their predecessor. The collapse in 2020 of Blackmore Bonds, a firm dealing in high-risk mini-bonds, with £45 million of ordinary savers' money, after warnings about it had years earlier been conveyed to the FCA, does not encourage confidence.

scale investment. However, as enterprises grew in size, and were increasingly run by professional managers, the long-considered matter of risk-taking became more prominent. Adam Smith himself had warned of the danger of directors of 'joint-stock' companies not exercising the same vigilance over other people's money as they would their own. And once cross-border capital movements allowed the emergence of financial globalisation after the 1980s, instantaneous transactions could be undertaken, in contrast to the more rooted, static elements of capitalism. The expansion of venture capital and hedge funds, investing leveraged money in businesses with which they may have scant connection, has merely exacerbated risk and endangered all of us. As Adam Smith said, *... the interest of the dealers... is never the same with that of the public, who have generally an interest to deceive and even to oppress the public...*[38]*

Here also there is a lack of equity; if shareholders bear no responsibility when a firm damages the environment or its consumers, there is clearly a liability deficit. *The same goes for corporations that openly enrich shareholders, directors, and officers at the expense of their employees,* says Katharina Pistor.[39] She maintains that the problem lies with markets, *which simply* cannot *price risk adequately, because market participants are shielded from the harms that corporations inflict on others. This pathology goes by the name of "limited liability".* Changes need to be made so that greater balance exists between the protection enjoyed by shareholder-owners and that of other participants such as employees, trade unions, and consumer groups. And when things go wrong, the onus to pick up the economic pieces should not also be borne by the taxpaying public. The demise of Farepak Ltd in the UK exemplifies how the repercussions of excessive risk can adversely impact ordinary people. Farepak, a club into which savers regularly bought vouchers to spend at Christmas, collapsed in 2006 with the loss of around £40 million belonging to 120,000 people, mostly low-income earners. European Home Retail (EHR), Farepak's owners, had used the money of savers to buy booksales firm DMG in 2000, later reimbursing Farepak accounts with bank loans from HBOS. But when DMG made

---

* Smith ends the section from which this quotation is taken (Book I, Chapter XI) with these significant words: *I shall conclude this very long chapter with observing that every improvement in the circumstances of the society tends either directly or indirectly to raise the real rent of land, to increase the real wealth of the landlord, his power of purchasing the labour, or the produce of the labour of other people.* One can deduce from this what he would have thought of today's capitalist landlords, of the financial or business variety.

large losses and was then re-sold for a minimal price, HBOS called in the debt in the form of the savings paid into Farepak.

The example of EHR, an apparently stable and reputable company, using Farepak's savings for its own financial purposes was certainly risky and unwise, but was not illegal. There is no requirement obliging savings clubs of this kind to ring-fence their funds. However, the situation was made worse by Farepak being forced by HBOS to continue accepting money from savers, at about £1 million a week, for several months after shares in the parent company had been suspended and it was clear that the Christmas savings club would go bust. However, the judge in the later court case made it clear that the bank had not acted illegally, although suggested that the public might not find its behaviour acceptable. Under limited liability, EHR and Farepak cannot be held accountable for their companies' decisions; yet their directors have earned substantial sums, and leave with insured pensions, while HBOS's £31 million loan was repaid in full. But thousands of modest savers eventually collected just 15p for every £1 they had previously saved. Nevertheless, apparently nobody can be held to account for the Farepak débâcle, the consequence of everyday financial wheeling and dealing in a system of commerce which cannot bring itself to protect the ordinary citizen. Thus it is the task of the political authorities to establish proper financial regulation to build a responsible, social capitalism to provide order and justice.

It is remarkable that scandals such as that of Farepak, which emerge from time to time, still evoke surprise when they hit the headlines, as if anyone was under the impression that neo-liberal commerce contained savings safety-nets. Setting up insurance policies to protect modest savers from reckless, speculative adventurism or financial empire-building would no doubt be seen as obstructionism by the advocates of *light-touch* regulation – taking some of the fun out of the financial merry-go-round. But further supervision of investment markets must be brought in, with binding norms, in order to contain risk and prevent it from imposing costs on society at large. It is invidious that financial hardship is visited upon ordinary citizens who have no idea that their savings are being gambled. Leaving matters to the workings of the market – as the neo-liberals would have us accept – should now be recognised as an absurdity; 'market perfectibility' is merely an empty slogan. Furthermore, the time has come to review limited liability itself, and consider what form of regulatory improvement might provide greater protection for the victims of collateral damage when firms collapse. While it is impossible to protect all the casualties of corporate failure, a form of insurance system, based on socially agreed criteria, could well be an answer to what is a systemic failure of capitalism. Many economists have pointed out the tendency of limited liability to encourage risk-taking, but not until the emergence of neo-liberalism did the need for regulation become so urgent.[40]

Project Four: Improving the conduct of free market capitalism

While enhanced regulation is a vital ingredient in creating a more socially beneficial economy, just as important is the manner in which business and commerce are conducted. The whole emphasis in neo-liberal capitalism is on short-term profit, with a concentration on shareholders and those already holding capital, so that the interests of employees, third-party suppliers, and even consumers are relegated. This has fostered a culture, especially in Anglo-Saxon capitalism, which encourages rent-seeking and the pursuit of ruthless efficiencies to the exclusion of more socially responsible considerations. The production of goods and services has a wider impact on society than is reflected in the manner or costs of producing them, both in added value which is often hidden, and in externalities which result from, for example, waste or pollution. But the other significant impact is on people, whether those employed in production or the wider public, most of whom have an important stake in capitalism. Neo-liberalism ignores these elements. A reformed 'social capitalism' will assume greater social responsibility for all these concerns. This was not unknown to British business in days gone by: it was not so long ago (although clearly pre-neo-liberalism) that industrialist Samuel Courtauld declared, *The quality of the workers who leave the factory doors every evening is even more important than the quality of the products which it delivers to the customers.*[41]

However, have there been signs more recently of changing times; perhaps business is starting to appreciate that the single-minded pursuit of shareholder value is not the be-all and end-all? Here is Jack Welch, former CEO of General Electric, speaking in 2009 after the financial crash: *Shareholder value is a result, not a strategy. Your main constituencies are your employees, your customers and your products.*[42] Many entrepreneurs and chief executives adopt this more progressive, but also more appropriate approach; the more enlightened are aware that the so-called 'shareholder primacy' model of corporate practice can damage the long-term interests of corporations and shareholders themselves, as well as society in general. To ensure that greater social responsibility on the part of companies becomes the norm is not easy in liberal societies, but with globalisation and a myriad of different business jurisdictions, the task is hugely multiplied. The UN has taken the initiative with its Global Compact, encouraging businesses to adopt socially responsible policies, with an emphasis on accountability, sustainability and transparency. But the voluntary Corporate Social Responsibility Agreements which it invites companies to sign up to have so far been adopted by relatively few of the 70,000-odd transnational corporations. Considerable work needs to be done between governments, and in international bodies, to encourage firms to adhere to global standards of responsible corporate governance.

Forging international agreements is ultimately the only way to inculcate common global practices. In an increasingly unified, homogenised, world business environment this has to be the way forward. Once recovery from the Covid-19 pandemic has been achieved, globalisation is likely to proceed, re-energised, but the ongoing preoccupation with climate change will undoubtedly concentrate minds on the need for international standards to meet the emergency. Here the impact on free market enterprises will be significant, especially regarding Sustainability, one of the UN planks of its Global Compact initiative. But the other two – Accountability and Transparency – are equally important, and self-reinforcing. If corporations are willing to adopt socially responsible policies, to subscribe to the idea of creating 'shared value' and eschewing the fixation with narrow profit-maximisation, they will have no need to shy away from transparency. But the success of these approaches internationally will depend on multi-lateral agreements, for which the current prevalence of populist leaders and political division is not at all auspicious. It has become clear that global warming will be combated effectively only by international agreement, and the same route will have to be followed with business practices as regards their accountability to wider society – including some measure of alignment on taxation to prevent footloose corporations from avoiding local, domestic regulatory restrictions.

The financial crash of 2007/08 has made greater international agreement and co-ordination even more urgent to address global crises, whether environmental or financial. It has been emphasised in earlier chapters of this work how individuals pursuing their self-regarding paths can often be to the detriment of their own and their communities' interests. The same counter-productive (and perhaps counter-intuitive) effects will inevitably result from individual nations adopting a selfish, isolationist approach to matters like taxation and business regulation. In an ever-shrinking world, no longer can single-minded, unilateral strategies be expected to produce the desired outcomes, without collateral damage as well as harm to nations themselves. Whether regarding global warming, depletion of fish stocks, corporation tax levels, business standards, or species loss, only international agreement and co-ordination will favour long-term national interests, and it is perverse self-delusion to think otherwise. International regulation and monitoring are essential to achieve this, but face the power of huge transnational corporations, some of which endeavour to thwart progressive policy. Exxon Mobil, the world's largest oil and gas company, for example, was shown to have understood the science behind global warming over forty years ago, yet has consistently opposed reducing greenhouse gas emissions and has challenged the scientific evidence on which it is based.[43]

The case of climate change, and Exxon Mobil's role in it, highlight the very question of the degree to which free market capitalism is aligned with long-term human and social interests, or under neo-liberalism is even compatible with them.* When corporate decision-making, often supported by partisan national governments, is focused almost exclusively on short-term profit, then sustainability – environmental or even corporate – will be neglected. As for transparency, Exxon Mobil went to great lengths in the United States to conceal the fact of their knowledge of the impact of their business on the health of the planet – even to the extent of invoking the right, under the First Amendment of the American Constitution, *not* to speak or be obliged to reveal information to regulators about what it had known – in effect, trying to use constitutional powers to prevent evidence coming to light which could give rise to fraud charges. This is testimony to the implicit rejection of corporate responsibility on the part of some multi-nationals, the size of which, in many cases, makes it almost impossible to hold them to account. And if

---

* Exxon Mobil was a member of the lobby group Global Climate Coalition (disbanded in 2002), a collection of businesses opposed to a reduction of greenhouse gas emissions, and which challenged the science behind global warming.

national governments condone corporate disregard for public accountability, effectively supporting a 'race to the bottom', in a throwback to outdated Mercantilism, then the consequence will be environmental crisis before long, as well as an internal, existential threat to capitalism itself.

However, the extent of corporate hubris under neo-liberal capitalism has led it to claim further rights in the United States on the basis of the First Amendment. Since a US Supreme Court case in 2010, corporations have been emboldened to assert the same constitutional rights as natural-born persons – a clear distortion of the concept of rights – in numerous fields, often stretching the notion of free speech to an absurd degree. The case of Citizens United v. The Federal Electoral Commission in 2010, which held that the corporate funding of independent political broadcasts in elections should not be restricted, has been the catalyst for egregious challenges to common practices. On the strength of the idea that they are 'associations of citizens', companies have, for example, contested whether they should be obliged to attach labels to food products. The consequences of such claims, not as yet brought on this side of the Atlantic, could be the further consolidation of corporate power at the expense of the national community and its political advocates. These trends move us in an entirely contrary direction to the one needed to foster social and ecological improvement and, ultimately, to the one which will safeguard the interests of companies themselves and the people they 'serve'. International supervision of the ambitions of transnational corporations, where they do not exercise self-control, is vital for public accountability.

Of course where governments, especially populist democratic ones, allow too much latitude to large corporations, progress may well be hampered. If the wealth of major conglomerates – sometimes with economies larger than small states – is used to influence political leaders it will rarely be for the benefit of society as a whole. The revolving door of movement between politics and company boardrooms is not in the interests of the wider population; it simply enmeshes politicians and corporate bosses in a symbiotic relationship which enriches those with experience of government and gives undue political influence to large corporations. Independent bodies are needed to provide oversight to regulate such practices much more tightly, and perhaps to prevent firms from political involvement of any kind. As things stand, many capitalist regimes and tax systems allow companies to build inordinate levels of wealth, as well as to exercise inappropriate advocacy in the democratic political process. Only progressive politics is likely to reverse these trends. But greater responsibility will also have to be borne by businesses and consumers. Environmental emergency has shown the need to moderate consumerism, to look to the long term with a much broader perspective on how we live, highlighting the reality that we cannot continue on our current, wasteful, profligate course. The Covid-19 pandemic should also have proved to us that in our interconnected world sustainability is a long-term project.

Companies will have to moderate their policies in similar fashion, to shed the short-termism of much corporate practice, which has demanded immediate returns and quick profits. This has become a mindset under neo-liberalism, resulting in less innovation and reduced investment in research and development, as well as in human capital. Paradoxically this is not in the best interests of companies, but the desire for short-term profits often steers policy in that direction. By continuing to maximize shareholder value – perhaps by reducing capital expenditure, cutting jobs, or even buying back its own shares, thus maintaining their market price – companies will generate higher profits and appear successful, even while they are weakening their own long-term prospects.* Such practices cannot be legislated against; the culture in boardrooms and amongst CEOs has to change, just as the novelty-driven, short-term culture of consumerism must be moderated, both for social and environmental reasons. The drive for efficiency and quick returns can have another effect: it can reduce 'slack' in the system. When successful companies are accused of inefficiency, of being 'bloated' and wasteful, it is often said that they should have cut back their corporate 'fat'. But a revealing book has pointed out that some slack in the system can be beneficial, even if sometimes wasteful. It is possible to increase the efficiency of an organisation without improving it; removing slack can reduce flexibility, limit breathing space, and restrict strategic thinking.[45]

Improving corporate governance by instituting long-term strategies which take in economic sustainability, the environment, and the everyday concerns of society at large would transform the culture of business. It would imply inclusivity, narrow corporate preoccupations being abandoned in favour of a model which embraces stakeholders,

---

* Economist Ha-Joon Chang points out that for decades up to the 1980s, share buybacks were less than 5% of US corporate profits, but subsequently rose steadily, reaching a gigantic 90% in 2007, and what he calls *an absurd* 280% in 2008.[44]

most of whom have a vital interest in the success of the private sector. It matters to consumers, taxpayers, to the retired with their pensions invested in private companies, and especially to employees, that free market capitalism thrives. None of these wish to see tax avoidance, shoddy expensive goods, exploited workers not paid a living wage, or company policy which results in costly negative externalities which society has to bear – and all so that executives and shareholders enrich themselves. To support responsible corporate practice, there has to be wider participation in company boardrooms, in the shape of worker and community representation. After all, one of the main reasons that maximizing shareholder value is bad for companies is that shareholders are the ones least committed to the long-term future of enterprises; they are able more easily to leave, whereas employees and suppliers generally have more of their livelihoods invested in firms.* Above all, the productive economy should be seen as a collaborative endeavour, and nations which put this into practice generally have more successful economies.**

The legitimacy of free market capitalism rests on it serving an array of participants. Private sector companies have a recognised place in society, and as such owe a responsibility to the community of which they are part; they benefit from a successful economy but also 'serve' it. Incidents where firms shed labour while consolidating their power and awarding themselves large bonuses as their share prices rise – these exemplify the worst of neo-liberalism. It is down to capitalists and politicians alike to abandon this model if they wish the free market economy to thrive. Judging by the economic landscape of recent years, with crippling austerity, greater economic deprivation, rising social inequality and escalating bosses' bonuses, the signs are not encouraging. Whether the impact of Covid-19 can bring about lasting change remains to be seen. Already opportunities have been squandered: the initial rescue package to alleviate the worst of the Coronavirus crisis prompted by the economic 'lockdown' provided 63 of some of Britain's major companies with £18 billion of loans at interest rates of between 0.3% and 0.7%,

---

* It has been pointed out that in 1970 American stocks were held on average for five years; forty years later the average was a mere five days.[46]

** 'Codetermination' in post-war West Germany was one of the building blocks of the German 'economic miracle' in the 1950s. A decentralised trade union structure established in the late-1940s, with employees on company boards, helped Germany avoid some of the worst excesses of neo-liberal practice. Codetermination was initially introduced in its current form in the iron and steel industries by the post-war British military command; it is regarded as an important element in later German industrial democracy.

much lower than that charged to other businesses. However, unlike policies in some European nations, the Covid Corporate Financing Facility (CCFF) – public money from the Bank of England – attached no meaningful conditions to the hand-out, beyond *requesting* borrowers to show restraint on senior pay and the size of dividends paid to shareholders.

Thus, while some continental countries attached binding conditions to the money which their governments allowed companies, the Bank of England's view was that it would be inappropriate to impose requirements on firms already struggling. The French and Dutch authorities, on the other hand, believed that this was precisely the moment to apply constructive conditions to cheap government money provided to their airlines – such as the stipulation to cut costs, accept pay cuts at all levels, to rule out bonuses or dividends until the loans were repaid, and to limit the night flights of their carriers. This stands in stark contrast to the aversion the British have towards anything which smacks of regulation, even though much of the CCFF money was given to high-carbon sectors. It was reported that British Airways accepted £300 million of public money but proposed initially to cut 12,000 jobs, while chemicals company BASF drew £1 billion from the CCFF before proceeding with a £3 billion dividend payment to shareholders: so much for corporate restraint.[47] And in spite of the magnitude of the economic crisis brought on by Coronavirus, the UK public are clearly dissatisfied with the lack of conditionality demanded of companies receiving money. Almost two-thirds of those polled believed that strings should have been attached to the bailouts, and only 5% thought that no conditions should have been applied[48] – by no means the first time the government has found itself out of step with the general public on the economy.

Project 5: Devising sensible taxation for the public good

Since free market capitalism is a component of modern society, and not *vice versa*, it is important that a consensus is arrived at on the role it should be allowed to play in the pluralistic social arena. Governing authorities need to gain public approval for the nature of what is essentially a social compact between human beings and the economic forces which surround them and influence so much of their lives. An agreed social compact must involve recognition that profits from capitalism not be excessive, and that enterprises behave in socially responsible ways, which means abiding by the same social and moral norms as the broader community of which it is a part. And a vital element in that agreement is taxation – the levy on the productive forces of capitalism which enables government and society to function for the general welfare. After all, capitalism itself benefits from the structure and institutions which society has built, and paid for publicly, especially in terms of law and education, as was outlined in earlier chapters. In mature societies the relationship between the market and the people will have gained general social approval, including the level and nature of taxation. But in nations where neo-liberalism dominates, the tension and division over what should be taxed and by how much are more prominent; where populist tendencies prevail, governments frequently assume an anti-tax stance, siding with high-earning firms and individuals as if they would like to abolish taxes entirely.

However, regardless of how the issues may be framed by those with a political axe to grind, all know how important taxation is for maintaining the infrastructure of a developed society. Politicians' rhetoric may claim taxes are a burden, but would hardly deny they are needed when pot-holes scar major roads or fire services require urgent equipment. But their reluctance to acknowledge the true level of taxation needed to fund decent social provision is testimony to their craven populism. Of course taxation has to fall in line with social norms, but those are conditioned by a variety of factors such as political and media influence, ideological persuasion, and ideas of fairness. These can and do vary over time; it is remarkable how quickly society adjusts to a new fiscal environment. In the early 1980s income tax rates – especially 'marginal' top levels – were substantially higher than today,* especially in the *Anglo-Sphere*, whereas in continental Europe they have been lower, and vary far less. Yet today's lower rates are taken by many to be entirely appropriate, as if to raise them would be unheard-of radical policy. In recent years, tax taken in the UK as a proportion of national income has been lower than in the vast majority of European states, as well as consistently below the OECD average, with an especially marked discrepancy in the level of social security contributions or pay roll taxes.[49]

It is not the task here to give a detailed outline of tax reform

---

* The Thatcher government taking office in 1979 reduced the top income tax rate from 83% to 60%, and then down to 40% in 1988. In the USA rates came down from 70% to 35% in the early '80s. These countries are conspicuous outliers amongst the G20 nations in transforming income tax rates for the benefit of high earners.

proposals, but to provide a general indication of principles, as well as of possible routes to achieving a fairer and more appropriate tax regime. The tax system in Britain certainly needs to be improved in a number of ways, a major priority being to make it less regressive. The less well-off contribute a much higher proportion of their income in taxes; even if they do not earn enough to pay income tax, they will add to the public purse through VAT, which affects them adversely far more than the better-off. And with the top rates of income tax and corporation tax having been reduced, the capacity for the super-rich and footloose companies to benefit has been greatly enhanced. Will Hutton highlights the ability of high-earners to reduce their tax bills; he suggests that those on incomes of £100,000 claim deductions of around 10%, and those earning £1 million about 30%.[50] By managing to limit their tax liability through tax relief, permitted deductions and avoidance, the rich cost the UK treasury billions each year.* The National Audit Office estimated that around £2 billion in revenue is lost just from a group of about half a million super-rich taxpayers alone,[52] largely the consequence of the efforts of an army of accountants working to minimize their clients' tax liabilities – the tip of a sizeable iceberg. As a result, many rich individuals and perhaps a quarter to a third of companies manage to get away with paying no tax at all.

Considerable work would be required to deal with the degree of tax evasion and avoidance prevalent in the UK. But with the cuts in staff and resources which the tax authorities, HMRC, had to bear under austerity, they simply do not now have the capacity to deal adequately with the problem. This reckless, counterproductive policy of reducing staff, who could recoup more than they cost, is evidence yet again of the lack of political will of populist leaders, their disdain for proper regulation, and a disregard for fiscal inequality.** With the extensive tax loopholes, and the lack of rigour in ensuring that all tax due is paid, the reputation of the British tax authorities in some quarters is that how much tax you pay pretty much depends on your personal moral scruples; this has to be addressed. Internationally, the situation is notoriously worse. The labyrinth of tax havens and other off-shore centres allow transnational

---

* Using figures of the Tax Justice Network, Will Hutton suggests that £12.9 billion of tax revenue might be lost in this way.[51]

** The HMRC investigation into the affairs of Airbnb, which led to that company receiving an extra tax bill of £1.8 million in 2020, to add to an earlier £1.1 million bill it paid on its reported £5.6 million profits in 2019, could be replicated many times over if it had a level of resources adequate to the size of the problem.

companies routinely to minimize their tax liability on a grand scale: tax, if any, is paid in ultra-low tax regimes on profits derived from products sold in developed countries where prices are high, while costs incurred will be off-set wherever it is advantageous to do so. Thus the benefits are transferred to shareholders and capitalists in the rich world, with little tax liability anywhere. The Financial Secrecy Index has estimated that there is between US$21 and 32 trillion of private financial wealth sitting off-shore, untaxed or very lightly so, in a variety of *secrecy jurisdictions* out of reach of democratic societies.[53]

In a global environment of fluid financial movement and instantaneous transactions, arriving at a suitable tax regime is going to be a long, tortuous procedure. But since numerous other agreements govern areas like diplomacy, weapons, human rights, and the oceans, under the auspices of various international bodies or bilateral treaties, it is only a matter of time before global tax succumbs to some degree of regulatory system. As the world of commerce becomes increasingly intertwined, and nations – especially poorer ones – more aware than ever of the dangers of unchecked competition and the perilous 'race to the bottom', the demands for international coordination will become more pressing. Going it alone may appear to offer the greatest benefit for individual nations, asserting their fiscal competitive advantage to the exclusion of others, but this free-for-all would ultimately damage all economies to some degree, even the largest. It is clearly important that corporations contribute to the public finances of nations where they have major business interests, especially in view of the benefits they derive from the infrastructure of the places where they trade, as well as their limited liability advantages there. One suggested solution has been the "minimum tax" idea, which would limit the tax relief corporations could claim for deductions like interest payments.[54]

But corporation tax is a levy towards which nations often have schizophrenic attitudes. On the one hand states are desperate to bring in more tax revenue, while at the same time bending over backwards to offer fiscal and other sweeteners to attract firms to set up within their borders, thus adding to local investment and employment. However, if countries continue to lower tax rates in a competitive tussle to lure business, the consequence will be the ongoing drain on many nations' finances to the enduring benefit of large corporations, which delight in such divisive competition. This does not stop company bosses from complaining about what they claim to be high tax levels restricting their profitability. Yet according to the IMF, corporation tax rates internationally have halved since 1980. In the UK the 52% tax in 1980 became 20% by 2015, while other European nations, as well as Japan and Australia lowered their rates significantly.[55] And then there is the considerable aid provided to major companies by government in the form of subsidies and research and development, outlined in Chapter 5. As far as the USA is concerned, although it does not have one of the lowest rates of corporate tax, the actual federal tax take has been calculated as 13% of reported worldwide income.[56] But until there is full international coordination of taxation, companies will succeed in playing off governments against one another as nations sue for corporate favours.*

Thus it is vital that wealthy nations modernize their corporate tax affairs in order to stabilize revenues. Until there is international agreement on business taxation and systems to prevent large scale avoidance, nations would be advised to rationalize their own tax arrangements without surrendering to corporate pressure and abdicating authority to the private sector. The largest companies build complex webs of entities to minimize their tax liabilities, setting up firms within the companies of their corporate group. This allows them to transfer their assets, profits and income, within their corporate umbrella, to these other companies in lower tax jurisdictions. As such, the subsidiary companies resident in different nation states are taxed differently. It has been said that more than half of global trade takes place within these transnational groups, rather than between them, while Guy Standing has pointed out that almost three quarters of the Fortune 500 list of largest US companies have tax haven subsidiaries.[58] Nevertheless, while it is easy to shift funds around the world, concrete plants and investments tend to be more rooted, which is why reform could be applied by having corporations pay taxes based on their local economic activity including production, sales and even research.** Furthermore, a system of variable taxes could be devised which offered lower rates to companies which could show they were investing in the local economy.

Recognition is growing of the need for enhanced international co-operation on tax. Setting up a World Tax Administration is still a long

---

* Research has estimated that corporate concessions (what have been termed 'corporate welfare') cost the UK treasury about £44 billion in tax benefits every year.[57]

** Ha-Joon Chang maintains that few corporations are in fact truly international, and that most still produce the majority of their output in their home nations. *Capital has a nationality*, he says.[59]

way off, but as world economies become more integrated, governments have begun to see its advantages, and most are aware that a global 'wild west' of evasion and exploitation cannot last. The G20 nations declared the end of banking secrecy in 2009, after which there was a trend towards more rigorous standards of transparency. The Global Forum on Transparency and Exchange of Information for Tax Purposes, under the OECD, has led the fight against off-shore tax evasion, so that pressure is building, albeit slowly. In 2020 negotiations took place among almost 140 nations, organised by the OECD, to reach agreement on a global digital tax on technological companies. But discussions ended in June that year when the USA withdrew from the talks, leaving the UK and EU to consider bringing in their own tax. In the new digital environment, and with vast resources devoted to hacking, computer piracy, and breaking down cyber barriers, governments are becoming aware of the difficulty of keeping data secret. The Foreign Account Tax Compliance Act (FATCA) in the USA in 2010, requiring foreign banks to report to the US authorities funds held abroad by US citizens and residents, was a major step forward. Other countries are bringing in similar measures. It will eventually be seen to be in the interests of all nations to collaborate through agreement at international level, just as in times gone by systems of tariffs and tolls were harmonized within national jurisdictions.*

A significant fact about today's rich nations is their enormous amounts of private wealth, which is so often at the expense of the public arena. In his *Capital in the Twenty-First Century*, Thomas Piketty cited a

---

* The difficulty of achieving international uniformity in corporate tax matters was exemplified by the case of Apple in Ireland. In 2016 the European Commission decided that Apple's transfer of around €110 billion in European sales to two subsidiaries in Ireland (though non-resident for tax there) was in fact illegal state aid. It ordered the Irish government to pay almost €14 billion in unpaid taxes. But in 2020 the court of the European Union overturned the ruling, noting that although Ireland may have allowed Apple to avoid tax, the operation was not illegal. In the absence of common laws prohibiting tax avoidance – whether in the EU or in the wider world – small nations will continue to assist large corporations in return for their presence in their countries. However, a landmark was reached in October 2021 when over 130 countries and jurisdictions, under the auspices of the OECD, finalized an international tax plan on a global minimum corporation tax, affecting firms earning more than £635 billion worldwide. Due to come into force in 2023, this agreement will tax companies at 15% – where they operate and earn profit, not necessarily where they have a physical presence.

remarkable statistic: the top 1% of the European population owns around 25% of the total wealth, amounting to about 125% of European GDP.[60] This has been the culmination of developments from the late 1970s, reversing trends of the earlier post-war period when the ratio of wealth to GDP fell. The rise in the value of assets – particularly those of property and share prices – as well as tax changes, have led to huge economic inequalities. Drawing on research by Khoman and Weale, Anthony Atkinson cites data for the period 1995 to 2006, for example, which show that house prices rose 3% per year faster than gross disposable income, and that share prices had risen 4.7% per year in real terms.[61]* The inequalities are especially marked in Britain where much of the population has seen little benefit in terms of disposable wealth even if house prices have risen substantially. (And personal savings have certainly not been responsible for increasing wealth; the household savings ratio has been declining since the 1970s.) Piketty maintains that when the private rate of return on capital is higher for long periods than the rate of growth and output – as has been the case over several decades – then this can be a destabilizing force, and a threat to democracy and lasting social values. Here is the main contradiction of capitalism, he says, that while a free market economy may provide many benefits, it can also display powerful forces of divergence which can represent an existential danger to the whole system.[62]

This is not the first time in history that the accumulation of wealth in society has been so grossly unequal, with its inherent dangers for the social and economic order. And just as relevant today are warnings from earlier periods, such as when Supreme Court Justice Louis Brandeis wrote in the 1930s of the danger to American democracy of a concentration of wealth in the hands of a minority. The same accumulation of wealth has been allowed to develop in Britain over the last forty years, so that the time has now come to apply a progressive annual wealth tax on individual assets. While the exorbitant levels of income tax of the 1950s and '60s would not be applicable today, a tax on capital would now be appropriate to help to address gross, damaging inequalities. It should be noted that the nations applying the greatest reductions to top tax rates since that time are those in which the top earners' share of national income has increased the most. Annual

---

* ... reinforcing the argument for a more effective capital gains tax – addressing the recent imbalance between remuneration from earnings and that from capital – to sit alongside a wealth tax.

wealth taxes have worked well elsewhere, such as in Spain and France. Such a measure in Britain would make a contribution to fiscal equity, and could even diminish or replace capital gains and inheritance taxes, and thus lead to a simplification of the tax system. Of course, wide transparency would need to accompany such a major fiscal change, and until greater international agreement on this had developed there would inevitably be considerable tax evasion. But as Piketty has pointed out, the automatic provision of banking data should have been part of the liberalization of capital movements in the 1980s.[63] This has to be the way forward.*

To a progressive wealth tax must be added a return to more progressive rates of income tax. The cuts in personal taxation since the 1970s have led to extreme social and income inequalities on both sides of the Atlantic, and the 'super-rich' 1% pulling away from the rest of their societies in egregious fashion. There is no convincing argument against an increase in top rates of tax, in spite of the specious rationalizing of neo-liberals and others. The amount of taxable income going to the top 1% of earners in the UK (about 540,000 people) has recently been revised up to a figure of almost 17% of national income,[65] whereas in the United States the equivalent is over 20%. Neither globalisation nor domestic economic reasons can justify these extremes of remuneration; other wealthy nations in the OECD, mostly with only modest fiscal alterations, have not experienced the same increasing inequalities over the past forty years. Prior to the 2019 General Election Britain's Labour Party proposed making the top 45% rate of personal income tax payable at £80,000 (affecting around 5% of income earners), instead of the current £150,000, as well as a higher rate of 50% starting at £125,000. This would raise an extra amount of anywhere between £3 and £10 billion, depending on assumptions as to its effect on behaviour, such as attempts at further tax evasion. However, as the Institute for Fiscal Studies said, pointing out the obvious, revenue might be maximized if avoidance opportunities were fewer.

Much discussion has been undertaken regarding the effects on revenue raised of different marginal top rates of tax, with estimations of

---

* In the United States, while campaigning for the Democratic Party nomination for the 2020 presidential election, Senators Elizabeth Warren and Bernie Sanders both advocated a tax on individual wealth of $50 million. Meanwhile, a 2019 opinion poll for the *New York Times* found that more than two-thirds of Americans, including a majority of Republicans, supported a 2% tax on households worth over that amount of wealth.[64]

the optimum rate varying between 56% and 80%.* There will inevitably be an inclination of top-rate taxpayers to minimize their liability – such as opting to take more of their remuneration in the form of dividends, or even as capital gains, both of which are taxed at lower rates for such earners.** Thus greater realignment of the tax system in Britain would be needed to bring in the required extra revenue, and to contribute to greater social equality. But modest increases in tax such as those cited above would still not bring Britain to the levels of fiscal equity seen in most of Europe. However, tax increases would find favour with a majority of the British people: in 2018, a survey indicated the greatest support in fifteen years for tax rises and increases in public spending, at just over 60%.[68] But even though more than half of Conservative supporters polled thought taxes should rise, the government of Boris Johnson is taken with the erroneous notion that lowering taxes encourages entrepreneurship, raises business activity, and even brings in more revenue. As regards investment, his view is contradicted by the IMF, which says that the sensitivity of investment to tax changes has declined internationally over the last thirty years mainly due to the rise in market power of big corporations.[69]

Nevertheless, economists on the right persist with their claim that tax cuts will boost economic performance. The evidence that lower taxes would lead to a demand for longer working hours or more overtime and that there is much pent-up energy for a wave of ambitious entrepreneurship just does not exist. In fact, to the contrary, for some time before the Covid-19 crisis surveys indicated a desire for a better work-life balance, and that reducing working hours was an aspiration for many employees. The famous Laffer Curve, originally advocated by economist Arthur Laffer when Ronald Reagan was in the White House, has seduced Johnson's neo-liberals, even though it has often been discredited. Laffer's main idea was that lowering rates is the route to greater tax revenues.*** But the consensus on the corollary, that raising

---

* There is a detailed discussion by Anthony Atkinson of the arguments around the effects of top tax rates.[66]

** Significantly, one poll indicated that 61% of respondents (and as many as 67% of Conservative voters!) thought investment income should be liable to the same rate of tax as income earned from work.[67]

*** The citizens of the American state of Kansas, who in 2012 were subjected to what was in effect a test of the efficacy of Laffer's theory, will be well aware of the downsides of lowering taxes: cuts of around a third led to a fall in revenue which impacted health care and education in the state, but not to more jobs being created. The scheme was later abandoned,

taxes is counter-productive in that it leads to a fall in revenue, is that it applies only in very limited circumstances, such as when income taxes reach levels of perhaps 75-80%. However, there is considerable uncertainty about these calculations. But there is no uncertainty as to the benefits for economic growth from lowering taxes: for example, after much research, Emmanuel Saez and Thomas Piketty declared:

> ... data show that there is no correlation between cuts in top tax rates and average annual GDP per capita growth since the 1970s. ... the bottom line is that rich countries have all grown at roughly the same rate over the past 30 years – in spite of huge variations in tax policies.[70]

Cuts in top income tax rates appear to promote rent-seeking but not economic growth.

It is time to herald these realities. The British tax system, like that of the United States, is less progressive now than it was for much of the twentieth century; the richest in the land have got considerably richer, while at the same time they have been taxed less. Income tax rates for the highest earnings need to be raised. In America taxes have been lowered several times over recent generations, always with promises of the benefits they would bring, including the latest cut by President Trump in 2017. That, like the others, failed to realise the promised benefits, as the IMF testified.* The political right likes to laud the tax contribution of the rich – to which the retort is yes, of course, that is the natural consequence of the exorbitant salaries paid to high earners. It would be a scandal if they were paying any less, and in any case the current tax rates mean they are still contributing less than they should. To prepare the ground to have these raised it is necessary to 'frame' the debate with two themes: fairness and social infrastructure. The first is a subject familiar to the people of the UK, who can see the injustice of vastly unequal standards of living and levels of tax. The second is already well known in that there is a popular clamour for more money for education and health, while the years of austerity have left the country with an

---

although its supporters maintained that it had not worked because it had not been fully implemented.

* Viz: the two IMF papers cited in Endnote 67. Even a traditional, conservative institution like the IMF agrees that excessive salaries and high income inequality are bad for mature economies and their social welfare.

AN ALTERNATIVE PROGRESS

all too visible decaying material infrastructure. These criteria must be the rationale for raising income tax rates, avoiding any sense of envy or punitive measures.

These suggestions are all intended to point to a fairer, more appropriate system without detracting from the ambition and enterprise of individuals and businesses. There was considerable energy and entrepreneurship in the Western world after World War II, but with much more equitable tax regimes, before countries intoxicated with neo-liberalism diverged from the rest and went off down their own misguided path. The ideas outlined above would help re-position these aberrant nations, and are designed to operate in 'normal' economic times. Of course, the current Coronavirus pandemic will delay the adoption of many of these reforms; the vast sums borrowed by governments to cope with the Covid crisis have been emergency measures to forestall even further economic damage. The degree of debt which this has led to – frightening as it may appear to many – will need to be managed (certainly assisted by historically low rates of interest). But nations like the United States, the United Kingdom and Japan, with their own sovereign currencies, are able to withstand the burden of debt, especially if they can borrow internally. After all, the increase in debt in Britain and America in 2020, incurred by the response to the pandemic, has still not reached the level of that of Japan, now standing at more than 250% of GDP.* When the worst of the current Covid crisis is over, taxes will inevitably have to rise, and considerable sums devoted to a fiscal re-balancing, and to increasing social and income equality.

Project Six: Re-evaluating work: its purpose and reward

On a late winter's day in March 1992, the Princess Royal formally opened The Centre for Process Systems Engineering at Imperial College, London. This institution, dealing in process engineering, was established to transfer brain capacity into a machine in order to employ the power and speed of computers to find the best way of making things. The production methods of items ranging from processed foods to nuclear technology would be able to take considerable work out of the hands of

---

* Japan has seen figures for national public debt of more than 200% of GDP since the 1990s, while the UK endured levels above 100% of GDP throughout the post-war period until the early 1960s.

the engineers; the majority of the tasks would be carried out by computers within 10 to 15 years, according to the Centre's Director Roger Sargent, though adding that engineers would not be made completely redundant (!). Heralding the opening of the Centre and the march of technological progress it apparently represented, one national newspaper reported the institution's function as ... *designed to free humans from work*.[71] During the same month, it was announced that Royal Mail's introduction of machines able to read handwritten postcodes would lead to the loss of some 15,000 post office jobs over a three-year period. At a cost of £250 million, 'optical character recognition equipment' was to be installed, thus making the existing character recognition 'equipment' – the human sorters – largely superfluous. What better examples of humans submitting themselves to technological autonomy? What better proof of the inviolability of narrow economic efficiency?

Where do we think our civilization is leading? It is as if the rampant march of materialistic forces is driving the human species to transcend itself and its fundamental nature through the ever more complex fruits of its own ingenuity. And this process appears to lead inexorably to the decay of many basic values of common humanity, while a new mechanistic race rises further and further from their remains. This may be seen as the logical result of two centuries of scientific progress since Western civilization was emancipated by the forces of the Enlightenment. However, there is nothing inevitable about the dehumanisation of mankind. The periodic social upheavals of the last two hundred years, particularly the rise of socialism, testify to a refusal to accept the meagre vision of a functional future lacking values. The critical danger in this early stage of the 21st century is that events and protagonists conspire to promote value-free political objectives; the demise of state communism and the hitherto apparent failure of a more humane capitalism have served to divert popular thinking towards reliance on a single-minded materialistic drive. The search for common denominators has largely bypassed social ideals, and in the process the common toil, the daily routine of people endeavouring to earn a living and support themselves and those closest to them has been devalued; work has become merely a means to a dehumanised function of serving the prevailing economic system.

Capitalism, like other belief systems, is based on much myth and dogma, a doctrine which in the end comes to be seen as normal, predictable. No doubt many of its adherents cannot help thinking that its working practices must be the way things, if not should be, then inevitably must be. The notion, put forward in a paper of 1930 by John Maynard Keynes, that people would be working around fifteen hours a week within a hundred years, may appear to many to be quaint but idealistically absurd. And the idea of a future age of leisure, commonly circulating up to the 1960s, could be put down to a lack of realism or an imperfect understanding of how capitalism works. But such assumptions are part of the myth of the market – commonplace views, hardly thought about consciously, which completely misinterpret the nature and potential of human beings. Extreme free market societies have wandered into a predicament in which long working hours, drives for efficiency, job insecurity, 'presenteeism', vastly unequal levels of pay, and a greatly impaired quality of life have become common to today's working world. While some capitalist economies, notably in Scandinavia, have managed to resist the worst of these consequences, they are seen to varying degrees elsewhere and are typical in the *Anglo-Sphere*. They appear predicated on another assumption, that they are inevitable features of capitalism over which we have no control, and that our prosperity and our economic success (such as it is) depends on our submitting to their demands.

It is time to reverse this absurd abdication of human and social responsibility. The path out of this conceptual cul-de-sac will not be easy, because it involves a major change of outlook. But Coronavirus has provided an opportunity: in forcing a variety of changes to work habits and routines, it has allowed organisations to recognize possibilities which they might not otherwise have contemplated. Work-sharing, working from home, and greater flexibility of hours have all been shown to be feasible, even if adopted under duress. The normal daily pressure, with limited time to consider imaginative amendments to working practices, inhibits sufficient 'blue-sky' thinking, but a deadly virus has forced our hand and made us see other priorities. We have even begun to re-assess the meaning of work – something long overdue. After all, it is more than just a livelihood; it is a way of structuring our world, giving it purpose – a means of acquiring a sense of oneself beyond human relationships, and a chance to form a reassuring social image.[72] The capacity to gain self-respect and dignity through work, a very personal, unspoken value, is lost when one is unemployed – a form of deprivation largely ignored.* How could anyone possibly imagine that systems ... *designed to free humans*... from this important role would have any merit whatsoever?

Paid employment is the principal route to participation in society; being made redundant, so often a blow to confidence and self-esteem, can be the trigger to further disengagement from communal involvement.** But government authorities must adapt to the new working environment, in which jobs will inevitably be lost to increasing automation and artificial intelligence. There are those who maintain that new jobs will always be created, that fears of mass unemployment expressed in days gone by have not materialised. But while it is true that we cannot now imagine the nature and variety of future productive enterprises, which will require their own new types of employment, nevertheless in a fast-changing world there will inevitably be periodic dislocation in different sectors, which will need creative management. Policies need to be developed to deal with employees moving from one kind of employment to another, and to cope with increased leisure, whether involuntary or chosen. And the focus must be on employment from a worker's perspective, on the process of creating satisfying work, NOT on the effort to shoe-horn people into jobs for the macro-economic purpose of increasing productivity and promoting growth. Employment policy must be person-focused; the energy and enterprise which may be generated through more workers having rewarding work, and a shorter working week, would make a valuable – incidental – contribution to greater productivity.

Surveys and opinion polls over the years have repeatedly shown that one of the key demands of workers is for more autonomy in employment, more control over their hours of work and working practices – features which more highly-paid employees often take for granted. In employment studies, the lack of freedom and autonomy at work frequently loom larger than low pay as a key complaint, although demands for pay rises take precedence, being an easier focus of discontent with a greater chance of garnering support. Conditions of work

---

* – especially by those who – content in their own satisfying, well-remunerated jobs – assume that more menial employment has no intrinsic value to those who carry it out.

** Under neo-liberalism, macro-economic policy has treated inflation as more dangerous than unemployment, in spite of the fact that rapidly rising prices in Britain, even in the inflationary 1970s, have never produced the human misery and social dislocation which accompany high unemployment. But this has been the stance of the privileged – to discriminate in favour of those with capital to the detriment of employees.

AN ALTERNATIVE PROGRESS 455

and the nature of the working environment would be an important concern of employee-centred policies. But although the quality of jobs is often highlighted, this is mainly lip service being paid to aspects which fail to gain public prominence. Nevertheless they need urgent attention; the quality of much employment has deteriorated over recent years, particularly under the austerity regime since 2010 which has led to the increasing intensity of work. A major study by the RSA revealed the extent of the dissatisfaction: 72% of those surveyed found work stressful, 40% were worried about being dismissed without good reason, 47% said they felt depressed or unhappy at work, and more than half regularly felt they were being monitored more than was necessary.[73] This damning picture of working conditions demonstrates the urgent need for a transformation of attitudes and policies.

A major contribution to changing such attitudes will have to come from employers, who themselves are under severe financial and time constraints. But the more enlightened of them will realise that improving the working environment will result in a more productive staff. Emphasis on the workplace, and the process, from the employee's perspective, will help engender greater unity of purpose between workers and management, resulting in better outcomes for all concerned; it is no accident that this is more often achieved in small businesses where employees are less remote from their bosses. But the other vital change needed is to reduce working hours. Even under existing conditions, a shorter working week would improve the quality of work for many. Almost 30% of employees have expressed a wish to work fewer hours, and 10% of all surveyed would be willing to do so for less pay.[74] As automation and artificial intelligence develop, the future will see less need for the human component, and the prospect of increased leisure – Keynes' vision of the future in the 1930s – can become a reality. This itself will help improve the work-life balance, often spoken of but so rarely achieved. A shorter working week is to be expected, and work-sharing will become more common, and while less 'stuff' may be produced, the reduction is likely to be far less than the loss in working time, (just as the well-known three-day week in 1974 did not result in a commensurate loss of output).*

Support for a shorter working work has been growing rapidly in

---

*   In spite of the working week having been reduced by 40% in the early months of 1974, the decline in production had been variously estimated at 6% and between 10 and 15%.

developed nations, the main preference appearing to be for a four-day week. Movements have sprung up in parts of continental Europe, such as Germany and Spain, with some firms deciding to go ahead with a shorter week. The company Software Delsol, in southern Spain, opted for a four-day week, declaring that gains in improved mental health, less absenteeism, and a smaller carbon footprint could be combined with maintaining productivity at previous levels.[75] The New Zealand Prime Minister has urged corporate bosses to consider reducing working hours for their staff, while in the UK the Labour Party, Green Party and the TUC have all advocated a four-day week. However, this is by no means a left/right issue, since the awareness of the benefits of working fewer hours is growing on all sides. While the more conservative company bosses may fear a financial disadvantage in trying to maintain wage levels for fewer hours, the results of trials of a shorter working week have not shown much change in productivity, and can even lead to a better quality product. In many white-collar jobs where 'presenteeism' is a way of gaining kudos in the workplace, reduced working hours would likely see little difference in the amount of work accomplished. But in any case, it is becoming clear that if the world is to forestall environmental and social disaster we must all produce less and consume less, which should start with working less.

Proposals of this kind will inevitably prompt opposition from those so wedded to the *status quo* that they do not appreciate that it cannot last. And the knee-jerk reaction of many bosses, appealing as they think to a conclusive argument, is that an unacceptable cost would have to be borne by taxpayers. This, of course, ignores the gains which would accrue from fewer sick days taken, reduced burn-out from current working conditions, and less staff turnover. These problems, which impose their own considerable costs, have become endemic in many sectors of the economy, and whilst hard to quantify, would be mitigated by a shorter working week. And in a potential example of joined-up policy-making, another advantage could flow from this: cutting a fifth of the working week would be environmentally beneficial by reducing travelling, as long as the reduced hours were not spread across the five days.* Furthermore, utilizing changes forced on us by the pandemic,

---

* In fact, if government policy were truly co-ordinated, there would be attempts to use changes in employment to drive the environmental agenda required by our international obligations under the Paris Agreement on climate change: long private transport commutes could be penalised, and/or living close to one's workplace rewarded.

which has widened horizons, some work could continue to be done from the home (where facilities were adequate), work-sharing could be developed further, and more part-time employment taken up – and not just by female workers. Flexibility has to be embedded into work practices so that a variety of work regimes are accepted – but this is not the 'flexible economy', which limits corporate responsibility and sees the gains going mainly to management.

So often the interests of employers are not seen to coincide with those of their employees. It is if the tension which can exist between the two exemplifies a struggle where employers endeavour to wring the most from their workers, who give as little as they can get away with. This is an image of an outdated industrial age. It is evident to many that when employees are well treated and motivated they and their employers are more likely to achieve good outcomes. But the economic downsides of a situation where management cannot appreciate this seem not conspicuous enough to promote rapid change. Coercion and pressure have been features of too many workplaces under neo-liberalism, as management has felt its own pressures in an increasingly austere landscape. This is due to top-down policy which objectifies the rank and file and neglects to get them on board in a common endeavour. We have been getting things the wrong way round for too long; the best interests of management, or even of the economy as a whole, will be better served by concentrating on the welfare of the majority, which involves better working conditions, a shorter working week, flexible working arrangements to suit employees, proper training, including 'lifelong learning' for career changes when unemployment occurs, and above all being treated with dignity and respect.*

Another reason to maintain that a shorter working week, at existing rates of pay, must be afforded is that it would be a form of recompense for the loss of reward over many years of neo-liberalism. The productivity gains of several decades represent a huge shortfall of earnings, especially in manufacturing, where workers were not rewarded, either in shorter working time or appropriately higher pay. The takings were leeched upwards in prodigious returns to capital and in grossly

---

* With automation, robotics and new forms of artificial intelligence many types of employment will be greatly reduced in the coming years. Being made redundant must not carry any stigma since it will become much more the norm, as workers move from one type of employment, through re-training and further education, to something new. Underpinned with decent financial protection, this need not be devastating for those involved.

inflated top salaries. Meanwhile, workers' wages stagnated, demand for traditional labour fell, and jobs were lost.* This represents a substantial backlog of productivity gains which have enriched capital and its executives. *The fairness and justice case for workers to share the gains of future automation is amplified by the fact that for decades those gains have not been shared.*[76] Then there is the extent of unpaid overtime which has been gifted to society by those in many public services who have contributed in selfless dedication well beyond what they have been paid, which in terms of medical staff and carers during the Covid-19 pandemic has been truly extraordinary. This constitutes another form of productivity backlog not remunerated, equivalent to many years of service. This is common practice where neo-liberalism has dominated: routine attempts to get away with having modern public services of all kinds, but on the cheap.

In spite of all the forecasts from various experts in the last century, the leisure revolution has not materialized. In fact, the smart modern image is often presented of professionals, usually in finance or other 'clean' jobs, always on the move and working long hours without a minute to spare; having time on your hands – the experience of the rich through the ages (and the unemployed and the feckless today) – is no longer fashionable. But this is the future for which we should be preparing. The long-hours culture, with all its stresses and strains, must be transformed by having a shorter working week as standard, and a retreat from the hyper-consumerist society which we have created – and which developing countries often wish to emulate. If economic growth does experience a revival, then the rewards should be taken in terms of leisure time, not in further consumption. It is no coincidence that the nations currently working the longest hours are the ones with the greatest income and social inequality. The change will inevitably involve a psychological adjustment, perhaps even greater than an economic one, to add to the other forms of adaptation which will be required by the recommendations outlined through this chapter. If the economic challenges which this work has advocated can be met, resulting in greater

---

* Connected here is a practice which should be ended – that of giving subsidies and tax breaks to companies investing in automation and robotics if it is to the financial benefit of firms because workers are laid off. In addition to the 'corporate welfare' involved, it results in further expense to the public in terms of unemployment costs, and possibly expenses of retraining. Aid to private companies has to be demonstrated to be for the public benefit, not just in subsidies to create cheaper consumer products and which further enrich the private sector.

social equality, then a dividend of extra leisure time will be available. The task will then be to learn how to use it, for the benefit of all.

Of course, adapting to a shorter working week will be a gradual, step-by-step process, managed by political leaders who believe in the new vision of capitalism of which this is a part.* And as preparation for more free time – but mostly without the extra income to exploit it in traditionally consumerist fashion – education must reflect the new demands of a re-structured working environment. Society will need to learn that 'more' has to be replaced by 'better', and that devoting some of the available extra time to absorbing, fulfilling pursuits can improve quality of life. This itself is a process of self-education, encompassing the realisation that personal identity can be found in unpaid pursuits – pastimes, voluntary work and civic involvement – as well as at work. Formal education will also have to adapt to the needs of a population whose daily concerns will go beyond careers, workplace matters, and income security. A broader curriculum will eventually be needed to find more time for education in the arts, less academic subjects, and 'life skills' which the functional, prescriptive regime under neo-liberalism has neglected. Policy-makers so often assume that materialism will keep the populace satisfied, but a society with more leisure time will need more than 'bread and circuses'. Already, brought on by lockdown in the time of Covid, there is a changed social atmosphere. Perhaps it takes transcendental events such as defeat in war or a devastating viral pandemic to remind people of what really matters.

As regards remuneration for work carried out, the situation under neo-liberalism has been stark: excessive pay for top salaries, stagnating wages further down the pay scales and ever greater income inequality resulting in a massive social divide. This was highlighted in Chapter 5 and has been documented so widely in society that it is a notoriously familiar picture, on both sides of the Atlantic, which has become established in popular folklore. The fact that it is unhealthy, economically counter-productive, acutely anti-social, and unjustifiable

---

* Daniel Susskind, in his book *A World Without Work*, says that in a future with less work policies will need to focus on leisure, not just think of it as an add-on, when other areas of the economy have been organised. Official planning will have to include leisure policies, just as today we have labour market policies.[77]

has not managed to impact business leaders or conservative politicians sufficiently to bring about real change.* It was as if those in power were so out of touch with grass-roots feelings during the recession and the policies of austerity that they were content with the *status quo*. And it appears that, in spite of the calamity of the Brexit vote and the electoral success of Donald Trump in the USA, with their implications as regards popular attitudes, they have still not got the message. So we find ourselves in the middle of a pandemic during which the richest individuals have become even richer: one source reported that the wealth of global billionaires increased by 27.5% to $10.2 trillion between April and July 2020.[78] This mirrored trends of recent years before Covid-19. In Britain executive earnings of FTSE 100 companies continued escalating, rising six times faster than average worker salaries, which went up by just 1.7% in 2017 – in spite of more votes against the remuneration reports of company boards than in previous years.**

While the growing income and wealth divides have been a feature of several developed countries this century, it is places where neo-liberalism has been dominant that have seen the most severe effects. For example, in Britain the income gulf is wider than in almost all of the EU; according to the High Pay Centre, average workers would have to multiply their earnings 144 times to match those of current CEOs of FTSE 100 companies, with a median income of £3.46 million. And 3,500 bankers in the UK – more than in any EU nation – are paid in excess of €1 million annually.[79] But there is an ambivalence in Britain towards the richest members of society. On the one hand, there is definite support for tax increases on the wealthy, and yet as a survey by the Tax Justice Network concluded ... *bashing the rich doesn't increase support for progressive policies*; they thought this was down to people's belief in the importance of *aspirational ambition*.[80] On the other hand many workers say they feel demotivated at work by the excessively high pay of their bosses – in one survey almost 60% of those polled expressed this view.[81] Whether people say they believe the rich should be

---

* And of course the problem was highlighted before the financial crash of 2007/08 when the neo-neo-liberal (New) Labour Party were in power, and has endured the years of Coalition and Conservative governments so that one might conclude that its existence has cross-party approval.

** Typical of these was the opposition of shareholders in 2018 to a salary of £2.7 million for the incoming head of privatised Royal Mail, and the £900,000 'golden parachute' payment to its outgoing CEO. The 70% vote against the board at the AGM was, however, only 'advisory'.

'bashed', or be allowed to enrich themselves further, depends in part on how questions are phrased, but there is certainly support – at company AGMs as well as in the nation as a whole – for some form of intervention from without.

Astronomical figures for executive pay frequently make the headlines, but they have now mostly become commonplace, part of popular culture, even though they still have the power to shock. When Janet Gornick, a New York City University professor, mentioned at an event in 2019 that the top 25 hedge fund managers made an average of $850 million a year, though correct, it was regarded with disbelief.[82] The degree of much corporate remuneration has become so extraordinary as to be almost fictional. And how it relates to the contributions of executives is distinctly problematic. The fact that the link between the pay of CEOs and company performance is mostly negligible was mentioned in Chapter 5, as was the evidence that if paid less there would not be widespread executive flight abroad to regimes where they could earn more. In fact, it is hard to find valid reasons to justify the salaries many CEOs receive. Certainly, the assertion that they earn their money in value added to their firms is less and less credible. A report by the Institute of Chartered Financial Analysts pointed out the *erratic* nature of the level of the value creation of FTSE 350 companies following the financial crash, and that although performance improved after 2010, the median firm still generated less than 1% economic return on invested capital.[83] From such meagre results, one can only conclude that few chief executives provide value for money and that companies are being exploited.

So one may wonder how on earth they have managed to glean salaries and bonuses of such extraordinary magnitude. As with so many aspects of society and the economy, it has much to do with image – in this case a picture of success which is entirely at odds with reality. After all, business leaders and politicians have been getting it all so wrong for decades. The financial boom of the opening years of this century accompanied reckless financial practices, from which top bankers pocketed escalating rewards, while average pay rose very modestly. However, duped by the appearance of economic success, the IMF concluded in 2007, just before the collapse of Lehman Brothers, that … *the worst news is behind us*, and that the USA would avoid serious recession.[84] Gordon Brown, about to become British Prime Minister in June 2007, exhibited similarly misplaced confidence in declaring that we were witnessing … *an era that history will record as the beginning of a new* *golden age for the City of London.*⁸⁵ He and others were entirely misled by stories of business success which, apart from being built on illusory foundations, ... *consistently exaggerate the impact of leadership style and management practices on firm outcomes*, as Daniel Kahneman maintains.⁸⁶ Kahneman believes that those factors are no reliable guide to successful outcomes because the element of luck plays a major role in company performance, and itself would be an equally good indicator as to how a business might perform.*

So in the absence of any convincing justification to the contrary, the time has come for a mandatory limiting of some salaries. With such extraordinary figures quoted for those of the elite at the top, it is hard to come to a reasoned assessment as to maximum amounts without accusations of being anti-capitalist, 'killing the golden goose', or just envy. But from what has been laid out in this work, it is clear that these must be ignored, and attention paid to sensible, moderate attitudes. Here is the founder of employee-owned John Lewis speaking in 1957, lamenting even then the discrepancies of remuneration:

> *Capitalism has done enormous good and suits human nature far too well to be given up as long as human nature remains the same. But the perversion has given us too unstable a society. Differences of reward must be large enough to induce people to do their best but the present differences are far too great. If we do not find some way of correcting that perversion of capitalism, our society will break down...*⁸⁸

The *differences of reward* in the 1950s and '60s, though seemingly large at the time, would suit capitalism very well today, when the *perversions* of the free market have been grossly exacerbated under neo-liberalism. Human nature is much the same today as when Lewis was speaking, but the hubristic tendencies always latent in it have led to the current extremes. The free market ethos of untrammelled freedom has added to the consolidation of attitudes against regulation – but it will have to come.

---

* Kahneman also believes that entrepreneurial optimism plays a part in how management is seen, because if prominent it can give an *illusion of control*, making leaders overly confident in their opinions. But he goes on to cite a study of *Fortune's* 'Most Admired Companies', which found that over a twenty-year period the firms with the worst ratings went on to earn much higher stock returns than the most admired firms.⁸⁷

Ideas as to how to calculate top salaries are varied indeed: whether to fix figures for upper limits, settle on a multiple of national average wages, or tie amounts to an worker's performance, all have merits as well as disadvantages.* Performance-related pay, once fashionable, has distinct shortcomings, particularly in measuring success in management roles where responsibilities are varied and where policies may pay off only in the long term. Before World War I, after a similar period of escalating pay and vast increases in wealth, banker J. P. Morgan suggested that CEOs should not receive more than twenty times the wage of the humblest workers in a company[89] – which if followed would represent a severe shock to many modern executives. Concentrating on the top echelons of the pay hierarchy, data show that if the top 1% of earners experienced modest reductions, then nine million middle and low income workers would have their pay enhanced.[90] Also, polling has found that more than half of the public would support the introduction of a maximum salary; £100,000 is the most popular limit, which would adversely affect only 2.85% of earners in the UK. But almost 70% of respondents would support a cap of either that figure, or £200,000 or £300,000.[91] While we are repeatedly told of the value of the highly-paid so-called 'wealth creators', it is time to moderate their remuneration and ensure that all those other 'wealth creators' (in the fullest sense) receive due reward for their dedication.

It is this dedication and service, particularly in a public sector that people rarely enter for its pay levels, which has to be recognised. And when high-fliers in private companies are over-remunerated – often in fields that do not obviously benefit the general welfare – the notoriety of their exorbitant pay can undermine those who choose careers for vocational reasons. Public service is too often denigrated, but even the most menial of such employment can bring pride and self-respect to those who work in it, as Richard Sennett has described.** It is here also that much wealth can be created – Social Capital. In a society of varying abilities, levels of ambition, motivation and inclination, there will inevitably

---

* And in any case such discussions exclude unearned income, whose recipients in the UK were making around £40,000 a year on average prior to the Covid-19 pandemic – much of it taxed at lower rates than earned income.

** Sennett highlights the importance workers so often attach to doing a good, useful job. However basic it may appear, ... *the work itself provides objective standards of feeling oneself worthwhile*. And while 'service' matters to public sector workers, ... *the craft aspect of usefulness helps people persevere under conditions in which their honour is frequently impugned*.[92]

be differences of income and wealth. But it is the magnitude of the differences and their effects on dignity, morale, and community values which have implications for social well-being, and should concern us all. As such, we must accept the need for regulation of pay, for the public good. At the same time, those who continually aspire to great wealth should appreciate that it is not the route to general well-being because, as Fred Hirsch emphasised, *What each of us can achieve, all cannot.* The limit on the supply of 'positional goods' will always deliver frustration to some who aim for wealth and exclusivity.* They would be better served by looking for intrinsic satisfaction from work itself or focus on 'experiential' goods rather than luxury commodities or high status.

Project Seven: Creating a more just society

A form of remuneration which has received much attention over recent years is the universal basic income (UBI). The idea of providing everyone in society of working age with a guaranteed income, regardless of other considerations such as whether or not they do paid work, has been around for many decades – even going back to Tom Paine in the eighteenth century. At one time it found supporters across the political spectrum, including even figures on the right such as Friedrich Hayek, the resolute classical liberal.** Proposals to give everyone a basic income, which it was thought could eliminate poverty, rose to prominence in the 1960s and '70s, and were even tried in limited pilot studies in countries like Canada and Finland. Experiments of this kind produced quite positive results, especially in that they did not lead to a marked reduction in people doing paid work, and at least in the short term appeared affordable. Above all, the projects had the effect of energizing communities, raising overall morale. Perhaps surprisingly, the idea found favour in the United States where in 1970 President Nixon attempted to put it into legislation with the Family Assistance Plan. Although the bill

---

* This 'paradox of affluence' was discussed in Chapter 4, explaining the limitations on the availability of 'positional goods' regardless of the extent of one's ambition or one's wealth. What is possible for a single individual is not possible for all, and would not be possible even if all possessed equal talent.

** Since Hayek's support for UBI was somewhat opaque, others, such as Professor Matt Zwolinski, have attempted to interpret it, usually along the lines that since freedom was so important to Hayek, receiving UBI would give one a better chance of living without fear of domination or coercion by an employer or the state.[93]

had widespread support from economists, it eventually failed to pass in the Senate, where the Democrats advocated starting with a higher level of basic income than that proposed. Nevertheless, a poll conducted in 1969 found that almost 80% of Americans supported a guaranteed basic income.[94]

The appeal of UBI, sometimes called a Citizens' Income, is many faceted. It would give much greater flexibility as regards paid employment and the number of hours worked, while being cheap and easy to administer. It would also provide more autonomy to carers trying to balance varied responsibilities and to people trying to start businesses. Many claim that it would enhance social cohesion and end the stigma associated with many state benefits. The tax and benefit systems would need to be reshaped, and more money raised, but fraud could be greatly reduced. Concerns about induced idleness are often voiced when a guaranteed income is suggested. But if it had some impact on the incentives to work and the urge to consume – for a future when there may be less of the former and we will need to reduce the latter – then it would not be unwelcome. However, attractive as the notion may be, the contention here is that it has important disadvantages, and that developing universal basic services (UBS) must take precedence. That is not to say that such schemes will not be worth considering; in a world where employment in the future is likely to undergo massive change, there may yet be a role for a secure, 'unearned' regular income, whether unconditional or based on some form of civic or social involvement, as proposed by economist Anthony Atkinson.*

A guaranteed basic income has the same appeal as schemes to give cash directly to the poor and destitute. On the basis that poverty is fundamentally a lack of money, why not just give it to those in dire need? The simple attractiveness of that idea is backed by the efficacy of numerous schemes around the world where it has been tried.[96] Most testify to the fact that so-called 'free money' does not induce people to work less hard, in fact to the contrary. However, cash hand-outs in whatever form do not address the wider socio-economic problem of neo-liberalism's iniquitous consequences. They would operate within the same economic parameters as market fundamentalism, doing little

---

* He calls his proposal a *participation income*, which would be paid not on the basis of citizenship, but on one's contribution to society, which could take the form of paid or voluntary work, education or training, or acting in a caring role, or a combination of these. One would qualify by making a social contribution, in the widest sense.[95]

to narrow income disparities or help build social cohesion. And UBI would be too expensive to be generous enough to allow people to refuse work; in fact, it is likely to maintain a brake on wages and consolidate the control of employers. In the absence of greater trade union power, and with increasing automation, it would leave employees in the same weak, subservient position in an economy of precarious work, and with public money still needed to subsidise low paid jobs. As Anna Coote has said, *The idea of giving public money to individuals sits comfortably with the neo-liberal claim that services are better when markets provide and customers choose.*[97] Universal basic services, however, are different, in that they undercut this ideology and reinforce the collective ideal.

What is required today is an extension of the so-called 'Five Giants', the five major social ills which were identified in the Beveridge Report as obstacles to people bettering themselves. When William Beveridge's report was published in 1942 it listed want, ignorance, idleness, disease and squalor as the problems holding people back from realising their full potential. Great strides were taken in addressing two of these – with the 1944 Education Act, and in setting up the NHS – while idleness was tackled with post-war near-full employment (even if not guaranteed today)*. However, the ongoing poverty and homelessness today are testimony to the failure of successive governments to deal with want or squalor in a now immeasurably richer nation. What the United Kingdom now needs is fresh dedication to Beveridge's ideals, to eradicate twenty-first-century poverty and ensure a home for everyone. But matters must also be taken further, to encompass the other modern needs of advanced society such as access to transport, energy, information services, child care and legal aid, all free or at nominal cost. (Outlined in the early part of this chapter, under Project Two.) And as Beveridge envisaged in his report, services should be universal and available without means-testing, which he was against. The sentiments which inspired Beveridge eighty years ago must now be combined with a recognition of the vital modern services needed to navigate society today – universal provision which all can support.

The social capital of the nation can be enlarged by extending access to the current norms and customs of society, which can best be done through removing the financial barrier to access, and providing services

---

* And to these were added the Family Allowances and National Insurance Acts of the late 1940s.

free or at nominal cost. This would help level the social playing field for participation in everyday, expected activities and widen autonomy for thousands of citizens. So the 'Five Giants' of Beveridge's era must now be broadened to form a longer list of social requirements – an illustration of the more complex, inter-related needs which have become an integral part of life for so many in this modern age. And although Britain is a more pluralistic society than in the 1940s, expectations have become more uniform as regards the services required and the standards demanded in an increasingly common culture. These needs can best be met by universally available services – those 'basic' to twenty-first-century life in a developed economy – but collectively provided according to need, which can give much better value for money than if supplied by the market. Furthermore, since the repercussions of the Covid pandemic are set to increase unemployment and likely to exacerbate social inequalities, it is even more vital to allow open access to the services outlined above, to forestall even greater social divisions. And as Anna Coote says, *Services revolve around everyday relationships in people's homes and neighbourhoods. ... they manifest the collective ideal.*[98]

After the battering which communal values have suffered under years of neo-liberal governments, of all stripes, it is vital to rebuild social solidarity. Especially in recent years, the policies of austerity have sowed division, creating scapegoats and setting people against one another – all exacerbated by Brexit. At the same time, funds for public services have been drastically reduced, impoverishing many, while the rich have moved on largely unscathed. It is not just budget cuts themselves that have had a serious impact; the language of 'welfare dependence' and 'skivers', and the hostile environment around unemployment and low pay have all corroded solidarity and poisoned public debate.* Establishing a range of goods and services accessible to all citizens without demeaning qualifications or cumbersome barriers to entry would mark a step towards repairing social solidarity. Ideally they should be organised on the basis of subsidiarity, provided at the lowest feasible administrative level, and by a variety of bodies and agencies – local authorities,

---

*   In an economy in which those without qualifications or experience are offered, in coercive fashion, only precarious, menial employment at basic rates of pay to suit the flexible, ever-changing requirements of corporate bottom-lines – and then need their low incomes subsidised by government tax credits – a hostile, counter-productive labour market is the inevitable result. This is neo-liberalism and it benefits nobody but the rich. The vast majority of people do not have an aversion to work, but it is as if current working conditions are to be made as unpalatable as possible to put this to the test.

trusts, voluntary organisations and perhaps co-operatives. The state would not be the provider of services, but the ultimate guarantor, facilitating operations, setting standards and ensuring the proper use of public money on a not-for-profit basis. Such public provision could amount to a 'social wage' amounting to over £500 a month per person, depending on the extent of individual take-up.*

Universal basic services as here described would make a positive contribution to reducing inequality, since the pooling of public funds to be drawn on for goods and services would be highly distributive. The charity Oxfam calculates that a 'social wage' of this kind could reduce income inequality by as much as 20%.[100] But as well as having an obvious economic impact it would, once it became established and accepted, alter the narrative in society by fostering the collective ideal, which would bring within the communal tent many who had previously been excluded or marginalized. It would also redress the balance between the public and the private, and demonstrate a potential for unifying a disparate, divided nation. Beyond the provision of common goods and services, there would be ample scope for the market to flourish, but it would not be at the expense of the basic essentials which allow normal participation in society. The intention would not be to prohibit private provision of services, but market forces would nevertheless have a much lower profile in their operations. At the same time, as Anna Coote has emphasised, such public services would not be

... *owned and controlled by the local or national state, or managed by professionals who see people as 'problems' to be solved by the application of expertise.*[101] Reforms along these lines are preferable to a universal basic income; they would have the potential to bring the community together beyond the reach of the divisive influences of the free market, while helping to limit its pervasive scope.**

---

* See the discussion of UBS as proposed by the Social Prosperity Network at the Institute for Global Prosperity, at UCL, outlined earlier in this chapter under Project 2. Anna Coote has noted that the technical analysis of Jonathan Portes and colleagues at the Institute has led them to conclude that these universal services can be financed through fairly modest adjustments to the tax system; how modest would inevitably depend on the range of services included.[99]

** Writing over thirty years ago, Charles Handy made the simple case for our reciprocal position as citizens of a nation: ... *we are both entitled to an income from our collective property, society, as well as obliged to pay a portion of our individual earnings for the maintenance of that society.* The case can equally be made for, in lieu of a citizens' income, a range of goods and services provided to all, which would form the basis of what people have a right to expect in a modern, developed economy.[102]

AN ALTERNATIVE PROGRESS

The thriller writer Lee Child has called the early 1980s ... *a dramatic hinge in history*.[103] This description encapsulates the change of direction which governments on both sides of the Atlantic – and in other corners of the 'Anglo-Saxon' world – took under leaders who wanted to break away from the troubles of the 1970s. But there was sufficient apparent continuity of policy to ensure that the dramatic changes underway did not alert the population to the prospect of revolution. After all, this was still free market capitalism, was it not? And many constituents believed that direct, forceful measures were required to re-energize economies after the doldrums of the '70s. Few could have foreseen the social consequences of the new trajectory and the world it would introduce, while those not paying attention might have thought nothing much was changing – beyond war in the South Atlantic, the chance to buy cut-price shares in new private companies, rising unemployment, but more consumer 'goodies' in the shops. Lee Child's perennial American hero Jack Reacher could sense an old world disappearing, and he was increasingly uncomfortable with the new ways he felt coming. As Child says, Reacher was *a creature of the old America*, the America people instinctively picture, of the famed American century, although Child says in reality it was only half a century – roughly 1930 to 1980.[104] For in the USA, as in Britain, a new age was dawning, and it was to be distinctly uncomfortable for many.

This work has endeavoured throughout to make clear that free market capitalism is not one monolithic economic system, but a variety of forms which have operated differently at different times in varying national jurisdictions. Capitalism as practised in modern Scandinavian countries, as well as in Japan, operates a more socially-focused system, with greater emphasis on protecting the welfare of ordinary citizens, in a similar fashion to the way free market operations in Britain and most of western Europe after 1945 still allowed the promotion of welfare states and the target, at least, of full employment. Both of these situations stand in stark contrast to the neo-liberal capitalism which has become established over the last forty-five years in certain regimes, above all in the UK and the USA. Anti-capitalists aspire to destroy the current economic system, but with no reference to these complexities, and mostly without a clear model of a post-capitalist future. There is a huge amount to object to in neo-liberalism, as outlined above and in Chapter 3, but the alternative is not a planned economy – as this work has argued. Of course, calling for the complete demolition of the system is a simple rallying cry, and asking for a more discriminating approach does not have the same uncomplicated appeal. However, though free market capitalism is not – quite – a broken system, it is the dangerous hubris and myopic fallibility of the human species which has brought it into question.

And since human ambition, imprudence and mismanagement have led to the current predicament, it is humanity – in the form of progressive, accountable, democratic government – that must put it right. Resolutely circumscribing and guiding market forces, as outlined above, will put economies on the correct path; only governments can take the lead and manage the transition to a more responsible capitalism with sensible regulation. But private corporations, the key players in the market, must follow with socially-orientated and environmental, sustainable policies instead of a single-minded focus on profit. The productive marketplace should be a collaborative enterprise with common objectives, not an adversarial arena with only zero-sum options. In this respect, risk should have a shared role, so that suppliers of major companies are not treated as fodder and exploited in order to satisfy the 'bottom line' of buyers with their overweening purchasing power. The preferred model has similarities to 'Rhenish' capitalism, in which a participatory, shared approach to business is the norm, and stakeholders have a role in decision-making. After all, the aims of workers and management are basically the same: that companies prosper so that the latter can make a decent profit, in order to be able to pay living wages to the former, as well as to invest in firms for future success and prosperity.

This picture of commercial businesses as collaborative projects, with all sides contributing to a common endeavour, is the way to get the best out of the human elements involved. It leaves room for suitable competition, but not of the cut-throat variety, since total commercial superiority tends to vanquish opponents and vitiate the continuation of the *infinite game* – as explained in Chapter 3. Companies like Google and Amazon exercise hegemony in their respective fields, which tends only towards unhealthy extremes and ultimately exploitation. Neo-liberalism actively fosters such developments through rigid, uncompromising corporate policy, which breeds income inequality and social division. Just as German and Scandinavian forms of capitalism do not inevitably pitch elements of the economy against one another, so East Asian models also practice co-operation as well as, crucially, looking to the long-term in business and financial development. Even Islamic trading practices – albeit in very economically unequal societies – emphasize fair dealing in trade, with a belief that capital should be socially constructive and employed as a medium of exchange only, not to be traded as a commodity. Consequently, in contrast to the tendencies of the *Anglo-Sphere*, risk is less of a feature of Islamic economies. All these models of free market operations are preferable to a system that encourages confrontation, excess, and a winner-take-all mentality that results in extreme social inequality.

In the world of sport, particularly in fields of elite, professional competition, a common concept is the 'small margins' idea. By adopting carefully planned but minor changes to on-field formations, playing styles, or training ground manoeuvres, more might be achieved by the same set of players, whether it be in football, rugby or other team games. And in highly competitive professional sports, limited modifications of a practical or psychological nature can make the difference between triumph and mediocrity. In the economy and society as a whole, even small changes of attitude and practice could also bring about a transformation in outcomes, refashioning neo-liberal regimes. The potential for such change is already evident – in the nature of existing society (already outlined in earlier chapters), in the immense misery caused by poverty and inequality, in the emergency caused by global warming, and in the desire on the part of so many for a different way of doing things. An economy does not have to be run as if it were an insatiable machine to be fed, placated and served. It would not require a transformation of outrageous proportions to tame it and allow dutiful humans back in charge. For capitalism needs mainly modest adjustments of the kinds outlined earlier in this chapter to redirect its course, as well as to relegate it to the subservient – though important – place it should occupy in wider society.

Part of the necessary transformation, already alluded to, is a conceptual one. Under neo-liberalism, the free market has taken on the aura of a secular faith, with the same kinds of myths and dogmas familiar to more conventional belief systems. The fact that these are hard to relinquish is an impediment to the changes which will have to come. But a vital element of the new capitalism will have to be a concentration on the needs of human beings and not on ideologies and systems – i.e. a focus on ends and not theoretical means, which have simply not done the job. When neo-liberalism was forged in the late 1970s, it was set *against* what were seen as obstacles to progress: powerful trades unions, a sluggish economic performance, Keynesian values, and government involvement. The future, 'social capitalism', must involve a campaign *for* people, sustainability, enterprise, high standards, looking to the long term, and community values. This is not a 'Third Way', between socialism and free market fundamentalism, although the term might be appropriate if earlier claimants had not so discredited it.* And it is not so far from Keynes' view that both extreme *laissez-faire* liberalism and socialism were wrong, and that something in between, with strong government action, decentralisation and institutional safeguards, was far preferable. Social capitalism represents a positive assertion of human and communal values in this context; this must take precedence, so that the free market can flourish within that framework of principles, and guided by them.

In the reformed capitalism of the future, there will still be scope for enterprise of all kinds – artistic, entrepreneurial, sporting – and competition will still have room to thrive. But without the zero-sum, hostile environment of market fundamentalism, a more constructive approach will prevail. Profit will not come at the expense of the well-being of community, or of those who can cope least well materially.** Although profit has long been seen as an indispensable purpose of economic activity, many organisations operate largely without it, while for entrepreneurs there are often many other *raisons d'être*. In 1974, in the early days of a new Labour government, a *Sunday Times* Business News article appeared with the title *Can we have a Non-Profit Society?* It was followed in June of that year by a conference on 'The Practical Implications of the Non-Profit Economy', at which participants were invited to accept that profit as a mainspring for British business was already dead. But the '70s represented the *hinge* of the neo-liberal era, as sentiments of that kind soon dissolved and a more divisive business model came to the fore. Under Social Capitalism, there will exist enterprises of all types; the presumption of profit as a driving force will weaken, as the full range of personal and social impulses becomes eligible. Capitalism

---

* Tony Blair's idea of New Labour being a Third Way between 'old' Labour socialism and neo-liberal Conservatism was as bogus as the pretence that Thatcherism represented a similar mid-point – *capitalism with socialist underwear*, as it was once called.[105] Even Spain's General Franco in the 1930s saw his right-wing crusade as something between conventional capitalism and communism.

** There is also the question of how profits are used. An interesting new book by Dr Catherine Casson and colleagues shows with detailed research how successful entrepreneurs in 13th-century Cambridge used their wealth to benefit the local community.[106]

is a primitive force, lacking nuance or subtlety, and in its neo-liberal form not worthy of the status of the human race. Thus it has to be kept in its place, and know its role.

The current mode of free market capitalism cannot last. This is not merely because of the concept of mankind which it entails, though one might wish it were so, but principally because on its own terms its efficacy is weakening as its flaws become more prominent. As the world emerges from the Coronavirus pandemic, there will be those determined to force more and more out of an ageing economic machine, who would willingly preach the rigours of efficiency and discipline until the engine ran into the ground. There will also be those striving to extend the market further and increase the commercial scope of life, a trend which will inevitably heighten the struggle for material advancement, leading only to further market dysfunction, greater economic inequality and more social division. Yet all that is unlikely to prevent the neo-liberal fundamentalists from proclaiming that we should leave it to the market to offer its own self-correcting remedies. But recent history has shown us that the richer we have become in a macro-economic sense, the less effective market mechanisms have become in sharing out the increased wealth. The greatest political and economic expertise the world can muster – Nobel Prize-winning economists, brilliant central bankers and fund managers, innovative entrepreneurs, and top political leaders – have all failed when faced with economic repercussions of the huge challenges of our age: financial crash, viral pandemic and global climate disaster. So as Ha-Joon Chang concludes, *The upshot is that we are simply not smart enough to leave the market alone.*[107]

The future has to place its focus on 'people', on human societies doing their 'strutting and fretting', for whom all this 'sound and fury' is ostensibly intended. Here so much has already been sacrificed: work and livelihoods which hardly recovered from the effects of the financial crash over a decade ago have since been hit by the havoc wrought by Covid-19. And as automation and AI take their toll on employment, even greater strains will be felt by those trying to earn a living and guide their lives. This was foreshadowed over sixty years ago by Michael Young in *The Rise of the Meritocracy,* where he wrote of the problems of late twentieth-century capitalism – automation taking over and unskilled workers becoming unemployable.[108] Persisting with unrestrained market forces will only exacerbate this and allow the benefits of future technological advance to bypass the majority of citizens. So we must change course; priorities have become skewed and values cramped; consciousness has been partially anaesthetised as mankind marches up a blind alley, searching in vain for the economic and technological elixir. Present trends are unsustainable; they will ultimately drain the economy dry of the dedication, loyalty and professionalism which are vital ingredients of a humane working society and ... *corrode... those qualities of character which bind human beings to one another and furnish each with a sense of sustainable self.*[109] Thus it is we, the people, who will be the chief focus of the conclusion in the final chapter.

END NOTES

i   Ralph Waldo Emerson's view of the country after two visits to England, which he said ... *subsists by antagonisms and contradictions* – in *English Traits*, Unit Library Ltd, London, 1902, pp. 54-5.

ii   From 'Utility in Architecture', final year thesis by a London architectural student, 1970, quoted in Martin Pawley, *The Private Future: Causes and consequences of community collapse in the West*, Thames and Hudson, London, 1973, p. 38.

iii   John Gray, *Heresies: Against Progress and Other Illusions*, Granta Books, London, 2004, p. 3.

iv   A 'Reddit' post by Stephen Hawking in 2015, at https://www.reddit.com/r/science/comments/3nyn5i/science_ama_series_stephen_hawking_ama_answers/cvsdmkv/

v   Luke Hildyard, Director of Britain's High Pay Centre, commenting on Amazon CEO Jeff Bezos, whose reputed net worth is greater than the GDP of the Ukraine, at https://highpaycentre.org/how-can-we-change-public-opinion-about-the-super-rich/

1. Mikael Klintman, *Knowledge Resistance: How we avoid insight from others*, Manchester University Press, Manchester, 2019.
2. Professor John Carey, in *The Sunday Times*, London, 10/8/1986.
3. Richard Douthwaite, *The Growth Illusion*, Green Books, Bideford, Devon, 1992, pp. 314-5.
4. Robert & Edward Skidelsky, *How Much Is Enough? The Love of Money, and the Case for the Good Life*, Penguin Books, London, 2013, p. 89.
5. Zygmunt Bauman, from *Liquid Life*, 2005, quoted in ibid., p. 171.
6. Martin Pawley, *The Private Future: Causes and consequences of community collapse in the West*, Thames and Hudson, London, 1973, p. 45.
7. James Tobin, 'On Limiting the Domain of Inequality', *Journal of Law and Economics*, Vol. 13, No. 2, University of Chicago, Oct. 1970, pp. 264-5.
8. Ibid, p. 276.
9. See Michael Walzer's, *Spheres of Justice*, Basic Books, New York, 1983.
10. Will Hutton, *Them and Us: Changing Britain – Why We Need a Fair Society*, Little, Brown, London, 2010, p. 55.
11. As explained by Stephen Armstrong in his *The Road to Wigan Pier Revisited*, Constable, London, 2012, p. 34.
12. Ibid. p. 31.
13. See an interesting paper, 'We Need Fare-Free Buses!' a Radical Transport Policy document at http://transportforqualityoflife.com/radicaltransportpolicytwopagers/
14. https://assets.publishing.service.gov.uk/government/uploads/system/uploads/attachment_data/file/787488/tsgb-2018-report-summaries.pdf
15. In *The Independent*, London, 6/7/1997.

16 According to official statistics, at **https://www.gov.uk/government/organisations/ department-for-transport/series/bus-statistics**

17 According to the report 'Building a World Class Bus System for Britain' by Ian Taylor & Lynn Sloman at http://www.transportforqualityoflife.com/ policyresearch/publictransport/. See Section 3 of the Extended Summary Report. In Section 2, the authors quote the 1984 Buses White Paper which outlined the rosy future forecast for privatised bus services: *Without the dead hand of restrictive regulation fares could be reduced now on many bus routes and the operator would still make a profit. New and better services would be provided. More people would travel* – as in so many policy areas involving public provision by private companies, an almost fraudulently unrealistic scenario.

18 The *New Statesman* article quoted here also pointed out that this was not unusual, in that companies Abellio, Arriva and RATP, which are wholly owned by the Dutch, German and French governments respectively, operate 37% of London's buses. See – **https://www.newstatesman.com/spotlight/ transport/2018/06/municipal-bus-companies-can-public-ownership-be-profitable**

19 From *The Financial Times*, 11/9/2019, citing research by Opus Restructuring, the social care analysts, at **https://www.ft.com/content/ eab8c4c4-d49a-11e9-8367-807ebd53ab77**

20 Report from the Pre-school Learning Alliance and Mumsnet, reported in *The Independent*, 4/9/2018, at **https://www.independent.co.uk/news/education/ education-news/parents-nursery-fees-30-hours-free-childcare-england-government-funding-mumsnet-a8521421.html**. The situation has not improved: by December 2019, hundreds of pre-schools, nurseries and child minders had left the scheme and de-registered.

21 'The Health Effects of Sure Start', June 2019, at **https://www.ifs.org.uk/uploads/ R155-The-health-effects-of-Sure-Start.pdf**

22 Frank Cottrell Boyce, in *The Observer*, London, 8/4/2018. The well-regarded Sutton Trust charity similarly lamented the decline in children's centres in the Sure Start programme, in its report 'Stop Start: Survival, Decline or Closure? Children's centres in England, 2018'. See **https://www.suttontrust.com/ wp-content/uploads/2018/04/StopStart-FINAL.pdf** It suggested that centres *... should reconnect with their original purpose.*

23 Jonathan Portes, Howard Reed, Adam Percy, 'Social prosperity for the future: A Proposal for Universal Basic Services', a Social Prosperity Network Report, 2017, for the Institute for Global Prosperity (IGP) at UCL, at **https://ubshub.files. wordpress.com/2018/03/social-prosperity-network-ubs.pdf**

24 According to a BBC Panorama programme, 'What Britain Wants: Somewhere to Live', first aired on BBC1, 9/3/2015, prior to the 2015 general election.

25 Jonathan Portes, Howard Reed, Adam Percy, op. cit.

26 See **https://www.housing.org.uk/news-and-blogs/news/1-in-7-people-in-england-directly-hit-by-the-housing-crisis/**. The research was carried out by Heriot-Watt University for the National Housing Federation, including analysis of figures from the major Understanding Society survey, to examine the scale of different types of housing need.

27 Cited by Anna Coote at **https://neweconomics.org/2017/12/ universal-public-services-answer-europes-widening-inequalities**

28 Jonathan Portes, Howard Reed, Adam Percy, op. cit.

29 According to a BBC news report, 'Malnutrition causing thousands of hospital admissions', 23/11/2015, at https://www.bbc.co.uk/news/uk-england-34777348
30 Tim Jackson, *Prosperity Without Growth: Foundations for The Economy of Tomorrow*, 2nd Edn., Routledge, London, 2017, p. 221.
31 Leopold Kohr, 'Appropriate Technology', in *The Schumacher Lectures*, Blond & Briggs, London, 1980, p. 85.
32 George Lakoff, *Don't Think of an Elephant: Know Your Values and Frame the Debate*, Chelsea Green Publishing, White River Junction, Vt., USA, 2014, p. 19.
33 See Daniel Kahneman, *Thinking, Fast and Slow*, Penguin Books, London, 2012, p. 216.
34 See 'A Bit Rich: Calculating the real value to society of different professions', by Eilis Lawlor, Helen Kersley, Susan Steed, New Economics Foundation, 14/12/2009, at https://neweconomics.org/2009/12/a-bit-rich. The authors suggest that childcare workers generate between £7 and £9.50 worth of benefits to society for every £1 that they are paid, partly through releasing earnings potential by allowing parents to continue to work. And for every £1 that hospital cleaners are paid, they generate £10 in social value. By contrast, they calculate that for a salary of between £75,000 and £200,000 tax accountants destroy £47 value for every £1 in value they create.
35 Robert Peston and Laurence Knight, *How Do We Fix This Mess? The Economic Price of Having It All and the Route to Lasting Prosperity*, Hodder & Stoughton, London, 2013, p. 366.
36 In Will Hutton, op. cit., pp. 178-9.
37 In Robert Peston and Laurence Knight, op. cit., p. 225.
38 Adam Smith, *An Inquiry into the Nature and Causes of the Wealth of Nations*, 1776, (1981), Vol. I, Book I, Chapter XI, Conclusion to Part III.
39 Katharina Pistor, of Project Syndicate, 5/2/2020, at https://www.project-syndicate.org/commentary/limited-liability-corporate-shares-by-katharina-pistor-2020-02?barrier=accesspaylog
40 In their book on the financial crash and its aftermath, Robert Peston and Laurence Knight, op. cit., give a revealing account of *casino capitalism* and the startling hubris of financial institution, notably in Chapter 3.
41 Samuel Courtauld speaking in the 1940s, quoted in Martin J. Wiener, *English Culture and the Decline of the Industrial Spirit, 1850-1980*, Cambridge University Press, Cambridge, 1982, p. 144.
42 From an interview, quoted in Will Hutton, op. cit., p. 216.
43 An investigation in 2015 indicated that Exxon Mobil fully understood the science behind climate change, partly from their own research into it, as early as 1977, reported in Scientific American, at https://www.scientificamerican.com/article/exxon-knew-about-climate-change-almost-40-years-ago/
44 Ha-Joon Chang, *23 Things They Don't Tell You about Capitalism*, Allen Lane, London, 2010, pp. 19-20.

45. Sendhil Mullainathan and Eldar Shafir make a convincing case against drives for excessive efficiency, in *Scarcity: The True Cost of Not Having Enough*, Penguin Books, London, 2014, particularly Chapter 9. *Cut too much fat, remove too much slack, & you are left with managers who will mortgage the future to make ends meet today*, they say (p. 189). The authors also highlight the work of Tom DeMarco, *Slack: Getting Past Burnout, Busywork, and the Myth of Total Efficiency* (Broadway, New York, 2002), in which he points out that by making an organisation a bit less efficient you can, in fact, improve it enormously.
46. By Rutger Bregman, in *Utopia For Realists: And How We Can Get There*, Bloomsbury, London, 2018, p. 168, from a 2012 article by Sam Ro, 'Stock Market Investors Have Become, Absurdly Impatient'.
47. In a report by 'Positive Money', at **https://positivemoney.org/2020/07/new-report-where-are-the-conditions-for-the-bank-of-englands-broken-bailout-scheme/**
48. Reported in *City A.M.*, 2/7/2020 at **https://www.cityam.com/two-thirds-of-brits-think-Coronavirus-bailouts-should-have-strings-attached/**
49. According to Britain's Institute for Fiscal Studies, using 2016 figures, at **www.ifs.org.uk/publications/14258** and **www.ifs.org.uk/publications/14256**
50. Will Hutton, op. cit., p. 296.
51. Idem.
52. See NAO data at **https://fullfact.org/economy/benefit-fraud-tax-inspectors-numbers/**
53. Data from the Financial Secrecy Index at the Tax Justice Network, at **https://fsi.taxjustice.net/en/**
54. Anthony Atkinson has outlined such a scheme in a detailed account of the fiscal reforms needed to move towards responsible global tax arrangements, in Anthony B. Atkinson, *Inequality: What Can Be Done?* Harvard University Press, Cambridge, Mass., USA, 2015, Chapter 7.
55. Cited by Guy Standing in *The Corruption of Capitalism: Why Rentiers Thrive and Work Does Not Pay*, Biteback Publishing, London, 2017, p. 89.
56. According to Joseph Stiglitz in *The Great Divide*, Penguin Books, London, 2016, p. 111.
57. Reported in a paper by K. Farnsworth of the University of Sheffield, cited in Guy Standing, op. cit., p. 108.
58. From a report for Citizens for Tax Justice, cited in Guy Standing, op. cit., p. 103.
59. Ha-Joon Chang, op. cit., title of Chapter 8.
60. Thomas Piketty, *Capital in the Twenty-First Century*, The Belknap Press of Harvard University, Cambridge, Mass., USA, 2017, p. 682.
61. Anthony Atkinson, op. cit., p. 200.
62. Thomas Piketty, op. cit., p. 746.
63. Ibid. p. 674. Thomas Piketty has suggested a wealth tax on fortunes above €1 million, which would affect around 2.5% of the European population (2013 figures). This would bring in a revenue equivalent to about 2% of European GDP.
64. Data from a poll for the *New York Times* conducted by the research firm Survey Monkey in the summer of 2019. See **https://www.nytimes.com/2019/10/01/us/politics/sanders-warren-wealth-tax.html**

65 According to the Resolution Foundation, May 2020, which stressed the importance of including capital gains in such calculations: https://www.resolutionfoundation.org/publications/who-gains/
66 In Anthony Atkinson, op. cit., pp. 183-7.
67 At www.taxjustice.uk/blog/conservative-voters-shift-in-favour-of-tax-rises-under-lockdown
68 According to results in the reputable annual British Social Attitudes Survey, at http://natcen.ac.uk/news-media/press-releases/2018/september/support-for-more-tax-spend-at-fifteen-year-high/
69 At https://blogs.imf.org/2019/08/08/us-business-investment-rising-market-power-mutes-tax-cut-impact/. In another, fairly conclusive comment an IMF paper says, *The growing economic wealth and power of big companies—from airlines to pharmaceuticals to high-tech companies—has raised concerns about too much concentration and market power in the hands of too few. In particular, in advanced economies, rising corporate market power has been blamed for low investment despite rising corporate profits, declining business dynamism, weak productivity, and a falling share of income paid to workers.* Found at https://blogs.imf.org/2018/06/06/chart-of-the-week-the-rise-of-corporate-giants/
70 From their *Guardian* article 'Why the 1% should pay tax at 80%', 24/10/2013, originally, with Stafanie Stantcheva, at https://voxeu.org/article/taxing-1-why-top-tax-rate-could-be-over-80
71 *The Daily Telegraph*, London, 9/3/1992. (Free humans to do what?!)
72 Raymond Williams (in *Culture and Society, 1780-1950*, Penguin, London, 1963) and André Gorz (*Capitalism, Socialism, Ecology*, Verso, London, 1994) both well understood and explained the significance of work – ideas which have been diluted and devalued under neo-liberalism.
73 This 1918 survey of the British workforce by the RSA, carried out in partnership with Populus, explored the state of 'good work' in the UK, focusing on two important factors in employment – economic security and a rewarding experience. See https://www.thersa.org/reports/seven-portraits-of-economic-security-and-modern-work-in-the-uk/. The remarkably high incidence of stress recorded in this research can be put alongside the figure for 2015 from the 33rd annual British Social Attitudes report, in which 37% of workers surveyed said they experienced stress at work 'always' or 'often'. This itself is an incidence of stress which must impact the quality of work produced and most probably absenteeism. See https://bsa.natcen.ac.uk/latest-report/british-social-attitudes-33/work.aspx
74 According to the reputable Labour Force Survey, at https://www.ons.gov.uk/employmentandlabourmarket/peopleinwork/employmentandemployeetypes/datasets/underemploymentandoveremploymentemp16
75 An example provided by the New Economics Foundation, which cites some UK companies which have reduced working hours for employees, including CMG Technologies, Indycube, Pursuit Marketing, Legacy Events, Radioactive PR, Curveball Media, and Aizle Restaurant, at https://neweconomics.org/2020/06/making-up-for-lost-time
76 Ibid.
77 Daniel Susskind, *A World Without Work: Technology, Automation, and How We Should Respond*, Allen Lane, London, 2020, pp. 226-7.

78 See https://highpaycentre.org/as-billionaires-get-richer-the-uk-public-express-broad-support-for-a-maximum-wage/
79 According to a report on high earners by the European Banking Authority, 11/3/2019, at https://eba.europa.eu/
80 At https://www.taxjustice.uk/uploads/1/0/0/3/100363766/talking_tax_how_to_win_support_for_taxing_wealth.pdf
81 Cited by the Chartered Institute of Personnel and Development, at https://www.cipd.co.uk/about/media/press/181215-exec-pay
82 Mentioned by *NYT* columnist Paul Krugman in his article, 'Bernie Sanders and the Myth of the 1 Percent', *The New York Times*, New York, 18/4/2019.
83 According to the CFA's 2016 Executive Remuneration Report (27/12/2016) at https://www.cfauk.org/media-centre/cfa-uk-executive-remuneration-report-2016#gsc.tab=0. The report concluded, *Despite relentless pressure from regulators and governance reformers over the last two decades to ensure closer alignment between executive pay and performance,* the association between CEO pay and fundamental value creation in the UK remains weak. (My emphasis.)
84 In Robert Peston & Laurence Knight, op. cit., p. 124.
85 Brown's now well-known claim, part of his speech at the 2007 annual Mansion House dinner, quoted in ibid. p. 127.
86 Daniel Kahneman, op. cit., p. 206.
87 Ibid. p. 207.
88 Quoted in Will Hutton, op. cit., p. 66.
89 Ibid. p. 67.
90 At https://highpaycentre.org/paying-for-covid-capping-excessive-salaries-to-save-industries/
91 Data from the High Pay Centre working with Autonomy, and results from recent polling by market research firm Survation, at ibid.
92 In Richard Sennett, *Respect: The Formation of Character in a World of Inequality*, Penguin Books, London, 2004, p. 202.
93 See Zwolinski's argument at https://www.libertarianism.org/columns/why-did-hayek-support-basic-income
94 A Harris poll cited in Rutger Bregman, op. cit., p. 42. Bregman gives an account of the arguments around UBI in the USA, how much support it received, and details of some trials of UBI carried out there, in Chapters 2 & 4.
95 See Anthony Atkinson, op. cit., pp. 218-223. He compares the two conditions – citizenship and participation – to qualify for UBI, and eventually comes down on the side of the latter, whereas the Citizen's Income Trust in Britain favours the former, at www.citizensincome.org
96 Rutger Bregman, op. cit., outlines a number of schemes around the world where UBI has been tried or free cash provided, in 'Why We Should Give Free Money to Everyone', Chapter 2.
97 See Anna Coote's article from the New Economics Foundation, under https://neweconomics.org/2018/02/better-fairer-ways-spreading-prosperity-ubi. She also argues that though UBI may appear feasible, it is *a creature of the moment*. She quotes Daniel Zamora, that UBI is … *not an alternative to neo-liberalism, but capitulation to it.*

98 See her article at https://braveneweurope.com/anna-coote-are-universal-public-services-the-answer-to-europes-widening-inequalities
99 Ibid.
100 Cited by Anna Coote in her New Economics Foundation article, op. cit.
101 In Anna Coote, article at https://braveneweurope.com op. cit.
102 Charles Handy, *The Age of Unreason*, Arrow Books, London, 1990, pp. 192-3.
103 Lee Child (James Grant) speaking on 'Broadcasting House', BBC Radio 4, Sunday 1/3/2020.
104 Idem.
105 Alasdair Palmer in *The Sunday Telegraph*, London, 20/9/1998.
106 Catherine Casson, Mark Casson, John S. Lee, Katie Phillips, *Compassionate Capitalism: Business and Community in Medieval England*, Bristol University Press, Bristol, 2020. The authors examine the property market in medieval Cambridge, showing how wealthy merchants consistently gave some of their profits to local religious houses and hospitals. As an example, one family – the Dunnings – continued with donations of land despite getting into debt.
107 Ha-Joon Chang, op. cit., p. 173.
108 Michael Young, *The Rise of the Meritocracy, 1870-2033*, Thames & Hudson, London, 1958, p.96. Young's futurist (?!) society includes a government body, the Clauson Committee, which – reporting in 1988 – found that about a third of all adults were unemployable in the ordinary economy.
109 Says Richard Sennett, *The Corrosion of Character; The Personal Consequences of Work in the New Capitalism*, W. W. Norton & Co., New York, 1998, p. 27.

Chapter 8
WE, THE PEOPLE – THE ULTIMATE 'RESOURCE'

The 'social state', that crowning of the long history of European democracy and until recently its dominant form, is today in retreat.
ZYGMUNT BAUMAN[i]

One of the singular facts of our present technology and its derivative economy of abundance is that no-one seems to know how to keep it running without making it go faster and faster and spreading its activities ever wider.
LEWIS MUMFORD, in 1960[ii]

…progress is seen as a matter of indefinitely increasing the number of tasks that can be carried out by machine. The final triumph is achieved when all the human components have been exchanged for electrical or mechanical ones.
HENRY BRAVERMAN[iii]

Science enlarges human power. It cannot make human life more reasonable, peaceful or civilized, still less enable humanity to remake the world.
JOHN GRAY[iv]

My fellow Americans, 'trickle-down' economics has never worked.
PRESIDENT JOE BIDEN, April 2021

AS the spring of 2022 approaches, as the dark Covid winter offers its glimmer of light with vaccinations to halt the pandemic, and devastated economies and populations throughout the world begin to hope, a watershed has been reached. Where does the world go from here, and who will guide its onward trajectory? Will we at last see a flowering of our race, the prospect of realising the promise inherent in Enlightenment values, or are our days as the species we recognize numbered? Can we make the most of what it means to be human, to draw on our finest sentiments as well as our prodigious intellect, or are we to proceed blindly into a future where we will be subsumed by an insatiable materialistic drive and by our own technological brilliance? Here is one view: *If we just stay as ordinary humans, we're going to be taken over by machines. Therefore if we upgrade by linking with technology maybe we can still stay in the driving seat.*[1] So says cybernetics expert Professor Kevin Warwick, on the potential for connecting technology directly to the human nervous system. This appears the latest stage in the development of a kind of 'cyborg' which will be technologically superior to normal human beings. The future for robots in the economy was forecast back in 1983: *the role of humans as the most important factor of production is bound to diminish.*[2] We may have adjusted to that notion, but going beyond, to human beings driven by technology and market forces, who need to be upgraded in order to retain their role as the dominant species on the planet – well then, we truly are in trouble.

For let us be in no doubt, the future is in the hands of the human agent to resolve. The choices taken by policy-makers and their constituents in the coming generations will determine the viability of *Homo sapiens*, or whether some other race of superior beings will steadily supersede the world's current inhabitants. If, with enlightened leadership, we take the right measures in the years ahead we will have the chance to remain as *ordinary humans*– opting for moderation and sustainability, reining in the avaricious grasp of the free market, applying a brake to the technological imperative, and putting our faith in the finest characteristics of our species. To forestall the dangers of *singularity,* technological dominance becoming irreversible, requires success in exercising control over science and technology, so that they serve humankind and do not come to master it. The prerequisite for this will be a reorientation in thinking, creating the social and economic conditions for reform by inhibiting the destructive forces of rampant free market capitalism, and introducing policies which promote the building of a more equal society. Science does not have the answers here; of course, scientific progress is real enough, demonstrating the glory of human virtuosity, but as John Gray says, *The illusion is in the belief that it can effect any fundamental alteration in the human condition.*[3] Only human beings can bring about the changes which the global village requires.

The years ahead – as employment is increasingly threatened by automation and heightened artificial intelligence, and by an ongoing struggle between community and market fundamentalism (assuming, that is, the recommendations in this work are not comprehensively embraced!) – have the potential to be the age when humans finally come into their own. The unique nature and the deep humanity of the race have the opportunity to contribute with the special qualities that no other beings – or artificial versions of them – can match. Up until now, the potential which human beings possessed – highlighted by the possibilities inspired by Enlightenment thought and by the scientific advances of the last three centuries – have nevertheless remained just that: possibilities, contingent on humans exploiting their essential humanity, instead of principally their ingenuity, which has never been in doubt. Whereas in centuries gone by our principal threats came from without, in the present age we humans are a danger to ourselves. We have created societies dependent on technologically-driven economies of abundance which, if sustained, will transform the planet's eco-system and threaten our very existence. However, now, when there are more people on the planet than ever before, and with less and less productive employment available due to the efficiency and over-production of developed economies, the time has come to use the essence of humanity, the goodwill and open-heartedness of millions, to serve other human beings instead of only money.

The example has been provided for us by the extraordinary response in many countries to the demands of the Coronavirus pandemic which has dominated 2020-22. Nations were fearful of their health resources becoming overwhelmed by the numbers succumbing to the virus, while millions of people were confined to their homes with their societies locked-down to limit its spread, or self-isolating to protect themselves or others. This resulted not just in an heroic level of effort and dedication on the part of health professionals, but in a tidal wave of their compatriots offering assistance to fellow citizens. Volunteers emerged to carry out a myriad of tasks such as shopping, collecting medication, getting in touch with vulnerable neighbours by phone or email, while video calls and websites were set up to establish contact with the isolated and console especially those living alone. The first half of 2020 saw the spectacle in Britain of people emerging from their homes on Thursday evenings to clap in unison outside their front doors in gratitude for the unstinting dedication of NHS and key workers; this might also be interpreted as a token of thanks to one another for their own contributions to their neighbours during a national crisis. The power of the selfless efforts of millions was on display during an unprecedented health and social emergency which was answered not only by professionals and scientists, but also in impressive fashion by ordinary people.

It is vital that this fundamental, human response be drawn on in the future. Where are resources most in need in neo-liberal societies like the United Kingdom? It is not in productive capacity of either industry or commerce; there may be shortages of commodities in some sectors, but in modern consumer societies there is generally an over-abundance, particularly of non-essential items, and an obsession with novelty and excess. Neither is it in the insufficiency of technological innovation – except perhaps in the response to climate change. But in societies where markets have been allowed to run riot, especially in the so-called *Anglo-Sphere*, the conspicuous shortage is in human services – other than those offered by the private sector, usually at considerable cost. There is currently a dearth of mental health professionals, police, prison and probation officers, nursing staff, and youth workers. And in practically every situation the lack of sufficient personnel puts an extra burden on existing staff, who have to do more with fewer resources – leading to absenteeism, greater staff turnover and experienced professionals abandoning their careers. This scenario has been greatly exacerbated by a decade of austerity – cuts to social provision and local authorities fraudulently imposed by central government, which has meanwhile pretended that services can be maintained at more or less the same level. The result has been a poorer, shabbier social landscape littered with the human consequences of political hypocrisy. Meanwhile, a successful economy is loudly proclaimed.

The future has to be one in which people are catered for by people, both well-resourced professionals and trained or informal volunteers. Self-evidently the health service needs increased numbers of doctors and nurses, highlighted yet again by the Covid-19 crisis.* Meanwhile, the

---

* In late 2020 it was widely reported that, according to the Royal College of Nursing,

social care sector must be better resourced, and as regards domiciliary care, fully professionalised and adequately staffed. It is too important an area to be left in the hands of private providers to profit from – as cited earlier in the last chapter. As regards youth services in Britain, austerity policy resulted in cuts of almost 70% by 2019,[4] during a time of surging street violence and knife crime – and that was before the pandemic led to the closure of local boxing gyms affecting young people in inner cities. No matter what Britain looks like from the outside, its social environment is being impoverished by a concentration on money and the market. This is nowhere more evident than in the failed part-privatisation of the Probation Service in 2014; eight out of ten private firms working for it were rated 'inadequate' in its 2019 report, and the numbers returning to prison for breaching licence conditions had risen sharply.* Yet again the public were being made to pay – financially, and in this case also in a less safe environment. Society as a whole is losing out, its interests sacrificed to ideology and an obsession with macro-economic appearance, the casualties of which will take years to heal.

We may have a shortage of many things, but we do not have an insufficiency of people. The years ahead will be times when they have to be called upon. There is scope for thousands of citizens, many already retired who would like to make a social contribution, some doing part-time work perhaps, and others who have had to take enforced redundancy who may be waiting to be re-employed, or perhaps are no longer employable in the market economy. With training, an army of willing personnel could be available to work in supporting roles in child care, youth services, fostering children, working as teaching assistants or on environmental projects, helping the elderly, taking on mentoring roles with, for example, ex-prisoners. In some of these areas, considerable training would be needed – in others, no more than is currently involved in being inducted as a volunteer for charity work, where even now thousands of people give of their time and expertise to help others.

---

there were 40,000 vacancies for registered nurses. As regards doctors, Britain still has fewer *per capita* than most European countries, and has tried for too long to get away with running its prized health service on the cheap.

* There were other startling revelations in that report, such as the fact that 22% of offenders left prison without knowing where they would sleep on the first night of their release. The Chief Inspector of Probation, Dame Glenys Stacey, concluded that the population would be safer if supervision of prisoners were returned to public ownership.[5] According to the National Audit Office, the flawed part-privatisation of probation resulted in £500 million of additional taxpayers' money. As so often, the triumph of dogma over sensible practice has financial as well as human costs.[6]

To develop this selfless dedication further, a form of national social service – not over-bureaucratised or over-regimented – could provide a framework in which people choose their field of interest. For example, the tragedy of teenagers, often excluded from school, being drawn into gangs – with terrible personal consequences – could be addressed by a comprehensive network of youth services, with professionals as well as social mentors to maintain contact and work to keep young people out of trouble.

Along similar lines, a mentoring system could be developed for prisoners on release. The current appalling state of the British penal system destroys lives, families and livelihoods, without making society safer. The hostile, punitive atmosphere around crime has resulted in England and Wales having more citizens incarcerated, *per capita*, than any other nation in Western Europe, and an almost doubling of the prison population in the last thirty years. The incidence of mental health and literacy issues in prison has not been tackled, overcrowding is still dangerously high, the numbers of suicides and levels of self-harming are scandals given scant publicity, while inadequate rehabilitation results in high levels of recidivism – and all at an average annual cost of around £38,000 to keep someone locked up. To this can be added the additional expenses, financial and social, of probation costs, family breakdown, lost taxes, increased state benefits, and often permanent loss of earnings. Reducing the prison population by handing down more community sentences, supervised and monitored, is an urgent requirement and would contribute to a safer environment. And prisoners released from custody would need the support of dedicated mentors to facilitate their reintegration into society, including help finding employment; for those given community sentences, supervision and extended follow-up would help keep them away from crime. It is only personal intervention by committed individuals – 'people power' – which can meet these demands.*

---

* Proposals along these lines would contribute to a major reduction in the prison population and eventually to the closing of a number of prisons. Such savings could then be re-invested in the kinds of supervision and monitoring suggested above. QC Chris Daw has recently made a valuable contribution to this debate with his excellent book.[7] The prison population has grown hugely during a period when crime generally has not; what have risen are demands for higher sentences and a hostile penal environment, at a time when neo-liberalism has exacted severe, unforgiving demands on all, especially the vulnerable and weak. After all, many criminals start off as victims. For a 'modern' nation like Britain this panorama suggests an immature, mean, backward-looking culture which can only have counter-productive results.

Of course, many of these activities will require funding. However, the goodwill of many people with the time to spare to give to others need not come at prohibitive cost – in some cases, they would receive only necessary expenses. What often inhibits involvement in such voluntary work is excessive bureaucracy and an over-emphasis on free market mechanisms, which can undermine the contribution of those freely giving their time. Capitalist operations have come to dominate so many social activities that those which do not carry a price are often not considered as valuable as private provision. But the important distinction here is between services for people, by people, as opposed to those seen as commodities, bought and sold in the marketplace. Furthermore, an outcome of 'people' services which would clearly be cost-effective is the vast sums in welfare payments, child services, police resources, and in the courts and prison system which could be saved by pre-empting many social problems that otherwise develop. As conventional employment contracts in the decades to come, so the services of people of all ages and backgrounds can – not supplant necessary, professional social provision – but support and reinforce it. But it is vital that this 'people's' involvement be accorded formal status – the dignity of valuable participation and giving to the national community. And, also important, this could help avoid human misery and recrimination – often a legacy when dedicated, hard-pressed public services come up short in attempting to solve major problems on the cheap.

The Social Capitalism which this work advocates encompasses a society in which 'people' will occupy centre stage. Economic theory, political ideology, the presumption in favour of high-tech solutions, and the empty vainglory of political leaders trying to make a name for themselves – these all need to be repudiated in the interests of the well-being of the people and the mechanisms by which they can be promoted. This will be a tall order in nations where neo-liberalism has come to dominate; principles such as the primacy of market forces, the sanctity of the growth imperative, or the prejudice against government involvement in the economy will not be easy to undermine. These and others have become shibboleths for generations of the political right, clung to with almost evangelical fervour to the extent that they take precedence over the concerns of ordinary people and the practical, commonplace means of serving them. It is ironic, especially in a Britain renowned for its pragmatism, that theory is held to with such resolve. But this is to a large extent because it embodies assumptions which – as was laid out in Chapter 1 – become *inevitable categories of the human mind*, through which related ideas are viewed. As a consequence, issues are not properly examined, only cursorily observed through the veil of long-held presumptions and prejudices. They are rarely tested, merely challenged by loud, partisan politics and rhetorical deceit.

As a result of the devastation caused by the financial crash over a decade ago, and now the effects of the Covid pandemic, the welfare of the mass of the population has at last received greater attention. But that does not mean that those bearing the brunt of these calamities have had their concerns properly addressed. After all, the Coronavirus pandemic has seen jobs destroyed and businesses extinguished while many of the richest individuals and companies have become wealthier. Governments have had to resort to major financial relief through furlough schemes and grants, to protect at least some employment and stave off economic catastrophe. The results have been patchy and inconsistent, due in part to the extraordinary disruption wrought by Covid-19, but also down to the ideological resistance of right-wing regimes to providing comprehensive government relief.* Thus poverty and hardship are likely to persist, particularly since in Britain and America the flimsy safety-nets which do exist are no bulwark against destitution. The dire expedient of the middle classes visiting food banks – a phenomenon already evident after the financial crash – is apparently still not enough to shame authorities into effective action. Besides, neo-liberal societies have become all too accustomed to the zero-sum environment with its familiar casualties, the notorious collateral damage of market fundamentalism.

However, a proper 'social state' would not find itself so ill-prepared if suddenly faced with a global pandemic of unprecedented impact.**

---

*   In Britain even meeting the requirements for receiving state assistance is often problematic. The many adults who in 2020 had to resort to applying for Universal Credit, having lost other sources of income through no fault of their own, would first have to eat up much of any savings they had accumulated over £16,000 before qualifying. Such a scenario, for a family with perhaps a modest nest-egg assiduously put aside over many years to buy a house, would immediately consign them to long-term renting, and possibly a lengthy period on state hand-outs, including housing benefit, in the hope that worthwhile employment would became available again.
** It should not need reiterating that the term 'social state' has nothing to do with socialism. It signifies a role for government in the safeguarding of individuals in community, and is a far cry from the domination of economy and society by the executive. The social

The ground would already have been laid so that emergency assistance for the needy would be accepted as routine: a normal extension of common humanity. But the adversarial environment of neo-liberal regimes is antagonistic to what are often seen as 'hand-outs' to the feckless, a perennial fear of allowing people 'to get something for nothing'. The extremes in such societies display a lack of generosity of spirit and a tendency to blame those in need for their misfortune – something far less evident in the 'social state'. This punitive approach is allied to a raw individualism incorporating the mistaken view that the interests of individuals can only be served by each of us alone looking after our affairs, and eschewing a communal path. This has been taken even further in the United States where the concentration on the self and one's nearest is accompanied by a growing insecurity, a fear of the outside and 'the other'. Even in the post-Trump age, with threats from white supremacists and QAnon conspiracies, there is a tendency to withdraw from what is seen as a dangerous wider society – an implicit rejection of community. Martin Pawley identified this phenomenon in its infancy fifty years ago: *The fear of the private citizen is continually reinforced, and with it his desire to strengthen the walls of his own privacy by dissociating himself from any remaining strands of obligation that still reach out into the public arena...*[8]

Of course, the 'social state' implies the dilution of the forces of the market, as described earlier, but not instead to empower other agencies, public or private. The containment of the market already outlined in previous chapters would place the provision of the basic commodities and services of a modern society beyond the reach of normal market rules. This reining-in of pervasive economic forces would allow a widening of personal and social autonomy, and thus the emancipation of whole swathes of poorer sections of the population. This is where Universal Basic Services (UBS), outlined in the last chapter, would have a crucial role to play. These services would not only inhibit the malign effects of the market in areas of basic need, but would also embody that social insurance which would afford citizens security and status, thereby facilitating their fuller participation in society as equal stakeholders. The late Zygmunt Bauman wrote at length, in several works, about the importance of such a process:

---

state encompasses social capitalism, which – as this work has tried to show – would be a form of free market capitalism with the emphasis on community and welfare.

> *A state is 'social' when it promotes the principle of 'communally endorsed', collective insurance against individual misfortune and its consequences… The social state is the ultimate modern embodiment of the idea of community.*[9]

Bauman relates this to Lord Beveridge's plans in 1940s Britain for an extension of the welfare state – insurance for all, collectively approved – and to Franklin Roosevelt's declaration of war on fear in the 1930s. (Roosevelt's little known proposals for a major extension of social rights in 1944 – cited in Chapter 3 – are in the very same tradition.)

In the process of rowing back the divisive apparatus of neo-liberalism, a more constructive social environment will need to be fostered. The seeds of this inclusive community already exist; they were there in the immediate post-war period of the 1950s, but since the 1970s have remained largely concealed beneath the surface, even if nurtured by many in ordinary vernacular life. The attractions of the market and its beguiling consumerism have undermined shared values and subverted concern for the common good. But such solidarity is at the heart of humanity and survives, to be resuscitated by emergencies like a viral pandemic, and by effective advocacy. Market fundamentalism thrives on a confrontational, even hostile atmosphere which pits individuals against one another. It is no coincidence that hostility has recently emerged in different guises. During Theresa May's time as Home Secretary, especially after 2012, a hostile environment was deliberately fostered to limit illegal immigration, but this soon morphed into a campaign against immigration generally, culminating in the Windrush scandal when people originally from the Caribbean with every right to live in the UK were wrongly deported. The criminal justice arena has also seen a more confrontational atmosphere develop, what has been called … *a shift of emphasis from the welfare to the penal modality* – in which security and punishment are more prominent. *The welfare mode has become … more offence centred, more risk conscious.*[10]

In the light of such developments there will need to be a considerable *shift* in the other direction. The hard-edged, reductionist form of capitalism corrodes social intercourse and spuriously raises disquiet in the population to potential dangers around them, which then become self-fulfilling prophecies as the need is felt for the security of the state to raise its game. This 'toughening-up' response, often encouraged by the media, has been partly responsible for the increased levels of incarceration in Britain over a thirty-year period when overall crime has not seen a commensurate rise. These trends have helped weaken common solidarity and convert the UK into what may be termed an *exclusionary state*: an intolerant setting which embodies the danger of making an enemy of anyone or anything which does not declare itself your ally, or is not economically productive, or to whom you cannot sell something. It sees risks presented by people who are different; sympathy does not extend to those perceived as outcasts – the underclass, convicted criminals, the homeless, any of those who are 'not like us'. Such a discriminatory society does not allow for the reintegration of those outside, which is partly why the rehabilitation of ex-offenders into the social mainstream has become so problematic. The social state has to combat these tendencies and reinforce the unifying principle of mutual sympathy for others who, regardless of prejudice, discrimination, and even 'fake news', are in fact just like us.

Under social capitalism, society will also need to be prepared to counter the trend towards further segregation of groups into their own separate silos. The gated communities and exclusive retirement 'villages' described in an earlier chapter are a symbol of a growing desire to keep 'the other' at a distance, by withdrawing into homogeneous enclaves which appear to offer protection against a world which cannot be trusted. This propensity also has elements of a self-fulfilling prophecy; the higher the walls of these rarefied enclosures, the greater the antipathy and covetousness of 'outsiders' are likely to be towards the inhabitants. Neo-liberal capitalism has fostered a society where people have grown apart. Britain has long been an unequal nation divided on class lines, but with physical separation an organic development, not based purely on money or the ideology of affluence, as now. Today's segregationist bias rests on a desire to live a separate existence, but in a society with an increasingly egalitarian ethos. There is no easy future for a community where some individuals believe, based on what they feel they have achieved, that they deserve to live apart, shielded from others of their kind. Material affluence does not change who we are, no matter how much we believe, or hope that it does. It will be a task of social capitalism to oversee a major reduction in economic and social inequality which, eventually, will make it easier to identify with others in society, regardless of who they are.

The development of separate, exclusive communities of, mainly, the rich has gone along with the steady invasion of the public domain by private interests. When a public area is bought up or taken over by a free market, private concern there is a narrowing of the communal realm belonging to us all. The so-called *res communis*, in which we all have a stake, is increasingly vulnerable to moneyed interests, as was outlined in Chapter 5. The overweening wealth of the private sector often cannot be resisted by central or local government which, particularly in times of austerity, no doubt regards the surrender of pieces of otherwise marginal public space as a small price to pay for a much-needed injection of funds. And a blurring of the line between private and public is often contrived so that the significance of the loss is conveniently concealed, almost always to the advantage of private concerns. This is a dangerously subversive path, leading to the shrinking of our collective heritage for short-term, usually modest gain. When school playing fields or local parks are sold off, there is a significant loss to the community, disproportionately impacting its poorer members who cannot afford to pay for alternative facilities.* Local green spaces were an important feature of the municipal infrastructure developed in the late-nineteenth and early twentieth centuries by public-spirited civic authorities – part of the so-called 'municipal socialism' of Joseph Chamberlain and his like, which was a source of great pride to many towns and cities of the time.

With municipal services now apparently vulnerable to the predations of private interests, it is crucial to speak up for the value of the public realm. One must be on guard against an overly relaxed attitude here, taking for granted facilities which have long been part of the landscape, especially since local authorities do not have a statutory obligation to provide amenities like municipal parks. But it was not foreseen that attempts would be made to extract private profit from public 'works' which had in most cases been created by public money. Defence of the public domain has never before been such a critical issue; in fact, in the social state it will need to be extended, with more facilities available free or at nominal cost, since they belong to all of us as part of our national patrimony. This is an important part of efforts towards a more egalitarian society in which our common inheritance is shared and sacrosanct.

---

* A few years ago, Battersea Park replaced its old adventure playground for children with new swings-and-slides equipment. Go Ape, the company contracted to build and manage the site, opened the new facility in late 2015. But instead of the previously free adventure area, climbing sessions were now available at a cost of between £18 and £33 per child. Thus the marketing of ordinary children's play as a commodity is apparently regarded as a suitable vehicle to bring in extra money for a cash-strapped local council.[11]

There is so much private wealth, adding greatly to individual autonomy of the minority, but making our joint inherited resources properly accessible to all will further equality and increase life chances for the rest. These are social rights, which all in a social state possess, in addition to our political rights which, vital as they are, do not necessarily enhance social equality.* Democratic authorities must not be allowed to sell off facilities which ultimately belong to everyone and no-one in the national community.

Cohesion in modern societies depends on a close reciprocal relationship between the public and the private. In nations like the United Kingdom, recent times have seen the private sector eulogized as the engine of wealth, the repository of energy and innovation, the assurance of our future prosperity, while the public arena has been denigrated. This deceit has been propagated while private interests – especially large corporations and their leaders – have steadily enriched themselves. However, when disaster strikes, in the form of a financial crisis or a devastating viral pandemic, from where do saviours emerge to rise to the occasion? They come from the public, in the form of political authorities, statutory agencies, public money, the NHS, charities, private companies collaborating with government-funded programmes, and of course huge numbers of ordinary people. States are national communities which thrive on the goodwill and effort of the mass of the population; ordinary citizens are their essence. So, as was explained earlier, it is to the community of people that we will need to look in the future to support our institutions and each other. Yet it is so often the case in a modern economy that revenue can be increased by large organisations 'letting people go', divesting themselves of labour, an expensive factor of production.** No responsibility need be accepted for externalizing

---

* In those democracies where people have fewer social rights – that is, especially in nations with great economic inequality – there will be a tendency to ignore political rights and thus not take part in the democratic process. If exercising one's vote never seems to make a difference to one's social or material conditions, then there will inevitably be a loss of faith in political means to improvement.

** Soon after German re-unification, economist Robert Bischof reflected on the differences between the British economy and the Rhineland model of capitalism practised in Germany, pointing out the more stable, forward-looking nature of the latter. He suggested that Britain's flexible labour laws, short notice periods, low redundancy payments and pressure for quick profits all encourage firms to *off-hire* promptly in a recession – but result in more volatile, self-destructive economic cycles. Almost 30 years on what, one may ask, has changed?[12]

costs at the public's expense, as firms go about their business of maximizing profits.

This is not responsible, social capitalism; it treats people as merely superfluous, exchangeable elements in the productive process, rather than as the heart of our society. We have to learn how better to 'employ' people, in the widest sense. Much of the dissatisfaction with current free market capitalism stems from the lack of human involvement – the frustrating efforts trying to get a personal response from companies, the time spent on the phone waiting for customer services to answer, and having to use self-service check-outs in stores with insufficient staff, in order to avoid queues. This is all so that companies can dispense with labour and reduce services for their own benefit. As this is exacerbated by further automation in the years ahead, the relationship between people and the organisations which 'serve' us must be re-examined; the economy is supposed to be working for citizens, not the other way round.* The signs of a successful society do not derive from macro-economic figures, large corporate profits, or the number of rich entrepreneurs, but from the satisfaction of its members with their living conditions, their security, and their life chances. Much of this depends on relationships with other people. The experience of 'lockdown' brought on by Coronavirus, and the restrictions required by the emergency, have emphasised to many the need for human contact, a yearning to reconnect and be part of a cause beyond ourselves which will tie us in to a wider community.

None of these sentiments is designed to undermine free market capitalism – only its neo-liberal iteration, which fosters a materialistic society empty of communal and inter-personal values. One might hear it said that there is no demand for an alternative – a specious argument, since that is never on offer in the amoral, socially-neutral arena of the marketplace. But there is plenty of evidence of the clamour for something more than materialism and rugged individualism, which leave a values deficit that no amount of affluence can replenish. As people, we need to impose ourselves on our economic system and bend it to our human requirements, rather than allow it to go its own rapacious way, free of responsibilities to us. Belonging to the national community is more than an economic function; it is above all a human and a social one. Political leaders need to appreciate this, and especially the respect

---

*   As Miatta Fahnbulleh, CEO of the New Economics Foundation has said, *Economic change for people can only be achieved by people.*[13]

for the dignity of their constituents which it implies. The social state involves a reciprocal relationship between authorities and the governed: the willing contribution of citizens in the collective interest, and the safeguarding of personal, individual concerns in the form of social insurance. The rationale for this was summed up some years ago by the Swedish Democratic Party:

> *Everyone is fragile at some point in time. We need each other. We live our lives in the here and now, together with others, caught up in the midst of change. We will all be richer if all of us are allowed to participate and nobody is left out. We will all be stronger if there is security for everybody and not only for a few.*[14]

So a capitalist economic system with free markets can still be an arrangement compatible with our fundamental interests – provided it is controlled and guided, and is subservient to transcendent human values. Society has guiding principles common to most; free markets are empty of moral and spiritual substance. Those demanding changes such as are recommended here must not be tarred with the anti-capitalist brush, although this will be attempted by many who resist modifications of any kind to the *status quo*. The future will have space for competition, but with limits; there is no reason for our ancestors' fight for survival to be revived, transformed into a contest for the basic requirements of everyday life, while society as a whole has more than enough to go round. There will always be differences of remuneration but, again, they should be only moderate, to allow for the dignity and morale of those less well paid to be preserved.* There must be room for ambition and enterprise, to allow the potential of individuals to be realised – but not so that they can assume an arrogance which sets them apart from their fellows. Economist Tim Jackson has summarized this neatly: as an economy of ... *simple first principles. Enterprise as service, work as participation, investment as a commitment to the future and money as a social good...*[15] These values represent the future, even if they may seem idealistic and impracticable set against the compelling attractions of market forces, consumerism, efficiency and growth. In the meantime,

---

* When reflecting on the vast wealth of the increasing numbers of the super-rich today one might recall Swift's comment: *Mankind may judge what Heaven thinks of riches by observing those upon whom it has been pleased to bestow them.*

leadership everywhere lacks vision, and is content to peddle populism and offer only more materialism to stir what is left of our dreams.

Times do change and attitudes do evolve. Although perhaps not seeming so, habits of mind are open to modifications, certainly to a greater extent than in the nineteenth century when John Stuart Mill wrote of *… the despotism of custom…* which may stand in the way of improvements being foisted on a reluctant population. For, stepping aside from the voracious machine of neo-liberalism would enable society to breathe again, re-examine priorities, and re-connect with the core of our humanity. This will be no easy project since, even if we are not entirely persuaded by the ideology of market fundamentalism, there is an intoxication with the lavish fruits of its productiveness – whether we have the means to pay for them or not. We feel we cannot live without these, and so must keep our noses to the grindstone, in the process of which we become slaves to new kinds of despots, from which we cannot easily emancipate ourselves. Nevertheless, the exhortation here is for us to break free, transform the mindset which has been developing over forty years, and return to an earlier, more humane, decent relationship with our economy and its protagonists. This is no clarion call to revolution, which would only return us to a worse version of the *status quo*, but an urgent demand to throw off subversive market dogmas and the beguiling myths they represent.

While there exists considerable demand for a gentler, less confrontational economy, moving from here to there will not be easy. Generations of Britons have grown up with an abrasive, winner-take-all *milieu*, and may take some convincing that there are other routes to success and prosperity. The stubbornness and recalcitrance of the British has long been noted; in 1881 Prime Minister Disraeli cautioned the writer and socialist H. M. Hyndman against expecting easily to change British attitudes: *It is a very difficult country to move … a very difficult country indeed, and one in which there is more disappointment to be looked for than success.*[17] Disraeli knew what should be recognised today, that the British are a people who, once they become set in their collective ways, are very difficult to budge. Contrary to appearances, there is much continuity in British social attitudes, the 'recent' superimposition of neo-liberal practices notwithstanding.* This may be partly due to the fact that for many centuries the nation has not experienced a break-up of associations which would likely be brought about by revolution, defeat in war, or invasion.** This has allowed lasting characteristics stubbornly to endure, even if at times concealed behind more high-profile postures. Over two centuries ago Edmund Burke understood this, when he wrote of the *cold sluggishness* of the national character. In spite of colourful rhetoric to the contrary, the sinews of values and vernacular practice bind one generation to the next, undergoing only a slow, piecemeal transfiguration.

So what is advocated here is not to transform ourselves entirely into something radical and new, but to take on a fresh approach, including reasserting old values and traditional ways. This will involve change, at least in a reorientation of attitudes and priorities. Change is something which politicians often call on their constituents to embrace, believing that is what their audiences want to hear. But it is also exploited by leaders determined to bring about reform. When Tony Blair announced to his first Labour Party conference as Prime Minister ... *Change is in the blood and bones of the British...*, he was congratulating the country on being ready for change – which New Labour were set on introducing – as well as implying a denigration of what had gone before.[19] But like other leaders he also suggested that 'change' was good, and would benefit the country. The enthusiasm which greeted the new government led to optimism as regards the new policies, in spite of the fact that the social upheavals of previous generations had often left people breathless for continuity and less political turmoil – something the seismic events since 2016 have only reinforced. Change is not always welcome, particularly when it involves measures with little connection with what went before. But in many cases society has learnt to expect constant

---

* This is but one of the many paradoxes of civilization in these islands, where the superficial often conceals a different disposition. Contradictory as it may appear, behind the fascination with modern technology and the allure of affluence and celebrity culture lies a humbler, less flashy tradition. Appearances can be deceptive. For example, in spite of becoming a mainly urban population by halfway through the 19th century, the English (especially) still have a strong anti-urban strain in their culture and an enduring idealization of rural life. D. H. Lawrence pointed out that ... *the English character has failed to develop the real 'urban' side of man*.[18] This was one of Emerson's anomalies, from his *English Traits*, cited in the opening to Chapter 7.

** Being defeated or invaded can often force a break in the lines of continuity and lead to the dismantling of old structures. France after 1871 and Germany after 1945 are conspicuous examples. Unlike victory, defeat in war creates the right psychological conditions for national renewal. But as the poet Dryden once said, *Even victors are by victory undone*.

motion, even if it has never given its consent to the revolution in its lives, families and communities which has been the pattern of the last fifty years.

Rapid change can be destructive, especially when – as in the case of the imposition of neo-liberal practices in the 1980s – it leads to confrontation, social divisiveness and human casualties. It does not help that those reforms were adopted on the basis of a misreading of history, misinterpreting the problems of the 1970s as well as the nature of British society and its suitability for market fundamentalism. And the British economy, having hitched itself to the bandwagon of neo-liberalism, has since found it difficult to uncouple itself, regardless of the incompatibility of such an anti-social regime with inherent national values. Once the strident new dogma had become established, it became inevitable that it should override communal concerns and traditional sentiments. And with macro-economic productiveness and prosperity being held up as the be-all-and-end-all, it became difficult to scale back expectations. So the result has been a country riding a tigerish economy largely out of control, a free-wheeling society which treats social concerns as if they can be addressed by economic solutions. It is only when the brakes are occasionally applied from without, by financial crash or global pandemic, that the machine is forced to slow down, before the same familiar efforts at economic maximization are later redoubled – that being the only approach that its leaders believe will satisfy their electorates.

It is true that people usually expect their salvation to derive from ever greater autonomy and affluence. But this is because they have been persuaded that is the way society progresses, and that is what everybody else desires. Constant change is built in to future expectations, and part of that is faith in yet higher standards of living, which is patently irreconcilable with the current crises of climate change and gross social inequalities, which decades of higher GDP have not solved. But how often does one hear that it is natural to expect the next generation to be better-off than the current one? By fraudulently conveying the idea that in the future we can enjoy greater prosperity, we are not only condoning the notion of constant movement, but blithely raising expectations that we cannot justify. Meanwhile, we implicitly devalue the familiar, that closer to home or nearer the present – which is where our focus should be applied. In fact, our obligations to the future must not involve assumptions of higher material standards – simply a duty to remedy matters here, today, by eradicating the gross disparities afflicting society, increasing opportunities for the poor and marginalized, reining in our insatiable economic forces, and tackling climate change. Then we might have some expectation of leaving to our descendants a future which may not be wealthier, but will certainly be better.

In fact, if we could effectively tackle the major environmental, economic and social problems of the day, we would be able to bring about change of a far more welcome, beneficial nature – and not change ourselves in the process. This is an endeavour which needs international co-operation, as was emphasised in earlier chapters. Climate change and cross-border finance are just two of the obvious issues which cannot be solved in an insular manner. Other kinds of nationalistic rivalry such as military or diplomatic confrontation should also be consigned to history; in an increasingly interconnected world, attempting to dominate by force has no future, since it could lead to global disaster. And economic competition is similarly outdated if it is waged on a winner-take-all basis in order to ruin a trading competitor. Healthy rivalry allows viable firms to survive, and it is in the interests of all that they should live to compete another day, as was outlined in detail in Chapter 5. Competition need not be mutually destructive and has its place, even if it is not the *sine qua non* of economic activity or social life. It is only the reductionist slant of those pretending that we are above all a selfish species that suggests that it is. Most people's existence is not ruled by constant rivalry, and need not suffer by its absence. In any case, there are many other areas of life where the competitive spirit may flourish without the pernicious consequences that extreme capitalist markets tend to produce.*

One of the problems with competition, as the philosopher Bertrand Russell once observed, is where it is practised: *The competitive habit of mind easily invades regions to which it does not belong.* And seeing life as a contest, he said, *leads to an undue cultivation of the will at the expense of the senses and the intellect.*[21] Dynamic exercise of the will certainly has far too prominent a place in neo-liberalism, so that economic competition tends to override other human, communal considerations. But striving for superiority or pre-eminence can be a

---

* Five years ago, before the political, economic and medical upheavals which have so consumed us, George Monbiot's analysis of neo-liberalism put it as the dominant influence behind current problems, and tellingly, *Neo-liberalism sees competition as the defining characteristic of human relations*, he said.[20]

benign ambition which need not be socially divisive. Struggling against human adversity often involves this resolve, but many other forms of commitment can be to the benefit of both the individual and the community. Even inspired by a competitive impulse, inventing useful new products, devising innovative social projects, dedication to artistic endeavour, contributing to the service of the community, as well as pushing one's own individual boundaries – any or all of these may improve lives and life chances, as well as bringing personal reward. None of them needs be at the expense of fellow human beings; aiming to excel can be socially constructive, and elite performance should not be disparaged. In the current climate emergency, after all, the brilliance of the best human minds is needed to help combat global warming, and competition would certainly not be out of place here. But in this respect, as more widely, life is not a zero-sum project.

Part of the problem with these issues, already alluded to, is the confusion of ends with means. The ingenuity of the human species has created a dazzling, complex world, an objective 'man-made' reality – both functional and dangerous. But through becoming intoxicated by the elaborate virtuosity of their methods and techniques – the means – it is all too easy for humans to lose sight of the ends. And the fertile inventiveness of technology has led to such an abundance of means that it is hardly surprising that their purpose is often lost. As Bertrand Russell once pointed out, the efficiency of what he called *practical men* is only one half of wisdom. Of the other half, concerned with ends, he went on to say,

> *... the economic process and the whole of human life take on an entirely new aspect. We ask no longer: what have the producers produced, and what has consumption enabled the consumers in their turn to produce? We ask instead: what has there been in the lives of consumers and producers to make them glad to be alive?*[22]

The scientific revolution of early modern history saw human beings, God's creation, as ends, and the natural world as a means of satisfying human needs. This dualism was an accepted vision for western civilization until recent times; the natural environment was counted not for its intrinsic, but its instrumental value. However, as exploitation of the natural world has grown ever more sophisticated and ingenious, there is a sense in which the old dualism has been reversed; advanced societies are increasingly being used to serve a civilization whose prowess has become a function of elaborate systems and complex technology. The ends have become the means, and vice versa.

Such is modernity – in which, for many, ends are shrouded in ambiguity and uncertainty, if they are contemplated at all. And with the decline of religion there is less consolation to be gained from the view that the passage through this life is but a stepping stone to a purer future, and so can serve a higher purpose. In an age of rampant materialism, minds are directed to the possibility of marginal improvements in living standards, the acquisition of gadgets and devices to occupy leisure hours, and the manufacture of fascination for artificial communities and virtual worlds. But in spite of the lack of an over-arching purpose, there is nevertheless a relentless looking forward to some indefinable future – a continual searching, not for something better but for more expedients which will add to our wealth and our means of excitement. Revolutions are predicted for this or that field which will, it is said, transform the way we live. There is a restless clamour for novelty, ... *the insane cult of the future...* the Mexican writer Octavio Paz called it.[23] This impatience to see desires realized is part of a pathological short-termism which rules macro-policy as well as at a personal level, implicitly expecting immediate results. It is a form of modernity which, as Zygmunt Bauman puts it, ... *is a state of perpetual emergency,*[24] in which the promise is that, through science and technology, solutions will eventually be found for all human problems, so that human achievement is indeed raised to where it aspires to be – the ultimate conclusion, one might say, to the fulfilment of Enlightenment potential.

There is an irony here in that even as we subscribe to these aspirations, we feel that something is lacking, something is false. After all, we know at heart that most worthwhile projects in life take time to mature, whether it be in personal ambition, affective relationships, or family life. That does not stop us getting caught up in the impatient, forward-looking desire to be modern, not to be left behind by the bandwagon of something called 'progress'. There really does seem no alternative. The power of the neo-liberal myth and its false promise has so captivated audiences, in spite of the fact that the realization of affluence for all, the ultimate prosperity which market economics is supposed to provide, is far from being achieved – and has no prospect of being achieved under neo-liberalism. For most it is simply a mirage, a dim spectre on the horizon which can never be made real, but that does not appear to undermine the myth. The success in sustaining the fiction is a tribute to the sophistry of political leaders, as well as to the enduring faith in plausible but empty economic dogma. Another strange irony with this philosophy of materialism is that, while the world has an overall sufficiency for global sustenance and well-being, the inexorable drive for greater affluence in the already rich 'North' has done little to spread equality, and in fact now presents a danger to human existence itself.

Much of this work has been about the myths by which we live, and the faith in them which allows us to pursue misguided ambitions – introduced in Chapter 1. Whether it is in the economic values which guide society, the confusion over the relationship between community and the individual, the role of economic growth, the inability to distinguish between goods and commodities, or in the extent to which we should tolerate social inequality – much illusion and self-deception have developed over recent decades. In a world which has more information at its disposal than ever before, we nevertheless seem governed by fallible myths which soon become part of our enduring perspective on life, through which we then judge our problems and our uncertainties. We may even doubt the authority of scientific data; the views of experts themselves may be rejected, especially if they do not conform to widespread prejudice and assumption – as was outlined in Chapter 1.* So the confusion of outlook, the mixture of illusion and authenticity, realism and self-deception, which have become so pervasive in recent times are powerful forces governing how society moves forward. And while there may be considerable opposition to myths of all kinds, governments frequently collude in their influence.

But perhaps the *mother* of all assumptions is a faith in the future, the over-arching belief that there is a promised land towards which, in spite of difficulties along the way, we are fitfully moving. The 'end of history' notions in the 1990s gave a sense of arrival at a destiny – at least in political terms – while the promise of affluence for all at some indefinable point in the future, provided by the productivity of free market capitalism, sustains faith in a seriously flawed economic system and a confusion of values. This relentless, forward-looking compulsion is nurtured by both commercial interests and government, which endeavour to keep

---

* Fabricated theories may carry more weight with some groups in society than any amount of authoritative evidence – viz. the belief that the 2020 US Presidential election was stolen from Donald Trump, together with associated conspiracies which a large proportion of the American right believes.

eyes trained ahead – helping to camouflage the iniquities of the moment with false optimism. Thus demand for new products is stimulated and fresh consumer markets created; needs are manufactured where none previously existed. So hope is continually promoted that the future will be better. This ambitious drive is encouraged by those who have benefited from neo-liberal capitalism, as well as by those who think they can profit by others subscribing to it. It is a soulless belief which exploits the dreams of humanity and abases their aspirations, inducing them to accept that abandoning the materialist treadmill would spell disaster. As a result, all that is left of a vision for mankind, beyond the purely functional, is a narrow focus on money and an addiction with technological novelty.

Finally, then, how do we look ahead, what can we find to inspire us? The answer, of course, is above all to improve the lot of all of contemporary humanity; this would be progress indeed. But no, this is not the principal project in hand; we would rather employ resources developing super-intelligent robots or sending spacecraft to Mars, than try to address the earthly scourges of war, oppression and poverty. It is through technology that we look for salvation; it transpires that – since there are no plausible *ends* on the horizon – we can only search for redemption through the *means* of our complex civilization. Lost in this confusion is any sense that there might be over-development, that, as Leopold Kohr contends, technological progress beyond a certain point can become an obstacle to social advancement.[25] Although there is an empty obsession with moving forward, what Octavio Paz called a never-ending gallop toward a promised land, attentions are not focused on destinations. In any case, according to Paz, that final point is not *solid earth* but ... *an evanescent substance: time*.[26] This is what *homo sapiens* has been reduced to – an intent pre-occupation with the complex expedients of the built civilization, but without ultimate purpose. The writer Wyndham Lewis described progress as *time-worship*;[27] it is the passage of time and our frantic resolve to occupy it that allows us to avoid contemplating where it will lead.

    A serious impediment to any reassessment of values or purpose, to moderating the insatiable appetite for affluence without integrity, is the powerful notion of human change as evolutionary, to which neo-liberalism has smoothly accommodated itself. The myth of history as progress has taken hold over the last two centuries or so, so that today there exists the vague conviction that the world is involved in a gradual, if at times fitful, advance from darkness into light. The negative social side-effects of this process, driven on by technological advance and political inaction, are treated as the necessary price of reaching out for new levels of human consciousness and achievement. They are never allowed to force a fundamental questioning of the course of development. Connections were made between the idea of history as progress on the one hand, and Darwin's theories of evolution and a hierarchy among species on the other, from which the former drew credibility. The Victorian belief in the superiority of Christian, scientific civilization, and the discounting of traditionalist native peoples as having made no contribution to these achievements, have been important in consolidating the view of an ever growing, ever improving human species – part of an ever expanding universe. And the Social Darwinism of Herbert Spencer, and his phrase *survival of the fittest,* appeared to corroborate the idea of an evolutionary human development, against which the notion of cyclically fluctuating human progress had no hope of gaining traction.*

At the height of Victorian self-confidence, the idea of perfection would have involved higher ideals, with religion at their core. Today, however, the culmination of the chiefly secular march forward – if given any serious consideration – would be seen as some form of technological *nirvana* run by *homo economicus*. But because plausible 'final ends' have been largely removed from our horizon, we can only busy ourselves with the here and now, with a vague sense that we are moving towards something better. However uncertain and indistinct, a promised land, we believe, does lie ahead. It does not have the countenance of the kingdom of heaven, except for those of some specific faith, and nor is it like a classless society, the endpoint of Marxists. But it does have a similarity to those belief systems in the sense that the golden age is in the future, and our flawed strivings towards it are not expected to bear fruit in the short term.** In fact, in this imperfect

---

* It was Spencer who asserted: *The ultimate development of the ideal man is logically certain, as certain as any conclusion in which we place the most implicit faith.*[28] Spencer would have had a concept of the ideal man, but today attempts to try to conceive of a human ideal are far more problematic.

** The irony here is that while the culmination of our efforts will always be ahead of us,

world any failings along the way can be understood, since we know a state of 'perfection' is unattainable in this life, even as we are compelled to continue to search for it; ultimate fulfilment is always in the future. Thus the perfectibility of human kind, an ideal since the early days of the Western Enlightenment, has experienced a bizarre transmutation with any Utopian conception removed from sight, to be replaced by the aspiration of little more than continual material improvement.

Oscar Wilde wrote that ... *Progress is the realisation of Utopias.*[29] In actual fact, progress does not signify their realisation, but the ongoing quest for a concept which lies half-hidden, half-formed on the far horizon. Utopia is more of a prop, there to inspire or encourage, giving us at least some *raison d'être* for our struggle which might otherwise be hard to justify. So we can take refuge in the shady spectre of some kind of 'better world', though without defining it further. However, the lack of meaningful purpose has left a vacuum at the heart of much of neo-liberal society, and democratic authorities are unable to provide solace because they rarely lift their eyes to see beyond the materialism they believe their constituents crave. So they cannot offer a vision of a better future; pledges of lower taxes or cheaper consumer goods will not truly inspire society. This was recognized in the early days of neo-liberalism, when former Conservative cabinet minister Lord Prior pointed out that such promises were more an aspiration than a vision. Prior, never fully in tune with Thatcherism, declared,

> *A vision is how you see society as a whole, what sort of society you want to create in Britain... I don't believe that enabling people to own their own shares and their own houses, however desirable those things are, is in fact a visionary concept of what a society ought to be.*[30]

Visions to be realized – these rarely figure in politicians' pronouncements even if they use the term; they are far too nebulous and imprecise.

So where does all this leave 'progress' – the renowned journey on which the world is embarked? It certainly embodies constant change, to which we are exhorted to adapt, and it is reputed to be an exciting improvement on the present. But since the future is essentially

---

(and even perhaps because of that) we are so desperately impatient to benefit from short-term political gains.

indefinable, it signifies mere possibility, potential opportunity, and yet without a trace of a humane vision. We are obliged to go along with this endless forward movement because we see no other choice. So, as Brian Appleyard put it some years ago, ... *in spite of ourselves, we embrace this fiction of the flux,* in which ... *our state of being is forever provisional, always available to be changed into something else.*[31] We have taken on trust that we are on an endless course of self-improvement and so have discarded – or are forever discarding – any *unnecessary* ballast, any fixed points which might encumber us. Cultural or ethical norms to which we might cling come to be regarded as a hindrance, and so are dispensable in the march towards future time. Nothing is any longer irreverent. In the end, as Brian Appleyard points out, there are no fixed points from which society's principles can be defended. *Everything is reduced by the idea of progress and change.*[32] The sense of projecting ourselves forward has become an integral element in modern society's outlook, but this has degraded our enduring values and corrupted our view of the past.

That 'past' has become increasingly devalued by modern societies; it amounts to little more than a collection of symbols indicating the path to the present. It is not exactly *bunk*, as was once famously said, but can be examined as *stations of progress*, a resource for appreciating the glories of today. For, *'Progress' stands not for any quality of history, but for the self-confidence of the present*, emphasised Zygmunt Bauman. *Progress does not elevate or ennoble history. 'Progress' is a declaration of belief that history is of no account and of the resolve to leave it out of account.*[33] The tendency to belittle the past and its attainments stems from the belief in progress. And the focus on the present as a means to future triumphs is in the process of doing the same to what we do and who we are now. We sometimes hear the phrase 'standing on the shoulders of giants', as a deceptive hint that our successes today are built on the achievements of our forefathers. But this is a mere nod in the direction of the titans of history who, for good and bad, helped produce our world – a gesture made even while we devalue their significance by implying that they were simply stepping stones to our contemporary glory. After all, history as a subject now has a much reduced place in modern education, as if it serves no instructive purpose for today.* It is as if everything starts from here and now, with little appreciation of how we arrived.

So history is cast aside; a thin veneer of expertise and learning, sophisticated technique without bearings or roots, are apparently all that will be required for the tasks ahead. The future centres on the immutable connection between science and the idea of progress – a fairly modern phenomenon – now closely allied to current free market capitalism, whose proponents speak the language of expansion and growth, of competitiveness and efficiency, of high-tech enterprise and the liberation of humanity through scientific ingenuity. Business and commerce see their success based on continual technological modernisation, as science and its derivatives move ever forward, and the ambitions of neo-liberal economics are tied to this endless drive. This path to the future is presented at the same time as desirable and inevitable, both as the natural way forward and an exciting prospect. But this whole materialist edifice has one major flaw: the absence of a place for essential human concerns. Wisdom, spirituality, ethics, inter-personal relations, social affairs, artistic inspiration, and appreciation of the natural world – time-honoured values of all peoples everywhere simply do not figure here. But should they? Their roles vary, according to changing cultural norms and social attitudes; they do not follow a steady upward trajectory. Indeed, we cannot say that they have gained any ground in the conduct of human affairs since the time of the ancient Greeks, while science has since marched ahead.

However, these immaterial, aesthetic, cerebral, psycho-social qualities are the essence of what it means to be human. They are lasting, indispensable features of our race and are not amenable to being 'upgraded' by advances in science. They contain the truths which artists and philosophers, as well as ordinary people, have sought throughout the ages. But a civilization dominated by science and technology conveys the message that the only valid truths, on which all can agree, are scientific ones, and – as current fashion dictates – that they can best come to fruition through capitalist market economics. (After all, money and innovation are inextricably woven together.) And the advance of

---

* It is perhaps no coincidence that as the course of modern society in neo-liberal economies takes on a more distasteful complexion, there is a growing interest in national heritage and family history, which represent enduring qualities that in any case cannot make demands on us.

science carries the implication that society beyond can, and should, likewise progress. But as John Gray makes clear, *Ethics and politics do not advance in line with the growth of knowledge, not even in the long run.*³⁴ Essentially, human beings do not change as their inventions and discoveries expand. Science may enhance the capacity and power of the species, but ... *it cannot make human life more reasonable, peaceful or civilized.*³⁵ Nevertheless, modern science poses as a benign force which will eventually benefit all aspects of society, even though there is little prospect of harmonisation between technological virtuosity and ethical and cultural values, and no likelihood of consigning physical science to a role by which it did not purport to represent human progress.*

In actual fact, as was suggested earlier in this chapter, the advance of science and technology – rather than representing holistic progress – can be an obstacle to the betterment of society. Evidence has been presented in this work of the anti-social effects of the inappropriate application of technological innovation, particularly when the market sees an opportunity for gain. And the march of advanced civilization in the late twentieth century and since, driven by focus on extreme free market economics, has placed the planet in serious jeopardy. The dangers of such 'progress' were already highlighted much earlier: *Progress is bent on the 'destruction of life'. It attacks it in all its forms...* said the German philosopher and poet Ludwig Klages in 1913.³⁶ And ... *it degrades such living creatures as it spares...* he went on. We are even more familiar with these destructive consequences today. But though we are increasingly aware of the risks to the planet of unrestrained scientific expansion, coupled with economic growth, it is unlikely that the modern romance – even obsession – with technological progress will be abandoned soon. The current sense of ourselves as a species is so bound up with it. Nevertheless, Western post-Enlightenment society, as well as global civilization as a whole, will not fully come of age until its scientific endeavour and economic impetus is devoted to producing a better quality of life – in all its diverse forms – rather than greater affluence and technological sophistication.

The most ominous aspect of the direction of contemporary science is the speed of development of artificial intelligence. The words of Professor Kevin Warwick at the beginning of this chapter suggest that

---

*   It is interesting that the advance of science in the ancient world did not signify the march of society as a whole, but was more akin to a compensation for the vagaries of life.

humans will need eventually – they don't know how soon! – to upgrade themselves by being 'cybernetically' linked to some kind of machine. The contention is that if we wish to remain as purely 'human', we will be at a disadvantage compared with intelligent machines – in other words, second-class citizens in our originally human world. This will, of course, provide tempting commercial opportunities which could help drive developments further and faster, unless decisions are taken by authorities to regulate such trends. John Gray does not believe the signs are auspicious: *Humans are no more masters of machines than they are of fire or the wheel,* he said twenty years ago. *The forms of artificial life and intelligence they are constructing today will elude human control just as naturally occurring forms of life have done.*[37] Gray termed this Posthuman Evolution.* Is this the Utopian future to inspire humankind, one which would represent the final divergence between our humanity and our scientific ingenuity? If not, can it be forestalled? Until now, neither fears for the planet's eco-system, nor disquiet at the spiritual vacuum at the heart of economic development, not even dismay at huge economic inequalities have been urgent enough to induce a proper re-evaluation of human progress.

Kurt Vonnegut's prescient, satirical dystopian novel *Player Piano* was published nearly seventy years ago. It depicts a society, in the not too distant future, dominated by machines and automation in which the scientists and managers in charge are also cogs in the organisational wheel. They believe in the system which has been created, but are nonetheless themselves victims of an inhuman regime which most feel is better than any alternative. The social control imposed from the top manages to maintain order, against which a few 'deviants' – notably the 'hero', Paul Proteus – are resolved to rebel.** Proteus encapsulates his opposition to the system when giving testimony at his own trial: *The main business of humanity is to do a good job of being human beings, not to serve as appendages to machines, institutions and systems.*[39] What better

---

*   The matter of control was precisely the question which Stuart Russell highlighted in his recent book on AI, *Human Compatible*. Since we do not always know our own objectives, if artificial machines are given too much autonomy they may reach endpoints which humans would find horrifying. Russell believes that building devices that are more intelligent than us would be a huge event in human history – but potentially the last.[38]

** The main character of Vonnegut's novel has similarities to The Savage in Huxley's *Brave New World* (though Huxley set his society several hundred years in the future). But both represent the essential qualities of humanity struggling against a bureaucratised and computerised tyranny which the ingenuity of mankind has foolishly created.

argument for our contemporary, flawed civilization, even as we move it steadily in the direction of Vonnegut's dystopian tyranny? Today, there are leaders the world over who appear to believe in the computerised, technological, free market society to come; many have a vested interest in the enterprise, while others see it as a 'least worst' option, even if not to their taste. But all are moving blindly into a post-human world, foolishly succumbing to the ultimate hubris. So perhaps now is the time to accept the recommendation of Vonnegut's protagonist, and abjure:

> ... *intemperate faith in lawless technological progress – namely, that man is on earth to create more durable and efficient images of himself, and hence, to eliminate any justification at all for his own continued existence.*[40]

Global civilization today is a kind of free-wheeling roller coaster. Its science and technology contingents are moving ahead inexorably, for good and ill, while its economic models are driven by consumerism and by corporate imperialism. Allowing scientific ambition the freedom to pursue its own path, perhaps laudable in itself, takes no account of the long-term implications for human welfare. And in economic terms, the liberty to profit from success in the free market is exercised with scant regard for the wider interests of the community, and especially of those who, with modest resources, themselves contribute to such gain. In both respects it is the general well-being which ought to take priority over the freedom of action – whether well meaning or not – of a minority. As this work has laboured to show, in its market fundamentalist version capitalism has reached a point where vast economic and social inequalities have become familiar – even accepted, where economic growth does not produce a better society, where much hardship and social dislocation is tolerated, and where an endless quest for even greater affluence consumes preoccupations. But this has become the notional *status quo*, the narrow lens through which we view society. It is our contemporary *truth*, rationalised purely by our current habit of looking at life as a materialistic struggle in which some will win and some must lose. It is a matter of perception; it need not be this way – and in the future it will not be.

The uncomfortable truth, for many, is that we know how to improve society; it is the fixation with ideology and theory which blinds political decision-makers and conveys to others the falsehood that our present path is the only way forward. The 'promised land' is not in the future; it is in the fruits of moderate, progressive policies undertaken here and now – the course recommended in these chapters. However, an outlook which prioritises equality and sustainability, investment in human resources and community, and which puts its trust in the present, may appear uninspiring to a civilization reared on the idea that the golden age is yet to come. And behind suspicion of such policies is the fear of not being modern, not keeping up, of missing out on yet greater bounty. For, while we cast about for the stability and harmony which humankind has sought since its earliest days, society is dominated by a restlessness which can have no end. The constant forward movement of the present age is toward material improvement – which under current practice cannot possibly benefit everyone – and this will be the experience of the next age, and the one after that, unless the absurd process is arrested. And if there is no end in view, then everything is means, and as Bryan Appleyard concludes, ... *I am destined to live and die for a cause that can never be triumphant.*[41]

So, in true pragmatic fashion, let us now, today, put our faith in society in all its diverse, vernacular, multi-faceted potential. We do not need Utopias; searching for visionary ideals to inspire us undermines faith in existing human potential. Believing in improvements to ordinary quality of life may not present itself as an exciting purpose to motivate people, but that seemingly humble objective is a project of immense power and significance to which we must now turn, in place of the high-flown rhetoric favouring grand schemes which have a curious habit of serving an affluent minority. Besides, to a century of lost faiths and disillusioned ideals, less grandiose goals – ones that do not dissolve into the distance as they are approached – represent a more appropriate vision for the future. But they must be aims which incorporate lasting values – altruism and trust, for example – not the ever-changing modes of contemporary capitalist society. As was said more than a generation ago, *Markets must be kept in their place because they encourage egoism over altruism and rational calculation of advantage over trust.*[42] Considering the poverty of expectation – the legacy of decades of fine words and equivocal policy – ameliorating the lives and lifestyles of the majority of society would represent an illustrious achievement. This cannot be managed by shabby, disreputable neo-liberalism.

The time must inevitably come when, from some future vantage point, people will look back in astonishment at an age when method and arbitrary rules about technological society and the free market dominated policy and attitudes. It will no doubt be viewed as incredible that 'man-made' norms were so precious that they could not be overridden even in the face of immense hardship and loss. In future historical analysis, it may well be equated with the terrible past crimes committed in the name of religion. In the latter case, there was always hope of salvation in the afterlife; in terms of the worldly expectations of today, all that can be promised for the poor and disadvantaged is that redemption is to come, for some unknown generation, at some indefinite point in the future. In the meantime, hope must take refuge in suspect dreams. It is not the job of government, or the free market, or big business, or media power, to condition human society and teach it how to live; it must be left to its own devices, to be as creative and fulfilled as it needs, and above all as human as it can be. We must look at ourselves and the world which we have built in recent generations, and we must declare – *it is not enough*. This cannot be the fulfilment of *homo sapiens*. Only then will we have the chance to find the resolve to vote with our hearts, with our feet, and with our money, for something better. Only then will we be able to drive out the incubus which has devitalized our soul for an age. And then, as R. H. Tawney wrote, *When the false gods depart there is some hope, at least, of the arrival of the true.*

END NOTES

i Zygmunt Bauman, *Wasted Lives: Modernity and its Outcasts*, Polity Press, Cambridge, UK, 2004, p. 89.
ii Lewis Mumford, in 'The New Yorker', New York, 8/10/1960.
iii Henry Braverman, in *Labour and Monopoly Capital*, 1976, quoted in Richard Douthwaite, *The Growth Illusion*, Green Books, Bideford, Devon, 1992, p. 133.
iv John Gray, *Heresies: Against Progress and Other Illusions*, Granta Books, London, 2004, p. 4.
v President Joe Biden in his first address to Congress, at the end of his first 100 days in office, effectively signalling his abandonment of a key element of neo-liberal economics.

1 Professor Kevin Warwick, speaking on BBC Radio 4, in 'Has Technology Rewired our Brains?' 27/1/2015, in the series 'History of Ideas'.
2 According to Nobel laureate Wassily Leontief in 1983, quoted in Rutger Bregman, *Utopia for Realists, and How We Can Get There*, Bloomsbury, London, 2018, p. 177.
3 John Gray, op. cit., p. 3.
4 According to *The Independent*, London, 24/9/2019.
5 Reported in March 2019 by the law and justice magazine *The Justice Gap*, at https://www.thejusticegap.com/part-privatisation-of-probation-irredeemably-flawed-says-chief-inspector/
6 National Audit Office data, reported 1/3/2019 at https://www.bbc.co.uk/news/uk-47409350. The NAO said that the payment-by-results model by which the service had been privatised was inappropriate for probation.
7 Chris Daw, *Justice on Trial: Radical Solutions for a System at Breaking Point*, Bloomsbury, London, 2020.
8 Martin Pawley, *The Private Future: Causes and Consequences of Community Collapse in the West*, Thames & Hudson, London, 1973, p. 99.
9 Zygmunt Bauman, *Does Ethics Have A Chance In A World Of Consumers?* Harvard University Press, Cambridge, Mass., USA, 2008, pp. 139 & 141.
10 David Garland had already identified this transformation twenty years ago, in his *The Culture of Control: Crime and Social Order in Contemporary Society*, OUP, 2001. These quotes are taken from Zygmunt Bauman, 2004, op. cit., p. 68. Bauman highlights Garland's thesis at length in Chapter 3.
11 A report by the Heritage Lottery Fund in 2014 revealed that 45% of local authorities at that time were considering either selling parks and green spaces or transferring their management to others. It also noted that large numbers of residents – rising to 81% of those with children – said that spending time in their local park was important, or essential to their quality of life. See https://www.heritagefund.org.uk/news/public-parks-under-threat

12 Robert Bischof, 'Why German cycles give a better ride', in *The Guardian*, London, 27/12/1994.
13 In 'An Economy For the People by the People: Stepping stones to a new economy', by The New Economics Foundation, 2018, at <https://neweconomics.org/2018/09/an-economy-for-the-people-by-the-people>
14 Part of the Swedish Social Democratic Programme of 2004, quoted in Zygmunt Bauman, 2004, op. cit., p. 142.
15 Tim Jackson, *Prosperity Without Growth: Foundations for the Economy of Tomorrow*, 2nd. Edn., Routledge, Abingdon, Oxon., 2017, pp. 157-8.
16 John Stuart Mill, 'On Liberty', in *Utilitarianism, Liberty and Representative Government*, Everyman's Library, J. M. Dent & Sons, London, 1910, p. 127.
17 Quoted in Martin J. Wiener, *English Culture and the Decline of the Industrial Spirit 1850-1980*, Cambridge University Press, Cambridge, 1981, p. 157.
18 Quoted in Raymond Williams, *The Country and the City*, Hogarth Press, London, 1985, p. 267.
19 Prime Minister Tony Blair, speech at the Labour Party Conference, Brighton, 30/9/1997.
20 In George Monbiot, 'Neo-liberalism – the ideology at the root of all our problems', *The Guardian*, London, 15/4/2016.
21 Bertrand Russell, *The Conquest of Happiness*, Unwin Books, London, 1965, pp. 34, 36.
22 In Bertrand Russell, *Authority and the Individual*, Unwin Books, London, 1965, p. 87.
23 In Octavio Paz, *One Earth, Four or Five Worlds*, Paladin Books, London, 1992, p. 27.
24 Zygmunt Bauman, 2004, op. cit., p. 30.
25 Leopold Kohr, 'Appropriate Technology' in *The Schumacher Lectures*, Blond & Briggs, London, 1980, Appendix 2, p. 186.
26 Octavio Paz, op. cit., p. 22.
27 Cited by John Gray, in *Straw Dogs: Thoughts on Humans and Other Animals*, Grant Books, London, 2003, p. 194.
28 Herbert Spencer, quoted in Daniel Bell, *The End of Ideology: On the Exhaustion of Political Ideas in the Fifties*, Collier Books, New York, 1961, p. 243.
29 Oscar Wilde in 'The Soul of Man under Socialism', 1891, quoted in Rutger Bregman, op. cit., p. 249.
30 James Prior, quoted in Hugo Young, Anne Sloman, *The Thatcher Phenomenon*, BBC, London, 1986, p. 134.
31 Brian Appleyard, *Understanding the Present: Science and the Soul of Modern Man*, Pan Books, London, 1993, p. 236.
32 Ibid. p. 237.
33 Zygmunt Bauman, *Liquid Modernity*, Polity Press, Cambridge, UK, 2000, p. 132.
34 John Gray, 2004, op. cit., p. 107.
35 Ibid. p. 4.
36 Ludwig Klages, quoted in Robert and Edward Skidelsky, *How Much Is Enough? The Love of Money, and the Case for the Good Life*, Penguin Books, London, 2013, p. 133.
37 John Gray, 2003, op. cit., p. 185.

38　Stuart J. Russell, *Human Compatible: AI and the Problem of Control*, Allen Lane, London, 2019.
39　Kurt Vonnegut Jr., *Player Piano*, Paladin/Grafton Books, London, 1990, p. 293.
40　Ibid. p. 282.
41　Brian Appleyard, op. cit., p. 236.
42　K. Hoover & R. Plant, *Conservative Capitalism in Britain and the United States: A Critical Appraisal*, Routledge, London, 1989, p. 51.

INDEX

Abbey, Edward 218
Adair, James 327
Airbnb 109, 443
Akerlof, George 249
Amazon (company) 125, 470, 475
American Association of Retired Persons 306
American Declaration of Independence 324
'American Dream', The 54, 68, 143, 145, 329
American Economics Association 82, 159, 355
American Environmental Protection Agency 241
American Federal Reserve 148, 213
American Recovery and Reinvestment Act (2009) 19
Anne, HRH The Princess Royal 451
Apple 446
Arendt, Hannah 354, 387
Argent (property firm) 271, 313
Aristotle 269
Armstrong, Sir Robert 240
Armstrong, Stephen 408, 475
Arnold, Matthew 328
Asch, Solomon 20
Atkinson, Anthony 447–448, 465, 478–480
Atos 253
Auden, W. H. 28, 33
austerity 39, 51, 63, 67, 138–139, 144–145, 153, 202, 224, 232, 239, 244, 252, 265, 269, 280–281, 285–288, 295, 301, 356, 377, 379, 381, 393–394, 406, 413, 416, 425, 440, 443, 450, 455, 460, 467, 485–486, 493

Bacon, Francis 32
Bagehot, Walter 32, 72, 77, 336, 384
Baggini, Julian 15, 32
Bahn, Paul 88
Bahramipour, Bob 141
Balfour, Arthur 318, 384
Bank of England 441
Barchester Healthcare 417
Barwise, Dr Patrick 121
Basel Rules 285
BASF 441
Bauman, Zygmunt 16, 32, 60–61, 66, 74, 76–77, 123, 126, 136, 162, 218, 352, 368, 379, 388–389, 391, 401, 475, 490, 502, 507, 514–515
Becker, Gary 97, 160
Beeching, Dr Richard 411
Bentham, Jeremy 114
Berlin, Isaiah 227, 338, 386
Besley, Professor Tim 314
Bet365 357
Beveridge Report 466
Beveridge, Sir William 66, 466
Biden, President Joe 29, 482, 514
BIDs (Business Improvement Districts) 270
Bischoff Inquiry 431
Blackmore Bonds 432
Blackwell and Seabrook 123

Blair, Tony 57, 65, 472, 498, 515
Boehm, Christopher 326, 385
Boeing 737 247
Booth, Charles 427
Boyce, Frank Cottrell 421, 476
Brandeis, Justice Louis D. 309
Bregman, Rutger 381, 391, 478, 480, 514–515
Bretton Woods 168
Brexit 25, 79, 171, 212, 243, 280, 334, 343, 356, 394, 460, 467
British Academy 284, 314
British Airways 261, 441
'British Disease', The 186
British Gas 409–410
British Medical Journal 337, 386
British Social Attitudes Survey 144, 388–389, 479
Brown, Gordon 18, 170, 287, 461
Brundtland Commission 196
BSkyB 276
BT 409
Buchanan, Professor Neil 248
Buffett, Warren 69, 77, 292
Burgess, Anthony 330, 386
Burns, Arthur 229
Bush, George W. 23, 187, 292
Bus Services Act, 2017 413
bus transport 412–415

517

Butler, R. A. 403
Butskellism 53, 403
Byrne, Liam 221, 287

Cable, Vince 254
Cairncross, Frances 121, 162
Cameron, David 64–65, 77, 198, 242–243, 258, 271, 289, 314
Cantril Ladder 199
capitalism
  and community 100–101, 107
  modes of 93–96
  the future 84–88
  theory 88–92
Care Quality Commission 264, 417
Care UK 417
Carey, Professor John 396, 475
Carnegie, Andrew 347
Carrillion 295
Carse, James P. 94
'casino capitalism' 282, 360, 430, 432, 477
CASSE (Center for the Advancement of the Steady State Economy) 209, 221
Casson, Dr Catherine 472, 481
CBI (Confederation of British Industry) 243
CCFF (Covid Corporate Financing Facility) 441
Centre for European Reform 247, 311
Centre for Process Systems Engineering 451
Centrica 410
CFA (Chartered Financial Analyst Institute) 297, 315, 480
Chadwick, Edwin 114
Chamberlain, Neville 372
Chang, Ha-Joon 22, 33, 42, 68, 75, 93, 118, 160–162, 185–186, 201, 219–220, 251, 284, 296, 299, 311, 314–315, 346, 355, 387–388, 439, 445, 473, 477–478, 481
Chernobyl 260
Cherokees 327
child care – early years 418–421
Childcare Act, 2017 (UK) 419
Child, Lee 469, 481
choice 45–46, 119–123
Chomsky, Noam 14, 32
Churchill, Winston 273, 372
CIPD (Chartered Institute of Personnel and Development) 315, 480
Circle Health 263–264
citizenship 65–66
City of London 116, 240, 282, 431, 461
Clinton, President Bill 102, 187, 240, 406, 429
Club of Rome 169, 218
Coates, Denise 357, 388
Cobb, John 45, 71, 196, 338
Codetermination (West Germany) 440
cognitive ease 13, 21, 189, 211, 216, 364, 378
Cohen-Portheim, Paul 317, 384, 386
Cold War 39
Coleridge, Samuel Taylor 159
Collins, Chuck 376
commercialization of public domain 130–131
Commission on the Measurement of Economic Performance and Social Progress 198
commodification 132–135, 236, 401
'commons, the' 266–270, 273–276
  and the NHS 279–280
  and sport 276–279

communal amenities 57–60
community 42–43, 45, 50–52, 73–75
Competition and Markets Authority 96
Conservative Party (UK) 232, 240, 293, 309
consumer sovereignty 124–127
consumerism 135–137
containment of the free market 397–403, 424–426
Conway, Kellyanne 27
Cook, Dr Sarah 385
Cook, Philip J. 161, 220, 388
Coote, Anna 424, 466–468, 476, 480–481
Coronavirus 27, 29, 64, 80, 149, 171, 293, 350, 355–356, 359, 367, 375, 379–380, 382, 394–395, 410, 423, 440–441, 451, 453, 473, 484, 489, 495
corporate conduct/responsibility 435–441
Corporate Social Responsibility Agreements 436
Courtauld, Samuel 435, 477
Covid-19 29, 106, 171, 188, 212, 279–280, 293, 356, 374, 380–381, 394, 397, 402, 406, 409, 422–423, 427, 436, 439–440, 449, 458, 460, 463, 473, 485, 489
Crimea 26
Crosland, Anthony 81

Dahrendorf, Ralf 169, 218
Daily Telegraph, The 76, 147, 163, 188, 219, 271, 313, 386, 479
Daly, Herman 45, 47, 50, 71, 196, 209, 338

INDEX

DARPA (Defense Advanced Research Project Agency) US 255
D'Aveni, Richard 94
Dawkins, Richard 70, 101
de Botton, Alain 16, 20, 61, 76, 218, 232
de-growth 180–181
Deliveroo 141
Department for Transport 246
De Tocqueville, Alexis 22, 33, 36, 384
Dilnot Commission 418
Disney World 136
Disraeli, Benjamin 385, 427
Dorling, Danny 362, 389
Douthat, Ross 354, 388
Douthwaite, Richard 475, 514
Duke of Westminster 268
Durkheim, Emile 37, 75

Easter Island 87
Easterlin, Richard 191
economic austerity 281–282, 285–289
economic growth
  and climate change 174–178
  and government spending 185
  and human well-being 167–168, 188–195
  and inequality 200–203, 365–366
  and living standards 178–182
  and the welfare state 184–185, 186–187
Economic Policy Institute 103
Edelman Trust Barometer 300
EHR (European Home Retail) 433–434
Electoral College 29
Elstein, David 276, 313
Emerson, Ralph Waldo 84, 159, 392, 475
employment
  consequences of flexible economy 144–146, 454–456
  significance 142–144, 453–454
  the market and the flexible economy 138–142
Enlightenment 29, 38, 41, 96, 101, 146, 192, 307–308, 326–328, 349, 368, 382, 452, 483–484, 502, 506
Enron 245
equality
  and income 323–324, 353–354
  and mental health 368
  and mortality 368–369
  history 324–329
  of being 335–336, 373–376
  of opportunity 340–343, 344–347
  versus liberty 336–338
EU Referendum in UK 13, 23, 25, 156, 243, 330, 393
European Commission 446
European Working Time Directive 139
expenditure cascades 357
Exxon Mobil 437, 477

FAA (Federal Aviation Authority) 247
Facebook 121
Fairburn, Carolyn 243
Fairburn, Jeff 296
fake news 15, 202, 492
Fankhauser, Peter 295, 297
Farage, Nigel 23
Farepak 433–434
Farnsworth, Kevin 259, 312
FATCA (Foreign Account Tax Compliance Act) US 446
Fat Cat Day 300

FCA (Financial Conduct Authority) 243, 311, 432
Federal Electoral Commission (US) 438
Federation of Small Businesses 289
Feed-in Tariff 259
feudalism 61–62, 273
financial boom and bust 281–285
Financial Secrecy Index 444, 478
Financial Services Modernization Act 240
First Amendment (US Constitution) 437–438
Fisher, Irving 249, 355
Fitoussi, Jean-Paul 198
Flenley, John 88
Foreign Office 305
Forestry Commission 273
Forster, E. M. 120, 162
Fortune 500 445
Four Seasons Health Care 417
Francis, Pope 27
Franklin, Benjamin 327
Frank, Robert H. 161, 220, 388
free markets 80–84
Freud, Sigmund 40, 142
Friedman, Milton 83, 226, 229–230, 301, 345, 387
Fromm, Erich 21, 33, 90–91, 160
FSA (Financial Services Authority) 432
FTSE (Financial Times Stock Exchange, now FTSE Russell Group) 295–298, 300, 315, 460–461
Fukushima 260
Fuller, Professor Steve 14

G4S 253
Gabor, Dennis 169, 178, 218–219

Gaitskell, Hugh 403
Galbraith, J. K. 58, 124
Galston, William 153
Garland, David 67, 77, 514
Gates, Bill 69, 77
Gatwick Airport 242
GDP (Gross Domestic Product) 103, 126, 165–168, 172–177, 179–180, 184–199, 201–203, 207, 214, 216, 219–221, 241, 257, 280, 288, 291, 293–294, 322, 361, 366, 369, 382, 418, 422, 447, 450–451, 475, 478, 499
GDP calculations and their problems 172–174
GDP growth: historical aspects 168–172
General Electric 435
Gini index 377
Gladstone, William Ewart 427
Glasgow University 26
GlaxoSmithKline 256, 297
Global Climate Coalition 437
Global Compact (UN) 436
Global Forum on Transparency and Exchange of Information for Tax Purposes (OECD) 446
Global Prosperity Institute 422
GNH (Gross National Happiness – Bhutan) 199
GNP (Gross National Product) 116, 166, 168, 173, 196–197, 221
Goffman, Erving 310
Golden Age of Capitalism 103, 355
Goldman Sachs 258, 299
Goodwin, (Sir) Fred 295

Google 26, 256, 258, 470
Gornick, Professor Janet 461
Gorz, André 122, 142–143, 162–163, 479
Gove, Michael 23, 58
government aid to private sector 254–256
government intervention 113–118, 250–253
GPI (Genuine Progress Indicator) 197
Gray, John 114, 149, 159, 161, 164, 228, 309, 475, 484, 509–510, 514–515
Grayling, Chris 414
Green, David 38
Greenhalgh, Liz 162
Green Party (UK) 456
Greenspan, Alan 148, 164, 241, 283, 310, 314
Grenfell Tower 242, 244, 428
Guardian, The 75, 77, 218, 221, 311–313, 315, 388, 391, 515
Gummer, John (Lord Deben) 100, 161
Guterres, António 176
GWR (Great Western Railway) 246

H/2 Capital Partners 417
Hackett, Dame Judith 244
Hammond, Philip 266
Hammond, Stephen 243
Hampden-Turner, Charles 94, 160
Hampton, Sir Philip 358
Handy, Charles 468, 481
Harari, Yuval Noah 30, 34
Hardin, Garrett 268
Hattersley, Roy 332
Hawking, Stephen 475
Hawkins, Merritt 145
Hayek, Friedrich 170, 226, 230, 464
HBOS 433–434

HC-One 417
HDI (The UN's Human Development Index) 198
Headmasters Conference 292
Heath, Edward 82
Heffernan, Margaret 147, 163
Helliwell, Professor John 200
Hennessey, Professor Peter 314
Henry VII 37
High Pay Centre 296, 298, 300, 460, 475, 480
Hildyard, Luke 392, 475
Hinchingbrooke Hospital 263
Hinkley Point C 259
Hirsch, Fred 50, 76–77, 105–107, 155–156, 160–162, 164, 204–205, 220, 270, 464
HMRC (Her Majesty's Revenue & Customs) 294, 443
Hodgson, Geoff 44–45, 75, 124, 162, 341, 387
Holmes Jr., Oliver Wendell 11, 32, 79, 150
Holocaust, The 26, 374
homo economicus 40, 45, 50, 71, 395–396, 505
household economics 230–232
housing 421–424
housing benefit 423, 489
Howell, David 85, 159
Hulme, T. E. 16, 32, 161, 366, 395
Hume, David 101
Hunt, Jeremy 293
Hurd, Douglas 329, 331
Hutton, Will 20, 33, 77, 86, 139, 162–163, 336, 338, 340, 371, 386–387, 408, 431, 443, 475, 477–478, 480
hypocognition 289, 314

INDEX

521

IFS (Institute for Fiscal Studies) 168, 292–293, 314, 476, 478
Illich, Ivan 133–134, 162
ILO (International Labour Organisation) 103, 201
IMF (International Monetary Fund) 22, 83, 287, 365, 389, 445, 449–450, 461, 479
Imperial College, London 451
Independent, The 101, 130, 244, 286, 300, 313, 475–476, 514
individualism 21, 36, 38, 40–46, 48–51, 54, 61, 64, 67, 70, 74, 81, 112, 123, 150, 155–156, 215, 226, 228–229, 235, 239, 308, 331, 339, 371, 374, 376, 378, 490, 495
   and altruism 70–73, 101–102
   and entrepreneurs 68–69
   and interdependence 61–62
inequality of income
   and child well-being 361–362
   and social well-being 361–362
   and self-enhancement bias 362–364
Inglis, Bob 24, 33
Institute of Chartered Financial Analysts 461
Intel 258
'invisible hand', the 48–49, 57, 73, 91–92, 100–102, 106, 227, 270, 283, 337, 343, 398, 415
IPCC (Intergovernmental Panel on Climate Change) 175
Ipsos MORI 290, 312
Iroquois Confederacy 327
ISEW (Index of Sustainable Economic Welfare) 196–197

Jackson, Tim 92, 131–132, 159–160, 162, 178, 192, 195, 210, 219–221, 299, 303, 315, 372, 390, 428, 477, 496, 515
James, Oliver 146, 349, 386–387
Javid, Sajid 242
Jefferson, Thomas 327, 385
John Lewis Partnership 237
Johnson, Boris 23, 293, 344, 346, 371, 449
Johnson, Harry 99
Johnson, Luke 213, 221
Johnson, Paul 391
Joseph, Keith 41, 82
J. P. Morgan 463
Ju 327, 385
Judt, Tony 32, 40, 69, 75, 81, 117, 159, 161, 250, 263, 311–312, 334–335, 373, 376, 386, 390

Kafka, Franz 218
Kahneman, Daniel 13, 21, 32, 364, 378, 389, 429, 461, 477, 480
Kaletsky, Anatole 86
Kaus, Mickey 317, 384
Kay, John 238, 310, 398
Kennedy, President John F. 27, 185
Kennedy, Senator Robert 217
Keynesianism 19, 201, 226
Keynes, John Maynard 63, 76, 208, 221, 287, 320, 452
Kings College, London 349
Klintman, Mikael 395, 475
Knight, Laurence 33, 159, 241, 310–311, 314–315, 388, 477, 480
Kobe Steel 93

Kohr, Leopold 138, 163, 429, 477, 504, 515
Krugman, Paul 18, 32, 188, 202, 219–220, 231, 283, 285, 288, 301, 309, 314–315, 371, 480
Kuznets, Simon 168, 218
Kyoto Climate Change Conference 413

Labour Force Survey 479
Laffer, Arthur 428, 449
Laffer Curve 449
laissez-faire 39, 89, 92, 96, 113–115, 117, 120, 146, 185, 250, 300, 353–354, 427, 472
Lakoff, George 232, 243, 274, 276, 281, 286, 289, 310, 313–314, 376, 390, 429, 477
Lamont, Michele 387
Latouche, Serge 215, 221
Lawson, Lord (Nigel) 25
Layard, Professor Richard 200
Leadsom, Andrea 243
Lebow, Victor 78, 159
Lee, Richard B. 327, 385
Lehman Brothers 245, 461
Le Pen, Marine 23
Lewandowsky, Steven 14, 32
Liberal Democrats 413
liberalism 38, 41, 43–44, 89, 101, 115, 148, 206, 227, 230, 238, 330, 472
light-touch regulation 140, 282, 285, 434
limited liability 432–435
Linklater, Andro 37, 75, 160, 240, 273, 310, 313–314, 385
Littler, Jo 388
London North Eastern Railway 246
Luttwak, Edward 170, 218
Lytton, Lord (Robert Bulwer-Lytton) 23

Macmillan Committee 432
Macmillan, Harold 81, 159, 169
Madison, James 328, 385
Major, John 65
Malcolm, Janet 31
Malik, Kenan 342, 387
market domains 403–405, 408–424, 426–427
market forces and values 97–99, 99–100
markets and individual choice 104–107
markets-orientated thinking 97
Markovits, Daniel 342, 387
Marquand, David 45, 51, 66, 75, 77
Marrakech 223
Marshall, Alfred 45
Marxism 147
Mason, Paul 85, 160
materialism and insatiability 183–184
Max-Neef, Manfred 173, 191, 218–219
May, Theresa 65, 281, 491
Mazzucato, Mariana 149, 164, 254, 256, 311–312
McCloskey, Professor Deirdre 371, 390
McGahern, John 183
McKibben, Bill 210, 221
measurements of human well-being 196–200
medieval society 37, 62
Meek, James 274–275, 313, 407
Melrose Industries 296
meritocracy 342–344, 354–355
Michaelson, Juliet 213, 221
Middle East 25, 292
Milburn, Alan 340
Miliband, Ed 18, 371

Mill, John Stuart 39, 43, 75, 99, 157, 207–208, 210–211, 218, 221, 399, 497, 515
Minford, Professor Patrick 25
Ministry of Defence 273
Minton, Anna 313
Mishan, E. J. 212, 221
Moore, Michael 151, 164, 403
Mount, Ferdinand 55, 76, 359, 385, 388
Mulgan, Geoff 160, 162
Mullainathan, Sendhil 388, 478
Mumford, Lewis 137, 163, 482, 514
Murray, Charles 53, 76

Nairn, Tom 334, 386
narrative fallacy 18
NASA (National Aeronautics and Space Administration) US 185
National Housing Federation 423, 476
Natural Law 38, 327
Neiman, Susan 71, 77
Network Rail 254
New Deal, The 185
New Economics Foundation 213, 424, 431, 477, 479–481, 495, 515
New Harmony 237
New Labour 17, 59, 65–66, 102, 128, 143, 145, 170, 198, 245, 262, 264–266, 282–283, 286–287, 381, 404, 406, 413, 420, 472, 498
New Lanark 237
New Right 17, 45–46, 75, 128, 169, 226, 228, 377
New Statesman, The 476
New York Times 220, 229, 311, 315–316, 388, 390, 448, 478, 480

NIH (National Institutes of Health) US 255
Nordhaus, William 196, 220
Northern Rock 245, 252, 285
Northumberland Healthcare NHS Foundation Trust 265
Nossiter, Bernard 302
Nozick, Robert 230
NPPF (National Planning Policy Framework) 271–272
Nuclear Decommissioning Authority 260

Obama, President Barak 187–188
Obermatt 297–298
Oborne, Peter 54, 76
OECD (Organisation for Economic Co-operation and Development) 179, 198, 219–220, 247, 280, 290, 311, 322–323, 368, 375, 377, 380, 384–385, 389–391, 442, 446, 448
Ofcom 410
Ofgem 410
On Liberty (Mill) 39, 515
ONS (Office for National Statistics) 174, 313, 391, 479
Opus Restructuring 476
Orwell, George 27, 43, 75, 224, 309, 320, 330, 333, 352, 384, 386, 388
Osborne, George 67, 254, 260, 286–287
Ostrom, Elinor 132, 268, 313
Outer Space Treaty 267
overseas investment 116–117
Owen, Robert 237
Oxfam 390, 424, 468

Paine, Tom 332, 386, 464
Paris Agreement 49, 175, 456

INDEX

Pawley, Martin 130, 162, 167, 218, 402, 475, 490, 514
pay
  and meritocracy 343
  and remuneration 294–302, 353, 356–360, 459–464
Peckham, Simon 296
Peel, Sir Robert 329
per capita 165, 179, 188, 192, 194–195, 197, 216, 251, 253, 280, 319, 322, 361, 368, 382, 450, 486–487
Percy, Adam 476
Persimmon 296
Peston, Robert 33, 83, 85, 159, 241, 250, 310–311, 314–315, 358, 388, 431, 477, 480
Pettifor, Ann 67
PFIs (Private Finance Initiatives) 264–266
Pickett, Kate 77, 202, 220–221, 324, 336, 361, 366, 384–390
Piketty, Thomas 59, 76, 103, 161, 180, 219, 288, 293, 296, 303, 314–316, 344, 353, 356, 385, 387–388, 446, 450, 478
Pinker, Steven 192, 220, 382, 391
Pirie, Madsen 124, 162
Pistor, Katharina 433, 477
planning and development 271–273
Plato 12
Polanyi, Karl 86
Portes, Jonathan 422, 468, 476
positional goods 106, 111–112, 155–156, 204, 464
precariat 139, 141
Prescott, John 198
Priestley, J. B. 159, 161, 184, 219, 386
private-public spaces 270
private wealth 446–448

privatisation of the public realm 261–264, 271–273
Prudential Regulation Authority 432
psychology of scarcity 351–353
Public Accounts Committee 245
Public Assistance Committees 352
public domain and market forces 128–130
public space 58–60
Public Spaces Protection Orders 59

QAnon 27–29, 490

RBS (Royal Bank of Scotland) 245, 252
Reacher, Jack 469
Reagan, President Ronald 18, 23, 83, 113, 170, 185, 187, 197, 228, 240, 257, 449
Reed, Howard 476
Reformation, The 37
regulation of the economy 427–435, 441
regulation of the market 239–250
Reich, Professor Robert 52
Reilly, Jacquie 270
Renaissance, The 37, 197
Republican Party (USA) 85, 248
res communis 267, 274, 279, 407, 422, 493
Resolution Foundation 479
Reuters 26
Rhoads, Stephen 71
Ricardo, David 72, 146
Richardson, Nigel 292
Right to Buy 423
Ritholtz, Barry 18, 32, 285
Ritzer, George 136, 163
Rogers, Will 102, 252

Roosevelt, President Franklin D. 151
Roszak, Theodore 32, 79, 159, 161, 228, 281, 309, 313, 365
Roubini, Nouriel 92
Rousseau, Jean-Jacques 327
Rowntree, Seebohm 408
Royal Bank of Scotland 117, 252, 295
Royal Institution 313, 328
Royal Mail 253–254, 262, 452, 460
RSA (Royal Society of Arts) 455, 479
Rubinstein, W. D. 116, 161

Sachs, Professor Jeffrey 200
Saez, Emmanuel 450
Sahlins, Marshall 326, 333, 349, 385–386
Sainsbury plc 358
Salisbury, Lord (Robert Arthur Talbot Gascoyne-Cecil) 23, 33, 115
Sandel, Michael 56, 76, 97–98, 160, 233, 279, 303–304, 306, 310, 313, 315–316
Sanders, Senator Bernie 315, 376, 448, 480
Santayana, George 329, 386
Sargent, Roger 451
SBIR (Small Business Innovation Research) US 255
Schumpeter, Joseph 94, 170, 397
Schwartz, Barry 121, 162
Schwarz, Walter 174, 215, 218, 221
Scruton, Roger 79, 159
Self, Peter 149, 153, 164, 227, 229, 309
Sen, Amartya 87–88, 157, 160, 164, 198, 390

Sennett, Richard 62–63, 75, 143–144, 159, 163, 238, 310, 361–362, 374, 389–390, 463, 480–481
Serco 253, 311
Shafir, Eldar 351, 388, 478
Shiller, Robert 20, 33, 249, 311
Sinclair, Upton 20
Skidelsky, Edward 99, 161, 183–184, 190, 193, 219–221, 226, 309, 401, 475, 515
Skidelsky, Robert 99, 161, 183–184, 190, 193, 226, 401, 515
Smith, Adam 38–39, 41, 48, 57, 70, 75, 83, 85, 87–89, 92, 98–102, 106, 113, 117, 124, 146, 157, 159–160, 226–227, 229, 234, 249, 270, 309, 372, 402, 407, 433, 477
Smith, Yves 80, 82–83, 101, 159, 161, 229, 309
social capitalism 3, 397, 434–435, 472, 488, 490, 492, 495
social care (adult) 416–418
social cohesion 64–65, 329–336
social comparisons 348–351
social-evaluative threat 350
Social Limits to Growth 76, 160, 220
social mobility 347–348
Social Prosperity Network 422–423, 425, 468, 476
social segregation 54–57, 375–376
social state 66–67
social trust 332–333, 366–368
Software Delsol 456
Soros, George 147–148, 163–164, 398
souk 223

Southern Cross 416
Spirit Level, The (Wilkinson & Pickett) 71, 77, 194, 213, 220, 324, 336, 366, 384
Sport England 278
Springford, John 247, 311
stakeholder capitalism 65, 94
Standing, Guy 33, 141, 163, 288, 312, 314, 445, 478
Stanford University 24
stationary state 99, 165, 208, 212
status quo bias 20
steady-state economy 202, 209, 211
Stepner, Michael 390
Stern, Baron Nicholas 175
Stiglitz, Joseph 198, 201, 254, 256, 294, 311–312, 315, 340, 345, 360, 387, 478
Stone, Jeanne 331
Stone, Lawrence 386
Streeck, Wolfgang 85, 160
subsidies to private firms ('corporate welfarism') 257–261
Suetonius 137
Sunday Times, The 159, 162, 164, 258, 312, 472, 475
Sure Start programme 237, 420, 426, 476
surveillance capitalism 121
Susskind, Daniel 459, 479
Suzman, James 385

Taleb, Nassim Nicholas 18, 32, 297
Tawney, R. H. 180, 309, 328–329, 338–339, 384–386, 392, 513
Tax Justice Network 443, 460, 478
taxation 152, 187–188, 289–294, 432, 441–451
Taylor, A. J. P. 64, 77

Taylor, Gordon Rattray 302, 315
technological imperative 137–138
Templeton Foundation 305
Terra Firma Capital Partners 417
Thatcher, Margaret 17, 41, 43, 83, 150, 164, 170, 197, 226, 228, 309, 359, 387
The Theory of Moral Sentiments (Smith) 38, 98
'Third Way' 150, 472
Thirteen Colonies 327
Thomas Cook 295
Thurow, Lester 48, 76
Time magazine 229
Titmuss, Richard 306
Tobin, James 196, 220, 403, 405, 475
Todd, Chuck 27
Toffler, Alvin 162, 189, 223, 309
Toller, Ernst 18
Tooze, Adam 164, 187, 219, 315, 385
tourism 107–113
Toynbee, Polly 290, 300, 314–315, 358, 388
transport 411–415
'trickle-down' economics 67, 102–104, 151, 180, 200, 203, 291, 323, 337, 353, 359, 382, 389, 482
Trollope, Anthony 309
Trump, Donald 13–14, 23, 27–29, 33, 79, 171, 187, 343, 460, 503
truth 11–15, 26–31.
TUC (Trades Union Congress) 163, 245, 456
Turner, Baron Adair 216, 218
Twain, Mark 80

Uber 140
UBI (Universal Basic Income) 464–466

INDEX

UBS (Universal Basic Services) 465–468
UNICEF 322, 361, 384–385
United Nations Sustainable Development Solutions Network 200
Universal Credit 404, 489
Universal Declaration of Human Rights 62
Uslaner, Eric 367
US Supreme Court 309, 438
U Thant 133, 162, 183, 219
Utilitarianism 39, 75, 515
utilities 409–411

Varoufakis, Yanis 158, 164, 235, 310, 317, 384
Vespasian, Emperor 137
Virgin Trains East Coast 246
Volkswagen 241
Voltaire (Arouet, François-Marie) 17
Von Mises, Ludwig 75

Walker, David 290, 300, 314–315, 358, 388

Wallich, Henry 213
Walmsley, Emma 297
Walzer, Professor Michael 305, 316, 404, 475
Warren, Senator Elizabeth 448
Watson, George 89, 160, 384
Wealth of Nations, The (Smith) 75, 98, 159, 309, 477
Weber, Max 36
Weizsäcker, Ernst von 172, 218, 220
Welch, Jack 435
welfare state 63, 83, 100, 114, 185–186, 319, 355, 372, 403, 491
Whitehead, Alfred North 71
Whitelegg, John 415
Whitfield, Dexter 266, 313
Wicks, Nigel 240
Wiener, Martin J. 477, 515
Wilkinson, Richard 77, 202, 220–221, 324, 336, 361, 366, 384–390

Willets, David 240
Williams, Raymond 335, 386, 479, 515
Williams, Tennessee 119, 162
Wilson Committee 432
Winthrop, Governor John 37
Wittgenstein, Ludwig 9
Witty, Andrew 256
WMDs 13
Woolard, Christopher 244
working hours 452–453, 455–459
WorldCom 245
World Happiness Report 200
Worpole, Ken 162
Wright, Ronald 82, 87, 159–160, 214, 221, 385
Yellen, Janet 231, 309
Young, Cristobal 298, 315
Young, Michael 167, 218, 342, 344, 387, 473, 481

zero-hours contracts 138
Zuckerberg, Mark 121
Zwolinski, Professor Matt 464